Bibliography of Canadiana
Published in Great Britain,
1519–1763

Bibliographie des ouvrages
sur le Canada publiés en
Grande-Bretagne entre 1519 et 1763

Bibliography of Canadiana Published in Great Britain, 1519–1763

FREDA FARRELL WALDON

Bibliographie des ouvrages sur le Canada publiés en Grande-Bretagne entre 1519 et 1763

Revised and edited by   Révisé et revu par
WILLIAM F.E. MORLEY

National Library of Canada   Bibliothèque nationale du Canada

E C W   P R E S S

Copyright © Minister of Supply and
Services Canada – 1990

Catalogue number: SN 3-240/1988

© Ministre des Approvisionnements et
Services Canada – 1990

Numéro de catalogue: SN 3-240/1988

CANADIAN CATALOGUING IN PUBLICATION DATA

Waldon, Freda Farrell, 1898–1973.
Bibliography of Canadiana published in Great Britain, 1519–1763 =
Bibliographie des ouvrages sur le Canada publiés en Grande-Bretagne entre 1519 et 1763

Text in English and French.
Co-published by the National Library of Canada.
Title of original manuscript: Canadiana published in Great Britain, 1519–1763.
Includes index.
ISBN 1-55022-087-X

1. Canada – History – To 1763 (New France) – Bibliography. 2. Canada – History – To 1763 (New France) – Bibliography – Union
lists. 3. Great Britain – Imprints. 4. Great Britain – Imprints – Union lists. 5. Catalogs, Union – Canada. I. Morley, William F. E.,
1920– . II. National Library of Canada. III. Title. IV. Title: Bibliographie des ouvrages sur le Canada publiés en Grande-Bretagne
entre 1519 et 1763. V. Title: Canadiana published in Great Britain, 1519–1763.

Z1365.W34 1990   016.97101   C88–095231–8E

DONNÉES DE CATALOGAGE AVANT PUBLICATION (CANADA)

Waldon, Freda Farrell, 1898–1973.
Bibliography of Canadiana published in Great Britain, 1519–1763 =
Bibliographie des ouvrages sur le Canada publiés en Grande-Bretagne entre 1519 et 1763

Texte en anglais et en français.
Publ. en collab. avec la Bibliothéque nationale du Canada.
Titre du manuscrit originale: Canadiana published in Great Britain, 1519–1763.
Comprend un index.
ISBN 1-55022-087-X

1. Canada – Histoire – Jusqu'à 1763 (Nouvelle-France) – Bibliographie. 2. Canada – Histoire – Jusqu'à 1763 (Nouvelle-France) –
Bibliographie – Catalogues collectifs. 3. Grande-Bretagne – Imprimés. 4. Grande-Bretagne – Imprimés – Catalogues collectifs. 5.
Catalogues collectifs – Canada. I. Morley, William F. E., 1920– . II. Bibliothèque nationale du Canada. III. Titre. IV. Titre:
Bibliographie des ouvrages sur le Canada publiés en Grande-Bretagne entre 1519 et 1763.
V. Titre: Canadiana published in Great Britain, 1519–1763.

Z1365.W34 1990   016.97101   C88–095231–8F

French-language translations by *CLC Ltée*, Hull, Quebec.
Key-entry by *Avant-Garde Word Processing*, Embro,
Ontario. Design and imaging by *ECW Type & Art*, Syden-
ham, Ontario. Don McLeod, M.L.S., production co-
ordinator for the publishers.

Published by ECW Press Ltd. in cooperation
with the National Library of Canada and
the Canadian Government Publishing Centre,
Supply and Services Canada.

Traduction par *CLC Ltée*, Hull, Québec.
Composé par *Avant-Garde Word Processing*, Embro,
Ontario. Design et préparation par *ECW Type & Art*, Syden-
ham, Ontario. Don McLeod, M.L.S., coordonnateur
à la production pour l'éditeur.

Publié par ECW Press Ltd. conjointement avec la
Bibliothèque nationale du Canada et le Centre
d'édition du gouvernement du Canada,
Approvisionnements et Services Canada

Freda Farrell Waldon, 1898–1973

It gives me a special pleasure to be asked to write a few words to launch my sister's bibliography. Dr. Freda Waldon worked on the compilation for over three decades, but she was unable to find a publisher. Canada was not yet ready for so detailed a study of bibliographical introspection. The present volume provides a fitting memorial to my late sister, and I am proud to send it forth with my blessing.

Mabel Thompson

C'est pour moi un honneur et un privilège que de pouvoir écrire ces quelques mots à l'occasion de la publication de la bibliographie de ma soeur. Mme Freda Waldon a travaillé pendant plus de trente ans à la compilation de cet ouvrage, mais elle n'a jamais pu trouver d'éditeur pour le faire publier. Il semble qu'on n'était pas prêt à recevoir une étude bibliographique aussi détaillée. La publication de l'oeuvre de ma soeur constitue un hommage à sa mémoire et c'est avec fierté que nous en lançons aujourd'hui le projet.

Mabel Thompson

TABLE OF CONTENTS • TABLE DES MATIÈRES

SPECIMEN PAGES • FEUILLES À L'EXAMEN

FOREWORD • AVANT-PROPOS

At the time Freda Waldon began compiling this bibliography, in 1931 and 1932, she and I were both frequenting the reading room of the British Museum. No doubt now and then we were under the famous dome at the same time. But we never met, and we did not become personally acquainted until 1946, when she was elected president of the Canadian Library Association (CLA) at the founding conference in Hamilton. To my considerable surprise, as I had been unable to get to Hamilton, and was far away at UBC, I was elected first vice-president and president-elect.

A National Library for Canada was a prime objective of the CLA, and Freda led the campaign to press the matter upon the attention of the government. By the autumn of 1946 a determined little group — Freda herself, Madge Gill, Elizabeth Dafoe, and Elizabeth Morton — were writing and speaking about it at every opportunity. I joined the fray, and the earliest surviving evidence of my participation seems to be an unsigned article entitled "Why Ask for a National Library?" that appeared in the November issue of the *Ontario Library Review*.

À l'époque où Mme Freda Waldon commençait sa bibliographie, vers 1931 ou 1932, elle et moi étions des assidus de la salle de lecture du British Museum. Il est à peu près certain que nous avons dû nous trouver dans ce monument célèbre au même moment. Pourtant, nous ne nous y sommes jamais rencontrés et ce n'est qu'en 1946 que nous avons fait connaissance. Cette année-là, elle avait été élue présidente de la Canadian Library Association (CLA) à la conférence de fondation qui avait lieu à Hamilton. À ma grande surprise, j'avais été élu premier vice-président et président désigné alors même que je n'avais pu assister à la conférence et que je me trouvais à l'Université de Colombie-Britannique.

La création d'une bibliothèque « nationale » était l'objectif premier de la CLA et c'est Freda Waldon qui a mené la campagne pour faire avancer notre cause auprès du gouvernement. C'est ainsi qu'à l'automne de 1946, un petit groupe de femmes déterminées – Freda Waldon, Madge Gill, Elizabeth Dafoe et Elizabeth Morton – écrivait ou donnait des conférences à ce sujet dès que l'occasion de le faire se présentait. Je me suis alors joint au groupe et la marque la plus ancienne de ma participation semble avoir été un article non signé intitulé « Why Ask for a National Library ? » (Créer une bibliothèque nationale ?) paru dans le numéro de novembre de l'*Ontario Library Review*.

Freda's approach to the problem struck me as being eminently practical and sensible. None of us had any expectation that the government would consider making an immediate large investment; the important thing was to bring a nucleus into being from which a full-fledged library could grow. It was at this time that I realized how fundamental bibliography was to Freda's approach to both reference services and to collection building. "Start with Services" became the campaign slogan. As Freda herself expressed it in a CBC broadcast in August 1947, "start the National Library *now*, right away, as soon as the practical details can be worked out, as an information bureau and bibliographical centre — and let it grow from these into the complete institution."

A vital part of a bibliographic centre would be a national union catalogue, which I remember declaring, in those immediate postwar times, would "mobilize the book resources of the nation." The sequence of Freda's thinking is clear: a growing collection of national and subject bibliographies would indicate what was available on a topic; the union catalogue would reveal which of the titles were available in Canada and where copies were located. Building up a substantial book collection would take years, but meanwhile first priority should be given to publishing a current national bibli-

Freda Waldon a fait preuve d'un sens pratique extraordinaire dans sa façon de faire face au problème. Personne d'entre nous ne s'attendait à ce que le gouvernement fît un investissement important à court terme ; ce qui comptait alors, c'était de créer un noyau à partir duquel pourrait éventuellement se constituer petit à petit une véritable bibliothèque nationale. C'est à cette époque-là aussi que je me suis rendu compte à quel point Freda Waldon accordait de l'importance à la science bibliographique pour la constitution de services de référence et la création de collections. « Des services d'abord » (Start with Services) était devenu le slogan de sa campagne. Comme Freda Waldon l'indiquait au cours d'une émission de la CBC (réseau anglais de la radio d'État) en août 1947, « jetons les bases d'une bibliothèque nationale dès maintenant, dès que les détails techniques peuvent être réglés. Autrement dit, créons un bureau de renseignements et un centre bibliographique. De ce germe pourra fleurir une institution véritable ».

L'organe principal du centre bibliographique devait être un catalogue collectif qui, comme je l'avais affirmé en ces années d'après-guerre, « mobiliserait toutes les ressources de la nation ». La stratégie de Freda Waldon était bien simple : grâce à une collection de bibliographies nationales et par sujets constamment mises à jour, il serait possible de déterminer quels ouvrages étaient disponibles sur tel ou tel sujet. Grâce au catalogue collectif, on pourrait savoir quels titres se trouvent au Canada et dans quelles bibliothèques. Il faudrait mettre des années pour constituer une collection digne de ce nom, mais, à cette époque, on s'était fixé comme objectif de publier une bibliographie nationale courante qui comprenne

ography that would list all new publications relating to Canada. This was essentially the plan that the government accepted in the autumn of 1948, and the Canadian Bibliographic Centre came formally into existence on 1 May 1950. In July, Freda gave the centre a copy of her bibliography, *Canadiana Published in Great Britain, 1519–1763*. It was the first gift received by the centre, and none could have been more appropriate.

It is the work of a scholar and a true-blue bibliographer — one of the devoted little band who are intrigued by some subject, area, or period and seek to run to the ends of the earth to uncover every publication relating to it. It reflects the endless patience, persistence, and detective instincts that such a quest requires.

Freda was well aware that a bibliography is rarely definitive; additional items are virtually certain to come to light from time to time. A note on the copy she gave to the National Library describes it modestly as an "unfinished manuscript." But recent events happen to have demonstrated how thorough her search for titles had been. In 1935, as noted in the introduction, she published the entries relating to the famous visit of the four "Indian Kings" to England in 1710. The "Kings" were received by Queen Anne, who commissioned portraits of them. The four paintings were acquired recently by the Public

tous les nouveaux ouvrages sur des sujets canadiens. Voilà essentiellement le plan que le gouvernement canadien a accepté à l'automne de 1948 et, le 1ᵉʳ mai 1950, le Centre bibliographique canadien voyait le jour. En juillet, Freda Waldon faisait don de sa bibliographie, *Canadiana Published in Great Britain, 1519–1763*, au Centre bibliographique. C'était le premier don au Centre, un don on ne peut plus approprié.

Cette bibliographie est l'œuvre d'une érudite et d'une bibliographe de la plus pure tradition. Freda Waldon faisait partie d'un petit groupe de personnes dévouées et déterminées qui, une fois intéressées par un sujet, par une région, par une période, pouvaient remuer ciel et terre pour dénicher toutes les publications qui s'y rapportaient. La bibliographie de Freda Waldon est l'expression concrète de la patience infinie, de la persévérance et des qualités de détective que pareille recherche suppose.

Freda Waldon savait bien qu'une bibliographie n'était jamais définitive ; il était à peu près certain, en effet, que de nouvelles notices viendraient s'y ajouter. Dans la note accompagnant la bibliographie dont elle a fait don, Freda Waldon faisait remarquer, avec beaucoup de modestie, qu'il s'agissait là d'un « manuscrit inachevé ». Cependant, on a pu constater dernièrement à quel point sa recherche des titres avait été exhaustive. Comme on le fait remarquer dans l'introduction, elle a publié en 1935 les titres se rapportant à l'importante visite des quatre « rois indiens » en Angleterre en 1710. Les « rois » ont été reçus par la reine Anne qui commanda alors des portraits d'eux. Les Archives publiques du Canada ont acheté les quatre portraits dernièrement et, à cette

Archives of Canada, and this has prompted the publication of an elaborate monograph (*The Four Indian Kings*) that includes a bibliography. After half a century it supersedes the 1935 listing, but it is noteworthy that of the dozen or so new items it includes, all but one were found in libraries that Freda had included in her search. They must either have been uncatalogued at the time of her visitation, or have been acquired since.

As this suggests, *Canadiana Published in Great Britain, 1519–1763* has stood the test of time exceptionally well. Those who consulted it during the long period when it languished in manuscript recognized that it was a basic reference in the making, and this revised and enlarged version, prepared by William F.E. Morley, increases its coverage and authority. Its publication is most welcome, and is both a tribute to Dr. Waldon and an important addition to Canadian bibliography.

W. Kaye Lamb

occasion, on a publié une monographie élaborée, *Les quatre rois indiens*, qui comprend aussi une bibliographie. Cinquante ans plus tard, on ne se sert plus de la liste de 1935, mais il est intéressant de noter que des douze nouveaux titres mentionnés, tous sauf un proviennent de bibliothèques que Freda Waldon avait incluses dans sa recherche. . . Ou bien les titres n'avaient pas été catalogués à l'époque de sa visite, ou bien ils ont été acquis depuis.

Il n'est pas exagéré de dire que la bibliographie de Freda Waldon a subi avec grand succès l'épreuve du temps. Ceux et celles qui ont eu à la consulter pendant cette trop longue période où elle n'a existé que sous forme de manuscrit savaient que l'ouvrage ferait autorité. La présente version, revue et augmentée par William F.E. Morley, en accroît encore la portée et l'autorité. Cette publication est des plus opportunes et constitue à la fois un hommage à Freda Waldon et un apport essentiel à la science bibliographique canadienne.

W. Kaye Lamb

PREFACE • PRÉFACE

One of the primary functions of a national library is to identify and record information on the country's published heritage, and thus promote the knowledge and use of that heritage. *Bibliography of Canadiana Published in Great Britain, 1519–1763* provides information valuable to scholars and researchers working in a range of disciplines. The work was compiled by Dr. Freda Waldon, who travelled to Great Britain in the 1940s and 1950s to carry out research on British publications relevant to her country. During the same period she, like many other Canadians, petitioned the Government of Canada to establish a national library. During the institution's first decade, she presented the manuscript of the bibliography to the National Librarian.

Dr. Waldon's work has been revised, enlarged and edited by William F.E. Morley, former Head of Special Collections at Queen's University, Kingston, Ontario. Scholars and researchers studying Canada's history and culture will benefit from their labours, since a knowledge of our past will help us to plan and shape more

L'une des principales fonctions d'une bibliothèque nationale consiste à recenser et enregistrer les informations portant sur le patrimoine de l'édition d'un pays, et à promouvoir la connaissance et l'utilisation de ce patrimoine. La publication *Bibliography of Canadiana Published in Great Britain, 1519–1763* fournit à cet égard des renseignements très utiles aux spécialistes et chercheurs travaillant dans un grand nombre de disciplines. Cette oeuvre a été réalisée par Mme Freda Waldon, qui a fait de nombreux voyages en Grande-Bretagne dans les années 1940 et 1950 afin d'effectuer des recherches sur les publications britanniques traitant de son pays. À la même époque, elle a été parmi les signataires, avec de nombreux autres Canadiens, d'une pétition demandant au gouvernement du Canada de créer une bibliothèque nationale. Au cours de la première décennie de l'existence de cet établissement, elle a soumis le manuscrit de sa bibliographie au directeur général de la Bibliothèque nationale.

L'oeuvre de Mme Waldon a été révisée, augmentée et éditée par M. William F.E. Morley, ancien chef du service descollections spéciales à l'Université Queen, de Kingston (Ontario). Les spécialistes et chercheurs qui s'intéressent à l'histoire et à la culture canadiennes pourront donc bénéficier du travail de ces deux personnes et seront ainsi plus en mesure de préparer et

effectively our future. The National Library is proud to have played a role in publishing this major contribution to Canadian Studies.

Marianne Scott
National Librarian

façonner efficacement notre avenir. La Bibliothèque nationale est donc fière d'avoir joué un rôle dans la publication de cette importante étude sur le Canada.

Marianne Scott
Le directeur général de la Bibliothèque nationale du Canada

BIOGRAPHICAL INTRODUCTION
•
NOTICE BIOGRAPHIQUE

FREDA FARRELL WALDON, 1898–1973

"The right person, in the right place, at the right time." Although Albert Bowron wrote these words about Freda Farrell Waldon in connection with her share in the long campaign to establish a National Library for Canada, they may with equal justice be applied to many other aspects of her life.

She was born in Winnipeg on 29 August 1898, but always considered herself a daughter of Hamilton, where she lived from the age of one year. Her mother's family had settled in Hamilton in 1827; her great-grandfather, William Hardy, built the first stone court house in Hamilton, the first firehall, and the first city hall. The third generation of her family to attend Central Public School, she went on to the Hamilton Collegiate Institute, and then to the University of Toronto, where she obtained her Bachelor of Arts degree in 1919. The first position of which we have any record was that of assistant employment manager for the Imperial Cotton Company. Here one of her responsibilities was editing and contributing articles to the company organ, *The Fabricator*. She resumed her education at Columbia University

« La personne qu'il fallait, là où il le fallait, au moment où il le fallait. » Même si Albert Bowron a employé ces mots pour décrire la contribution de Freda Farrell Waldon à la longue campagne qui a débouché sur la création de la Bibliothèque nationale du Canada, on pourrait aussi bien les appliquer à de nombreux autres aspects de sa vie.

Née à Winnipeg le 29 août 1898, Freda Farrell Waldon a toujours considéré Hamilton comme sa ville d'origine, où elle a d'ailleurs vécu à partir de l'âge d'un an. La famille de sa mère s'était établie à Hamilton en 1827. Son arrière grand-père, William Hardy, y a construit le premier palais de justice en pierre, la première caserne de pompiers et le premier hôtel de ville. Faisant partie de la troisième génération de sa famille à fréquenter la Central Public School, elle a ensuite étudié au Hamilton Collegiate Institute, puis à l'Université de Toronto, dont elle obtenait le baccalauréat en arts en 1919. D'après les dossiers que nous avons, le premier poste qu'elle a occupé était celui de directrice adjointe du service d'emploi à l'Imperial Cotton Company. L'une de ses responsabilités à ce titre était de rédiger et de réviser des articles pour le journal de la compagnie, *The Fabricator*. Elle a repris ses études à l'Université Columbia à l'automne de 1924 ; elle a terminé sa

in the fall semester of 1924, completing her course work for an M.A. in English in the 1925–26 academic year. Alexander Henry (the elder) was the subject of her thesis, completed in 1930, and her degree was awarded in 1931.

In the meantime Miss Waldon had returned to Hamilton due to her mother's ill health and, fortunately for Canadian librarianship, took a position as a substitute in the Circulation Department of the Hamilton Public Library in November 1926. The following January she was appointed head of the Cataloguing Department. At this time the Hamilton Public Library was in the throes of a reorganization along modern lines, necessitated by a devastatingly critical report by the inspector of public libraries, W.O. Carson, in 1922. Although some progress had already been made, there remained much to be done and the new staff member joined the fray with enthusiasm. A lack of formal library training was no hindrance; only the then chief librarian, Miss Lurene McDonald (Mrs. Norman W. Lyle), had a full year of professional education, and for this omission at that time an academic background more than compensated. Only two other recent recruits to the staff had university degrees; few had even the basic three-month course in librarianship. However, it was not long before she herself recognized the need for professional knowledge, and in 1930 Miss Waldon obtained leave of absence for two years, first to attend the School of Librarianship at the

scolarité de maîtrise en anglais pendant l'année scolaire 1925–1926. Alexander Henry L'Ancien était le sujet de sa thèse, terminée en 1930. Elle a reçu son diplôme en 1931.

Entre-temps, Freda Waldon était retournée à Hamilton au chevet de sa mère malade et, pour le plus grand bonheur de la bibliothéconomie au Canada, a accepté le poste de remplaçante au service de prêt de la bibliothèque publique de Hamilton en novembre 1926. En janvier suivant, elle était nommée chef du service de catalogage. À l'époque, la bibliothèque municipale de Hamilton était en pleine réorganisation et devait se moderniser, conformément aux recommandations d'un rapport extrêmement sévère de l'inspecteur des bibliothèques publiques, W.O. Carson, en 1922. Même si des progrès avaient déjà été réalisés, beaucoup restait à faire et c'est avec enthousiasme que la nouvelle employée s'était jointe au groupe. Le fait de ne pas avoir de formation en bibliothéconomie ne posait pas de problèmes. En effet, seule la bibliothécaire en chef, Mlle Lurene McDonald, qui épousa plus tard M. Norman W. Lyle, avait reçu une formation professionnelle qui avait duré un an. À cette époque, une formation académique générale compensait largement cette lacune. Seulement deux des dernières recrues détenaient un diplôme universitaire. Rares étaient les employés qui possédaient même la formation de base de trois mois en bibliothéconomie. Cependant, Freda Waldon s'est vite rendue compte qu'une formation professionnelle était nécessaire. C'est ainsi qu'en 1930, elle obtenait un congé de deux ans d'abord pour suivre la formation de l'école

University of London, from which she received her diploma in 1931, and secondly, to take up a Carnegie Fellowship in 1931–32, in order to prepare a bibliography of Canadiana published in Great Britain up to 1763.

This research topic was chosen in consultation with W. Stewart Wallace, then librarian at the University of Toronto, who supported her application for a Carnegie Fellowship. Miss Waldon worked extensively at the British Museum and her original work slips, with the source of information noted on the reverse, attest to her careful attention to bibliographic detail. Although she did not consider herself a "real" bibliographer, she much enjoyed the pursuit of answers to the puzzles set by variant copies and editions of some of the relevant titles. Most entertaining of the many bibliographies and lists checked was the transcript of the Stationers' Register from 1557 to 1640; possibly the thrill of coming across the first item associated with Shakespeare was recompense for the frustration of finding records of licenses issued for the printing of broadsides and ballads in her field which had long since perished. She also had access to a number of other libraries in London, as well as the Bodleian, Cambridge University Library, the National Library of Scotland, the John Rylands Library in Manchester, and Sir Leicester Harmsworth's collection.

de bibliothéconomie de l'Université de London, qui lui décernait son diplôme en 1931, et, ensuite, pour préparer une bibliographie des œuvres sur le Canada publiées en Grande-Bretagne jusqu'en 1763, projet pour lequel elle a reçu le Carnegie Fellowship en 1931–1932.

Freda Waldon a choisi son sujet de recherche en collaboration avec le regretté W. Stewart Wallace, alors bibliothécaire à l'Université de Toronto, qui a appuyé sa demande de bourse au Carnegie Fellowship. Freda Waldon a consacré beaucoup de ses efforts au British Museum. Ses fiches de travail originales révèlent un souci marqué du détail bibliographique ; Freda Waldon notait systématiquement la source de ses renseignements au verso de sa fiche. Même si elle ne se considérait pas comme une véritable bibliographe, elle prenait plaisir à essayer de résoudre l'énigme que pouvait poser l'existence de divers exemplaires ou éditions de certains des titres qui l'intéressaient. Parmi les nombreuses bibliographies et listes vérifiées par Freda Waldon, on note l'amusante transcription du Stationers' Register de 1557 à 1640 ; la jubilation qu'elle a dû ressentir à la découverte du premier titre lié à Shakespeare a sûrement compensé la frustration associée à la découverte de registres de permis émis pour l'impression de feuillets et de ballades disparus depuis longtemps. Elle avait aussi accès à d'autres bibliothèques à Londres, ainsi qu'à la bibliothèque Bodleian, la bibliothèque de l'Université de Cambridge, la bibliothèque nationale d'Écosse, la bibliothèque John Rylands de Manchester et la collection de Sir Leicester Harmsworth.

The Hamilton Public Library
La bibliothèque publique de Hamilton
1946

On her return to Canada she was once again caught up in the task of transforming the catalogue of the Hamilton Public Library from a very unreliable tool into one so useful and complete that she could consider it to be one of the achievements for which she would wish to be remembered. The other was the book collection, a testament to her belief that "the aim of public libraries is to build good collections and to organize them for use," and it was a lasting grief that straitened circumstances during the Great Depression had deprived the collection of the second copy of good titles necessary if they were to survive.

In spite of her demanding duties as chief cataloguer, Miss Waldon did not neglect the bibliography. In 1933 she visited the Public Archives in Ottawa, the New York and Detroit public libraries, and the Newberry Library in Chicago. She also worked with a private collection in Hamilton, and checked references to such distant libraries as the Huntington in California by mail. The following year she again used her holidays for this work, concentrating on the Toronto Public Library's *Bibliography of Canadiana*, the depository catalogue of the Library of Congress, the catalogue of Queen's University Library, and Philéas Gagnon's catalogue for the Montreal Public Library. In the spring of 1935 she took a leave of absence for four months and returned to England to put her work in shape, and in September the *Canadian Historical Review* published

À son retour au Canada, Freda Waldon se retrouvait de nouveau face à la tâche de modifier le catalogue de la bibliothèque publique de Hamilton et d'en faire un outil utile et complet, l'une des réalisations pour lesquelles elle souhaitait laisser sa marque. Elle espérait aussi léguer une généreuse collection de livres, témoin tangible de ce que Freda Waldon croyait être la raison d'être des bibliothèques publiques : « se constituer de bonnes collections et les organiser pour qu'on puisse s'en servir ». Or, le fait que, pendant les dures années de la grande crise économique, la bibliothèque n'ait pas pu se permettre le deuxième exemplaire de bons titres nécessaire à leur survie a été l'objet d'une constante affliction chez elle.

Malgré les exigences de son poste de chef-catalogueur, Freda Waldon ne négligeait pas sa bibliographie. En 1933, elle visitait les Archives nationales à Ottawa, les bibliothèques publiques de New York et de Détroit, ainsi que la bibliothèque Newberry de Chicago. Elle a pu consulter une collection privée à Hamilton et a vérifié des références « par correspondance » auprès de la bibliothèque Huntington en Californie. L'année suivante, elle consacrait de nouveau ses vacances à ce travail, concentrant ses efforts sur la *Bibliography of Canadiana* de la bibliothèque publique de Toronto, le catalogue du dépôt légal de la Bibliothèque du Congrès, le catalogue de la bibliothèque de l'Université Queen's et le catalogue de Philéas Gagnon de la bibliothèque publique de Montréal. Au printemps de 1935, elle a pris quatre mois de congé et s'est rendue en Angleterre mettre la dernière main à son travail. En septembre de cette année-là, la *Canadian Historical Review* publiait « Queen Anne and 'The Four Kings

"Queen Anne and 'The Four Kings of Canada': A Bibliography of Contemporary Sources," based on the materials she had found of what she considered a most amusing body of literature, the visit of four Indian chiefs to Queen Anne in 1710. Any hope there may have been of having the manuscript published in its entirety vanished with the outbreak of war.

By February 1940, Miss Waldon did not expect to find many more titles of importance, and had typed up most of her original slips, one item and its attendant notes to each sheet, thus allowing for the insertion of other titles later. She planned to use part of her vacation that year to finish typing the latest entries, mainly the result of her work at the John Carter Brown Library in Providence, Rhode Island. Presumably sheets for any new items gained from the completion of Sabin's *Dictionary of Books Relating to America* were already prepared. Increasing responsibilities due to the recurring illness of the chief librarian, and to more than a year spent, first as the head of the largest branch and then in reopening the oldest branch which had been closed for three years due to the Depression, had left her with little time or energy for the bibliography. This had been a worry to her and it must have been a great relief to feel that she had done all that she could with the sources then available to her.

of Canada': A Bibliography of Contemporary Sources » (« La reine Anne et les quatre rois du Canada : Bibliographie de sources contemporaines »), article rédigé à partir d'ouvrages qu'elle considérait des plus amusants : la visite de quatre chefs indiens à la reine Anne en 1710. Tout espoir de voir le manuscrit publié intégralement s'évanouit avec le début de la guerre.

En février 1940, Freda Waldon, ne prévoyant pas trouver d'autres titres intéressants, avait dactylographié la plupart de ses fiches de travail originales ; elle ne rédigeait qu'une notice par page, acompagnée des notes afférentes, pour permettre l'insertion éventuelle de nouveaux titres. Elle avait prévu prendre une partie de ses vacances cette année-là pour finir de taper les dernières notices, produit de son travail à la bibliothèque John Carter Brown de Providence au Rhode Island. Vraisemblablement, elle avait déjà préparé les notices obtenues à partir de la version complète du *Dictionary of Books Relating to America* de Sabin. Les nouvelles responsabilités qui lui avaient échu en raison de la maladie prolongée de la bibliothécaire en chef et celles qu'elle a dû assumer, pendant plus d'un an, d'abord à titre de chef de la succursale centrale et, ensuite, pour rouvrir la succursale la plus ancienne qui avait été fermée pendant trois ans à cause de la grande crise économique, ne lui laissaient que peu de temps et d'énergie pour sa bibliographie. Elle s'en inquiétait, d'ailleurs. Mais elle savait qu'elle avait tiré tout ce qu'elle pouvait des sources qui lui étaient alors disponibles et cette seule pensée avait suffi à l'apaiser.

Freda Waldon became the acting chief librarian of the Hamilton Public Library in June 1940 and was appointed to the position on 1 October. World War II was already changing the demands made upon the library, and immediate tasks were to make the library responsive to the needs of expanding war industries and to provide information for every type of war effort. Equally important was the response to an anxious and, at times, disheartened population, first by instilling pride through organizing an exhibition of everything that was accomplished in Hamilton during the 1914–18 war, and secondly, by providing reading that would offer refreshment and respite from the war. She was one of the first to show a concern to help the foster parents of British Child Guests. In addition, she expected her staff to show calm and confident faces and to discourage gloomy talk.

Miss Waldon's administration of the Hamilton Public Library was marked by a steady growth in prestige and usefulness. During the war years and afterwards serious attention was paid to increasing the library's holdings so that, before her retirement, the collection was the fourth largest in a public library in Canada, circulation had grown to the third largest, and a nation-wide reputation had been gained for the quality of the reference service offered. Equally arduous but less successful was the effort to keep pace with the expanding city. In 1948–49 a modern branch library on Hamilton Mountain

Freda Waldon est devenue bibliothécaire en chef par intérim de la bibliothèque publique de Hamilton en juin 1940 ; le 1er octobre, elle était nommée officiellement bibliothécaire en chef. En raison de la guerre, les exigences posées à la bibliothèque changeaient. Il a fallu s'organiser pour que la bibliothèque puisse répondre aux besoins des industries militaires en pleine expansion et fournir des renseignements pour tous les genres d'effort de guerre. Il fallait aussi répondre à une population angoissée et, parfois, démoralisée ; la bibliothèque a donc organisé une exposition sur les réalisations de Hamilton pendant la Première guerre mondiale pour relever la fierté des citoyens, et a offert du material de lecture divertissant pour essayer de faire oublier la guerre. Freda Waldon a été l'une des premières personnes à aider les familles qui accueillaient des enfants britanniques. Par ailleurs, elle s'attendait de son personnel qu'il affiche calme et sérénité et qu'il décourage le pessimisme.

Sous l'administration de Freda Waldon, la bibliothèque publique de Hamilton a vu son prestige et ses services s'accroître sans cesse. Pendant la guerre, et aussi après, on s'est attaché plus particulièrement à augmenter la collection de la bibliothèque si bien que, avant la retraite de Freda Waldon, la bibliothèque publique de Hamilton se situait au quatrième rang des bibliothèques publiques canadiennes pour sa collection et au troisième rang pour le nombre de prêts. La bibliothèque avait acquis une réputation nationale pour la qualité de ses services de référence. Par contre, il a été plus difficile pour la bibliothèque de maintenir le rythme de croissance de la ville même. En 1948–1949, une succursale moderne a été

replaced a long outgrown rented store, and in the never-to-be-forgotten nightmare period from August 1951 to November 1952, the main library was completely renovated to make better use of available space. Survivors were proud to recall that service was disrupted for less than two weeks.

In those days of few, if any, libraries in grade schools, Miss Waldon became an expert at pleading successfully the reading needs of children before the board of control, emphasizing the danger that in some districts they would grow up without the enrichment in their lives which a library can bring. Over the years she was able to open four small children's branches in outlying schools, and to establish a system of book boxes for selected grades in other schools more than a mile from a branch. Possibly the memory of her own childhood search for good reading in a library with just a few shelves for children, where she considered herself lucky to find a "pennyworth of good reading among an intolerable deal of tripe," lent eloquence to her pleas for additional funds for juvenile books. It was not as easy to persuade Council that adults too were entitled to library service within reasonable distance from their homes, and it was not until late in 1956 that the Travelling Branch went on the road, stopping at schools and shopping centres, and serving both children and adults. It was located at, and shared the staff and adult book collection of, the modern

érigée sur la colline Hamilton en remplacement de l'ancienne bibliothèque située dans ce qui était un magasin. De plus, entre août 1951 et novembre 1952, période cauchemardesque s'il en fût, la bibliothèque principale était rénovée de fond en comble. Les « survivants » de cette époque se rappellent avec fierté que les services n'avaient été suspendus que pendant moins de deux semaines.

À cette époque, rares étaient les écoles primaires à posséder une bibliothèque. Freda Waldon est passée maître dans l'art de plaider devant la commission scolaire la cause des enfants qui, dans certains secteurs, risquaient d'être privés des bienfaits d'une bibliothèque dans leur vie. C'est ainsi qu'au fil des années, elle faisait ouvrir quatre petites succursales dans des écoles éloignées du centre-ville et elle réussissait à établir un système de boîtes de livres destinés à certains niveaux dans d'autres écoles situées à plus d'un mille d'une succursale. Le souvenir de la soif de lire qu'elle éprouvait, enfant, alors que les bibliothèques ne comptaient que quelques rayons pour enfants et qu'elle s'était considérée chanceuse de pouvoir trouver une « perle dans la boue », y est sans doute pour quelque chose dans la vigueur de sa croisade afin d'obtenir des fonds supplémentaires pour les livres pour la jeunesse. Il ne lui a pas été facile non plus de convaincre le conseil que les adultes avaient, eux aussi, droit à des services de bibliothèque à proximité de chez eux. Ce n'est qu'à la fin de l'année 1956 que la succursale itinérante était lancée ; elle s'arrêtait tantôt dans les écoles, tantôt dans les centres commerciaux, desservant aussi bien enfants et adultes. Elle était située à la succursale moderne et attrayante Western, ouverte en juin 1957, qui abritait aussi la succursale scolaire ; elle

and attractive Western Branch Library, opened in June 1957, which also housed the Schools Branch. This combination of services exemplified Dr. Waldon's concern to build only where the size of the population justified the expense of full-time staff and a satisfactory book collection. Her last project along these lines was the planning of a replacement for the city's first branch library, which had given service for almost fifty years in a former YMCA building. Not completed until a few months after her retirement, it bears her trademark of providing an attractive and serviceable building without extravagance.

Dr. Waldon's view of library service to the community extended far beyond the provision of information and good reading. With Dr. C.H. Stearn, director of Extension Services of McMaster University, she organized Hamilton's first adult education conference in 1942. Thirty-five organizations sent representatives and from this grew the Hamilton Adult Education Council, which had a positive influence in many areas of the community. Its first accomplishment was to persuade the Board of Education to re-establish their English classes for the foreign-born. The council shared her view of adult education as any leisure time activity with some intellectual or artistic content; it established a study group on postwar reconstruction and worked vigorously, but unsuccessfully, towards the building of a civic centre. It also began the agitation which resulted in a new art gallery for

partageait avec la Western le personnel et la collection des livres pour adultes. En offrant ce genre de services partagés, Freda Waldon démontrait le souci qu'elle avait d'exploiter au maximum les ressources disponibles et de ne construire de nouveaux locaux que là où la population justifiait l'embauche de personnel à temps plein et l'existence d'une collection satisfaisante. Le dernier projet de ce genre que Freda Waldon a entrepris a été la planification du déménagement de la première succursale logée pendant presque cinquante ans dans un ancien YMCA. L'immeuble, achevé quelques mois après la retraite de Freda Waldon, témoigne de son souci d'offrir des services dans un cadre à la fois attrayant, commode et sobre.

Pour Freda Waldon, le rôle d'une bibliothèque dans la communauté dépassait la simple prestation de renseignements ou même de livres. En effet, en collaboration avec C.H. Stearn, directeur des services d'éducation permanente de l'Université McMaster, elle organisait la première conférence sur l'éducation permanente en 1942. Trente-cinq organismes y ont envoyé des représentants ; de cet exercice devait naître le conseil de l'éducation permanente de Hamilton, qui a eu un effet bénéfique dans bien des secteurs de la vie de Hamilton. Le premier bon point marqué a été de persuader le conseil scolaire de reprendre les cours d'anglais pour les étrangers. Le conseil croyait, comme Freda Waldon, qu'il fallait, dans le cadre d'un programme d'éducation permanente, offrir un passe-temps ayant une certaine valeur intellectuelle ou artistique. Le conseil a aussi créé un groupe d'étude sur la reconstruction d'après-guerre et a investi beaucoup d'efforts, en vain, pour la construction d'un centre municipal. Le conseil a mené une campagne qui a

Hamilton; opened in 1953, this gallery has already been outgrown, razed, and replaced. Dr. Waldon also helped to found the Hamilton Recreation Council and the Hamilton branch of the National Film Forum, which she served as programme chair for several years. In 1950 she initiated the first Programme Planners Institute in Canada, held at the Hamilton Public Library, at which was presented, with the co-operation of several other organizations, a survey of the resources of the community and the services of the library.

Books and bookmobiles, buildings and a catalogue — however perfect the last might be — and excellent community programming were not the only requirements for the kind of library service Dr. Waldon wished to offer. She was well acquainted with the principles of good personnel practice and had a sincere concern for the well-being of her staff. She worked long and hard to raise salaries to an adequate level, and to produce an equitable classification and pay plan; she was warmly appreciative of staff efforts and considered it important that their work should not be so tiring that they would not enjoy it; she tried always to make working conditions as comfortable as possible while maintaining high standards of public service. Firmly committed to the belief that the first principle of library service is to know one's community and to provide the materials that the citizens

débouché sur la création du nouveau musée des beaux-arts de Hamilton ; ouvert en 1953, ce musée a déjà été rasé et relogé parce qu'il ne suffisait plus. Freda Waldon a aussi contribué à fonder le conseil récréatif de Hamilton et la section locale du National Film Forum ; elle a d'ailleurs été présidente du secteur des programmes de ce groupe pendant de nombreuses années. En 1950, elle a lancé le premier Programme Planners Institute au Canada, tenu à la bibliothèque publique de Hamilton et au cours duquel a été présentée, en collaboration avec de nombreux autres organismes, une enquête sur les ressources communautaires et les services offerts par les bibliothèques.

Des livres, des bibliothèques ambulantes, des immeubles, un catalogue – aussi excellent fût-il – et une programmation complète n'étaient pas les seuls éléments du service que Freda Waldon entendait offrir. Elle connaissait bien les principes qui encouragent de bonnes relations avec le personnel et elle avait à coeur le bien-être de ses employés. Elle s'est démenée pendant longtemps pour obtenir que les salaires soient relevés à un niveau adéquat et pour en arriver à une classification et à un régime de salaire équitables. Elle savait apprécier à sa juste valeur la contribution de son personnel et considérait que le travail ne devrait pas être épuisant au point qu'on ne puisse plus s'y plaire. Freda Waldon s'efforçait de toujours maintenir à la fois de bonnes conditions de travail pour ses employés et des normes de service élevées pour le bénéfice du grand public. Convaincue que le premier principe à respecter pour offrir un service de qualité, c'est de bien connaître le public auquel on s'adresse et de fournir ce dont il a besoin dans la vie de tous les jours, Freda

need to help them in their daily lives, Dr. Waldon's aim was to instill this principle in all staff members. They admired and respected their chief and were proud of her accomplishments.

From the beginning of her library career Freda Waldon was active in professional organizations. Even before she attended the School of Librarianship she became a charter member of the Ontario Regional Group of Catalognuers and was elected to the executive. Elected again on her return to Canada, she served as chair for the 1935–36 year. A position as councillor of the Ontario Library Association (OLA) followed, and in due course she served as president, 1941–42, and organized the 1942 conference in Hamilton around the theme of public relations. Over the years she served on every major OLA committee and was either convener or chair of those dealing with war libraries, library records, salaries, and the provincial library. She was also a member of the special committee appointed in 1945 to revise the brief "Library Needs in the Province of Ontario," and headed the delegation which presented it to the Royal Commission on Education. When the OLA Executive needed "someone with lots of experience and uncommonly good judgement in the interests of the profession" as chair of a new committee to make an award to librarians who give valuable service to the profession, Freda Waldon was their unanimous choice.

Waldon s'est efforcée d'inculquer ce principe à ses employés qui, pour leur part, admiraient et respectaient leur chef, et étaient fiers de ses succès.

Dès les débuts de sa carrière comme bibliothécaire, Freda Waldon a été active dans les cercles professionnels. Avant même de fréquenter l'école de bibliothéconomie, elle est devenue membre agréée du groupe des catalogueurs de la région de l'Ontario, et a été élue au comité exécutif. Élue de nouveau à son retour au Canada, elle a été présidente de l'organisme en 1935-1936. Elle a ensuite occupé le poste de conseillère à l'Ontario Library Association (OLA) ; elle en est devenue la présidente en 1941-1942 et a organisé la conférence sur les relations avec le public qui a eu lieu en 1942 à Hamilton. Freda Waldon a, au fil des ans, siégé à tous les comités importants de l'OLA ; ou bien elle se chargeait de convoquer les réunions, ou bien elle assurait elle-même la présidence des comités qui portaient sur les bibliothèques de guerre, les dossiers de bibliothèque, les salaires et la Bibliothèque provinciale. Elle a aussi été membre du comité spécial nommé en 1945 pour réviser le mémoire sur les besoins de l'Ontario en matière de bibliothèques ; Freda Waldon était chef de la délégation qui a présenté le mémoire à la Commission royale sur l'enseignement. Lorsque le comité exécutif de l'OLA avait besoin de « quelqu'un avec une vaste expérience et un jugement sûr pour tout ce qui touche la profession » afin d'assurer la présidence d'un nouveau comité créé pour décerner des prix à des bibliothécaires pour leur insigne contribution à la profession, il était unanime dans son choix : Freda Waldon.

For many years Dr. Waldon was a tireless worker in the campaign for the organization of a national association of librarians and the provision of a national library service. Known and respected across the country for what Dr. F. Dolores Donnelly recognized as her "professional experience, breadth of interest, an active social conscience, and a great capacity for single-minded devotion to an idea or a cause," she was the natural choice of her fellow librarians for the demanding position of first president of the Canadian Library Association. Elected at the organizational conference held in Hamilton in June 1946, Dr. Waldon and other members of the council began their work towards a National Library by inviting representatives from learned societies and other national organizations to join in planning a campaign that could not fail to produce an immediate response from the federal government. The final outcome of this meeting was a detailed and comprehensive brief, prepared by representatives of the Canadian Library Association, the Royal Society of Canada, the Canadian Political Science Association, the Canadian Historical Association, and the Social Science Research Council of Canada. For the first time the government was fully informed of the purpose of a national library, of its functions, and of its potential benefit to the people of Canada. Included also was the practical suggestion that the National

Pendant de nombreuses années, Freda Waldon a œuvré sans relâche dans une campagne en vue de l'organisation d'une association nationale des bibliothécaires et de la prestation d'un service de bibliothèque nationale. Reconnue et respectée partout au pays pour ce que F. Dolores Donnelly appelait son « expérience professionnelle, ses multiples intérêts, sa conscience sociale et sa grande capacité à se dévouer corps et âme pour une idée ou une cause », Freda Waldon a été le choix évident de ses collègues bibliothécaires lorsqu'il s'est agi d'élire le premier président de la Canadian Library Association. Freda Waldon, élue présidente lors de la conférence de fondation en juin 1946, et d'autres membres du conseil ont commencé leur travail pour obtenir la création d'une bibliothèque nationale et ont invité des représentants de sociétés savantes et d'autres organismes nationaux à se joindre à eux dans une campagne qui ne pouvait pas manquer de faire réagir le gouvernement fédéral. C'est ainsi que la Canadian Library Association, la Société royale du Canada, l'Association canadienne des sciences politiques, la Société historique du Canada et le Conseil canadien de recherche en sciences sociales ont préparé un mémoire très détaillé pour faire valoir leur cause. Pour la première fois, le gouvernement était informé des détails de l'objectif d'une bibliothèque nationale, de ses fonctions et de ses avantages possibles pour la population canadienne. On proposait d'offrir les services tant attendus quitte à construire l'immeuble à une date ultérieure, à la convenance du gouvernement. Même si elle a assuré la présidence du comité qui a présenté ce mémoire, Freda Waldon

Library start with much needed services, and that the building itself be delayed until a later time convenient for the government. Although chair of the committee which prepared the brief, Dr. Waldon took no credit for it, citing the contributions of the more than fifty persons consulted. It is unnecessary to repeat here the record of her major involvement in the eventually successful campaign; this has been amply covered in F. Dolores Donnelly's history, *The National Library of Canada*. In her own words she "walked on air for the first few days after the news came out," the news being the appointment of Dr. W. Kaye Lamb as dominion archivist with the special assignment of laying the foundations of the National Library, and a copy of the typed sheets of her bibliography was the first gift to the new institution. Her part in this long campaign, both in an official capacity and as a private citizen, was cited in May 1954, when she received an honorary Doctor of Laws degree from McMaster University in recognition of her contribution to Canadian librarianship. It was recognized also in two appointments to the National Library Advisory Council.

In addition to these services to her provincial and national associations, Dr. Waldon served for four years on the American Library Association Council and for three years as a director of the ALA Division of Public Libraries. She attended ALA midwinter meetings for a number of

n'en a tiré aucune gloire personnelle, citant plutôt l'apport de la cinquantaine de personnes consultées. Inutile de répéter ici le détail du rôle qu'elle a joué dans cette entreprise qui devait finalement être couronnée de succès : F. Dolores Donnelly en a parlé largement dans l'ouvrage historique *The National Library of Canada*. Selon les mots mêmes de Freda Waldon, elle « planait » les premiers jours après l'annonce de la nouvelle de la nomination de W. Kaye Lamb au poste d'archiviste fédéral qui, à ce titre, devait jeter les bases de la Bibliothèque nationale. Freda Waldon, elle, remettait le premier cadeau que la nouvelle institution a reçu : le manuscrit de sa bibliographie. Le rôle de Freda Waldon dans cette longue campagne, à titre officiel et à titre de simple citoyenne, a été cité en mai 1954 lorsqu'elle a reçu un doctorat honorifique en droit de l'Université McMaster en reconnaissance de sa contribution dans le domaine des bibliothèques du Canada. Deux nominations au Conseil consultatif de la Bibliothèque nationale sont aussi venues confirmer ce rôle.

En plus des services qu'elle a rendus à ses associations provinciales et nationales, Freda Waldon a siégé pendant quatre ans au conseil de l'American Library Association (ALA) et a tenu le poste de directrice pendant trois ans à la division des bibliothèques publiques de ce même organisme. Elle a assisté aux réunions d'hiver de l'ALA pendant

years and always returned with new ideas for services or programmes to be considered at the library.

In her tribute to Freda Waldon on the occasion of her retirement, Board chair Mrs. Mabel Taylor referred to her support of every cultural activity in the city. Ten years earlier a previous chair, Dr. Lawrence Cragg, had similarly acknowledged "the contributions she makes in so many ways to the cultural life of the city — and indeed of the province and dominion." Neither writer exaggerated. Dance, film, fine arts, history, international and public affairs, nature, recreation, and the theatre, all were of vital importance to this "Renaissance woman" as she was called during the bestowal of one of her several honours. During her early years in Hamilton there were few cultural amenities and she worked during her lifetime to make the city a place where "one could live the good life with beautiful things to see and interesting things to do and a great variety of human nature to observe and take delight in." Although one result of her involvement would be that the services offered by the library could become well known in all areas of the community, Dr. Waldon's personal interests were equally well served. As a founding member of the Head-of-the-Lake Historical Society she promoted research about the early days of the community to which she was so deeply committed. She was also a founding member of the Women's Committee of the Art Gallery of Hamilton. Her "more than

plusieurs années et en revenait toujours avec de nouvelles idées de services ou de programmes.

Dans son hommage à Freda Waldon à l'occasion de sa retraite, la présidente du conseil, Mme Mabel Taylor, a cité l'appui de Freda Waldon à toutes les activités culturelles de la ville. Dix ans auparavant, le président de l'époque, Lawrence Cragg, reconnaissait « l'apport généreux de Mme Waldon à la vie culturelle de la ville et aussi de la province et du pays ». Ces louanges n'avaient rien d'exagéré. Danse, cinéma, beaux-arts, histoire, affaires internationales et affaires publiques, nature, loisirs et théâtre, voilà ce qui constituait la palette de cette femme « des lumières », comme on l'a si bien décrite lors d'un des nombreux honneurs qu'on lui a rendus. Pendant la jeunesse de Freda Waldon, Hamilton n'offrait que très peu de divertissements culturels ; toute sa vie durant, elle s'est efforcée de faire de Hamilton une ville « où il fait bon vivre, où il y a de jolies choses à voir, des choses intéressantes à faire et toute une foule de créations et de réalisations à admirer ». Même si elle a consacré beaucoup de son énergie aux services offerts par la bibliothèque dans tous les secteurs de la communauté, Freda Waldon a su aussi s'occuper de ses intérêts personnels. À titre de membre fondateur de la société historique Head-of-the-Lake, elle s'est occupée de promouvoir une recherche sur les débuts de la localité à laquelle elle avait consacré déjà beaucoup. Elle était aussi membre fondateur du comité des femmes du musée des beaux-arts de Hamilton. Pendant plus de trente-cinq ans, elle a été membre de l'Association des Nations Unies et était une ardente partisane des idéaux et des aspirations des Nations Unies et de son

thirty-five years of active membership and staunch support of the ideals and aspirations of the United Nations and its antecedent, the League of Nations" were recognized by the Hamilton branch of the association in naming her the first recipient of their Award for Meritorious Service. Her concern for the preservation of Hamilton's architectural treasure made her a natural choice for membership on the Dundurn Castle Restoration Committee, and she was responsible for much of the historical research which preceded the restoration of the fine Regency mansion of Sir Allan MacNab, one-time premier of the United Canadas. After its completion she continued to serve as a member, and ultimately chair, of the Dundurn Castle Committee, a position held almost until her death.

Although space does not permit even a listing of the many organizations of which she was a valued member, mention must be made of the Hamilton Association for the Advancement of Literature, Science, and Art, of which she became the first woman secretary in 1941 and, in 1955, the first woman president in its ninety-eight year history. Her presidential address was a brilliant review, "The Massey Report: Three Years After." For many years too she enjoyed the Discussion Group of this association, at which members in turn researched and discussed literary and political issues of the day.

prédécesseur, la Ligue des Nations ; d'ailleurs, la section de Hamilton de l'Association reconnaissait le rôle important de Freda Waldon dans ce domaine et lui remettait le premier prix qu'elle ait accordé pour services éminents. Le souci de Freda Waldon de préserver le trésor architectural de Hamilton faisait d'elle une candidate de premier choix à la fonction de membre du comité de restauration du château Dundurn ; elle a d'ailleurs été chargée de la recherche historique qui a précédé la restauration du manoir de style régence ayant appartenu autrefois à Sir Allan Mac-Nab, ancien premier ministre du Canada-Uni. Après la fin des travaux de restauration, elle est restée membre du comité du château Dundurn, et en a assumé la présidence presque jusqu'à sa mort.

Si nous ne pouvons faire ici la liste de tous les organismes dont elle a été un membre fort apprécié, il faut mentionner l'association pour l'avancement de la littérature, des sciences et des arts de Hamilton ; en 1941, elle devenait la première femme à occuper le poste de secrétaire et, en 1955, la première femme à prendre la présidence de cette association qui avait été fondée quatre-vingt-dix-huit ans auparavant. Le discours qu'elle a prononcé lors de son élection comme présidente constituait une critique brillante du rapport Massey, « The Massey Report: Three Years After ». Pendant de nombreuses années, elle a participé avec enthousiasme au groupe de discussion de l'association, dont les membres étaient invités à faire une recherche sur les questions politiques et littéraires du jour, et à en discuter.

On the national scene, she served on the councils of the Canadian Association for Adult Education, the Canadian Institute on Public Affairs, and the Canadian Council for Reconstruction through UNESCO.

Freda Waldon was one of those fortunate persons whose career provides them with the opportunity to do those things they most enjoy. Being "one of those who find greater satisfaction in putting words together so they sound well than in almost anything else in life," she enjoyed public speaking and did it very well. She was in demand not only at library conferences but also by numerous other organizations. Naturally her topics frequently concerned library matters, but her other interests were also reflected. A travelogue on Greece in 1932 was a forerunner of several in later years when she had the opportunity to visit many distant countries. "The Status of Women," "Adult Education and Town Planning," "Hamilton as We Want It" all found receptive audiences, as did several accounts of the report of the Massey Commission. Trans-Canada broadcasts on the need for a national library and on the first hundred years of the Hamilton Association gave her a wider audience than the listeners to the local stations, where she spoke on various occasions about library affairs. She was also expert in the give-and-take of discussion and no long and embarrassing silence ever followed a request for questions and comments if Dr. Waldon was in the audience.

Sur la scène nationale, elle a été membre des conseils de l'association canadienne pour l'éducation permanente, de l'Institut canadien des affaires publiques et du Conseil canadien pour la reconstruction par l'UNESCO.

Freda Waldon est l'une de ces rares personnes à avoir eu le bonheur de voir sa carrière lui offrir l'occasion de faire ce qu'elle aimait le plus. Une de ses plus grandes satisfactions était l'harmonie et l'agencement des mots ; elle adorait l'art oratoire et y excellait. Elle était sollicitée non seulement par les organisateurs de conférences en bibliothéconomie, mais aussi par de nombreux autres genres d'organismes. Bien sûr, elle parlait fréquemment de sujets liés à la bibliothéconomie, mais elle avait bien d'autres sujets d'intérêt. Le récit de son voyage en Grèce en 1932 a été le premier d'une série qu'elle allait donner au fil des ans chaque fois qu'elle avait visité un pays lointain. « La situation des femmes », « Éducation permanente et planification urbaine », « Hamilton, une ville à construire à notre image » sont autant de conférences qui ont remporté un très grand succès, ainsi que de nombreux exposés sur le rapport de la Commission Massey. Elle a participé à des émissions radiophoniques retransmises partout au pays sur la nécessité d'établir une bibliothèque nationale et sur les cent premières années d'existence de l'association de Hamilton, en plus des nombreuses émissions locales où elle parlait de questions relatives aux bibliothèques. Vive et alerte, elle saisissait l'occasion de faire ses remarques ou d'apporter des éclaircissements chaque fois qu'on la lui offrait.

She was equally effective in print. Although she had a story published in *Saturday Night* and won both an award for a short story in her teens and a *Canadian Forum* competition for a "short, short" vacation story in 1937, her real gift lay in the clear exposition of the principles, services, and ideas in which she believed. She was a frequent contributor to professional journals and other periodicals, and wrote articles on the history of the Hamilton Public Library for *The Hamilton Centennial, 1846–1946* and on several occasions for the *Hamilton Spectator*. She contributed the entry on Alexander Henry (the elder) to the *Encyclopedia Canadiana* and the article on Archibald Macallum to Volume X of the *Dictionary of Canadian Biography*. A larger work was *The History of the First Hundred Years of the Hamilton Association, 1857–1957*.

It is in her files of correspondence that those who worked closely with Freda Waldon can still hear her voice. Detailed replies of practical advice were sent to fellow librarians who needed information about such items as book cards or buildings, staff training, or supplies of furniture. Residents of small communities received a regretful refusal of direct mail service, an explanation of inter-library loans, and an exposition of the great need for and value of a provincial library service; indeed the whole long story of the campaign for a provincial library, in which she played so important a role, can be gleaned from her correspondence of the period. Courteous pressure for the

Freda Waldon avait aussi une très belle plume. Même si elle a vu un de ses écrits publié dans *Saturday Night* et qu'elle a reçu un prix pour une nouvelle alors qu'elle était adolescente et un prix du *Canadian Forum* pour un « très, très bref » récit de vacances en 1937, c'était surtout dans l'exposé des principes, des services et des idées qui lui tenaient à coeur qu'elle excellait. Elle collaborait fréquemment à des revues spécialisées et à d'autres périodiques ; elle a rédigé des articles sur l'histoire de la bibliothèque publique de Hamilton pour le *Hamilton Centennial 1846–1946* ainsi que des articles divers pour le *Hamilton Spectator*. Elle a rédigé l'article sur Alexander Henry L'Ancien dans l'édition revue et corrigée de l'*Encyclopedia Canadiana* et l'article sur Archibald Macallum dans le volume X du *Dictionnaire biographique du Canada*. Mentionnons aussi un travail plus volumineux : *The History of The First Hundred Years of the Hamilton Association, 1857–1957*.

C'est dans la correspondance de Freda Waldon que ses collaborateurs peuvent toujours entendre sa voix. Elle envoyait à ses collègues bibliothécaires des réponses détaillées et des conseils pratiques sur notamment les cartes de livre, les immeubles, la formation du personnel ou même l'ameublement. C'est à regret que Freda Waldon a dû refuser aux citoyens des petites localités un service de prêt par la poste : dans une lettre à leur intention, elle leur explique le service de prêt inter-bibliothèques et leur expose la valeur d'une bibliothèque provinciale. En fait, la longue croisade en vue de la création d'une bibliothèque provinciale, dans laquelle elle a joué un rôle de premier plan, peut être retracée dans sa correspondance de l'époque. Dans une autre lettre, elle presse, avec beaucoup

full payment of provincial grants was included in a grateful acknowledgement to the minister of education of the new regulations which increased them but did not provide full funding. Congratulatory letters were sent for new appointments or new publications; warm encouragement for a young author may be contrasted with a firm rebuke to an established one who depicted librarians as drab and uninspired. A long essay on public libraries and their place in adult education went to the director of the Department of Education after the appointment of an Adult Education Board consisting only of university members! Some insight into the breadth of her interests can be gained by a glance through her letters to the editor of various newspapers and periodicals over the years. An especially fine issue of the *Canadian Historical Review* is commended; the *Library Journal*'s reference to the American Library Association as the world's first library association is courteously refuted with a description of the Association of Mechanics Institutes of Ontario; the destruction of wild flowers, the loss of green space, the demolition of historic buildings, are all deplored. The *Saturday Review* receives a suggestion about its Doublecrostics competition and *Saturday Night* an appreciation of Robertson Davies. Whatever the topic, the writer's point of view is expressed forthrightly and without unnecessary length. Equally revealing are the

de tact, le ministre de l'Éducation de verser la totalité des subventions provinciales tout en le remerciant pour la mise en place du nouveau règlement prévoyant l'augmentation de ces subventions – sans assurer le financement intégral de la bibliothèque. Elle a envoyé des lettres de félicitations à l'occasion de nominations et de la parution de nouvelles publications. Elle savait encourager les jeunes auteurs et, en même temps, faire des remontrances aux auteurs connus qui disaient des bibliothécaires qu'ils étaient ennuyants et manquaient d'imagination. Freda Waldon a envoyé une longue dissertation sur les bibliothèques publiques et sur leur rôle dans l'éducation permanente au directeur du ministère de l'Éducation après la nomination d'une commission sur l'éducation aux adultes composée seulement d'universitaires! C'est à ses lettres aux rédacteurs en chef de diverses publications qu'on peut constater la variété de ses intérêts. Elle louange un numéro particulièrement réussi de la *Canadian Historical Review* ou réfute poliment l'assertion du *Library Journal* selon laquelle l'American Library Association est la première association des bibliothèques dans le monde, et décrit l'Association of Mechanics Institutes of Ontario. Elle déplore par ailleurs la destruction de la flore, la perte d'espaces verts et la démolition d'édifices historiques. Freda Waldon a envoyé ses suggestions sur le concours Doublecrostics à la *Saturday Review* et une appréciation de Robertson Davies à la *Saturday Night*. Quel que fût le sujet de son écrit, Freda Waldon savait être directe et concise. Les « bulletins annuels » du temps des Fêtes qu'elle a envoyés à son large cercle d'amis pendant plus de quinze

annual Christmas reports sent out to her wide circle of friends for over fifteen years. Mixed in with accounts of major professional events are those of her major pleasures: travel with one or more close friends and/or her sister, Mabel Thompson; visits with or from good friends, of whom she had so wide a circle; Nice Long Walks in the Nice Fresh Air; art lessons; the Couchiching Conference; and the recurring theme of visits to the theatre.

This last was among her greatest pleasures, both as a participant and a spectator. According to a contemporary review of her first recorded vehicle, a one-act play during her collegiate years, she possessed "real histrionic ability" and evoked applause from the audience whenever she appeared on stage. In Toronto she acted with the University College Alumnae Dramatic Club, and, on her return to Hamilton, won praise as the director of the Blue Triangle Players in a group of three one-act plays. As a student in London she made time, not only to attend the theatre regularly but also to send home to a local newspaper, *The Herald*, her "London Letters" which included criticism and appreciation of current productions. Some of her happiest memories were of her acting days with the Attic Theatre Club, which disbanded in the early days of World War II. Although she did not act again, and her ballet lessons were strictly for exercise, she continued to attend performances wherever they were available. An ardent supporter of a national theatre,

ans sont aussi très révélateurs. Elle y décrivait non seulement ses activités professionnelles, mais aussi ses passe-temps les plus chers : voyages avec un ou deux de ses amis intimes ou avec sa soeur, Mabel Thompson ; visites, promenades, leçons d'art ; la conférence Couchiching et, bien sûr, ses nombreuses sorties au théâtre.

Le théâtre était l'un de ses plus grands plaisirs, aussi bien comme actrice que comme spectatrice. Selon une critique parue à l'occasion de ses débuts sur les planches dans une pièce en un acte alors qu'elle fréquentait le collège, Freda Waldon possédait « un véritable talent de comédienne » et soulevait les applaudissements de la foule chaque fois qu'elle apparaissait sur la scène. À Toronto, elle a joué avec le club d'art dramatique des anciennes du collège universitaire et, à son retour à Hamilton, a reçu des éloges pour sa mise en scène de trois pièces en un acte des Blue Triangle Players. Lorsqu'elle étudiait à London, elle prenait le temps non seulement d'aller au théâtre régulièrement, mais aussi d'envoyer au journal local, *The Herald*, ses « Lettres de London », dans lesquelles elle faisait la critique des productions de l'heure. Elle gardait un souvenir impérissable de sa participation au groupe d'art dramatique Attic Theatre Club, qui s'est dispersé au début de la Deuxième guerre mondiale. Bien qu'elle ne soit plus remontée sur les planches par la suite et qu'elle ne prît des cours de ballet que pour le bénéfice de l'exercice, elle a continué à fréquenter le théâtre aussi souvent qu'elle le pouvait. Ardente partisane

she was writing to promote this cause in *The Canadian Student* thirty years before the Stratford Festival gave aspiring Canadian actors an opportunity to remain at home. The November 1944 issue of *Saturday Night* included another plea for a national theatre, not a building but a Canadian equivalent of Britain's Council for the Encouragement of Music and the Arts, to take responsibility for ensuring that Canadian dramatists would have an opportunity to try out their talents on a Canadian stage and that gifted Canadian actors would not have to leave the country to become professional. Similarly, a warmly congratulatory letter to Vida Peene on her appointment to The Canada Council made a case, among other suggestions, for the encouragement of professional touring companies by guaranteeing travelling expenses for those which had already proved themselves in their own communities. She likened this to a subsidy to overcome Canada's distances, just as had been done for canals, freight rates, and the CBC.

Reading, too, was a delight. Although books were always important in her home, it was not until her grandfather's library card gave her access to the public library that she had enough to read. Since there was no real provision for children or young people it is interesting to examine a list of almost five hundred books, recorded over several years of her youth, and to try to identify which titles reflect her own taste and which were read only for lack of something

de la création d'un théâtre national, Freda Waldon publiait des articles pour promouvoir cette cause dans *The Canadian Student* trente ans avant que le Festival de Stratford ne donne aux jeunes comédiens canadiens la possibilité de se produire au pays. Le numéro de novembre 1944 de *Saturday Night* contenait un autre appel pour la création d'un théâtre national – non pas la construction d'un immeuble, mais l'établissement de l'équivalent canadien du Conseil britannique pour la musique et les arts. L'organisme pourrait s'assurer que les pièces de dramaturges canadiens puissent être montées au pays et que les acteurs doués n'aient pas à s'exiler pour devenir professionnels. Dans une lettre de félicitations adressée à Vida Peene pour sa nomination au Conseil des arts du Canada, Freda Waldon proposait, entre autres, de favoriser la création de troupes itinérantes en défrayant les déplacements des troupes professionnelles bien établies. Pour elle, ce genre d'aide était assimilable aux subventions accordées pour faciliter les communications dans ce vaste pays : canaux, tarifs spéciaux pour le transport de marchandises et la Société Radio-Canada.

Freda Waldon aimait la lecture passionnément. Bien que cette activité ait toujours été encouragée à la maison, ce n'est vraiment que lorsqu'elle a pu fréquenter la bibliothèque publique grâce à la carte de son grand-père qu'elle a pu enfin lire à satiété. Comme il n'y avait pas grand-chose pour les jeunes à cette époque, il serait intéressant d'examiner les quelque cinq cents titres qu'elle a empruntés au fil de ses années de jeunesse et d'essayer de déterminer lesquels elle a lus parce qu'elle en avait vraiment envie et lesquels elle a lus faute de mieux.

more suitable. Since her adult reading reflected her other activities it was widely diversified, and books on theatre, art, and the ballet vied for her time along with biography, history, new Canadian titles, and well-written fiction reflecting the human experience.

Freda Waldon lived during an exciting period of Canadian librarianship, in the course of which she saw a profession "created by unselfseeking people out of janitorial and clerical jobs." It is a sad loss to the literature of that profession that she did not accept Jack McClelland's serious suggestion that she should write her memoirs as a Canadian librarian to include her professional career, her views on librarianship, its future development, and the standards and principles needed. There is no hint among her papers that she gave any consideration to this idea, either in 1966 or in the year preceding her death when it was again proposed. What a treasure house of information, inspiration, and wisdom we should have had!

Kathleen R. Mathews
Co-ordinator, Special Collections
Hamilton Public Library
Hamilton, Ontario
June 1985

Les lectures de Freda Waldon une fois adulte reflétaient ses autres intérêts et étaient diversifiées : théâtre, arts, ballet, biographies, histoire, nouveaux titres canadiens et romans bien écrits portant sur l'expérience humaine.

Freda Waldon a vécu à une époque stimulante de la bibliothéconomie au Canada. Elle a vu naître une profession « créée par des personnes dévouées et généreuses formées sur le tas ». La profession a perdu beaucoup quand Freda Waldon a refusé l'offre de Jack McClelland de rédiger ses mémoires et d'écrire sur sa vie professionnelle, ses vues sur la profession, son évolution, les normes et principes requis. Rien n'indique dans ses papiers qu'elle ait même songé à cette idée, ni en 1966, ni l'année qui a précédé sa mort, année où on lui a renouvelé la proposition. De quel puits de renseignements, d'inspiration et de sagesse nous voilà désormais privés !

Kathleen R. Mathews
Coordonnatrice, Collections spéciales
Bibliothèque publique de Hamilton
Hamilton (Ontario)
juin 1985

The basis of this project is an unpublished typescript of detailed bibliographical notes, compiled by Dr. Freda Farrell Waldon. Dr. Waldon was the chief librarian of Hamilton Public Library from 1940 to 1963 but, as Kathleen Mathews has told us so well in her "Biographical Introduction," she was active all her busy life in a variety of important local and national affairs and worthy causes, and had established a sound reputation as a scholar and a library administrator. Over a period of many years, particularly during the 1930s and 1940s, Dr. Waldon had also been working as time permitted on a "full-dress" bibliography of Canadiana with British imprint published up to 1763 (in *The Canadian Who's Who* volumes for the 1960s and early 1970s it is described as a "Bibliography of Canadiana to 1763 published in Great Britain"). Nothing quite like it had ever been attempted before. The idea of displaying bibliographically how the Old World reacted in print to the discoveries and events in the New World preceded publication of the first volume of the John Carter Brown Library's *European Americana* by almost fifty years. Dr. Waldon was unstinting in her attention to detail: she indicated line-endings, for

Le présent ouvrage a été rédigé à partir du tapuscrit non publié des notes bibliographiques détaillées compilées par Freda Farrell Waldon. Mme Waldon a été bibliothécaire en chef à la bibliothèque publique de Hamilton de 1940 à 1963. Comme Mme Kathleen Mathews l'écrit si bien dans sa notice biographique, Freda Waldon a appuyé activement toute sa vie durant une foule de causes importantes et nobles –tant à l'échelle nationale que locale – et s'est acquis une réputation solide sur les plans académique et professionnel. Pendant de nombreuses années –plus particulièrement dans les décennies 1930 et 1940 – Freda Waldon a travaillé, quand le temps le lui permettait, à une bibliographie complète des ouvrages publiés en Grande-Bretagne jusqu'en 1763 et qui portaient sur des sujets canadiens. Dans le *Canadian Who's Who* des années 1960 et du début des années 1970, on dit qu'il s'agit d'une « Bibliographie des documents sur le Canada, son histoire publiés en Grande-Bretagne jusqu'en 1763 ». Rien de semblable n'avait été entrepris auparavant. L'idée de faire une bibliographie des ouvrages portant sur la façon dont l'Ancien Monde voyait les découvertes et l'histoire du Nouveau Monde a précédé de cinquante ans environ la publication du premier volume de la série *European Americana* de la bibliothèque John Carter Brown. Freda Waldon était très méticuleuse : elle indiquait, par exemple, les

example, and sought to represent a "type facsimile" form of typescript of the title-pages, and often she provided collations by signatures. On her visits to Canadian, American, and British libraries, she always found time for work on her bibliography and, as Ms. Mathews indicates, Dr. Waldon's correspondence in connection with this work was extensive; but the years passed without its completion, for so massive an undertaking must have required countless hours of painstaking endeavour. She achieved the impressive total of about 600 titles within her established parameters, and the record shows that she tried hard to attract a publisher; but I believe that during the last years of her life the task of bringing the vast body of material she had gathered into publishable order was beyond her will, for it lay fallow for several years before her death in 1973.

It was quite by accident that I became aware of Dr. Waldon's gigantic labours: an article by Dr. W. Kaye Lamb ("Seventy-Five Years of Canadian Bibliography," in the Royal Society of Canada's *Transactions* 3rd ser. 51 [June 1957]: Sec. 2, p. 10) describes the work briefly, saying it was "the first gift received by the National Library," and that, though some work remained to be done, "it should be ready for printing before too long." That was in 1957! Upon reading Dr. Lamb's reference, I was sufficiently motivated to make inquires about the location and status

fins de ligne et essayait de réaliser un « fac-similé » à la machine à écrire des pages de titre. Souvent, elle fournissait les collations par signatures. Si elle avait l'occasion de visiter une bibliothèque canadienne, américaine ou britannique, elle trouvait toujours le temps de travailler à sa bibliographie et, comme l'indique Mme Mathews, sa correspondance à ce sujet est volumineuse. Pendant des années, le travail est resté en plan ; l'entreprise était colossale et exigeait un nombre incalculable d'heures de travail ardu. Freda Waldon a recueilli la somme impressionnante de 600 titres suivant les paramètres qu'elle s'était fixés. Elle a bien essayé d'attirer les éditeurs, en vain. Je crois, en fait, qu'au cours des dernières années de sa vie, elle s'est rendue compte qu'organiser ce matériel pour qu'il soit publiable était une tâche qui allait bien au-delà de ce qu'elle voulait faire; le projet resta en friche de nombreuses années et ce, jusqu'à sa mort en 1973.

C'est le hasard qui m'a dirigé vers l'œuvre de Freda Waldon. W. Kaye Lamb, le premier directeur général de la Bibliothèque nationale, dans son article « Soixante-quinze ans de bibliographie au Canada », paru dans *Transactions* de la Société royale du Canada, 3e série 51, juin 1957, Section 2, p. 10, décrivait brièvement la bibliographie et en parlait comme du « premier don fait à la Bibliothèque nationale » ; s'il restait un peu de travail à faire, « la bibliographie pourrait néanmoins être publiée sous peu ». C'était en 1957 ! L'article de W. Kaye Lamb avait piqué ma curiosité ; j'ai donc fait quelques recherches pour récupérer le tapuscrit. Moins mes

of the typescript. My curiosity deepened as difficulties mounted, and not the least of these was the news that the National Library's copy of the typescript had been misplaced (subsequently and most fortunately it was recovered). I tried to reach Dr. Waldon directly, only to receive another setback with the sad news that she had but recently died. Eventually I was able to make contact with Dr. Waldon's elderly sister, Mabel Thompson, in Hamilton. I asked her if she would possibly be able to examine Dr. Waldon's papers and effects for anything that might be the elusive bibliography. Dr. Waldon's sister was herself unwell, and most of our exchanges were conducted through the good offices of my friend, the gentle but persistent Katherine Greenfield, then special collections librarian at Hamilton Public Library. It was only after the passage of some months, and the receipt of several gloomy communications, that a jubilant letter arrived from Ms. Greenfield announcing Ms. Thompson's success. I arranged to acquire a photocopy of what turned out to be a carbon typescript of the bibliography. When the National Library's copy was recovered a few years later I obtained a facsimile, and found that it differed from the typescript from the Waldon papers. I suspect this is evidence that Dr. Waldon continued to work on her typescript after 1950, when she gave her other copy to the National Library.

démarches étaient fructueuses, plus ma curiosité augmentait ; tout d'abord, l'exemplaire de la Bibliothèque nationale avait été égaré (il était heureusement retrouvé quelques années plus tard). Ensuite, j'ai essayé de rejoindre Freda Waldon directement et je devais essuyer un autre revers : Freda Waldon venait de mourir. J'ai pu enfin communiquer avec la soeur aînée de Freda Waldon, Mme Mabel Thompson, à Hamilton. Je lui ai demandé d'examiner les documents de sa soeur dans l'espoir de trouver la fameuse bibliographie. La soeur de Freda Waldon ne se portait pas très bien elle-même et la plupart de nos échanges ont été relayés par mon amie Katherine Greenfield, bibliothécaire chargée des collections spéciales à la bibliothèque publique de Hamilton. Ce n'est qu'après des mois d'efforts soutenus mais courtois auprès de Mme Thompson et la réception de plusieurs notes décourageantes que Mme Greenfield m'annonçait le succès de Mme Thompson. J'ai réussi alors à tirer une photocopie de la copie au carbone du tapuscrit. Lorsque l'exemplaire de la Bibliothèque nationale a enfin été retrouvé quelques années plus tard, j'en ai fait tirer un fac-similé et j'ai constaté que cet exemplaire différait du tapuscrit découvert par Mabel Thompson. Il n'est donc pas impossible que Freda Waldon ait continué à travailler au tapuscrit après 1950, année où elle a fait don de l'autre exemplaire à la Bibliothèque nationale.

My thought then, as now, was that the bibliography should be published as a memorial to the skilled and patient endeavours of Dr. Waldon. In this, I obtained the blessing of Ms. Thompson (who, at my suggestion, provided a brief note to launch the project just before she too died), and the support of Dr. W.M. Thompson in Vancouver, Mabel Thompson's brother-in-law. Through the kind arrangement of Judith McAnanama, the present chief librarian of Hamilton Public Library, Kathleen Mathews prepared the "Biographical Introduction" to enhance the memorial aspect of the work. Dr. W. Kaye Lamb and Katherine Greenfield, with whom I have been in correspondence over the years, have both given me constant encouragement to prepare the typescript for the press. Dr. Lamb, whose article provided the initial information and who personally received the gift of Dr. Waldon's typescript, has now crowned the work by generously composing the foreword. In more affluent years, the former national librarian, Dr. Guy Sylvestre, agreed to publish the completed volume. I was most appreciative. Now, I am particularly grateful to Dr. Marianne Scott, the present national librarian, for continuing this support in such difficult times. Through both administrations I have enjoyed the co-operation of Flora Patterson, director of the Public Services Branch of the National Library, and I thank her for her vital efforts as liaison officer with the project.

Je croyais alors – et je crois encore aujourd'hui – que la bibliographie devrait être publiée en hommage à la mémoire de Freda Waldon pour sa précieuse contribution. Cette entreprise obtenait la bénédiction de Mme Thompson qui, à ma demande, a accepté de rédiger une note pour lancer le projet, juste un peu avant de mourir. Nous avons aussi obtenu l'appui de W.M. Thompson, beau-frère de Mabel Thompson, de Vancouver. Grâce aux bons offices de Judith McAnanama, bibliothécaire en chef actuelle à la bibliothèque publique de Hamilton, Mme Kathleen Mathews a préparé la notice biographique pour mettre en valeur le fait qu'il s'agit d'une publication à la mémoire de Freda Waldon. W. Kaye Lamb et Katherine Greenfield, avec qui je corresponds depuis des années, m'ont aidé, par leurs encouragements, à préparer le tapuscrit pour la publication. W. Kaye Lamb, qui, par son article, nous a aiguillé et qui a personnellement reçu le don du tapuscrit de Freda Waldon, nous a fait l'honneur de rédiger l'avant-propos. À une époque de vaches grasses, l'ancien directeur général de la Bibliothèque nationale, M. Guy Sylvestre, acceptait de publier le volume une fois achevé. Nous lui en savons gré. Aujourd'hui, nous sommes particulièrement heureux que l'actuelle directrice générale de la Bibliothèque nationale du Canada, Mme Marianne Scott, nous prête toujours son concours malgré les temps difficiles. Sous les deux directeurs, nous avons eu la joie de collaborer avec Mme Flora Patterson, directrice des Services au public de la Bibliothèque nationale, et nous la remercions pour le rôle essentiel qu'elle a joué comme agente de liaison pour ce projet.

The typescript from the Waldon family has been in my possession for over a decade now — since 1973. During the first years, I tried to persuade a dozen different bibliographically minded persons to undertake the editing or at least the preliminary checking of the work. I was fully engaged on other projects, but I stood ready to advise and assist so far as I was able. For each of these busy people (they are gratefully identified below) sorting out the profusion of detail and scholarly notes, and identifying the highly abbreviated sources, proved to be an implacable deterrent, only aggravated when the work had to bear someone else's name. At this impasse, about five years later, I came to the desperate realization that, if "Waldon" were ever to reach publication, a radical simplification of the descriptions would be necessary. The difficulty has been I think that Dr. Waldon, in an analytic spirit which is more at home in the nineteenth than the twentieth century, was *too* thorough, her descriptions too extensive, to attract publication funds easily in the postwar era. I believe that nowadays, when a scholar requires such details as relate to line-endings, signature anomalies, and title-page typography, he seeks access to photocopies, or better still in this age of rapid transit, to a personal examination of the actual work. The *Short-Title Catalogue*, distinguishing editions and issues but with minimal descriptive information, is

Nous avons en main le tapuscrit de la famille Waldon depuis plus de dix ans maintenant (1973). Au début, nous avons essayé de convaincre une douzaine de personnes s'intéressant à la bibliographie d'entreprendre la révision ou, au moins, la vérification préliminaire du tapuscrit. Nous étions occupé à d'autres projets, mais étions prêt à donner conseils et avis dans la mesure où nous pouvions le faire. Toutes ces personnes occupées (dont nous reconnaissons la contribution plus loin) se trouvaient placées devant une tâche insurmontable : mettre de l'ordre dans cette profusion de détails et de notes savantes, et identifier les sources abrégées. En plus de ces difficultés d'ordre technique, le travail qu'elles devaient y mettre ne serait pas reconnu et c'est un nom autre que le leur qui apparaîtrait dans la publication. Devant, cinq ans plus tard, faire face à cette impasse, il nous a fallu nous rendre à l'évidence : si la bibliographie de Freda Waldon devait être publiée, il faudrait simplifier radicalement les descriptions qu'elle contient. Selon nous, la capacité d'analyse de Freda Waldon avait davantage à voir avec le XIXe siècle qu'avec le XXe siècle; sa recherche était trop détaillée, ses descriptions étaient trop poussées pour intéresser les éditeurs d'après-guerre. Aujourd'hui, lorsqu'un chercheur a besoin de renseignements sur des détails comme les fins de ligne, les signatures divergentes, la typographie de la page de titre, il consulte des photocopies ou, mieux encore, en cette époque de transport rapide, il se rend sur les lieux examiner l'original. Le *Short-Title Catalogue*, qui distingue éditions et numéros grâce à une information minimale, est sans doute l'un

still one of the most useful bibliographical tools for the period it covers. In Canada, the same can be said of R.E. Watters's *A Checklist of Canadian Literature and Background Materials, 1628–1960* and Bruce Peel's *A Bibliography of the Prairie Provinces to 1953.* Emboldened by these thoughts, I drew up a prescription which would eliminate much of the scholarly apparatus in Dr. Waldon's typescript, but yet preserve or introduce notes on editions, translations, and other relationships, and on the Canadian connection, while distinguishing all new information.

I will be the first to admit that some valuable information will be lost from a version that has been edited in this way, though not lost entirely in the present case, for the typescript is still available at the National Library. Even so, some losses are only partial: where Dr. Waldon's notes are incomplete, for example, or where the identification of the sources of her titles and descriptions are given with tantalizing brevity (see the list following "Abbreviations Used," under "Sources Cited," below), or in the frequent cases where locations of the copies she saw are implied rather than specified (if not omitted altogether). To have this bibliography in people's hands in the forseeable future, some drastic editorial compromises had to be made. The degressive principle applies: better an incomplete but usable work than a perfect one that is beyond reach. So, after discussing the editorial plan with colleagues (and persuading one of them to assist in the

des outils bibliographiques les plus utiles pour la période sur laquelle il porte. On peut en dire de même du *Checklist of Canadian Literature and Background Materials, 1628–1960* de R.E. Watters et de la *Bibliography of the Prairie Provinces to 1953* de Bruce Peel. Encouragé par cette perspective, nous avons élaboré une prescription qui éliminerait la plupart des accessoires savants du tapuscrit de Freda Waldon, mais qui préserverait ou présenterait les notes sur les éditions, les traductions et autres relations, et sur le lien avec le Canada, tout en distinguant tout nouveau renseignement.

Nous admettons d'entrée de jeu que nous perdrions ainsi quelques renseignements précieux, quoiqu'ils ne soient pas vraiment perdus puisque le tapuscrit existe toujours à la Bibliothèque nationale. D'ailleurs, certaines des « pertes » ne le sont pas vraiment : dans certains cas, les notes de Freda Waldon étaient de toute façon incomplètes ; parfois, les sources des titres et des descriptions étaient trop brèves (se reporter à la liste suivant la rubrique Abréviations utilisées sous Sources citées, plus bas) ; il arrivait encore que l'emplacement des divers exemplaires consultés était cité implicitement plutôt qu'explicitement, quand il n'était pas carrément omis. Pour que la bibliographie soit publiée, il fallait faire des révisions importantes. La loi du compromis devait s'appliquer : mieux valait un ouvrage imparfait et utilisable qu'un ouvrage parfait et hors de portée. Donc, après avoir discuté d'un plan de révision avec des collègues – et en avoir convaincu un de collaborer au projet – nous avons obtenu une modeste subvention de Conseil canadien de recherche en sciences humaines et avons

project), I gained a small grant from SSHRCC and picked up the threads of the project again, but now with fewer other distractions.

remis le travail sur le métier et, cette fois-ci, avec moins de distractions.

Methodology and Scope of the Book

Méthodologie et portée

For over six years, such leisure as I could command has been devoted, with the assistance of Stewart Renfrew, to the revision of what we have come to refer to simply as "Waldon." It must be understood first of all that the editing process here is *not* based on the personal examination of the actual works themselves, though occasionally it has been necessary to examine original titles when problems of reconciling Waldon with NUC or BLC entries have arisen. The editing has been founded on the checking of entries against standard bibliographies, which are always identified (there may be half a dozen entries where Waldon titles could not be verified, and this has been stated). Dr. Waldon has, clearly in most cases, already examined actual copies — thus obeying the first rule of bibliography. The project's aim has been for the bibliographical editing of the original entries, for undertaking supporting research where necessary, and for the revision (and incidental enlargement) of the typescript, in preparation for the press. Yet, if simplification were the watchword, this plan of taking information at second hand has not been without

Pendant six ans, nous avons consacré nos temps libres à la révision, en collaboration avec Stewart Renfrew, de ce que nous appellerons désormais le « Waldon ». Signalons d'abord que le processus de révision n'est pas fondé sur un examen des ouvrages mêmes, bien que nous ayons dû, à l'occasion, examiner les titres originaux lorsque les entrées du Waldon ne correspondaient pas aux notices du NUC ou du BLC. Pour la révision, nous avons vérifié chaque notice du Waldon par rapport aux bibliographies standard, qui sont toujours identifiées – il y a une demi-douzaine de notices du Waldon dont les titres n'ont pu être vérifiés (ceux-là sont identifiés comme tels). Dans la plupart des cas, Freda Waldon avait examiné les exemplaires originaux, respectant ainsi la première règle bibliographique. Nous poursuivions un triple objectif par ce travail : la révision bibliographique des notices originales, la recherche quand elle s'imposait et la révision (et l'augmentation) du tapuscrit en vue de la publication. Si simplifier devenait notre mot d'ordre, le travail n'en comportait pas moins des difficultés inévitables. C'est ainsi que, d'ordinaire, le NUC n'inscrit, pour prénom de l'éditeur, que l'initiale ; ici, nous nous sommes permis de rajouter, entre crochets, le reste du prénom – utilisant le *Dictionary* de Plomer – pour marquer qu'il s'agit bien

unavoidable difficulties. For example, publishers' forenames are customarily represented by initials in NUC entries, but I have expanded these (usually by reference to Plomer's *Dictionary*), placing the expanded part in square brackets to indicate matter added; yet the full forenames may actually have been present on the title-page, so that the brackets give a false indication. Again, following the principles enunciated by Ronald B. McKerrow in *An Introduction to Bibliography for Literary Students* (Oxford, 1965: p. 154, and Appendix 3), in transcribing Waldon or NUC entries I have not rendered a medial capital *V* into a lower-case *v*, but into a *u*; yet, since I have not usually seen the original title-page, I cannot know whether a letter so rendered in NUC, or in Waldon titles published after about 1700 (when she stopped using type-facsimile transcription) *was* all in capitals (*e.g.* "DIUIDED" into "Divided," not "Diuided"). The capital *I* for both *I* and *J*, and the lowercase *i* for *i* and *j*, have been preserved as in the original.

During the process of revising and editing, many titles and editions apparently unknown to Dr. Waldon have been encountered and added (indicated by an asterisk preceding the entry), although augmentation has not been a primary objective. No systematic search for new titles has been made, though quite certainly a good many relevant titles had not yet been discovered by Dr. Waldon at the time her work on the bibliography ceased. It should be borne in mind

d'un ajout par rapport au Waldon original ; or, il se peut que le prénom en toutes lettres ait en fait figuré sur la page de titre de l'ouvrage. Dans ce cas, les crochets nous donnent une fausse indication. Suivant les principes énoncés par Ronald B. McKerrow dans *An Introduction to Bibliography for Literary Students* (Oxford, 1965, p. 154 et Annexe 3), pour la transcription des notices du Waldon ou du NUC, nous avons rendu la majuscule médiale *V* non par la minuscule *v*, mais par un *u*. Cependant, comme nous n'avons pu, dans la plupart des cas, consulter la page de titre de l'original, il nous est impossible de savoir si une lettre ainsi transcrite dans le NUC, ou dans les titres du Waldon publiés après 1700 (notices pour lesquelles elle n'utilisait plus la technique du fac-similé) *était* ou non écrite en majuscules (p.ex., DIUIDED –Divided et non Diuided). Nous avons conservé la majuscule *I* pour le *I* et le *J* et la minuscule *i* pour le *i* et le *j*, telles qu'elles figurent dans l'original.

Au cours du processus de révision, nous avons pris connaissance de titres et d'éditions que ne connaissait vraisemblablement pas Freda Waldon ; nous les avons ajoutés, bien que notre objectif premier n'ait pas été d'augmenter le nombre des notices et avons dans ces cas-là utilisé l'astérisque. Nous n'avons fait aucune recherche systématique de nouveaux titres, même si un bon nombre de titres intéressants n'avaient pu être relevés par Freda Waldon lorsqu'elle a mis un terme à ses travaux. Il faut se rappeler que Freda Waldon n'avait pas les moyens et les

that Dr. Waldon worked under many handicaps. There was a great paucity of those bibliographies and research tools relating to Canada which we take for granted today, and few Canadian bibliographers from whom to seek information. There was no all-embracing *National Union Catalog*, nor anything comparable to the present *British Library Catalogue*. Moreover, Dr. Waldon worked in a library that possessed few of the titles that interested her, and travel was arduous and expensive, with few opportunities for grants-in-aid. Electronic communication, photo-copying, and much of today's technical equipment useful to bibliographers were unknown. In light of these difficulties, Dr. Waldon's accomplishment is even more remarkable! The task of compiling a record of *all* British imprints of Canadian interest, however, if so definitive a work is even possible, must be left to others.

Some titles in Waldon have been deliberately excluded by the editor, however. One such excluded category is manuscripts, a form of text quite incongruous in a bibliography describing publications and imprints. Similarly, *parts* of works seem inappropriate, so I have arbitrarily excluded articles from journals, extracts, and other parts of larger works not published separately, as well as periodicals, such as the *London Magazine*. Other Waldon entries I have included reluctantly; examples are ballads and maps, and assuredly there are *very* many of the latter which Waldon might eventually have found.

outils dont nous disposons aujourd'hui : les bibliographies et les outils de recherche portant sur le Canada tels que nous les connaissons de nos jours étaient plutôt rares, comme, d'ailleurs, le nombre de bibliographes auprès desquels demander conseils et avis. Il n'existait ni *National Union Catalog* ni *British Library Catalogue*. De plus, Freda Waldon travaillait dans une bibliothèque où les titres qui l'intéressaient n'étaient pas très nombreux. Les déplacements étaient difficiles et coûtaient cher, et étaient rarement subventionnés, même en partie. Les outils techniques dont se servent les bibliographes de nos jours – communications électroniques, photocopie – n'existaient pas encore. Compte tenu de toutes ces embûches, le travail de Freda Waldon est donc d'autant plus remarquable. Quoi qu'il en soit, la compilation de *tous* les titres publiés en Grande-Bretagne sur un sujet canadien – si cela est possible – est une tâche qu'il faudra laisser à d'autres.

Certains des titres du Waldon ont été délibérément éliminés par le réviseur. C'est ainsi que nous n'avons pas retenu les manuscrits, type de document qui ne se prête pas à une bibliographie qui décrit des publications et des ouvrages imprimés. De même, certaines *parties* d'ouvrages nous semblaient inappropriées ; nous avons décidé arbitrairement de ne pas retenir les articles de revues, les extraits et les autres sections d'ouvrages plus volumineux qui n'ont pas fait l'objet d'une publication distincte, ainsi que les périodiques, tels le *London Magazine*. C'est avec une certaine réticence que nous avons retenu certaines notices : ballades, cartes (que Freda Waldon aurait certainement fini par trouver en très

Broadsides and broadsheets *have* been included (though there must be hundreds of these ephemeral items which escaped Dr. Waldon), because these are unquestionably complete works. (A "broadside" is distinguished from a "broadsheet," the latter being printed on both sides.) It will be noticed that many early works relate to Newfoundland, but (while on the subject of omissions) it is quite certain that Dr. Waldon has not exhausted the field; however, the recently published *Bibliography of Newfoundland*, largely the work of Agnes O'Dea and a comprehensive gathering, undoubtedly supplies the missing titles. Finally, while works printed outside the British Isles are excluded, British imprints of translations, reprints, and other works originally published elsewhere (particularly in France, the Netherlands, and what is now the United States) are included — always providing they have a Canadian connection.

The result is a bibliography of printed works published in Britain (some originally published elsewhere) to 1763 (the Treaty of Paris), which concern in some way any part of the present area of Canada. It should be of interest to Canadians and others for its records of both French and English activities in Canada throughout the period of New France. It is a source book of the earliest published works of Canadiana. With its titles chronologically ordered, the work will also

grand nombre). Les feuilles imprimies nonpliées d'un seul côté ou des deux côtés ont ité incluses – même si des centaines de ces articles éphémères ont pu échapper à Freda Waldon – car il s'agit de toute évidence d'œuvres complètes. Fait intéressant à signaler : beaucoup des titres les plus anciens portent sur Terre-Neuve, mais puisque nous discutons des omissions, il est certain que Freda Waldon n'a pas épuisé le sujet. Cependant, la *Bibliography of Newfoundland*, qui vient de paraître et qui est due, en grande partie, à Mme Agnes O'Dea, fournit les titres manquants. Enfin, alors que certains ouvrages publiés hors des Îles britanniques ont été exclus, les traductions, les réimpressions et même certains ouvrages publiés à l'origine dans d'autres pays – notamment en France, en Hollande et aux États-Unis – et portant une adresse bibliographique britannique ont été retenus, en autant qu'ils traitaient d'un sujet canadien.

C'est ainsi qu'on en est arrivé à une bibliographie des ouvrages publiés en Grande-Bretagne (dont certains avaient d'abord été publiés dans d'autres pays) jusqu'en 1763, année où le Traité de Paris fut signé, et qui portent sur un sujet canadien ou sur une région de ce qui constitue aujourd'hui le Canada. Notons, pour le bénéfice des Canadiens surtout, que la bibliographie porte sur l'activité des Français et des Anglais pendant la période de la Nouvelle-France. Il s'agit d'un ouvrage de référence sur les premiers titres à avoir été

be useful as a perspective of those important events which gave rise to comment in print, from proclamations and treaties to navigators' accounts and explorers' and traders' narratives, and from descriptions of the aborigines to the contemporary works of historians and geographers. Since very little was published within the bounds of Canada up to 1763 (thirty-five of over 1,200 titles in Marie Tremaine's *A Bibliography of Canadian Imprints, 1751–1800*), this compilation is an original reference to the background materials (often primary sources) for this early period in our history. Sabin's *Bibliotheca Americana* covers the whole of North and South America, while catalogues of former private libraries such as those of Church, Rich, and John Carter Brown are equally general. *A Bibliography of Canadiana* (TPL) contains some 360 titles up to 1763, but the arrangement is chronological by date of *subject*, and many titles listed for this period were published much later. Even Bishop White Kennett's *Bibliothecae Americanae Primordia* (London, 1713), while in chronological order, covers a shorter period, of course, but also again a broader field: all America, including the West Indies.

An examination of the bibliography for its inferences will no doubt prove rewarding. For example, one might be surprised at the consistent interest of the Dutch in Canadian

publiés sur le Canada, son histoire. La bibliographie étant organisée en ordre chronologique, elle donne aussi un aperçu des événements importants qui ont justement donné lieu à des écrits : proclamations, traités, récits de navigateurs, d'explorateurs et de commerçants ; descriptions des aborigènes et œuvres contemporaines d'historiens et de géographes. Comme très peu d'ouvrages ont été imprimés au Canada jusqu'en 1763 – seulement trente-cinq des quelques 1 200 titres cités par Marie Tremaine dans *A Bibliography of Canadian Imprints, 1751–1800* – cette bibliographie constitue une référence originale aux ouvrages, le plus souvent des sources primaires, portant sur les débuts de notre histoire. La *Bibliotheca Americana* de Sabin porte sur l'ensemble de l'Amérique du Nord et du Sud, et les catalogues de bibliothèques privées, telles la Church, Rich et John Carter Brown, sont de portée tout aussi générale. La *Bibliography of Canadiana* (TPL) contient quelque 360 titres jusqu'à 1763, organisés par ordre chronologique de sujet ; en fait, beaucoup des titres ont été publiés plus tard. Même la *Bibliothecae Americanae Primordia* (London, 1713) de Bishop White Kennett – bien qu'organisée elle aussi par ordre chronologique – porte sur une période plus courte et un domaine plus vaste, toute l'Amérique, y compris les Antilles.

L'ouvrage de Freda Waldon est intéressant non seulement par sa valeur bibliographique, mais par les conclusions historiques qu'on peut en tirer. C'est ainsi que le lecteur constatera l'intérêt soutenu

events, and one also notes the mounting British attention to New France and the area now called Canada as the eighteenth century advanced. This British interest, notably but certainly not exclusively in Newfoundland and Hudson Bay, existed from the earliest times, culminating in the 1750s. The terms of the peace at the close of the Seven Years' War were debated extensively and furiously, and in print. These publications constitute almost a genre of their own, with the pamphlet controversy on "Guadeloupe or Canada" forming a lively subgroup. Here are some random areas of possible future research, and even of bibliographical investigation.

des Hollandais pour le Canada ; il remarquera aussi l'attention accrue des Britanniques au cours du XVIIIe siècle pour la Nouvelle-France et la région qu'on appelle maintenant le Canada. L'intérêt des Britanniques – particulièrement, mais non exclusivement, pour Terre-Neuve et la Baie d'Hudson – datait des premiers temps de la colonie et a culminé dans les années 1750. Les conditions du traité de paix à la fin de la guerre de Sept Ans ont été débattues vigoureusement et en profondeur dans des écrits. Ces documents constituent un genre en soi, les pamphlets sur la « Guadeloupe ou le Canada » formant un sous-groupe fort coloré. Voilà autant de possibilités de recherche et même d'enquête bibliographique.

Arrangement and Explanation of Entries

The arrangement of Dr. Waldon's original typed sheets is preserved here, as they were received. That is, titles are arrayed alphabetically by main entry (title, or author when known), grouped under the year of publication, the groups being in chronological order by date of British publication, from 1519 to 1763. Multiple-volumed works published over a period of two or more years are arranged under the publication year of the first volume.

Organisation et explication des notices

Nous avons préservé la présentation des fiches dactylographiées de Freda Waldon telles que nous les avons reçues. Les titres sont organisés en ordre alphabétique, par notice principale (titre ou auteur, s'il est connu) et regroupés selon l'année de publication en Grande-Bretagne ; la bibliographie porte sur la période entre 1519 et 1763. Les titres comportant plus d'un volume et publiés sur une période de plus d'un an sont classés suivant l'année de publication du premier volume.

Each entry consists of a basic framework. First is the bibliographic description, beginning with the author's name, when known, following the *National Union Catalog* (NUC) usage for the most part, but calling upon the *Dictionary of National Biography* (DNB) as needed, and always preferring the form and spelling of the *Dictionary of Canadian Biography* (DCB). The search for the authorship of works with title entries in Waldon rarely extended beyond NUC, the *British Library General Catalogue* (BLC), and Halkett and Laing. Titles and imprints are taken from the Waldon sheets but verified in NUC or BLC (or other standard sources if not in these); frequently, however, the Waldon titles are more complete than those in NUC. The forenames of printers and publishers, usually represented as initials only in NUC, are completed from Waldon if given, otherwise from the appropriate volume of Plomer's *Dictionary*. Roman numbers in dates, and usually elsewhere too (excepting when so given to distinguish preliminary paging), are transcribed into Arabic numerals. All Old Style imprint dates are, when information is sufficient, rendered into New Style dates, *e.g.* January 1733–34 is given as "1734 [N.S.]," and thus filed. Waldon's collations by pages are not in the standard form of today, but they are often informative. For example, Dr. Waldon usually indicates "t.-p." (title-page) instead of "p. l." (preliminary leaf), and often identifies a terminal section as "index" or a final page as "list" (the

Chaque notice est présentée selon le même modèle : d'abord la description bibliographique – nom de l'auteur s'il est connu, suivant l'usage du *National Union Catalog* (NUC) dans la plupart des cas. Nous nous sommes servi aussi du *Dictionary of National Biography* (DNB) le cas échéant, et avons préféré la graphie et l'orthographe proposées par le *Dictionnaire biographique du Canada* (DBC). Pour ce qui est de la recherche des auteurs des titres du Waldon, nous nous sommes limités au NUC, au *British Library General Catalogue* (BLC) et au Halkett et Laing. Les titres et les adresses bibliographiques ont été transcrits à partir des fiches de Freda Waldon et vérifiés dans le NUC ou le BLC (ou dans une autre source standard). Les titres du Waldon sont souvent plus complets que ceux du NUC. Les prénoms des imprimeurs et des éditeurs, représentés seulement par des initiales dans le NUC, sont écrits en toutes lettres dans le Waldon, quand ils existent et s'ils diffèrent du volume approprié du *Dictionary* de Plomer. Les chiffres romains utilisés notamment pour les dates – sauf ceux qui servent à distinguer les pages liminaires –ont été transcrits selon la numérotation arabe. Toutes les dates d'adresse bibliographique données selon le calendrier julien ont été traduites suivant le calendrier grégorien lorsque les données étaient suffisantes. Par exemple, janvier 1733–34 est devenu « 1734 [C.G.] ». Les collations par page de Freda Waldon ne sont pas la norme aujourd'hui, mais elles fournissent beaucoup de renseignements intéressants. Par exemple, Freda Waldon emploie « t.-p. » (title-page – page de titre) au lieu de « p.l. » (preliminary leaf – page liminaire) ; souvent, elle appelle « index » la dernière section d'un ouvrage ou « list » la page finale où sont

publisher's list of current titles) within her collations. I have used the standard form of pagination, transferring the other information to the notes. Under my original prescription of simplification, collations by signatures were eliminated, and where the pagination is clear this stands; but in rare cases where pagination is inadequate, collation by signatures has been employed for elucidation. Dr. Waldon's format by sheet-folds, rather than NUC's size in centimetres, has been retained (unless unavailable) because for these early books format by signatures conveys information on make-up and proportions. However, Waldon's "s.sh." (single sheet), from BLC usage, has been translated into the more obvious term "broadside," and her "f." into "fol." for folio.

In the bibliographical description, matter such as the price of the book is enclosed within angle brackets (< >) when it appears within square brackets ([ ]) in the original. The angle brackets are used in Waldon's notes when the matter so enclosed was placed in square brackets by Dr. Waldon. Square brackets themselves are used, as is customary, to indicate supplied matter *not* found in the original.

Following the statement of format, and placed always at the right following the bibliographic description, is presented the main source of verification of the Waldon entry: the symbol for the bibliography or catalogue (*see* "Sources Cited," below), and the location within that source. It is from this and other verifying

présentés les titres disponibles chez l'éditeur. Nous avons utilisé la pagination standard, reportant les autres renseignements dans les notes. Selon la formule de simplification que nous avions proposée au début, les collations par signatures ont été éliminées ; lorsque la pagination est simple, cette règle vaut toujours. Mais dans les rares cas où la pagination n'est pas appropriée, nous avons utilisé les collations par signatures afin d'éclaircir la situation. Le format en feuillet – plutôt que le format métrique du NUC – utilisé par Freda Waldon a été conservé, sauf si ce n'était pas possible, car le format par signatures de ces livres anciens nous renseigne sur la composition et les proportions. Cependant, le terme « s.sh. » (single sheet – page) du BLC a été remplacé par le terme « broadside » – in-plano – beaucoup plus explicite ; l'abréviation « f. » a été remplacée par « fol. » (folio – in-folio).

Dans les descriptions bibliographiques, les renseignements tels le prix du livre ont été inscrits entre les empattements triangulaires (< >) lorsqu'ils figurent entre crochets ([ ]) dans l'original. Les signes d'infériorité et de supériorité ont remplacé dans le présent ouvrage les crochets utilisés par Freda Waldon. Selon la convention, les crochets servent à indiquer les ajouts qui ne se trouvent *pas* dans l'original.

Après les indications sur le format, toujours placées après la description bibliographique, figure la source principale de vérification de l'entrée du Waldon : abréviation de la bibliographie ou du catalogue (se reporter à Sources citées, plus loin) et la page. Ce sont de ces sources de vérification que nous avons pu tirer les nouveaux titres et éditions au cours du

sources that I have usually derived new titles and editions, discovered (often by Stewart Renfrew) during the ordinary checking process. Many of these sources are of recent publication, such as NUC and BLC, and therefore were not available to Dr. Waldon. The new entries are distinguished (by an asterisk) from those already listed as separate entries in Dr. Waldon's typescript, though sometimes she simply gave the dates of other editions within her notes to the first edition. A rough survey yields a count of about 600 entries in the Waldon typescript and 265 new entries, for a total of about 865 entries for titles and editions in this bibliography.

The second element in the basic framework of the entries consists of the notes. In a few cases the only note may be "No further information discovered," and this almost always means that the search for verification has been conducted through a few standard works only, though the occasional interlibrary loan or letter of inquiry has been made. To allocate further time, tempting though it always was, would have contravened the prescription of simplification adopted earlier. The usual order of the notes, by subject, is: errata (if any); notes on the author or the authorship, the title, imprint, collation, and verifying source; notes on the subject of the work, with its Canadian connection; discussion of the textual relationships ("a reply to," "answered by," "this is further to" or "further to this is," and translations), followed by

processus de vérification ordinaire. (C'était le fait souvent de M. Stewart Renfrew). Il s'agit très souvent de publications récentes, comme le NUC et le BLC, que, par le fait même, Freda Waldon n'avait pu consulter. Les nouvelles notices, marquées d'un astérisque, constituent une catégorie distincte dans le tapuscrit de Freda Waldon, bien qu'elle ait parfois inscrit les dates des autres éditions dans ses notes sur l'édition originale. Un calcul rapide révèle la présence de 600 notices environ dans le tapuscrit de Freda Waldon et 265 nouvelles notices, pour un total de quelque 865 notices pour les titres et éditions de la présente bibliographie.

Deuxième élément du modèle : les notes. Dans quelques cas, la seule note qui apparaisse est « Aucun autre renseignement » ; ceci signifie que la vérification a été faite à partir de quelques ouvrages standard seulement dans la plupart des cas. Il est arrivé cependant qu'il ait fallu faire un prêt inter-bibliothèques ou faire faire une recherche. Si nous avions accordé davantage de temps à cette étape, comme c'était d'ailleurs tentant de le faire, nous aurions été à l'encontre du principe même de simplification que nous avions adopté au début. L'ordre habituel des notes, par sujet, est le suivant : erreurs (le cas échéant) ; notes sur l'auteur (ou les auteurs) ; titre ; adresse bibliographique ; collation et source de vérification. Suit une note sur le contenu de l'ouvrage et l'intérêt qu'il a pour le Canada. Figurent ensuite les notes de renvoi à d'autres documents (en réponse à, réponse de, pour faire suite à et traduction de) et à d'autres éditions (mention des titres qui ont

the bibliographical relationships of editions with references to changed titles. These notes and the cross-references will enable the user to place the work in hand within its literary and historical context (works to which it responded, and which responded to it) as well as relating it within the bibliography to other editions, issues, variant titles, and translations of the same work, up to 1763 (though later editions and translations are often noted). It should be observed, while on this topic, that for economy of presentation the successive editions are described only briefly within their respective entries, and users are referred back to the principal entry — most commonly the first edition — for more complete information. These abridged titles in subsequent editions, however, always record wording, spelling, punctuation, abbreviation, and other variations from the principal or immediately previous edition; the only notes given are those specific to the later edition, the user being referred to the principal edition for general notes as well as for the list of other editions. The bibliography's index will, of course, assist in this process of making connections.

All these edited notes (and to some extent the bibliographic descriptions that precede them), while drawing primarily on the Waldon typescript, are freely extended from other sources when new information was judged to be of Canadian or bibliographical interest, and are sometimes adapted or reconciled

été modifiés). Grâce aux notes et aux renvois, le lecteur pourra mettre l'ouvrage dans son contexte littéraire et historique (œuvres qui précèdent et suivent le titre en question) et repérer dans la bibliographie les autres éditions, numéros, variantes de titre et traductions du même ouvrage parues jusqu'en 1763 – bien que des éditions et traductions ultérieures soient souvent signalées. Pour des questions d'économie d'espace, les éditions subséquentes d'un ouvrage sont décrites brièvement dans des notices distinctes et on renvoie le lecteur à la notice principale – le plus souvent, la notice de l'édition originale – pour plus de détails. Les titres abrégés des éditions subséquentes, cependant, comportent toujours ce qui les distingue de l'édition principale ou de l'édition précédente : notamment les variantes graphiques ou orthographiques, les variantes dans la ponctuation, les abréviations. Les notes qui figurent alors sont celles qui s'appliquent spécifiquement à l'édition récente ; le lecteur peut se reporter à l'édition principale pour les notes générales et la liste des autres éditions. L'index de la bibliographie permet aussi d'établir les correspondances.

Toutes les notes révisées – et, jusqu'à un certain point, les descriptions bibliographiques qui les précèdent – ont été rédigées à partir, bien sûr, du tapuscrit de Freda Waldon, mais comportent certains ajouts dont le contenu a été tiré d'autres sources lorsqu'on jugeait qu'il présentait une certaine valeur bibliographique ou qu'il portait sur un sujet canadien ; les notes ont

when one or another source was judged to be a more accurate statement. New notes, quite often taken verbatim from the NUC entries, are offset in italic from the Waldon notes, and changes in Waldon's own notes are indicated by omission marks and enclosure in square brackets.

It is fervently hoped that this eclecticism has never created a bibliographical "ghost," though considering that only a very few of the works listed have been examined by the editor (in original or facsimile), the possibility does exist.

The final element in the framework of each entry is the paragraph giving the locations of copies in Canada (American locations can be found in NUC), using the standard symbols as established by the National Library. I have not provided a table expanding these because the list is extensive and constantly developing, but copies of the publication *Symbols of Canadian Libraries* (under continual revision) are available in most libraries, and are obtainable free of charge from the National Library in Ottawa. The great majority of these location symbols, at the end of the entries, have very kindly been provided by the National Library from its master list, the Canadian Union Catalogue. A selection of locations only is given, representative of the regions of Canada from east to west. It could never have been expected that very many of these early works would be available in Canadian libraries; had this been different, Dr. Waldon's work would have been considerably

parfois été adaptées quand une autre source semblait plus juste. Les nouvelles notes, souvent transcrites telles quelles du NUC, figurent en retrait par rapport aux notes de Freda Waldon et les changements apportés à ses notes sont indiqués par des points de suspension entre crochets.

Il est à souhaiter que cet éclectisme ne donnera pas lieu à une stérilité bibliographique ; même si seulement quelques ouvrages (en forme originale ou fac-similé) de la liste ont été examinés par le réviseur.

Le dernier élément à considérer est le paragraphe sur les bibliothèques qui possèdent des exemplaires de l'ouvrage au Canada (les bibliothèques américaines figurent dans le NUC) ; les sigles standard de la Bibliothèque nationale du Canada ont été utilisés. Nous n'en avons pas fait la liste ici, car elle est exhaustive et qu'on la modifie constamment. Il est possible, cependant, de consulter un répertoire des *Sigles des bibliothèques canadiennes* (en révision constante) dans la plupart des bibliothèques au Canada et qu'on peut s'en procurer un exemplaire gratuit auprès de la Bibliothèque nationale du Canada à Ottawa. La plupart de ces sigles, figurant à la fin de la notice, nous ont été fournis aimablement par la Bibliothèque nationale qui a eu recours à son catalogue collectif. Seulement quelques bibliothèques sont mentionnées, qui représentent les régions du Canada d'un océan à l'autre. L'on ne pouvait pas s'attendre qu'un grand nombre de ces œuvres anciennes se trouvent dans les bibliothèques canadiennes ; si cela avait été le cas, la tâche de Freda Waldon n'aurait pas été aussi lourde. Or, grâce au programme de l'Institut canadien de

1

reduced! However, the splendid programme of the Canadian Institute for Historical Microreproductions in making microfiche of early Canadiana will change the whole picture, so far as availability of texts is concerned — it has, in fact, already accomplished a great deal to make life simpler for scholars in Canadian studies. The institute's work will no doubt increase the usefulness of this bibliography, and quite possibly the bibliography will in turn provide the institute with some new titles and editions.

A word on orthography. The so-called "long *s*," or "*ſ*" (which is not an *f* at all) is represented throughout as a "short *s*" (*i.e.*, *s*). The transcription of *V* to *v* and *u*, and of *I* to *I* and *J* (its swash form), and of *i* to *i* and *j*, according to the principles of R.B. McKerrow, have been described above. The letter *VV*, when intended as a *W*, is so given when the original or a facsimile, if seen, has a space between the adjacent serifs of the two *V*s; otherwise, it is represented as a *W*. Spellings (and misspellings) are transcribed as given in the originals. Asterisks, hyphens, or other marks of omission used on many title-pages to disguise (often thinly) names, are transcribed as given, with the same number of marks, but the full name is supplied in brackets when not obvious. The retention of this orthography and such mannerisms is required bibliographically but also adds a contemporary flavour to the representation of old works. In

microreproduction historique, dont l'objet est la production sur microfiches d'ouvrages anciens portant sur des sujets canadiens, l'accès aux documents sera désormais tellement plus facile – en fait, la tâche des canadianistes s'est déjà beaucoup simplifiée grâce à ce programme. Les travaux actuels de l'institut feront certainement ressortir l'utilité de cette bibliographie ; il est possible, par ailleurs, que, grâce à la bibliographie, l'institut puisse mettre la main sur de nouveaux titres ou de nouvelles éditions.

Passons maintenant à la question de l'orthographe. La lettre qu'on appelle « *s* long » ou « *ſ* » (en fait, qui n'est pas un *f*) est représentée partout dans la bibliographie par un « *s* court » (« *s* »). Le protocole de translittération du *V* majuscule en *v* ou en *u* minuscules, du *I* majuscule en *I* et *J* majuscules (forme historiée) et du *i* minuscule en *i* et *j* minuscules selon les principes de R.B. McKerrow a été décrit plus haut. La lettre *VV*, quand il s'agit d'un *W*, n'a pas été modifiée si, sur l'original ou le fac-similé, nous avons constaté la présence d'une espace entre les séries adjacents des deux *V* ; sinon, nous avons employé le *W* ordinaire. L'orthographe des mots a été conservée telle quelle même s'il y avait des erreurs. Les astérisques, traits d'union et autres signes orthographiques utilisés pour signaler une omission sur de nombreuses pages de titre et employés ici pour masquer (souvent sans succès) les noms, ont été transcrits sans modification, avec le même nombre de marques ; le nom au complet a été noté entre crochets s'il n'était pas évident. Il est nécessaire, d'un point de vue

unquoted matter, I have rendered spellings of names according to modern Canadian usage (*e.g.,* "Louisbourg," not "Louisburg"), drawing heavily upon the *Dictionary of Canadian Biography* (DCB), the source also of personal dates when in dispute.

One great hazard of working from another's text is that of compounding errors: first those of the original compiler, accepted unknowingly or without change even if known because the apparent error may be taken verbatim from the original; and then in addition the editor's own errors, equally inevitable. A more elaborate project, in which the bibliographer will return to an examination of the actual originals, and seek deliberately to expand the number of titles, must be considered desirable; but regrettably it must await the co-operation of agencies with time and funds to support a project so massive — yet so eminently worthwhile!

bibliographique, de conserver l'orthographe et les signes orthographiques originaux ; cette exigence présente l'avantage de mettre en valeur le caractère ancien de ces ouvrages séculaires. Nous nous en sommes tenu à l'usage canadien moderne pour l'orthographe des noms propres figurant dans les notes qui ne sont pas des citations (p.ex. Louisbourg et non Louisburg) et avons eu recours au *Dictionnaire biographique du Canada* (DBC), source de dates sur les auteurs en cas de divergences.

Le fait de travailler le texte d'une autre personne présente un grand danger : celui d'ajouter un second niveau d'erreurs. Il y a, à un premier niveau, les erreurs de l'auteur même, qu'elles soient inconscientes ou conscientes – si l'erreur provient de l'ouvrage étudié ; et il y a, à un second niveau, les erreurs du réviseur, qui se glissent inévitablement. Il serait préférable, évidemment, que le projet fût de plus grande envergure et que le bibliographe réexaminât les ouvrages originaux et qu'il cherchât délibérément à augmenter le nombre des titres ; malheureusement, même si le projet est éminemment utile, il faudra attendre l'aide humaine et financière d'organismes intéressés pour pouvoir réaliser une entreprise de pareille envergure.

Acknowledgements

In addition to those persons whose invaluable contributions I mentioned earlier, I would like to acknowledge and thank the following institutions and individuals for their assistance and support.

Remerciements

En plus des personnes dont nous avons déjà souligné la précieuse collaboration, nous aimerions remercier les institutions et les personnes suivantes.

Firstly, I am especially appreciative of the financial assistance, and the confidence in the project it expressed, from the Social Sciences and Humanities Research Council of Canada. Bibliography is labour-intensive, and even the moderate funds awarded have proved invaluable in easing the burden of bibliographical checking and typing. I would also like to thank the School of Graduate Studies and Research of Queen's University for administering the award, and for material help earlier for bibliographical assistance, with a Queen's Research Award. Of those who have helped personally, I must record special thanks to my colleague Stewart Renfrew for his invaluable research assistance over several hard winters and hot summers; his was indeed a labour of love. To Margot McBurney, Chief Librarian of Queen's University, and Lin Good, Associate Librarian, I am indebted for their encouragement, and for the use of library facilities. Maureen Tasker has my fullest appreciation for her patient typing of exacting material from impenetrable handwriting. To Beth B. Watters, for her encouragement and very practical aid, I am deeply grateful; and a proud father is happy to acknowledge the laborious work of Vivian C. Morley in compiling the index. Some bibliographical checking was undertaken, starting many years ago and for varying periods, by Jane Graves, Elsie de Bruijn, Robert Cupido, Rinolde Van Weringh, Wendy Spettigue, and particularly by my colleague Barbara St.

Tout d'abord, nous tenons à souligner l'apport financier et moral au projet du Conseil canadien de recherche en sciences humaines. Pour produire une bibliographie, il faut d'abord et avant tout pouvoir compter sur la main-d'œuvre : les subventions, même modestes, ont été précieuses et ont allégé le fardeau de la frappe et de la vérification des notices bibliographiques. Nous aimerions aussi remercier l'École des études supérieures et de la recherche de l'Université Queen's pour la bourse et pour l'aide matérielle accordée aux premiers stades du projet et pour la bourse de recherche de Queen's. Nous aimerions aussi souligner plus particulièrement l'étroite collaboration de notre collègue Stewart Renfrew pour le travail précieux accompli beau temps, mauvais temps, un travail exigeant qu'il a fait par plaisir. Nous remercions Mme Margot McBurney, chef bibliothécaire à l'Université Queen's, et Mme Lin Good, bibliothécaire adjointe, pour leur encouragement et pour nous avoir laissé utiliser les ressources de la bibliothèque. Nous tenons à remercier Madame Maureen Tasker pour la patience dont elle a fait preuve pour la transcription de données arides et souvent très difficiles à déchiffrer. Madame Beth B. Watters nous a aussi été d'un très grand secours, tant par son encouragement que par son aide pratique. C'est avec fierté que nous soulignons le travail laborieux de notre fille Vivian C. Morley dans la compilation de l'index. Enfin, voilà de nombreuses années, Jane Graves, Elsie de Bruijn, Robert Cupido, Rinolde Van Weringh et Wendy Spettigue ont entrepris, pour des périodes variables, la vérification de la bibliographie ; notre collègue Barbara St. Remy (maintenant Teatero) a effectué des recherches poussées et s'est occupée des prêts

Remy (now Teatero), whose intensive research and arrangement of interlibrary loans was conducted with marvellous bibliographical exactitude.

To all the foregoing, my warmest appreciation for their assistance with preparing Dr. Waldon's *magnum opus* for publication; may the worthiness of the project long be their satisfaction and recompense.

WFEM
Special Collections
Queen's University Library
Kingston, Ontario
September 1985

inter-bibliothèques, et ce, avec un grand souci d'exactitude.

Nous avons une dette de gratitude envers toutes ces personnes qui nous ont aidé à préparer l'œuvre magistrale de Freda Waldon en vue de sa publication ; que la valeur de ce projet soit leur satisfaction et leur récompense.

WFEM
Collections spéciales
Bibliothèque de l'Université Queen's
Kingston (Ontario)
Septembre 1985

SOURCES CITED • SOURCES CITÉES

A few other sources besides those listed here, when they are cited only once or twice throughout the bibliography, appear within the entries with full information. General works of reference, such as encyclopedias and Oxford *Companions*, consulted only for orientation in a field, are excluded. It is hoped that the abbreviations used in the citations will be recognizable to most users as they stand, without constant reference to this list. The form of the location part of the citations is usually obvious, referring to volume number then to page, column, or item number, separated by a colon. Because the volumes of the British Library *Catalogue*, cited as "BLC(to 1975)," were still in process of publication during the editing of this bibliography, it sometimes happened that the volume wanted was not yet published and recourse had to be had to the old "BM(to 1955)" *Catalogue*. Citation of BM or BLC will therefore depend upon the stage of publication of BLC at the moment the check of that source was made.

Les ouvrages de référence qui ont été cités seulement une ou deux fois dans la bibliographie, ne figurent pas dans la liste ci-après ; nous les avons cités plutôt dans les notices comme telles avec tous les renseignements nécessaires. Nous avons exclus de la présente liste les ouvrages généraux, tels les encyclopédies et les Oxford *Companions*, que nous avons consultés simplement pour nous mettre sur la piste. Nous espérons que le lecteur pourra reconnaître les abréviations utilisées dans les citations sans avoir à se reporter constamment à la liste. Les notes sur l'emplacement des ouvrages sont habituellement explicites ; figurent consécutivement et séparés par un deux-points le numéro du volume, le numéro de la page, l'indicateur de la colonne ou le numéro de l'article. Parce que les volumes du *Catalogue* de la British Library, appelé BLC(to 1975) dans le présent ouvrage, étaient en cours de publication pendant la révision de la bibliographie, il est arrivé que nous ayons dû avoir recours au *Catalogue* BM(to 1955) parce que le volume recherché de la nouvelle édition n'était pas encore publié. Les sources citées, donc, dépendent du stade de publication du BLC au moment où la vérification a été faite.

Arber • Arber, Edward. *The term catalogues, 1668–1709 A.D.; with a number for Easter term, 1711 A.D.* . . . London: 1903–06. 3 vols.

Arber • Arber, Edward. *The term catalogues, 1668–1709 A.D. ; with a number for Eastern term, 1711 A.D.* . . . Londres, 1903–1906, 3 vol.

BLC(to 1975) • British Library. Department of Printed Books. *The British Library general catalogue of printed books to 1975.* London: 1979–87. 360 vols.

BM • British Museum Catalogues (in general). *See also* BM under "Abbreviations Used," below.

BM(to 1955) • British Museum. Department of Printed Books. *General catalogue of printed books. Photolithographic edition, to 1955.* London: 1965–66. 263 vols.

BN • Bibliothèque nationale. Département des Imprimés. *Catalogue général des livres imprimés . . . . Auteurs.* Paris: 1897–1981. 231 vols.

Casey • Casey, Magdalen. *Catalogue of pamphlets in the Public Archives of Canada, 1493–1877.* Ottawa: 1931. Vol. one.

Church • Cole, George Watson. *A catalogue of books relating to the discovery and early history of North and South America, forming a part of the library of E.D. Church.* New York: 1951. 5 vols.

DCB • *Dictionary of Canadian biography.* Toronto: 1966– . 12 vols. (publication in progress).

DNB • *Dictionary of national biography. . . . From the earliest*

BLC (to 1975) • British Library. Department of Printed Books. *The British Library general catalogue of printed books to 1975.* Londres, 1979–1987, 360 vol.

BM • British Museum Catalogues (en général). Se reporter à BM sous la rubrique Abréviations ci-après.

BM (to 1955) • British Museum. Department of Printed Books. *General catalogue of printed books. Photolithographic edition, to 1955.* Londres, 1965–1966, 263 vol.

BN • Bibliothèque nationale. Département des Imprimés. *Catalogue général des livres imprimés . . . . Auteurs.* Paris, 1897–1981, 231 vol.

Casey • Casey, Magdalen. *Catalogue of pamphlets in the Public Archives of Canada, 1493–1877.* Ottawa, 1931. Vol. 1.

Church • Cole, George Watson. *A catalogue of books relating to the discovery and early history of North and South America, forming a part of the library of E.D. Church.* New York, 1951, 5 vol.

DBC • *Dictionnaire biographique du Canada.* Toronto, 1966– , 12 vol. (en cours de publication).

DNB • *Dictionary of national biography . . . . From the earliest times to 1900.*

times to 1900. London: 1967–68. 21 vols. and *Suppl.* (1 vol., 1968).

Dionne • Dionne, Narcisse E. *Inventaire chronologique* . . . . Québec: 1905–09. 4 vols. and *Suppl.* (1912).

Evans • Evans, Charles. *American bibliography . . . 1639 down to and including the year 1820* . . . . Chicago: 1903–34. 12 vols. 1639 to 1799; continued by Clifford K. Shipton to 1800 (Worcester, Mass.: 1955), and with index, vol. 14, by Roger Pattrell Bristol (Worcester, Mass.: 1959).

Faribault • Faribault, Georges B. *Catalogue d'ouvrages sur l'histoire de l'Amérique* . . . . Québec: 1837. 1 vol., in 3 pts. (general, anon. works, maps and prints).

Harmsworth • Canada. Public Archives. *The Northcliffe Collection; presented to the Government of Canada by Sir Leicester Harmsworth* . . . . Ottawa: 1926. Presented as a memorial to Harmsworth's brother, Viscount Northcliffe. The abbreviated citation "Harmsworth" is used by Waldon, but it is uncertain to which of the numerous catalogues of parts of Sir Leicester's great library she refers (cf. NUC(Pre–56) 231:282–83).

Londres, 1967–1968, 21 vol. et suppl. (1 vol., 1968).

Dionne • Dionne, Narcisse E. *Inventaire chronologique.* . . . Québec, 1905–1909, 4 vol. et suppl. (1912).

Evans • Evans, Charles. *American bibliography . . . 1639 down to and including the year 1820* . . . . Chicago, 1903–1934, 12 vol. 1639 à 1799, terminés par Clifford K. Shipton jusqu'à 1800 [Worcester (Mass.)], 1955 ; index ; vol. 14 par Roger Pattrell Bristol [Worcester (Mass.)], 1959.

Faribault • Faribault, Georges B. *Catalogue d'ouvrages sur l'histoire de l'Amérique* . . . . Québec, 1837, 1 vol. en 3 parties (généralités, ouvrages, cartes et gravures anonymes).

Harmsworth • Canada. Archives publiques. *The Northcliffe Collection ; presented to the Government of Canada by Sir Leicester Harmsworth* . . . . Ottawa, 1926. Hommage à la mémoire du frère de Harmsworth, le vicomte Northcliffe. Waldon utilise le vocable « Harmsworth », mais ne précise pas à quel des nombreux catalogues des parties de la grande bibliothèque de sir Leicester elle fait référence. [cf. NUC(Pre–56) 231:282–83].

JCB(1) • Brown University. John Carter Brown Library. *Bibliotheca americana. A catalogue of books relating to North and South America . . .* by John Russell Bartlett. Providence, R.I.: 1865–71. 3 pts. in 4 (or 7) vols. (pt. 3: 2 or 5 vols.). Pt. 1: 1493–1600; pt. 2: 1601–1700; pt. 3: 1701–1800. (Also Kraus reprint, 1963.)

JCB(2) • Brown University. John Carter Brown Library. *Bibliotheca americana. A catalogue of books . . .* by John Russell Bartlett. Second ed. Providence, R.I.: 1875–82. 2 pts. in 2 (or 5) vols. (Pt. 1: 2 vols.; pt. 2: 3 vols.) Pt. 1: 1482–1600; pt. 2: 1601–1701 (t.-p. dates are incorrect). 1482–1701.

JCB(3) • Brown University. John Carter Brown Library. *Bibliotheca americana. Catalogue of the John Carter Brown Library* . . . . Third ed. Providence, R.I.: 1919–31. 3 pts. in 5 vols. 12th cent. to 1674.

JCB(4) • Brown University. John Carter Brown Library. *Bibliotheca americana. Catalogue of the John Carter Brown Library* . . . . *Books printed 1675–1700.* Providence, R.I.: 1973. Continues JCB(3), the third ed.

Kennett • Kennett, White. *Bibliothecæ americana primordia*

JCB (1) • Brown University. John Carter Brown Library. *Bibliotheca americana. A catalogue of books relating to North and South America . . . Par John Russell Bartlett. Providence (R.I.), 1865–1871, 3 parties en 4 (ou 7) vol. (partie 3: 2 ou 5 volumes). Partie 1 : 1493–1600 ; partie 2 : 1601–1700 ; partie 3 : 1701–1800. (Aussi réimpression Kraus, 1963.)*

JCB (2) • Brown University. John Carter Brown Library. *Bibliotheca americana. A catalogue of books . . . Par John Russell Bartlett. 2e édition. Providence (R.I.), 1875–1882, 2 parties en 2 (ou 5) vol. (Partie 1 : 2 vol. ; partie 2 : 3 vol.) Partie 1 : 1482–1600 ; partie 2 : 1601–1701 (les dates des pages de titre sont incorrectes). 1482–1701.*

JCB (3) • Brown University. John Carter Brown Library. *Bibliotheca americana. Catalogue of the John Carter Brown Library . . . . 3e édition. Providence (R.I.), 1919–1931, 3 parties en 5 vol., XIIe siècle à 1674.*

JCB (4) • Brown University. John Carter Brown Library. *Bibliotheca americana. Catalogue of the John Carter Brown Library . . . . Books printed 1675–1700.* Providence (R.I.), 1973, suite de JCB (3), 3e édition.

Kennett • Kennett, White. *Bibliothecæ americana primordia . . . . Londres,*

.... London: 1713. Said to be the first bibliography of North America in English.

London Library • Wright, C.T. Hagberg, and C.J. Purnell. *Catalogue of the London Library, St. James's Square, London.* London: 1913–14. 2 vols. and *Suppl.*, 1913– (London: 1920–).

Morgan, BBH • Morgan, William T. *A bibliography of British history, 1700–1715.* Bloomington, Ind.: 1934–42. 5 vols.

NUC(Pre–56) American Library Association. *The national union catalog, pre–1956 imprints* .... London: 1968–80. 685 vols., and *Suppls.* 1980–81, vols. 686–754.

Plomer • Aldis, H.G., Robert Bowes, . . . and H.R. Plomer. *A dictionary of printers and booksellers in England, Scotland and Ireland . . . 1557–1640.* General editor: R.B. McKerrow. London: 1910. Plomer, Henry R. *A dictionary of the booksellers and printers . . . 1641 to 1667.* London: 1907. Plomer, Henry R., et al. *A dictionary . . . 1668 to 1725.* Oxford: 1922. Plomer, H.R., et al. *A dictionary . . . 1726 to 1775.* Oxford: 1932.

1713. On dit qu'il s'agit de la première bibliographie publiée en anglais sur l'Amérique du Nord.

London Library • Wright, C.T. Hagberg et C.J. Purnell. *Catalogue of the London Library, St. James's Square, London.* Londres, 1913–1914, 2 vol. et suppl., 1913– (Londres, 1920–).

Morgan, BBH • Morgan, William T. *A bibliography of British history, 1700–1715.* Bloomington (Ind.) : 1934–1942, 5 vol.

NUC (Pre–56) • American Library Association. *The national union catalog, pre–1956 imprints* .... Londres, 1968–1980, 685 vol. et suppl. (1980–1981, vol. 686–754).

Plomer • Aldis, H.G., Robert Bowes, . . . et H.R. Plomer. *A dictionary of printers and booksellers in England, Scotland and Ireland . . . 1557–1640.* Éditeur général : R.B. McKerrow. Londres, 1910. Plomer, Henry R. *A dictionary of the booksellers and printers . . . 1641 to 1667.* Londres, 1907. Plomer, Henry R., [etc.]. *A dictionary . . . 1668 to 1725.* Oxford, 1922. Plomer, Henry R., [etc.]. *A dictionary . . . 1726 to 1775.* Oxford, 1932.

Rich • Rich, Obadiah. *Bibliotheca Americana nova; a catalogue of books . . . relating to America printed since the year 1700 . . . .* London: 1835–46. 2 vols.

STC • Pollard, A.W., and G.R. Redgrave. *A short-title catalogue of books printed in England, Scotland, & Ireland . . . 1475–1640.* London: 1926. Continued by Donald Wing, *Short-title catalogue . . . 1641–1700.* New York: 1945–51. 3 vols.

Sabin • Sabin, Joseph. *A dictionary of books relating to America, from its discovery to the present time.* New York: 1868–1936. 29 vols.

Somers Tracts • *A collection of scarce and valuable tracts . . . .* 2d ed., rev., augm., and arr. by Walter Scott. London: 1809–15. 13 vols. Catalogue of materials in various public and private libraries, particularly the seventeenth and eighteenth century library of Lord John Somers.

TPL • Toronto. Public Library. *A bibliography of Canadiana . . . .* Eds. Frances M. Staton and Marie Tremaine. Toronto: 1934. 1 vol. and *Suppls.*

Rich • Rich, Obadiah. *Bibliotheca Americana nova ; a catalogue of books . . . relating to America printed since the year 1700 . . . .* Londres, 1835–1846, 2 vol.

STC • Pollard, A.W. et G.R. Redgrave. *A short-title catalogue of books printed in England, Scotland & Ireland . . . 1475–1640.* Londres, 1926. Poursuivi par Donald Wing, *Short-title catalogue . . . 1641–1700.* New York, 1945–1951, 3 vol.

Sabin • Sabin, Joseph. *A dictionary of books relating to America, from its discovery to the present time.* New York, 1868–1936, 29 vol.

Somers Tracts • *A collection of scarce and valuable tracts . . . .* 2e éd., revue, augmentée, et arrangée par Walter Scott. Londres, 1809–1815, 13 vol. Catalogue des ouvrages publiés au XVIIe et au XVIIIe siècle de la bibliothèque de Lord John Somers.

TPL • Toronto. Public Library. *A bibliography of Canadiana . . . .* Frances M. Staton et Marie Tremaine. Toronto, 1934. 1 vol. et suppl.

Bowers, Fredson. *Principles of bibliographical description.* Princeton: 1949 (esp. chap. 2).

Halkett, Samuel, and John Laing. *Dictionary of anonymous and pseudonymous English literature.* New and enl. ed. by James Kennedy *et al.* Edinburgh: 1926–34. 7 vols. (incl. *Suppls.*)

McKerrow, Ronald B. *An introduction to bibliography for literary students.* Oxford: 1927.

Steinberg, Sigfrid H. *A new dictionary of British history.* London: 1963.

Bowers, Fredson. *Principles of bibliographical description.* Princeton, 1949 (surtout chap. 2).

Halkett, Samuel et John Laing. *Dictionary of anonymous and pseudonymous English literature.* Édition nouvelle par James Kennedy [etc.]. Edimbourg, 1926–1934, 7 vol. (suppl. y compris).

McKerrow, Ronald B. *An introduction to bibliography for literary students.* Oxford, 1927.

Steinberg, Sigfrid H. *A new dictionary of British history.* Londres, 1963.

Abbreviations Used • Abréviations utilisées

Common abbreviations, such as *sic* and *e.g.*, are not included here. In the bibliography, an asterisk (*) appears after the bibliographic citation in the entries when that source lists more than one edition of the work.

arr. • arranged

augm. • augmented

BM • Department of Printed Books, British Museum (now the British Library)

cf. • confer, consult

corr. • corrected

ed. • edition

engr. • engraved

Les abréviations usuelles, telles *sic* et *p. ex.*, n'ont pas été incluses dans la présente liste. Dans la bibliographie, un astérisque figure après la citation bibliographique des notices lorsque la source donne plus d'une édition de l'ouvrage.

aj. • ajout, ajouté(e)

augm. • augmenté(e)

BM • Département des livres imprimés, British Museum (aujourd'hui la British Library)

cf. • conférer, consulter

c. g. • calendrier grégorien ; le calendrier grégorien a commencé à être utilisé officiellement en Grande-Bretagne le 3 septembre 1752, ce qui exigeait une correction immédiate de 11 jours d'avance ; il a commencé à être utilisé de façon non officielle bien avant. La nouvelle année commençait le 25 mars avant l'instauration du calendrier grégorien. *Voir aussi* c. j.

c. j. • calendrier julien ; calendrier utilisé officiellement jusqu'au 3 septembre 1752 en Grande-Bretagne. L'année civile, écclésiale et légale commençait alors le 25 mars, même si, de façon non officielle, l'année historique commençant le 1er janvier avait été instaurée en 1582. *Voir aussi* c. g.

corr. • corrigé(e), correction

éd. • édition

enl. • enlarged

f. • feuillet (s'il est suivi d'un chiffre)

facsim. • facsimile

fac-sim. • fac-similé

f. l. • feuillet liminaire

fol. • folio

fol. • folio

incl. • includes, including

introd. • introduction

in–4° • in-quarto

in–8° • in-octavo

in–8°(in 4s) • 4 feuillets par signature (probablement des demi-feuillets)

l. • leaf, leaves (when followed by a number)

MF • microformat: microfilm, microcard, microfiche (used especially after location symbol)

mic. • microfiche, microfilm, microforme

ms(s). • manuscript(s)

man. • manuscrit

n. • note

N.S. • New Style; refers to the Gregorian calendar, used in Britain from 3 Sept. 1752, O.S. (which required an immediate correction of eleven days advance), but often unofficially earlier. Before that date the new year began officially on 25 March. *See also*: O.S.

no(s). • number(s) (Note: Roman numerals are usually changed into the more familiar arabic numerals.)

orig. • origine

O.S. • Old Style; refers to the Julian calendar, used in Britain officially till 3 Sept. 1752, O.S., when the civil, ecclesiastical, and legal years

began 25 March, though the
historical year had begun
unofficially on 1 Jan. since 1582. *See
also*: N.S.

p. • page, pages

p. l. • preliminary leaf or leaves

p. de t. • page de titre

PRO • Public Record Office,
London, England

PRO • Public Record Office, Londres

pref. • preface

pt(s). • part(s)

part. • partie

pseud. • pseudonym

pseud. • pseudonyme

pub. • publisher, published

publ. • publication, publié(e)

q.v. • *quod vide*: which see; the
special usage here, after a title, is to
indicate that this title is listed
separately elsewhere.

q.v. • *quod vide* : qui voit. L'usage
particulier qu'on fait de cette abréviation
ici indique que le titre est répertorié
ailleurs.

rev. • revised

rév. • révisé(e)

s. d. • sans date

s. p. • sans page

sig(s). • signature(s), or signature
mark(s)

suppl(s). • supplement(s)

t.-p. • title-page

transl. • translated, translation

trad. • traduction, traduit(e)

v. or vol(s). • volume(s)

vol. • volume

4° • quarto

8° • octavo

8°(in 4s) • 4 leaves to the
signature (probably in half-sheets)

Identification of Some Abbreviations Used by Dr. Waldon
Quelques abréviations utilisées par Mme Waldon

Bodleian Library, Oxford University	• *Bod.* •	Bodleian Library, Université d'Oxford
Church Catalogue (*see* Sources Cited)	• *C.* •	Church Catalogue (*voir* Sources citées)
Canadian Archives (*see* Sources Cited, "Casey")	• *CA* •	Archives du Canada (*voir* Sources citées, "Casey")
The library of Sir Leicester Harmsworth, London. (The Northcliffe Collection, a memorial to his brother Viscount Northcliffe, is in PAC, Ottawa.)	• *Harmsworth* •	Bibliothèque de sir Leicester Harmsworth, Londres. (La collection Northcliffe, en mémoire à son frère le vicomte Northcliffe, se trouve aux APC, Ottawa.)
Cambridge (or Collection of) Harvard College, Cambridge, Mass.?	• *C.H.C.* •	Cambridge (ou collection de) Harvard College, Cambridge (Massachusetts)?
Henry E. Huntington Library, San Marino, California	• *HN* •	Bibliothèque Henry E. Huntington, San Marino (Californie)
Royal Empire Society Library, London	• *R.E.S.* •	Bibliothèque de la Royal Empire Society, Londres
Sabin (*see* Sources Cited)	• *S.* •	Sabin (*voir* Sources citées)
Stationers' Register (London. Stationers' Company. *A transcript of the registers . . . 1554-1640* . . . . Edited by Edward Arber. London, 1875–77; Birmingham, 1894. 5 vols.)	• *S.R.* •	Stationers' Register (London. Stationers' Company. *A transcript of the registers . . . 1554-1640* . . . . Édité par Edward Arber. Londres, 1875–1877; Birmingham, 1894. 5 vol.)

Bibliography of Canadiana
Published in Great Britain,
1519–1763

Bibliographie des ouvrages
sur le Canada publiés en
Grande-Bretagne entre 1519 et 1763

1519

[Rastell, John], *ca./vers* 1475–1536, *supposed author/auteur présumé*. Nature of the four elements. A new iuterlude [*sic*] and a mery of the nature of the iiij. elements declarynge many proper poynts of phylosophy naturall and of dyuers straunge landys and of dyuers straunge effects & causis whiche interlude yf ye hole matter be playd wyl conteyne the space of an hour and a halfe but yf ye lyst ye may leue out muche of the sad mater as the messengers pte and some of naturys parte and some of expervens pte & yet the matter wyl depend conuenyently and than it wyll not be paste thre quarters of an hour of length .... [London? 1519?] 1 v., unpaged. 8°

NUC (Pre–56) 481:669

This play contains the first description of America printed in English (p. ci–cii). The passage is supposed to reflect the experience of Cabot. In 1517, John Rastell, a printer and publisher, attempted a voyage to Newfoundland, apparently with the same purpose as the Gilberts and Frobisher later: to establish a colony on Newfoundland to serve as a base for exploration to find the Northwest Passage. These plans were frustrated by a mutinous crew, but he may have written and printed this play as one tangible result of his interest in the New World. ¶ *Waldon notes "Frequently reprinted"; but not, apparently, before 1764. ¶ For a note on the orthography of this and similar title-pages of this period, see the Introduction.*

Cette pièce contient la première description de l'Amérique imprimée en anglais (p. ci–cii). Ce passage est censé refléter l'expérience de Cabot. En 1517, l'imprimeur et éditeur John Rastell entreprit un voyage pour Terre-Neuve, en caressant le même projet que, plus tard, Gilberts et Frobisher : établir à Terre-Neuve une colonie destinée à servir de base aux activités d'exploration visant à découvrir le passage du Nord-Ouest. La mutinerie de l'équipage contrecarra l'entreprise, mais il est possible que Rastell ait écrit et imprimé cette pièce comme preuve tangible de son intérêt pour le Nouveau Monde. ¶ *Waldon indique « fréquentes réimpressions » ; mais apparemment pas avant 1764. ¶ À propos de l'orthographe des pages de titre de cette époque*, voir *l'introduction du présent ouvrage.*

Eden, Richard, 1521?–1576, *ed. and trad./rév. et trad.* The decades of the newe worlde or West India, conteynyng the nauigations and conquestes of the Spanyardes, with the particular description of the most ryche and large landes and ilandes lately founde in the west ocean; perteynyng to the inheritaunce of the kinges of Spayne. In the which the diligent reader may not only consyder what commoditie may hereby chaunce to the hole Christian orld in tyme to come, but also learne many secreates touchynge the lande, the sea, and the starres, very necessarie to be knowē to al such as shal attempte any nauigations, or otherwise haue delite to beholde the strange and woonderfull woorkes of God and nature. Wrytten in the Latine tounge by Peter Martyr of Angleria, and translated into Englysshe by Rycharde Eden. Londini. In aedibis Guilhelmi Powell. Anno. 1555. [24] p.l., 361, [13] numb. l., fol. diagrs. 4°

NUC (Pre–56)155:415*

Colophon: Imprynted at London in Paules Churchyarde at the signe of the Byble by Richarde Jug. Anno Dñi M.D.LV. ¶ William Powell printed this book for Robert Toy, Edwarde Sutton, and Wyllam Seres, and perhaps others, as well as for Richarde Jug, and each had his name separately inserted in the colophon of his quota of copies; some copies may have had no colophon at all. [This is a paraphrase of Dr. Waldon's notes, in which she also remarks on one copy with a map laid in and another with a portrait; she refers the reader to Church 1:236–41 for a facsimile title-page, full collation, and valuable notes.] ¶ *NUC copy has an extra leaf inserted between leaves 309 and 310.* ¶ The title is in black-letter, excepting "The decades" and the imprint, and all is within an ornamental border. ¶

This is the third English book on America and the first English collection of voyages and discoveries. This is the first English book with any real description relevant to our purpose, however. ¶ There is a reference to "the woorthy owlde man yet lyuing Sebastiane Cabote" in "The preface to the Reader" (C1ᵃ) and several other references in the text; an account of his voyage to "Baccallaos" in the sixth book of the third Decade (fol. 118ᵇ–119ᵃ) and "Of the lande of Bacoaleos cauled Terra Baccalearum, situate on the North syde of the firme lande" (fol. 213ᵇ). The most important passages referring to Canada occur in the fourth Decade, in the section headed (fol. 249): Of Moscouie and Cathay. A discourse of Dyuers vyages and wayes by the whiche Spices, Precious stones, and golde were brought in owlde tyme India into Europe and other partes of the world. Also of the voyage to Cathay and East India by the north sea: And of certeyne secreates touchynge the same vyage, declared by the duke of Moscouie his ambassadoure to an excellent lerned gentelman of Italia, named Galeatius Butrigarius. Lykewyse of the vyages of that woorthy owlde man Sebastian Cabote, yet liuynge in Englande, and at this present the gouernour of the coompany of the marchantes of Cathay in the citie of London. ¶ "Of Moscouie and Cathay" (fol. 249) refers to Cartier's voyage, the Northwest Passage and Cabot; "of the landes of Laborador and Baccalaos, lyinge west and northwest from le tout est encadré par une bordure décorative. ¶ Il s'agit du troisième livre anglais traitant de l'Amérique et du premier recueil anglais de voyages et de découvertes. Quoiqu'il en soit, c'est le premier livre anglais offrant une description pertinente pour notre recherche. ¶ On fait mention de « Sébastien Cabote, ce vénérable vieillard toujours vivant » dans « The preface to the Reader » (C1ᵃ) et dans quelques autres passages du texte ; on fait mention de son voyage au « Baccallaos » dans le sixième livre de la troisième décade (fol. 118ᵇ–119ᵃ) et « De la terre de Bacoaleos appelée Terra Baccalearum, située du côté nord de la terre ferme », (fol. 213ᵇ). Les passages les plus importants se rapportant au Canada se trouvent dans la quatrième décade, dans la partie intitulée (fol. 249) « Of Moscouie and Cathay ». Un traité sur les divers périples et routes ayant permis de rapporter des Indes anciennes vers l'Europe et d'autres parties du monde, des épices, des pierres précieuses et de l'or. À propos également du voyage à Cathay et aux Indes orientales via la mer du nord : et de certains secrets concernant le même voyage révélé par l'ambassadeur du duc de Moscou à un excellent et érudit gentilhomme de l'Italie nommé Galeatius Butrigarius. Aussi des voyages de Sébastien Cabote, ce vénérable vieillard toujours vivant en Angleterre, et, à l'heure actuelle, gouverneur de la Compagnie des marchands de Cathay dans la cité de Londres. ¶ « Of Moscouie and Cathay », (fol. 249), fait mention du voyage de Cartier, du passage du Nord-Ouest et de Cabot ; l'article « of the landes of Laborador and Baccalaos, lyinge west and northwest from Englande, and beinge parte of the firme lande of the West Indies » (fol. 317 et 318ᵇ), fait de nouveau mention de Cabot. ¶ *Première*

Englande, and beinge parte of the firme lande of the West Indies" (fol. 317 and 318 ^{b}) again refers to Cabot. ¶ *First edition; another edition* 1577; see also *1612, 1626, 1628, under Anghiera, Pietro M. d'.*

édition ; autre édition, 1577 ; voir aussi 1612, 1626, 1628, sous Anghiera, Pietro M. d'.

1559

Lanquet, Thomas, 1521–1545. An epitome of cronicles. Conteyninge the whole discourse of the histories as well of this realme of England as al other coūtreys, with the succesion [sic] of their kinges . . . and what notable actes they did . . . gathered out of most probable auctours. Firste by Thomas Lanquet, from the beginning of the worlde to the incarnacion of Christe, secondely to the reigne of . . . King Edward the sixt by Thomas Cooper, and thirdly to the reigne of . . . Quene Elizabeth, by Robert Crowley. Londini, In aedibus Thomae Marshe, 1559. 28 p.l., 280 fol., 30 l. 4°

NUC (Pre–56)315:499*

Colophon: Imprinted at London by VVilliam Seres . . . 1559. ¶ P.l. 28 blank. ¶ Many folios wrongly numbered; Waldon's collation is: t.-p., [26], 280, [26] fol. 4°. ¶ There is a reference to Cabot, "An englisheman, borne at Bristow, but a genoways [*i.e.* Genoan's] sonne" (4E3 ^{b}). This passage was added in 1559 to the first edition of Cooper's *Chronicle,* 1549, without his authorization, but was retained by him, with alterations in his 1560 and 1565 editions [*q.v.* under Thomas Lanquet, *Coopers Chronicle,* below]. ¶ *The first ed. of the* Chronicle, *by Thomas Cooper, bp. of Winchester (1517?–1594), was pub. (presumably with no Canadian reference) under the*

Colophon : Imprinted at London by VVilliam Seres . . . 1559. ¶ F. p. 28 blanc. ¶ Beaucoup de feuillets numérotés incorrectement. Collation de Waldon : p. de t., [26], 280, [26] fol. in-4°. ¶ On y fait mention de Cabot, « Un Anglais, né à Bristow, mais fils d'un Génois » (4E3 ^{b}). Ce passage fut ajouté en 1559 à la première édition de Chronicle de Cooper, datant de 1549, sans son autorisation ; toutefois, celui-ci le conserva en le modifiant dans les éditions de 1560 et de 1565 [q.v. Thomas Lanquet, Coopers Chronicle, plus bas]. ¶ La première édition de Chronicle par Thomas Cooper, évêque de Winchester (1517 ?–1594) fut publiée (probablement sans matériel concernant le Canada) sous le titre An epitome of cronicles gathered fyrst, by Thomas Lanquet, from the beginnyng of the world to the

title: An epitome of cronicles gathered fyrst, by Thomas Lanquet, from the beginnyng of the world to the incarnation of Christ, and now continued by Thomas Cooper. *London, 1549. The third source mentioned in the title, by Robert Crowley (1518?–1588), has not been positively identified, and may not have been published separately, but possibly it is contained in* The select works of Robert Crowley, printer, archdeacon of Hereford (1559–1567), vicar of St. Lawrence, Jewry, &c. &c .... *London, pub. for the Early English Text Soc., by N. Trübner, 1872 (extra series, no. 15) — cf. NUC(Pre–56) 128:264.*

to the incarnation of Christ, and now continued by Thomas Cooper. *Londres, 1549. La troisième source mentionnée dans le titre et attribuée à Robert Crowley (1518 ?–1588) n'a pas été identifiée avec certitude et n'a peut-être pas fait l'objet d'une publication distincte. Toutefois, elle fait probablement partie de* The select works of Robert Crowley, printer, archdeacon of Hereford (1559–1567), vicar of St. Lawrence, Jewry, &c. &c. .... *Londres, publié pour la Early English Text Soc., par N. Trübner, 1872 (collection supplémentaire, nº 15) –cf. NUC(Pre–56)128:264.*

1560

*[Lanquet, Thomas], 1521–1545. Coopers chronicle, conteininge the whole discourse of the histories as well of this realme, as all other countreis, with the succession of their kynges, the time of their raigne, and what notable actes were done by them, newly enlarged and augmented, as well in the first part with diuers profitable histories, as in the latter ende with the whole summe of those thinges that Paulus Iouius and Sleidane hath written of layte yeres, that is, from the beginnyng of Kyng Henrie the Eightes raigne vnto the late death of Queene Marie, by me Thomas Cooper. Londini, 1560. 30 p.l., 377 numb. l, 1 l. 4°(?)

NUC(Pre–56)315:497*

Colophon: Imprinted at London in Flete strete, in the house late Thomas Berthelettes ... anno 1560. ¶ Title within ornamental border; black-letter. ¶ On verso of t.-p. is "An

Colophon : Imprinted at London in Flete strete, in the house late Thomas Berthelettes ... anno 1560. ¶ Titre encadré par une bordure décorative ; écriture gothique. ¶ Au verso de la page de titre, on peut lire « An

admonicion to the reader," warning him against the piratical edition published by Marsh and Seres in 1559. ¶ First edition pub. as: *An epitome of cronicles . . . by Thomas Lanquet . . . and now continued by Thomas Cooper*. London, 1549; but Canadian references first appeared, apparently, in Thomas Lanquet, *An epitome of cronicles*. London, 1559, the pirated edition mentioned above — *q.v.* for other notes and editions. A later issue of the 1560 edition appeared the same year — *see* next entry.

admonicion to the reader » (un avertisse-ment au lecteur) qui met celui-ci en garde contre l'édition pirate publiée par Marsh et Seres en 1559. ¶ La première édition fut publiée à Londres en 1549 sous le titre *An epitome of cronicles . . . by Thomas Lanquet . . . and now continued by Thomas Cooper*. Il semble, toutefois, que les premiers passages se rapportant au Canada aient été introduits dans l'édition pirate mentionnée ci-dessus : Thomas Lanquet, *An epitome of cronicles*. Londres, 1559 (*q.v.* pour d'autres notes et éditions). Une version ultérieure de l'édition de 1560 parut la même année (*voir* notice suivante).

*[Lanquet, Thomas]**, 1521–1545.   Coopers chronicle . . . newly enlarged and aug-mented from the beginnyyng of Kyng Henrie the Eightes raigne unto the late death of Queene Marie, by me Thomas Cooper. Londini, 1560. [60] p., 376 numb. l., [16] p. 4°(?)

NUC(Pre–56)315:497*

See preceding entry. ¶ Other entries appear in NUC, with 1560 date, and variant spellings and collations, some possibly being different issues.

Voir notice précédente. ¶ D'autres notices figurent au NUC pour l'année 1560, présentant des variantes orthographiques et descriptives du même ouvrage ; dans cer-tains cas, il peut s'agir de tirages différents.

AN EPITOME

OF CRONICLES.

Conteyninge the whole discourse
of the histories as well of this realme of England as al other coūtreys, with the succession of their
kinges, the time of their reigne, and what notable
actes they did: much profitable to be redde, namelye
of Magistrates, and such as haue auctoritee in com-
mō weales, gathered out of most probable auctours.
Firste by Thomas Lanquet, from the beginning of the worlde to the incarnacion
of Christe, Secondely to the reigne of
our soueraigne lord king Edward,
the sixt by Thomas Cooper,
and thirdly to the reigne of
our soueraigne Ladye,
Quene Elizabeth, by
Robert Crow-
ley.

Anno . 1 5 5 9 .

LONDINI,

In ædibus Thomæ Marshe.

Thomas Lanquet. *An epitome of chronicles.* London/Londres, 1559.

1563

Ribaut, Jean, *fl.* 1520–1565. The VVhole and true discouerye of Terra Florida, (englished [as] the Florishing lande.) Conteyning as well the wonderfull straunge natures and maners of the people . . . neuer founde out before the last yere 1562. Written in Frenche by Captaine Ribauld the fyrst that whollye discouered the same. And nowe newly set forthe in Englishe the .xxx. of May, 1563. Prynted at London by Rouland Hall, for Thomas Hacket [1563]. 23 l. 8°

NUC(Pre–56)492:147*

Reference to Cabot, under 1498: (A2–A3). The author holds that God reserved America for France because France will convert the natives to Christianity. ¶ *Transl. from his* Histoire de l'expedition française en Floride. *London, 1563; English transl. reprinted as "The true and last discouerie of Florida, made by Captain John Ribault in the yeere 1562 . . . transl. into Englishe by one Thomas Hackit" (in Richard Hakluyt,* Divers voyages touching the discovery of America. *London, 1582,* q.v.; *reprinted London, Hakluyt Soc., 1850); reprinted as his* Narrative of the first voyage of Jean de Ribault *(in B.F. French,* Historical collections of Louisiana and Florida. *New York, 1875, 2d ser., p. 159–89); further reprinted as* Jean Ribaut's discoverye of Terra Florida. *[London? 1917], itself a reprint from* English historical review, *April 1917.*

Il est fait mention de Cabot à propos de l'année 1498 : (A2–A3). L'auteur prétend que Dieu a réservé l'Amérique à la France parce que la France convertira les indigènes au christianisme. ¶ *Traduction de l'ouvrage de Ribaut intitulé* Histoire de l'expedition française en Floride. *Londres, 1563 ; la traduction anglaise fut réimprimée sous le titre « The true and last discouerie of Florida, made by Captain John Ribault in the yeere 1562 . . . transl. into Englishe by one Thomas Hackit »* (dans Richard Hakluyt, Divers voyages touching the discovery of America. *Londres, 1582,* q.v. ; *réimpression à Londres, Hakluyt Soc., 1850) ; réimpression de l'ouvrage sous le titre* Narrative of the first voyage of Jean de Ribault *(dans B.F. French,* Historical collections of Louisiana and Florida. *New York, 1875, deuxième coll., p. 159–89) ; réimpression ultérieure sous le titre* Jean Ribaut's discoverye of Terra Florida. *[Londres ? 1917], ce document étant lui-même une réimpression de* English historical review, *avril 1917.*

1565

*[Lanquet, Thomas], 1521–1545. Coopers chronicle contenynge the vvhole discourse of the histories as well of thys realme, as all other countreis. With the succession of theyr kynges, the tyme of theyr reign, and what notable actes were done by thē [i.e. them] newely enlarged and augmented, as well in the first parts wyth diuers profitable historries. As in the latter ende wyth the whole summe of those thynges that Paulus Jouius and Sleigdane hath written of late yers that is, now lately ouersene and with great dilligence corrected and augmented vnto the .vii. yere of the raigne of our most gracious Quene Elizabeth that nowe is. [London] Anno. 1565. the first day of Auguste. 30 p.l., 376 numb. l., 8 l. 4°

NUC(Pre–56)315:498*

First edition pub. as *An epitome of cronicles . . . by Thomas Lanquet . . . and now continued by Thomas Cooper.* London, 1549; but Canadian references first appeared, apparently, in Thomas Lanquet, *An epitome of cronicles.* London, 1559, *q.v.* for other notes and editions. Also, the following variant.

Première édition publiée sous le titre *An epitome of cronicles . . . by Thomas Lanquet . . . and now continued by Thomas Cooper.* Londres, 1549 ; toutefois, on trouve les premiers passages se rapportant au Canada dans Thomas Lanquet, *An epitome of cronicles.* Londres, 1559, *q.v.* pour d'autres notes et éditions. *Voir aussi* la variante suivante.

*[Lanquet, Thomas], 1521–1545. Coopers chronicle conteinyng the whole discourse of the histories, as vvell of thys realme, as all other countreys, with the succession of their kings . . . vnto the .vii. yeare of the reigne of . . . Queene Elizabeth, that now is. [London] Anno Domini 1565. xx. die Mens. Aprili. 30 p.l., 378 [i.e. 380] numb. l., 4 l. 4°(?)

NUC(Pre–56)315:498*

For notes, *see* preceding entry, another issue, and compare variant spellings, collations, and months of printing. Other entries appear in NUC, with 1565 date, variant spellings

Voir les notes de la notice précédente, qui présente un autre tirage de cette publication, et comparer les variantes orthographiques et descriptives, ainsi que les mois d'impression. D'autres notices figurent au NUC pour

and collations, some possibly being issues; one is on MF.

l'année *1565*, présentant des variantes orthographiques et descriptives du même ouvrage (dans certains cas, il peut s'agir de tirages différents), dont une reproduction sur mic.

*Stow, John, 1525?–1605. A summarie of Englyshe chronicles, conteynyng the true accompt of yeres, wherein euery kyng of . . . England began theyr reigne, howe long they reigned: and what notable thynges hath bene doone durynge theyr reygnes. . . . Collected . . . in the yere . . . 1565 . . . In aedibus Thomae Marshi. 247 l. 8°

NUC(Pre–56)572:36*

Colophon: Imprinted at London by Thomas Marshe. 1565. ¶ Collation from BM(to 1955)231:52. ¶ This is the first edition under this title, of a work later issued in more complete form as his *The chronicles of England.* London, 1580, *q.v.* for other notes. *A breviat chronicle contaynynge all the kynges [of England].* Canterbury, J. Mychell [1561], is not an earlier ed. but a different work (cf. DNB, "Stow, John"). The text of *A summarie* was republished in MF, in STC series (no. 15586, carton 356), Ann Arbor, Mich., University Microfilms, and in hard copy by the same publisher, 1966 (cf. NUC); other editions under this title: 1566, 1567, 1570, 1573, 1575, 1579, 1584, 1587, 1590, 1598, 1604.

Colophon : Imprinted at London by Thomas Marshe. 1565. ¶ Collation du BM(to 1955)231:52. ¶ Il s'agit de la première édition publiée sous ce titre; un ouvrage parut ultérieurement sous une forme plus complète et intitulée *The chronicles of England.* Londres, 1580, *q.v.* pour d'autres notes. *A breviat chronicle contaynynge all the kynges [of England].* Canterbury, J. Mychell [1561], n'est pas une édition antérieure, mais un ouvrage différent (cf. DNB sous Stow, John). Le texte de *A summarie* a été reproduit sur mic. dans la collection du STC (n° 15586, carton 356), Ann Arbor (Mich.), University Microfilms ; il a aussi été reproduit sur papier par le même éditeur, 1966 (cf. NUC) ; autres éditions sous le même titre : 1566, 1567, 1570, 1573, 1575, 1579, 1584, 1587, 1590, 1598, 1604.

1566

Stow, John, 1525?–1605. A summarie of ur Englysh chronicles. Diligently collected by Iohn Stowe . . . 1566. . . . London, imprinted by T[homas]. Marshe [1566]. 12 p.l., 281 (*i.e.* 279) numb. [l]., 13 [l]. 16°(?)

NUC(Pre–56)572:36*

A 1566 ed. with variant title: BM(to 1955)231:51. ¶ First ed.: London, 1565, *q.v.* for other notes.

Édition de 1566 avec variante dans le titre : BM(to 1955)231:51. ¶ Première édition : Londres, 1565, *q.v.* pour d'autres notes.

1567

Stow, John, 1525?–1605. A summarie of Englishe chronicles, . . . abridged and continued til this present moneth of Nouember . . . 1567. By J.S. London, imprinted by Thomas Marshe [1567]. [12], 200, [2] [l]. 16°

BM(to 1955)231:51*

Leaves 177–200 misnumbered 77–100. ¶ First ed.: London, 1565, *q.v.* for other notes.

Feuillets 177 à 200 numérotés par erreur 77 à 100. ¶ Première édition : Londres, 1565, *q.v.* pour d'autres notes.

1568

Grafton, Richard, *d./déc.* 1572? This seconde volume [chronicle of Briteyn], beginning at William the Conquerour, endeth wyth . . . Queene Elizabeth . . . . [London], 1568. vol. 2.

See vol. 1, under title *A chronicle at large* . . . , London, 1569, for other notes.

Pour d'autres notes, *voir* le vol. 1, sous le titre *A chronicle at large* . . . , Londres, 1569.

Thevet, André, 1502–1590. The new found vvorlde, or Antarctike, wherein is contained wõderful and strange things, as well of humaine creatures, as beastes, fishes, foules, and serpents, trees, plants, mines of golde and siluer: garnished with many learned aucthorities, trauailed and written in the French tong, by that excellent learned man, Master Andrevve Thevet. And now newly translated into Englishe, wherein is reformed the errours of the auncient cosmographers. Imprinted at London, by Henrie Bynneman, for Thomas Hacket. And are to be sold at his shop in Poules church-yard, at the signe of the key [1568]. 8 p.l., 138 numb. [l]., [3] p. 4°

NUC(Pre–56)589:544*

Transl. by Thomas Hacket from *Les singvlaritez de la France Antarctique, avtrement nommée Amerique* . . . . Paris, 1557. ¶ *Title within ornamental border; Dedicatory epistle to Sir Henrie Sidney (signed Thomas Hacket), in italics, text in Gothic type.* ¶ *Colophon: Imprinted at London, in Knight-rider strete, by Henry Bynneman, for Thomas Hacket 1568.* ¶ Several folios misnumbered. ¶ *Text of this edition republished in MF, Ann Arbor, Mich., University Microfilms, no. 15640, carton 360 (STC:23950)* — *cf. NUC. Numerous editions in French, Spanish: cf. NUC.* ¶ *OTP*

Traduction par Thomas Hacket de *Les singvlaritez de la France Antarctique, avtrement nommée Amerique.* . . . Paris, 1557. ¶ *Titre encadré par une bordure décorative ; épître dédicatoire à l'intention de sir Henrie Sidney (signée Thomas Hacket), en italiques, texte en caractères gothiques.* ¶ *Colophon : Imprinted at London, in Knight-rider strete, by Henry Bynneman, for Thomas Hacket 1568.* ¶ Plusieurs feuillets numérotés incorrectement. ¶ *Le texte de cette édition a été reproduit sur mic., Ann Arbor (Mich.), University Microfilms, n° 15640, carton 360 (STC:23950)* –*cf. NUC. De nombreuses éditions en français et en espagnol : cf. NUC.* ¶ *OTP*

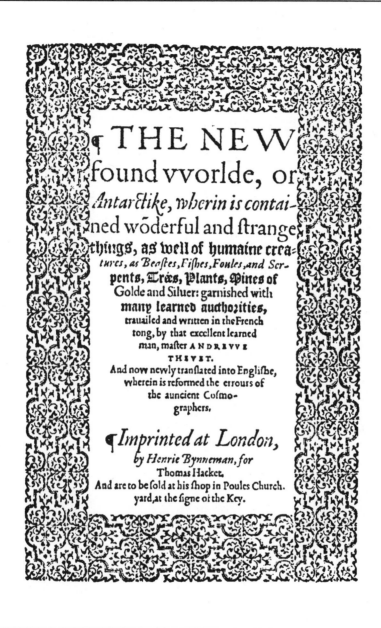

¶ THE NEW
found vvorlde, or
Antarctike, wherin is contai-
ned wōderful and ſtrange
things, as well of humaine creatures, as *Beaſtes, Fiſhes, Foules, and Ser-*
pents, Trées, Plants, Mines of
Golde and Siluer: garniſhed with
many learned authozities,
trauailed and written in the French
tong, by that excellent learned
man, maſter A N D R E V V E
T H E V E T.
And now newly tranſlated into Engliſhe,
wherein is reformed the errours of
the auncient Coſmo-
graphers.

¶ *Imprinted at London,*
by *Henrie Bynneman, for*
Thomas Hacket.
And are to be ſold at his ſhop in Poules Church.
yard, at the ſigne of the Key.

André Thevet. *The new found vvorld, or Antarctike* .... London/Londres, 1568.

1569

[**Grafton, Richard**], *d./dec.* 1572? A chronicle at large, and meere history of the affayres of Englande, and kinges of the same, deduced from the creation of the worlde, vnto the first yere of the reigne of ... Queene Elizabeth: collected out of sundry aucthors .... [London, imprinted by H[enry]. Denham, for R[ichard]. Tottyl and H[umphrey]. Toye] 1569 [–1568]. 2 v. in 1. illus. 4°(?)

NUC(Pre–56)209:379*

Vol. 2 has title: This seconde volume, beginning at William the Conquerour .... *London, 1568, q.v., above.* ¶ New edition, [London, printed for J. Johnson etc.] 1809, v. 2, p. 393, has reference to Cabot under <1527, May>. [The work was reprinted by University Microfilms, Ann Arbor, Mich., ca. 1950, as no. 14215 (cf. NUC).]

Le deuxième volume porte le titre This seconde volume, beginning at William the Conquerour .... *Londres, 1568, q.v. plus haut.* ¶ Une nouvelle édition, [imprimée à Londres pour J. Johnson etc.] en 1809, vol. 2, p. 393, contient une mention concernant Cabot sous <1527, May>. [Reproduction sur mic., Ann Arbor (Mich.), University Microfilms, v. 1950, sous le n° 14215 (cf. NUC).]

1570

*Stow, John, 1525?–1605. A summarye of the chronicles of Englande, from the first comminge of Brute into this lande, vnto this present yeare ... 1570. Diligentlye collected and nowe newly corrected and enlarged .... Imprinted in London by Thomas Marshe. [1570.] 8°

NUC(Pre–56)572:36*

NUC has three issues, each with variant collations by signatures. ¶ First ed.: London, 1565, *q.v.* for other notes; text republished in MF in the

Le NUC donne trois exemplaires, la collation par signature étant différente pour chacun d'eux. ¶ Première éd. : Londres, 1565, *q.v.* pour d'autres notes ; reproduction sur mic.

STC series, by University Microfilms, Ann Arbor, Mich. (no. 23332 [*i.e.* 23322], carton 356 — cf. NUC). dans la collection du STC, Ann Arbor (Mich.), University Microfilms, (n° 23332 [*c.-à-d.* 23322] carton 356 –cf. NUC).

1573

*Stow, John, 1525?–1605. The summarye of the chronicles of Englande. Lately collected, newly corrected, abridged and continued, vnto this present yeare of Christ 1573. By I.S. Imprinted at London by Thomas Marshe. [1573.] [532] p. 16°

NUC(Pre–56)572:36*

Format from BM(to 1955)231:51. ¶ First ed.: London, 1565, *q.v.* for other notes. Format du BM(to 1955)231:51. ¶ Première édition : Londres, 1565, *q.v.* pour d'autres notes.

1575

*Stow, John, 1525?–1605. A summarie of the chronicles of England, from the first coming of Brute into this land, vnto this present yeare of Christ 1575 .... London, Richard Cottle [*i.e.* Tottle?] and Henry Binneman [1575]. viii [l]., 570 p., xxviii [l]. 8°

NUC(Pre–56)572:36*

Numerous errors in pagination. ¶ Imprint and collation from BM(to 1955)231:51. ¶ First ed.: London, 1565, *q.v.* for other notes. Nombreuses erreurs de pagination. ¶ Adresse bibliographique et collation du BM(to 1955)231:51. ¶ Première édition : Londres, 1565, *q.v.* pour d'autres notes.

1576

Gilbert, Sir **Humphrey**, 1539?–1583. A discourse of a discouerie for a new passage to Cataia. VVritten by Sir Humfrey Gilbert, Knight. Quid non? Imprinted at London by Henry Middleton for Richarde Ihones. Anno Domini. 1576. Aprilis 12. 14 p.l., [60] p. fold. map. 4°

NUC(Pre–56)199:437*

"Faultes escaped in the printing" at end. ¶ *Title within ornamental border; the text in black-letter, woodcut initials.* ¶ *Waldon has pagination as [84] p.* ¶ *Booklist on verso of colophon.* ¶ "The book, which is an essay to prove the practicability of the Northwest Passage, is credited with giving a new impulse to English explorations" (Church:117). ¶ *First edition; reprinted, Richard Hakluyt,* Voyages, *London, 1589, vol. 3, p. 597–610, and (says Waldon) "frequently, thereafter,"* sometimes with the title Voyage to Newfoundland *(cf. NUC and BLC); also at Ann Arbor, University Microfilms, no. 14161.*

Errata à la fin. ¶ *Titre encadré par une bordure décorative ; texte en caractères gothiques, initiales xylographiées.* ¶ *Waldon dénombre [84] pages.* ¶ *Liste de livres au verso du colophon.* ¶ « Le livre, qui est un essai visant à prouver la praticabilité du passage du Nord-Ouest, est reconnu pour avoir donné un nouvel élan aux explorations anglaises » (Church:117). ¶ *Première édition ; réimpressions : Richard Hakluyt,* Voyages, *Londres, 1589, vol. 3, p. 597–610, et, selon Waldon, « à de nombreuses reprises par la suite », parfois sous le titre* Voyage to Newfoundland *(cf. NUC et BLC), ainsi qu'à Ann Arbor, University Microfilms, n° 14161.*

Eden, Richard, 1521?–1576, *ed. and tr./rév. and trad.* The history of trauayle in the VVest and East Indies, and other countreys lying eyther way, towardes the fruitfull and ryche Moluccaes. As Moscouia, Persia, Arabia, Syria, Aegypte, Ethiopia, Guinea, China in Cathayo, and Giapan: VVith a discourse of the Northwest passage. In the hande of our Lorde be all the corners of the earth. Psal. 94. Gathered in parte, and done into Englyshe by Richarde Eden. Newly set in order, augmented, and finished by Richarde VVilles. Imprinted at London by Richarde Iugge. 1577. Cum privilegio. 10 p.l., 466 numb. l., 6 l. diagr. 4°

NUC(Pre–56)155:416*

Many leaves irregularly numbered. ¶ *Eden's* Decades of the newe worlde, *1555, rearranged, some parts omitted, and a number of translations added. Church notes that Oviedo's* History of the West Indies *is also included, points out that Eden had died the year before, and lists all the passages in the 1555 edition which are here omitted.* ¶ Contents relating to Canada: "Of the lande of Baccalos, called Terra Baccalearum, situate on the north syde of the firme land": fol. [*i.e.* leaf] 225; "Of the landes of Laborador and Baccalaos, lying in the West and northwest from England and being part of the firme lande of the VVest Indies": fol. 227 ᵇ–228 ᵇ; "For M. Cap. Fvrbyshers [*i.e.*, Frobisher's] Passage by the Northvvest. Of China in Cathayo . . . By Richarde Willes." (Addressed to Lady Anne, Countess of VVarwyke): fol. 230–36; "Of the Northeast frostie Seas . . . likewise of the viages of that worthie old man Sebastian Cabote,

Numérotation irrégulière pour beaucoup de feuillets. ¶ *Il s'agit d'un remaniement des* Decades of the newe worlde *d'Eden; l'édition a éte amputée de certaines parties et augmentée de plusieurs traductions. Church signale l'insertion de* History of the West Indies *par Oviedo, souligne le décès d'Eden un an auparavant, et donne la liste de tous les passages de l'édition de 1555 qui ont été retranchés.* ¶ Qui portent sur le Canada : « Of the lande of Baccalos, called Terra Baccalearum, situate on the north syde of the firme land » : fol. [*c.-à-d.* feuillet] 225 ; « Of the landes of Laborador and Baccalaos, lying in the West and northwest from England and being part of the firme lande of the VVest Indies » : fol. 227 ᵇ –228 ᵇ ; « For M. Cap. Fvrbyshers [*c.-à-d.* Frobisher's] Passage by the Northvvest. Of China in Cathayo . . . By Richarde Willes. » (Dédié à Lady Anne, comtesse de VVarwyke) : fol. 230–36 ; « Of the Northeast frostie Seas . . . likewise of the viages of that worthie old man Sebastian Cabote, sometymes governour of the companie of the Merchantes of Cathay, in the Citie of

Sebastian Cabote, sometymes governour of the companie of the Merchantes of Cathay, in the Citie of London": fol. 254 [*i.e.*, 261]. The most interesting material not contained in the 1555 edition is the letter to the Countess of Warwick. ¶ *See* 1555 (Eden, *The decades*).

London » : fol. 254 [*c.-à-d.* 261]. Le document le plus intéressant parmi ceux ne faisant pas partie de l'édition de 1555 est celui dédié à la comtesse de Warwick. ¶ *Voir* 1555 (Eden, *The decades*).

Fuller, _____, *fl.* 1577. Ffullers ffarewell to master Ffourbousier and the other gentlemen adventurers whoe labour to discouer the right passage to Catay. Licensed to John Jugge, May 20, 1577, charge, "iiij d and a copie." [London, 1577.] [No collation or format given.]

"S.R., v. 2, fol. 139b, p. 312."

Dr. Waldon's source is: London. Stationers' Company. A transcript of the registers of the Company of Stationers of London; 1554–1640 .... Edited by Edward Arber. London, 1875–77; Birmingham, 1894. 5 vols.; vol. 2, l. 139b. ¶ Waldon observes that no copy is apparently extant, and that it was probably a ballad or a broadside.

Source de Waldon : Londres. Stationers' Company. A transcript of the registers of the Company of Stationers of London; 1554–1640 .... Édité par Edward Arber. Londres, 1875–1877 ; Birmingham, 1894, 5 vol. ; vol. 2, f. 139b. ¶ Waldon fait observer qu'il n'y a apparemment plus d'exemplaire conservé et qu'il s'agissait probablement d'une ballade sur in-plano.

Settle, Dionyse. A true reporte of the laste voyage into the West and Northwest regions, &c. 1577. worthily atchieued by Capteine Frobisher of the sayde voyage the first finder and Generall. With a description of the people there inhabiting, and other circumstances notable. Written by Dionyse Settle, one of the companie in the sayde voyage, and seruant to the Right Honourable the Earle of Cumberland. Nil mortalibus arduum est. Imprinted at London by Henrie Middleton. Anno. 1577. 24 [l]. 8°

NUC(Pre–56)539:511*

Title within ornamental border. ¶ *"A rythme decasyllabicall, upon this last luckie voyage of worthie Capteine Frobisher. 1577"* (verso of t.-p.) signed: *Abraham Fleming.* ¶ Settle accompanied Frobisher on his second voyage. His account differs from that of Best [George Best, d. 1584?] who also accompanied Frobisher, and who published an account of all three voyages in 1578 [*A Trve discovrse of the late voyages of discouerie* .... London, 1578]. ¶ A second issue in the same year has some slight variations and additions to the text... a photostat is included in the Americana series of the Mass. Hist. Soc., no. 140 .... Reprinted [Richard] Hakluyt, [*The principall navigations* .... London.] 1589, v. 3, p. 622–30, and J[ohn]. Pinkerton, *A general collection of voyages,* [17 vols. London, 1807–14], v. 12, 1808: also privately reprinted by John Carter Brown, Providence, R.I., 1868. ¶ *BVAU · BVIPA (1868)*

Titre encadré par une bordure décorative. ¶ *"A rythme decasyllabicall, upon this last luckie voyage of worthie Capteine Frobisher. 1577"* (verso de la p. de t.) signé : *Abraham Fleming.* ¶ Settle a accompagné Frobisher lors de son deuxième voyage. Son compte rendu diffère de celui de Best [George Best, déc. 1584?] qui accompagna également Frobisher et publia un compte rendu des trois voyages faits en 1578 [*A Trve discovrse of the late voyages of discouerie* .... Londres, 1578]. ¶ Un deuxième tirage présente quelques variations et additions au texte... le n° 140 de la collection Americana de la Mass. Hist. Soc. en présente une photocopie .... Réimpression [Richard] Hakluyt, [*The principall navigations* .... Londres.] 1589, vol. 3, p. 622–30, et J[ohn]. Pinkerton, *A general collection of voyages,* [17 vol. Londres, 1807–1814], vol. 12, 1808: et une réimpression privée par John Carter Brown, Providence (R.I.), 1868. ¶ *BVAU · BVIPA (1868)*

A thinge touchinge Ffourboyser. Licensed to Andrew Manssell ... July 1, 1577, charge, "iiij d and a copie." [London, 1577.] [No collation or format.]

"S.R., v. 2, fol. 140b, p. 314."

Dr. Waldon's source: The stationers' register (see note to Fuller, 1577, above, for full citation). She notes that no copy is apparently extant, and that it was probably a ballad or broadside.

Source de Waldon : The stationers' register (voir plus haut la note de la notice sur Fuller, 1577, pour référence complète). Waldon fait observer qu'il n'y a apparemment plus d'exemplaire conservé et qu'il s'agissait probablement d'une ballade sur in-plano.

1578

[**Best, George**], *d./déc.* 1584? A true discourse of the late voyages of discouerie, for the finding of a passage to Cathaya, by the northvveast, vnder the conduct of Martin Frobisher Generall: deuided into three bookes. In the first wherof is shewed, his first voyage. Wherein also by the way is sette out a geographicall description of the worlde, and what partes thereof haue bin discouered by the nauigations of the Englishmen. Also, there are annexed certayne reasons, to proue all partes of the worlde habitable, with a generall mappe adioyned. In the second, is set out his second voyage, with the aduentures and accidents thereof. In the thirde, is declared the strange fortunes which hapned in the third voyage, with a seuerall description of the countrey and the people there inhabiting. VVith a particular card therevnto adioyned of Meta Incognita, so farre forth as the secretes of the voyage may permit. At London, imprinted by Henry Bynnyman, seruant to the right Honourable Sir Christopher Hatton Vizchamberlaine. Anno Domini. 1578. 8 p.l., 52, 39, 68 p. illus., 2 fold. maps. 4°

NUC(Pre–56)51:205

Dedication signed: George Best. ¶ Colophon: At London, Printed by Henry Bynnyman. Anno Domini. 1578. Decembris. 10. ¶ The maps are by James Beare, Frobisher's principal surveyor. ¶ Waldon gives detailed notes on variants. ¶ Best here describes Sir Martin Frobisher's three voyages (1576, 1577, 1578), in which Frobisher explored the coast of Labrador and discovered Frobisher Bay and Hudson Strait. ¶ First edition; reprinted in: Richard Hakluyt, The third and last volume of the voyages ... *London, 1600* (q.v., *below*), *and* Collection of voyages, *vol. 3, London, 1810* (cf. NUC); *also in MF, Ann Arbor, Mich., University Microfilms, no. 10940* (case 33, carton 196), *and in STC series, no. 1972.*

Dédicace signée George Best. ¶ Colophon : At London, printed by Henry Bynnyman. Anno Domini. 1578. Decembris. 10. ¶ Les cartes sont de James Beare, géomètre principal de Frobisher. ¶ Waldon fournit des notes détaillées sur les variantes existantes. ¶ Best fait ici la description des trois périples de sir Martin Frobisher (1576, 1577, 1578) au cours desquels celui-ci explora la côte du Labrador et découvrit la Baie de Frobisher et le Détroit d'Hudson. ¶ Première édition ; réimpressions : Richard Hakluyt, The third and last volume of the voyages ... *Londres, 1600* (q.v. plus bas), *ainsi que* Collection of voyages, *vol. 3, Londres, 1810* (cf. NUC) ; *reproductions sur mic., Ann Arbor* (Mich.), *University Microfilms, n° 10940* (boîte 33, carton 196), *ainsi que dans la collection du STC, n° 1972.*

Churchyard, Thomas, 1520?–1604. A discourse of the Queenes Maiesties entertainement in Suffolk and Norffolk: ... Deuised by Thomas Churchyarde, Gent. ... Wherevnto is adioyned a commendation of Sir Humfrey Gilberts ventrous iourney. At London, imprinted by Henrie Bynneman, seruante to the right Honourable Sir Christofer Hatton Vizchamberlayne. [1578.] Unpaged, 44 l., signed: A-K⁴ [K4 blank], L⁴ 4°

NUC(Pre–56)109:317*

Title within ornamental border. ¶ Dedicated to "Maister William Iarret, the Queenes Maiesties Attourney Generall." ¶ *Signature L (4 leaves) contains a poem, "A welcome home to Master Martin Frobusher, and all those gentlemen and souldiers, that haue bene with him this last iourney, in the countrey called (Meta Incognita) whiche welcome was written since this booke was put to the printing, and ioyned to the same booke ....*" ¶ "A matter touching the Iourney of Sir Humfrey Gilbarte Knight": H2–K3; "A welcome home to Master Martin Frobusher": L⁴. These are both poems followed by a prose passage beginning: "Thus have I playnely expressed with pen, what portion of good will I beare to all those that valiantly and worthily are workers to the enriching and honour of our common wealthe." ¶ First edition; a variant [Church:120B describes both] has dedication addressed to "Maister Gilbert Gerard, the Queenes Maiesties Attourney Generall" and address to reader typographically different, otherwise the same; other editions: London, J.G. Bell, 1851, 27 p., 8° (sixty copies only; cf. BLC(to 1975)62:269), which Waldon says is "from ms. copy of Bynneman's edition, 1579 [*i.e.* 1578; Sabin:13032 has

Titre encadré par une bordure décorative. ¶ Dédié à « Maître William Iarret, Procureur Général de sa Majesté la Reine ». ¶ *Le cahier L (4 feuillets) contient un poème « Heureux retour à maître Martin Frobusher ainsi qu'aux gentilshommes et soldats qui l'ont accompagné lors de ce dernier voyage au pays appelé (Meta Incognita), le présent souhait de bienvenue ayant été écrit alors que le présent livre était sous presse, puis joint audit livre ....* » ¶ « A matter touching the Iourney of Sir Humfrey Gilbarte Knight » : H2–K3 ; « A welcome home to Master Martin Frobusher » : L⁴. Ces deux titres coiffent deux poèmes qui sont suivis par un passage en prose commençant ainsi : « Aussi ai-je pris la plume pour exprimer simplement tout le bien que je pense de ceux qui ont vaillamment et dignement travaillé au profit et pour l'honneur de l'intérêt commun ». ¶ Première édition ; il existe une variante en tout point semblable [Church:120B décrit les deux versions] sauf pour une dédicace adressée à « Maître Gilbert Gerard, Procureur Général de sa Majesté la Reine » ainsi qu'une autre dédicace adressée au lecteur et dont la typographie est différente ; autres éditions : Londres, J. G. Bell, 1851, 27 p., in-8°(seulement 60 exemplaires ; cf. BLC(to 1975)62:269), que Waldon identifie comme une copie manuscrite de l'édition de Bynneman, 1579 [*c.-à-d.* 1578 ; le Sabin: 13032 indique « vers 1788 » !], sans les

"about 1788"!], without the poems to Gilbert and Frobisher"; Boston, Mass. Hist. Soc., 1922, Americana series no. 79, one of ten photostat copies from the Huntington Library original (NUC).

poèmes à Gilbert et Frobisher ; Boston, Mass. Hist. Soc., 1922, collection Americana n° 79, une des dix photocopies de l'original de la Huntington Library (NUC).

Churchyard, Thomas, 1520?–1604. A prayse, and reporte of Maister Martyne Forboishers voyage to Meta Incognita. (A name given by a mightie and most great personage) in which praise and reporte is written diuers discourses neuer published by any man as yet. Now spoken by Thomas Churchyarde Gentleman, and dedicated to the right honorable M. Secretarie Wilson, oue [*i.e.*, one] of the Queenes Maiesties most honorable Priuie Counsell. Imprinted at London [by John Kingston, cf. NUC] for Andrew Maunsell in Paules Church-yard at the signe of the Parret. [The tenth of Maye. 1578.] 1 p.l., [46] p. 8°

BLC(to 1975)62:270; NUC(Pre–56)109:319* (facsims. only)

Black-letter. Initials, head and tail pieces. ¶ Title from facsim. t.-p., Church:120A; imprint completed from colophon. ¶ Refers to Martin Frobisher's second voyage, May-Sept. 1577, to what he named Meta Incognita, probably the southern part of Baffin Island. He had brought back a quantity of ore from his first expedition, which gave (false) prospect of gold, thus aiding Frobisher in mounting this second voyage. This report was published before he sailed on his third voyage. ¶ "A discourse of the valiant voyage to Meta Incognita" begins (A5ᵃ): "The first labour and verses in the behalfe of Maister Forboyshers voyage, procured my pen after the farewell giuen to him (and his valliant companions) to salute them with a welcome home, likewise in verse, so soone as thei here seuerally and saffely ariued." This evidently refers to the

Écriture gothique. Initiales, tête et fin de chapitre. ¶ Titre reproduit à partir d'un fac-similé du p. de t., Church:120A ; adresse bibliographique complétée à partir du colophon. ¶ Le texte traite du deuxième voyage de Martin Frobisher de mai à septembre 1577, vers la région qui correspond probablement à la partie sud de la terre de Baffin et qu'il nomma Meta Incognita. Il avait ramené, de sa première expédition, une quantité de minerai, ce qui avait fait naître l'espoir (faux) de trouver de l'or. Cette perspective avait aidé Frobisher à préparer son deuxième voyage. Ce compte rendu fut publié avant qu'il entreprenne son troisième voyage. ¶ « A discourse of the valiant voyage to Meta Incognita » (A5ᵃ) commence ainsi : « La première oeuvre et les premiers vers à l'occasion du voyage de maître Forboysher ont inspiré à ma plume, par suite des adieux faits à celui-ci (ainsi qu'à ses valeureux compagnons), un salut sous la forme d'un souhait de bienvenue, également en vers, à l'occasion

verses in Churchyard's *A discourse of the Queenes Maiesties entertainement.* London, 1578, *q.v.,* above. ¶ *First edition; Boston, Mass. Hist. Soc., 1922, Americana series no. 70, photostat reproduction from the original in BLC; Ann Arbor, Mich., University Microfilms, no. 11763, MF facsimile (both in NUC).*

du retour ici de chacun d'entre eux sain et sauf ». Cette phrase fait évidemment référence aux vers qu'on retrouve dans l'ouvrage de Churchyard *A discourse of the Queenes Maiesties entertainement.* Londres, 1578, *q.v.* plus haut. ¶ *Première édition ; photocopie de l'original du BLC : Boston, Mass. Hist. Soc., 1922, collection Americana n° 70 ; reproduction du fac-similé sur mic., Ann Arbor (Mich.), University Microfilms, n° 11763. (Les deux derniers documents figurent au NUC.)*

A discription of the purtrayture and shape of those strange kinde of people whiche the worthie master Martin Ffourbosier brought into England in Anno 1576 and 1577. Licensed to John Aldee, Jan. 30, 1578. charge "iiij d and a copy." [London, 1578.] [No collation or format.]

"S.R., v. 2, fol. 145, p. 323."

Dr. Waldon's source: The stationers' register (see *note to Fuller, 1577, above, for full citation). She notes that no copy seems to be extant.*

Source de Waldon : The stationers' register (voir *plus haut la note de la notice sur Fuller, 1577, pour référence complète). Selon Waldon, il semble qu'il n'existe plus aujourd'hui d'exemplaire conservé.*

Ellis, Thomas, *sailor/marin.* A true report of the third and last voyage into Meta incognita: atchieued by the worthie Capteine, M. Martine Frobisher Esquire. Anno. 1578. Written by Thomas Ellis sailer and one of the companie. Imprinted at London, at the three Cranes in the Vintree, by Thomas Dawson. [1578.] 20 l. fold. plate (4 woodcuts, facing t.-p.). 8°

NUC(Pre-56)158:546*

Title within ornamental border. ¶ Black-letter, with marginal notes in italics. ¶ *Meta Incognita is the name given by Frobisher to the southern part of Baffin Island.* ¶ *First edition (the only complete copy is in the Huntington Library, San Marino, California; Church:120C); an edition of ten photostatic copies was issued as no. 60 in the Americana series, Boston, Mass. Hist. Soc., 1922 (this is the work described in NUC, cited above), and subsequently a microfilm of the work was issued, Ann Arbor, Mich., University Microfilms, no. 12555 (case 49, carton 290).*

Titre encadré par une bordure décorative. ¶ Écriture gothique et notes dans les marges en italiques. ¶ *Meta Incognita est le nom donné par Frobisher à la partie sud de la terre de Baffin.* ¶ *Première édition (le seul exemplaire complet se trouve dans la Huntington Library, San Marino (Californie) ; Church:120C) ; une édition constituée de 10 photocopies a paru sous le n° 60 de la collection Americana, Boston, Mass. Hist. Soc., 1922 (il s'agit de l'ouvrage décrit par le NUC et cité plus haut). Reproduction ultérieure sur mic., Ann Arbor (Mich.), University Microfilms, n° 12555 (boîte 49, carton 290).*

Fourboysers voiage. Printed without license by John Charlwood, 1 Dec. 1578. [London, 1578.] [No collation or format given.]

Hazlitt, W. Carew . . . (see note).

Dr. Waldon's source: William Carew Hazlitt, Second series of bibliographical collections and notes on early English literature, 1474–1700. *London, 1882, p. 237. No copy, she says, appears to be extant.*

Source de Waldon : William Carew Hazlitt. Second series of bibliographical collections and notes on early English literature, 1474–1700. *Londres, 1882, p. 237. Selon Waldon, il semble qu'il n'existe plus aujourd'hui d'exemplaire conservé.*

A pamphlet in the praise of master Captaine Ffrobisher in forme of A farewell at his third voiage in Maye. 1578. by the northe[a]st seas toward the iland of Cataea. Licensed to Richard Jones, May 13, 1578, charge, "iiij d and a copie." [London, 1578.] [No collation or format given.]

"S.R., v.2, fol. 147, p. 327."

Dr. Waldon's source: The stationers' register (see *note to Fuller, 1577, above, for full citation*). *No copy, she says, appears to be extant.*

Source de Waldon : The stationers' register (voir *plus haut la note de la notice sur Fuller, 1577, pour référence complète*). *Selon Waldon, il semble qu'il n'existe plus aujourd'hui d'exemplaire conservé.*

1579

Eden, Richard, 1521?–1576. The epistle dedicatorie. To the ryght woorshipfull Syr Wylliam Wynter, Knyght, Maister of the Ordinaunce of the Queenes Maiesties Shippes, and Surveyor of the sayd shippes. Richarde Eden wysheth health and prosperitie. (In Joannes Taisnier, b. 1509. *A very necessarie and profitable booke concerning navigation, comp. in Latin . . . . Translated into Englishe, by Richarde Eden.* Imprinted at London by Richarde Iugge. [1579?] 4°. Reprinted in Edward Arber, *The first three English books on America.* Westminster, A. Constable & Co., 1895.)

NUC(Pre–56)155:417*

According to Arber, p. xlvi, this translation was made in 1574, and printed four or five years later; the Epistle Dedicatorie contains the only account of Cabot's death. The reference (third p.l.ᵃ) is as follows: "By whiche description [of an invention] some doo understand that the knowledge of the longitude myght so be founde, a thyng doubtlesse greatly to be desyred, and hytherto not certaynely knowen, although Sebastian Cabot on his death bed tolde me that he had the knowledge thereof by diuine reuelation, yet so, that he myght not teache any man. But I thinke that the good olde man, in that extreme age, somewhat doted, and had not yet euen in the article of

Selon Arber, p. xlvi, cette traduction fut rédigée en 1574 et imprimée quatre ou cinq ans plus tard ; l'épître dédicatoire contient la seule mention concernant le décès de Cabot. En voici le contenu (troisième f. l.ᵃ) : « Par laquelle description [d'une invention] certaines personnes comprennent que la connaissance de la longitude puisse être acquise, une information, sans aucun doute, hautement recherchée et qui, jusqu'ici n'est pas connue, bien que Sébastien Cabot m'ait confié sur son lit de mort, qu'il en avait eu connaissance par une révélation divine même s'il ne pouvait la divulguer à personne. Je crois, toutefois, que le cher vieillard, parvenu à cet âge extrême, radotait quelque peu et qu'il ne s'était pas encore, même à l'article de la mort, vraiment détourné des vanités terrestres. » L'ensemble de l'épître

death, utterly shaken of all worldlye vayne glorie." The whole Epistle is reproduced by Arber, p. xlvi–xlviii.

est reproduit par Arber, p. xlvi–xlviii.

*Stow, John, 1525?–1605. The summarie of the chronicles of England. Diligently collected . . . vnto this present yeare . . . 1579 . . . . Imprinted at London by Richard Tottle, and Henry Binneman [1579.] 16°

NUC(Pre–56)572:36*

Collation given in signatures only in NUC. ¶ First ed.: London, 1565, q.v. for other notes; text republished in MF in the STC series, by University Microfilms, Ann Arbor, Mich. (no. 23325, carton 506 — cf. NUC).

Collation du NUC par signature seulement. ¶ Première éd. : Londres, 1565, q.v. pour d'autres notes ; reproduction sur mic. dans la collection du STC, Ann Arbor (Mich.), University Microfilms, (n° 23325, carton 506 –cf. NUC).

1580

Cartier, Jacques, 1491–1557. A shorte and briefe narration of the two nauigations and discoueries to the northwest partes called Newe Fraunce, first translated out of French into Italian by Gio. Bapt. Ramutius and now turned into English by Iohn Florio . . . . Imprinted at London by H[enry]. Bynneman, dvvelling in Thames streate, neere vnto Baynardes Castell. Anno Domini. 1580. [6], 78, [2] p. 4°

NUC(Pre–56)97:247*

Though Hakluyt's name does not appear in the volume and his share in the work has been generally over-looked, he was responsible for this translation, the first publication in English of Cartier's narrative — cf. Parks [George B., Richard Hakluyt and the English voyages. New York, Amer.

Bien que son nom n'apparaisse pas dans l'ouvrage et que sa contribution ait été le plus souvent passée sous silence, c'est Hakluyt qui a commis cette traduction qui constitue la première publication en anglais du récit de Cartier – cf. Parks [George B., Richard Hakluyt and the English voyages. New York, Amer. Geog. Soc., 1928] p. 64 [où il est

Geog. Soc., 1928], p. 64 [where it says only that Hakluyt "caused" Cartier "to be translated" partly at his own expense]. The original ms. of the first voyage, long lost, was found in 1867. It differs from the earliest version, that in the third volume of Ramusio's *Nauigationi*, Venice, 1556, fol. 435–40. The second voyage was published in Paris, 1545 — cf. Church, v. 1, p. 284–85 [no. 125. Church also says that the present translation of the second voyage *was* by John Florio, that it was in turn translated into French and printed at Rouen, 1598, and that this is one of the earliest books relating to Canada]. ¶ *Page 65 numbered 95 in error. Waldon has the title-leaf preceding the [6] prelim. pages.* ¶ The second voyage was reprinted in Richard Hakluyt, *The principal navigations*. London, 1600, vol. 3, p. 212–32, *q.v.* below under Cartier, 1600; and this first and second voyage in photostatic reproduction from the New York Public Library copy, 1920 (cf. NUC). Waldon also notes New York, 1906, and Ottawa, 1924, reprints of the three voyages together.

seulement dit que Hakluyt est à l'origine de la traduction de l'ouvrage de Cartier et ce, en partie à ses propres frais]. Le manuscrit original relatant le premier voyage, longtemps égaré, fut retrouvé en 1867. Il diffère de la version la plus ancienne, celle du troisième volume de l'ouvrage de Ramusio, *Nauigationi*. Venise, 1556, fol. 435–40. Le récit du deuxième voyage fut publié à Paris en 1545 – cf. Church, vol. 1, p. 284–85 [n° 125. Church indique également que cette traduction du deuxième voyage *est* de John Florio, et que celle-ci fut à son tour traduite en français et imprimée à Rouen en 1598, et qu'il s'agit de l'un des plus anciens livres traitant du Canada]. ¶ *La page 65 porte par erreur le numéro 95. Waldon note que le feuillet de titre précède les [6] pages liminaires.* ¶ Le récit du deuxième voyage fut réimprimé dans Richard Hakluyt, *The principal navigations*. Londres, 1600, vol. 3, p. 212–32, *q.v.* plus bas la notice sur Cartier, 1600 ; cet ouvrage relatant le premier et le deuxième voyage a été reproduit sur mic. à partir de l'exemplaire de la New York Public Library, 1920 (cf. NUC). Waldon signale également les tirages de New York, 1906, et d'Ottawa, 1924, qui reprennent ensemble les trois voyages de Cartier.

Stow, John, 1525?–1605. The chronicles of England, from Brute vnto this present yeare of Christ. 1580. Collected by Iohn Stow citizen of London. Printed at London by Ralphe Newberie, at the assignment of Henrie Bynneman. Cum Priuilegio Regiae Maiestatis. [1580.] 16 p.l., 1223 p. incl. port. 4°

NUC(Pre–56)572:35*

On page 875 is given the passage relating to Cabot from Fabian's *Chronicle* [*i.e.* Robert Fabyan, *The newe cronycles of Englande and of Fraunce*. London, Richard Pynson, 1516 — cf. NUC(Pre–56)165:357], later printed in [Richard] Hakluyt's *Divers voyages*. [London] 1582, *q.v.*, but with some variations. ¶ This is apparently the first edition of the *Chronicles* in the complete form, of which his *Summarie*, 1565 (*q.v.*) had formed a prelude (cf. BM), and which later appeared under the title *The annales of England*, 1592 (*q.v.*). Text republished in MF, Ann Arbor, University Microfilms, no. 15588, carton 356 (STC:23334); a similar though different work appeared under the first four words of this title in 1587, *q.v.*

À la page 875, on retrouve le passage concernant Cabot et tiré de l'ouvrage de Fabian intitulé *Chronicle*, [*c.-à-d.* Robert Fabyan, *The newe cronycles of Englande and of Fraunce*. Londres, Richard Pynson, 1516 – cf. NUC(Pre–56)165:357], publié plus tard dans [Richard] Hakluyt, *Divers voyages*. [Londres] 1582, *q.v.*, avec quelques modifications toutefois. ¶ Il s'agit apparemment de la première édition des *Chronicles* dans leur forme complète, pour lesquelles le *Summarie* de l'auteur en 1565 (*q.v.*) a constitué un prélude (cf. BM) et qui fut publié sous le titre *The annales of England* en 1592 (*q.v.*). Reproduction sur mic., Ann Arbor, University Microfilms, n° 15588, carton 356 (STC:23334) ; un ouvrage similaire quoique différent a paru sous les quatre premiers mots du titre ci-dessus, en 1587, *q.v.*

1582

[Hakluyt, Richard], 1552?–1616. Divers voyages touching the discouerie of America, and the ilands adiacent vnto the same, made first of all by our Englishmen, and afterward by the Frenchmen and Britons: and certaine notes of aduertisements for obseruations, necessarie for such as shall heereafter make the like attempt, with two mappes annexed heereunto for the plainer understanding of the whole matter. Imprinted at London for Thomas VVoodcocke, dwelling in paules Church-yard, at the signe of the blacke beare. 1582. 60 l. 2 fold. maps. 4°

NUC(Pre–56)226:474*

"The Epistle Dedicatorie" signed: R.H. ¶ *With colophon.* ¶ Maps: 1. Map of the world, 1527, made by or for Robert

« *L'épître dédicatoire* » *est signée : R. H.* ¶ *Colophon.* ¶ Cartes : 1. Carte du monde, 1527, faite par ou pour Robert Thorne, afin

Thorne, to accompany his own book; 2. Map of America, made for this book by Michael Lok [or Lock, merchant, traveller, and principal investor in the Frobisher voyages, which virtually ruined him], with inscription: Illustri Viro, Domino Philippo Sidnaeo Michael Lok Civis Londinensis Hanc Chartam Dedicabat:1582. ¶ [Partial] contents: ... "A verie late and great probabilitie of a passage by the Northwest part of America, in 58. degrees of northerly latitude"; "Letters patentes of Henry VII to Iohn Gabate [Cabot] and his three sons, Latin and English"; "A note of Sebastian Gabotes voyage of discouerie, taken out of an old chronicle written by Robert Fabian ... Iohn Baptista Ramusius in his Preface to the thirde volume of the nauigations, writeth thus of Sebastian Gabot"; "The relation of Iohn Verarzanus [Verrazzano, who sailed along the Atlantic coast of Canada, 1524] ..."; "The names of certaine commodities growing in part of America ... fro Florida northward, gathered out of the discourses of Verarzanus, Thorne, Cartier, Ribalt, Thevet, and best ...." ¶ This is Hakluyt's first publication. He gathered all the material he could find on the Cabots and the English title to America and combined it with other chronicles as an incentive to further exploration and discovery. The letters patent to the Cabots are the most important documents in the book. ¶ Reprinted as Hakluyt Society publication no. 7, London, 1850 [and in various other

d'accompagner son livre ; 2. Carte de l'Amérique, faite pour le présent livre par Michael Lok (ou Lock, marchand, voyageur et principal investisseur dans les voyages de Frobisher, qui l'ont pratiquement ruiné), portant l'inscription : Illustri Viro, Domino Philippo Sidnaeo Michael Lok Civis Londinensis Hanc Chartam Dedicabat:1582. ¶ Liste partielle des chapitres portant sur le Canada : ... « A verie late and great probabilitie of a passage by the Northwest part of America, in 58. degrees of northerly latitude » ; « Letters patentes of Henry VII to Iohn Gabate [Cabot] and his three sons, Latin and English » ; « A note of Sebastian Gabotes voyage of discouerie, taken out of an old chronicle written by Robert Fabian ... Iohn Baptista Ramusius in his Preface to the thirde volume of the nauigations, writeth thus of Sebastian Gabot » ; « The relation of Iohn Verarzanus [Verrazzano qui navigua le long de la côte atlantique du Canada en 1524]... » ; « The names of certaine commodities growing in part of America ... fro Florida northward, gathered out of the discourses of Verarzanus, Thorne, Cartier, Ribalt, Thevet, and best .... » ¶ Il s'agit de la première publication de Hakluyt. Il a rassemblé tout le matériel qu'il pouvait trouver sur les Cabot et sur les prétentions anglaises en Amérique, matériel qu'il a combiné à d'autres chroniques propres à susciter les explorations et les découvertes futures. Les lettres patentes délivrées à Cabot sont les documents les plus importants de l'ouvrage. ¶ Réimpression (publication n° 7 de la Hakluyt Society) à Londres en 1850 [ainsi qu'ultérieurement, sous différentes formes de reproduction, cf. NUC ; Waldon signale d'autres réimpressions de différentes parties de ce recueil ainsi

facsimile forms subsequently, cf. NUC; Waldon indicates other reprints of various parts of this collection, and sources of further information].

que des sources d'information supplémentaires].

Parmenius, Stephanus, *Budaeus, d./déc.* 1583. De navigatione illustris et magnanimi equitis aurati Humfredi Gilberti, ad deducendam in novum orbem coloniam susceptâ, carmen Epibatikon [*transliterated from Greek/transcrire du grec*] Stephani Parmenii Budeii. Londini, apud Thomam Purfutium. An. 1582. 1 p.l., [13] p. 4°

NUC(Pre–56)443:6*

Parmenius was a learned Hungarian of Buda, who accompanied Gilbert to Newfoundland in 1583. Both were lost on the return voyage. The only other writing of Parmenius extant is the Latin letter to Hakluyt from St. John's port, Nfld., dated 6 August 1583, descriptive of the voyage and the island, published by Hakluyt in 1589. ¶ *Reproduced on MF: Ann Arbor, Mich., University Microfilms, [post-World War II], case 65, carton 387. Also:* ¶ Reprinted [in Richard] Hakluyt, second ed., 1600 [presumably his *The third and last volume of the voyages, navigations, traffiques .... London, 1600, q.v.,* below]. *See also* "Memoir of Parmenius" in Mass. Hist. Soc. *Collections,* 1804, v. 9, p. 55–75, where both English and Latin versions are reproduced.

Parmenius était un Hongrois érudit de Buda qui accompagna Gilbert à Terre-Neuve en 1583. Ils se perdirent en mer pendant le trajet de retour. Le seul autre écrit de Parmenius qui nous soit parvenu est une lettre en latin de Saint-Jean (Terre-Neuve) datée du 6 août 1583 et décrivant le voyage et l'île. Hakluyt la publia en 1589. ¶ *Reproduction sur mic. : Ann Arbor (Mich.), University Microfilms, [postérieure à la Seconde guerre mondiale], boîte 65, carton 387.* ¶ Réimpression : [Richard] Hakluyt, deuxième éd., 1600 [probablement *The third and last volume of the voyages, navigations, traffiques ....* Londres, 1600, q.v. plus bas]. *Voir aussi* « Memoir of Parmenius » dans Mass. Hist. Soc. *Collections.* 1804, vol. 9, p. 55–75, dans lequel les deux versions, en anglais et en latin, sont reproduites.

1583

[**Peckham**, Sir **George**], *d./déc.* 1608. A trve reporte, of the late discoueries, and possession, taken in the right of the crowne of Englande, of the Newfound landes: by that valiaunt and worthye gentleman, Sir Humfrey Gilbert knight. Wherein is also breefely sette downe, her highnesse lawfull tytle therevnto, and the great and manifolde commodities, that is likely to grow thereby, to the whole realme in generall, and to the aduenturers in particular, together with the easines and shortnes of the voyage. Seene and allowed. At London, printed by I[ohn]. C[harlwood]. for Iohn Hinde, dwelling in Paules Church-yarde, at the signe of the golden Hinde. Anno. 1583. 5 p.l., [50] p. 4°

NUC(Pre–56)447:111*

Dedication signed: G.P. ¶ This exists in at least three states with the same title-page, no two copies examined being exactly alike. Possibly the explanation is that corrections were made and additional matter set up while the book was in the press, and corrected and uncorrected sheets bound up with the additional matter indiscriminately. [Waldon then describes the three states or issues she has found.] ¶ *Reprinted in Richard Hakluyt,* The principall navigations .... *London, 1589, p. 701–18,* q.v *for notes and other editions of Hakluyt; also Tarrytown, N.Y., W. Abbatt, 1920 (in* The magazine of history with notes and queries, *extra no. 68, [pt. 1], and the Americana series, photostat reproductions, Boston, Mass. Hist. Soc., 1927, no. 183 (cf. NUC).*

Dédicace signée : G. P. ¶ Ce document existe en au moins trois variantes portant la même page de titre; toutefois, chacune d'entre elles s'est révélée, après examen, quelque peu différente des autres. On peut avancer comme explication que des corrections et des ajouts furent introduits alors que le livre était sous presse, les feuillets corrigés et non corrigés de même que ceux portant les ajouts étant reliés ensemble sans distinction. [Waldon décrit ensuite les trois états ou versions qu'elle a relevés.] ¶ *Réimpressions : Richard Hakluyt,* The principall navigations .... *Londres, 1589, p. 701–18* q.v. *pour notes et autres éditions de Hakluyt, ainsi que Tarrytown (N.Y.), W. Abbatt, 1920 (dans* The magazine of history with notes and queries, *n° spécial 68, [première partie], et dans la collection Americana, photocopies, Boston, Mass. Hist. Soc., 1927, n° 183 (cf. NUC).*

1584

*Stow, John, 1525?–1605. A svmmary of the chronicles of England. Diligently collected ... vnto ... 1584. London, imprinted by R[alph]. Newbery and H[enry]. Denham, 1584. 488 p. 1 illus. 16°(?)

NUC(Pre–56)572:36*

First ed.: London, 1565, q.v. for notes.

Première éd. : Londres, 1565, q.v. pour notes.

1587

*Stow, John, 1525?–1605. The chronicles of England, from the yeare ... 1576, where Raphaell Holinshed left, supplied and continued to this present yeare 1586; by John Stow and others. [London] 1587 [n.s.]. vol. 3 (of 3). fol.

BM(to 1955) 231:50

This is apparently vol. 3 of the second edition of Raphael Holinshed's *Chronicle* (first ed. 1578), edited and continued by John Hooker to 1586, with some sections completed by three others: John Stow, Francis Thynne, and Abraham Fleming (cf. DNB, "Holinshed"); vol. 3 here is a work different from Stow's *Chronicles* and the predecessor, his *A summarie of Englyshe chronicles*, 1565 (q.v.), etc., but founded upon it; a fourth vol. by Stow and others was pub. in 1808 (cf. BM(to 1955)231:50–51). ¶ First ed. by Stow, under this title: London, 1580 (q.v.); subsequent editions of Stow's

Il semble qu'il s'agisse du troisième volume de la deuxième édition de l'ouvrage de Raphael Holinshed *Chronicle* (première éd. 1578), édité par John Hooker qui a poursuivi le travail jusqu'en 1586, avec la collaboration, pour certaines des parties du travail, de John Stow, de Francis Thynne et d'Abraham Fleming (cf. DNB sous Holinshed) ; ce troisième volume est différent de l'ouvrage de Stow *Chronicles* et de celui qui l'a précédé *A summarie of Englyshe chronicles*. 1565 (q.v.), etc., quoiqu'il s'en inspire ; un quatrième volume par Stow et al. fut publié en 1808 (cf. BM(to 1955)231:50–51). ¶ Première éd. par Stow sous le même titre : Londres, 1580 (q.v.) ; des éditons ultérieures de l'ouvrage

work appeared under the title *The annales of England*, from 1592 (*q.v.*) onwards.

de Stow furent publiées sous le titre *The annales of England*, à partir de 1592 (*q.v.*).

*Stow, John, 1525?–1605. A summarie of ur Englysh chronicles . . . . London, printed by R[alph]. Newberrie, at the assignment of H[enry]. Denham, 1587. [14] l., 505 p., [16] l. 16°

NUC(Pre–56)572:36*

BM(to 1955)231:51 has a variant 1587 title. ¶ First ed.: London, 1565, *q.v.* for other notes.

Le BM(to 1955)231:51 donne un document de 1587 avec variation dans le titre. ¶ Première éd. : Londres, 1565, *q.v.* pour d'autres notes.

1589

Hakluyt, Richard, 1552?–1616. The principall navigations, voiages and discoveries of the English nation . . . . Imprinted at London by George Bishop and Ralph Newberie, deputies to Christopher Barker, printer to the Queenes most excellent Maiestie, 1589. [16], 505, [1], 506–643,[12], 644–825,[10] p. fold. map. fol.

NUC(Pre–56)226:476*

Paging and signatures irregular (cf. NUC). Contents relating to Canada: Cabot material (including the passages already published in *Divers voyages* as well as material from the *Decades* of Peter Martyr): p. 509–15; "The voiage of the two ships . . . 1527. for the discouerie of the North partes.": p. 517; "The voyage of

Pagination et signatures irrégulières (cf. NUC). Qui portent sur le Canada : textes sur Cabot (comprenant les passages déjà publiés dans *Divers voyages* de même que des textes des *Decades* de Peter Martyr) : p. 509-15 ; « The voiage of the two ships . . . 1527. for the discouerie of the north partes. » p. 517 ; « The voyage of master Hore and diuers other Gentlemen, to Newfoundland, and

master Hore and diuers other Gentlemen, to Newfoundland, and Cape Breton, in the yeare 1536 ....": p. 517–19; "The large pension graunted by K. Edward the 6. to Sebastian Cabota, constituting him grand Pilot of England.": p. 519–20; "An acte against the exaction of money or any other thing by any officer for licence to trafique into Iseland; and Newfoundland, made in An. 2. Edwardi Sexti.": p. 521; "A discourse written by Sir Humfrey Gilbert Knight, to prooue a Passage by the Northwest to Cathaia, and the East Indies.": p. 597–610; "Certaine other reasons, or arguments to prooue a passage by the Northwest, learnedly written by M. Richard Willes Gentleman.": p. 610–15; "The first voyage of M. Martine Frobisher, to the Northwest for the search of the straight or passage to China, written by Christopher Hall, and made in the yeare of our Lord 1576.": p. 615–22; "The second voyage of Master Martin Frobisher, made to the VVest, and Northwest Regions, in the yeare, 1577. with a description of the Countrey, and people: Written by Dionise Settle.": p. 622–30; "The third and last voyage into Meta Incognita, made by M. Martin Frobisher, in the yeere 1578. VVritten by Thomas Ellis.": p. 630–35; "The report of Thomas Wiars passenger ... in the last voyage of Master. Martin Frobisher, 1578. concerning the discouerie of a great Island ....": p. 635; "Notes framed by M. Richard Hakluit of the middle Temple Esquire, giuen to certaine Gentlemen

Cape Breton, in the yeare 1536 ....» : p. 517–19 ; « The large pension graunted by K. Edward the 6. to Sebastian Cabota, constituting him grand Pilot of England » : p. 519–20 ; « An acte against the exaction of money or any other thing by any officer for licence to trafique into Iseland; and Newfoundland, made in An. 2. Edwardi Sexti » : p. 521 ; « A discourse written by Sir Humfrey Gilbert Knight, to prooue a Passage by the Northwest to Cathaia, and the East Indies » : p. 597–610 ; « Certaine other reasons, or arguments to prooue a passage by the Northwest, learnedly written by M. Richard Willes Gentleman » : p. 610–15 ; « The first voyage of M. Martine Frobisher, to the Northwest for the search of the straight or passage to China, written by Christopher Hall, and made in the yeare of our Lord 1576 » : p. 615–22 ; « The second voyage of Master Martin Frobisher, made to the VVest, and Northwest Regions, in the yeere, 1577. with a description of the Countrey, and people : Written by Dionise Settle » : p. 622–30 ; « The third and last voyage into Meta Incognita, made by M. Martin Frobisher, in the yeere 1578. VVritten by Thomas Ellis » : p. 630–35 ; « The report of Thomas Wiars passenger ... in the last voyage of Master. Martin Frobisher, 1578. concerning the discouerie of a great Island ....» : p. 635 ; « Notes framed by M. Richard Hakluit of the middle Temple Esquire, giuen to certaine Gentlemen that went with M. Frobisher in his Northwest discouerie, for their directions ....» : p. 636–38 ; « A letter written to M. Richard Hakluyt of the middle Temple, conteining a report of the true state and commodities of New found land, by M. Anthonie Parkhurst Gentleman, 1578 » : p. 674–77 ; « The Letters Patents graunted

that went with M. Frobisher in his Northwest discouerie, for their directions ....": p. 636–38; "A letter written to M. Richard Hakluyt of the middle Temple, conteining a report of the true state and commodities of New found land, by M. Anthonie Parkhurst Gentleman, 1578.": p. 674–77; "The Letters Patents graunted by her Maiestie to Sir Humfrey Gilbert knight, for the inhabiting and planting of our people in America.": p. 677–79 ; "A report of the voyage and successe thereof, attempted in the yeere of our Lord, 1583. by Sir Humfrey Gilbert knight ... written by M. Edward Haies Gentleman ....": p. 679–97; "Letter from Steuen Parmenius of Buda to Richard Hakluyt (Latin and English): p. 697–99; "A relation of Richard Clarke of Weymouth, master of the shippe called the Delight, going for the discouerie of Norumbega with Sir Humfrey Gilbert 1583 ....": p. 700–01; "A true report of the late discoueries, and possession taken in the right of the Crowne of England of the Newfound Lands, By ... Sir Humfrey Gilbert Knight...Written by Sir George Pecham [i.e., Peckham] Knight ....": p. 701–18; "A letter written from M. Thomas Aldworth merchant, and then Maior of the citie of Bristow, to the right honourable Sir Francis Walsingham principall Secretarie to her Maiestie, concerning a Westerne voiage intended for discoueries in America." [1583, offering 1000 markes to fit out a ship]: p. 718; "A briefe and summarie discourse upon the intended voyage to

by her Maiestie to Sir Humfrey Gilbert knight, for the inhabiting and planting of our people in America » : p. 677–79 ; « A report of the voyage and successe thereof, attempted in the yeere of our Lord, 1583. by Sir Humfrey Gilbert knight ... written by M. Edward Haies Gentleman .... » : p. 679–97 ;« Letter from Steuen Parmenius of Buda to Richard Hakluyt [en latin et en anglais] : p. 697–99 ;« A relation of Richard Clarke of Weymouth, master of the shippe called the Delight, going for the discouerie of Norumbega with Sir Humfrey Gilbert 1583 .... » : p. 700–01 ; « A true report of the late discoueries, and possession taken in the right of the Crowne of England of the Newfound Lands, By ... Sir Humfrey Gilbert Knight ... Written by Sir George Pecham [c.-à-d. Peckham] Knight .... » : p. 701–18 ; « A letter written from M. Thomas Aldworth merchant, and then Maior of the citie of Bristow, to the right honourable Sir Francis Walsingham principall Secretarie to her Maiestie, concerning a Westerne voiage intended for discoueries in America » [1583, il offre 1000 marks pour armer un navire] : p. 718 ; « A briefe and summarie discourse upon the intended voyage to the hithermost parts of America: written by captaine Carlill in Aprill, 1583 .... » : p. 718–25 ; « The Letters patents of the Queenes Maiestie, graunted to Master Adrian Gylbert and others, for the search and discouerie of the Northwest Passage to China » : p. 774–76 ; « The first voyage of Master Iohn Dauis, vndertaken in Iune 1585. for the Discouerie of the Northwest Passage, written by Iohn Ianes Marchant .... »: p. 776–80 ; « The second voyage attempted by Master Iohn Dauis with others, for the discouerie of the Northwest passage, in Anno 1586 » : p. 781–86 ; « The

the hithermost parts of America: written by captaine Carlill in Aprill, 1583 . . . .": p. 718–25; "The Letters patents of the Queenes Maiestie, graunted to Master Adrian Gylbert and others, for the search and discouerie of the Northwest Passage to China.": p. 774–76; "The first voyage of Master Iohn Dauis, vndertaken in Iune 1585. for the Discouerie of the Northwest Passage, written by Iohn Ianes Marchant . . . .": p. 776–80; "The second voyage attempted by Master Iohn Dauis with others, for the discouerie of the Northwest passage, in Anno 1586.": p. 781–86; "The relation of the course which the Sunshine . . . and the North starre . . . being two vessels of the fleet of M. Iohn Dauis held after he had sent them from him to discouer the passage betweene Groenland and Island, written by Henry Morgan . . . .": p. 787–89; "The third voyage Northwestward, made by Iohn Dauis . . . for the discouerie of a passage . . . in the yeere, 1587. Written by Iohn Ianes . . . .": p. 789–92. ¶ Hakluyt performed an inestimable service in making this collection. Among the items of interest to us here are some never before published, as well as reprints of narratives, copies of which have now become very rare. Hakluyt should be read in the text of the first edition; it is a delightful book, conveying an atmosphere that modern reprints lack. ¶ *First edition, first issue; NUC has another copy with slightly varying collation, and also a second issue of the same year (see next entry); other editions: 1598–1600 (3 vols.), 1599–*

relation of the course which the Sunshine . . . and the North Starre . . . being two vessels of the fleet of M. Iohn Dauis held after he had sent them from him to discouer the passage betweene Groenland and Island, written by Henry Morgan . . . . » : p. 787–89 ; « The third voyage Northwestward, made by Iohn Dauis . . . for the discouerie of a passage . . . in the yeere, 1587. Written by Iohn Ianes . . . . » : p. 789–92. ¶ Hakluyt a rendu un inestimable service en produisant ce recueil. Parmi les documents d'intérêt pour nous, certains n'ont jamais été publiés auparavant, d'autres sont des réimpressions de récits dont les exemplaires sont aujourd'hui très rares. Hakluyt gagne à être lu dans le texte de la première édition ; il s'agit d'un ouvrage très agréable qui nous plonge dans une ambiance dont les réimpressions modernes sont dépourvues. ¶ *Première édition, premier tirage : le NUC donne un autre exemplaire dont la collation est légèrement différente ainsi qu'un deuxième tirage pour la même année (voir notice suivante) ; autres éditions : 1598–1600 (3 vol.), 1599–1600 (3 vol.), ainsi que de nombreuses éditions ultérieures, oeuvres choisies, publications d'extraits, etc., à ce jour. ¶ BVIPA*

1600 (3 vols.), and numerous later editions, selections, extracts, etc., to the present day. ¶ *BVIPA*

*Hakluyt, Richard, 1552?–1616. The principall navigations.... Imprinted at London by George Bishop . . ., 1589. 8 p.l., 643, [12], 644–825(*i.e.* 822), [10] p. fol.

NUC(Pre–56)226:476*

Paging irregular (cf. NUC). ¶ First edition, second issue.

Pagination irrégulière (cf. NUC). ¶ Première édition, deuxième tirage.

1590

*Stow, John, 1525?–1605. A summarie of the chronicles of England, from the first arriuing of Brute in this island, vnto . . . 1590: first collected, since inlarged, and now continued by Iohn Stow . . . . Imprinted at London by Ralph Newbery. Anno Domini 1590. 8 p.l., 760, [8] p. 8°

NUC(Pre–56)572:36

First ed.: London, 1565, *q.v.* for notes.

Première édition. : Londres, 1565, *q.v.* pour notes.

1592

*Stow, John, 1525?–1605. The annales of England, faithfully collected out of the most autenticall authors, records, and other monuments of antiquitie, from the first inhabitation vntill this present yeere 1592, by John Stow . . . . London, imprinted by R[alph]. Newbery [1592]. 12 p.l., 1305, [1] p. 4°

"Faultes escaped": [1] p. at end. ¶ Format from BM(to 1955)231:50. ¶ This is a new edition of Stow's *The chronicles of England*. London, 1580 (*q.v.*), issued with this new title; it reappeared in 1600, 1601, 1605 (the year of Stow's death), and in 1615 and 1631, *q.v.*; the 1592 text was republished in MF, Ann Arbor, Mich., University Microfilms, no. 15588, carton 356 (STC:23334).

Errata : [1] p. à la fin. ¶ Format du BM(to 1955)231:50. ¶ Il s'agit d'une nouvelle édition de *The chronicles of England*. Londres, 1580 (*q.v.*), publiée sous ce nouveau titre ; elle fut publiée de nouveau en 1600, 1601, 1605 (année de la mort de Stow), ainsi qu'en 1615 et en 1631, *q.v.* ; le document de 1592 a été reproduit sur mic., Ann Arbor (Mich.), University Microfilms, n° 15588, carton 356 (STC:23334).

1595

Davys, John, 1550?–1605. The worldes hydrographical discription. Wherein is proved not onely by aucthoritie of writers, but also by late experience of trauellers and reasons of substantiall probabilitie, that the worlde in all his zones [,] clymats and places, is habitable and inhabited, and the seas likewise vniuersally nauigable without any naturall annoyance to hinder the same whereby appeares that from England there is a short and speedie passage into the South Seas, to China, Molucca, Phillipina, and India, by northerly nauigation, to the renowne [,] honour and benefit of her Maiesties state, and communalty. Published by I [*i.e.* J, John]. Dauis of Sandrudge [*i.e.* Sandridge] by Dartmouth in the Countie of Deuon. Gentleman. Anno. 1595. May 27. Imprinted at London by Thomas Dawson dwelling at the three cranes in the vinetree. And are there to be sold. 1595. 24 l. 8°

NUC(Pre–56)135:226*

Black-letter, excepting for title-page, head-lines, and running title, in roman. "The Epistle Dedicatorie" is to the Privy Council. ¶ Davys was the discoverer of Davis Strait [between Baffin Island and Greenland], and he here describes his three voyages in search of the Northwest Passage. ¶ *First edition; reprinted in Richard Hakluyt,* The principal navigations, *London, 1598–1600 (etc., q.v., below; see also the 1589 edition for earlier voyages by Davys), and in* The voyages and works of John Davis, *ed. with introd. and notes by Albert Hastings Markham, London, Hakluyt Soc., 1880, 2 v. (This contains also "The first and third voyage of J. Davis, written by John Jane," and Davys's "The seamans secrets."); it also appeared in photostatic form from the Huntington Library copy, in microfilm by University Microfilms, Ann Arbor,*

Écriture gothique sauf pour la page de titre, les en-têtes et le titre courant qui sont en romain. L'épître dédicatoire est à l'intention du Conseil privé. ¶ *Davys fut le découvreur du Détroit de Davis [qui sépare la terre de Baffin du Groenland]. Il décrit ici ses trois voyages d'exploration à la recherche du passage du Nord-Ouest.* ¶ *Première édition ; réimpressions : Richard Hakluyt,* The principal navigations. *Londres, 1598–1600 (etc., q.v. plus bas ; voir aussi l'édition de 1589 portant sur les voyages antérieurs de Davys), ainsi que* The voyages and works of John Davis, *édité, préfacé et annoté par Albert Hastings Markham, Londres, Hakluyt Soc., 1880, 2 vol. (cet ouvrage contient également « The first and third voyage of J. Davis, written by John Jane » ainsi que « The seamans secrets » de Davys.) ; l'ouvrage a également été reproduit par photocopie à partir de l'exemplaire de la Huntington Library, sur mic., Ann Arbor (Mich.), University Microfilms, n° 12086, et par photocopie*

Mich., no. 12086, and in photostat in the Americana series, Boston, Mass. Hist. Soc., 1925, from the BM copy (cf. NUC).

dans la collection Americana, Boston, Mass. Hist. Soc., 1925, à partir de l'exemplaire du BM (cf. NUC).

1598

*Stow, John, 1525?–1605. A summarie of the chronicles of England. Diligently collected...vnto...1598 .... London, imprinted by Richard Bradocke, 1598. [30], 460, [31] p. 16°

NUC(Pre–56)572:36*

Format from BM(to 1955)231:52. ¶ First ed.: London, 1565, q.v. for other notes.

Format du BM(to 1955)231:52. ¶ Première édition : Londres, 1565, q.v. pour d'autres notes.

1598–1600

*Hakluyt, Richard, 1552?–1616. The principal navigations, voiages, traffiqves and discoueries of the English nation .... Imprinted at London by George Bishop, Ralph Newberie and Robert Barker, 1598[–1600]. 3 v. in 2. map. fol.

NUC(Pre–56)226:476*

For a note on the cancelled t.-p., cf. NUC. ¶ Many errors in paging. ¶ Vol. 2 has title: "The second volume of the principal navigations ... to the south and south-east parts of the world, at any time within the compass of these 1600 yeres ...."; vol. 3: "The third

Pour une note concernant la p. de t. qui a été supprimée, cf. NUC. ¶ Nombreuses erreurs de pagination. ¶ Le volume 2 porte le titre : « The second volume of the principal navigations ... to the south and south-east parts of the world, at any time within the compass of these 1600 yeres

and last volume of the voyages ... of the English nation ...." (*q.v.*, under 1600). ¶ *See* 1589.

.... » ; vol. 3 : « The third and last volume of the voyages ... of the English nation .... » (*q.v.* 1600). ¶ *Voir* 1589.

1599

[Abbot, George, *abp. of Canterbury/aev. de Canterbury*], 1562–1633. A briefe description of the whole worlde. Wherein is particularly described, all the monarchies, empires, and kingdomes of the same: with their seuerall titles and scituations thereunto adioyning. At London: printed by T. Iudson for Iohn Browne, and are to be sould at the signe of the Bible in Fleete-streete. 1599. 34 l. 4°(in 8s).

NUC(Pre–56)1:307*

Signatures: A–D⁸, E²; NUC has a 1599, [63] p. variant signed: A–H⁴. ¶ New France and Northwest Passage: D8ᵇ–E1; p. 298–301 in 1664 ed. The section on America was considerably enlarged in later editions. ¶ *First edition; other printings and editions: 1600, 1605, 1608 (third), 1617 (fourth), 1620 (fifth), 1624 (sixth), 1634, 1635, 1636, 1642, 1656, 1664, and transl. into French as (apparently, see* BM(to 1955)51:579) Description abrégée des principales régions de la terre. *Paris, 1728.*

Signatures : A–D⁸, E² ; le NUC *donne une variante de [63] p. de 1599 dont la signature est A–H⁴.* ¶ Nouvelle France et passage du Nord-Ouest : D8ᵇ – E1 ; p. 298–301 dans l'édition de 1664. La partie traitant de l'Amérique fut considérablement augmentée dans les éditions ultérieures. ¶ *Première édition ; autres réimpressions et éditions : 1600, 1605, 1608 (troisième), 1617 (quatrième), 1620 (cinquième), 1624 (sixième), 1634, 1635, 1636, 1642, 1656, 1664. L'ouvrage aurait également été traduit en français, (voir le* BM(to 1955)51:579) *sous le titre* Description abrégée des principales régions de la terre. *Paris, 1728.*

1600

*[Abbot, George, *abp. of Canterbury/aev. de Canterbury*], 1562–1633.   A briefe description of the whole worlde . . . . At London printed by R[ichard]. B[radock]. for Iohn Browne, 1600. 32 l. 4°

NUC(Pre–56)1:307*

See 1599.   *Voir* 1599.

*[Cartier, Jacques], 1491–1557.   A shorte and briefe narration of the nauigation made by the commandement of the King of France, to the islands of Canada, Hochelaga, Saguenay, and diuers others which now are called New France, with the particular customes, and maners of the inhabitants therein. [London, 1600.] (*In* Richard Hakluyt, [*The principal navigations*.] London, 1600, v.3, p. 212–32.)

NUC(Pre–56)97:248*

The second of Cartier's voyages, first pub. in English as *A short and briefe narration of the two nauigations* . . . . London, 1580, *q.v.*, above. It was reprinted in Hakluyt's *Collection of . . . voyages.* London, 1810, v. 3, p. 262–85.

Récit du deuxième voyage de Cartier, publié pour la première fois en anglais sous le titre *A short and briefe narration of the two nauigations* . . . . Londres, 1580, *q.v.* plus haut. L'ouvrage fut réimprimé dans Hakluyt, *Collection of . . . voyages.* Londres, 1810, vol. 3, p. 262–85.

Hakluyt, Richard, 1552?–1616. The third and last volume of the voyages, navigations, traffiques, and discoueries of the English nation, and in some few places, where they haue not been, of strangers, performed within and before the time of these hundred yeeres, to all parts of the newfound world of America, or the West Indies, from 73. degrees of northerly to 57. of southerly latitude: as namely to Engronland, Meta Incognita [S. Baffin Is.], Estotiland [Canada E. of Hudson Bay], Tierra de Labrador, Newfoundland, vp the grand bay, the gulfe of S. Laurence, and the Riuer of Canada to Hochelaga and Saguenay . . . And from thence on the backside of America, along the coastes, harbours, and capes of . . . California, Noua Albion, and more northerly as farre as 43. degrees . . . . Collected by Richard Hakluyt preacher, and sometimes student of Christ-Church in Oxford. Imprinted at London by George Bishop, Ralfe Newberie, and Robert Barker. Anno Dom. 1600. 1 p.l., [14], 868 p. double map. fol.

NUC(Pre–56)226:476*

NUC has in contents note only, as vol. 3 to The Principal navigations . . . , *London, 1598–[1600], and 1599–1600.* ¶ "The English voyages, . . . (intended for the finding of a Northwest passage) to the North parts of America . . .": p. 4–128; "The voyages of the English nation to Nevv-fovndland, to the Isles of Ramea, and the Isles of Assumption . . . and to the coastes of Cape Briton, and Arambec, corruptly called Norunbega [esp. Nova Scotia & New England], . . .": p. 129–201; "Certaine voyages containing the discouerie of the Gulfe of Sainct Laurence to the west of Newfoundland, and from thence vp the riuer of Canada to Hochelaga, Saguenay, and other places . . .": p. 201–42. ¶ These three sections include the following items not already published in the first edition, the third section being entirely new: "A true Discourse of the three Voyages of discouerie, for the finding of a passage to Cathaya, by the Northwest, vnder the conduct of Martin Frobisher . . . . Penned by

Le NUC n'a qu'une note de contenu présentant cet ouvrage comme le vol. 3 de The Principal navigations . . . , *Londres, 1598–[1600] et 1599–1600.* ¶ « The English voyages, . . . (intended for the finding of a Northwest passage) to the North parts of America . . . » : p. 4–128 ; « The voyages of the English nation to Nevv-fovndland, to the Isles of Ramea, and the Isles of Assumption . . . and to the coastes of Cape Briton, and Arambec, corruptly called Norunbega [principalement la Nouvelle-Écosse et la Nouvelle-Angleterre], . . . » : p. 129–201 ; « Certaine voyages containing the dis-couerie of the Gulfe of Sainct Laurence to the west of Newfoundland, and from thence vp the riuer of Canada to Hochelaga, Saguenay, and other places . . . » : p. 201–42. ¶ Voici les articles qui n'avaient pas été publiés dans la première édition et que comprennent les trois parties citées plus haut, la troisième partie n'étant constituée que de matériel inédit : « A true Discourse of the three Voyages of discouerie, for the finding of a passage to Cathaya, by the Northwest, vnder the conduct of Martin Frobisher . . . . Penned by Master George

Master George Best . . .": p. 47–60; "A true report of such things as happened in the second voyage of Captaine Frobisher, pretended for the discouerie of a new passage to Cataya, China, and the East Indies, by the Northwest. Ann. Dom. 1577": p. 60–73; "The third voyage of Captaine Frobisher, pretended for the discouerie of Cataia, by Meta Incognita, Anno. Do. 1578": p. 74–96; "A Traverse-Booke made by M. Iohn Davis in his third voyage for the discouerie of the Northwest passage. Anno 1587.": p. 115–18; "A report of Master Iohn Dauis of his three Voyages made for the discouery of the Northwest passage, taken out of a Treatise of his, Intituled The worlds Hydrographicall description": p. 119–20; "De Nauigatione Illustris & Magnanimi Equitis Aurati Humfredi Gilberti . . . Carmen . . . Stephani Parmenii Bvdeii": p. 137–42; Letters from Sir Francis Walsingham, March 11, 1582, to R. Hakluyt and Thomas Aldworth, respectively: p. 143–88; "A relation of the first voyage and discouerie of the Isle Ramea, made by Monsieur de La court Pre Rauillon, and Grande Pre, with the ship called the Bonauenture . . . 1591": p. 189–90; "A letter sent to . . . Lord Burghley . . . from M. Thomas Iames of Bristoll, concerning the discouerie of the Isle of Ramea . . . 1591": p. 191; "A briefe note on the Morsse and the vse thereof": p. 191; "The voyage of the ship called the Marigold of M. Hill of Redrife vnto Cape Briton and beyond to the latitude of 44 degrees and an half, 1593. Written by Richard

Best. . . » : p. 47–60 ; « A true report of such things as happened in the second voyage of Captaine Frobisher, pretended for the discouerie of a new passage to Cataya, China, and the East Indies, by the Northwest. Ann. Dom. 1577 » : p. 60–73 ; « The third voyage of Captaine Frobisher, pretended for the discouerie of Cataia, by Meta Incognita, Anno. Do. 1578 » : p. 74–96 ; « A Traverse-Booke made by M. Iohn Davis in his third voyage for the discouerie of the Northwest passage. Anno 1587. » : p. 115–18 ; « A report of Master Iohn Dauis of his three Voyages made for the discouery of the Northwest passage, taken out of a treatise of his, Intituled The worlds Hydrographicall description » : p. 119–20 ; « De Nauigatione Illustris & Magnanimi Equitis Aurati Humfredi Gilberti . . . Carmen . . . Stephani Parmenii Bvdeii » : p. 137–42 ; Lettres de Sir Francis Walsingham, l'une à l'intention de R. Hakluyt et l'autre, de Thomas Aldworth, et datées du 11 mars 1582 : p. 143–88 ; « A relation of the first voyage and discouerie of the Isle Ramea, made by Monsieur de La court Pre Rauillon, and Grand Pre, with the ship called the Bonauenture . . . 1591 » : p. 189–90 ; « A letter sent to . . . Lord Burghley . . . from M. Thomas Iames of Bristoll, concerning the discouerie of the Isle of Ramea . . . 1591 » : p. 191 ; « A briefe note on the Morsse and the vse thereof » : p. 191 ; « The voyage of the ship called the Marigold of M. Hill of Redrife vnto Cape Briton and beyond to the latitude of 44 degrees and an half, 1593. Written by Richard fisher . . . » : p. 191–93 ; « A briefe note concerning the voyage of M. George Drake of Apsham to the Isle of Ramea in the aforesayd yere 1593 » : p. 193 ; « The voyage of the Grace of Bristol of M. Rice Iones . . . vp into the Bay of Saint

fisher . . .": p. 191–93; "A briefe note concerning the voyage of M. George Drake of Apsham to the Isle of Ramea in the aforesayd yere 1593": p. 193; "The voyage of the Grace of Bristol of M. Rice Iones . . . vp into the Bay of Saint Laurence to the Northwest of Newefoundland . . .": p. 194–95; "The voyage of M. Charles Leigh, and diuers others to Cape Briton and the Isle of Ramea.": p. 195–201; Florio's translation of Jacques Cartier's two voyages (first pub. 1580): p. 201–32; "The third voyage of discouery made by Captaine Jaques Cartier, 1540. vnto the Countreys of Canada, Hochelaga, and Saguenay.": p. 232–36; Two letters to M. Iohn Growte from Iaques Noel, nephew of Cartier: p. 236; "Here followeth the course from Belle Isle, Carpont, and the Grand Bay in Newfoundland vp the Riuer of Canada for the space of 230. leagues, obserued by Iohn Alphonse of Xanctoigne chiefe Pilote to Monsieur Roberual. 1542.": p. 237–40; "The Voyage of Iohn Francis de la Roche, knight, Lord of Roberual, to the Countries of Canada, Saguenai, and Hochelaga . . . 1542 . . .": p. 240–42.¶ This is the first year in which this form of the text was published; the first edition appeared as *The principall navigations* . . ., London, 1589 (*q.v.*, above).

Laurence to the Northwest of Newefoundland . . . » : p. 194–95 ; « The voyage of M. Charles Leigh, and diuers others to Cape Briton and the Isle of Ramea. » : p. 195–201 ; traduction du récit des deux voyages de Jacques Cartier par Florio (première publication en 1580) : p. 201–32 ; « The third voyage of discouery made by Captaine Jaques Cartier, 1540. vnto the Countreys of Canada, Hochelaga, and Saguenay. » : p. 232–36 ; Deux lettres adressées à M. Iohn Growte par Iaques Noel, neveu de Cartier : p. 236 ; « Here followeth the course from Belle Isle, Carpont, and the Grand Bay in Newfoundland vp the Riuer of Canada for the space of 230. leagues, obserued by Iohn Alphonse of Xanctoigne chiefe Pilote to Monsieur Roberual. 1542. » : p. 237–40 ; « The Voyage of Iohn Francis de la Roche, knight, Lord of Roberual, to the Countries of Canada, Saguenai, and Hochelaga . . . 1542 . . . » : p. 240–42.¶ Il s'agit de la première année où ce document fut publié sous cette forme ; la première édition a paru sous le titre *The principall navigations* . . . . Londres, 1589 (*q.v.*, plus haut).

*Stow, John, 1525?–1605. The annales of England, from the first inhabitation untill 1600. London, R[alph]. Newbery [1600]. 1315 p. 4°

NUC(Pre–56)572:34*

Collation and format from BM(to 1955)231:50, where the title is given as: *The annales of England, faithfully collected out of the most autenticall authors ... lately corrected, encreased and continued, from the first inhabitation untill this present yeere 1600 ...*, which title is similar to that of the first appearance of *The annales*, under this title, 1592, *q.v.* for other notes.

Collation et format du BM(to 1955)231:50, dans lequel le titre se lit comme suit : *The annales of England, faithfully collected out of the most autenticall authors ... lately corrected, encreased and continued, from the first inhabitation untill this present yeere 1600 ...*, lequel titre est semblable à celui de la première publication de *The annales*, sous le même titre en 1592, *q.v.* pour d'autres notes.

1601

Galvão, Antonio, *d./déc.* 1557. The discoveries of the world from their first originall vnto the yeare of our Lord 1555. Briefly written in the Portugall tongue by Antonio Galvano, gouernour of Ternate, the chiefe island of the Malucos: Corrected, quoted, and now published in English by Richard Hakluyt .... Londini, impensis G[eorge]. Bishop. 1601. 6 p.l., 97 p. 4°

NUC(Pre–56)190:64*

Cabot: p. 32–33; Cortereal: p. 35–36; Cartier: p. 76. ¶ *First edition; this was reprinted in the following collections:* Thomas Osborne, A collection of voyages and travels, *London, 1745, q.v. (under Galvão);* A collection of voyages and travels, *London, 1747, q.v. (under Galvão); Awnsham Churchill,* A collection of voyages and travels, *London, 1752, q.v. (under Galvão);*

Cabot : p. 32–33 ; Cortereal : p. 35–36 ; Cartier : p. 76. ¶ *Première édition ; ce document fut réimprimé dans les recueils suivants :* Thomas Osborne, A collection of voyages and travels, *Londres, 1745, q.v. Galvão ;* A collection of voyages and travels, *Londres, 1747, q.v. Galvão ; Awnsham Churchill,* A collection of voyages and travels, *Londres, 1752, q.v. Galvão ; James S. Clarke,* The progress of maritime discovery, *Londres, 1803,*

James S. Clarke, The progress of maritime discovery, *London, 1803, Appendix; Richard Hakluyt,* Hakluyt's collection of the early voyages, *London, 1812, v. 4, BVIPA; Richard Hakluyt,* A selection of curious, rare and early voyages, *London, 1812, p. 1–50, BVIPA; Hakluyt Society,* Works, *London, 1862, no. 30, BVAU · BVIPA.*

annexe ; Richard Hakluyt, Hakluyt's collection of the early voyages, *Londres, 1812, vol. 4, BVIPA ; Richard Hakluyt,* A selection of curious, rare and early voyages, *Londres, 1812, p. 1–50, BVIPA ; Hakluyt Society,* Works, *Londres, 1862, nº 30, BVAU · BVIPA.*

*Stow, John, 1525?–1605. The annales of England. Faithfully collected out of the most autenticall authors . . . lately corrected, encreased, and continued . . . vntill . . . 1601. By Iohn Stow . . . . Imprinted at London by Ralfe Newbery [1601]. 4°

NUC(Pre–56)572:34*

Collation given in signatures only. ¶ First published under this title: London, 1592, and again in 1600, *q.v.* for a fuller title and other notes.

Collation donnée par signature seulement. ¶ Première publication sous ce titre à Londres en 1592, puis à nouveau en 1600, *q.v.* pour un titre plus complet et d'autres notes.

1602

Brereton, John, *fl.* 1603. A brief and true relation of the discouerie of the north part of Virginia . . . made this present yeere 1602, by Captaine Bartholomew Gosnold, Captaine Bartholowmew Gilbert, and diuers other gentlemen their associats, by the permission of the honourable knight, Sir Walter Ralegh, &c. Written by M. Iohn Brereton one of the voyage. Whereunto is annexed a treatise conteining important inducements for the planting in those parts, and finding a passage that way to the South sea, and China. Written by M. Edward Hayes, a gentleman long since imploied in the like action. Londini, impensis Geor[ge]. Bishop. 1602. 24 p. 4°

NUC(Pre–56)74:404*

Transcribed from facsimile title-page in Church:325. ¶ Hayes wants to give up the idea of finding a passage through the frozen north and hopes to find a way, part overland, part by rivers and lakes, in more temperate regions. He wants to follow the rivers to the middle of the continent where they take their rise in mountains, arguing that there must be more rivers flowing the other way, down the other side of the mountains to the South Sea. He proposes that ships from Cathay come to the head of navigation, whence pack animals or "salvages" can carry the goods over the mountains to the ships on the other side. Ships from Europe would reverse the process. ¶ *First edition; facsimile reprints in* The Bibliographer, *New York, vol. 1, Oct.–Dec.1902, and New York, Dodd, Mead, 1903, and Boston, 1905, and New York, 1906 (all in NUC); "second impression," also 1602 (see next entry).*

Transcription à partir d'un fac-similé de la page de titre dans Church:325. ¶ Hayes veut abandonner l'idée de trouver un passage à travers les glaces du nord et espère plutôt trouver une voie, en partie par la terre ferme, en partie via les rivières et les lacs des régions plus tempérées. Il veut remonter les rivières jusqu'aux montagnes du milieu du continent, là où elles prennent leur source ; il soutient qu'il doit y avoir encore un plus grand nombre de rivières coulant dans l'autre sens, de l'autre côté des montagnes, en direction des mers du sud. Il propose que des vaisseaux en provenance de Cathay viennent jusqu'à la limite des eaux navigables, d'où bêtes de somme et « sauvages » porteraient les marchandises à travers les montagnes jusqu'aux vaisseaux européens, de l'autre côté, qui prendraient la relève de l'opération. ¶ *Première édition ; réimpressions d'après fac-similés dans* The Bibliographer, *New York, vol. 1, oct.–déc. 1902, New York, Dodd, Mead, 1903, Boston, 1905 et New York, 1906 (tous au NUC) ; aussi, deuxième impression en 1602, (voir notice suivante).*

Brereton, John, *fl.* 1603. A briefe and true relation of the discouerie of the north part of Virginia . . . . Whereunto is annexed a Treatise, of M. Edward Hayes, conteining important inducements for the planting in those parts, and finding a passage that way to the South sea, and China. With diuers instructions of speciall moment newly added in this second impression. Londini, impensis Geor[ge]. Bishop, 1602. 48 p. 4°

NUC(Pre–56)74:404*

The additions, p. 25–48, are taken from Richard Hakluyt, Fernando de Soto, René Laudonnière, Thomas Herriot, and

Les ajouts des pages 25 à 48 sont tirés de Richard Hakluyt, Fernando de Soto, René Laudonnière, Thomas Herriot et autres. ¶ Le NUC donne aussi

others. ¶ *NUC has also a "second edition"(74:405), 1602, perhaps the same as this "second impression." ¶ See first edition, preceding entry.*

une deuxième édition (74:405), datée de 1602; il s'agit peut-être du même document que ce deuxième tirage. ¶ Voir la première édition, à la notice précédente.

1603

Great Britain. Sovereigns, etc., 1603–1625 (James I). By the King. A proclamation for the due and speedy execution of the statute against rogues, vagabonds, idle, and dissolute persons .... Giuen at ... Woodstocke the seuenteenth day of September, 1603 .... Colophon: Imprinted at London by Robert Barker, printer to the Kings most Excellent Majestie. Anno 1603. Two broadsheets. fol.

NUC(Pre–56)215:273

Waldon notes, within the title: Banishing vagabonds to Newfoundland and the West Indies, 17 Sept. 1603.

Waldon note, dans le titre : déportation de vagabonds vers Terre-Neuve et les Antilles, le 17 septembre 1603.

1604

*Stow, John, 1525?–1605. A summarie of the chronicles of England. Diligently collected ... vnto ... 1604.... London, imprinted by Iohn Harison. 1604. [16], 459, [30] p. 16°

NUC(Pre–56)572:36*

Format from BM(to 1955)231:52. ¶ First ed.: London, 1565, *q.v.* for other notes.

Format du BM(to 1955)231:52. ¶ Première éd. : Londres, 1565, *q.v.* pour d'autres notes.

1605

[**Abbot, George,** *abp. of Canterbury/aev. de Canterbury*], 1562–1633. A briefe description of the whole worlde . . . . newly augmented and enlarged . . . . London: printed for Iohn Browne, 1605. 82 l. 4°

NUC(Pre–56)1:307*

See 1599.   *Voir* 1599.

*Stow, John, 1525?–1605. The annales of England. Faithfully collected . . . since encreased . . . vntil . . . 1605. By Iohn Stow . . . . Imprinted at London for G[eorge]. Bishop and T[homas]. Adams [1605]. [1410] p. 4°

NUC(Pre–56)572:35*

Format from BM(to 1955)231:50. ¶ Various pagings. ¶ Black-letter; initials. Title within ornamental border. ¶ "Authors out of whom these annales are collected": p. [7–8]. ¶ First published under this title: London, 1592, *q.v.* for fuller title and other notes.

Format du BM(to 1955)231:50. ¶ Paginations multiples. ¶ Lettres gothiques ; initiales. Titre encadré par une bordure décorative. ¶ « Auteurs des oeuvres parmi lesquelles ces annales ont été recueillies » : p. [7–8] ¶ Publié pour la première fois sous ce titre : Londres, 1592, *q.v.* pour un titre plus complet et d'autres notes.

1607

[Stafford, Robert], 1588–1618. A geographicall and anthologicall description of all the empires and kingdomes, both of continent and ilands in this terrestriall globe. Relating their scituations, manners, customes, prouinces, and gouernements .... London, printed by T.C. for S[imon]. VVaterson, dwelling at the signe of the Crowne in Paules Church-yard. 1607. 4 p.l., 67, [5] p. tables. 4°

NUC(Pre–56)563:583*

Dedication signed: Rob. Stafforde. ¶ "Of the unknown parts of the Earth" (arctic and antarctic regions): p. 4–5; "Norumbega, Nova Francia, Terra Cortealis, Estotiland, Newfoundland": p. 62–63. These sections remained unchanged in the later editions. ¶ *First edition; other eds.: 1618, 1634, q.v.; text republished in MF, in the STC series (no. 23135, carton 939 — cf. NUC).*

Dédicace signée : Rob. Stafforde. ¶ « Of the unknown parts of the Earth » (arctique et antarctique) : p. 4–5 ; « Norumbega, Nova Francia, Terra Cortealis, Estotiland, Newfoundland » : p. 62–63. Ces sections restent les mêmes dans les éditions ultérieures. ¶ *Première édition ; autres éd. : 1618, 1634, q.v. ; reproduction sur mic. dans la collection du STC (n° 23135, carton 939 – cf. NUC).*

*Stow, John, 1525?–1605. The abridgement or summarie of the English chronicle, first collected by master Iohn Stow, and after him augmented with sundry memorable antiquities, and continued with maters forrein and domesticall, vnto this present yeare 1607. By E[dmond]. H[owes]., gentleman. London, printed for the Companie of Stacioners [1607]. [14], 616, [38] p. 8°

NUC(Pre–56)572:34*

Black-letter. ¶ "To the honest and friendly reader" signed: Edmond Howes. ¶ "This is another edition of the original work [Stow's *The chronicles of England* .... London, 1580, q.v.], not of 'Summarie ... abridged,'" *i.e., A summarie of*

Lettres gothiques. ¶ « Au lecteur honnête et amical » signé : Edmond Howes. ¶ « Ceci est une autre édition de l'oeuvre originale de Stow [*The chronicles of England*.... Londres, 1580, q.v.] et non du « Summarie ... abridged », c.-à-d. *A summarie of Englyshe chronicles*.... Londres, 1565, q.v. (cf. BM(to

Englyshe chronicles . . . . London, 1565, *q.v.* (cf. BM(to 1955)231:52). ¶ This is the first appearance under this title; the work was subsequently published in 1611 and 1618 (cf. below).

1955)231:52). ¶ Il s'agit de la première parution sous ce titre ; l'oeuvre fut ultérieurement publiée en 1611 et en 1618 (cf. plus loin).

1608

*[Abbot, George, *abp. of Canterbury/aev. de Canterbury*], 1562–1633. A briefe description of the whole worlde. . . . Newly augmented and enlarged . . . . The third edition. At London printed for Iohn Browne, and are to be sold at his shoppe in Saint Dunstans Church-yard in Fleetstreet. 1608. A–V⁴ 4°

NUC(Pre–56)1:307*

Printed by Richard Bradock (*see* NUC, where a variant(?) is signed: A–V⁸). ¶ *See* 1599.

Imprimé par Richard Bradock (*voir* NUC, qui donne une variante (?) numérotée A–V⁸). ¶ *Voir* 1599.

*[Botero, Giovanni], 1540–1617. Relations, of the most famous kingdoms and common-weales thorough the world. Discoursing of their scituations, manners, customes, strengthes and pollicies. Translated into English and enlarged, with an addition of the estates of Saxony, Geneva, Hungary, and the East Indies, in any language never before imprinted. London, printed [by William Iaggard] for Iohn Iaggard, dvvelling in Fleetstreet, at the Hand and Starre, betweene the two Temple gates, 1608. [116], 113–330 p. 4°

NUC(Pre–56)68:557*

First edition in English under this title. ¶ *See* 1630.

Première édition en anglais parue sous ce titre. ¶ *Voir* 1630.

1609

[**Lescarbot, Marc**], *ca.* 1570–1642. Nova Francia: or the description of that part of Nevv France, which is one continent with Virginia. Described in the three late voyages and plantation made by Monsieur de Monts, Monsieur du Pont-Graué, and Monsieur de Poutrincourt, into the countries called by the French men La Cadie, lying to the southwest of Cape Breton. Together with an excellent seuerall treatie [*sic*] of all the commodities of the said countries, and maners of the naturall inhabitants of the same. Translated out of French into English by P[ierre]. E[rondelle]. Londini, Imponsis [*sic*] Georgii Bishop. 1609. 1 p.l., 16, 307 p. 4°

NUC(Pre–56)328:113*

The author's dates are those in DCB, *which differ from those in* NUC. ¶ NUC *has only the microfilm of this listed, and the Andrew Hebb 1609 edition (see next entry).* ¶ A translation at the request of Hakluyt, of the fourth and sixth books [Church:341 says from Book 2, Chap. 31, "to the end of the Third and last"] of Lescoubat's [*i.e.* Lescarbot's] *Histoire de la Nouvelle-France*, first published [Paris] 1609. The map which is sometimes found with the work does not properly belong with it, but is inserted from the French edition. ¶ *This and the variant following are the first English translations; it appeared in German in 1613, and in other English editions in ca. 1625, 1745, 1747, and 1752, q.v. It was also reprinted in Toronto by the Champlain Society, 1907–14, 3 vols., in London by Routledge in 1928, and in New York by Harpers in 1928.*

Les dates de l'auteur sont celles que l'on retrouve dans le DBC, *elles diffèrent de celles contenues dans le* NUC. ¶ *Le* NUC *ne donne que le microfilm ainsi que l'édition Andrew Hebb de 1609, (voir la notice suivante).* ¶ Une traduction, faite à la demande de Hakluyt, des quatrième et sixième livres [Church:341 indique du Livre 2, Chap. 31), « jusqu'à la fin du troisième et dernier » livre] de l'*Histoire de la Nouvelle-France* de Lescoubat [c.-à-d. Lescarbot] fut d'abord publiée [à Paris] en 1609. La carte que l'on retrouve parfois dans l'oeuvre anglaise n'en fait pas proprement partie, il s'agit d'une insertion provenant de l'édition française. ¶ *Cet ouvrage ainsi que la variante qui suit sont les premières traductions en anglais. Il parut en allemand en 1613 et dans d'autres éditions anglaises v. 1625, 1745, 1747, et 1752, q.v. Il fut aussi réimprimé à Toronto par la Société Champlain, 1907–1914, 3 vol. ; à Londres par Routledge en 1928 ainsi qu'à New York par Harpers en 1928.*

[Lescarbot, Marc], ca. 1570–1642. Nova Francia, or the description of that part of Nevv France, which is one continent with Virginia. Described . . . by . . . Monsieur du Pont-Graué, and Monsieur de Poutriucourt [*sic*], into the countries called by the French-men La Cadie . . . . London. Printed for Andrew Hebb, and are to be sold at the signe of the Bell in Pauls Church-yard. [1609.] 9 p.l., 307 p. 4°

NUC(Pre–56)328:113*

Waldon has collation as: t.-p., 14, 307 p. ¶ NUC notes that this "covers only the part [of the original French edition] relating to the voyages and settlements of de Monts, Pontgrave and Poutrincourt, with the book on the Indians." ¶ For other notes and editions, see *preceding entry.*

Collation de Waldon : p. de t., 14, 307 p. ¶ Le NUC note que l'ouvrage « ne comprend que la partie [de l'édition française originale] qui traite des voyages et des efforts de colonisation par de Monts, du Pontgravé et de Poutrincourt ainsi que le livre traitant des Indiens ». ¶ Pour d'autres notes et éditions, voir *la notice précédente.*

1611

*[Botero, Giovanni], 1540–1617. Relations, of the most famous kingdoms . . . with an addition of the estates of Venice, Saxony . . . . London . . . 1611 [*see* 1608 ed.]. 2 p.l., 437 [*i.e.* 435] p. 4°(?)

NUC(Pre–56)68:557*

Numbers 93, 94, 378, 379 omitted in paging; 431, 432 repeated in page numbering. ¶ First edition in English under this title: 1608, *q.v.*, above. ¶ See 1630.

Les numéros 93, 94, 378, 379 ont été omis dans la pagination ; les numéros 431 et 432 sont répétés. ¶ La première édition en anglais parue sous ce titre : 1608, *q.v.* plus haut. ¶ *Voir* 1630.

[Digges, Sir Dudley], 1583–1639. Fata mihi totum mea sunt agitanda per orbem. Imprinted at London by W[illiam]. White for Iohn Barnes. 1611. 1 p.l., 26 p. 8°

NUC(Pre–56)143:662

NUC has collation: [15] l. ¶ Digges was a pupil of Dr. George Abbot, afterwards archbishop of Canterbury, and one of the founders of a company, incorporated in 1612, for the purpose of trading on the northwest passage, and which promoted five voyages: Hudson (1610–11), Button (1612–13), Gibbons (1614), Bylot and Baffin (1615 and 1616). This book may have been written to reassure the public after Hudson's failure and death. ¶ *This seems to have been the first ed., and NUC also has the same title but with the printer given only as "W.W."; another edition appeared in 1612 (q.v. below), and the work was reprinted with notes in* Bibliographical miscellany, *London, no. 2–3, 15 Dec. 1853–20 Jan. 1854 (Sabin:5195), in photostat form from the Huntington Library copy (cf. NUC), and again in photostat from the Mass. Hist. Soc. copy, Boston, 1921, which copy has the t.-p. date altered in ms. from 1612 to 1632 (cf. NUC, note to 1612 ed.).*

Collation du NUC : [15] f. ¶ Digges fut un élève du Dr George Abbot qui devint par la suite archevêque de Canterbury. Il fut aussi l'un des fondateurs d'une compagnie constituée en 1612 afin de commercer le long du passage du Nord-Ouest. Celle-ci fut à l'origine de cinq voyages : celui d'Hudson (1610–11), de Button (1612–13), de Gibbons (1614), de Bylot et de Baffin (1615 et 1616). Ce livre a peut-être été écrit pour rassurer le public après l'échec et la mort d'Hudson. ¶ *Il semble s'agir de la première édition. Le NUC note aussi le même titre mais l'imprimeur n'est identifié que par les initiales « W.W. ». Une autre édition fut publiée en 1612 (q.v. plus loin) et une version annotée fut réimprimée dans* Bibliographical miscellany. *Londres, n° 2–3, 15 déc. 1853–20 janv. 1854 (Sabin:5195), à partir de la photocopie de l'exemplaire de la Huntington Library (cf. NUC) et, à nouveau, à partir de la photocopie de l'exemplaire appartenant à la Mass. Hist. Soc., Boston, 1921, et dont la date de la p. de t. a été modifiée à la main de 1612 à 1632 (cf. NUC, note se rapportant à l'éd. de 1612).*

*Stow, John, 1525?–1605. The abridgement of the English Chronicle, first collected by M. Iohn Stow, and after him augmented with very many memorable antiquities, and continued with matters forreine and domesticall, vnto the end of the yeare 1610. By E[dmond]. H[owes]., gentleman. There is a briefe table at the end of the booke. Imprinted at London for the Company of Stationers, 1611. 7 p.l., 510, [20] p. 8°

NUC(Pre–56)572:34*

Black-letter; title within ornamental border; initials. ¶ Format: from BM(to 1955)231:52. ¶ Numerous paging errors (cf. NUC). ¶ "Of the vniversities in England ...": [14] p. following p. 510. ¶ "This is another edition of the original work," Stow's *The chronicles of England.* London, 1580 (*q.v.*): cf. BM (as cited above). ¶ First pub. under this title: London, 1607, *q.v.* (Stow); text republished in MF, in the STC series (no. 23331, carton 1221).

Lettres gothiques ; titre encadré par une bordure décorative ; initiales. ¶ Format du BM(to 1955)231:52. ¶ Nombreuses erreurs de pagination (cf. NUC). ¶ « Des universités d'Angleterre ... » : [14] p. suivant la p. 510. ¶ « Il s'agit d'une autre édition de l'ouvrage original », *The chronicles of England* de Stow, Londres, 1580 (*q.v.*) : cf. BM (cité ci-dessus). ¶ Première publ. sous ce titre : Londres, 1607, *q.v.* (Stow) ; reproduction sur mic. dans la collection du STC (n° 23331, carton 1221).

1612

Anghiera, Pietro Martire d', 1455–1526. De nouo orbe, or The historie of the West Indies, contayning the actes and aduentures of the Spanyardes, which haue conquered and peopled those countries, inriched with varietie of pleasant relation of the manners, ceremonies, lawes, gouernments, and warres of the Indians. Comprised in eight decades. Written by Peter Martyr a Millanoise of Angleria .... Whereof three, haue beene formerly translated into English by R. Eden, whereunto the other fiue, are newly added by ... M. Lok .... London[.] Printed for Thomas Adams. 1612. 5 p.l., 318 numb. l. 4°

NUC(Pre–56)17:14*

With the addition of Michael Lok's translations, this is the first complete English edition of the eight Decades. The four translated by Eden had appeared as early as 1555 (q.v.), and again in 1577 (q.v.) with an abridgement of Decades five to eight. ¶ The West Indies included North America and its

Avec les traductions de Michael Lok, il s'agit de la première édition anglaise complète des huit Décades. Les quatre traduites par Eden parurent dès 1555 (q.v.), et à nouveau en 1577 (q.v.) avec un abrégé des Décades cinq à huit. ¶ Les Antilles incluaient l'Amérique du Nord et les Indiens qui y habitaient. Traduction à la demande de Hakluyt à partir de son édition de Paris,

Indians. Translated at Hakluyt's instance from his Paris edition, 1587. Reprinted in vol. 5 of the 1809 Hakluyt. ¶ There are several references to Cabot "my very frende, whom I vse familiarly, and delight to haue him sometimes keepe mee companie in my owne house," the longest being the account of his discoveries in the sixth chapter of the third Decade, fol. 124 b–125 b. ¶ *First edition; other editions: 1626, 1628, under his* The historie of the West-Indies, *and* The famovs historie, *respectively.*

1587. Réimpression dans le vol. 5 de l'édition Hakluyt de 1809. ¶ L'on y trouve plusieurs mentions concernant Cabot « mon véritable ami, que je traite familièrement et qu'il me fait grand plaisir de recevoir parfois chez moi », la plus longue étant le compte rendu de ses découvertes que l'on retrouve dans le sixième chapitre de la 3ᵉ Décade, fol. 124 b–125 b. ¶ *Première édition ; autres éditions : 1626 et 1628, sous les titres respectifs suivants :* The historie of the West-Indies *et* The famovs historie.

*[Digges, Sir **Dudley**], 1583–1639. Fata mihi totum mea sunt agitanda per orbem. London(?), 1612.

See this entry, 1611, for notes.

Voir notes à la notice de 1611.

[Digges, Sir **Dudley**], 1583–1639. Of circumference of the earth: or, A treatise of the northeast [*i.e.* northwest] passage. Imprinted at London by W[illiam]. W[hite]. for Iohn Barnes. 1612. 1 p.l., 26 p. 8°

NUC(Pre–56)143:662*

Title within decorative border. ¶ *Incorrectly attributed in Mass. Hist. Soc. catalogue to "E. Hows"; see* MHS *Collections, ser. 4, v. 6, p. 480, and Proceedings, v. 52, p. 277 (cf. NUC).* ¶ The text is the same as in the 1611 ed. with Latin title, but the type has been reset, partially at least. ¶ *First pub. as:* Fata

Titre encadré par une bordure décorative. ¶ *Incorrectement attribué à « E. Hows » dans le catalogue de la Mass. Hist. Soc. ; voir* MHS *Collections. coll. 4, vol. 6, p. 480, et Proceedings. vl. 52, p. 277 (cf. NUC).* ¶ Le texte est identique à celui de l'édition de 1611 avec titre latin, mais il s'agit, du moins en partie, d'une recomposition typographique.

mihi totum . . . . *London, 1611,* q.v., *above, for notes.* ¶ *BVIP*

¶ *Publ. à l'orig. sous le titre* Fata mihi totum . . . . *Londres, 1611,* q.v. *plus haut, pour d'autres notes.* ¶ *BVIP*

1613

Purchas, Samuel, 1577?–1626. Purchas his pilgrimage. Or, Relations of the world and the religions observed in all ages and places discouered, from the creation vnto this present. In foure partes. This first containeth a theologicall and geographicall historie of Asia, Africa, and America, with the ilands adiacent. Declaring the ancient religions before the flovd, the heathnish, Jewish and Saracenicall in all ages since . . . . By Samuel Purchas, minister at Estwood in Essex. . . . London, printed by William Stansby for Henrie Fetherstone, and are to be sold at his shoppe in Pauls Churchyard at the signe of the Rose. 1613. 14 p.l., 752 [*i.e.* 754], [20] p. fol.

NUC(Pre–56)475:489*

Pagination irregular (cf. NUC for details). ¶ *Index: [20] p. at end.* ¶ "Of the North parts of the New World (Groenland, Estotiland, Meta Incognita, and other places) unto New Fraunce": p. 617–25. ¶ "Of Newfound-Land, Noua Francia, Arambec, and other countries of America, extending to Virginia": p. 625–30. ¶ *First edition; text republished in MF, in the STC series (no. 20505, carton 1184 — cf. NUC); subsequent editions appeared in 1614 (second ed.), 1617 (third), 1626 (fourth), and in* Purchas his pilgrimes *in 1625,* q.v.; *and a Dutch transl. in Amsterdam, 1655.* Purchas his pilgrim. Microcosmvs, or The historie of man, *London, 1619 and 1627, is a different work, theological in subject.*

Pagination irrégulière (cf. NUC pour plus de renseignements). ¶ *Index : [20] p. à la fin.* ¶ « Of the North parts of the New World (Groenland, Estotiland, Meta Incognita, and other places) unto New Fraunce » : p. 617–25. ¶ « Of Newfound-Land, Noua Francia, Arambec, and other countries of America, extending to Virginia » : p. 625–30. ¶ *Première édition ; reproduction sur mic. dans la collection du STC (n° 20505, carton 1184 –cf. NUC) ; des éditions ultérieures parurent en 1614 (deuxième éd.), en 1617 (troisième éd.), en 1626 (quatrième éd.), et dans* Purchas his pilgrimes *en 1625,* q.v. ; *et dans une trad. hollandaise parue à Amsterdam en 1655.* Purchas his pilgrim. Microcosmvs, or The historie of man. *Londres, 1619 et 1627, est une oeuvre différente dont l'orientation est théologique.*

1614

Purchas, Samuel, 1577?–1626. Pvrchas his pilgrimage. Or, Relations of the world and the religions observed in all ages and places discouered, from the creation vnto this present. In fovre parts. . . . The 2d ed., much enlarged with additions through the whole worke; by Samvel Pvrchas . . . . London, printed by William Stansby for Henrie Fetherstone, and are to be sold at his shop in Pauls church-yard at the Signe of the Rose. 1614. 14 p.l., 918 [*i.e.* 910], [36] p. fol.

NUC(Pre–56)475:489*

Nos. 330–31 duplicated and 852–61 omitted in paging. ¶ "The catalogue of the authors [mentioned]": p.l. 11–14. ¶ Index: [36] p. at end. ¶ "Of the discoueries of the North parts of the New World, and toward the Pole, and of Greenland, Groenland, Estotiland, Meta Incognita, and other places vnto New France": p. 735–46; "Of Newfound-land, Nova Francia, Arambec, and other Countries of America, extending to Virginia": p. 746–48. The account of Hudson (p. 743–45) is fuller than in the first edition. ¶ *First edition: 1613,* q.v. *for fuller title and other editions besides: 1617 (third) and 1626 (fourth); reprinted London, 1915, 20 vols. (Meclehose edition, cf. NUC).*

N° 330–31 en double et n° 852–61 omis dans la pagination. ¶ « Le catalogue des auteurs [mentionnés] » : f. l. 11–14. ¶ Index : [36] p. à la fin. ¶ « Of the discoueries of the North parts of the New World, and toward the pole, and of Greenland, Groenland, Estotiland, Meta Incognita, and other places vnto New France » : p. 735–46 ; « Of Newfound-land, Nova Francia, Arambec, and other Countries of America, extending to Virginia » : p. 746–48. Le récit d'Hudson (p. 743–45) est plus complet que dans la première édition. ¶ *Première édition : 1613,* q.v. *pour un titre plus complet et d'autres éditions : 1617 (troisième) et 1626 (quatrième) ; réimprimé à Londres, 1915, 20 vol. (édition Meclehose, cf. NUC).*

John Stow. *The annales, or Generall chronicle of England* .... London/Londres, 1615.

1615

*Stow, John, 1525?–1605. The annales, or Generall chronicle of England, begun first by maister Iohn Stow, and after him continued and augmented with matters forreyne, and domestique, auncient and moderne, vnto the ende of this present yeere 1614. by Edmond Howes, gentleman. Londini impensis Thomae Adams. 1615. 10 p.l., 988, [30] p. fol.

NUC(Pre–56)572:35*

Format from BM(to 1955)231:50, where the imprint is given as: Imprinted by Thomas Dawson for Thomas Adams: London, 1615. ¶ Numerous errors in paging (cf. NUC). ¶ Black-letter; initials. Title within ornamental border. ¶ In double columns. ¶ Colophon: Imprinted in London at the Three Cranes in the Vintree, by Thomas Dawson, for Thomas Adams. Anno 1615. [Evidently the colophon is the source of the BM imprint.] ¶ First published under this title: London, 1592, q.v. for other notes.

Format du BM(to 1955)231:50, où l'on donne l'adresse bibliographique suivante : Imprinted by Thomas Dawson for Thomas Adams : London, 1615. ¶ Nombreuses erreurs de pagination (cf. NUC). ¶ Lettres gothiques ; initiales. Titre encadré par une bordure décorative. ¶ Sur deux colonnes. ¶ Colophon : Imprinted in London at the Three Cranes in the Vintree, by Thomas Dawson, for Thomas Adams. Anno 1615. [De toute évidence, le colophon est la source de l'adresse bibliographique notée par le BM.] ¶ Publ. à l'orig. sous ce titre : Londres, 1592, q.v. pour d'autres notes.

1616

*[Botero, Giovanni], 1540–1617. Relations, of the most famous kingdoms ... their scituations, manners, customes, strengths, greatnesse, and policies .... London, printed for Iohn Iaggard ... betweene the two Temple-gates. 1616 [see 1608 ed.]. 2 p.l., 437, [3] p. 4°(?)

NUC(Pre–56)68:557*

First edition in English under this title: 1608, *q.v.*, above. ¶ *See* 1630.

Première édition en anglais sous ce titre : 1608, *q.v.* plus haut. ¶ *Voir* 1630.

1617

*[Abbot, George, *abp. of Canterbury/aev. de Canterbury*], 1562–1633. A briefe description of the whole VVorld. . . . Newly augmented and enlarged . . . . The 4th ed. London, printed for I. Browne, 1617. 1 p.l., [168] p. 4°

NUC(Pre–56)1:308*

Signatures: A–Y⁴ ¶ *See* 1599.

Signatures : A–Y⁴ ¶ *Voir* 1599.

Purchas, Samuel, 1577?–1626. Pvrchas his pilgrimage, or Relations of the vvorld and the religions observed in al ages and places discouered, from the creation vnto this present. Jn fovre parts. The first contayneth a . . . historie of . . . America, . . . religions . . . heathenish, Jewish, and Saracenicall in all ages since . . . . 3d ed., much enl. with additions through the whole worke; by Samvel Pvrchas . . . . London, printed by William Stansby for Henry Fetherstone . . . 1617. 19 p.l., 1102 [*i.e.* 1096], [40] p. fol.

NUC(Pre–56)475:489*

Paging irregular: 1052–57 omitted in numbering; Waldon appears to have 20 p.l. (t.-p., [38] . . . p.). ¶ "Of the Discoueries of the North parts the New-World": p. 915–29; "Of New-found-Land, Nova Francia, Arambec, and other Countries of America, extending to Virginia": p. 929–36. ¶ *First edition: 1613,* q.v. *for fuller title*

Pagination irrégulière : omission des numéros de page 1052–57 ; Waldon aurait 20 f. l. (p. de t., [38] . . . p.) ¶ « Of the Discoueries of the North parts the New-World » : p. 915–29 ; « Of New-found-Land, Nova Francia, Arambec, and other Countries of America, extending to Virginia » : p. 929–36. ¶ *Première édition : 1613,* q.v. *pour un titre plus complet et d'autres éditions outre celles de 1614*

and other editions besides: *1614 (second) and 1626 (fourth); text republished in MF, in the STC series (no. 20507, carton 1215 — cf. NUC).*

(deuxième) et de 1626 (quatrième) ; reproduction sur mic. dans la collection du STC (n° 20507, carton 1215 — cf. NUC).

1618

*[**Stafford, Robert**], 1588–1618. A geographicall and anthological description of all the empires and kingdomes . . . . London, printed by N[icholas]. O[kes]. for I[ohn]. Parker, 1618. 4 p.l., 27 [*i.e.* 67], [5] p. 4°(?)

NUC(Pre–56)563:583*

Dedication signed: Rob. Stafforde. ¶ For a fuller title, and other notes and editions, *see* first ed., London, 1607. Republished in MF: Ann Arbor, Mich., University Microfilms, 1974 (cf. NUC); another issue follows. ¶ BVAU

Dédicace signée : Rob. Stafforde. ¶ Pour un titre plus complet et d'autres notes et éditions, *voir* première éd., Londres, 1607. Reproduction sur mic., Ann Arbor (Mich.), University Microfilms, 1974 (cf. NUC) ; autre tirage ci-dessous. ¶ BVAU

*[**Stafford, Robert**], 1588–1618. A geographicall and anthological description of all the empires and kingdomes . . . . London, printed by Nicholas Okes for S[imon]. W[aterson]., 1618. 4 p.l., 27, [1] [*i.e.* 67, [1]] p., 2 l. 4°

NUC(Pre–56)563:583*

Dedication signed: Rob. Stafforde. ¶ Page 67 wrongly numbered 27. ¶ Consists of the same sheets as those of the preceding entry, except for the new t.-p. ¶ First ed.: 1607 (*q.v.* for

Dédicace signée : Rob. Stafforde. ¶ Page 67 incorrectement numérotée 27. ¶ Constituée des mêmes feuillets que ceux de la notice précédente, exception faite de la nouvelle p. de t. ¶ Première éd. : 1607, (*q.v.* pour un

fuller title, and other notes and editions); republished in MF: Ann Arbor, Mich., University Microfilms, 1974 (cf. NUC). ¶ BVAU

titre plus complet et d'autres notes et éditions) ; reproduction sur mic. : Ann Arbor (Mich.), University Microfilms, 1974 (cf. NUC). ¶ BVAU

*Stow, John, 1525?–1605. The abridgement of the English chronicle . . . continued . . . vnto the beginning of the yeare, 1618. . . . Imprinted <by E[dward]. Allde?> for the Company of Stationers, 1618. 6 p.l., 568, [41] p. 8°

NUC(Pre–56)572:34*

Black-letter; title within ornamental border; initials. ¶ Format: from BM(to 1955)231:52. ¶ Errors in paging. ¶ "To the honest and friendly reader" signed: Edmond Howes. ¶ "Of the vniversities in England": p. [1–14] at end. ¶ First pub. under this title: London, 1607, *q.v.* (Stow) and 1611, *q.v.* for a fuller title. (STC:23332)

Lettres gothiques ; titre encadré par une bordure décorative ; initiales. ¶ Format du BM(to 1955)231:52. ¶ Erreurs de pagination. ¶ « Au lecteur honnête et amical » signé : Edmond Howes. ¶ « Des universités d'Angleterre » : p. [1–14] à la fin. ¶ Publ. à l'orig. sous ce titre : Londres, 1607, *q.v.* (Stow) et 1611, *q.v.* pour un titre plus complet. (STC:23332)

1620

*[Abbot, George, *abp. of Canterbury/aev. de Canterbury*], 1562–1633. A briefe description of the whole VVorld. . . . Newly augmented and enlarged . . . . The fift [*sic*] edition. London: printed for Iohn Marriot, 1620. 88 l. 4°

NUC(Pre–56)1:308

First leaf blank except for signature mark. ¶ *See* 1599.

Premier feuillet vierge, à l'exception de la signature. ¶ *Voir* 1599.

[Mason, John], 1586–1635. A briefe discourse of the Nevv-found-land, with the situation, temperature, and commodities thereof, inciting our nation to goe forward in that hopefull plantation begunne . . . . Edinburgh, printed by Andro Hart. 1620. 1 p.l., [12] p. 4°

NUC(Pre–56)367:140*

"To the reader" signed: Iohn Mason. ¶ The modern facsimiles in NUC have collation: [14] p. ¶ Reprinted Edinburgh, 1869 (Bannatyne Club pubs., no. 114), in Boston in 1887 (edited by J.W. Dean; both of these, says Waldon, "have the map of Newfoundland made from Mason's surveys, pub. in [William] Vaughan's Golden Fleece, [London] 1626 [cf. DNB, Wm. Vaughan, 1577–1641]," and Boston, 1938, as well as in MF (STC series, no. 17616, carton 996 — cf. NUC).

« Au lecteur » signé : Iohn Mason. ¶ Collation du NUC à partir des fac-similés modernes : [14] p. ¶ Réimpression à Édimbourg, 1869 (Éd. Bannatyne Club, n° 114), à Boston, 1887 (dir. par J.W. Dean). Selon Waldon, ces deux éditions « comprennent la carte géographique de Terre-Neuve tracée à partir des relevés de Mason publiés dans Golden Fleece de [William] Vaughan, [Londres] 1626 [cf. DNB, Wm Vaughan, 1577–1641] », et Boston, 1938, ainsi que sur mic. (collection du STC, n° 17616, carton 996 – cf. NUC).

*Whitbourne, Sir Richard, fl. 1579–1626. A discourse and discovery of Nevv-found-land, with many reasons to prooue how worthy and beneficiall a plantation may there be made, after a far better manner than now it is. Together with the laying open of certaine enormities and abvses committed by some that trade to that countrey, and the meanes laide downe for reformation thereof. Written by Captaine Richard Whibourne of Exmouth, in the county of Deuon, and published by authority. Imprinted at London by Felix Kyngston, for William Barret, 1620. 9 p.l., 69, [4] p. 4°(?)

NUC(Pre–56)659:501*

First edition; German transls. pub. Frankfurt am Main, 1629 (two, cf. NUC); reprinted in Samuel Purchas, Pilgrimes. London, 1625 (q.v.), vol. 4, bk. 10, p. 1882–88; an abstract was pub. under the title Westward hoe for Avalon. London, 1870 (cf. NUC), and it appeared in MF in the STC series (no.

Première édition ; trad. allemandes publ. à Francfort-sur-le-Main, 1629 (deux, cf. NUC) ; réimpression dans l'ouvrage de Samuel Purchas, Pilgrimes. Londres, 1625 (q.v.), vol. 4, livre 10, p. 1882–1888 ; un résumé fut publié sous le titre Westward hoe for Avalon. Londres, 1870 (cf. NUC), et, reproduit sur mic. dans la collection du STC

25372, carton 945 — cf. NUC). Other editions were pub. in 1622 and 1623, *q.v.*, below.

(n° 25372, carton 945 – cf. NUC). D'autres éditions furent publ. en 1622 et en 1623, *q.v.* plus loin.

1621

[Heylyn, Peter], 1599–1662. Microcosmus, or A little description of the great world. A treatise historicall, geographicall, politicall, theologicall. By P.H. [Two-line motto from Martial, then Oxford university arms]. At Oxford, printed by Iohn Lichfield, and Iames Short printers to the famous Universitie. 1621. 8 p.l., 317 [*i.e.* 417], [3] p. 4°

NUC(Pre–56)244:507*

Norumbega [Nova Scotia], Nova Francia, Terra Corterialis [probably eastern Newfoundland], Estotiland [Newfoundland and Labrador]: p. 408–09; Bacaleos [also Newfoundland]: p. 416. These passages are condensed from Purchas and are chiefly interesting as showing how little was known at this date. The same passages will be found [in] p. 786–88 and p. 805 in the eighth edition, 1639. ¶ *First edition, this also appeared in MF (STC series, no. 13276, carton 962 — cf. NUC); other editions (with their titles in Greek letters): 1625, 1627 (third ed. rev.), 1629 (fourth ed.), 1631 (fifth ed.), 1633 (sixth ed.), 1636 (seventh ed.), and 1639 (eighth ed.), q.v., below.*

Norumbega [Nouvelle-Écosse], Nouvelle France, Terra Corterialis [probablement l'est de Terre-Neuve], Estotiland [Terre-Neuve et le Labrador] : p. 408–09; Bacaleos [aussi Terre-Neuve] : p. 416. Ces extraits condensés, tirés de Purchas, donnent une bonne indication du peu de connaissance sur le sujet à cette époque. L'on retrouve ces mêmes passages [aux] p. 786–88 et 805 de la huitième édition, 1639. ¶ *Première édition ; reproduction sur mic. (collection du STC, n° 13276, carton 962 – cf. NUC) ; autres éditions (avec titre en caractères grecs) : 1625, 1627 (troisième éd. rév.), 1629 (quatrième éd.), 1631 (cinquième éd.), 1633 (sixième éd.), 1636 (septième éd.), et 1639 (huitième éd.), q.v. plus loin.*

Winne, Edward. A letetr [*sic*] written by Captaine Edvvard Winne, to the Right Honourable, Sir George Caluert, knight, his Maiesties principall Secretary: from Feryland in Newfoundland, the 26. of August. 1621. [London?] Imprinted 1621. 1 p.l., 21 p. 8°

BM(to 1955)259:411*

BM, Waldon's only given source, has an abridged title. ¶ Includes: "Another letter of the 28. of August, from the said Captaine Winne, vnto Master Secretary Caluert.... Signed Edward Winne. From Ferryland, the 28. of August 1621": p. 19–21. ¶ Winne left "Plimmoth" on June 26 and arrived Aug. 4 at Feryland, the "beautifullest Coast and the pleasantest Sea cant that ever mine eyes beheld" (p. 31). He found (p. 3–4) "A very Champion Country. without any Hill, and appearing either within Land, or vpon the Coast.... Of the fertility of the Soyle I can say nothing onely that it is very probable that much or most part thereof may proue very good with the help of mans industry." He saw (p. 6–7) "Wheate, Barly and Rye, growing full eared & kerned, the which had been accidentally shed out of Salt Mats among Stone & Grasse." He is optimistic also in regard to salt making and the growing of hemp and flax for cordage and thread, and hops. Tar, iron, and timber will be needed for building and he begs redress for certain abuses, some of the settlers not being considerate of the rights of others and the good of the country. (For action in regard to lawlessness in Newfoundland *see* 1633: Great Britain. *A commission . . .* [*i.e.*, Great Britain. Laws,

Le BM, la seule source qu'ait donnée Waldon, fait état d'un titre abrégé. ¶ Inclut : « Another letter of the 28. of August, from the said Captaine Winne, vnto Master Secretary Caluert. . . . Signed Edward Winne. From Ferryland, the 28. of August 1621 » : p. 19–21. ¶ Winne, ayant quitté « Plimmoth » le 26 juin, arriva le 4 août à Feryland, « la plus belle côte et la mer la plus agréable que j'aie jamais vues » (p. 31). Il trouva (p. 3–4) « un pays formidable, sans aucune colline, autant à l'intérieur des terres que sur la côte . . . . Pour ce qui est de la fertilité de la terre, je puis seulement dire que la plus grande partie de celle-ci se révélera, avec le travail de l'homme, probablement très bonne. » Il vit (p. 6–7) « poussant dans l'herbe et parmi les pierres, du blé, de l'orge et du seigle, portant épis et grains parfaits, venant de semences accidentellement tombées des paillassons à sel ». Il envisage aussi avec optimisme la production du sel et la culture du chanvre et du lin pour fabriquer de la corde et du fil ainsi que celle du houblon. Du goudron, du fer et du bois seront nécessaires pour la construction, et il plaide le redressement de certains torts causés par les colons ne respectant ni les droits d'autrui, ni le bien du pays. (Pour ce qui est des mesures prises pour contrer la délinquance à Terre-Neuve, *voir* 1633 : Great-Britain. *A commission . . .* [c.-à-d. Great-Britain. Laws, Statutes, etc., 1625–1649 (Charles I) *A commission . . .* London, 1634]). Winne donne aussi les

statutes, etc., 1625–1649 (Charles I) *A commission* ... London, 1634]). Winne also gives particulars of building undertaken, and asks for guns. ¶ Other letters from Winne appeared in Sir Richard Whitbourne, *A discourse and discovery*. London, 1622 and 1623 [and, in BM, Whitbourne's *A discourse containing a loving invitation*, 1622]. ¶ *Reprinted in the STC microfilm series, no. 25854, and extracts of similar letters in: Samuel Purchas, Pilgrimes. London, 1625, q.v., below.* ¶ OKQ(MF) · OOU(MF) · OLU(MF) · BVAU(MF)

particularités des constructions entreprises et demande qu'on lui fournisse des armes à feu. ¶ D'autres lettres de Winne ont paru dans l'ouvrage de sir Richard Whitbourne, *A discourse and discovery*. Londres, 1622 et 1623 [et, au BM, *A discourse containing a loving invitation*, 1622]. ¶ *Reproduction sur mic. dans la collection du STC, n° 25854, et extraits de lettres similaires dans l'ouvrage de Samuel Purchas, Pilgrimes. Londres, 1625, q.v. plus loin.* ¶ *OKQ (mic.) · OOU (mic.) · OLU (mic.) · BVAU (mic.)*

1622

[Waterhouse, Edward], *fl.* 1622. A declaration of the state of the colony and affaires in Virginia. ... And a treatise annexed, written by that learned mathematicien Mr. Henry Briggs, of the Northwest passage to the South Sea through the continent of Virginia, and by Fretum Hudson. ... Published by authoritie. Imprinted at London by G[eorge]. Eld, for Robert Mylbourne, and are to be sold at his shop, at the great South doore of Pauls. 1622. 3 p.l., 54 p. fold. front. 4°

NUC(Pre–56)650:443*

Dedication signed: Edvvard Waterhovse. ¶ *"A tract on the Northwest Passage" by Briggs has, says DNB, "only his initials prefixed."* ¶ *Text republished in MF, in the STC series (no. 25104, carton 944), and in MF (negative): Louisville, Ky., Lost Cause Press, 1975 (Selected Americana from Sabin's Dictionary), and also in micro-opaque, in* Travels in the Old South *series, 1:171 — cf. NUC;*

Dédicace signée : Edvvard Waterhovse. ¶ *Selon le DNB, « A tract on the Northwest Passage » de Briggs « ne porte que ses initiales au début ».* ¶ *Reproduction sur mic. dans la collection du STC (n° 25104, carton 944), sur mic. (négatif) : Louisville (Ky.), Lost Cause Press, 1975, (Selected Americana from Sabin's Dictionary), et aussi sur microfiche dans la collection* Travels in the Old South, *1:171 – cf. NUC ; réimpression : New York, DaCapo Press, 1970, 54 p.*

it was reprinted: New York, DaCapo Press, 1970, 54 p. ¶ NBFU(1970) · OOCC(1970) · SRU(1970)

¶ *NBFU(1970) · OOCC(1970) · SRU(1970)*

*Whitbourne, Sir **Richard**, *fl.* 1579–1626. A discourse and discovery of Nevv-found-land .... Written by Captaine Richard Whitbourne ... and published by authority. As also, an inuitation: and likewise certaine letters sent from that countrey; which are printed in the latter part of this booke. Imprinted at London by Felix Kingston, 1622. 11 p.l., 107, [5], 15 p. 4°(?)

NUC(Pre–56)659:501*

Page 35 is incorrectly numbered 3; p. 70 and 71 are correctly numbered in NUC copy. ¶ Second edition; first ed.: London, 1620, *q.v.* for fuller first half of title, and other eds. Text reproduced in MF from a transcript, in *Canadiana in the Toronto Public Library* series, Toronto, ca. 1960.

La page 35 est incorrectement numérotée p. 3 ; les p. 70 et 71 sont correctement numérotées dans l'exemplaire du NUC. ¶ Deuxième édition ; première éd. : Londres, 1620, *q.v.* pour une transcription plus complète de la première moitié du titre et d'autres éditions. Reproduction sur mic. à partir d'une transcription, dans *Canadiana dans la collection de la Toronto Public Library*, v. 1960.

*Whitbourne, Sir **Richard**, *fl.* 1579–1626. A discourse containing a loving invitation both honourable, and profitable to all such as shall be aduenturers, either in person, or purse, for the advancement of His Maiesties most hopefull plantation in the Nevv-fovnd-land, lately vndertaken. Written by Captaine Richard Whitbovrne of Exmouth, in the county of Deuon. Imprinted at London by Felix Kyngston, dwelling in Pater-noster-row, 1622. 4 p.l., 46 p. 4°(?)

NUC(Pre–56)659:502*

For notes on some variants, and contents, cf. NUC. ¶ Text republished in MF, in the STC series (no. 25375, carton 945 — cf. NUC).

Pour des notes sur quelques variantes et sur les titres, cf. NUC. ¶ Reproduction sur mic. dans la collection du STC (n° 25375, carton 945 – cf. NUC).

[Scott, Thomas], 1580?–1626. An experimentall discoverie of Spanish practises. Or the counsell of a well-wishing souldier, for the good of his prince and state. Wherein is manifested from known experience, both the cruelty, and policy of the Spaniard, to effect his own ends. Chiefly swelling with multiplicity of glorious titles, as one of the greatest monarchs of the earth, that being admired of all, his greatnesse might amaze all, and so by degrees seeking covertly to tyrannize over all. When as indeed and truth, the greatest part of his pretended greatnesse, is but a windy crack of an ambitious minde. [London?] printed, anno 1623. 1 p.l., 54 p. 4°

NUC(Pre–56)534:257*

This is often catalogued as being in two parts [as in NUC], but *A second part of Spanish practises. Or, a relation of more particular wicked plots . . . of the Spaniards. . .*, 1624, is now catalogued by BM as a separate publication. ¶ The author claims America for England by the discovery of the Cabots, and warns [Prince] Charles to deal firmly with Spain. War, he thinks, may be necessary to make a good peace (p. 35–47). ¶ *Prince Charles was pursuing the hand of the infanta of Spain, and this was opposed by Scott in many works, though he had been chaplain to James I. Scott sought refuge in Holland late in 1623, becoming preacher to the English garrison at Utrecht, where the second edition of the present work was printed (cf. DNB, "Scott"). ¶ First edition; reprinted 1624, and under a new title,* The Spaniards cruelty, *1656*, q.v.

Dans les catalogues, on donne souvent cette édition en deux parties [p. ex. comme dans le NUC], mais *A second part of Spanish practises. Or, a relation of more particular wicked plots . . . of the Spaniards. . .*, 1624, est maintenant cataloguée par le BM comme une publication distincte. ¶ En raison de la découverte par les Cabot, l'auteur revendique l'Amérique en tant que possession anglaise et conseille au [prince] Charles de traiter fermement avec l'Espagne. La guerre s'avérera peut-être nécessaire à l'établissement d'une paix avantageuse (p. 35–47). ¶ *Le prince Charles projetait d'épouser l'Infante d'Espagne. Scott s'y opposa dans de nombreux ouvrages, bien qu'il ait été l'aumônier de Jacques I*. À la fin de 1623, Scott chercha refuge en Hollande et devint prédicateur auprès de la garnison anglaise d'Utrecht où fut publiée la deuxième édition de cet ouvrage (cf. DNB, « Scott »). ¶ Première édition ; réimpression en 1624, et sous un autre titre,* The Spaniards cruelty, *1656*, q.v.

A Short discourse of the new-found-land: contaynig [*sic*] diverse reasons and inducements, for the planting of that countrey. Published for the satisfaction of all such as shall be willing to be adventurers in the said plantation. Dublin, printed by the Societie of Stationers. 1623. [30] p. 4°

NUC(Pre–56)544:417*

Waldon has [27] p. ¶ Contents: ... "To the Right Honourable Henry Lo: Cary, Viscount of Falkland"; "A discourse of the Nevv-Found-Land" [ended by "Finis"]; "Conditions propounded by the right honorable the Lord Viscount Falkland, Lo: Deputie general of the Kingdome of Ireland; to all such as wil joine with him for the plantation of a Colonie in the South-East parts of Newfoundland"; "Post-script," verso blank. ¶ The author quotes Captain Winne's letters of 17 Aug. 1622. It is possible that he took his information chiefly from [Sir Richard] Whitbourne [*Discourse and discovery of New-foundland*. London, 1620, *q.v.*, above]; he speaks in the Dedication of "This short Discourse, or rather, an abstract of a Discourse." ¶ The conditions provided that £100 would purchase a share in the fisheries and other enterprises, half a harbour, and 2,000 acres of land, for a yearly rent of one penny per 100 acres, hold in fee a place to build "a stage and necessarie roomes to salt fish on." In return the grantee must, within three years after date of grant, maintain eight persons upon the land and pay yearly rent of 10 shillings. For £200 one obtained a whole harbour, 4,000 acres, and other rights to correspond. Other amounts

Collation de Waldon : [27] p. ¶ Qui portent sur le Canada : ... « To the Right Honourable Henry Lo: Cary, Viscount of Falkland » ; « A discourse of the Nevv-Found-Land » [se termine par « Finis »] ; « Conditions propounded by the right honorable the Lord Viscount Falkland, Lo: Deputie general of the Kingdome of Ireland; to all such as wil joine with him for the plantation of a Colonie in the South-East parts of Newfoundland » ; « Postscript », verso en blanc. ¶ L'auteur cite les lettres du Capitaine Winne, datées du 17 août 1622. Il se peut que sa principale source d'information ait été [sir Richard] Whitbourne, [*Discourse and discovery of New-found-land*. Londres, 1620, *q.v.* plus haut]. Dans la dédicace, il parle de « Ce court écrit, ou plutôt cet écrit sommaire ». ¶ Les conditions stipulaient que 100 £ donnaient droit à une part dans les pêcheries et d'autres entreprises, à la moitié d'un havre, et à l'utilisation de 2 000 acres de terre dont le loyer annuel serait d'un penny les 100 acres. De plus cette somme garantissait un endroit pour la construction d'une « plate-forme et des pièces nécessaires au salage du poisson ». En échange du droit d'exploitation, le concessionnaire devait, dans un délai de trois ans, entretenir huit personnes sur cette terre et payer une rente annuelle de 10 shillings. Pour 200 £, l'on obtenait un havre entier, 4 000 acres et d'autres droits correspondants. D'autres

brought varying benefits in proportion. Labourers were to receive good wages and grants of land after five years' service. It is interesting to note that this was an Irish scheme. ¶ *Text pub. on microfilm: Ann Arbor, Mich., University Microfilms, 1973 (Early English books, 1475–1640, reel 1301 — cf. NUC).* ¶ *BVAU(MF)*

mises de fonds donnaient droit à des bénéfices proportionnels. Les travailleurs devaient recevoir de bons salaires et des terres leur seraient octroyées après cinq ans de service. Il y a lieu de noter qu'il s'agissait d'un projet irlandais. ¶ *Reproduction sur mic., Ann Arbor (Mich.), University Microfilms, 1973 (Early English books, 1475–1640, bande 1301 –cf. NUC).* ¶ *BVAU (mic.)*

---

*Whitbourne, Sir **Richard,** *fl.* 1579–1626. A discourse and discovery of Nevv-Found-Land .... Written by Captaine Richard Whitbourne .... As also a louing inuitation: and likewise the copies of certaine letters .... London, imprinted by Felix Kingston, 1623. 9 p.l., 97, [1] p., 8 l. 4°

NUC(Pre–56)659:502*

Pages 34–35 wrongly numbered 35–36. ¶ "The second motive and indvcement added to my former Discourse, as a louing inuitation": p. [63]–97 (with caption title: A loving invitation) contains part of the text of his *A discovrse containing a loving invitation.* London, 1622 (*q.v.*), with variations in wording, and slight variations also from the text as included in the 1622 edition of *A discovrse and discovery* (*q.v.*, above). ¶ "A conclusion to the former Discourse, with a Relation of something omitted .... As also of a strange creature seene": p. [98–101]; "The coppy of a letter from Captaine Edward Wynne, Gouernour of the Colony at Ferriland ... in New-found-land" and other letters, 1622: p. [103–114] (cf. NUC, where other

Les pages 34–35 sont incorrectement numérotées 35–36. ¶ « The second motive and indvcement added to my former Discourse, as a louing inuitation » : p. [63]–97 (avec titre de départ : A loving invitation) contient une partie du texte de son *A discovrse containing a loving invitation.* Londres, 1622, (*q.v.*), avec des variantes dans la formulation et quelques variantes par rapport au texte de l'édition de 1622 de *A discovrse and discovery* (*q.v.* plus haut). ¶ « A conclusion to the former Discourse, with a Relation of something omitted .... As also of a strange creature seene » : p. [98–101] ; « The coppy of a letter from Captaine Edward Wynne, Gouernour of the Colony at Ferriland ... in New-found-land » et autres lettres, 1622 : p. [103–114] (cf. NUC, où l'on trouve d'autres titres). ¶ Semble être la troisième éd. ; première éd., 1620, et deuxième éd., 1622, *q.v.* pour un titre plus complet et

items of contents are also given). ¶ Appears to be the third ed.; first ed., 1620, and second ed., 1622, *q.v.* for fuller title and other notes; reprinted in MF in STC series (no. 25374, carton 1088 — cf. NUC).

d'autres notes ; reproduction sur mic. dans la collection du STC (n° 25374, carton 1088 –cf. NUC).

1624

*[Abbot, George, *abp. of Canterbury/aev. de Canterbury*], 1562–1633. A briefe description of the whole world. . . . Newly augmented and enlarged . . . . The sixt [*sic*] edition. London, printed [by A. Mathewes] for I. Marriot, 1624. 1 p.l., [172] p. 4°(?)

NUC(Pre–56)1:308*

See 1599.

Voir 1599.

Eburne, Richard. A plaine path-way to plantations: that is, A discourse in generall, concerning the plantation of our English people in other countries. Wherein is declared, that the attempts or actions, in themselues are very good and laudable, necessary also for our country of England. Doubts thereabout are answered: and some meanes are shewed, by which the same may, in better sort then hitherto, be prosecuted and effected. Written for the perswading and stirring vp of the people of this land, chiefly the poorer and common sort to affect and effect these attempts better then yet they doe. With certaine motiues for a present plantation in New-foundland aboue the rest. Made in the manner of a conference, and diuided into three parts, for the more plainnesse, ease and delight to the reader. By Richard Eburne of Hengstridge in the countie of Somerset. [London] Printed by G.P[urslow]. for Iohn Marriot, 1624. 1 p.l., [15], 120 p. 4°

NUC(Pre–56)154:620*

NUC *has collation 127 l., but notes: Typewritten copy.* ¶ Dedication (A2-A4) to Bishop of Bath and Wells, and Bishop of Bristol, signed: Richard Eburne. ¶ *A modern microreproduction by University Microfilms, Ann Arbor, Mich. (no. 20632) is described in* NUC *with the slight t.-p. variation:* A plaine path-way to plantations . . . in other countrie[s].

Scott, Thomas, 1580?–1626. The workes of the most famous and reverend divine Mr. Thomas Scot. Batcheler in diuinitie: sometimes preacher in Norwich. Printed at Vtrick. 1624. 24 pts. in 1 v. front. (port.), illus., plates. 4°

NUC(Pre–56)534:261*

NUC *lists the contents, including* An experimentall discoverie of Spanish practises, *and* A second part of Spanish practises, *both of which it says are not by Scott (the former "not Scott's? possibly by Henry Hexham"); Waldon notes the former as the "1623 edition reset."* ¶ *Second appearance in print; see 1623 for first ed. and other notes; also pub. posthumously under title:* The Spaniards cruelty, *1656,* q.v.

Stirling, William Alexander, *1st earl of/1ᵉʳ comte de,* 1567?–1640. An encouragement to colonies. By Sir William Alexander, knight. . . . London, printed by William Stansby. 1624. 4 p.l., 47 p. fold. map. 4°

NUC(Pre–56)570:94*

74

Waldon has collation as: t.-p., [3], 47 p. ¶ The unsold sheets of this were reissued, without dedication, as The mapp and description of New-England. *London, 1630* (q.v.) — cf. Church:400. ¶ This is the record of the Earl of Stirling's unsuccessful attempt to found a Scottish colony along feudal lines in Nova Scotia, to which he gave its name. The work also gives some account of the French settlement in New France (cf. NUC and Church, as cited above). ¶ First edition; reissued *London, 1625* (q.v.), in *1630* under the new title (q.v., as above), and in Edinburgh, Bannatyne Club, 1867, and Boston, Prince Society, 1873.

Collation de Waldon : p. de t., [3], 47 p. ¶ Les feuilles invendues furent remises en circulation, sans dédicace, sous le titre The mapp and description of New-England. *Londres, 1630* (q.v.) – cf. Church:400. ¶ Récit de l'échec du projet du comte de Stirling en vue d'établir une colonie écossaise de régime féodal sur ce territoire qu'il baptisa la Nouvelle-Écosse. L'ouvrage donne aussi un compte rendu de la colonisation française en Nouvelle France (cf. NUC et Church, cités ci-dessus). ¶ Première édition ; réimpression : *Londres, 1625* (q.v.), en *1630* (q.v.) sous le nouveau titre susmentionné, et à Édimbourg, Bannatyne Club, 1867, et à Boston, Prince Society, 1873.

1625

[Camden, William], 1551–1623. Annales. The true and royall history of the famous empresse Elizabeth, Queene of England, France and Ireland, &c., true faith's defendresse of diuine renowne and happy memory. Wherein all such memorable things as happened during hir blessed raigne, with such acts and treaties as past betwixt Hir Matie and Scotland, France, Spaine, Italy, Germany, Poland, Sweden, Denmark, Russia, and the Netherlands, are exactly described. London, printed for B[enjamin]. Fisher . . ., 1625. 2 v. 47 p.l., 435 p.; 292 p. port. 4°

NUC(Pre–56)91:505*

The translation of "The French epistle dedicatory" is signed: P.D.B.; "The epistle dedicatory" is signed: Abraham Darcie (to whom the King's authority was granted). ¶ Volume 2 has imprint: London, printed by Tho. Harper and are to be sold by W[illiam?]. Web . . ., 1629. These volumes form Parts 1–4

La traduction de « L'épître dédicatoire française » est signée : P.D.B.; « L'épître dédicatoire » est signée : Abraham Darcie (investi de l'autorité du Roi). ¶ Le volume 2 porte l'adresse bibliographique : London, printed by Tho. Harper and are to be sold by W[illiam ?]. Web . . ., 1629. Ces volumes forment les parties 1–4 [NUC : livres 1–3,

[NUC has: books 1–3, 1558–88, about two-thirds of the whole] of Camden's *Annales rerum Anglicarum [et Hibernicarum regnante Elizabetha*, transl. by Abraham Darcie from the French version by Paul de Bellegent, of the original Latin]. ¶ Contains many references to the first settlements in America. Frobisher's voyage in 1576: vol. 1, p. 363–65. ¶ First edition in English.

1558–1588, soit les deux tiers de l'ensemble] de l'ouvrage de Camden, *Annales rerum Anglicarum [et Hibernacarum regnante Elizabetha*, trad. en anglais par Abraham Darcie, d'après la version française, elle-même traduite du latin (langue originale) par Paul de Bellegent]. ¶ Contient de nombreuses mentions relatives aux premières colonies d'Amérique. Le voyage de Frobisher en 1576 : vol. 1, p. 363–65. ¶ Première édition en anglais.

Gordon, Sir **Robert**, *of/de Lochinvar, d./déc.* 1627? Encouragements. For such as shall have intention to bee vnder-takers in the new plantation of Cape Briton, now New Galloway in America, by mee, Lochinvar . . . . Edinburgh, printed by Iohn Wreittoun. Anno. Dom. 1625. 2 p.l., [30] p. 4°

NUC(Pre–56)207:139*

The dedication (leaf following the title leaf) is to Sir William Alexander and the "remnant the noble-men, and knights baronets in Scotland, under-takers in the plantations of New Scotland, in America," and to those who favour inhabiting Cape Briton [i.e. Breton], now New Galloway. ¶ Waldon notes that Sabin:41715 has Edinburgh 1620 and 1624 eds., but that she has found no confirmation of this; the work was reprinted in Edinburgh, 1867 (Bannatyne Club, pub. no. 114), and in Boston, 1938 (Photostat Americana, Mass. Hist. Soc., 2d series, no. 59).

La dédicace (suivant le feuillet de titre) est adressée à sir William Alexander et « aux autres hommes de noblesse et baronnets d'Écosse, aux exploitants de plantations de Nouvelle-Écosse, Amérique, » ainsi qu'à ceux préférant habiter « Cape Briton » [c.-à-d. Breton] maintenant appelé New Galloway. ¶ Waldon note que le Sabin:41715 donne les éd. d'Édimbourg de 1620 et de 1624, mais que ses recherches n'ont pu le confirmer ; cet ouvrage fut réimprimé à Édimbourg, 1867 (Bannatyne Club, publ. n° 114) et à Boston, 1938 (Photostat Americana, Mass. Hist. Soc., deuxième collection, n° 59).

*Heylyn, Peter, 1599–1662. [Mikrokosmos: *title transliterated from Greek/le titre transcrit du grec.*] A little description of the great world. Augmented and revised . . . . Oxford, printed by Iohn Lichfield and William Turner, and are to be sold by W[illiam]. Turner and T[homas]. Huggins, An. Dom. 1625. 8 p.l., 812 [*i.e.* 802], [2] p. fold. table. 4°(?)

NUC(Pre–56)244:507*

Numbers 381 and 390 omitted in paging. ¶ First edition pub. under title *Microcosmus*, 1621, *q.v.*; this appears to be the second edition. ¶ BVIPA

Omission des numéros de page 381 et 390. ¶ Première édition publiée sous le titre *Microcosmus*, 1621, *q.v.* ; il semble s'agir de la deuxième édition. ¶ BVIPA

*[Lescarbot, Marc], *ca.* 1570–1642. Nova Francia or the description of that part of Nevv France, which is one continent with Virginia. Described in the . . . voyages . . . by . . . Monsieur de Poutriucourt [*sic*] into the countries called by the French-men La Cadie . . . . Together with seuerall treatie [*sic*] . . . . London, printed for Andrew Hebb [1625?] 10 p.l., 307 p. 4°

NUC(Pre–56)328:113*

Consists of the same sheets, except the t.-p., as the edition with imprint: London [*i.e.* Londini], Impensis [*i.e* Imponsis] Georgii Bishop, 1609 (NUC). ¶ Waldon notes a reprint of this in: *Purchas his pilgrimes*, 1625, v. 4, p. 1620–41 (abridged). ¶ For other notes and editions, *see* the 1609 editions.

À l'exception de la p. de t., les feuillets sont identiques à ceux de l'édition portant l'adresse bibliographique : London [*c.-à-d.* Londini], Impensis [*c.-à-d.* Imponsis] Georgii Bishop, 1609 (NUC). ¶ Waldon en note une réimpression dans : *Purchas his pilgrimes*, 1625, vol. 4, p. 1620–41 (abrégé). ¶ Pour d'autres notes et éditions, *voir* les éditions de 1609.

Purchas, Samuel, 1577?–1626. Purchas his pilgrimes. Jn five bookes. The first, contayning the voyages and peregrinations made by ancient kings . . . . The second, a description of all the circum-nauigations of the globe. The third, nauigations and voyages of English-men, alongst [*sic*] the coasts of Africe . . . . The fourth, English voyages beyond the East Indies . . . . The fifth, nauigations, voyages, traffiques, discoueries, of the English nation in the easterne parts of the world . . . . London, printed by William Stansby for Henrie Fetherstone, and are to be sold at his shop in Pauls Church-yard at the signe of the Rose. 1625. 4 v. illus. (incl. maps), fold. maps. fol.

Church:401; NUC(Pre–56)475:489* (short title)

Each vol. has separate t.-p.; vol. 1 has added t.-p. engraved (and this Waldon uses for her entry): Hakluytus posthumus or Purchas his pilgrimes. Contayning a history of the world . . . . ¶ *Vols. 1–2 and 3–4 paged continuously, except Book I, vol. 1, which is paged separately. Many errors in paging.* ¶ *NUC notes that* Purchas his pilgrimage. Or relations of the world . . . , *fourth ed., London 1626* (q.v., *below) is bound uniformly with this set and lettered:* Purchas's pilgrims. Vol. v. *Waldon regards it as a separate work.* ¶ *Contains much material on America, the titles of which and contents relating to Canada are as follows:* ¶ "A briefe Discouerie of the Northerne Discoueries . . ." (including voyages of Frobisher, Humfrey Gilbert, Davis, from Hakluyt): p. 462–73. ¶ "Divers voyages and Northerne Discoueries of . . . Master Henry Hvdson . . . . Written partly by Iohn Playse one of the Company, and partly by H. Hvdson" (from Hakluyt): p. 567–74. ¶ "The Third Voyage of master Henrie Hvdson toward Nova Zembla, and at his returne to New-found Land . . . . Written by Robert

Chaque volume a une p. de t. distincte ; la p. de t. supplémentaire du vol. 1 est une estampe (que Waldon utilise pour sa notice) : Hakluytus posthumus or Purchas his pilgrimes. Contayning a history of the world . . . . ¶ *Les vol. 1–2 et 3–4 sont paginés de façon continue sauf le livre I, vol. 1, qui est paginé séparément. Nombreuses erreurs de pagination.* ¶ *Le NUC note que* Purchas his pilgrimage. Or relations of the world . . . , *quatrième éd., Londres 1626* (q.v. *plus loin) est relié uniformément à cet ensemble et ainsi rédigé :* Purchas's pilgrims. Vol. v. *Waldon le considère comme un ouvrage distinct.* ¶ *Il contient de nombreuses informations sur l'Amérique et, notamment, sur le Canada :* ¶ « A briefe Discouerie of the Northerne Discoueries . . . » (incluant les voyages de Frobisher, Humfrey Gilbert et Davis tirés de Hakluyt) : p. 462–73. ¶ « Divers voyages and Northerne Discoueries of . . . Master Henry Hvdson . . . . Written partly by Iohn Playse, one of the company, and partly by H. Hvdson » (tiré de Hakluyt) : p. 567–74. ¶ « The Third Voyage of master Henrie Hvdson toward Nova Zembla, and at his returne to New-found Land . . . . Written by Robert Ivet de Lime-house » (tiré de Hakluyt) : p. 581–95. ¶ « An Abstract of the Iournall of Master Henry Hvdson, for the discouerie of the

Ivet of Lime-house" (from Hakluyt): p. 581–95. ¶ "An Abstract of the Iournall of Master Henry Hvdson, for the discouerie of the North-west Passage . . . 1610 (from Hakluyt); A larger Discourse of the same voyage, and the successe thereof, written by Abacvk Pricket; A note found in the Deske of Thomas Wydowse . . . one of them who was put into the Shallop": p. 596–610. ¶ "Discoueries made by English-men to the north-west: voyages of Sir Sebastian Cabot, Master Thorne and other Ancients, and of Master Weymouth" (partly from Hakluyt): p. 806–14. ¶ "The voyage of Master Iohn Knight . . . for the Discouvery of the North-west Passage . . . 1606" (from Hakluyt): p. 827–31. ¶ "A true Relation of such things as happened in the fourth Voyage for the Discouerie of the North-west Passage . . . 1615. Written by William Baffin" (partly from Hakluyt): p. 836–42. ¶ "To the Right Worshipfull master Iohn Wostenholme Esquire, one of the chiefe Adventurers for the discouerie of a passage to the North-west; A briefe and true Relation . . . of the fifth voyage, for the discouerie of a passage to the North-west . . . 1616 by William Baffin": p. 843–48; "A briefe Discourse of the probabilitie of a passage to the Westerne or South Sea . . . by Master Brigges" (partly from Hakluyt): p. 848–53. ¶ *Waldon also gives the title of vol. 4:* Purchas his pilgrimes. In five bookes. The sixth, contayning English voyages, to . . . America, *and the contents relating to Canada, thus:* ¶ "The first voyages

North-west Passage . . . 1610 (tiré de Hakluyt) ; A larger Discourse of the same voyage, and the successe thereof, written by Abacvk Pricket ; A note found in the Deske of Thomas Wydowse . . . one of them who was put in the Shallop » : p. 596–610. ¶ « Discoueries made by English-men to the north-west: voyages of Sir Sebastian Cabot, Master Thorne and other Ancients, and of Master Weymouth » (partiellement tiré de Hakluyt) : p. 806–14. ¶ « The voyage of Master Iohn Knight . . . for the Discouvery of the North-west Passage . . . 1606 » (tiré de Hakluyt) : p. 827–31. ¶ « A true Relation of such things as happened in the fourth Voyage for the Discouerie of the North-west Passage . . . 1615. Written by William Baffin » (partiellement tiré de Hakluyt) : p. 836–42. ¶ « To the Right Worshipfull master Iohn Wostenholme Esquire, one the chiefe Adventurers for the discouerie of a passage to the North-west; A briefe and true Relation . . . of the fifth voyage, for the discouerie of a passage to the North-west . . . 1616 by William Baffin » : p. 843–48. « A briefe Discourse of the probabilitie of a passage to the Westerne or South Sea . . . by Master Brigges » (partiellement tiré de Hakluyt) : p. 848–53. ¶ *Waldon donne aussi le titre du vol. 4 :* Purchas his pilgrimes. In five bookes. The sixth, contayning English voyages, to . . . America ; *ainsi que les titres suivants qui portent sur le Canada :* ¶ « The first voyages made to divers parts of America by Englishmen, Sir Sebastian Cabot, Sir Tho. Pert: also of . . . many others: collected briefly out of Master Camdem, Master Haklvyt, and other writers. » Cabot : p. 1177. ¶ « Notes of Voyages and Plantations of the French in the Northerne America : both in Florida and Canada » : p. 1603–05. ¶ « The voyage of Samvel

made to divers parts of America by Englishmen, Sir Sebastian Cabot, Sir Tho. Pert: also of . . . many others: collected briefly out of Master Camden, Master Haklvyt, and other writers." Cabot: p. 1177. ¶ "Notes of Voyages and Plantations of the French in the Northerne America: both in Florida and Canada": p. 1603–05. ¶ "The voyage of Samvel Champlaine of Brouage, made into Canada in the yeere 1603 . . ." (Hakluyt): p. 1605–19. ¶ "The Patent of the French King to Monsieur de Monts for the inhabiting of the Countries of La Cadia Canada, and other places in New France; The voyage of monsieur de Monts into New France, written by Marke Lescarbot": p. 1619–41. ¶ "Collections out of a French Booke, called Additions to Nova Francia; containing the Accidents there, from the yeere 1607 to 1611": p. 1642–45. ¶ "Noua Scotia. The Kings Patent to Sir William Alexander Knight, for the Plantation of New Scotland in America, and his proceedings therein; with a description of Mawooshen for better knowledge of those parts" (description of Mawooshen from Hakluyt): p. 1871–75. ¶ "The beginning of the Patent for New-found-land; and the Plantation there made by the English, 1610. delivered in a letter dated thence from M. Gvy, to M. Slany: Also of the weather the three first Winters, and of Captaine Weston: With other remarkable occurrents" (from Hakluyt): p. 1876–82. ¶ "Captaine Richard Whitbourne's voyages to New-found-land, and observations

Champlaine of Brouage, made into Canada in the yeere 1603 . . . » (Hakluyt) : p. 1605–19. ¶ « The Patent of the French King to Monsieur de Monts for the inhabiting of the Countries of La Cadia Canada, and other places in New France; The voyage of monsieur de Monts into New France, written by Marke Lescarbot » : p. 1619–41. ¶ « Collections out of a French Booke, called Additions to Nova Francia; containing the Accidents there, from the yeere 1607 to 1611 » : p. 1642–45. ¶ « Noua Scotia. The Kings Patent to Sir William Alexander Knight, for the plantation of New Scotland in America, and his proceedings therein; with a description of Mawooshen for better knowledge of those parts » (la description de Mawooshen est tirée de Hakluyt) : p. 1871–75. ¶ « The beginning of the Patent for New-found-land; and the Plantation there made by the English, 1610. delivered in a letter dated thence from M. Gvy to M. Slany: Also of the weather the three first Winters, and of Captaine Weston: With other remarkable occurrents » (tiré de Hakluyt) : p. 1876–82. ¶ « Captaine Richard Whitbourne's voyages to New-found-land, and observations there, and thereof; taken out of his Printed Booke » : p. 1882–88. ¶ « The Names of Divers honorable persons and others who have vndertaken to helpe advance his Maiestie's Plantation in the New-found-land: Written by the said R.W. with extracts of certaine Letters written from thence by Capt. Edward Winne, and N.H. » : p. 1888–91. ¶ *La bibliographie de cet ouvrage est complexe, mais documentée et dépouillée en détail dans le Sabin:66683–85. ¶ Première édition de Purchas his pilgrimage. Londres, 1613, q.v. pour le titre complet et d'autres éditions : 1614 (deuxième), 1617 (troisième), et 1626 (quatrième), q.v. L'édition*

there, and thereof; taken out of his Printed Booke": p. 1882–88. ¶ "The Names of Divers honorable persons and others who have vndertaken to helpe advance his Maiestie's Plantation in the New-found-land: Written by the said R.W. with extracts of certaine Letters written from thence by Capt. Edward Winne, and N.H.": p. 1888–91. ¶ *The bibliography of this work is complex, but given extensively in Sabin: 66683–85, with detailed contents. ¶ First edition of* Purchas his pilgrimage: *London, 1613,* q.v. *for full title and other editions besides: 1614 (second), 1617 (third), and 1626 (fourth),* q.v. *The 1625 ed. was reprinted with the Hakluyt Soc. pubs., extra series, 1905–07, 20 v., and the text also appeared in MF, in the STC series (no. 20509, cartons 972, 973, 973A, 973B).* ¶ *BVIPA*

de 1625 à été réimprimée dans les publ. de la Hakluyt Soc., collections supplémentaires, 1905–1907, 20 vol. ; reproduction sur mic. dans la collection du STC (n° 20509, cartons 972, 973, 973A, 973b). ¶ *BVIPA*

---

*Stirling, William Alexander, *1st earl of/1ᵉʳ comte de,* **1567?–1640.** An encouragement to colonies. . . . London, printed by William Stansby, 1625. 3 p.l., 47 p. 4°

A reissue of the first ed., London, 1624 (*q.v.* for other notes), but without the map; both NUC and Waldon (in her 1624 entry) note that the map is lacking in this issue, and the BM copy Waldon saw showed signs of a map having been torn out.

Une réimpression de la première éd., Londres 1624, (*q.v.* pour d'autres notes), mais sans la carte ; le NUC et Waldon (dans sa notice 1624) notent que la carte manque dans cette édition, de plus, une carte semblait avoir été arrachée de l'exemplaire du BM examiné par Waldon.

Vaughan, William, 1577–1641. Cambrensium Caroleia. Quibus nuptie regales cele-brantur, memoria Regis Pacifici renouatur, & precceptā necessaria ad rempublicam nostram foeliciter administrandam intexuntur: reportata a Colchide Cambriola ex Australissima Novae Terrae plaga, Opera & studio Orphei iunioris [pseud.] Londini, Excudebat Gulielmus Stansbeius. 1625. [A] ⁴B–G⁸H ⁴. fold. map. 8°

NUC(Pre–56)631:54*

Of the three variant spellings of "intex-untur" in the three NUC entries, this one is correct. ¶ Latin verse. ¶ Dedication to the King signed: Gulielmus Vau-hannus. ¶ *Contains the map by John Mason said to be the first English map of Newfoundland; it also appears in his* The golden fleece, 1626, q.v. ¶ *This edition issued in facsimile in Americana series, photostat reproductions, no. 169, Boston, Mass. Hist. Soc. 1926, and in MF, in STC series, no. 24604 (carton 943) — cf. NUC; another edition: London, 1630, q.v.* ¶ *NFSM(MF) · OOU(MF) · BVIV(MF)*

Des trois variantes orthographiques de « intexuntur » dans les 3 notices du NUC, celle-ci est la forme correcte. ¶ Vers latins. ¶ Dédicacé au roi et signé : Gulielmus Vauhannus. ¶ *Contient la carte de John Mason qu'on croit être la première représentation anglaise de Terre-Neuve. Carte aussi incluse dans* The golden fleece, 1626, *du même auteur, q.v.* ¶ *Repro-duction par fac-similé dans la collection Ameri-cana, reproduction par photocopie, n° 169, Bos-ton, Mass. Hist. Soc., 1926 et sur mic., collection du STC, n° 24604 (carton 943) –cf. NUC ; autre édition : Londres, 1630, q.v.* ¶ *NFSM (mic.) · OOU (mic.) · BVIV (mic.)*

*Winne, Edward. Extracts of a letter from Captaine Edward Winne, Gouernour of the colony at Ferryland . . . . vnto the Right Honourable Sir George Calvert . . . July 28, 1622. Another letter to Master Secretary Calvert, from Captain Winne, of the seuenteenth of August 1622. London, 1625. (In Samuel Purchas, *Pilgrimes.* London, 1625, vol. 4, book 10, p. 1889–90.)

NUC(Pre–56)668:181

Purchas his pilgrimes, London, 1625, with detailed contents, appears above.

Le titre et la description de *Purchas his pil-grimes,* Londres, 1625, figurent plus haut.

A PROSPECT
OF
THE MOST FAMOVS
Parts of the VVorld.

VIZ.

| Afia, | 3 | }{ | Europe, | 7 |
| Affrica, | 5 | | America. | 9 |

WITH

Thefe Kingdomes therein contained,

Grecia,	11		Denmarke,	29
Roman Empire,	13		Poland,	31
Germanie,	15		Perfia,	33
Bohemia,	17		Turkifh Empire,	35
France,	19	}{	Kingdo: of China,	37
Belgia,	21		Tartaria,	39
Spaine,	23		Sommer Ilands,	41
Italie,	25		Ciuill Warrs, in England,	
Hungarie,	27		Wales, and Ireland.	

You fhall find placed in the beginning of the
fecond Booke marked with thefe ⁎.⁑ and (5)

TOGETHER

With all the Prouinces, Counties and Shires, contained in that large
THEATER of Great BRITTAINES Empire.

Performed

BY

I OHN S PEED

LONDON
Printed by *Iohn Dawfon* for *George Humble*, and are to be fold at his
Shop in Popes-head Pallace. 1 6 2 7.

John Speed. *A prospect of the most famovs parts of the vvorld* . . . . London/Londres, 1627.

Anghiera, Pietro Martire d', 1455–1526. The historie of the West-Indies, containing the actes and aduentures of the Spaniards, which haue conquered and peopled those countries, inriched with varietie of pleasant relation of the manners, ceremonies, lawes, gouernments, and warres of the Indians. Published in Latin by Mr. Hakluyt, and translated into English by M. Lok.... London, Printed for Andrew Hebb, and are to be sold at the signe of the Bell in Pauls Church-yard. [1626?] 5 p.l., 318 numb. l. 4°

NUC(Pre–56)17:14*

Another issue of the 1612 edition, *q.v.*, with new title. Hebb took over Adams's stock of copyrights 6 May 1625. There are no previous entries for Hebb, so this edition [*i.e.* issue] must not be earlier than 1625. The dedication to James [I], who died in 1625, is omitted. BM gives:[1626?]. ¶ *BVIPA*

Autre tirage de l'édition de 1612, *q.v.*, avec un nouveau titre. Hebb reprit les droits d'auteur de Adams le 6 mai 1625. Aucune autre notice pour Hebb existe antérieurement à cette date; cette édition [*c.-à-d.* ce tirage] ne doit donc pas dater d'avant 1625. La dédicace à Jacques [Iᵉ], qui mourut en 1625, manque. Le BM donne : [1626 ?]. ¶ *BVIPA*

Purchas, Samuel, 1577?–1626. Purchas his pilgrimage. Or Relations of the world and the religions obserued in all ages and places discouered from the creation vnto this present. Contayning a theologicall and geographicall historie of Asia, Africa, and America .... The 4th ed., much enl. with additions, and illustrated with mappes through the whole worke: and three whole treatises annexed, one of Russia ... the second of the gulfe of Bengala ...; the third of the Saracenicall empire .... By Samvel Pvrchas .... London, printed by William Stansby for Henrie Fetherstone ... 1626. 20 p.l., 1047 (*i.e.* 1051), [34] p., 1 l. illus. (incl. maps), fold. map. fol.

NUC(Pre–56)475:489*

NUC notes: *Bound uniformly with the author's* Purchas his pilgrimes, *London, 1625 (q.v., above), lettered: Purchas's pilgrims. Vol. v. ¶ Paging irreg-*

Note du NUC : *relié en un seul volume avec l'ouvrage* Purchas his pilgrimes, *Londres, 1625 (q.v. plus haut) du même auteur et transcrit :* Purchas's pilgrims. Vol. v. ¶ *Pagi-*

ular: numbers 241–42 and 635–36 repeated; Waldon has: t.-p., [38] . . . p., so agrees with 20 p.l. in this edition (cf. note to 1617 ed.). ¶ "The catalogve of the avthors [mentioned]": 16–19 p.l. ¶ Index: [34] p. at end; Waldon has [35] p. ¶ This is often regarded as vol. 5 of Purchas his pilgrimes, 1625 [q.v.], but it is a separate work. ¶ "Of the discoueries of the North parts of the New-World . . .": p. 807–21; "Of Newfoundland, Nova Francia, Arambec . . .": p. 821–28. ¶ First edition: 1613, q.v. for fuller title and other editions besides: 1614 (second), and 1617 (third); text republished in MF, in the STC series (no. 20508, carton 1150 — cf. NUC).

nation irrégulière : les numéros 241–42 et 635–36 se répètent ; Waldon donne : p. de t., [38] . . . p., ce qui correspond aux 20 f. l. de cette édition (cf. note de l'éd. de 1617). ¶ « The catalogve of the avthors [mentionné] » : 16–19 f. l. ¶ Index : [34] p. à la fin ; Waldon note [35] p. ¶ On considère souvent ce livre comme le vol. 5 de Purchas his pilgrimes, 1625 [q.v.], mais il s'agit bien d'un ouvrage distinct. ¶ « Of the discoueries of the North parts of the New-World . . . » : p. 807–21 ; « Of Newfoundland, Nova Francia, Arambec . . . » : p. 821–28. ¶ Première édition : 1613, q.v. pour un titre plus complet et les éditions autres que 1614 (deuxième) et 1617 (troisième) ; reproduction sur mic. dans la collection du STC (n° 20508, carton 1150 – cf. NUC).

[Vaughan, William], 1577–1641. The golden fleece diuided into three parts, under which are discouered the errours of religion, the vices and decayes of the kingdome, and lastly the wayes to get wealth, and to restore trading so much complayned of. Transported from Cambrioll Colchos, out of the southermost part of the iland, commonly called the Newfoundland, By Orpheus Iunior [pseud.] for the generall and perpetuall good of Great Britaine. London, printed for Francis Williams, and are to bee sold at his shop at the signe of the Globe, ouer against the Royall Exchange, 1626. [14] p.l., 149, 105, 96 p. fold. map. 4°

NUC(Pre–56)631:55*

Three parts in one volume. ¶ The map is of Newfoundland, "described by Captaine John Mason an industrious gent: who spent seven yeares in the country" (cf. NUC). ¶ The golden fleece is found in Newfoundland, where Vaughan tried to found a colony, 1617. The book is made up of prose and verse, fact and

Volume en trois parties. ¶ Carte de Terre-Neuve, « décrite par le capitaine John Mason, homme industrieux qui a passé sept ans dans le pays » (cf. NUC). ¶ La toison d'or est découverte à Terre-Neuve où Vaughan essaya de fonder une colonie en 1617. Livre mi-fictif, mi-réaliste, en prose et en vers, rédigé pour encourager la colonisation à

fiction, to induce settlement in Newfoundland. ¶ *An allegory with many interesting references to Vaughan's colony in Newfoundland . . . (NUC).* ¶ *Text reissued in MF (negative) of type-script: Louisville, Ky., Lost Cause Press, 1973, and in MF in the STC series (no. 24609, carton 943 — NUC).* ¶ *NFSM · OOU · OONL(MF)*

Terre-Neuve. ¶ *Allégorie comportant des mentions nombreuses et intéressantes sur la colonie de Vaughan à Terre-Neuve. . . (NUC).* ¶ *Reproduction sur mic. (négatifs) à partir d'un tapuscrit : Louisville (Ky.), Lost Cause Press, 1973, et sur mic. dans la collection du STC (n° 24609, carton 943 –NUC).* ¶ *NFSM · OOU · OONL (mic.)*

1627

*Heylyn, Peter, 1599–1662 [Mikrokosmos: *title transliterated from Greek/le titre transcrit du grec.*] A little description of the great world. The 3d ed. rev. . . . Oxford, printed by I[ohn]. L[ichfield]. and W[illiam]. T[urner]. for William Turner and Thomas Huggins, 1627. 10 p.l., 807 [*i.e.* 809], [3] p. fold. table 4°(?)

NUC(Pre–56)244:507*

First edition pub. under title *Micro-cosmus*, 1621, *q.v.*; this 1627 edition reissued by University Microfilms, Ann Arbor, Mich., as microfilm no. 17542.

Première édition publiée sous le titre *Microcosmus* en 1621, *q.v.* ; cette édition publiée de nouveau par University Micro-films, Ann Arbor (Mich.), microfilm n° 17542.

*Speed, John, 1552?–1629. A prospect of the most famovs parts of the vvorld . . . . Together with all the prouinces, counties and shires, contained in that large theater of Great Brittaines empire. London, printed by Iohn Dawson for G[eorge]. Humble, 1627. 44 [*i.e.* 86], 5–8 [*i.e.* 6] p. 22 maps (3 col.) fol.

NUC(Pre–56)561:149*

First(?) edition; for a somewhat fuller title, and other editions and notes, *see* the editions of 1631 and 1646.

Première édition (?) ; *voir* titre un peu plus complet et autres notes et éditions dans les éditions de 1631 et de 1646.

1628

Anghiera, Pietro Martire d', 1455–1526. The famovs historie of the Indies: declaring the aduentures of the Spaniards, which haue conquered these countries, with varietie of relations of the religions, lawes, gouernments, manners, ceremonies, customes, rites, warres, and funerals of that people. Comprised into sundry decads. Set forth first by Mr. Hackluyt, and now published by L.M. Gent. The second edition. London: printed for Michael Sparke dwelling at the signe of the blue Bible in Green-Arbor. 1628. 3 p.l., 318 numb. l. 4°

NUC(Pre–56)17:16

Many errors in foliation. ¶ *"Save for title and dedication to Sir Julius Caesar this is identical with the Adams issue of 1612":* JCB(3)2:217 *(1612 issue: JCB(3) 2:86–87).* ¶ Another issue of the 1612 edition, *q.v.*, with first sheet cancelled and new title-page.

Nombreuses erreurs de foliotage. ¶ « *Exception faite du titre et de la dédicace à sir Julius Caesar, cette édition est identique à celle d'Adams parue en 1612* » : JCB(3)2:217 *(tirage de 1612 : JCB (3)2:86–87).* ¶ Autre tirage de l'édition de 1612, *q.v.*, sauf pour la page de garde qui a été supprimée et une nouvelle page de titre.

[Hayman, Robert], 1575–1629. Quodlibets, lately come over from New Britaniola, Old Newfound-land. Epigrams and other small parcels, both morall and diuine. The first foure bookes being the authors owne: the rest translated out of that excellent epigrammatist, Mr. Iohn Owen, and other rare authors: with two epistles of that excellently wittie doctor, Francis Rablais: translated out of his French at large. All of them composed and done at Harbour-Grace in Britaniola, anciently called Newfound-Land. By R.H. Sometimes Gouernour of the plantation there. London, printed by Elizabeth All-de, for Roger Michell, dwelling in Pauls Church-yard, at the signe of the Bulls-head. 1628. 4 p.l., 64 p. 1 illus. 4°

NUC(Pre–56)236:503*

Dedication signed: Robert Hayman. ¶ Hayman was an Oxford graduate, and is perhaps better known as a poet and epigrammatist; but he was an adventurer, too, and became governor of Bristol's Colony in Newfoundland for many years —his visits may have spanned a period as long as 1617 to 1628. Hayman was an enthusiastic promoter of the Newfoundland plantations. Bristol's Colony was in Conception Bay, and the name survives in Bristol's Hope. The verse and translations here were actually written in Newfoundland, and the book is amongst the very earliest publications in English to be written in Canada. Hayman died while on an expedition to Guyana. "Quodlibet" is Middle English from Latin: "What-pleases," and here refers to Hayman's poetic epigrams. ¶ The second part appears to be missing from the copy described by Waldon. NUC has the same collation, but notes "the second part is wanting, containing 'Certaine Epigrams Out Of The First Foure Bookes Of The Excellent Epigrammatist Master Iohn Owen . . .,' " etc. (q.v., next entry), with special title-pages. A microfilm reprint (note below) of an apparently complete copy has collation: 4 p.l., 64, [4],

Dédicace signée : Robert Hayman. ¶ Diplômé d'Oxford, Hayman est peut-être mieux connu comme poète et auteur d'épigrammes, mais il fut également un aventurier. En effet, il fut gouverneur de la colonie de Bristol à Terre-Neuve pendant de nombreuses années – ses visites s'y sont échelonnées entre 1617 et 1628. Hayman fut un promoteur dynamique des colonies de Terre-Neuve. La colonie de Bristol se trouvait à Conception Bay et son nom s'est perpétué dans Bristol's Hope. Les présents poèmes et traductions furent écrits à Terre-Neuve, le livre se plaçant parmi les toutes premières publications en anglais écrites au Canada. Hayman mourut lors d'une expédition en Guyane. « Quodlibet » vient du moyen anglais d'origine latine, qui signifie « Ce-qui-plaît », et se rapporte aux épigrammes poétiques de Hayman. ¶ La deuxième partie du volume semble manquer dans l'exemplaire décrit par Waldon. Le NUC, dont la collation est la même, note : « la deuxième partie manque qui contient 'Certaine Epigrams Out Of The First Foure Bookes Of The Excellent Epigrammatist Master Iohn Owen . . .' », etc. (q.v. la notice suivante), avec pages de titre distinctes. Pour une reproduction sur microfilm (note plus loin) d'un exemplaire apparemment complet, on donne la collation : 4 f. l., 64, [4], 58 p. (cf. NUC), les deux ouvrages se trouvant ainsi réunis en 1 vol. Waldon note que la deuxième partie, « Certaine

58 p. *(cf. NUC), thus having both works in one vol. The second part, "Certaine Epigrams," is "identical with the separate copy of this work, except for the omission of the tail piece on the verso of A3 . . .," says Waldon.* ¶ NUC *lists a microfilm reproduction: Ann Arbor, Mich., University Microfilms, 1941 (American Culture series, reel 4.27), 35 mm.* ¶ NFSM *(facsim., BM original) OKQ (facsim., RPJCB original) — both bound with* Certaine epigrams, *probably as issued.*

Epigrams », *est identique à la copie séparée de cet ouvrage, sauf pour le cul-de-lampe qui manque au verso de A3.* ¶ Le NUC *cite entre autres une reproduction sur mic. : Ann Arbor (Mich.), University Microfilms, 1941 (collection American Culture, bobine 4.27), 35 mm.* ¶ Le NFSM (fac-sim., le BM original) le OKQ (fac-sim., le RPJCB original) —les deux reliés avec Certaine epigrams, *probablement comme ils ont été publiés.*

Owen, John, 1560?–1622. Certaine epigrams out of the first foure bookes of the excellent epigrammatist, Master Iohn Owen: Translated into English at Harbor-Grace in Bristols-Hope in Britaniola, anciently called New-found-land: By R.H. At London imprinted for Roger Michell, and are to be sold at the signe of the Bulshead in Pauls Church-yard. 1628. 3 p.l., 58 p. 4°

NUC(Pre–56)436:70

Dedication (second p.l.), "To the far-admired admirably faire, vertuous and witty beauties of England," signed by the translator: Robert Hayman. ¶ *Transl. by Robert Hayman, from . . .* Epigrammatum Libri Tres. *London, 1606, and* Epigrammatum . . . Liber Singularis. *London, 1607.* ¶ NUC *collation: 3 p.l., 51, 54–55, 58 p. (issued as part of* Quodlibets. *London, 1628, q.v., preceding entry).* ¶ *Waldon indicates that the BM copy has a second t.-p. on p. [41]:* Severall sententious epigrams, and witty sayings out of sundry authors. . . translated into English at Harbor-Grace, in Bristols-Hope, in Brittaniola, anciently called, New-found-

La dédicace (deuxième f. l.), « Aux beautés gracieuses, intelligentes et vertueuses d'Angleterre, admirées partout dans le monde », est signée par le traducteur : Robert Hayman. ¶ *Traduction de Robert Hayman de . . .* Epigrammatum Libri Tres. *Londres, 1606 et de* Epigrammatum . . . Liber Singularis. *Londres, 1607.* ¶ *Collation du NUC : 3 f. l., 51, 54–55, 58 p. (publication faisant partie de* Quodlibets. *Londres, 1628, q.v. notice précédente).* ¶ *Waldon précise que l'exemplaire du BM renferme une seconde page de titre à la p. [41] :* Severall sententious epigrams, and witty sayings out of sundry authors. . . translated into English at Harbor-Grace, in Bristols-Hope, in Brittaniola, anciently called, New-found-land ; by R.H. *Londres,*

land; by R.H. *London, 1628, and this is confirmed from the NFSM facsimile of the BM original, which collates for the entire work* (Hayman's Quodlibets, *1628,* q.v., *and* Certaine epigrams, *probably issued together): 4 p.l., 64, [4], 40, [2], 43–58 p., where the 4 p.l., 64 p. consist of* Quodlibets, *and [4], 40 p. the* Certaine epigrams *with a separate t.-p., while the [2], 43–58 [possibly 56, see next note] p. has the separate t.-p. (unpaged, but counted in paging):* Severall sententious epigrams, *as above (with thanks to Ms. Anne Alexander of NFSM).* ¶ *Another entry in NUC seems to describe the same work, excepting that it has 56 p.; however, the penult. p. is no. 55, and the no. on p. 58 is indistinct.* ¶ *NFSM (facsim., BM original) OKQ (facsim., RPJCB original) — both bound with* Quodlibets, *probably as issued.*

1628. Ceci se trouve confirmé dans le fac-similé du NFSM tiré de l'original du BM qui donne comme collation pour l'ouvrage complet (Quodlibets, *1628,* q.v., *et* Certaine epigrams *de Hayman, probablement parus en même temps) : 4 f. l., 64, [4], 40, [2], 43–58 p., où les 4 f. l., 64 p. constituent* Quodlibets, *les [4], 40 p.,* Certaine epigrams, *avec page de titre distincte ; les pages [2], 43–58 [vraisemblablement 56, voir la note suivante] comportent une p. de t. distincte (non paginée, mais comptée dans la pagination) :* Severall sententious epigrams, *comme ci-dessus (avec remerciements à Mᵐᵉ Anne Alexander du NFSM).* ¶ *Une autre notice du NUC semble décrire le même ouvrage, sauf qu'il ne renferme que 56 p. ; cependant, la p. pénult. est en position 55 et le n° inscrit sur la p. 58 n'est pas clair.* ¶ *Le NFSM (fac-sim., le BM original) le OKQ (fac-sim., le RPJCB original) — les deux reliés avec* Quodlibets, *probablement comme ils ont été publiés.*

1629

Heylyn, Peter, 1599–1662. [Mikrokosmos: *title transliterated from Greek/le titre transcrit du grec.*] A little description of the great world. The 4th ed. Revised. . . . Oxford: printed by W[illiam]. T[urner]. for William Turner, and Thomas Huggins, 1629. 10 p.l., 807 [*i.e.* 819], [1] p., 2 l. fold. table 4°

NUC(Pre–56)244:508*

Numbers 179–80, 501–10 repeated in paging. ¶ First edition pub. under title *Microcosmus,* 1621, *q.v.* for other notes. ¶ BVAU

Les numéros 179–80 et 501–10 se répètent dans la pagination. ¶ Première édition publiée sous le titre *Microcosmus,* 1621, *q.v.* pour d'autres notes. ¶ BVAU

1630

Botero, Giovanni, 1540–1617. Relations of the most famous kingdomes and common-wealths thorowout the world: discoursing of their situations, religions, languages, manners, customes, strengths, greatnesse and policies. Translated out of the best Italian impression of Boterus. And since the last edition by R[obert]. I[ohnson]. now once againe inlarged according to moderne observation; with addition of new estates and countries .... London, printed by Iohn Haviland, and are to be sold by Iohn Partridge, 1630. 4 p.l., 644, [3 (index)] p. front. (fold. map). 4°

NUC(Pre–56)68:557*

Revised edition of R. Johnson's translation (of Botero's Le relationi universali, Rome, 1591), editor not known. ¶ First English edition published, London, 1601, under title: The travellers breviat, or an historicall description of the most famous kingdomes in the world. This edition contains no description of America. ¶ Nova Francia: p. 636. ¶ Other editions: 1608, 1611, 1616, q.v., above.

Édition revue de la traduction de R. Johnson (de Le relationi universali, Rome, 1591, de Botero). Éditeur inconnu. ¶ Édition originale anglaise publiée à Londres en 1601 sous le titre The travellers breviat, or an historicall description of the most famous kingdomes in the world. Cette édition ne contient aucune description de l'Amérique. ¶ Nova Francia : p. 636. ¶ Autres éditions : 1608, 1611, 1616, q.v. plus haut.

Stirling, William Alexander, 1st earl of/1ᵉʳ comte de, 1567?–1640. The mapp and description of New-England; together with A discourse of plantation, and collonies: also, A relation of the nature of the climate, and how it agrees with our owne country England. How neere it lyes to New-found-Land, Virginia, Noua Francia, Canada, and other parts of the West-Indies. Written by Sr. William Alexander, knight. London, printed for Nathaniel Butter, An. Dom. 1630. 1 p.l., 47 p. fold. map. 4°

NUC(Pre–56)570:94*

Caption title, p. 1: An encouragement to colonies. ¶ This work consists of the unsold sheets of the author's An encouragement to colonies, London,

Titre de départ, p. 1 : An encouragement to colonies. ¶ Cet ouvrage rassemble les pages non vendues de An encouragement to colonies, Londres, 1624 (q.v.) du même auteur, mais sans

1624 (q.v.), *without the dedication, but issued with a new title-page (Church:414). ¶ Text republished in MF: Ann Arbor, Mich., University Microfilms (no. 3064, carton 609 — cf. NUC). ¶ NFSM*

la dédicace, avec une page de titre différente (Church:414). ¶ Reproduction sur mic. : Ann Arbor (Mich.), University Microfilms (n° 3064, carton 609 – cf. NUC). ¶ NFSM

*[Vaughan, William], 1577–1641. Cambrensium Caroleja. Quibus precepta necessaria ad rempublicam nostram foeliciter administrandam intrxuntur: opera & studio Gulielmi Vaughanni Militis. Londini, impensis Francisci Constable, in Caemiterio S. Pauli, 1630. 112 p. fold. map. 4°

NUC(Pre–56)631:54*

Assumed to be another edition of his 1625 title beginning with the same two words, q.v., above; reproduced in MF in the STC series, no. 24605 (carton 862) — cf. NUC.

Probablement une édition ultérieure à celle de 1625 du même auteur et commençant par les mêmes mots, q.v. plus haut : reproduction sur mic. dans la collection du STC, n° 24605 (carton 862) – cf. NUC.

Vaughan, William, 1577–1641. The Newlanders cure. Aswell [sic] of those violent sicknesses which distemper most minds in these latter dayes: as also by a cheape and newfound dyet, to preserue the body sound and free from diseases, vntill the last date of life, through extreamity of age. Wherein are inserted generall and speciall remedies against scuruy. Goute. Coughes. Collicke. Feauers. Sea-sicknesses, and other grieuous infirmities. Published for the weale of Great Brittaine, by Sir William Vaughan, Knight. . . . Imprinted at London by N[icholas]. O[kes]. for F[rancis]. Constable, and are to be sold at his shop in Pauls church at the signe of the craine. 1630. 1 p.l., [12], 143 p. 8°

NUC(Pre–56)631:56*

NUC has "free from all diseases" in the title, and "7 p.l." in the collation. ¶ A

Dans le NUC, le titre contient « free from all diseases » et la collation est « 7 f. l. ». ¶

medical work, treating of the complaints most prevalent in Newfoundland. The letter of dedication describes the author's efforts to colonize Newfoundland and his hopes for the island. ¶ *Contents: Of the bodies infirmities; Of the mindes infirmities [in verse]. ¶ The following entry for a microfilm is either a variant, or the same work erroneously transcribed.*

Ouvrage médical traitant des problèmes les plus courants à Terre-Neuve. La lettre dédicace décrit les efforts de l'auteur pour coloniser Terre-Neuve et les espoirs qu'il fondait sur l'île. ¶ *Titres : Of the bodies infirmities ; Of the mindes infirmities [en vers]. ¶ La notice suivante sur microfilm est ou une variante, ou le même ouvrage contenant des erreurs de transcription.*

*Vaughan, William, 1577–1641. The newlanders cure. . . . remedies against the scuruy. Coughes. Feauers. Goute. Collicke. Sea-sicknesses, and other grieuous infirmities. London, imprinted by N[icholas]. O[kes]. for F[rancis]. Constable . . . 1630. [No collation or format given.]

NUC(Pre–56)631:56*

STC:24619 (carton 1042). Microfilm. ¶ *See* preceding entry for other notes. ¶ OKQ · OLU · OOU · BVAU

STC:24619 (carton 1042). Microfilm. ¶ *Voir* notes à la notice précédente. ¶ OKQ · OLU · OOU · BVAU

1631

*Heylyn, Peter, 1599–1662. [Mikrokosmos: *title transliterated from Greek/le titre transcrit du grec.*] A little description of the great world. The 5th ed. . . . Oxford, printed for William Turner, and Robert Allott. 1631. 10 p.l., 807 [*i.e.* 809], [1] p. fold. table. 4°(?)

NUC(Pre–56)244:508*

Numbers 179 and 180 repeated in paging. ¶ First edition pub. under title *Microcosmus*, 1621, *q.v.* for other notes.

Les numéros 179 et 180 se répètent dans la pagination. ¶ Première édition parue sous le titre *Microcosmus*, 1621, *q.v.* pour d'autres notes.

Speed, John, 1552?–1629. A prospect of the most famous parts of the vvorld. Viz. Asia, Affrica, Evrope, America . . . . Together with all the prouinces, counties, and shires, contained in that large Theator of Great Brittaines empire. Performed by Iohn Speed. London, printed by Iohn Dawson for George Humble, and are to be sold at his shop in Popes-head Pallace. 1631. 2 pts.: 1 p.l., 44, [3] l.; [8], 146 [*i.e.* 144], [5] l. front. (port.), maps. fol.

NUC(Pre–56)561:149*

Index: [5] l. at end. Each map is double, with text printed on the reverse. Pt. 2 has separate t.-p.: The theatre of the empire of Great Britaine . . . 1627. ¶ Norumbega [Nova Scotia]; Nova Francia; Terra Laboratoris of Corterialis [Newfoundland]; Estotiland [Labrador peninsula]; Bacalaes [Newfoundland]: l. 10. The map is fairly detailed for the area of Canada. ¶ *First (?) edition: London, 1627; other eds.: 1646, 1662, 1665, 1668, 1675, and 1676, q.v. NUC also lists a [London, 1631?] edition, apparently in one volume, and two other entries for 1631 works, but both are pub. by G. Humble.*

Index : [5] f. à la fin. Toutes les cartes sont doubles avec texte imprimé au verso. La deuxième partie a sa propre p. de t. : « The theatre of the empire of Great Britaine. . . 1627. » ¶ Norumbega [Nouvelle-Écosse], Nova Francia, Terra Laboratoris de Corterialis [Terre-Neuve], Estotiland [péninsule du Labrador], Bacalaes [Terre-Neuve] : f. 10. La carte géographique fournit assez de détails sur la région de Canada. ¶ *Première (?) édition : Londres, 1627 ; autres éd. : 1646, 1662, 1665, 1668, 1675 et 1676, q.v. Le NUC donne également une édition [londonienne de 1631 ?], apparemment en 1 vol., et 2 autres notices pour des ouvrages de 1631, mais ces derniers ont été publiés par G. Humble.*

*Stow, John, 1525?–1605. Annales, or, A generall chronicle of England. Begun by John Stow: continved and augmented with matters forraigne and domestique, ancient and moderne, vnto the end of this present yere, 1631. By Edmvnd Howes . . . . Londini, impensis R[ichard]. Meighen, 1631. 10 p.l., 1050, [1055]–1062 p., 2 l., 1062–1087, [2] p. fol.

NUC(Pre–56)572:35*

Engraved t.-p.; head-pieces; initials. ¶ Gothic type; double columns. ¶ BM(to 1955)231:50 has imprint as: Printed by A.M. for R. Meighen: London, 1631. It also notes that the Appendix has a separate t.-p. with the date: 1632. ¶ First published under this title: London, 1592, q.v. for other notes; text republished in MF in the STC series (no. 23340, carton 1189 — cf. NUC). ¶ BVAU

Titre gravé ; vignettes d'en-tête ; initiales. ¶ Caractères gothiques ; sur deux colonnes. ¶ Le BM(to 1955)231:50 donne comme adresse bibliographique : Printed by A.M. for R. Meighen : London, 1631. Il spécifie également que l'appendice a une page de titre distincte, datée de 1632. ¶ Édition originale publiée sous ce titre à Londres en 1592, q.v. pour d'autres notes ; reproduction sur mic. dans la collection du STC (n° 23340, carton 1189 – cf. NUC). ¶ BVAU

1633

*Heylyn, Peter, 1599–1662. [Mikrokosmos: *title transliterated from Greek/le titre transcrit du grec.*] A little description of the great world. The 6th ed. . . . Oxford, printed for W[illiam]. Turner & R[obert]. Allott, 1633. 10 p.l., 807 p., 1 l. 4°(?)

NUC(Pre–56)244:508*

First edition pub. under title *Microcosmus*, 1621, q.v.; this 1633 ed. reissued in microfilm about 1950s (cf. NUC).

Première édition sous le titre *Microcosmus*, 1621, q.v. ; édition de 1633 reproduite sur microfilm dans les années 1950 (cf. NUC).

James, Thomas, 1593?–1635? The strange and dangerous voyage of Captaine Thomas Iames, in his intended discouery of the Northwest Passage into the South Sea. VVherein the miseries indured both going, wintering, returning; and the rarities obserued, both philosophicall and mathematicall, are related in this Iournall of it. Published by His Maiesties command. To which are added, a plot or card for the sayling in those seas. Diuers little tables of the author's, of the variation of the compasse, &c. VVith an appendix concerning longitude, by Master Henry Gellibrand .... And an Aduise concerning the philosophy of these late discoueryes. By W.W. London, printed by Iohn Legatt, for Iohn Partridge. 1633. 4 p.l., 120 p., 12 l. fold. map. 4°

NUC(Pre–56)276:645*

The "Aduise concerning the philosophy" (l. 8–12 at end) by William Watts is signed: X.Z. ¶ A portrait of the author appears on the map. ¶ Waldon's collation differs: t.-p., [4], 120, [6], 1 l., [16] p. ¶ The map shows Baffin Bay and adjacent coasts, with a portrait of Capt. James. ¶ *First edition; second ed., rev. and corr., under title:* The dangerous voyage of Capt. Thomas James. *London, 1740 (q.v.), and frequently reprinted in collections, e.g. John Harris,* Navigantium atque itinerantium bibliotheca. *London, 1705 (q.v.); Awnsham Churchill,* A collection of voyages. *London, 1732 (q.v.), etc.; Daniel Coxe,* A collection of voyages. *London, 1741 (q.v.);* The world displayed. *London, 1762–90, vol. 10 (1773), p. [151]–202. Waldon also notes some nineteenth- and twentieth-century reprints, and the Thomas James biog. in DNB concludes with a few reprints. ¶* BVAU · BVIPA

« Aduise concerning the philosophy » (f. 8–12 à la fin) de William Watts signé : X. Z. ¶ Portrait de l'auteur sur la carte. ¶ La collation de Waldon diffère : p. de t., [4], 120, [6], 1 f., [16] p. ¶ La carte représente la Baie de Baffin et les côtes environnantes ; elle comporte aussi le portrait du cap. James. ¶ Première édition ; deuxième éd. revue et corr., sous le titre The dangerous voyage of Capt. Thomas James. *Londres, 1740 (q.v.), réimprimée souvent dans des collections, p. ex. John Harris,* Navigantium atque itinerantium bibliotheca. *Londres, 1705 (q.v.) ; Awnsham Churchill,* A collection of voyages. *Londres, 1732 (q.v.), etc. ; Daniel Coxe,* A collection of voyages. *Londres, 1741, (q.v.) ;* The world displayed. *Londres, 1762–90, vol. 10 (1773), p. [151]–202. Waldon donne aussi quelques réimpressions du XIXe et XXe siècle et signale que la biographie de Thomas James dans le* DNB *se termine par quelques réimpressions. ¶* BVAU · BVIPA

1634

*Abbot, George, *abp. of Canterbury/aev. de Canterbury*, 1562–1633. A briefe description of the whole world. . . . kingdomes of the same, with their academies. Written by the Right Reverend Father in God, George, Late Archbishop of Canterburie. London, printed for W. Sheares, 1634. 2 p.l., 329, [3] p. 12°(?)

NUC(Pre–56)1:308*

Added t.-p., engr., with portrait of author. ¶ *See* 1599.	P. de t. ajoutée, gravée, avec portrait de l'auteur. ¶ *Voir* 1599.

Great Britain. Laws, statutes, etc., 1625–1649 (Charles I). A commission for the well governing of our people, inhabiting in New-found-land; or, traffiquing in bayes, creekes, or fresh rivers there. Imprinted at London by Robert Barker, printer to the Kings most excellent Majestie: and by the assigns of John Bill. 1633 [*i.e.* 1634 N.S.]. 1 p.l., 22 p. 4°

BLC(to 1975)95:415

Witnessed "the tenth day of February," 1634, N.S. ¶ Because laws have not hitherto been given, some lawless persons have thought that they could not be impeached in England, and injuries and abuses have arisen. Charles I now gives laws to prevent disorder in the future. For murder, or theft to the value of 40/-(carrying the death penalty), the offender may be brought before the Earl Marshall. Lesser crimes may be dealt with by the mayors of Southampton, Weymouth, Melcolmbe Regiis, Lynne, Foye, and Barnestable. The vice-admirals of Southampton, Dorset, Devon, and

Attesté devant témoins le dixième jour de février, en l'an de grâce 1634, c.g. ¶ Parce que des lois n'ont point encore été ici données, quelques personnes malhonnêtes ont cru qu'elles pourraient demeurer impunies en Angleterre. Des blessures ont été infligées et des abus commis. Charles Ier ordonne donc que des lois soient instaurées afin de contrer de futurs désordres. En cas de meurtre ou de vol pour une valeur de 40/- (encourant la peine de mort), le coupable peut être amené à comparaître devant le juge du comté. Les offenses moins graves pourront être jugées par les maires de Southampton, de Weymouth, de Melcolmbe Regiis, de Lynne, de Foye et de Barnestable.

Cornwall may proceed against those who commit offences at sea. The laws laid down suggest the kind of disputes that had actually arisen: conflicts over places to fish, the use of timber from a neighbour's stage to repair one's own, etc. It is also provided that divine service is to be read on Sundays. ¶ *Three apparent variants appeared in 1634 (see next entries), with other editions in 1669, 1745, and 1747 (q.v.), and a photostat reprint, Boston, Mass. Hist. Soc., 1929 (Americana series, no. 242).*

Les vice-amiraux de Southampton, de Dorset, de Devon et de Cornwall peuvent agir dans les cas de délits en mer. Les lois mises de l'avant font état du genre de disputes qui eurent cours : disputes sur les droits de pêche, utilisation du bois pris sur le quai d'un voisin pour réparer le sien, etc. On y dit également que l'office divin aura lieu tous les dimanches. ¶ *Il semble que trois versions différentes parurent en 1634 (voir notices suivantes) en plus des éditions ultérieures de 1669, 1745 et 1747 (q.v.) et une réimpression par photocopie, Boston, Mass. Hist. Soc., 1929 (collection Americana, n° 242).*

Great Britain. Laws, statutes, etc., 1625–1649 (Charles I). A commission for the well-governing of our people inhabiting in Newfoundland; or, trafficking in bays, creeks, or fresh rivers there. [London? 1633?] 3 p. fol.

Waldon cites only Casey, but Casey: 16 is different (see below), so Waldon must have seen a variant. The imprint date here is O.S. ¶ Witnessed, "the 10th day of February in the ninth year of our reign" [hence, 1634, Charles I having ascended to the throne in 1625]. ¶ See *preceding entry for other variants and editions.*

Waldon ne signale que Casey comme source, mais la notice Casey: 16 est différente (voir plus loin); la version de Waldon doit donc être une variante. Date d'impression selon le calendrier julien. ¶ Attesté devant témoins « le dixième jour de février de la neuvième année de notre règne » [alors, 1634, Charles Ier ayant monté sur le trône en 1625]. ¶ Voir *autres variantes et éditions à la notice précédente.*

*Great Britain. Laws, statutes, etc., 1625–1649 (Charles I). A commission for the well gouerning of our people, inhabiting in New-found-land; or traffiquing in bayes, creekes, or fresh riuers there. Imprinted at London by Robert Barker and by the assignes of Iohn Bill, 1633 [*i.e.* 1634 N.S.] 12 p. [? A–C⁴] 4°

NUC(Pre–56)213:437*

Given 10 Feb. 1634. ¶ *See* second entry preceding for other variants and editions.

Daté du 10 février 1634. ¶ *Voir* autres variantes et éditions deux notices plus haut.

*Great Britain. Laws, statutes, etc., 1625–1649 (Charles I). A commission for the well governing of our people inhabiting in New-found-land; or, traffiquing in bayes, creeks, or fresh rivers there. Imprinted at London by Robert Barker, printer to the Kings most excellent Majestie; and by the assigns of John Bill. [London?] 1633. 21 p. 12°

Casey:16 (photostat)

The date here is O.S., or 1634 N.S. ¶ *See* third entry preceding for other variants and editions.

Daté selon le calendrier julien, c.-à-d., 1634 suivant le calendrier grégorien. ¶ *Voir* autres variantes et éditions trois notices plus haut.

*[Stafford, Robert], 1588–1618. A geographicall and anthologicall description of all the empires and kingdomes .... London, printed by Nicholas Okes, for Simon Waterson, 1634. [64] p. [?] 4°

NUC(Pre–56)563:583*

Collation in NUC: A–H⁴. ¶ Dedication signed: Rob. Stafforde. ¶ First edition: London, 1607 (*q.v.* for fuller title, and other notes and editions); republished in MF: Ann Arbor, Mich.,

Collation du NUC : A–H⁴. ¶ Dédicace signée : Rob. Stafforde. ¶ Première édition : Londres, 1607 (*q.v.* pour un titre plus complet, d'autres notes et éditions) ; reproduction sur mic. : Ann Arbor (Mich.),

University Microfilms, 1974 (Early English books, 1475–1640, reel 1365; cf. NUC).

University Microfilms, 1974 (Early English books, 1475–1640, bobine 1365 ; cf. NUC).

1635

*Abbot, George, *abp. of Canterbury/aev. de Canterbury,* 1562–1633. A briefe description of the whole world. . . . kingdomes of the same, with their academies. . . . Written by the Right Reverend Father in God, George, late Archbishop of Canterburie. London, printed for W. Sheares, 1635. 2 p.l., 350, [5] p. 12°(?)

NUC(Pre–56)1:308*

Added t.-p., engr., with portrait of author, has imprint date 1634. ¶ *See* 1599.

P. de t. ajoutée, gravée, avec portrait de l'auteur, date d'impression : 1634. ¶ *Voir* 1599.

Fox, Luke, 1586–1635. North-vvest Fox, or Fox from the North-west passage. Beginning with King Arthur, Malga, Octhur, the two Zeni's of Iseland, Estotiland, and Dorgia; following with briefe abstracts of the voyages of Cabot, Frobisher, Davis, Waymouth, Knight, Hudson, Button, Gibbons, Bylot, Baffin, Hawkridge. Together with the courses, distance, latitudes, longitudes, variations, depths of seas, sets of tydes, currents, races, and over-falls; with other observations, accidents and remarkable things, as our miseries and sufferings. Mr. Iames Hall's voyages to Groynland, with a topographical description of the countries, the salvages lives and treacheries, how our men have been slayne by them there, with the commodities of all those parts; whereby the marchant may have trade, and the mariner imployment. Demonstrated in a polar card, wherein are all the maines, seas, and ilands, herein mentioned. With the author his owne voyage, being the XVIth. with the opinions and collections of the most famous mathematicians, and cosmographers; with a probabilitie to prove the same by marine remonstrations, compared by the ebbing and flowing of the sea, experimented with places of our owne coast. By Captaine Luke Foxe of Kingstone upon Hull, capt. and pylot for the voyage, in his Majesties pinnace the Charles. Printed by his Majesties command. London, printed by B[ernard]. Alsop and Tho. Favvcet, dwelling in Grubstreet, 1635. 5 p.l., 269, [3] p. front., illus. (map), fold. map. 4°

NUC(Pre–56)179:636*

Waldon has a long and broken pagination for what appears to be an imperfect copy. ¶ Fox prefixed to his own narrative, accounts of all previous voyages north-westward, most of them from Hakluyt and Pinchas [*i.e.* Purchas], but some original and of value. He is almost the sole source for the voyages of Gibbons, Hawkridge, and Britton. Christy [*see* below] considers "more than likely" C.R. Monkham's [*i.e.* Markham's] suggestion (*The voyages of William Baffin, 1612–1622,* p. 223) that Fox copied Baffin's lost map (suppressed by Purchas) for Baffin's Bay, which is shown correctly on Fox's map. ¶ *First edition; reprinted as* The voyages of Captain Luke Foxe of Hull, and Captain Thomas James of Bristol, in search of the Northwest Passage, in 1631-32, *edited with notes*

Waldon donne une longue pagination interrompue de ce qui semble n'être qu'une copie imparfaite. ¶ Fox introduit son propre travail par des comptes rendus de tous les voyages précédents à destination du Nord-Ouest, la plupart faits par Hakluyt et Pinchas (*c.-à-d.* Purchas), mais certains étant originaux et présentant une certaine valeur. Il est un des seuls à relater les voyages de Gibbons, de Hawkridge et de Britton. Christy (*voir* plus loin) pense que C.R. Monkham [*c.-à-d.* Markham] (*The voyages of William Baffin, 1612–1622,* p. 223) a « très probablement raison » quand il affirme que Fox copia la carte perdue de Baffin (supprimée par Purchas) de la Baie de Baffin, la baie étant représentée correctement sur la carte de Fox. ¶ *Première édition ; réimpression sous le titre* The voyages of Captain Luke Foxe of Hull, and Captain Thomas James of Bristol, in search of the Northwest Passage, in 1631-32, *édition*

and an introd. by Miller Christy. London, Hakluyt Soc., 1894, 2 v. Christy also prints, as appendices to v. 2, many related documents. ¶ OTP · OTU · BVIPA

annotée et présentée par Miller Christy. Londres, Hakluyt Soc., 1894, 2 vol. Christy ajoute en annexe au vol. 2 plusieurs documents pertinents. ¶ OTP · OTU · BVIPA

1636

*Abbot, George, abp. of Canterbury/aev. de Canterbury, 1562–1633. A briefe description of the whole world. . . . kingdomes of the same, with their academies. Written by the Most Reverend Father in God, George, late Arch-bishop of Canterbury. London, printed by T[homas]. H[arper]. and are to be sold by Wil. Sheares, at the signe of the Harrow in Brittaine Burse, 1636. [1] p.l., A–P¹² 12°

NUC(Pre–56)1:308*

Added t.-p., engr. by William Marshall (see NUC). ¶ See 1599.

P. de t. ajoutée, gravée par William Marshall (voir le NUC). ¶ Voir 1599.

*Heylyn, Peter, 1599–1662. [Mikrokosmos: title transliterated from Greek/le titre transcrit du grec.] A little description of the great world. The 7th ed. . . . Oxford, printed by W[illiam]. Turner, 1636. 10 p.l., 808 p., 1 l. front. (fold. map), fold. table. 4°(?)

NUC(Pre–56)244:508*

First edition pub. under title Microcosmus, 1621, q.v. for notes.

Édition originale publiée sous le titre Microcosmus, 1621, q.v. pour d'autres notes.

NORTH-VVEST FOX.

OR,

Fox *from the North-west passage*.

BEGINNING

With King ARTHVR, MALGA, OCTHVR,

the two ZENI's of *Iseland*, *Estotiland*, and *Dorgia* ;
Following with briefe Abstracts of the Voyages of *Cabot*,
Frobisher, *Davis*, *Waymouth*, *Knight*, *Hudson*, *Button*, *Gib-*
bons, *Bylot*, *Baffin*, *Hawkridge* : Together with the
Courses, Distance, Latitudes, Longitudes, Variations,
Depths of Seas, Sets of Tydes, Currents, Races,
and over-Falls; with other Observations. Accidents
and remarkable things, as our Miseries and
sufferings.

M.ͬ IAMES HALL's three Voyages to *Greynland*, with a
Topographicall description of the Countries, the *Salvages*
lives and Treacheries, how our Men have beene slayne
by them there, with the Commodities of all those
parts ; whereby the Marchant may have Trade, and
the Mariner Imployment.

Demonstrated in a Polar Card, wherein are all the Maines, Seas,
and flands, herein mentioned.

With the Author his owne Voyage, being the XVI.ᵗᵃ

with the opinions and Collections of the most famous Mathematicians, and Cosmographers ; with a Probabilitie to
prove the same by Marine Remonstrations, compared by the Ebbing and Flowing of the Sea, experimented
with places of our owne Coast.

By Captaine LVKE FOXE *of* Kingstone *vpon* Hull, *Capt.*
and Pylot for the Voyage, in his Majesties Pinnace
the CHARLES,

Printed by his Majesties Command.

LONDON,

Printed by B. ALSOP and THO. FAVVCET, dwelling in *Grubstreet*,
1635.

1639

*Heylyn, Peter, 1599–1662. [Mikrokosmos: *title transliterated from Greek/le titre transcrit du grec.*] A little description of the great world. The 8th ed. . . . Oxford, printed by William Turner, Ann. Dom. 1639. 10 p.l., 808 (*i.e.* 810) p., 1 l. 4°(?)

NUC(Pre–56)244:508*

Errors in paging: nos. 160 and 389 omitted; nos. 179–80 and 395–96 repeated. ¶ Illustrated t.-p.; head and tailpieces. ¶ First edition pub. under title *Microcosmus*, 1621, *q.v.* for other notes.

Erreurs de pagination : les numéros 160 et 389 ont été omis ; les numéros 179–80 et 395–96 se répètent. ¶ P. de t. illustrée ; vignettes. ¶ Première édition publiée sous le titre *Microcosmus*, 1621, *q.v.* pour d'autres notes.

1642

*Abbot, George, *abp. of Canterbury/aev. de Canterbury,* 1562–1633. A briefe description of the whole world. . . . kingdomes of the same, with their academies. Written by the Most Reverend Father in God, George, late Arch-bishop of Canterbury. London, printed by B. Alsop [s.d., 1642]. 2 p.l., 329, [3] p. 12°(?)

NUC(Pre–56)1:308*

Added t.-p., engr., with portrait of author, has imprint: printed for Will: Sheares at the Bible in Couen Garden. 1642. ¶ See 1599.

P. de t. ajoutée et gravée avec le portrait de l'auteur ; adresse bibliographique : printed for Will : Sheares at the Bible in Couen Garden. 1642. ¶ *Voir* 1599.

*Heylyn, Peter, 1599–1662. Cosmographie in four bookes. Containing the choro-
graphie and historie of the whole world . . . . By Peter Heylyn . . . . London, printed
for Henry Seile . . . 1642. 4 pts. in 1 v. 3 fold. maps, table. fol.

NUC(Pre–56)244:499*

Added t.-p., engraved. ¶ Numerous
errors in paging. ¶ Revised and
enlarged from his *Microcosmus*.
Oxford, 1621, *q.v.* ¶ First edition
under title *Cosmographie*; also published London, 1652, *q.v.* for other
notes and editions.

P. de t. ajoutée, gravée. ¶ Nombreuses
erreurs de pagination. ¶ Édition revue et
augmentée de *Microcosmus* du même auteur.
Oxford, 1621, *q.v.* ¶ Première édition parue
sous le titre *Cosmographie* ; ouvrage publié
aussi à Londres, 1652, *q.v.* pour d'autres
notes et éditions.

1644

Castell, William, *d./déc.* 1645. A short discoverie of the coasts and continent of America,
from the equinoctiall northward, and of the adjacent isles. By William Castell, minister
of the gospell at Courtenhall in Northamptonshire. Whereunto is prefixed the authors
petition to this present Parliament, for the propagation of the gospell in America;
attested by many eminent English and Scottish divines. And a late ordinance of Parliament for that purpose, and for the better government of the English plantations
there. Together with Sir Benjamin Rudyers speech in Parliament, 21. Jan. concerning
America. London, printed in the yeer 1644. 6 p.l., 48 (*i.e.* 44), 54 p. 4°

NUC(Pre–56)98:288*

*Pages 22, 23, and 44 (second count)
incorrectly numbered 23, 22, and 48
respectively.* ¶ *"An ordinance of the Lords
and Commons assembled in Parliament.
Whereby Robert Earle of Warwicke is
made Governour in Chiefe and Lord
High Admiral of all those ilands and other
plantations, inhabited, planted, or
belonging to any of His Majesties the King
of Englands subjects, within the bounds*

*Pages 22, 23 et 44 (deuxième numération)
numérotées incorrectement 23, 22 et 48
respectivement.* ¶ « *Ordonnance de la Chambre
des Lords et de la Chambre des Communes
réunies au Parlement et selon laquelle Robert,
comte de Warwicke, est promu Gouverneur en
Chef et Lord Grand Amiral de toutes les îles et
autres colonies habitées, colonisées ou appartenant aux sujets de Sa Majesté le roi d'Angleterre,
quels qu'ils soient, à l'intérieur des limites et sur*

and upon the coasts of America": p. [v–x]. "To the most high and honourable court of Parliament, now assembled, the humble petition of William Castell, parson of Courtenhall in Northamptonshire, for the propogating [sic] of the gospell in America" [also pub. separately, cf. NUC]: p. 1–8. "An introduction to the worke": p. 9–12. "The seconde book": 54 p. at end. ¶ "New-found-Land": p. 12–14; "Nova Francia": p. 15–18. ¶ First edition; other appearances of the text: 1745, 1752 (q.v.).

les terres d'Amérique » : p. [v–x]. « À la très haute et très honorable cour du Parlement en assemblée, l'humble requête de William Castell, pasteur de Courtenhall, Northamptonshire, pour la propagation de l'Évangile en Amérique » [aussi publ. séparément, cf. NUC] : p. 1–8. « An introduction to the worke » : p. 9–12. « The seconde booke » : 54 p. à la fin. ¶ « New-found-Land » : p. 12–14 ; « Nova Francia » : p. 15–18. ¶ Première édition ; autres tirages en 1745 et en 1752 (q.v.).

1646

Speed, John, 1552?–1629. A prospect of the most famous parts of the world. Viz. Asia Affrica Evrope America with kingdomes therein contained together vvith all the provinces, counties, and shires, contained in that large theater of Great Brittaines empire. London, printed by J[ohn]. Legatt for W[illiam]. Humble, 1646. 5 pts. in 1 v. front., ports., 89 double maps, coat of arms. fol.

NUC(Pre–56)561:149*

This is a variant of Waldon's edition, which appears in the next entry. ¶ [Parts 2–5] each have a special t.-p. ¶ [Part 2] has engraved t.-p.: The theatre of the empire of Great Britaine. 1627. ¶ Norumbega; Nova Francia; Terra Laboratoris or Corterialis; Estotiland: p. 51–52; Bacalaes: p. 55. The map of America is reduced from the first edition, with fewer names on it. ¶ First ed.: 1627; also: 1631 (q.v. for

Variante de l'édition de Waldon présentée à la notice suivante. ¶ [Les parties 2–5] ont chacune une p. de t. propre. ¶ [La partie 2] a un titre gravé : The theatre of the empire of Great Britaine. 1627. ¶ Norumbega, Nova Francia, Terra Laboratoris ou Corterialis, Estotiland : p. 51–52. Bacalaes : p. 55. Carte de l'Amérique de format réduit par rapport à celle de la première édition avec moins de noms dessus. ¶ Première édition : 1627 ; aussi : 1631 (q.v. pour une explication des noms

explanation of geographical names used in previous note); other eds.: 1662, 1665, 1668, 1675, and 1676, q.v.

géogr. utilisés dans la note précédente) ; autres éd. : 1662, 1665, 1668, 1675 et 1676, q.v.

*Speed, John, 1552?–1629. A prospect of the most famovs parts of the world. . . . London, printed by M.F. for W[illiam]. Humble, 1646. 1 p.l., 206 p. maps (in text) 8°

NUC(Pre–56)561:149*

Waldon has collation: 2 pts.: pt. 1, unpaged; pt. 2, 206 p. ¶ "This seems to be the earliest pocket edition of Speed's book of letterpress and maps" (cf. NUC). First(?) ed.: 1627; others: 1631, 1662, 1665, 1668, 1675, and 1676, *q.v.*

Collation de Waldon : 2 parties : la première non paginée et la deuxième comportant 206 p. ¶ « Il semble que cette édition du recueil de lettres et de cartes de Speed soit la première du genre en format de poche » (cf. NUC). Première (?) édition : 1627 ; autres éd. : 1631, 1662, 1665, 1668, 1675 et 1676, *q.v.*

1648

Remonstrance on behalf of the merchants trading to Spain, East Indies, and Newfoundland. London, 1648. [No collation.] fol.

Sabin:69584

Not in NUC, BLC, and no copy located in Canadian Union Catalogue. Possibly issued in the Selected Americana from Sabin's Dictionary *series, in microformat.* ¶ *BVAU(MF)*

Titre introuvable dans le NUC, le BLC ou le Catalogue collectif canadien. Paru probablement sur mic. dans le Selected Americana from Sabin's Dictionary. ¶ *BVAU (mic.)*

1650

Gardyner, George. A description of the new world . . . . Colophon: 1650.

This is a brief entry in NUC of the RPJCB copy. For fuller information, *see* the 1651 edition.

Courte notice du NUC tirée de l'exemplaire de la RPJCB. Pour plus de renseignements, *voir* l'édition de 1651.

1651

Gardyner, George. A description of the New World. Or, America islands and continent: and by what people those regions are now inhabited. And what places are there desolate and without inhabitants. And the bays, rivers, capes, forts, cities and their latitudes, the seas on their coasts: the trade, winds, the North-west passage, and the commerce of the English nation, as they were all in the year 1649. Faithfully described for information of such of his countrey as desire intelligence of these perticulars. By George Gardyner of Peckham, in the county of Surrey Esq. London, printed for Robert Leybourn, and are to be sold by Thomas Pirrepoint, at the Sun in S. Pauls churchyard, 1651. 8 p.l., 187 p., 1 l. 8°

NUC(Pre–56)191:315*

License, "November 18 1650. Imprimatur Nathanael Brent": 1 l. at end. ¶ "Of the Island of Newfoundland": chap. 4, p. 45–46;"Of the North-west Passage, and the Lands called Nova Britania, or Nova Framuncia": chap. 25, p. 83–90. ¶ *An entry in NUC has a brief title, and a colophon dated 1650; another entry is for a microfilm of this: Washington, D.C., Microcard Editions, 196–.* ¶ *BVAU*

Permis, « November 18 1650. Imprimatur Nathanael Brent » : 1 f. à la fin. ¶ « Of the Island of Newfoundland » : chap. 4, p. 45–46 ; « Of the North-west Passage, and the Lands called Nova Britania, or Nova Framuncia » : chap. 25, p. 83–90. ¶ *Une des notices du NUC comporte un court titre et un colophon daté de 1650 ; une autre notice porte sur l'édition sur microfilm : Washington (D.C.), Microcard Editions, 196–.* ¶ *BVAU*

1652

Heylyn, Peter, 1599–1662. Cosmographie in four bookes. Containing the chorographie and historie of the whole world, and all the principall kingdomes, provinces, seas, and isles thereof. By Peter Heylyn. London, printed for Henry Seile, and are to be sold at his shop over against Saint Dunstans Church in Fleetstreet. 1652. 4 pts. in 1 v.: 1 p.l., [9], 324; 274, [4]; 257, [1] p.; 1 l., 196, [1] p. 4 fold. col. maps. fol.

NUC(Pre–56)244:500*

Errata: [1] p. at end, followed by 17 p. of tables, unpaged. ¶ *Added t.-p., engraved.* ¶ America, Book IV, Part II, p. 95–185: "Of Estotiland" (including Terra Corterialis, New-Found-Land, Bacalaos): p. 103–05; "Of Canada": p. 106–08. Appendix, "Vnknown parts of the World," Book IV, p. 191–96: "Terra Incognita Borealis": p. 191–92. ¶ "Terra Incognita Borealis" summarizes accounts of Northern voyages, both east and west (Cabot, Frobisher, Davis, etc.) and concludes (p. 192): "I cannot choose but rank the hopes of these Northern Passages amongst those Adventures which are only commendable for the difficulties presented in them." ¶ In the 1703 edition the conclusion was reached (p. 1129): "As for any passage by the North-west, it has been so well searched, that we may conclude it highly improbable, if not impossible." ¶ *Revision and enlargement of his* Microcosmus. *Oxford, 1621, q.v.; the fourth bk., pt. 2, appears to have been issued in London, printed for Phillip Chetwind [1652?], as p. 1011–98 of another work, with a fold. map (cf. NUC(Pre–56)244:502).* ¶ *First edition*

Errata : [1] p. à la fin, suivie de 17 p. de tables non paginées. ¶ *P. de t. ajoutée, gravée.* ¶ Amérique, livre IV, partie II, p. 95–185 : « Of Estotiland » (Terra Corterialis, New-Found-Land et Bacalaos inclus) : p. 103–05 ; « Of Canada » : p. 106–08. Annexes : « Vnknown parts of the World », livre IV, p.191–96, qui comprend « Terra Incognita Borealis » : p. 191–92. ¶ « Terra Incognita Borealis » est un résumé des comptes rendus des voyages nordiques, tant vers l'est que vers l'ouest (Cabot, Frobisher, Davis, etc.) et conclut (p. 192) : « Je ne peux faire autrement que de classer les espoirs en ces passages au rang des entreprises louables en raison des difficultés qu'elles présentent. » ¶ Dans l'édition de 1703, on tire la conclusion suivante (p. 1129) : « Pour ce qui est d'un passage du Nord-Ouest, après de nombreuses expéditions, nous en venons à la conclusion qu'il est peu probable, voire impossible, qu'il existe. » ¶ *Version revue et augmentée de* Microcosmus *du même auteur, Oxford, 1621, q.v. ; il apparaît que le quatrième livre, partie 2, fut imprimé à Londres pour Phillip Chetwind [1652 ?], tout comme les p. 1011–98 d'un autre ouvrage doté d'une carte pliante (cf. NUC(Pre–56)244:502).* ¶ *Première édition parue sous le titre* Cosmographie. *Londres, 1642, q.v. Nombreuses éditions datant*

under title Cosmographie. *London, 1642,* q.v. *Numerous seventeenth-century editions up to 1703 (cf. NUC), principally as follows* (q.v.): *1657 (second ed.), 1660, 1665 (third), 1666 (fourth), 1669 (fifth), 1670 (sixth), 1674, 1677, 1682, 1702, and 1703 (seventh), the last two improved by Edmund Bohun. From the mixed make-up of dated parts and confused paginations, it seems evident that printing, collation of vols. from stock, and publication (sale) were continuous, over many years.* ¶ *BVAU · BVIPA*

du XVIIᵉ s. jusqu'à 1703 (cf. NUC), principalement celles-ci (q.v.) : *1657 (deuxième éd.), 1660, 1665 (troisième), 1666 (quatrième), 1669 (cinquième), 1670 (sixième), 1674, 1677, 1682, 1702 et 1703 (septième), les deux dernières améliorées par Edmund Bohun. La mise en page hétéroclite des parties datées et les paginations embrouillées laissent supposer que l'impression, la collation des volumes du fonds et la publication (vente) se sont étalées sur plusieurs années.* ¶ *BVAU · BVIPA*

1655

America: or An exact description of the West-Indies: more especially of those provinces which are under the dominion of the King of Spain. Faithfully represented by N.N. gent. London, printed by Ric[hard]. Hodgkinsonne for Edw[ard]. Dod, and are to be sold at the Gun in Ivy-lane. 1655. 7 p.l., 484 p., 1 l. fold. map. 8°

NUC(Pre–56)11:453*

In two parts, pt. 2 with title: America: The second part. Containing the topographicall description of the several provinces, both of the northern and southern part: with some other observations incident thereunto: by N.N. Printed by R. Hodgkinsonne for E. Dod. ¶ "Of Estotiland [Canada east of Hudson Bay, but esp. Newfoundland and Labrador], and the several Provinces which it containeth": Chap. II, p. 233–46 (including Labrador, Arctic regions and Newfoundland); "Of Canada and the

En deux parties. Partie 2 intitulée : America : The second part. Containing the topographicall description of the several provinces, both of the northern and southern part: with some other observations incident thereunto: by N.N. Printed by R. Hodgkinsonne for E. Dod. ¶ « Of Estotiland [le Canada à l'est de la Baie d'Hudson et plus particulièrement Terre-Neuve et le Labrador] and the several Provinces which it containeth » : chap. II, p. 233–46 (incluant le Labrador, les régions arctiques et Terre-Neuve) ; « Of Canada and the Countries belonging to it » : chap. III,

Countries belonging to it": Chap. III, p. 246–60 (including Nova Scotia). The map of North America shows the coast of Canada as far as "Fretum Davis" and "Groenland." ¶ *Another edition: 1657.*

p. 246–60 (incluant la Nouvelle-Écosse). Carte de l'Amérique du Nord représentant la côte canadienne jusqu'à « Fretum Davis » et même le « Groenland ». ¶ *Autre édition : 1657.*

Great Britain. Treaties, etc., 1649–1660 (Commonwealth). Articles of peace, friendship and entercourse, concluded and agreed between England & France, in a treaty at Westminster, bearing date the third of November, new stile, in the year of our Lord God, 1655. Printed and published by His Highness special command. London, printed by Henry Hills and John Field, printers to His Highness, 1655. 1 p.l., 161–78 p. fol.

NUC(Pre–56)215:500*

Waldon notes that in the BM copy, paging is not continuous with the items bound before and after this. ¶ Question of "Pemptacoet," S. Jean and Port Royal referred to commissioners: p. 177. ¶ *Reprinted in Edinburgh the same year:* see *next entry.*

Waldon note que, dans l'exemplaire du BM, la pagination ne constitue pas une suite continue avec les parties placées avant et après cet ouvrage. ¶ Question des forts de « Pemptacoet », de Saint-Jean et de Port-Royal soumise aux commissaires : p. 177. ¶ *Réimprimé à Édimbourg la même année :* voir *la notice suivante.*

***Great Britain. Treaties, etc., 1649–1660 (Commonwealth).** Articles of peace, friendship and entercourse . . . . Edinburgh, reprinted by C[hristopher]. Higgins, 1655. 12 p. 12°(?)

NUC(Pre–56)215:500*

A reprint of the first edition: *see* preceding entry.

Réimpression de la première édition : *voir* la notice précédente.

Great Britain. Treaties, etc., 1649–1660 (Commonwealth). Articles of the Treaty of Peace betwixt England and France, and a particular reference of the controversie betwixt both parties, touching the Forts of Penitacot, St. John, and Port-Royal, lately taken in America. With a Proclamation of the said Peace, by Oliver, Lord Protector. Given at Whitehall 20th of November 1655. [London? 1655?] [No pagination given.] 4°

Sabin:2151

Dr. Waldon notes only "From Kennet, p. 106. S2151," and gives the first fort as "Pemtacoct," though Sabin has this as above. "Kennet" is evidently Bibliothecae americanae primordia (London, 1713), by Bishop White Kennett, 1660–1728, the first English bibliography on America. ¶ *The articles of the treaty probably covered "peace, friendship and entercourse," as did the more general treaty concluded at Westminster, 3 November 1655 (N.S.); see the two preceding entries.*

Waldon note seulement « Tiré de Kennet, p. 106. S2151 » et donne « Pemtacoct » comme nom du premier fort, malgré l'orthographe notée dans le Sabin (plus haut). Bien entendu, « Kennet » renvoie à Bibliothecae americanae primordia (Londres, 1713), ouvrage de l'évêque White Kennett, 1660–1728, et première bibliographie anglaise portant sur l'Amérique. ¶ *Les articles du traité portaient sans doute sur « la paix, l'amitié et les relations », tout comme dans le cas du traité plus général conclu à Westminster le 3 novembre 1655 (c.g.) ; voir les deux notices précédentes.*

1656

*Abbot, George, *abp. of Canterbury/aev. de Canterbury,* **1562–1633.** A briefe description of the whole VVorld. . . . kingdomes of the same, with their academies. Written by the Most Reverend Father in God, George Abbott, late Archbishop of Canterbury. London: printed for W. Sheares, 1656. 2 p.l., 329, [1] [*i.e.* 337, (1)] p., 1 l. 12°

NUC(Pre–56)1:308*

Numbers 189–96 repeated in paging. ¶ Added t.-p. engr. by Will: Marshall. ¶ *See* 1599.

Les numéros 189 à 196 se répètent dans la pagination. ¶ P. de t. ajoutée, gravée par Will: Marshall. ¶ *Voir* 1599.

[Scott, Thomas], 1580?-1626. The Spaniards cruelty and treachery to the English in the time of peace and war, discovered, being the council of a person of honour to King James, then upon treaty of peace with them, for to insist upon a free trade in the West-Indies with some expedients for the subjecting of the Spaniards in America, to the obedience of England. Now tendered to the consideration of His Highness the Lord Protector, and his council. London. Printed by J.M. for Lodowick Lloyd and are to be sold at his shop, at the sign of the Castle in Cornhill, 1656. 2 p.l., 56 [i.e. 54] p., 1 l. 4°

NUC(Pre-56)534:259

Numbers 41-42 omitted in paging; Waldon omits the final leaf in her collation. ¶ Dedication signed: D.K. Attributed also to Daniel King (cf. NUC). ¶ Identical with his An experimentall discoverie, 1623 (q.v.), to p. 20, after which this has thirty-one lines to the page, the first ed. [having] thirty-two lines. ¶ First pub. London, 1623 (q.v.) as pt. 1 of his An experimentall discoverie of Spanish practises, q.v. for other notes; another ed. under the earlier title appeared in 1624, q.v.

Les numéros 41 et 42 manquent à la pagination ; dans sa collation, Waldon ne donne pas de feuillet final. ¶ Dédicace signée : D.K. Attribuée également à Daniel King (cf. NUC). ¶ Identique à l'ouvrage An experimentall discoverie du même auteur, 1623 (q.v.), jusqu'à la p. 20, après quoi l'ouvrage contient 31 lignes par page contrairement à la première éd. qui en compte 32. ¶ Publié pour la première fois à Londres en 1623 (q.v.) et constituant la première partie de An experimentall discoverie of Spanish practises, q.v. pour d'autres notes ; autre éd. portant le premier titre parue en 1624, q.v.

1657

*America: or An exact description of the West-Indies: . . . . London, printed by R.H. for Edw. Dod, 1657. 2 p.l., [12], 484, [2] p. fold. map, diagr. 8°

NUC(Pre-56)11:453*

See 1655.

Voir 1655.

A book of the continuation of foreign passages. That is, of the peace made between this common-wealth, & that of the United Provinces of the Netherlands, with all the articles of that peace. Apr. 5, 1654. And the articles of peace, friendship and entercourse agreed between England and Sweden, in a treaty at Upsall. May 9. 1654. As also the substance of the articles of the treaty of peace betwixt England and France. Given at White Hall the 20 of Novemb: 1655 .... London, printed by M.S. for Thomas Jenner at the south entrance of the Royall Exchange. 1657. 1 p.l., 61 p. 8 illus. (incl. 4 ports., 1 map) 4°

NUC(Pre–56)66:358

"A Proclamation of the Peace made between this Commonwealth, and France": p. 20–22. ¶ "Here followeth the substance of the Articles of the Treaty of Peace betwixt England & France. Nov. 20, 1655": p. 22–29. (Article XXV, p. 28, refers the question of forts Pemtacoet, Saint John, and Port Royal to the commissioners and arbitrators appointed to deal with prizes by Art. XXIV.)

« A Proclamation of the Peace made between this Commonwealth, and France » : p. 20–22. ¶ « Here followeth the substance of the Articles of the Treaty of Peace betwixt England & France. Nov. 20, 1655 » : p. 22–29. (L'article XXV, p. 28, renvoie la question des forts de Pemtacoet, de Saint-Jean et de Port-Royal aux commissaires et arbitres chargés de l'administration des prises en vertu de l'art. XXIV.)

*Clarke, Samuel, 1599–1683. A geographicall description of all the countries in the known world. As also of the greatest and famousest cities and fabricks which have been, or are now remaining: together with the greatest rivers, the strangest fountains, the various minerals, stones, trees, hearbs, plants, fruits, gums, &c. which are to bee found in every country. Unto which is added, a description of the rarest beasts, fowls, birds, fishes, and serpents which are least known amongst us. Collected out of the most approved authors, and from such as were eye-witnesses of most of the things contained herein. By Sa: Clarke, pastor of the church of Christ in Bennet Finck, London .... London, printed by R.I. for Thomas Newberry, at the three Lions in Cornhill, over against the Conduit. 1657. 2 p.l., 225, [8] p. fol.

NUC(Pre–56)111:358*

Half-title within ornamental border, engraved by R. Gaywood. ¶ Includes descriptions of Newfoundland and

Faux-titre encadré par une bordure décorative, gravé par R. Gaywood. ¶ Contient des descriptions de Terre-Neuve et de la

Nova Scotia: Waldon's entry notes its appearance in Clarke's *A mirrour or looking-glasse*, 1657, *see* next entry. ¶ First separate edition; *see* next entry for its publication with other works; also London, printed by T. Milbourn, 1671, *q.v.*; *see also* Clarke's *A new description of the world*. London, 1689, and other editions.

Nouvelle-Écosse ; dans sa notice, Waldon mentionne la présence de ce texte dans l'ouvrage de Clarke : *A mirrour or looking-glasse*, 1657, *voir* la notice suivante. ¶ Première édition distincte ; *voir* la notice suivante pour des renseignements sur la publication de cet ouvrage à l'intérieur d'autres recueils ; aussi imprimé à Londres par T. Milbourn en 1671, *q.v.*; *voir aussi A new description of the world*. Londres, 1689, de Clarke et autres éditions.

Clarke, Samuel, 1599–1683. A geographicall description of all the countries in the known world.... By Sa. Clarke .... London, printed by R.I. [Robert Ibbitson?] for Thomas Newberry, 1657. 2 p.l., 225, [8] p. fol. (In his *A mirrour or looking-glasse*.... 3d ed. London, 1657.)

NUC(Pre–56)III:358*

Added illus. t.-p. ¶ *Also pub. separately:* see *preceding entry.* ¶ "Newfoundland described": p. 184–89; "New-Scotland [Nova Scotia] described": p. 185. New-Scotland is considered an island. Norumbega [east coast of North America] and New-France are mentioned as provinces of "Mexicana" but not described. ¶ See *preceding entry.*

Ajout d'une p. de t. illustrée. ¶ *Aussi publié séparément :* voir *la notice précédente.* ¶ « Newfound-land described » : p. 184–89 ; « New-Scotland [Nouvelle-Écosse] described » : p. 185. On croit que la Nouvelle-Écosse est une île. On fait mention de Norumbega [côte est de l'Amérique du Nord] et de la Nouvelle France en tant que provinces de « Mexicana », mais on n'en donne pas de description. ¶ Voir *la notice précédente.*

*Heylyn, Peter, 1599–1662. Cosmographie in four books. . . . The 2d ed. . . . London, printed for H[enry]. Seile, 1657. 7 p.l., 1095 [*i.e.* 1099] p., 10 l. 4 maps. fol.

NUC(Pre–56)244:500*

Added illus. t.-p. signed: Rob. Vaughan sculp. ¶ Many pages wrongly numbered. ¶ Maps dated 1652. ¶ In six pts., each with special t.-p. Bks. 1–2 have imprint: London, printed by E.C. for H. Seile, 1656–57. Bk. 3, bk. 4, pt. 1, and "An appendix" have imprint: London, printed for H. Seile, 1656. Bk. 4, pt. 2 has imprint: London, printed for P. Chetvvind. NUC also lists a variant from a different setting of type, with undated maps; also other 1657 entries, which may be variants; as well as a 1656 entry, but this has t.-p. lacking. ¶ Revised and enl. from his *Microcosmus*. Oxford, 1621, *q.v.* ¶ First pub. under this title: London, 1642 (*q.v.*); also pub. London, 1652, *q.v.* for other notes.

Ajout d'une p. de t. illustrée et signée : Rob. Vaughan sculp. ¶ Nombreuses pages mal numérotées. ¶ Cartes datées de 1652. ¶ En 6 parties avec chacune une p. de t. individuelle. Adresse bibliographique des livres 1 et 2 : London, printed by E. C. for H. Seile, 1656–57. Le livre 3, le livre 4, partie 1 et l'appendice ont comme adresse bibliographique : London, printed for H. Seile, 1656. Le livre 4, partie 2 a comme adresse bibliographique: London, printed for P. Chetvvind. Le NUC donne aussi une autre version dont le jeu de caractères est différent et qui contient des cartes non datées ; autres notices de 1657 qui pourraient être des variantes ; notice de 1656 où la p. de t. manque. ¶ Version revue et augmentée de *Microcosmus* du même auteur. Oxford, 1621, *q.v.* ¶ Publié pour la première fois sous ce titre à Londres en 1642, (*q.v.*) ; publié également à Londres en 1652, *q.v.* pour d'autres notes.

1658

Fage, Robert. A description of the whole world, with some general rules touching the use of the globe, wherein is contained the situation of several countries. Their particular and distinct governments, religions, arms, and degrees of honour used among them. Very delightful to be read in so small a volume. By Robert Fage, Esq. . . . London, printed by J[ohn]. Owsley, and sold by Peter Stent . . ., 1658. 70, [2] p. fold. map, chart. 8°

NUC(Pre–56)165:487*

List of books: [2] p. at end. ¶ The parts of America are enumerated, but there is no real description of Canada (p. 68). The map shows a number of places in Canada. Because of this slight interest, the other editions are not listed separately [except as a reference from *Cosmography*, 1667] in this bibliography. It is listed here as having some interest as negative evidence. [Sabin notes: "Mostly related to America."] ¶ *First edition; later editions appeared as:* Cosmography or, A description of the whole world. *London, 1663 (cf. Sabin:23646), 1667, and 1671 (cf. NUC).*

Liste de livres : [2] p. à la fin. ¶ On y énumère les régions américaines, sans toutefois fournir de description du Canada (p. 68). La carte illustre un certain nombre de localités canadiennes. Étant donné la valeur plus ou moins significative de cet ouvrage, les autres éditions ne sont pas énumérées séparément dans cette bibliographie [sauf comme renvoi de *Cosmography*, 1667]. Ce titre est donné ici parce qu'il représente un certain intérêt en tant que preuve négative. [D'après le Sabin : « Plutôt d'intérêt américain ».] ¶ *Première édition ; les éditions ultérieures parurent sous le titre* Cosmography or, A description of the whole world. *Londres, 1663 (cf. Sabin : 23646), 1667 et 1671 (cf. NUC).*

*Gorges, Ferdinando, 1630–1718. America painted to the life. London, printed for Nath[aniel]. Brook, 1658. 4 pts., pts. 2 and 3; pts. 1 and 4 are dated 1659, *q.v.* for full entry and notes.

NUC(Pre–56)207:273*

Pt. 2 is entitled: *A briefe narration of the originall undertakings of the advancement of plantations. . . .*

Partie 2 intitulée *A briefe narration of the originall undertakings of the advancement of plantations. . . .*

*Gorges, Ferdinando, 1630–1718. A brief narration of the originall undertakings of the advancement of plantations . . . .

See preceding entry.

Voir la notice précédente.

1659

Gorges, Ferdinando, 1630–1718. America painted to the life. The history of the Spaniards proceedings in America, their conquests of the Indians, and of their civil wars among themselves. From Columbus his first discovery, to these later times. As also, of the original undertakings of the advancement of plantations into those parts with a perfect relation of our English discoveries, shewing their beginning, progress and continuance, from the year 1628 to 1658. . . . More especially, an absolute narrative of the north parts of America, and of the discoveries and plantations of our English . . . . Publisht by Ferdinando Gorges. London, printed for Nath[aniel]. Brook at the Angel in Cornhil, 1659. 4 pts.: [6], 51 p.; 1 p.l., 57 p.; 1 p.l., [2], 236, [4] p.; 1 p.l., [2], 52, [20] p. front., fold. map. 4°

NUC(Pre–56)207:273*

Pts. 2 and 3 are dated 1658; pt. 2 has title: A briefe narration of the original undertakings. . . . ¶ Lists of books: [4] p. at end of pt. 3; [3] p. at end of pt. 4, following a [17] p. index. ¶ Discovery of Newfoundland, Cartier's discovery of the "Island of the Assumption" in the "River Canada": pt. 1, p. 2; "Nova

Parties 2 et 3 datées de 1658 ; titre de la partie 2 : A briefe narration of the original undertakings. . . . ¶ Liste de livres : [4] p. à la fin de la partie 3 ; [3] p. à la fin de la partie 4, à la suite d'un index de [17] p. ¶ Découverte de Terre-Neuve ; Cartier découvre « l'Ile de l'Assomption » dans la « Rivière Canada » : partie 1, p. 2 ; « Nova Francia » :

Francia": pt. 1, p. 15–16. ¶ *First edition; pt. 2 reprinted as* A brief narration . . ., *Portland, Me., 1847 (in* Collections of the Maine Hist. Soc., *[1st ser.] vol. 2, [pt. 2], p. [v]–xiv, 15–71), and reprinted again by the Maine Hist. Soc., Portland, 1902 (cf. NUC); reproduced in MF, Ann Arbor, Mich., University Microfilms, 1941 (American Culture series, reel 6.61).*

partie 1, p. 15–16. ¶ *Première édition ; partie 2 réimprimée sous le titre* A brief narration. . . *à Portland (Me.), 1847 (dans les* Collections of the Maine Hist. Soc., *[1ʳᵉ collection] vol. 2, [partie 2], p. [v]–xiv, 15–71), et réimprimée de nouveau par la Maine Hist. Soc. à Portland en 1902 (cf. NUC) ; reproduction sur mic., Ann Arbor (Mich.), University Microfilms, 1941 (collection American Culture, bobine 6.61).*

Petau, Denis, 1583–1652. A geographical description of the world . . . . London, printed by John Streater, 1659. [2], 154, [5] p. map. fol.

Waldòn cites BM and Sabin, but both list as in next entry.

Index: [5] p. at end. ¶ Part 2 of his *The history of the world (q.v.,* next entry), with special t.-p. and separate pagination.

Index : [5] p. à la fin. ¶ La deuxième partie de son ouvrage *The history of the world (q.v.,* notice suivante), avec p. de t. spéciale et pagination distincte.

*Petau, Denis, 1583–1652. The history of the vvorld; or, An account of time. Compiled by the learned Dionisius Petavius. And continued by others, to the year of our Lord, 1659. together with A geographical description of Europe, Asia, Africa, and America. London, printed by J[ohn]. Streater, 1659. 4 p.l., [807] p. port., fold. map. fol.

NUC(Pre–56)452:413

BLC(to 1975)255:453 notes that the work is in two parts, and provides the format, folio; NUC indicates "many errors in paging," and "To the reader" signed "R.P.," who is

Dans la notice du BLC(to 1975)255:453 on indique que l'ouvrage est divisé en 2 parties et on en donne le format : in-folio ; le NUC signale de nombreuses erreurs de pagination et la dédicace « To the reader » signée

apparently responsible for the translation, continuation, and the "Geographical discription." The following are from Waldon's notes to *A geographical description* (preceding entry). ¶ *Encyclopedia Britannica*: Petau, Denys, better known as Dionysius Petavius, which is Sabin's entry. ¶ Norumbega [Eastern Canada]; New France; Terra Corterialis [Newfoundland]; Estotiland [Canada east of Hudson Bay]: p. 159–60, *i.e.*, p. 139–40. ¶ Another edition: *see* next entry. ¶ BVIP

« R. P. », à qui l'on doit probablement la traduction, la suite et la partie « Geographical discription ». Les renseignements suivants sont tirés des notes de Waldon sur *A geographical description* (notice précédente) : ¶ *Encyclopedia Britannica* : Petau, Denys, mieux connu sous le nom de Dionysius Petavius, ce qui correspond à la notice du Sabin. ¶ Norumbega [Est du Canada], Nouvelle France ; Terra Corterialis [Terre-Neuve] ; Estotiland [le Canada à l'est de la Baie d'Hudson] : p. 159–60, *c.-à-d.*, p. 139–40. ¶ Autre édition : *voir* la notice suivante. ¶ BVIP

Petau, Denis, 1583–1652. The history of the world. London: Humphrey Mosely. 1659. [8], 610 p. table, [34], Geographical description, [2], 154, [5] p. fol.

Sabin:61175*

This is the same collation as for the Streater ed., preceding.

Même collation que pour l'édition Streater, précédente.

Porter, Thomas, *fl.* 1659. A compendious view, or cosmographical, and geographical description of the whole world .... By Tho. Porter. [London] Are to be sold by Robert Walton, at the Globe and Compass, in S. Paul's Churchyard, on the North-side. 1659. 2 p.l., 138, [2, maps] p. front., fold. map. 8°

NUC(Pre–56)466:302

Estotiland [Labrador]; Terra-Corterealis [Newfoundland-Labrador]; Canada; New France; New-Scotland

Estotiland [Labrador], Terra-Corterealis [Terre-Neuve et Labrador], Canada, Nouvelle France, New-Scotland [Nouvelle-

[Nova Scotia]; Norumbega [Nova Scotia-New Brunswick]: p. 79; Newfoundland: p. 90.

Écosse], Norumbega [Nouvelle-Écosse et Nouveau-Brunswick] : p. 79 ; Terre-Neuve: p. 90.

1660

*Heylyn, Peter, 1599–1662. Cosmographie in foure bookes contayning the chorographie & historie of the whole world .... By Peter Heylyn. London, printed for P[hilip]. Chetwind, 1660. 4 v. in 5. 4 fold. maps. fol.

NUC(Pre–56)244:500*

Appendix has imprint: London, printed for P. Chetwinde, 1662. ¶ Paging irregular; v. 4, pt. 2: numbers 1089–95 repeated in paging. ¶ Revised and enl. from his *Microcosmus*. Oxford, 1621, *q.v.* ¶ First edition under this title: London, 1642; also pub. London, 1652, *q.v.* for other notes and editions. Part of this, the fourth bk., pt. 2, "containing the chorography & historie of America," was pub. separately, London, printed for P. Chetvvind [166-?]: cf. NUC(Pre–56) 244:502.

Adresse bibliographique de l'annexe : London, printed for P. Chetwinde, 1662. ¶ Pagination irrégulière : dans la partie 2 du vol. 4, les numéros 1089–95 se répètent. ¶ Version revue et augmentée de *Microcosmus* du même auteur. Oxford, 1621, *q.v.* ¶ Première édition parue sous ce titre : Londres, 1642 ; publ. aussi à Londres en 1652, *q.v.* pour d'autres notes et éditions. Une partie de cet ouvrage, la deuxième du quatrième livre, « containing the chorography & historie of America », fut publiée séparément à Londres pour P. Chetvvind [166- ?] : cf. NUC(Pre–56)244:502.

1662

*Speed, John,** 1552?–1629. A prospect of the most famous parts of the world. *Viz.* Asia . . . Africa . . . Europe . . . America . . . . Together with all the provinces, counties, and shires, contained in that large Theater of Great Britaines empire . . . . London, printed by M[athew]. and S[amuel]. Simmons, and are to be sold by R[oger]. Rea the elder and R[oger]. Rea the younger, 1662. 2 p.l., 42 numb. l., 43–44, [8] p., 94 [*i.e.* 97] numb. l., [2] p., 99–126 numb. l., [2] p., 131–52 numb. l., [2] p., 137–46 numb. l., [10] p. incl. double maps, coat of arms. fol.

NUC(Pre–56)561:150*

"The Theatre of the empire of Great Britaine," which has special engr. t.-p., dated 1650, bound before the general t.-p., is in four parts; pts. 2–4 have special t.-p.'s, dated 1662 (cf. NUC). ¶ First(?) ed.: 1627; other eds.: 1631, 1646 (to which this title is similar), 1665, 1668, 1675, and 1676, *q.v.* NUC has two other entries for this edition, with the same title and imprint, but variant collations; these may be examples of the variation in the composition of atlases with the same title at this time.

« The Theatre of the empire of Great Britaine », ouvrage daté de 1650, ayant sa propre p. de t. gravée et placée avant la p. de t. générale, est formé de quatre parties ; les parties 2 à 4 ont des p. de t. individuelles et sont datées de 1662 (cf. NUC). ¶ Première édition (?) : 1627 ; autres éd. : 1631, 1646 (dont le titre est semblable), 1665, 1668, 1675 et 1676, *q.v.* Le NUC donne 2 autres notices pour cette édition avec le même titre et la même adresse bibliographique, la collation étant différente : ces derniers pourraient constituer des exemples de variations dans la composition des atlas de même titre de l'époque.

1664

*Abbot, George, *abp. of Canterbury/aev. de Canterbury,* 1562–1633. A briefe description of the whole world. . . . kingdoms of the same, with their academies. . . . Written by the Reverend Father in God George Abbot, late Archbishop of Canterbury. The fifth eddition [*sic* in NUC]. London, printed for Margaret Sheares, and J. Playfere, 1664. 2 p.l., 340 p. 12°(?)

NUC(Pre–56)1:308*

Added t.-p. engr., with imprint: Printed for W. Sheares. ¶ New France and Northwest Passage: p. 298–301. ¶ *See* 1599.

P. de t. ajoutée et gravée, avec l'adresse bibliographique suivante : Printed for W. Sheares. ¶ Nouvelle France et passage du Nord-Ouest : p. 298–301. ¶ *Voir* 1599.

1665

*Heylyn, Peter, 1599–1662. Cosmographie in four books. Containing the chorographie and historie of the whole world . . . . 3d ed. London, printed for Philipp Chetwind, 1665. 1095 p. fold. maps. fol.

NUC(Pre–56)244:500*

Added illustrated t.-p., engraved: cosmographie. . . . Published for Philip Chetwind, 1660. ¶ Four bks. in five pts., each with special t.-p. Bk. 4, pt. 1 has date 1662, pt. 2 without date (though this may refer only to copy described in NUC). Evidently printing, collation from stock, and publication (sale) were continuous. ¶ Revised and enl. from his *Microcosmus*. Oxford, 1621, *q.v.* ¶ First edition under this title: London, 1642; also

P. de t. illustrée, ajoutée et gravée : cosmographie. . . . Published for Philip Chetwind, 1660. ¶ Quatre livres divisés en 5 parties ayant chacune une p. de t. individuelle. La partie 1 du livre 4 est datée de 1662, mais la partie 2 n'est pas datée (cependant, il est possible qu'elle ne renvoie qu'à l'exemplaire décrit dans le NUC). Il est évident que l'impression, la collation des volumes du fonds et la publication (vente) se sont étalées sur plusieurs années. ¶ Version revue et augmentée de *Microcosmus* du même

pub. London, 1652, *q.v.* for other notes and editions.

auteur. Oxford, 1621, *q.v.* ¶ Première édition sous ce titre, Londres, 1642 ; publiée aussi à Londres en 1652, *q.v.* pour d'autres notes et éditions.

*Speed, John, 1552?–1629. A prospect of the most famous parts of the world. London, printed by M.S. for Roger Rea, 1665. 206 p. maps 8°(?)

NUC(Pre–56)561:150*

First(?) ed.: London, 1627; other eds.: 1631 (*q.v.* for notes), 1646, 1662, 1668, 1675, and 1676, *q.v.*

Première édition (?) : Londres, 1627 ; autres éd. : 1631 (*q.v.* pour notes), 1646, 1662, 1668, 1675, et 1676, *q.v.*

1666

*Heylyn, Peter, 1599–1662. Cosmographie, in four books. Containing the chorographie and historie of the whole world . . . . With an accurate and an approved index of all the kingdoms, provinces, countries . . . much wanted and desired in the former, and now annexed to this last impression, revised and corrected by the author himself immediately before his death . . . . London, printed for Anne Seile, 1666. 7 p.l., 998 p., 1 l., 999–1088 p., 1 l., 1089–95, [39] p. 4 fold. maps. fol.

NUC(Pre–56)244:500*

Errors in paging. ¶ Added illus. t.-p., engraved: Cosmographie . . . . The 3d ed. corr. and enl. by the author. London, printed for Anne Seile, 1665. ¶ Bks. 1–3, the two pts. of bk. 4, and the Appendix, have each a special t.-p. dated 1665. ¶ The fourth ed. (cf. Sabin), being the third ed. (1665) with

Erreurs de pagination. ¶ P. de t. ajoutée, illustrée et gravée : Cosmographie . . . . The 3d ed. corr. and enl. by the author. London, printed for Anne Seile, 1665. ¶ Les livres 1 à 3, les 2 parties du livre 4 et l'annexe ont chacun une p. de t. individuelle datée de 1665. ¶ La quatrième éd. (cf. Sabin) est, en fait, pareille à la troisième (1665), mais elle

a new t.-p. and "an alphabetical and exact table [etc.]" added to it. A similar work, with variant collation, and pub. date "1666[–67]," and another with variant collation only, appear in NUC. ¶ Rev. and enl. from his *Microcosmus*. Oxford, 1621, *q.v.* ¶ First ed. under this title: London, 1642; also pub. London, 1652, *q.v.* for other notes and editions.

comporte une nouvelle p. de t. et « une table alphabétique détaillée [etc.] ». Le NUC donne un ouvrage semblable dont la collation est différente, et qui a été publié en « 1666[–67] », et un autre de collation différente seulement. ¶ Version revue et augmentée de *Microcosmus* du même auteur. Oxford, 1621, *q.v.* ¶ Première édition publiée sous ce titre à Londres en 1642 ; publ. aussi à Londres en 1652, *q.v.* pour d'autres notes et éditions.

1667

*Fage, Robert. Cosmography or, A description of the whole world. London, printed by S[arah]. Griffin for John Overton, 1667. 4 p.l., 3–166 p. front. 8°(?)

NUC(Pre–56)165:487*

First edition pub. as: *A description of the whole world*. London, 1658, *q.v.* for other notes and editions.

Première édition publiée sous le titre *A description of the whole world*. Londres, 1658, *q.v.* pour d'autres notes et éditions.

Great Britain. Sovereigns, etc. 1660–1685 (Charles II). By the King. A proclamation for publishing the Peace between His Majesty, and the French King. Given at our Court at Whitehall the 24th day of August, in the nineteenth year of our reign. God save the King. In the Savoy, [London] printed by the assigns of John Bill and Christopher Barker, printers to the King's most Excellent Majesty. 1667. Broadside. fol.

NUC(Pre–56)215:368*

Royal arms at head of title. ¶ The king is Charles II, and this concerns the Treaty of Breda (July 1667), which ended the second of the so-called Dutch Wars, 1665–67, the result of commercial rivalry. The French under Louis XIV had declared war on England in 1666, but they took little part in the war; under the Treaty, Acadia (which included present Nova Scotia and New Brunswick) was restored to France, it having been taken by a Cromwellian expedition in 1654. ¶ For another edition, Edinburgh, 1667, see next entry.

Titre orné des armoiries royales. ¶ Le roi dont il est ici question est Charles II et cet ouvrage se penche sur le traité de Bréda (juillet 1667) qui mit fin à la deuxième des guerres hollandaises, celle de 1665–1667, provoquée par la rivalité commerciale. Les Français, sous Louis XIV, avaient déclaré la guerre à l'Angleterre en 1666, mais ne s'engagèrent que très peu dans ce conflit ; en vertu du traité, l'Acadie (formée des provinces actuelles de la Nouvelle-Écosse et du Nouveau-Brunswick), de prise qu'elle avait été par une expédition de Cromwell en 1654, fut rendue à la France. ¶ Autre édition : Édimbourg, 1667, voir la notice suivante.

*Great Britain, Sovereigns, etc., 1660–1685 (Charles II). A proclamation, for publishing the Peace between His Majesty and the French King. Edinburgh, printed by Even Tyler, printer to the Kings most Excellent Majesty, 1667. Broadside. fol.

NUC(Pre–56)215:368*

"Given at our court at Whitehall, the twenty fourth day of August, one thousand six hundred and sixty seven . . . ." ¶ *See* preceding entry for other notes.

« Remise à notre cour de Whitehall, le vingt-quatrième jour du mois d'août en l'an de grâce mil six cent soixante-sept. . . ». ¶ *Voir* autres notes à la notice précédente.

Great Britain. Treaties, etc., 1660–1685 (Charles II). Articles of peace & alliance, between the most serene and mighty Prince Charles II. by the grace of God King of England, Scotland, France and Ireland, Defender of the Faith, &c. and the most serene and mighty Prince Louis XIV. the most Christian King. Concluded the 21/31 day of July, 1667. Published by His Majesties command. [London] In the savoy, printed by the assigns of John Bill and Christopher Barker, printers to the Kings most Excellent Majesty. [1667.] 1 p.l., p. 35–46. 4°

NUC(Pre–56)215:501

Waldon has collation: p. [33]–46. ¶ The peace was sealed by the Treaty of Breda (31 July 1667), ending the Second Dutch War, 1665–67, in which the Dutch had been joined by France in 1666. ¶ Nova Scotia was given to France.

Collation de Waldon : p. [33]–46. ¶ La paix fut conclue par le traité de Bréda (31 juillet 1667) qui mit fin à la seconde guerre hollandaise de 1665–1667 et au cours de laquelle la France s'était alliée à la Hollande en 1666. ¶ La Nouvelle-Écosse fut alors donnée à la France.

1668

*[Child, Sir **Josiah**], 1630–1699. Brief observations concerning trade, and interest of money. By J.C. London, printed for Elizabeth Calvert [etc.] 1668. 38 p. 16°(?)

NUC(Pre–56)106:636*

Canadian content unknown, but this was later pub. under the title *A new discourse of trade*. London, 1692 (etc.), *q.v.* ¶ Another ed.: London, E. Calvert, 1668. 20 p. Sm. 4° (cf. NUC).

Les titres portant sur le Canada ne sont pas connus. Ouvrage publié de nouveau quelques années plus tard sous le titre *A new discourse of trade*. Londres, 1692 (etc.), *q.v.* ¶ Autre éd. : Londres, E. Calvert, 1668. 20 p., petit in–4°(cf. NUC).

[Speed, John], 1552?–1629. A prospect of the most famous parts of the world. Viz. Asia, Africa, Europe, America .... London, printed for Roger Rea, 1668. 1 l., 206 p. incl. maps. 8°

NUC(Pre–56)561:149*

Maps are by Petrus Kaerius; two are dated 1646. ¶ Same as the 1646 edition, q.v. for fuller title; first(?) ed.: 1627; others: 1631, 1662, 1665, 1675, and 1676, q.v.

Cartes exécutées par Petrus Kaerius; deux d'entre elles sont datées de 1646. ¶ Même édition que celle de 1646, q.v. pour un titre plus complet; première édition (?) : 1627; autres éd. : 1631, 1662, 1665, 1675 et 1676, q.v.

1669

*Great Britain. Laws, statutes, etc., 1625–1649 (Charles I). A commission for the well-governing of our people inhabiting in New-foundland; or, trafficking in bays, creeks, or fresh rivers there. [London?] 1669. 2 p. 4°

Casey:34

First pub. 1634, *q.v.* for other variants and editions.

Publié pour la première fois en 1634, *q.v.* pour d'autres variantes et éditions.

*Heylyn, Peter, 1599–1662. Cosmographie in four books. ... revised and corrected by the author himself immediately before his death .... London, printed for Anne Seile: and are to be sold by George Sawbridg, Thomas Williams, Henry Broom, Thomas Basset, and Richard Chiswell, 1669. 4 v. in 1. 4 fold. maps. fol.

NUC(Pre–56)244:501*

Title in red and black. ¶ Added t.-p. engraved: *Cosmographie in foure books .... The 5th edition. Corrected and*

Titre en rouge et noir. ¶ Page de titre ajoutée, gravée : *Cosmographie in foure books .... The 5th edition. Corrected and inlarged by*

inlarged by the author. London, printed for Anne Seile over against St. Dunstans church in Fleetstreete, 1669. ¶ Bks. 1–3, the two pts. of bk. 4, and the Appendix, have each a special t.-p., with date 1668 for bks. 2–4. ¶ Revised and enl. from his *Microcosmus*. Oxford, 1621, *q.v.* ¶ First edition under this title: London, 1642; also pub. London, 1652, *q.v.* for other notes and editions. The fourth bk., pt. 2, was also pub. separately in 1668, cf. NUC(Pre–56) 244:502.

the author. London, printed for Anne Seile over against St. Dunstans church in Fleetstreete, 1669. ¶ Les livres 1 à 3, les 2 parties du livre 4 et l'annexe ont chacun une p. de t. individuelle. Les livres 2 à 4 sont datés de 1668. ¶ Version revue et augmentée de *Microcosmus* du même auteur. Oxford, 1621, *q.v.* ¶ Première édition sous ce titre : Londres, 1642 ; publ. à Londres en 1652, *q.v.* pour d'autres notes et éditions. La partie 2 du quatrième livre fut aussi publiée séparément en 1668, cf. NUC(Pre–56)244:502.

1670

Blome, Richard, *d./déc.* 1705. A geographical description of the four parts of the world taken from the notes and workes of the famous Monsieur Sanson, geographer to the French King, and other eminent travellers and authors. To which are added the commodities, coyns, weights, and measures of the chief places of traffick in the world; compared with those of England, (or London) as to the trade thereof. Also, a treatise of travel, and another of traffick . . . . The whole illustrated with variety of useful and delightful mapps and figures. By Richard Blome . . . . London, printed by T.N. for R. Blome, and are also sold by . . . [three others], 1670. 5 p.l., [461] p. col. plates, 25 fold. maps. fol.

NUC(Pre–56)61:492*

Five parts, separately paged, but with continuous signatures. [Waldon gives 2 p.l. and separate paging for each part, in her collation.] ¶ *Title in red and black.* America is treated in Book IV; Canada or New-France [New-Fovnd-Land, Estotiland]: p. 5–7. "A New Mapp of America Septentrionale, designed by Monsieur Sanson,

En cinq parties, paginées séparément, mais de signature continue. [Waldon signale 2 f. l. et une nouvelle pagination pour chaque partie dans sa collation.] ¶ *Titre en noir et rouge.* Le livre 4 traite de l'Amérique ; Canada ou Nouvelle France [New-Fovnd-Land, Estotiland] : p. 5–7. « A New Mapp of America Septentrionale, designed by Monsieur Sanson, Geographer to the

Geographer to the French King, and Rendred into English, and Illustrated by Richard Blome. By his Majesties Especiall Command. London, printed for Richard Blome, 1669.": opposite p. 2. ¶ "Monsieur Sanson in his Geographical Tables hath divided this America Septentrionalis into Canadiana, and Mexicana. Under the name of Canadiana is understood that part of America which is about Canada, where the English, French Hollanders, Danes and Swedes have divers Colonies: And under the name of Mexicana, that part of America which the King of Spain doth almost alone possess, and where he hath established abundance of Colonies, subdividing Canadiana into the Arctick Lands, and Canada or new France; and Mexicana into New Mexico, and Mexico or new Spain." ¶ *First edition; another entry in NUC differs only in the collation: 6 p.l., [472] p.; a so-called second part appeared in 1680 (q.v.). ¶ OKQ · ACG · BVIP*

French King, and Rendred into English, and Illustrated by Richard Blome. By his Majesties Especiall Command. London, printed for Richard Blome, 1669. » : en regard de la p. 2. ¶ « Dans ses relevés géographiques, M. Sanson divise l'America Septentrionalis en deux parties : Canadiana et Mexicana. Le Canadiana comprend la partie de l'Amérique englobant à peu près le Canada et où Anglais, Hollandais, Français, Danois et Suédois possèdent plusieurs colonies, tandis que le Mexicana représente la partie de l'Amérique dont le roi d'Espagne est presque l'unique possesseur et où il a établi nombre de colonies. Il subdivise le territoire du Canadiana en deux régions : les terres arctiques et le Canada ou Nouvelle France, et celui du Mexicana en deux parties également : le Nouveau Mexique et le Mexique ou Nouvelle-Espagne. » ¶ *Première édition ; une autre notice du NUC ne diffère que par sa collation : 6 f. l., [472] p. ; une deuxième partie aurait été publiée en 1680 (q.v.). ¶ OKQ · ACG · BVIP*

---

*Heylyn, Peter, 1599–1662. Cosmographie in four books. Containing the chorography and history of the whole world .... Rev., corr. and inlarged by the author himself immediately before his death .... London, printed for P[hilip]. Chetwind, 1670. 8 p.l., 1095 (*i.e.* 1099), [10] p., 1 l., [28] p., 1 l. 4 fold. maps. fol.

NUC(Pre–56)244:501*

Title in red and black. ¶ Added t.-p., engraved: Cosmographie .... The 3d ed. corr. & inlarged by the author. London, P. Chetwind, 1670. (The third ed. was pub. London, 1665, *q.v.*)

Titre en noir et rouge. ¶ P. de t. ajoutée, gravée : Cosmographie .... The 3d ed. corr. & inlarged by the author. London, P. Chetwind, 1670. (La troisième édition a été publiée à Londres en 1665, *q.v.*) ¶ La sixième

¶ The sixth ed., being the third ed. with a new t.-p. and "an alphabetical and exact table [etc.]" added to it. ¶ Bks. 1–3, the two pts. of bk. 4, and the Appendix each have a special t.-p., dated respectively: 1665; bk. 4, pt. 1, 1662, pt. 2, no date; Appendix, 1667. ¶ Paging irregular: nos. 745–60, 893–98,959–60 omitted; nos. 921–32, 1089–95 repeated in paging. ¶ Rev. and enl. from his *Microcosmus*. Oxford, 1621, *q.v.* ¶ First ed. under this title: London, 1642; also pub. London, 1652, *q.v.* for other notes and editions. NUC also has another entry dated 1670, with collation: "p. (14); (1110 paged 1095); (40); 4 maps," and no edition statement.

éd. se trouve formée de la troisième éd., plus une nouvelle p. de t. et une « table alphabétique détaillée [etc.] ». ¶ Les livres 1 à 3, les 2 parties du livre 4 et l'annexe ont chacun une p. de t. individuelle et sont datés respectivement de : 1665 ; livre 4, partie 1 : 1662 ; partie 2 non datée ; annexe : 1667. ¶ Pagination irrégulière : les n°s 745–60, 893–98,959–60 ont été omis ; les n°s 921–32, 1089–95 se répètent. ¶ Version revue et augmentée de *Microcosmus* du même auteur. Oxford, 1621, *q.v.* ¶ Première édition sous ce titre à Londres en 1642 ; publ. aussi à Londres en 1652, *q.v.* pour d'autres notes et éditions. On retrouve aussi une autre notice du NUC pour 1670 et dont la collation est la suivante : « p. (14) ; (p. 1110 numérotée 1095) ; (40) ; 4 cartes », sans note d'édition.

Montanus, Arnoldus, 1625?–1683. America .... London, 1670.

See Ogilby, John. America .... London, 1670.

Voir Ogilby, John. America .... Londres, 1670.

*Ogilby, John, 1600–1676. America: being an accurate description of the New World; containing the original of the inhabitants; the remarkable voyages thither: the conquest of the vast empires of Mexico and Peru, their ancient and later wars. With their several plantations, many, and rich islands; their cities, fortresses, towns, temples, mountains, and rivers: their habits, customs, manners, and religions, their peculiar plants, beasts, birds, and serpents. Collected and translated from most authentick authors, and augmented with later observations; illustrated with notes, and adorn'd with peculiar maps, and proper sculptures, by John Ogilby, Esq; .... London: printed by Tho. Johnson for the author ... 1670. [6], 629 p. plates, maps, plans. fol.

Sabin:50088

Sabin has this under Montanus, describing this English translation as an impudent plagiarism. ¶ Another issue: 1671, under Ogilby, *q.v.* for other notes.

Sabin donne ce titre sous Montanus, qualifiant cette traduction anglaise de plagiat éhonté. ¶ Autre tirage : 1671, sous Ogilby, *q.v.* pour d'autres notes.

Young, F. Remarks on the debate on the Newfoundland fishery. London, 1670.

"From C.H.C., p. 883"

No further information discovered.

Aucun autre renseignement.

Peter Heylyn. *Cosmographie in four books.* London/Londres, 1670.

1671

Clarke, Samuel, 1599–1683. A geographical description of all the countries in the known world .... Whereunto are now added, an alphabetical description of all the counties in England, and Wales; and of the four chiefest English plantations in America. Together with the rarest beasts, fowls, birds, fishes, and serpents .... Collected out of the most approved authors .... By Sa. Clarke .... London, printed by T[homas]. Milbourn for R[obert]. Clavel, T[homas]. Passinger [etc.], 1671. 1 p.l., 298, 85, 35 p. fol. (In his *A mirror or looking-glass* ... 4th ed. London, 1671. v. 1, [pt. 2–3].)

NUC(Pre–56)111:358*

Newfound-Land; New-Scotland: p. 287–119[?]. ¶ *"A true, and faithful account of the four chiefest plantations of the English in America.... Collected by Samuel Clarke .... London"* (printed for R. Clavel [etc.], 1670): *85, 35 p.* at end. ¶ *Originally published separately in 1657 (q.v., above), with variant title. Waldon also notes Sabin:13444, a separate edition, London, 1670–71, fol., with title not identical with the 1657 edition nor with the 1671 above.*

Newfound-Land ; New-Scotland : p. 287–119 [?]. ¶ *« Une description véridique et fidèle des quatre principales colonies des Anglais en Amérique .... Renseignements recueillis par Samuel Clarke .... Londres »* (imprimé pour R. Clavel [etc.] en 1670) : *85, 35 p. à la fin.* ¶ *À l'origine, publié séparément, 1657, (q.v. plus haut) sous un titre différent. Waldon signale également une édition distincte, le Sabin:13444, Londres, 1670–1671, fol., dont le titre diffère des éditions de 1657 et de 1671 plus haut.*

Meriton, George, 1634–1711. A geographical description of the world. With a brief account of the several empires, dominions, and parts thereof.... London, printed for William Leake, at the Crown in Fleet-Street, between the two Temple-gates, 1671. 9 p.l., 352, [6] p. 12°

NUC(Pre–56)377:266*

Added t.-p., engraved and illustrated. ¶ Format from Arber, 1:66. ¶ In Waldon's notes to the third ed., 1679, this work has references to Norumbega (roughly, the east coast of North America north of

P. de t. ajoutée, gravée et illustrée. ¶ Format tiré de Arber, 1:66. ¶ D'après les notes de Waldon sur la troisième éd. de 1679, cet ouvrage fait mention de Norumbega (en gros, la côte est de l'Amérique du Nord au nord de la Floride, mais

Florida, but esp. Nova Scotia and New England), Nova Francia (New France), Terra Corterealis (probably eastern Newfoundland), Estotiland (Canada east of Hudson Bay, esp. Labrador), and Newfoundland. ¶ First edition; second ed., enl. and amended, 1674, third ed. 1679, q.v.¶ OH(MF) · OOU(MF) · BVIP(MF)

plus spécialement la Nouvelle-Écosse et la Nouvelle-Angleterre), de Nova Francia (Nouvelle France), de Terra Corterealis (probablement la partie est de Terre-Neuve), d'Estotiland (le Canada à l'est de la Baie d'Hudson, plus particulièrement le Labrador) et de Terre-Neuve. ¶ Première édition ; deuxième éd. augmentée et corrigée, 1674 ; troisième éd., 1679, q.v. ¶ OH(mic.) · OOU(mic.) · BVIP(mic.)

Montanus, Arnoldus, 1625?–1683. America . . . . London, 1671.

See Ogilby, John. America . . . . London, 1671.

Voir Ogilby, John. America . . . . Londres, 1671.

Ogilby, John, 1600–1676. America: being the latest, and most accurate description of the New World; containing the original of the inhabitants, and the remarkable voyages thither. The conquest of the vast empires of Mexico and Peru, and other large provinces and territories, with the several European plantations in those parts. Also their cities, fortresses, towns, temples, mountains, and rivers. Their habits, customs, manners, and religions. Their plants, beasts, birds, and serpents. With an appendix containing, besides several other considerable additions, a brief survey of what hath been discover'd of the Vnknown South-Land and the Arctick Region. Collected from most authentick authors, augmented with later observations, and adorn'd with maps and sculptures, by John Ogilby . . . . London, printed by the Author, and are to be had at his house in White Fryers, 1671. 5 p.l., 674, [1] p. illus. 32 plates (part fold.), 6 ports., 19 maps (part fold.) fol.

NUC(Pre–56)427:602

Apparently based in part on Arnoldus Montanus's De Nieuwe en onbeken :e weereld: of beschryving van American en 't zuid-land, *which was granted*

Semble basé en partie sur l'ouvrage De Nieuwe en onbekende weereld : of beschryving van American en 't zuid-land *de Arnoldus Montanus auquel les droits d'auteur furent accordés*

135

copyright privileges in *July 1670*, and published in Amsterdam in *1671*. Sabin:50089 calls this a plagiarism, and enters it under Montanus. ¶ *Title in red and black.* ¶ *Waldon has collation: t.-p., [5]–674, [1] p.* ¶ Frobisher's expedition: p. 108; Estotiland [Newfoundland-Labrador], Terra Laboratoris [Labrador], Canada, Acadia, Norumbega [Nova Scotia]; p. 126–38; Several Attempts for the discovery of the North-West Passage: p. 672–74. Canada is shown on the general map of America, by John Ogilby, preceding p. 1. ¶ *BVIPA*

en juillet 1670 ; publié à Amsterdam en 1671. Le Sabin:50089 qualifie cet ouvrage de plagiat et le fait apparaître sous Montanus. ¶ *Titre en noir et rouge.* ¶ *Collation de Waldon : p. de t. [5]–674, [1] p.* ¶ *Expédition de Frobisher : p. 108 ; Estotiland [Terre-Neuve et Labrador], Terra Laboratoris [Labrador], Canada, Acadia, Norumbega [Nouvelle-Écosse] : p. 126–38 ; Several Attempts for the discovery of the North-West Passage : p. 672–74. Carte générale de l'Amérique exécutée par John Ogilby et représentant le Canada, placée avant la p. 1.* ¶ *BVIPA*

1672

Blome, Richard, *d./déc.* 1705. A description of the island of Jamaica; with the other isles and territories in America, to which the English are related . . . . Taken from the notes of Sr. Thomas Linch . . . governour of Jamaica; and other experienced persons in the said places . . . . Published by Richard Blome. London, printed by T[homas]. Milbourn, and sold by J[ohn]. Williams, jun., 1672. 4 p.l., 192 p. 2 fold. maps. 8°

NUC(Pre–56)61:492*

The maps are of Carolina and Virginia (cf. BM*(to 1955)21:1013).* ¶ New-Found-Land: p. 185–92; "A Draught of the Isle of Newfoundland" in lower right-hand corner of "A Draught of the Sea Coast and Rivers, of Virginia, Maryland, and New England. Taken from the latest Surveys. London, printed for Ric. Blome." The coast of Acadia is also shown. ¶ *First edition; other issues follow; also pub. in microcard*

Cartes de la Caroline et de la Virginie (cf. BM*(to 1955)21:1013).* ¶ *New-Found-Land : p. 185–92 ; « A Draught of the Isle of Newfoundland » dans le coin droit du bas de la carte « A Draught of the Sea Coast and Rivers, of Virginia, Maryland, and New England. Taken from the latest Surveys. London, printed for Ric. Blome ». La côte de l'Acadie est aussi représentée.* ¶ *Première édition ; autres tirages plus loin ; publiée aussi sur microcartes (cf. NUC) ; deuxième éd. : 1678*

ed. (cf. NUC); second ed.: 1678 (q.v.); transl. as Description de l'isle de la Jamaique (in Recueil de divers voyages .... Paris, 1684), as Richardi Blome Englisches America .... Leipzig, 1697, and as Description des isles et terres que l'Angleterre possède en Amérique .... Amsterdam, 1715.

(q.v.) ; traductions : « Description de l'isle de la Jamaique » (dans Recueil de divers voyages .... Paris, 1684), Richardi Blome Englisches America .... Leipzig, 1697 et Description des isles et terres que l'Angleterre possède en Amérique .... Amsterdam, 1715.

Blome, Richard, *d./déc.* 1705. A description of the island of Jamaica .... London, printed by T[homas]. Milbourn; sold by the book-sellers of London, & Westminster, 1672. [No collation given.] 8°

BM(to 1955)21:1013

The maps are of Barbados, Carolina, and Virginia.

Cartes de la Barbade, de la Caroline et de la Virginie.

Blome, Richard, *d./déc.* 1705. The history, or description, of the island of Jamaica; with other isles and territories in America, to which the English are related. *viz.* .... Newfound Land, taken from the notes of Sir Thomas Linch . . . and other experienced persons in the said places. Printed for Jo[hn]. Williams Junior in Cross Keys Court, in Little Britain. Price, bound, 2s. [London, 1672.] [No collation given.] 8°

Arber, 1:96

1673

Hudson's Bay Company. A list of the names and stocks, of the Governour and Company of the Adventurers of England, trading to Hudsons-Bay. Every hundred pound stock is to have one vote, and noe person not having two hundred pound stock are capable to be chosen of the Committee .... The names of the Governour, Deputy-Governour, and Committee, from November 1672. to November 1673. [London, 1673?] Broadside. fol.

BLC(to 1975)154:300

The list is headed by the Duke of York, with £300, and Prince Rupert, with £270, stock. The total amount subscribed is £8,720.

Liste des actionnaires de la compagnie avec, en tête, le duc de York, 300 £, et le prince Rupert, 270 £. Montant total investi : 8 720 £.

*Moxon, Joseph, 1627–1700. The English empire in America described in a map ... beginning eastward at Newfoundland, and proceeding westwards to New Scotland.... Set forth by Joseph Moxon ... and sold by him on Ludgate Hill, at the sign of the Atlas. Price, pasted on cloth and coloured, 16s. [London, 1673.] [No collation given.] fol.(?)

Arber, 1:141

Proceeds from Nova Scotia to the British American colonies and West Indies.

Description de la Nouvelle-Écosse, des colonies britanniques en Amérique et des Antilles.

1674

*Heylyn, Peter, 1599–1662. Cosmography, in four books. Containing the chorography and history of the whole world . . . . London, printed for Philip Chetwind and Anne Seile, 1674. 5 pts. in 1 v. 4 fold. maps. fol.

NUC(Pre–56)244:501*

Added illus. t.-p., engr.: Cosmographie. . . . The 5th ed. corr. & inlarged by the author. London, printed for Anne Seile . . . 1669. ¶ Bks. 1–3, the two pts. of bk. 4, and the Appendix, have each a special t.-p., dated 1673. ¶ Various pagings, and errors in paging. ¶ Revised and enl. from his *Microcosmus*. Oxford, 1621, *q.v.* ¶ First edition under title *Cosmographie*: London, 1642; also pub. London, 1652, *q.v.* for other notes and editions. ¶ The sixth ed. appeared in 1670 (*q.v.*); this appears to be a reprint of that but using pts. of other eds. and issues. NUC has other variants, too: London, printed for Anne Seile and Philip Chetwind, 1674, title in red and black; two other 1674 eds. have four pts. in one v., one with statement on added t.-p.: . . . Sixth ed., corr. and inlarged by the author. London, 1670. Evidently printing, collating from stock, and sale were continuous over many years, resulting in mixed make-ups.

P. de t. illustrée, ajoutée et gravée : Cosmographie. . . . The 5th ed. corr. & inlarged by the author. London, printed for Anne Seile . . . 1669. ¶ Les livres 1 à 3, les 2 parties du livre 4 et l'appendice ont chacun une p. de t. distincte et sont datés de 1673. ¶ Pagination disparate et erronée. ¶ Version revue et augmentée de *Microcosmus* du même auteur. Oxford, 1621, *q.v.* ¶ Première édition sous le titre *Cosmographie* : Londres, 1642 ; publ. aussi à Londres en 1652, *q.v.* pour d'autres notes et éditions. ¶ Sixième éd. parue en 1670 (*q.v.*) ; cette dernière semble être une réimpression de cette édition avec toutefois des ajouts d'autres éditions et tirages. Le NUC donne d'autres variantes : Londres, imprimé pour Anne Seile et Philip Chetwind, 1674, titre en noir et rouge ; 2 autres éd. de 1674 comprenant 4 parties en 1 vol., l'un des exemplaires renfermant les renseignements suivants sur sa p. de t. ajoutée : . . . Sixth ed., corr. and inlarged by the author. Londres, 1670. De toute évidence, l'impression, la collation à partir du fonds et la vente s'étalèrent sur plusieurs années, ce qui produisit une composition hétéroclite.

Meriton, George, 1634–1711. A geographical description of the world. With a brief account of the several empires, dominions, and parts thereof. As also the natures of the people, the customs, manners, and commodities of the several countreys. With a description of the principal cities in each dominion. Together with a short direction for travellers. The second edition enlarged and amended, with an addition of several islands countries, and places, not extant in the former impression. By G. Meriton gent. London, printed for William Leake, and John Leake, at the Crown in Fleet-street between the two Temple-gates, 1674. 14 p.l., 440,[4] p. 12°

NUC(Pre–56)377:266*

Added t.-p., engraved and illustrated. ¶ Format from Arber, 1:157. ¶ First ed., 1671, and third ed. 1679, q.v. for notes.

P. de t. ajoutée, gravée et illustrée. ¶ Format tiré de Arber, 1:157. ¶ Première édition : 1671, troisième éd. : 1679, q.v. pour notes.

1675

Josselyn, John, *fl.* 1630–1675. An account of two voyages to New-England.... London: G[iles]. Widdows, 1675. 4 p.l., 279 [*i.e.* 277], [3] p. 8°

Sabin:36672: cf. NUC(Pre–56)285:235*

Second ed., with new t.-p. only. ¶ *First ed.: London, 1674, q.v. for other notes; this second ed. reprinted Cambridge, Mass., Mass. Hist. Soc. Collections, 1833. Series 3, vol. 3, p. [211]–396, and this is the edition described in NUC; reprinted Boston, W. Veazie, 1865, with facsims. of t.-p.'s (cf. NUC).*

Deuxième éd. avec nouvelle p. de t. seulement. ¶ *Première édition : Londres, 1674, q.v. pour d'autres notes ; deuxième éd. réimprimée à Cambridge (Mass.), Mass. Hist. Soc. Collections, 1833. Collection 3, vol. 3, p. [211]–396, même édition que celle décrite dans le NUC ; réimpression à Boston, W. Veazie, 1865, avec fac-similés des p. de t. (cf. NUC).*

*Speed, John, 1552?–1629. A prospect of the most famous parts of the world. Viz. Asia . . . Africa . . . Europe . . . America . . . . London, by W.G., 1675. 1 p.l., 276 [*i.e.* 278] p. incl. 27 maps. 32°

NUC(Pre–56)561:150*

First(?) ed.: London, 1627; for a somewhat fuller title, and other editions and notes, *see* the editions of 1631 and 1646; this seems to have a similar (but shorter) title to that of the edition of 1662. W.G. also published a version of the 1676 edition: *see* note to that edition.

Première édition (?) : Londres, 1627 ; pour un titre plus complet et d'autres notes et éditions, *voir* les éd. de 1631 et de 1646 ; il semble que le présent ouvrage soit de titre similaire, mais plus court que l'édition de 1662. W.G. a également publié une version de l'édition de 1676 : *voir* la note de cette dernière édition.

1676

Speed, John, 1552?–1629. A prospect of the most famous parts of the world, viz. Asia, Africa, Europe, America . . . . By John Speed. To which are added in this new edition . . . the descriptions of His Majesty's dominions abroad; with a map fairly engraven to each description. Viz. New-England, New York . . . . London, printed for Thomas Basset at the George in Fleet-street, and Richard Chiswel at the Rose and Crown in St. Paul's Church-yard, 1676. . . . 1 p.l., 56 numb. l., [11] p. incl. 28 double maps (incl. illus., ports., coats of arms, diagrs., plans) fol. (Issued as Book [5] of his *The Theatre of the empire of Great-Britain*. London, 1676.)

NUC(Pre–56)561:150*

Waldon's entry has an abridged title and imprint, and the collation: t.-p., 56, [6] fol. [i.e. leaves], with the note: Pt. 2 of his The theatre of the empire of Great-Britain. . . . ¶ Index: [11] p. at end; "Advertisement" (corrigenda): last p. ¶ Text and numbers on alternate rectos and versos of leaves, with double

Waldon donne un titre et une adresse bibliographique abrégés et la collation : p. de t., 56, [6] fol. [c.-à-d. feuillets], et note : partie 2 de l'ouvrage The theatre of the empire of Great-Britain . . . . du même auteur. ¶ Index : [11] p. à la fin ; « Avertissement » (errata) : dernière p. ¶ Texte et numéros au recto et au verso des feuillets alternativement, plus des cartes

maps between (cf. NUC). ¶ The map of America is the same as in the edition of 1631, and very little has been added to the text relating to Canada (l. 9–10). ¶ Also pub.: London, by W.G., 1676 (with his England, Wales, Scotland and Ireland described, cf. NUC). ¶ First(?) ed.: 1627; other editions: 1631, 1646, 1662, 1665, 1668, and 1675, q.v.

doubles insérées (cf. NUC). ¶ La carte de l'A-mérique est pareille à celle de l'édition de 1631 ; très peu de texte a été ajouté à la partie traitant du Canada (f. 9–10). ¶ Publié aussi à Londres par W.G. en 1676 (accompagné de l'ouvrage England, Wales, Scotland and Ireland described du même auteur, cf. NUC). ¶ Première édition (?) : 1627 ; autres éditions : 1631, 1646, 1662, 1665, 1668 et 1675, voir ces dates.

1677

*Heylyn, Peter, 1599–1662. Cosmography in four books. Containing the chorography and history of the whole world . . . . London, printed by A.C. for P[hilip]. Chetwind and A[nne]. Seile, 1677. 4 v. in 1. 4 fold. maps. fol.

NUC(Pre–56)244:501*

Title in red and black. ¶ Added t.-p., engr.: Cosmographie in foure books . . . The fifth ed. . . . London, printed for A. Seile, 1677. This is, however, a reprint of the sixth ed., 1670 (q.v.), being the third ed., 1665 (q.v.) with a new t.-p. and "an alphabetical and exact table [etc.]" added to it. Bks. 1–3, the two pts. of bk. 4, and the Appendix, each have a special t.-p., that of pt. 3 dated 1676. NUC has two apparent variant t.-p.'s with the following after A. Seile in the imprint: . . . and are to be sold by T[homas]. Basset, J[ohn?]. Wright, R[ichard]. Chiswell, and T[homas]. Sawbridge . . . 1677. ¶ Revised and enl. from his Microcosmus. Oxford, 1621, q.v. ¶

Titre en noir et rouge. ¶ P. de t. ajoutée, gravée : Cosmographie in foure books . . . The fifth ed. . . . London, printed for A. Seile, 1677. Il s'agit ici, cependant, d'une réimpression de la sixième éd., 1670 (q.v.) publiée à partir de la troisième éd. de 1665 (q.v.) à laquelle fut ajoutée une nouvelle p. de t. et une « table alphabétique détaillée [etc.] ». Les livres 1 à 3, les 2 parties du livre 4 ainsi que l'appendice ont chacun une p. de t. distincte, celle de la partie 3 datée de 1676. Le NUC fait état de 2 p. de t. visiblement différentes où, après « A. Seile » dans l'adresse bibliographique, est inscrit : . . . and are to be sold by T[homas]. Basset, J[ohn ?]. Wright, R[ichard]. Chiswell, and T[homas]. Sawbridge. . . 1677. ¶ Version revue et augmentée de Microcosmus du même auteur.

First edition under title *Cosmographie*. London, 1642; also pub. London, 1652, *q.v.* for other notes and editions.

Oxford, 1621, *q.v.* ¶ Première édition sous le titre *Cosmographie*. Londres, 1642 ; publ. aussi à Londres en 1652, *q.v.* pour d'autres notes et éditions.

1678

Blome, Richard, *d./déc.* 1705. A description of the island of Jamaica . . . [and] New-Found-Land. Published by Richard Blome. Together with The present state of Algiers. London, printed by J.B. for Dorman Newman, 1678. 3 p.l., 88 p., 1 l., 17 p., 2 l. port., 4 fold. maps. 8°

NUC(Pre–56)61:492*

"The present state of Algiers," with special title-page, follows the 88 p. in the collation. ¶ *"A Description of New-Fovnd-Land": p. 85–88; map as in 1672 ed.* ¶ *NUC notes: The maps are of Jamaica, Barbados, Carolina & Virginia.* ¶ *Second edition; first ed.: 1672, q.v. for other notes; another issue follows.* ¶ *NBFU*

« The present state of Algiers », avec sa propre page de titre, vient après 88 p. dans la collation. ¶ *« A Description of New-Fovnd-Land » : p. 85–88 ; carte semblable à celle de l'éd. de 1672.* ¶ *Notes du NUC : cartes de la Jamaïque, de la Barbade, de la Caroline et de la Virginie.* ¶ *Deuxième édition ; première édition : 1672, q.v. pour d'autres notes ; autre notice ci-dessous.* ¶ *NBFU*

*Blome, Richard, *d./déc.* 1705. A description of the island of Jamaica, with other isles and territories in America to which the English are related, *viz.* . . . . Newfoundland. Published by Rich[ard]. Blome . . . . [London, 1678.] [No collation given.] 8°

Arber, 1:336

Another issue: *see* preceding entry.

Autre tirage : *voir* la notice précédente.

1679

[Bethel, Slingsby], 1617–1697. An account of the French usurpation upon the trade of England, and what great damage the English do yearly sustain by their commerce, and how the same may be retrenched, and England improved in riches and interest. London, printed in the year, 1679. 1 p.l., 24 p. 4°

NUC(Pre–56)51:299

Signed: J.B. ¶ Among other measures, the writer advocates setting up Royal fisheries as an aid to trade, and to train seamen for the navy. Encroachments of the French on the Newfoundland fisheries: p. 14.

Signé : J.B. ¶ L'auteur prône entre autres l'établissement de pêcheries royales comme mesure d'aide au commerce et aussi pour former des matelots pour la marine. Empiétement des Français sur les pêcheries de Terre-Neuve : p. 14.

Meriton, George, 1634–1711. A geographical description of the world.... The 3d ed. enl., and amended, with an addition of several islands, countries, and places, not extant in the former impression. By G. Meriton. London, printed for William Leake, and John Leake, at the Crown in Fleet-street, between the two Temple-Gates, 1679. [24], 388 [*i.e.* 384] p. 12°

NUC(Pre–56)377:266*

Added t.-p. engraved and illustrated. ¶ *Errors in paging (not noted by Waldon): p. 70–71 numbered 72–73; nos. 169–76 omitted in paging.* ¶ Norumbega, Nova Francia, Terra Cortelialis [*i.e.* Corterealis], Estotiland: p. 264–65; New Found Land: p. 382–83. ¶ *First ed., 1671,* q.v. *for notes; second ed., 1674,* q.v. *for full title.*

P. de t. ajoutée, gravée et illustrée. ¶ *Erreurs de pagination (non relevées par Waldon) : p. 70–71 numérotées 72–73, n°s 169–76 omis dans la pagination.* ¶ Norumbega, Nova Francia, Terra Cortelialis [*c.-à-d.* Corterealis], Estotiland : p. 264–65 ; New Found Land : p. 382–83. ¶ *Première édition : 1671,* q.v. *pour notes ; deuxième, 1674,* q.v. *pour le titre complet.*

1680

*Blome, Richard, d./déc. 1705. A geographical description of the world, taken from the works of the famous monsieur Sanson, late geographer to the present French King. To which are added, about an hundred geographical and hydrographical tables, of the kingdoms, countreys, and isles in the world, with their chief cities and sea-ports; drawn from the maps of the said monsieur Sanson, and according to the method of the said description. Illustrated with maps. The second part. By Richard Blome. [London, Samuel Roycraft.] Printed in the year. 1680. 1 p.l., 493 p. illus. (tables). 24 fold. maps. (Issued as a part of his *Cosmography and geography in two parts*, London, 1682.) fol.

NUC(Pre–56)61:493

An altered and expanded version of his *Geographical description of the four parts of the world*, first pub. London, 1670. ¶ Compiled and translated by Blome mostly from works of Nicholas Sanson.

Version revue et augmentée de *Geographical description of the four parts of the world* du même auteur et publiée pour la première fois à Londres en 1670. ¶ Ouvrage de compilation et de traduction par M. Blome établi surtout à partir des travaux de Nicholas Sanson.

[Petyt, William], 1636–1707. Britannia languens, or A discourse of trade: shewing the grounds and reasons of the increase and decay of land-rents, national wealth and strength. With application to the late and present state and condition of England, France, and the United Provinces .... London, printed for T[homas]. Dring [etc.], 1680. 4 p.l., 303 [*i.e.* 311], [8] p. 8°

NUC(Pre–56)454:7*

Preface signed: Philangius; wrongly ascribed to James Howell, notes Dr. Waldon, but Petyt's authorship confirmed in Arber, 1:520. ¶ Waldon indicates that this has a Newfoundland interest. ¶ A similar title beginning

Préface signée : Philangius ; selon Waldon, l'ouvrage fut attribué par erreur à James Howell, mais la paternité de Petyt se trouve confirmée dans Arber, 1:520. ¶ Waldon indique que le livre renferme des renseignements sur Terre-Neuve. ¶ Un ouvrage de titre similaire

Britannia languens, *and by the same author, pub. London, 1689 (q.v.), appears to be another edition.*

au début de Britannia languens *du même auteur et publié à Londres en 1689 (q.v.) pourrait être une autre édition.*

1682

Collins, John, 1625–1683. Salt and fishery, a discourse thereof . . . . By John Collins, accomptant to the Royal Fishery Company. London, printed by A[rthur]. Godbid and J[ohn]. Playford, and are to be sold by Mr. Robert Horne . . . [etc.], 1682. 4 p.l., 164, [4] p. 4°

Waldon has collation: [8], 164, [4] p. ¶ "Of the Newfoundland fishery": p. 93–101.

Collation de Waldon : [8], 164, [4] p. ¶ « Of the Newfoundland fishery » : p. 93–101.

*Heylyn, Peter, 1599–1662. Cosmography in four books. Containing the chorography and history of the whole world . . . . London, printed for P.C. T[homas]. Passenger at the Three Bibles on London-Bridge, B[enjamin]. Tooke at the Ship in St. Paul's Church-yard, and T[homas]. Sawbridge at the Three Flower de Luces in Little-Britain, 1682. 4 v. in 1. 4 fold. maps, 1 table. fol.

NUC(Pre–56)244:502*

Bks. 1–3, the two pts. of bk. 4, and the Appendix have each a special t.-p. ¶ Rev. and enl. from his *Microcosmus.* Oxford, 1621, *q.v.* ¶ First pub. under the above title: London, 1642; also pub. London, 1652, *q.v.* for other notes and editions. ¶ This is a reprint of the sixth edition, 1670 (*q.v.*); NUC has a variant with title in red and

Les livres 1 à 3, les 2 parties du livre 4 et l'appendice ont chacun une p. de t. distincte. ¶ Version revue et augmentée de *Microcosmus* du même auteur. Oxford, 1621, *q.v.* ¶ Publié pour la première fois sous le titre ci-dessus à Londres en 1642 ; publ. aussi à Londres en 1652, *q.v.* pour d'autres notes et éditions. ¶ Il s'agit ici d'une réimpression de la sixième éd. de 1670 (*q.v.*) ; le NUC donne

black, and an added t.-p., engr.: Cosmographie in foure books. The 6th edition.

un exemplaire similaire avec un titre en noir et rouge et une page de titre gravée : Cosmographie in foure books. The 6th edition.

1685

[**Crouch, Nathaniel**], 1632?–1725? The English empire in America: or A prospect of His Majesties dominions in the West-Indies. Namely, Newfoundland and New-England New-York [etc., the American, West Indian, and Bermuda colonies] . . . with an account of the discovery, scituation, product, and other excellencies of these countries. To which is prefixed a relation of the first discovery of the new world called America, by the Spaniards. And of the remarkable voyages of several Englishmen to divers places therein. Illustrated with maps and pictures. By R.B. [*pseud.*] . . . . London, printed by Nath. Crouch . . . 1685. 2 p.l., 209 p. 2 maps (incl. front.), 2 plates. 12°

NUC(Pre–56)128:173*

Crouch wrote under the pseudonym of Robert Burton and Richard Burton, and the initials R.B. Note also a similar work by Richard Blome, 1687. ¶ *Waldon has illus. as: front. (map), 3 plates.* ¶ Chap. II, The voyages and discoveries of several Englishmen into America, contains references to Canada: Sir Sebastian Cabot, p. 27–28; Sir Martin Frobisher, p. 28–32; Mr. John Davis, p. 32–33; Capt. George Weymouth, 1602, p. 33; Capt. James Hall, 1605, p. 34–35; Capt. Henry Hudson, p. 39–41. Chap. III, A prospect of New found-land, with the discovery, plantation, and product thereof: p. 60–66. ¶ *First edition; subsequent editions appeared in 1692, 1698, 1704, 1711, 1728, 1729, 1735, and 1739, q.v., below.*

Crouch écrit sous les pseudonymes de Robert Burton et de Richard Burton et sous les initiales R.B. Il existe aussi un ouvrage similaire de Richard Blome, 1687. ¶ *Waldon signale les illus. suivantes : frontispice (carte), 3 planches.* ¶ Qui portent sur le Canada : chap. II, « The voyages and discoveries of several Englishmen into America » (sir Sebastian Cabot : p. 27–28 ; sir Martin Frobisher: p. 28–32; M. John Davis : p. 32–33 ; cap. George Weymouth, 1602 : p. 33 ; cap. James Hall, 1605 : p. 34–35 ; cap. Henry Hudson : p. 39–41) ; chap. III, « A prospect of New found-land, with the discovery, plantation, and product thereof » : p. 60–66.¶ *Première édition ; éditions suivantes : 1692, 1698, 1704, 1711, 1728, 1729, 1735 et 1739, q.v. plus loin.*

1686

Great Britain. Treaties, etc., 1685–1688 (James II). Treaty of peace, good correspondence & neutrality in America, between the most serene and mighty Prince James II. by the grace of God, King of Great Britain, France and Ireland, Defender of the Faith, &c., and the most serene and mighty Prince Lewis XIV. the most Christian King: concluded the 6/16th day of Novemb. 1686. Published by His Majesties command. [London] In the Savoy: printed by Thomas Newcomb, one of His Majesties printers. 1686. 19, [1] p. 4°

NUC(Pre–56)215:507*

Waldon has collation: 19 p. ¶ *"An advertisement": [1] p. at end.* ¶ *NUC has note to the Latin edition (below): "Whitehall Treaty of Neutrality."* ¶ In regard to America, the sovereigns agree to respect each other's rights and territories and not to attack each other's forts and colonies, no help or supplies are to be given Indians with whom the French may be at war, and should a breach occur in Europe, the French and English in America are not to be at war. ¶ *This also appeared in Latin the same year (see next entry), and in French as* Traité de neutralité, conclu a Londres le 16. novembre 1686 .... *Paris, 1686.* ¶ *OTP*

Collation de Waldon : 19 p. ¶ *« Annonce » : [1] p. à la fin.* ¶ *Note du NUC pour l'édition latine (ci-dessous) : « Whitehall Treaty of Neutrality ».* ¶ En ce qui concerne l'Amérique, les souverains acceptent de respecter leurs droits et territoires respectifs et de ne point attaquer les forts et colonies de l'autre, aucune aide matérielle ou autre ne sera fournie aux Indiens avec qui les Français pourraient être en guerre et, s'il advenait qu'un conflit se produise en Europe, les Français et les Anglais d'Amérique ne devraient point se faire la guerre. ¶ *Cet ouvrage parut également en latin la même année (voir la notice suivante) et en français,* Traité de neutralité, conclu à Londres le 16. novembre 1686..., *à Paris en 1686.* ¶ *OTP*

*Great Britain. Treaties, etc., 1685–1688 (James II). Tractatus Pacis, Bonae Correspondentiae, Et Neutralitatis in America, Inter Serenissimum & Potentissimum Principem Jacobum II. Dei Gratiâ Magnae Britanniae, Franciae & Hiberniae Regem, Fidel Defensorem, &c. Et Serenissimum & Potentissimum Principem Ludovicum XIV. Eadem Dei Gratia Regem Christianissimum, Conclusus 6/16 Die Mensis Novembris, Anno Dom. 1686. Cum Privilegio. [Londini] Typis Thomae Newcomb, unius ex Typographis Regiis in vico vulgo dicto The Savoy, 1686. 1 l., 3–15 p. 4°

NUC(Pre–56)215:507*

Bookseller's advertisement: last page. ¶ For other notes, *see* English edition, preceding entry.

Annonce du libraire : dernière page. ¶ *Voir* l'édition anglaise (notice précédente) pour d'autres notes.

1687

[Blome, Richard], *d./déc.* 1705. The present state of His Majesties isles and territories in America, viz. Jamaica, Barbadoes, S. Christophers, Mevis, Antego, S. Vincent, Dominica, New-Jersey, Pensilvania, Monserat, Anguilla, Bermudas, Carolina, Virginia, New-England, Tobago, New-found-land, Mary-land, New-York. With new maps of every place. Together with astronomical tables, which will serve as a constant diary or calendar, for the use of the English inhabitants in those islands; from the year 1686, to 1700 . . . . London, printed by H[enry]. Clark, for Dorman Newman, at the Kings-Arms in the Poultrey, 1687. 4 p.l., 262, [36] p. front. (port.), 7 fold. maps, fold. diagr. 8°

NUC(Pre–56)61:493

Five of the maps are by Robert Morden. ¶ Pages 59, 257, 260, 261 erroneously numbered 65, 241, 244, 245. ¶ Transl. into French as: L'amerique angloise. Amsterdam, 1688 (and other editions), and into German as: Richardi Blome Englisches America. Leipzig, 1697 (and a similar work, Frankfurt, 1709: NUC(Pre–56)61:491). ¶ "A

Cinq des cartes sont de Robert Morden. ¶ Pages 59, 257, 260 et 261 numérotées fautivement 65, 241, 244 et 245. ¶ Traduction française : L'amerique angloise. Amsterdam, 1688 (et autres éditions) ; traduction allemande : Richardi Blome Englisches America. Leipzig, 1697 (ouvrage similaire publié à Francfort en 1709 : NUC(Pre–56)61:491). ¶ « A description of New-Found-Land » :

description of New-Found-Land": p. 239–46. Folded map of "The North-West part of America by Robt. Morden": opposite p. 239. ¶ First ed. to appear under this title, and to contain all the maps. A similar work by Blome under title: *A description of the island of Jamaica*, appeared in 1672 and 1678 (*q.v.*, and of which BM(to 1955)21:1013 describes *The present state* as being "another edition"), and in 1673 (as p. 325–41 of Blome's *Britannia*, London, T. Roycroft for R. Blome).

p. 239–46. Carte pliante « The North-West part of America by Robt. Morden » : en regard de la p. 239. ¶ Première éd. à être publiée sous ce titre et à contenir toutes les cartes. Un ouvrage similaire de Blome portant le titre *A description of the island of Jamaica* parut en 1672 et en 1678 (*q.v.*, dans le BM(to 1955)21:1013, on note que cet ouvrage *The present state* serait une « autre édition »), et aussi en 1673 (composant les p. 325–41 du livre *Britannia*, de Blome, Londres, T. Roycroft pour R. Blome).

1688

Great Britain. Sovereigns, etc., 1685–1688 (James II). By the King, a proclamation prohibiting His Majesties subjects to trade within the limits assigned to the Governour and Company of Adventurers of England, Trading into Hudson's Bay, except those of the Company. London, printed by Charles Bill, Henry Hills, and Thomas Newcomb, printers to the Kings most Excellent Majesty, 1688. Broadside. fol.

NUC(Pre–56)215:388

Royal arms at head of title. ¶ *Dated at end: 31 March, 1688.* ¶ Reprinted in the American Antiquarian Society (Worcester, Mass.) *Transactions*, 1911, vol. 12, p. 143–46.

Titre orné des armoiries royales. ¶ *Date à la fin : 31 mars 1688.* ¶ Réimprimé dans la revue *Transactions* de la American Antiquarian Society, Worcester (Mass.), en 1911, vol. 12. p. 143–46.

THE
ENGLISH PILOT,

THE
FOURTH BOOK.

DESCRIBING

The Sea-Coasts, Capes, Head-Lands, Rivers, Bays, Roads, Havens, Harbours, Streights, Islands, Depths, Rocks, Shoals, Sands, Banks, and Dangers from the River *Amazons* to *New-found-Land*; with all the *West-India* Navigation, and the Islands therein, as *Cuba Hispaniola, Jamaica, Barbadoes, Porto Rico,* and the rest of the *Caribbe* Islands.

WITH

A New DESCRIPTION of *New-found-Land, New-England, Virginia, Mary-Land, &c.*

SHEWING

The Courses and Distances from one Place to another, the Ebbing and Flowing of the Sea, the Setting of the Tides and Currents, &c.

By the INFORMATION of divers NAVIGATORS of our own, and other NATIONS.

LONDON,

Printed for *William Fisher* at the Postern on *Tower-Hill*, and *John Thornton* at the Plat in the *Minories*, MDCLXXXIX.

The English Pilot. The Fourth Book .... London/Londres, 1689.

Clarke, Samuel, 1599–1683. A new description of the world. Or a compendious treatise of the empires, kingdoms, states, provinces, countries, islands, cities and towns of Europe, Asia, Africa and America . . . . Faithfully collected from the best authors, by S. Clark. London, printed for Hen. Rhodes next door to the Swan Tavern, near Brides-Lane, in Fleet-Street, 1689. 3 p.l., 232 p. front. 12°

NUC(Pre–56)111:361*

On verso of t.-p.: Licensed, August the 11th. 1688. ¶ Estotiland [Canada east of Hudson Bay]: p. 184–85; New-Found-Land: p. 186–87; Canada: p. 187–88. ¶ *First edition; other editions* (see *below*): *London, 1696, 1708, 1712, 1719;* see also *his* A geographicall description. . . . *London, 1657, and other editions; the NUC note to the 1708 ed. (q.v.) states: Originally pub., 1657, under title:* A geographicall description . . . *(q.v.).* ¶ *BVIPA*

Au verso de la p. de t. : Licensed, August the 11th. 1688. ¶ Estotiland [le Canada à l'est de la Baie d'Hudson] : p. 184–85 ; New-Found-Land : p. 186–87 ; Canada : p. 187–88. ¶ *Première édition ; autres éditions* (voir *plus loin*) : *Londres, 1696, 1708, 1712, 1719 ;* voir aussi A geographicall description . . . . *du même auteur, Londres, 1657 et d'autres éditions ; note du NUC pour l'éd. de 1708 : publié pour la première fois en 1657 sous le titre* A geographicall description . . . (voir *ce titre*). ¶ *BVIPA*

The English pilot. The fourth book; containing charts of the north part of America, or Hudson's Bay &c., Newfoundland, the islands of Jamaica, Barbadoes, Bermuda, Hispaniola, &c., &c.; a general chart of the West Indies, a new map of Carolina, and maps of Virginia, Maryland, Pennsylvania, New Jersey, New-York, with parts of New-England. London, 1689. fol.

Sabin:22616

Waldon takes this from Sabin, where no other imprint or collational information is given. ¶ *First edition; numerous subsequent editions (q.v.) to 1763, and beyond: 1698, 1706, 1707, 1716, 1721,*

Waldon tire ses renseignements du Sabin, où aucun autre renseignement sur l'adresse bibliographique ou la collation n'est fourni. ¶ *Édition originale ; de nombreuses éditions ultérieures (q.v.) jusqu'en 1763 et plus tard : 1698, 1706,*

1725, 1729, 1732, 1737, 1742, 1745, 1748, 1749, 1751, 1755, 1758, 1759, 1760, 1761, 1763; for these and later editions (1764, 1765, 1767, etc., to 1794), see NUC(Pre–56)160:373–75.

1707, 1716, 1721, 1725, 1729, 1732, 1737, 1742, 1745, 1748, 1749, 1751, 1755, 1758, 1759, 1760, 1761, 1763 ; pour ces éditions et les plus récentes (1764, 1765, 1767, etc., jusqu'à 1794), voir le NUC(Pre–56)160:373–75.

Great Britain. Parliament, 1689. House of Commons. An address agreed upon at the Committee for the French war, and read in the House of Commons April the 19th. 1689. Licensed, and entred [*sic*] according to law. London, Printed for Richard Janeway in Queens-Head Alley in Pater-Noster-Row. 1689. [2], 6 p. fol.

NUC(Pre–56)214:546*

This reviews the many intrusions of the French, including their seizure of Hudson's Bay (p. 5), and assures the King that if he will declare war, the Committee will support it. ¶ *Reprinted London, 1808 (in* The Harleian Miscellany, *vol. 1, p. 54–56).* ¶ *OONL(MF) · OOU(MF) · OSTCB(MF)*

Cet ouvrage passe en revue les nombreuses invasions des Français, y compris la prise de possession par eux de la Baie d'Hudson (p. 5) et assure au roi que le Comité le soutiendra s'il déclare la guerre. ¶ *Réimprimé à Londres en 1808 (dans* The Harleian Miscellany, *vol. 1, p. 54–56).* ¶ *OONL (mic.) · OOU (mic.) · OSTCB (mic.)*

Great Britain. Sovereigns, etc., 1689–1694 (William and Mary). Their Majesties declaration against the French King. Given at our Court at Hampton Court, the seventh day of May, 1689. . . . London, printed by Charles Bill, and Thomas Newcomb, printers to the King and Queen's Most Excellent Majesties, 1689. Broadside. fol.

NUC(Pre–56)215:401

Among the causes of provocation enumerated are the encroachments of the French on Newfoundland and their invasion of Hudson's Bay.

Parmi les causes de la provocation énumérées se trouvent les déprédations des Français à Terre-Neuve et l'invasion par eux de la Baie d'Hudson.

*[Petyt, William], 1636–1707. Britannia languens: or, A discourse of trade, shewing that the present management of trade in England, is the true reason of the decay of our manufacturers, and the late great fall of land-rents; and that the increase of trade, in the method it now stands in, must proportionably decay England. Wherein is particularly demonstrated that the East-India Company, as now managed, has already near destroyed our trade in those parts, as well as that with Turky, and in short time must necessarily beggar the nation. Humbly offered to the consideration of this present Parliament. London, R[ichard]. Baldwin, 1689. 4 p.l., 303, [8] p. 8°

NUC(Pre–56)454:7*

For notes on what is probably another edition, and an improved collation, *see* under 1680, above.

Voir 1680 plus haut pour des notes sur ce qui constitue probablement une autre édition, et pour une meilleure collation.

1690

The case of the owners and proprietors of the ship and goods, *Charles*, seized by order of the Hudson's-Bay Company, as the said ship was sailing on the high seas, in or near Hudsons-straits. [London, 1690?] Broadside. fol.

NUC(Pre–56)97:631

Endorsed: The case of the owners of the ship Charles, seiz'd by the Hudson's-Bay Company. ¶ BLC(to 1975)154:302 notes: "[praying for a proviso in case of the confirmation of the Company's charter]." ¶ See also *other works under 1690 relating to this controversy, and the notes appended to those entries.*

Inscription officielle : The case of the owners of the ship Charles, seiz'd by the Hudson's-Bay Company. ¶ *Notes du BLC(to 1975)154:302 :* « [Requête d'une clause restrictive pour le cas où la charte de la Compagnie serait confirmée] ». ¶ Voir aussi *les autres ouvrages de l'année 1690 sur cette controverse, et les notes afférentes.*

Hudson's Bay Company. The case of the Felt Makers [Company] against the bill now depending, for confirming the charter of the Hudson's-Bay Company, humbly submitted to the Honourable House of Commons. [London, 1690?] Broadside. fol.

BLC(to 1975)154:301

See also *other works under 1690 relating to this controversy, and the notes appended to those entries.*

Voir aussi *les autres ouvrages de l'année 1690 sur cette controverse, et les notes afférentes.*

Hudson's Bay Company. The case of the Hudsons-Bay-Company. The kings of England, by right of discovery . . . have the sole rightful title . . . of all the seas, lakes . . . &c. as well as . . . territories within the entrance of the straits of Hudson . . . . [London? 169–] Broadside. fol.

cf. NUC(Pre–56)258:448

Assumed to be the same as the Waldon entry: The case of the Hudsons-Bay-Company. *[London, 1690?], with the note: "Begins: The kings of England"; cf. also a HBCo. entry with the same note, but dated [1687], in NUC(Pre–56) 258:450. ¶ This is very similar in title to several other works, one with the assigned date of 1690? (see preceding entry), and others of 1696, 1748, and 1749 (q.v.). ¶ Attributed [if this is the Waldon entry noted above] to [London, 1699] by the New York Public Library* Catalog, *and to [169–] by the LC* Catalog. *Text refers to "twenty years past." The Company was organized in 1670. ¶ First edition; reprinted [Boston, 1921] in the Photostat Americana series of the Mass. Hist. Soc., no. 52, from the original in the Public Record Office, London. This latter is the work descrbeed by both Waldon and NUC.*

On suppose qu'il s'agit d'une notice semblable à celle de Waldon : The case of the Hudsons-Bay-Company. *[Londres, 1690 ?], avec la note : « Begins: The kings of England » ; se reporter aussi à la notice du NUC(Pre–56) 258:450 sur la Compagnie de la Baie d'Hudson avec la même note, mais datée de [1687]. ¶ Ce titre est semblable à celui de nombreux autres ouvrages, dont l'un porte la date 1690 ? (voir la notice précédente), et d'autres ouvrages datés de 1696, 1748 et 1749 (q.v.). ¶ Le* Catalog *de la New York Public Library donne [s'il s'agit de la notice de Waldon susmentionnée] [Londres, 1699], tandis que le* Catalog *de la Library of Congress donne [169-]. Dans le texte, il est question des « vingt dernières années ». La Compagnie a été créée en 1670. ¶ Première édition ; réimpression à [Boston, 1921] dans la collection Photostat Americana de la Mass. Hist. Soc., n° 52, à partir de l'original du Public Record Office de Londres. Ce dernier est l'ouvrage décrit par Waldon et le NUC. ¶*

¶ See also *other works under 1690 relating to this controversy, and the notes appended to those entries.*

Voir aussi *les autres notices de l'année 1690 sur cette controverse, et les notes afférentes.*

Hudson's Bay Company. The case of the Hudsons-Bay Company. Reasons for the continuance of the former act. [London, 1690?] Broadside. fol.

BLC(to 1975)154:301

This is very similar in title to several other works, one with the assigned date of 169– (see following entry), and others of 1696, 1748, and 1749 (q.v.). ¶ Endorsed on verso: Case of the Hudson's-Bay Company. ¶ The Company claims to have made no dividend since the year 1690 and has run much in debt to "Support this Trade to the Nation," and fears being dispossessed by the French. "The Company hath sustained very great losses by the Invasions of the French in time of Peace, and during the late War, and hath ever since the making of the Act been hindered in the Prosecution of several probable and advantageous Discoveries and Improvements of the said Trade by the means beforementioned." Only a joint stock company can meet the difficulties of this trade. ¶ In 1690 the Company appealed to Parliament, asking confirmation of its charter for seven years. There was some opposition from the felt-makers company and other sources, but the Bill received Royal assent May 20, 1690, with a clause to protect the felt-makers. ¶

Ce titre est semblable à celui de nombreux autres ouvrages, dont l'un porte la date 169– (Voir la notice suivante), et d'autres ouvrages datés de 1696, 1748 et 1749 (q.v.). ¶ Inscription officielle : Case of the Hudson's-Bay Company. ¶ La Compagnie maintient n'avoir fait aucun profit depuis 1690 et s'être endettée pour « soutenir le commerce avec la nation », et craint d'être dépossédée par les Français. « La Compagnie a essuyé de très grandes pertes à la suite d'invasions par les Français en temps de paix et au cours de la dernière guerre ; elle a, depuis la promulgation de cette loi, été ralentie dans sa poursuite de nombreuses et avantageuses découvertes ou améliorations probables au niveau du commerce suivant les moyens susmentionnés. » Seule une société de capitaux peut affronter les difficultés que représente ce commerce. ¶ En 1690, la Compagnie faisait appel auprès du Parlement et demandait que sa charte soit confirmée pour une période de sept ans. Les fabricants de feutre, notamment, s'y sont opposés, mais le projet de loi recevait la sanction royale le 20 mai 1690 et comportait une disposition pour protéger les fabricants de feutre. ¶ Voir aussi *les autres notices de l'année 1690 sur cette controverse, et les notes*

See also *other works under 1690 relating to this controversy, and the notes appended to those entries, and also Hudson's Bay Company entries under 1696, 1748, and 1749.*

afférentes, ainsi que les notices de la Compagnie de la Baie d'Hudson des années 1696, 1748 et 1749.

Hudson's Bay Company. The case of the Hudsons-Bay. The kings of England, by right of discovery . . . . [London? 169–] Broadside. fol.

cf. NUC(Pre–56)258:448

Assumed to be the same as above.

On suppose qu'il s'agit d'un même.

Hudson's Bay Company. [A petition for continuance of their privileges, etc.] [London, 1690?] Broadside. fol.

BLC(to 1975)154:301

Headed: "Hudsons-Bay-Company." ¶ See also *other works under 1690 relating to this controversy, and the notes appended to those entries.*

En-tête : « Hudsons-Bay-Company ». ¶ Voir aussi *les autres ouvrages de l'année 1690 sur cette controverse, et les notes afférentes.*

An impartial account of the present state of the Hudson-Bay Company, as they stand incorporated in a charter granted them by King Charles the Second. [London? 1690?] Broadside. fol.

cf. NUC(Pre–56)265:187

Issued with: Hudson's Bay Company. The case of the Hudson's Bay Company of England, in referrence to the Canada Company of France. *[London?*

Publié avec : Hudson's Bay Company. The case of the Hudson's Bay Company of England, in referrence to the Canada Company of France *[Londres ? 1696 ?]* q.v., *à partir des*

1696?], q.v., from the originals in the Public Record Office, London. ¶ Text refers to "privileges enjoyed more than twenty years." The Company appealed to Parliament in 1690 [*see*: Hudson's Bay Company. *A petition .... London, 1690?, above*]. This is an attack on the Company. The writer opposes the address of the Company to Parliament for a "boundless charter." He sees no need for a joint stock company. ¶ *First edition; reprinted [Boston, 1921] in the Photostat Americana series of the Mass. Hist. Soc., no. 52, from the original in the Public Record Office, London. This latter is the work described in NUC, but Waldon appears to have seen the PRO original.* ¶ See also *other works under 1690 relating to this controversy, and the notes appended to those entries.*

originaux du Public Record Office, Londres. ¶ Le document traite des « privilèges qui existent depuis plus de vingt ans ». La Compagnie a fait appel devant le Parlement en 1690 [*voir* : Hudson's Bay Company. *A petition .... Londres, 1690 ?, plus haut*]. Il s'agit d'une attaque contre la Compagnie. L'auteur s'oppose à ce que la Compagnie demande au Parlement une « charte illimitée ». Il ne voit pas la nécessité de créer une société de capitaux. ¶ *Première édition ; réimpression [Boston, 1921] dans la collection Photostat Americana de la Mass. Hist. Soc., nᵒ 52, à partir de l'original du Public Record Office de Londres. Ce dernier est l'ouvrage décrit dans le NUC, mais Waldon semble avoir consulté l'original du PRO.* ¶ Voir aussi *les autres notices de l'année 1690 sur cette controverse, et les notes afférentes.*

Reasons humbly offered against the bill, for continuing a former act, for the confirming to the Hudson's-Bay Company, their priviledges and trade .... [London, 1690.] 3 p. fol.

NUC(Pre–56)483:512

Endorsed: Reasons against the Hudson's-Bay Company. ¶ Waldon has "privileges" and pub. date "[1690?]," which accords with a broadside, but otherwise similar work (it may, in fact, be the same work, differently described): see *next entry*. ¶ The writer protests against many abuses, and opposes the formation of a joint stock company.

Inscription officielle : Reasons against the Hudson's-Bay Company. ¶ Waldon note « privileges » et une date de publication « [1690 ?] » qui correspondent à un ouvrage similaire en tous points sauf que celui-là est un in-plano (il pourrait, en fait, s'agir du même ouvrage, décrit différemment). Voir *la notice suivante*. ¶ L'auteur s'élève contre les nombreux abus et s'oppose à la création d'une société de capitaux.

*Reasons humbly offered against the bill for continuing a former act, for the confirming to the Hudson's Bay-Company, their privileges and trade. [London, 1690?] Broadside. fol.

BLC(to 1975)154:301

See also other works relating to this controversy under 1690, and the notes appended to those entries (which refer also to other publication dates), but especially the preceding entry, which may be for the same work.	*Voir aussi* les autres ouvrages de l'année 1690 sur cette controverse, et les notes afférentes, qui se rapportent aussi à d'autres dates de publication ; la notice précédente pourrait bien se rapporter au même ouvrage.

1691

Boston. Citizens. To the King's Most Excellent Majesty, the humble address of divers of the gentry, merchants, and others, your Majesties most loyal and dutiful subjects inhabiting in Boston, Charles-town and places adjacent, within your Majesties territory and dominion of New-England in America. With a letter dated Charles-town, New-England, Novemb. 22. 1690, giving an account of the unfortunate expedition to Quebec in Canada, the inducements to it, &c. Signed L.H. Licensed Apr. 28th. 1691. [Colophon: Licensed April the 28th. 1691. London, printed by Henry Hills in Black-Fryars 1691.] 8 p. 4°

cf. NUC(Pre–56)68:171

Signed by Thom. Graffort, P. Bowden, Dav. Waterhouse, Laur. Hammond, and thirty others, p. 2. ¶ Address of a faction dissatisfied with the existing government of Massachusetts, because of its failure to protect the colony against the French and Indians, appealing to be taken into the "immediate care and protection" of the king. ¶ Waldon cites the similar title, Sabin: 6474 and Faribault: 161:	*Signé par Thom. Graffort, P. Bowden, Dav. Waterhouse, Laur. Hammond et trente autres personnes, p. 2. ¶ Mémoire d'un groupe de citoyens mécontents du gouvernement en place au Massachusetts en raison de son incapacité à protéger la colonie des Français et des Indiens, qui demandent « protection immédiate » de la part du roi. ¶ Waldon cite un titre similaire, Sabin:6474 et Faribault:161 : Address of the gentry and merchants of Boston, &c., giving*

Address of the gentry and merchants of Boston, &c., giving an account of the unfortunate expedition to Quebec, in Canada. *London, 1691, suggesting it as a "good example" of the mutilation of the "excellent catalogue" of Bishop White Kennett:* Bibliothecae americanae primordia *(London, 1713), referring to his entry on p. 153.* ¶ *NUC lists only the facsimile reprint of the Mass. Hist. Soc. [Boston, 1928].* ¶ *BVAU (facsim.)*

an account of the unfortunate expedition to Quebec, in Canada. *Londres, 1691, et laisse entendre qu'il s'agit d'un « bon exemple » de la mutilation dont est victime « l'excellent catalogue » de l'évêque White Kennett :* Bibliothecae americanae primordia *(Londres, 1713), se reportant à sa notice de la p. 153.* ¶ *Le NUC ne mentionne que la réimpression par fac-similé de la Mass. Hist. Soc., [Boston, 1928].* ¶ *BVAU (fac-similé)*

Echard, Laurence, 1670?–1730. A most compleat compendium of geography, general and special; describing all the empires, kingdoms, and dominions in the whole world. . . . By Laurence Eachard . . . . London: printed for Thomas Salusbury . . . 1691. 18 p.l., 168 p. 2 maps. 12°

Sabin:21760

This is Waldon's title; for a fuller title see next entry, and the complete title is given by Sabin (who gives 17 p. after the 168 p. for this edition). ¶ Canada: p. 144; Newfoundland: p. 160. ¶ *First edition; second ed., see next entry; also 1693 (third), 1697 (fourth), 1700 (fifth), 1704 (sixth), 1705 (seventh), 1713 (eighth) editions,* q.v.

Il s'agit du titre donné par Waldon ; un titre plus complet figure à la notice suivante. Le Sabin en cite le titre intégralement (qui donne 17 pages après les 168 de cette édition). ¶ Canada : p. 144 ; Terre-Neuve : p. 160. ¶ *Première édition ; deuxième édition :* voir *la notice suivante ; se reporter aux autres éditions : 1693 (troisième), 1697 (quatrième), 1700 (cinquième), 1704 (sixième), 1705 (septième), 1713 (huitième),* q.v.

*Echard, Laurence, 1670?–1730. A most compleat compendium of geography, general and special; describing all the empires, kingdoms, and dominions in the whole world. Shewing their bounds, situation, dimentions, ancient and modern names, history, government, religions, languages, commodities, divisions, sub-divisions, cities, rivers, mountains, lakes, with their archbishopricks, bishoppricks, and universities. . . . Collected according to the latest discoveries, and agreeing with the choicest and newest maps. The second edition, corrected, much improv'd, and enlarged above one quarter. By Laurence Eachard . . . . London: printed for Tho[mas]. Salusbury . . ., 1691. 8 p.l., 207 (*i.e* 227), [23] p. front., maps. 12°

NUC(Pre–56)154:608*

Page 227 incorrectly numbered 207. ¶ First edition published in the same year, 1691, *q.v.*, above.

La page 227 porte incorrectement le n° 207. ¶ Édition originale publiée la même année, 1691, *q.v.* la notice précédente.

Savage, Thomas, 1640–1705. An account of the late action of the New-Englanders, under the command of Sir William Phips, against the French at Canada. Sent in a letter from Major Thomas Savage of Boston in New-England, (who was present at the action) to his brother Mr. Perez Savage in London. Together with the Articles of war composed and agreed upon for that purpose. Licensed April 13, 1691. London, printed for Thomas Jones at the White Horse without Temple-Bar, 1691. 12, [3] p. 4°

NUC(Pre–56)522:228*

The unnumbered pages at the end contain "This indented bill of ten shillings," 1 p., and "A catalogue of books," 2 p. ¶ Savage was the officer in command of the militia in Phips's disastrous expedition against Quebec in 1690. This pamphlet is one of two narratives written by participants (cf. Church: 722). ¶ *Another ed. has collation: 1 l., [6] p. (i.e. 4 l.), but otherwise apparently the same (cf. BLC(to 1975)); reprinted in*

Les pages non numérotées à la fin comprennent « This indented bill of ten shillings » 1 p. et « A catalogue of books » 2 p. ¶ Savage commandait la milice lors de l'expédition désastreuse de Phips contre Québec en 1690. Cet opuscule est l'un des deux récits écrits par des participants (cf. Church:722). ¶ *Une autre éd. présente la collation suivante : 1 f., [6] p. (c.-à-d. 4 f.) mais, à part cela, il s'agit apparemment de la même édition (cf. BLC(to 1975)) ; réimpression dans le cadre de Photostat Americana,*

Photostat Americana, second series, no. 46, Boston, Mass. Hist. Soc., 1937 (cf. NUC). ¶ NSWA

deuxième collection, n° 46, Boston, Mass. Hist. Soc., 1937 (cf. NUC). ¶ NSWA

1692

*Child, Sir **Josiah**, 1630–1699. A new discourse of trade, wherein is recommended several weighty points relating to companies of merchants. The act of navigation. Naturalization of strangers. And our woolen manufactures. The balance of trade. And the nature of plantations, and their consequences in relation to the kingdom, are seriously discussed. Methods for the employment and maintenance of the poor are proposed. The reduction of interest of money to 4[l]. per centum is recommended. And some proposals for erecting a court of merchants for determining controversies, relating to maritine [sic] affairs, and for a law for transferance of bills or debt, are humbly offered. London, printed and sold by T[ace]. Sowle [1692.] 24 p.l., 238 p. 8°(?)

NUC(Pre–56)106:637*

A reply in part to: *Interest of money mistaken*. First pub. London, 1668, and Thomas Manly, *Usury at six percent examined*. First pub. London, 1669. ¶ Concerns Newfoundland fisheries, and is opposed to settlement. ¶ Apparently the first ed.; other editions and issues appeared in 1693, 1694, 1698, 1718, 1740, and 1751, *q.v.* for other notes; and also 1775 and 1804 (cf. NUC). Under an entry for the 1740 edition, NUC notes: First pub. under title *Brief observations concerning trade and interest of money*. London, 1668, *q.v.*

En partie, une réplique à : *Interest of money mistaken*. Première publ. Londres, 1668, et *Usury at six percent examined*. Première publ. Londres, 1669, de Thomas Manly. ¶ Traite des pêcheries de Terre-Neuve, et s'oppose à la colonisation. ¶ Apparemment la première éd. ; autres éditions et tirages en 1693, 1694, 1698, 1718, 1740, et 1751, *q.v.*, pour d'autres notes ; ainsi qu'en 1775 et 1804 (cf. NUC). Dans une notice pour l'édition de 1740, le NUC note : Première publ. sous le titre *Brief observations concerning trade and interest of money*. Londres, 1668, *q.v.*

[Crouch, Nathaniel], 1632?–1725?   The English empire in America: or, A prospect of Their Majesties dominions in the West-Indies.... By R.B. [*pseud.*] The second edition. London, printed for Nath. Crouch at the Bel in the Poultrey near Cheapside, 1692. 2 p.l., 184, [4] p. 2 plates, 2 maps (incl. front.) 12°

NUC(Pre–56)128:174*

Paging irregular. ¶ *First edition: 1685, q.v. for other information.*

Pagination irrégulière. ¶ *Première édition : 1685, q.v. pour d'autres renseignements.*

1693

Bayard, Nicholas, 1644?–1707, *and/et* C. Lodowick. A journal of the late actions of the French at Canada. With the manner of their being repuls'd, by His Excellency, Benjamin Fletcher, their Majesties governour of New-York. Impartially related by Coll. Nicholas Reyard [*sic*], and Lieutenant Coll. Charles Lodowick, who attended His Excellency, during the whole expedition. To which is added, I. An account of the present state and strength of Canada, given by two Dutch men, who have been a long time prisoners there, and now made their escape. II. The examination of a French prisoner. III. His Excellency Benjamin Fletcher's speech to the Indians. IV. An address from the corporation of Albany, to his Excellency, returning thanks for His Excellency's early assistance for their relief. Licensed, Sept. 11th, 1693. Edward Cooke. London, printed for Richard Baldwin, in Warwick-Lane, 1693. 2 p.l., 22 p., 1 l. 4°

NUC(Pre–56)40:485

Commonly known as Bayard's Journal (*cf. Church:727*). ¶ "Tis no more than what has been already printed at New-York by his Excellency's ... particular authority there," p. [iv]; [Church says this "is a reprint of that which is sometimes referred to as 'the lost Bradford Journal,' " and NUC has this as: *A narrative of an attempt made by the French of Canada* .... New York, 1693]. ¶ *Other editions: 1868*

Communément appelé Bayard's Journal (*cf. Church:727*). ¶ « Il ne s'agit rien de plus que ce qui a déjà été publié à New York par Son Excellence... qui fait spécialement autorité en la matière », p. [iv] ; [selon le Church, il « s'agit d'une réimpression de ce qu'on appelle parfois le Journal perdu de Bradford », tandis que le NUC répertorie cet écrit sous le titre *A narrative of an attempt made by the French of Canada* .... New York, 1693]. ¶ *Autres éditions : 1868 (New York,*

(New York, Sabin), NSWA, OTP, BVAU; 1903 (New York, facsim.). ¶ See also: following entry, Bayard's Narrative.

Sabin), NSWA, OTP, BVAU ; 1903 (New York, fac-sim.). ¶ Voir aussi Narrative de Bayard, à la notice suivante.

*[Bayard, Nicholas, 1644?–1707, and/et C. Lodowick.] A narrative of an attempt made by the French of Canada upon the Mohaques country being Indians under the protection of their Majesties Government of New-York. To which is added, 1. An account of the present state and strength of Canada, given by two Dutch-men, who have been prisoners there, and now made their escape. 2. The examination of a French prisoner. 3. His Excellency Benjamin Fletcher's speech to the Indians. 4. The answer of the five nations of the Mohaques to his Excellency. 5. Proposals made by the four chief Sachims of the five nations, to his Excellency. And his Excellency's reply thereto. 6. An address from the Corporation of Albany to his Excellency, returning thanks for his Excellency's early assistance for their relief, &c. New York: Printed and Sold by William Bradford, Anno 1693. 14 p. 4°(?)

NUC(Pre–56)40:486*

Caption title and colophon. ¶ The narrative has caption: A Journal kept by Coll. Nicholas Beyard and Lieut. Coll. Charles Lodwick, who attended his Excellency in this Expedition. ¶ An account of Frontenac's expedition against the Mohawks in 1692, and of Governor Fletcher's attempt to repulse their advance on Schenectady. Commonly known as Bradford's *Journal* (cf. Church:727). ¶ Perhaps the first book printed in New York, the only known copy is in the Public Record Office, London (cf. Church:727). ¶ First edition; other editions: 1903 (New York), 1922 (Boston), 1937 (Boston), 1940 (Boston). ¶ *See also:* preceding entry, Bayard's *Journal*.

Titre de départ et colophon. ¶ Le récit est assorti d'une légende : Journal tenu par le Col. Nicholas Beyard et le Lᵗ-col. Charles Lodwick, qui accompagnaient Son Excellence dans cette expédition. ¶ Un récit de l'expédition de Frontenac contre les Mohawks en 1692, et de la tentative du gouverneur Fletcher pour repousser leur avance sur Schenectady. Désignation courante : *Journal* de Bradford (cf. Church:727). ¶ Il s'agit peut-être du premier livre imprimé à New York, dont le seul exemplaire connu se trouve au Public Record Office, Londres (cf. Church:727). ¶ Première édition ; autres éditions : 1903 (New York), 1922 (Boston), 1937 (Boston), 1940 (Boston). ¶ *Voir aussi Journal* de Bayard, à la notice précédente.

Child, Sir **Josiah,** 1630–1699. A new discourse of trade, wherein is recommended several weighty points relating to companies of merchants. The act of navigation. Naturalization of strangers. And our woollen manufactures. The ballance of trade. And the nature of plantations, and their consesequences [*sic*] in relation to the kingdom, are seriously discussed. And some proposals for erecting a court of merchants for determining controversies, relating to maritime affairs, and for a law for transferrance [*sic*] of bills of debts, are humbly offered. By Sir Josiah Child. London, printed and sold by John Everingham, at the Star in Ludgate Street, in the year 1693. 27 p.l., 37, 234 (*i.e.* 238) p. 8°

NUC(Pre–56)106:637*

Waldon has pagination as: 2 p.l., 50, 234 p., but in any case this differs from the 1692 collation. ¶ "December 24, 1692. Imprimatur Edmund Bohum": verso of first p.l. ¶ "Concerning plantations": p. 164–208; Newfoundland: p. 195–204. The only value of Newfoundland lies in the fisheries. The author is opposed to settlement. ¶ *First ed. under this title appeared in 1692, and the so-called second ed. in 1694, but the title and collation here are different. Other eds.: 1698, 1718, 1740, and 1751,* q.v. ¶ "Concerning plantations" was reprinted as: *The nature of plantations and their consequence to Great Britain seriously considered,* by Sir Josiah Child (in: *Select dissertations on colonies and plantations.* London, printed and sold by W. Hay, 1875, 8°). A large part of the original, including the discussion of Newfoundland, is omitted from *A discourse concerning plantations,* by Sir Josiah Child, 1692 (in: *Select tracts relating to colonies.* London, J. Roberts, 174–?, p. 31–40).

Waldon indique pour pagination : 2 f. l., 50, 234 p., ce qui diffère en tout cas de la collation sous 1692. ¶ « December 24, 1692. Imprimatur Edmund Bohum » : verso du premier f. l. ¶ « Concerning plantations » : p. 164–208 ; Terre-Neuve : p. 195–204. La seule valeur de Terre-Neuve réside dans les pêcheries. L'auteur est contre la colonisation. ¶ *La première éd. sous ce titre parut en 1692, puis celle qu'on considère la deuxième éd. fut publiée en 1694, mais le titre et la collation diffèrent dans ce cas. Autres éd. : 1698, 1718, 1740, et 1751,* q.v. ¶ « Concerning plantations » fut réimprimé sous le titre *The nature of plantations and their consequence to Great Britain seriously considered* par sir Josiah Child (dans : *Select dissertations on colonies and plantations.* Londres, imprimé et vendu par W. Hay, 1875, in-8°). Une grande partie de l'original, y compris le débat sur Terre-Neuve, ne figure pas dans *A discourse concerning plantations* par sir Josiah Child, 1692 (dans : *Select tracts relating to colonies.* Londres, J. Roberts, 174–?, p. 31–40).

*Echard, Laurence, 1670?–1730. A most compleat compendium of geography, general and special . . . . The third edition, corrected and much improv'd . . . by Laurence Eachard . . . . London, printed for T[homas]. Salusbury . . . 1693. 8 p.l., 236, [12] p. 4 maps on 2 l. 12°

NUC(Pre–56)154:608*

Publisher's adverts: first p.l. and p. [246–48]. ¶ *See* first ed., 1691, for notes.

Réclames de l'éditeur : premier f. l. et p. [246–48]. ¶ *Voir* notes dans la première éd., 1691.

1694

Child, Sir **Josiah,** 1630–1699. A new discourse of trade, wherein is recommended several weighty points relating to companies of merchants . . . . And some proposals . . . relating to maritine [*sic*] affairs . . . . By Sir Josiah Child. The second edition. London, printed, and sold by Sam[uel]. Crouch, Tho[mas]. Horn, & Jos[eph]. Hindmarsh. 1694. 24 p.l., 238 p. 8°

NUC(Pre–56)106:637*

Waldon has pagination as: t.-p., 46, 238 p. ¶ *Same title as the 1693 edition, excepting "maritine" for "maritime."* ¶ Newfoundland [fisheries]: p. 195–204. ¶ *First pub. under this title: London, 1692; another edition appeared in 1693, but not called second ed.; further editions appeared in 1698, 1718, 1740, and 1751,* q.v. *for other notes. NUC has a variant 1694, with paging errors and no edition statement.* ¶ BVAU

Pagination de Waldon : p. de t., 46, 238 p. ¶ *Titre identique à celui de l'édition de 1693, à l'exception du mot « maritine » au lieu de « maritime ».* ¶ Terre-Neuve [pêcheries de] : p. 195–204. ¶ *Première publ. sous ce titre : Londres, 1692 ; une autre édition parut en 1693 mais n'est pas appelée deuxième éd. ; d'autres éditions furent publiées en 1698, 1718, 1740, et 1751,* q.v. *pour d'autres notes. Le NUC répertorie une variante de 1694, qui comporte des erreurs de pagination et ne comprend aucune mention d'édition.* ¶ BVAU

1695

Brewster, Sir Francis, *fl.* 1674–1702. Essays on trade and navigation. In five parts. The first part. By Sir Francis Brewster, k[t]. Licensed, January 3, 1694/5 [*i.e.,* 1695 N.S.]. London: printed for Tho. Cockerill . . . 1695. 1 p.l., xi p., 1 l., 126 p. 8°

NUC(Pre–56)75:39

"The first part only was published": DNB. ¶ *Arber, 2:540 completes the imprint: for T. Cockerill at the Three Legs, over against the Stocks market.* ¶ "Of the New-found-land Fishing": p. 68–74. The author contends that, the French interest having been predominant at the court of Charles II, no steps were taken to check French encroachments on the Newfoundland fisheries and that the French have grown great in their trade and navigation by their fishing. He proposes to develop the Newfoundland fisheries in the English interest.

« Seule la première partie fut publiée » : DNB. ¶ *Arber, 2:540 complète l'adresse bibliographique : for T. Cockerill at the Three Legs, over against the Stocks market.* ¶ « Of the New-found-land Fishing » : p. 68–74. Selon l'auteur, les intérêts français ayant occupé une place prépondérante à la cour de Charles II, aucune mesure ne fut prise pour empêcher les Français d'empiéter sur les droits de pêche de Terre-Neuve, et les Français sont devenus d'excellents commerçants et navigateurs grâce à la pêche. Il propose de développer les pêcheries de Terre-Neuve dans l'intérêt de l'Angleterre.

1696

*Clarke, Samuel, 1599–1683. A new description of the world . . . . By S. Clark. The second edition. London, printed for Hen. Rhodes at the Star the corner of Brides-lane, Fleet-Street, 1696. 3 p.l., 218, [2] p. front. 12°

NUC(Pre–56)111:361*

Booksellers' advert.: [2] p. at end. ¶ First pub. London, 1689, *q.v.*

Réclames des libraires : [2] p. à la fin. ¶ Première publ. Londres, 1689, *q.v.*

*Hudson's Bay Company. [Announcement. Begins:] Upon Wednesday the 18th day of November instant . . . . London, the thirteenth day of November, 1696. Broadside. fol.

NUC(Pre–56)258:447

An announcement of the forthcoming election of officers for the Hudson's Bay Company, no doubt including some who were, or would be serving, or had served, in Canada.

Une annonce de l'élection prochaine de membres du conseil d'administration de la Compagnie de la Baie d'Huson, dont, à n'en pas douter, un certain nombre qui servaient ou serviraient au Canada, ou y avaient servi.

Hudson's Bay Company. The case of the Hudson's Bay Company of England, in referrence [*sic*] to the Canada Company of France, and their servant Gabriel de la Forest. [London? 1696?] Broadside. fol.

cf. NUC(Pre–56)258:448

First edition; reprinted [Boston, 1921] in the Photostat Americana series of the Mass. Hist. Soc., no. 52, from the original in the Public Record Office, London. This latter is the work described by both Waldon and NUC. See also An impartial account of the present state of the Hudson-Bay Company. [London? 1690?].

Première édition ; réimpression [Boston, 1921] dans la collection Photostat Americana de la Mass. Hist. Soc., n° 52, d'après l'original du Public Record Office, Londres. Celui-ci est l'ouvrage décrit à la fois par Waldon et le NUC. Voir aussi An impartial account of the present state of the Hudson-Bay Company. [Londres ? 1690 ?].

1697

*Echard, Laurence, 1670?–1730. A most compleat compendium of geography, general and special. . . . Shewing their bounds, situation, dimensions . . . . The fourth edition, corrected and much improved. By Laurence Echard . . . . London, printed for J[ohn]. Salusbury . . . 1697. 7 p.l., 236, [9] p. map. 12°

NUC(Pre–56)154:608*

Advertisements: last page. ¶ *See* first ed., 1691, for notes.

Réclames : dernière page. ¶ *Voir* notes dans la première éd., 1691.

Great Britain. Lords Justices. By the Lords Justices, a proclamation for publishing the peace between His Majesty and the French King. Given at the Court at Whitehall the eighteenth day of October, 1697. In the ninth year of His Majesties reign . . . . London, printed by Charles Bill, and the executrix of Thomas Newcomb, deceas'd; printers to the Kings most Excellent Majesty. 1697. Broadside. fol.

NUC(Pre–56)214:116

The Peace of Ryswick, September 1697, ended the War of the Grand Alliance. ¶ *Reprinted in Scotland the same year:* see *next entry.*

Le traité de Ryswick, septembre 1697, mit fin à la guerre dite « de la Ligue d'Augsbourg ». ¶ *Réimpression en Écosse la même année :* voir *la notice suivante.*

*Great Britain. Lords Justices. By the Lords Justices . . . . Edinburgh, reprinted by the Heirs of A[ndrew]. Anderson, 1697. Broadside. fol.

BLC(to 1975)95:279

First pub. London, the same year: *see* preceding entry.

Première publ. Londres, la même année : *voir* la notice précédente.

Great Britain. Treaties, etc., 1694–1702 (William III). Articles of peace between the most serene and mighty Prince William the Third, King of Great Britain, and the most serene and mighty Prince Lewis the Fourteenth, the Most Christian King, concluded in the royal palace at Ryswicke the 10/20. day of September, 1697. By command of their excellencies the Lords Justices. London, printed by Charles Bill and the executrix of Thomas Newcomb, deceas'd; printers to the Kings most excellent Majesty. 1697. 17 p. fol.

NUC(Pre–56)215:508*

Proclamation of the Treaty of Ryswick (20 Sept. 1697, N.S.), by which France regained Acadia and retained most of the Hudson's Bay Company forts. ¶ Reprinted in Edinburgh, and in London in Latin (q.v.), and in Boston, Mass., all in the same year.

Proclamation du traité de Ryswick (20 sept. 1697, c.g.), en vertu duquel la France récupéra l'Acadie et conserva la plupart des forts de la Compagnie de la Baie d'Hudson. ¶ Réimpression la même année à Édimbourg, ainsi qu'à Londres en latin (q.v.), et à Boston (Mass.).

*Great Britain. Treaties, etc., 1694–1702 (William III). Articles of peace between the most serene and mighty Prince William the Third, King of Great-Britain, and the most serene and mighty Prince Lewis the Fourteenth . . . at Ryswicke . . . . [Edinburgh: reprinted by the heirs and successors of A[ndrew]. Anderson, printer to the King's most excellent Majesty, 1697.] 5 p. fol.

NUC(Pre–56)215:508*

Caption title and colophon. ¶ *See* preceding entry for other notes.

Titre de départ et colophon. ¶ *Voir* autres notes à la notice précédente.

Great Britain. Treaties, etc., 1694–1702 **(William III).** Articuli pacis inter . . . Gulielmum Tertium Magnae Britanniae regem, & . . . Ludovicum Decimum Quartum regem christianissimum, in domo regia Ryswicensi conclusae 10/20 die Septembris, anno 1697. Articles of peace between . . . William the Third, King of Great Britain, and . . . Lewis the Fourteenth . . . . London, printed by Charles Bill and the executrix of Thomas Newcomb, 1697. 16 p. 16°(?)

NUC(Pre–56)215:508*

Latin and English in parallel columns. ¶ See *preceding entry but one for other notes.*	En latin et en anglais sur des colonnes parallèles. ¶ Voir *autres notes à l'avant-dernière notice, plus haut.*

[Mather, Cotton], 1663–1728. Pietas in patriam: the life of his excellency Sir William Phips, knt. Late captain general, and governour in chief of the province of the Massachuset-Bay, New England. Containing the memorable changes undergone, and actions performed by him. Written by one intimately acquainted with him . . . . London: printed by Sam. Bridge in Austin-Friers, for Nath. Hiller at the Princes-Arms in Leaden-Hall Street, over against St. Mary-Ax, 1697, 6 p.l., 110, [6], 2 p. 12°

NUC(Pre–56)369:82

Waldon has collation as: t.-p., [8] p., 1 l., 110 [6, Poem; 2, Books] p. ¶ Phips's expeditions against the French and Indians: p. 30–54; 82–88. ¶ *NUC notes: Reprinted in 1699, and also included in Mather's* Magnalia Christi Americana. *London, 1702, and these are also recorded in Sabin:46455, but the 1699 reprint is not further identified in NUC or Sabin.*	*Collation de Waldon: p. de t., [8] p., 1 f., 110 [6, Poème ; 2, Livres] p.* ¶ Expéditions de Phips contre les Français et les Indiens : p. 30–54 ; 82–88. ¶ *Note du NUC : Réimpression en 1699, et insertion dans l'ouvrage de Mather,* Magnalia Christi Americana. *Londres, 1702. Ces ouvrages figurent également dans le Sabin:46455, mais la réimpression de 1699 ne fait pas l'objet d'autres précisions aussi bien dans le NUC que dans le Sabin.*

An account of Monsieur de la Salle's last expedition and discoveries in North America. Presented to the French king, and published by the Chevalier Tonti, governour of Fort St. Louis, in the province of the Illinois. Made English from the Paris original. Also the adventures of the Sieur de Montauban, captain of the French buccaneers on the coast of Guinea, in the year 1695. London, printed for J. Tonson at the Judge's Head, and S. Buckley at the Dolphin in Fleet-street, and R. Knaplock, at the Angel and Grown [*sic*] in St. Paul's church-yard. 1698. 1 p.l., 211, [1], 44 p. 8°

NUC(Pre–56)2:553*

Authorship of the work was denied by De Tonti, although it is apparently based on a narrative written by him: cf. Charlevoix, *Histoire . . . de la Nouvelle France*. Paris, 1744, v. 2, p. 260. ¶ At head of text, p. 1: A new account of the Northern America. ¶ The Montauban *Adventures* has separate pagination, but continuous signature marks. ¶ Transl. from: *Dernieres decouvertes dans l'Amerique Septentrionale de M. de La Sale*. Paris, 1697. ¶ First English edition; another edition: 1814.

De Tonti nia être l'auteur de cet ouvrage, qui serait toutefois basé sur un récit de sa propre plume : cf. Charlevoix, *Histoire . . . de la Nouvelle France*. Paris, 1744, vol. 2, p. 260. ¶ En marge de tête, p. 1 : A new account of the Northern America. ¶ L'ouvrage de Montauban, *Adventures*, comporte une pagination distincte quoique assortie de signatures continues. ¶ Trad. de : *Dernieres decouvertes dans l'Amerique Septentrionale de M. de La Sale*. Paris, 1697. ¶ Première édition anglaise ; autre édition : 1814.

Bernard, Jacques, 1658–1718, *ed./éd.* The acts and negotiations, together with the particular articles at large, of the general Peace, concluded at Ryswick, by the most illustrious Confederates with the French King. To which is premised, the negotiations and articles of the Peace, concluded at Turin, between the same prince and the Duke of Savoy. Translated from the original publish'd at the Hague [and edited by Jacques Bernard]. London: printed for Robert Clavel . . . and Tim. Childe . . . 1698. [12], 223, 74–142 (*i.e.* 290) p. 2 fold. plans. 8°

NUC(Pre–56)49:439*

Waldon enters under: Gt. Brit. Treaties, etc. ¶ *Transl. from:* Actes et mémoires des négociations de la paix de Ryswick. *La Haye, 1699 (and later eds.), collected by Jacques Bernard in four vols.* ¶ *Pages 224–90 misnumbered 74–142.* ¶ *The Peace of Ryswick, 20 Sept. 1697, ended the war of the Grand Alliance; by it, France recovered Acadia and retained all the Hudson's Bay Company forts excepting Fort Albany. (See under 1697 for editions of the treaty.)* ¶ *The several entries in NUC, each with the same title and imprint, and the various paginations all totalling about 290 p., may be different descriptions of the same edition.*

Répertorié par Waldon sous : Gt. Brit. Treaties, etc. ¶ *Trad. de :* Actes et mémoires des négociations de la paix de Ryswick. *La Haye, 1699 (et des éd. ultérieures), réunis en quatre vol. par Jacques Bernard.* ¶ *Erreur de pagination : les pages 224–90 portent les numéros 74–142.* ¶ *Le traité de Ryswick (20 sept. 1697) mit fin à la guerre dite « de la Ligue d'Augsbourg » ; grâce à ce traité, la France récupéra l'Acadie et conserva tous les forts de la Compagnie de la Baie d'Hudson sauf Fort Albany. (Voir sous 1697 pour des éditions du traité.)* ¶ *Les diverses notices du NUC, qui portent toutes le même titre et la même adresse bibliographique, ainsi que les différentes paginations, dont chacune représente environ 290 p., constituent peut-être des descriptions distinctes de la même édition.*

The Case of Captain Desborow against Captain Norris, in relation to Monsieur Ponti. [London? 1698.] Broadside. fol.

BLC(to 1975)81:187

Title from endorsation on back. ¶ Begins: "Captain Desborow, by his Petition to the Honourable House of Commons, sets forth, That he being Commander of the Mary-Galley, was the last Year, together with Fourteen other Ships, ordered to Newfoundland, under the Command of Captain John Norris." ¶ Desborow charges that (1) Norris denies him and his men their share of prizes taken near Newfoundland, (2) Norris had the chance to capture M. Ponti with five

Titre tiré de l'inscription officielle au verso. ¶ Commence par : « Dans sa requête à l'honorable Chambre des communes, le capitaine Desborow déclare qu'en sa qualité de commandant du Mary-Galley, il a reçu l'ordre l'année dernière de faire voile sur Terre-Neuve, avec quatorze autres navires, sous le commandement du capitaine John Norris ». ¶ Les accusations de Desborow sont les suivantes : 1) Norris a spolié Desborow et ses hommes de leur part des prises réalisées à proximité de Terre-Neuve, 2) la chance de capturer M. Ponti avec cinq

ships but the men-of-war were too crowded with prize-goods to fight, and (3) Norris used a prize-ship for fishing, and the king's stores, and men in fitting boats, etc. ¶ See also: *Peire, Monsieur*, A copy of Monsieur Peire's certificate. *[London? 1698?]*.

navires s'est offerte à Norris, mais les vaisseaux de guerre étaient trop encombrés des marchandises du butin pour livrer le combat, et 3) Norris s'est servi d'un bateau capturé pour pêcher, il a usé des entrepôts du roi et il a utilisé des hommes dans des chaloupes, etc. ¶ Voir aussi : *Peire, Monsieur*, A copy of Monsieur Peire's certificate. *[Londres ? 1698 ?]*.

Child, Sir **Josiah**, 1630–1699. A new discourse of trade, wherein is recommended several weighty points relating to companies of merchants. The act of navigation. Naturalization of strangers. And our woolen manufactures. The ballance of trade. And the nature of plantations, and their consequences in relation to the Kingdom, are seriously discussed. Methods for the employment and maintenance of the poor are proposed. The reduction of interest of money to 4[l]. per centum, is recommended . . . . By Sir Josiah Child. London, printed and sold by T[race]. Sowle . . . 1698. 24 p.l., 238 p. 8°

NUC(Pre–56)106:637*

Same title as the 1692 edition. ¶ Waldon has pagination as: t.-p., 46, 238 p. ¶ Newfoundland [fisheries]: p. 195–204. ¶ First pub. under this title: London, 1692; Sabin calls this the third edition, but see 1718 ed.; also 1693, 1694 (second), 1718, 1740, and 1751 eds., q.v.

Titre identique à celui de l'édition de 1692. ¶ Pagination indiquée par Waldon : p. de t., 46, 238 p. ¶ Terre-Neuve [pêcheries de] : p. 195–204. ¶ D'abord publ. sous ce titre : Londres, 1692 ; selon le Sabin, il s'agit de la troisième édition, mais voir l'éd. de 1718 ; autres éd. : 1693, 1694 (deuxième), 1718, 1740, et 1751, q.v.

[Crouch, Nathaniel], 1632?–1725? The English empire in America: or a Prospect of their Majesties dominions in the West-Indies . . . . Illustrated with maps and pictures. By R.B. [*pseud.*] The third edition. London, printed for Nath. Crouch at the Bell in the Poultry near Cheapside. 1698. 1 p.l., 178 p. illus., map. 12°

NUC(Pre–56)128:174*

Two plates printed on versos. ¶ *First edition: 1685, q.v. for other information; this third ed. also reprinted [San Francisco, 1940] — cf. NUC.*

Deux planches imprimées aux versos. ¶ *Première édition : 1685, q.v. pour d'autres renseignements ; cette troisième éd. a également été réimprimée [San Francisco, 1940] –cf. NUC.*

Degrave, John, *fl.* 1697. The case of John Degrave, Francis Minshall and others, owners of the seven sail of ships taken up in July, 1697. by the Commissioners of the Transport. Humbly presented to the Honourable House of Commons . . . . [London? 1698?] [No collation.] fol.

BLC(to 1975)79:224

Petition to the House of Commons to pay their bill for carrying provisions to Newfoundland at great risk. The settlers would have perished without their assistance. They were to have been paid out of "that Year's Funds," but accounts were settled and they were not paid, suggesting 1698 as date, as in Sabin, rather than "1700," as in BLC. ¶ *Possibly reprinted New York, Joseph Sabin, 18(65?), in Sabin reprints; also appeared in microcard and microfiche editions.* ¶ *BVAU(MF)*

Requête à la Chambre des communes afin d'obtenir le paiement de leur facture pour le transport de provisions jusqu'à Terre-Neuve à grands risques. Les colons auraient péri sans leur aide. Ils devaient être réglés à même « les fonds de l'année courante », mais les comptes ont été fermés et ils ne touchèrent rien, cette mention donnant à penser que cet écrit date de 1698, comme l'indique le Sabin, plutôt que de « 1700 ? », comme le mentionne le BLC. ¶ *Autre réimpression possible : New York, Joseph Sabin, 18(65 ?), dans le cadre des réimpressions du Sabin ; reproductions sur microcarte et microfiche.* ¶ *BVAU (mic.)*

*The English pilot. The fourth book. Describing the sea-coasts, capes, head-lands, rivers, bays, roads, havens, harbours, streights, islands, depths, rocks, shoals, sands, banks, and dangers from Hudson-Bay to the River Amazones, with all the West-India navigation, and all the islands therein. . . . With a new description of New-found-Land, New-England, New York. . . . Shewing the courses and distances from one place to another, the ebbing and flowing of the sea, the getting of the tides and currents, &c. . . . By the information of divers navigators of our own and other nations. London, printed for John Thornton and Richard Mount, 1698. 1 p.l., 62 p. illus., maps (part fold.). fol.

NUC(Pre–56)160:373*

First edition: 1689, *q.v.* for other editions.

Première édition : 1689, *q.v.* pour d'autres éditions.

*Hennepin, Louis, 1626–*ca.* 1705. A new discovery of a vast country in America, extending above four thousand miles, between New France and New Mexico. With a description of the Great Lakes, cataracts, rivers, plants, and animals: also, the manners, customs, and languages, of the several native Indians; and the advantage of commerce with those different nations. With a continuation: giving an account of the attempts of the Sieur de la Salle upon the mines of St. Barbe, &c. The taking of Quebec by the English; with the advantages of a shorter cut to China and Japan. Both parts illustrated with maps and figures, and dedicated to his Majesty K. William. By L. Hennepin, now resident in Holland. To which is added, several new discoveries in North-America, not publish'd in the French edition. London: printed for M. Bentley, J[acob]. Tonson, H[enry]. Bonwick, T[imothy]. Goodwin, and S[amuel]. Manship, 1698. 12 p.l., 299 p.; 16 p.l., 178 p., 1 l., 303–55 p. 2 fold. maps, 6 fold. plates. 4°(?)

NUC(Pre–56)240:546–47*

Engraved half-title: A new discovery of a large country in America by Father Lewis Hennepin. ¶ [Part 1] is a translation of the "Nouvelle découverte"; [pt. 2] of "Nouveau voyage," with special t.-p. and pagination: A continuation of the new

Faux-titre gravé : A new discovery of a large country in America by Father Lewis Hennepin. ¶ [La partie 1] est une traduction de « Nouvelle découverte » ; [la part. 2] une traduction de « Nouveau voyage », avec p. de t. et pagination individuelle : A continuation of the new discovery of a vast

discovery of a vast country in America, extending above four thousand miles, between New France and New Mexico .... By L. Hennepin .... London, 1698. ¶ Appended to the second part: Joliet's account, with half-title "An account of several new discoveries in North-America": 1 l., p. 303–06; "An account of M. la Salle's voyage to the river Mississippi ...": p. 307–17; "A discovery of some new countries and nations in the Northern-America. By Father Marquette": p. 318–55. ¶ First English edition; NUC also has another entry for the same year, but with a different collation: 11 p.l., 243 p., 1 l., [30], 228 p., and a frontispiece; also published in English: London, 1699 (*q.v.*), with later American editions, and an abridged English edition: *A discovery of a large, rich, and plentiful country, in the North America*. London, 1720 (*q.v.* for other notes). First pub. Utrecht, 1697, in French, succeeded by numerous other editions and translations in French (mostly pub. in Holland), German, Dutch, and Spanish. ¶ BVA · BVIPA

country in America, extending above four thousand miles, between New France and New Mexico .... Par L. Hennepin .... Londres, 1698. ¶ Annexé à la deuxième partie : le récit de Joliet, avec le faux-titre : « An account of several new discoveries in North-America » : 1 f., p. 303–06 ; « An account of M. la Salle's voyage to the river Mississippi. . . » : p. 307–17 ; « A discovery of some new countries and nations in the Northern-America. By Father Marquette » : p. 318–55. ¶ Première édition anglaise ; le NUC donne une autre notice pour la même année, mais avec une collation différente : 11 f. l., 243 p., 1 f., [30], 228 p., et un frontispice ; également publié en anglais : Londres, 1699 (*q.v.*), avec des éditions américaines ultérieures, et une édition anglaise abrégée : *A discovery of a large, rich, and plentiful country, in the North America*. Londres, 1720 (*q.v.* pour d'autres notes). Première publ. Utrecht, 1697, en français, suivie par de nombreuses autres éditions et traductions en français (surtout publ. en Hollande), en allemand, en hollandais et en espagnol. ¶ BVA · BVIPA

Peire, Monsieur. A copy of Monsieur Peire's certificate, sent by him to Captain Desborow; concerning Monsieur Ponti's five ships appearing off St. John's port in Newfoundland, translated into English from the original, which is ready to be produced. [London? 1698?] Broadsheet. fol.

BLC(to 1975)250:359

Printed on both sides. ¶ Dated: Dover, 28 Jan. 1698. ¶ *Monsieur Peire and his certificate, from which this apparently was translated, have not been identified, and the certificate may never have been published (not found in BN); but the French ships off St. John's were part of a series of attacks on the English settlements in Newfoundland under Frontenac and D'Iberville, from 1689 until the Peace of Ryswick, 1697, called a truce in the Grand Alliance War in Europe and restored most French possessions in Canada to France. ¶ Further to this are: Charles Desborow,* The humble address . . . . *[London,] 1699, and* The case of Captain Desborow. *[London? 1698],* q.v.

Imprimé sur les deux côtés. ¶ Date : Douvres, le 28 janv. 1698. ¶ *Monsieur Peire et son attestation, dont cet écrit semble être une traduction, n'ont pas été identifiés, et l'attestation n'a peut-être jamais été publiée (introuvable dans le BN) ; mais les vaisseaux français au large de St. John's prirent part à une série d'attaques contre les colonies anglaises de Terre-Neuve sous la commande de Frontenac et d'Iberville, de 1689 jusqu'au traité de Ryswick signé en 1697 qui mit fin à la guerre dite « de la Ligue d'Augsbourg » en Europe et restituèrent à la France la plupart de ses possessions au Canada. ¶ On trouve ensuite :* The humble address . . . . *[Londres] 1699, de Charles Desborow et* The case of Captain Desborow. *[Londres ? 1698],* q.v.

1699

Desborow, Charles. The humble address of the Lords Spiritual and Temporal to His Majesty, in relation to the petition of Charles Desborow, late captain of His Majesty's ship Mary-Gally, employ'd in the expedition to Newfoundland, in the year 1697, under the command of Captain John Norris: and His Majesty's most gracious answer thereto. [London,] printed for Charles Desborow, 1699. [4], 8 p. 4°

BLC(to 1975)81:187

Waldon has collation: t.-p., [2], 8 p. ¶ *Desborow's petition appears at the front.* ¶ The House of Lords supported Desborow's claim to have been "unjustly charged with Breach of Orders, and Neglect of Duty, and dismiss'd from his command," and requested that Captain Norris, the squadron

Collation de Waldon : p. de t., [2], 8 p. ¶ *La requête de Desborow est inscrite à la première page.* ¶ La Chambre des Lords appuya la déclaration de Desborow, suivant laquelle il avait été « injustement accusé d'avoir enfreint les ordres et manqué à son devoir, ainsi qu'injustement démis de son commandement », et elle demanda que le

commander, be summoned before the House to answer charges in connection with the failure to attack the French under Ponti off St. John's on 21 June 1697. ¶ *A work with a similar title*, The case of Captain Desborow against Captain Norris, in relation to Monsieur Ponti, *was published in London(?), 1698 (cf. BLC).* See also: *Peire, Monsieur*, A copy of Monsieur Peire's certificate. *[London? 1698?].*

Great Britain. Laws, statutes, etc. Anno regni Guilielmi III . . . decimo (undecimo). In the Parliament begun . . . 1698. (An Act to encourage the trade to Newfoundland.) [London] Charles Bill and the executrix of Thomas Newcombe, 1699. fol.

"From Harmsworth cat."

Perhaps from Sir R.L. Harmsworth, Catalogue of Americana *(type-script; unavailable to the editor); not found in* The Northcliffe Collection *in PAC (Ottawa, 1926); but NUC lists many other catalogues of parts of the great Harmsworth Library. This is similar to, perhaps the same as,* An Act to incourage the trade to Newfoundland, *[London?] 1700, q.v., under the same heading as above.*

Hennepin, Louis, 1626–*ca.* 1705. A new discovery of a vast country in America, extending above four thousand miles, between New France & New Mexico; with a deseription [*sic*] of the Great Lakes, cataracts, rivers, plants, and animals. Also, the manners, customs, and languages of the several native Indians. . . . With a continuation . . . . Both illustrated with maps, and figures; and dedicated to His Majesty King William . . . . To which are added, several new discoveries in North America, not published In [*sic*] the French edition. London, printed by [*sic*] for Henry Bonwicke, 1699. 2 v. in 1: 1 p.l., 18, 1–138, 155–70, 161–240; 1 l., 30–216 p. front., 6 fold. plates, 2 fold. maps. 8°

NUC(Pre–56)240:547*

The "Continuation" has a special t.-p. ¶ "The taking of Quebec by the English," 1629, has been added to the contents of the 1698 edition. ¶ *First pub. in English: London, 1698, q.v. for other notes and editions.* ¶ *OTP*

« La continuation » comporte une p. de t. distincte. ¶ *« La prise de Québec par les Anglais » en 1629 a été ajoutée à l'édition de 1698.* ¶ *Première publ. en anglais : Londres, 1698, q.v. pour d'autres notes et éditions.* ¶ *OTP*

*[Mather, Cotton], 1663–1728. Pietas in patriam: the life of his excellency Sir William Phips, Knt. . . . . London, 1699.

cf. NUC(Pre–56)369:82

This work is referred to in the NUC and Sabin:46455 notes to the first ed., 1697, *q.v.*

Le NUC et le Sabin:46455 renvoient à cet ouvrage dans leurs notes à la première édition de 1697, *q.v.*

A new account of North America, as it was lately presented to the French king; containing a more particular description of that vast country, and of the manners and customs of the inhabitants, than has been hitherto publisht. [London] printed for R[obert]. Knaplock at the Angel and Crown in St. Paul's Churchyard [1698, *i.e.,* 1699 N.S.]. [No collation given.]

Arber, 3:108

Waldon has this under 1698, the Old Style date, Arber's listing being under Feb. 1699, N.S. ¶ This . . . [title is] in the list of books, p. xx, at end of v. 6, [Awnsham] Churchill's *Collection of voyages and travels*. [London] 1746 [6 v., 1744–46 (also 8 v., 1744–47), *q.v.*, under 1744] where the imprint is London, 1698 [evidently O.S.], with note: "We have here a *French* account of those countries, but more particularly what belongs to them, more exact than any other has delivered." No copy has been located. It may be another translation, or the same translation with a different title-page, of [Henri de] Tonti's work *An account of Monsieur de la Salle's last expedition*. [London, 1698], *q.v.* Or it may be the same book, [with] an erroneous entry in *The term catalogues* having been copied in Churchill.

Waldon répertorie cet ouvrage sous 1698, selon le calendrier julien, tandis qu'Arber l'a classé sous février 1699, c.g. ¶ Ce . . . [titre est] dans la liste de livres, p. xx, à la fin du vol. 6, *Collection of voyages and travels*. [Londres], 1746, de [Awnsham] Churchill, [6 vol., 1744–1746 (aussi en 8 vol., 1744–1747), *q.v.*, sous 1744] où l'adresse bibliographique indique Londres, 1698 [manifestement selon le calendrier julien], avec la note : « Nous avons ici un rapport *français* sur ces contrées, qui indique plus particulièrement ce qui leur appartient, avec plus d'exactitude que tout autre auparavant ». Aucun exemplaire n'a été trouvé. Il peut s'agir d'une autre traduction, ou de la même traduction avec une page de titre différente, de l'ouvrage de [Henri de] Tonti, *An account of Monsieur de la Salle's last expedition*. [Londres, 1698], *q.v.* Ou peut-être s'agit-il du même livre, [avec] une notice dans *The term catalogues* qui est erronée et aurait été copiée d'après Churchill.

1700

Bray, Thomas, 1656–1730. A memorial, representing the present state of religion, on the continent of North-America. By Thomas Bray .... London: Printed by W. Downing, for the author, 1700. 12 [*i.e.,* 15] p. fol.

NUC(Pre–56)73:295*

Caption title: A memorial humbly laid before the Right Reverend the lord bishops of this kingdom, and other right noble, and worthy patrons of religion; representing the present state thereof, in the

Titre de départ : A memorial humbly laid before the Right Reverend the lord bishops of this kingdom, and other right noble, and worthy patrons of religion; representing the present state thereof, in the several provinces on the continent

several provinces on the continent of North America, in order to the providing a sufficient number of proper missionaries, so absolutely necessary to be sent at this juncture into those parts. ¶ Pages 13–15 wrongly numbered 9–10, 12. ¶ Addressed to the Archbishop of Canterbury; Newfoundland treated: p. 9–10. The first church was established in St. John's in 1699. ¶ Other issues appeared in 1700, and other editions in 1701, 1901, and 1916.

of North America, in order to the providing a sufficient number of proper missionaries, so absolutely necessary to be sent at this juncture into those parts. ¶ Erreur de pagination : les pages 13 à 15 portent les numéros 9, 10 et 12. ¶ Adressé à l'archevêque de Canterbury ; on y traite de Terre-Neuve : p. 9–10. La première église fut bâtie à St. John's en 1699. ¶ D'autres tirages parurent en 1700, et d'autres éditions en 1701, 1901 et 1916.

*Echard, Laurence, 1670?–1730. A most compleat compendium of geography, general and special . . . . The fifth edition, corrected and much improved. By Laurence Echard . . . . London, printed for J[ohn]. Nicholson, at the King's-Arms in Little-Britain. [1700.] 8 p.l., 236, [12] p. 2 maps 12°(?)

NUC(Pre–56)154:608*

"America": p. 184–211. ¶ Bookseller's adverts.: first p.l.b – eighth p.l., and p. [10–12] at end. ¶ See first ed., 1691, for notes.

« America » : p. 184–211. ¶ Réclames du libraire : premier f. l.b – huitième f. l., et p. [10–12] à la fin. ¶ Voir notes dans la première éd., 1691.

Great Britain. Laws, statutes, etc. An Act to incourage the trade to Newfoundland as beneficial to this kingdom, in its trade and navigation. [London?] Anno X & XI. Guil. III. [i.e., 1700] cap. XXV. [No collation or format.]

"From Kennett, p. 181"

Source: White Kennett, Bibliothecae americanae primordia. London, 1713. No other information discovered.

Source : Bibliothecae americanae primordia. Londres, 1713, de White Kennett. Aucun autre renseignement.

1701

Bowrey, Thomas, *fl.* 1650–1713. A dictionary of the Hudson's-Bay Indian language. 8 p. fol.

Sabin:7098

Caption title. ¶ In the Cree language, alphabetically arranged, containing about 600 words. ¶ *Sabin has the author's name as "Bowrie," and pub. date as "about 1776," but cites Allibone (Samuel A. Allibone,* A critical dictionary of English literature. *Philadelphia, 1859–71, 3 v.) for the Bowrey form, and for the date 1701. For "Bowrey" and 1701, Dr. Waldon cites Watt (Robert Watt,* Bibliotheca Britannica. *Edinburgh, 1824, 4 v.), vol. 1, p. 141.* ¶ The only copy I have seen, that in the British Museum, bears no evidence of authorship, date, or place of issue [but it is bound with a London, 1701, Maylayo-English-Maylayo dictionary by Bowrey]. ¶ *Possibly issued in the* Selected Americana *from Sabin's* Dictionary *series, in microformat.* ¶ *BVAU(MF)*

Titre de départ. ¶ En langue cri et en ordre alphabétique, comprend environ 600 mots. ¶ *Le Sabin donne « Bowrie » comme nom de l'auteur et « vers 1776 » comme date de publ., mais il cite Allibone (Samuel A. Allibone,* A critical dictionary of English literature. *Philadelphie, 1859–71, 3 vol.) pour le nom orthographié Bowrey et pour la date 1701. À cet égard, Waldon cite Watt (Robert Watt,* Bibliotheca Britannica. *Édimbourg, 1824, 4 vol.), vol. 1, p. 141.* ¶ Le seul exemplaire que j'ai vu, soit celui du British Museum, ne fournit aucune indication d'auteur, de date ou de lieu de publication [mais il est relié avec un dictionnaire malais-anglais-malais par Bowrey, Londres, 1701]. ¶ *A peut-être paru en microformat dans la collection* Selected Americana *d'après le Dictionnaire Sabin.* ¶ *BVAU (mic.)*

Bray, Thomas, 1658–1730. A memorial, representing the present state of religion . . . . [Second ed.] London, Printed by John Brudenell, for the Author, 1701.

See first ed., 1700, for notes.

Voir notes à la première éd., 1700.

A collection of several treaties, &c. since the late Revolution . . . . London, printed in the year 1701. 1 p.l., iv, 53 p. 4°

NUC(Pre–56)115:350*

"Their Majesties Declaration of War against the French King, May 7, 1689" [War of the Grand Alliance]: p. 8–10; "Articles of Peace Between the most Serene and Mighty Prince William the Third King of Great Britain, and the most Serene and Mighty Prince Lewis the Fourteenth the most Christian King, concluded in the Royal Palace at Ryswicke the ¹⁰/₂₀ day of September 1697" [Peace of Ryswick, ending the war]: p. 11–19. ¶ *Another edition appeared in the same year (next entry).*

« Their Majesties Declaration of War against the French King, May 7, 1689 » [guerre dite « de la Ligue d'Augsbourg »] : p. 8–10 ; « Articles of Peace Between the most Serene and Mighty Prince William the Third King of Great Britain, and the most Serene and Mighty Prince Lewis the Fourteenth the most Christian King, concluded in the Royal Palace at Ryswicke the ¹⁰/₂₀ day of September 1697 ». [Traité de Ryswick, qui mit fin à la guerre] : p. 11–19. ¶ *Une autre édition parut la même année (notice suivante).*

*A collection of several treaties, &c. . . . . . London: printed in the year, 1701. 47 (*i.e.* 43) p. 4°(?)

NUC(Pre–56)115:350*

Numbers 21–24 omitted in paging. ¶ Another edition appeared in the same year (preceding entry).

Omission dans la pagination : les numéros 21–24 manquent. ¶ Une autre édition parut la même année (notice précédente).

*Hudson's Bay Company. Sir, May it please you to be at the Hudson's Bay house, on the   day of   170   at   a clock in the   noon, at a committee there to be held. [London? 1701?] Broadside. 10.5 x 14.5 cm.

NUC(Pre–56)258:451

Blank form, filled out in ms. for a meeting held on Wednesday, 23 July 1701, at 8 a.m. ¶ An example of a meeting notice, though perhaps not of close Canadian relevance.

Formule vierge, remplie à la main pour une réunion tenue le mercredi 23 juillet 1701 à 8 h. ¶ C'est un modèle de convocation d'assemblée, qui n'a peut-être toutefois qu'un rapport lointain avec le Canada.

Moll, Herman, *d./déc.* 1732. A system of geography, or, A new & accurate description of the earth in all its empires, kingdoms and states. Illustrated with history and topography, and maps of every country, fairly engraven on copper . . . . By Herman Moll . . . . London: printed for T[imothy]. Childe . . . 1701. 2 pts. in 1 v.: 1 p.l., [32], 444 p.; 1 p.l., 230, [28, index], 4 [adverts.] p. front. (engr. t.-p.), maps. fol.

NUC(Pre–56)390:182

The "Introduction to geography" and a large part of the descriptive text in pt. 1 are by Robert Falconer. ¶ Pt. 2, chap. 2, "Arctick countries": p. 157; Chap. 3, "Canada and the adjacent islands": p. 158–60 (map, p. 161); "The Arctick or Northern countries" (relating to the Northwest passage): p. 220–23.

L'auteur de « Introduction to geography » ainsi que d'une bonne partie du texte descriptif figurant dans la part. 1 est Robert Falconer. ¶ Part. 2, chap. 2, « Arctick countries » : p. 157 ; chap. 3, « Canada and the adjacent islands » : p. 158–60 (carte, p. 161) ; « The Arctick or Northern countries » (se rapportant au passage du Nord-Ouest) : p. 220–23.

1702

Great Britain. Sovereigns, etc., 1702–1714 (Anne). Her Majesties declaration of war against France and Spain. London, printed by Charles Bill, and the executrix of Thomas Newcomb, decea'd; printers to the Queens most Excellent Majesty, 1702. Broadside. fol.

NUC(Pre–56)215:409

Royal arms at head of title. ¶ "Given at our court at St. James's the fourth day of May, 1702 ...." ¶ This was a revival under Queen Anne of the long war between England and France, which began in 1689 under William and Mary; in 1702 it was called the War of the Spanish Succession, and it was terminated by the Treaty of Utrecht, 1713.

Armoiries royales en tête du titre. ¶ « Given at our court at St. James's the fourth day of May, 1702 .... » ¶ Cette déclaration de guerre de la reine Anne fut l'une des péripéties qui marquèrent la longue guerre entre l'Angleterre et la France, laquelle débuta en 1689 sous le règne de Guillaume et de Marie ; en 1702, on l'appelait la guerre de la Succession d'Espagne, et le traité d'Utrecht y mit fin en 1713.

*Heylyn, Peter, 1599–1662. Cosmography in four books. Containing the chorography and history of the whole world .... Improved with an historical continuation of the present times, by Edmund Bohun, Esq. London, 1702. 4 pts. in 1 v. fol.

NUC(Pre–56)244:502*

The fourth bk. contains Chorography and history of America, p. 839–1132. ¶ Revised and enl. from *Microcosmus*. Oxford, 1621, *q.v.* ¶ First pub. under the above title: London, 1642; also pub. London, 1652, *q.v.* for other notes and editions.

Le quatrième livre comprend Chorography and history of America, p. 839–1132. ¶ Édition révisée et augm. de *Microcosmus*. Oxford, 1621, *q.v.* ¶ Première édition sous le titre ci-dessus : Londres, 1642 ; également publ. à Londres en 1652, *q.v.* pour d'autres notes et éditions.

Proposals for carrying on an effectual war in America, against the French and Spaniards .... London, printed for John Nutt ... 1702. 24 p. 4°

NUC(Pre–56)472:670*

The author proposes to make plunder of the conquered peoples pay for the war [War of the Spanish Succession, 1702–13], and thinks that "The taking of Canada may be easie enough if we

L'auteur propose de rançonner les peuples conquis à titre de dédommagement pour la guerre [guerre de la Succession d'Espagne, 1702–13] et croit que « la conquête du Canada peut s'effectuer assez facilement si

attack it at once both by Sea and Land": p. 18. ¶ Reprinted in the *Harleian Miscellany*, 1744, v. 1, p. 379–85; also *ibid.*, 1808, v. 1, and 1810, v. 10 for the 1808 reprint (cf. NUC, which has a more complete title than that above).

nous attaquons à la fois par voies de mer et de terre » : p. 18. ¶ Réimpression dans *Harleian Miscellany*, 1744, vol. 1, p. 379–85 ; aussi *ibid.*, 1808, vol. 1, et 1810, vol. 10 pour la réimpression de 1808 (cf. NUC, qui comporte un titre plus complet que le titre susmentionné).

1703

Burchett, Josiah, 1666?–1746. Memoirs of transactions at sea during the war with France; beginning in 1688, and ending in 1697. Most humbly dedicated to His Royal Highness Prince George of Denmark .... By Josiah Burchett, Esq; Secretary to the Admiralty. [London] In the Savoy: Printed by Edw. Jones, 1703. 22 p.l., 408 p. 8°

NUC(Pre–56)84:487*

Concerns the War of the League of Augsburg (or Grand Alliance). ¶ *Answered by: Luke Lillingston,* Reflections on Mr. Burchet's Memoirs *(London, 1704), to which Burchett responded with:* Mr. Burchett's justification of his naval-memoirs *(London, 1704); neither work relates to Canada.* ¶ "Monsieur Ponty's coming to Newfoundland, when the squadron commanded by Capt. Norris was there, and what happen'd thereupon": p. 374–82. ¶ *First edition; the text was also incorporated with his* A complete history of the most remarkable transactions at sea ... *(London, 1720), q.v., and transl. into French as* Memoires de tout ce qui s'est passé ... *(Amsterdam, 1704).* ¶ *OTP*

Se rapporte à la guerre de la Ligue d'Augsbourg (ou, en anglais, de la Grand Alliance). ¶ *Cet ouvrage a suscité la réplique suivante :* Reflections on Mr. Burchet's Memoirs *(Londres, 1704), de Luke Lillingston, ouvrage auquel Burchett répliqua par* Mr. Burchett's justification of his naval-memoirs *(Londres, 1704) ; ces deux ouvrages ne traitent pas du Canada.* ¶ « La venue de M. Ponty à Terre-Neuve, lorsque l'escadrille commandée par le cap. Norris s'y trouvait, et les événements qui se déroulèrent dès lors » : p. 374–82. ¶ *Première édition ; le texte fut également intégré à son ouvrage* A complete history of the most remarkable transactions at sea ... *(Londres, 1720), q.v., et trad. en français sous le titre* Memoires de tout ce qui s'est passé ... *(Amsterdam, 1704).* ¶ *OTP*

*Heylyn, Peter, 1599–1662. Cosmography in four books. Containing the chorography and history of the whole world . . . . By Peter Heylyn, D.D. Improv'd with an historical continuation to the present times, by Edmund Bohun, Esq.; with a large and more accurate index, than was in any of the former editions . . . . And five new-engrav'd maps . . . . London, printed for E[dward]. Brewster, R[ichard]. Chiswell, B[enjamin]. Tooke, T[homas]. Hodgkin and T[homas]. Bennet, 1703. 4 pts. in 1 v. 5 fold. maps, 2 tables. fol.

NUC(Pre–56)244:502*

Title-page in red and black. ¶ Added t.-p., engraved: Cosmography in foure bookes . . . . ¶ The 7th edition . . . . Four bks. in five pts., each with special t.-p. Bks. 1–3 dated 1701, the two pts. of bk. 4 dated 1702; the Appendix has caption title only. ¶ Paging irregular. ¶ Revised and enl. from his *Microcosmus*. Oxford, 1621, *q.v.* ¶ First pub. under above title: London, 1642 (*q.v.*); also pub. London, 1652, *q.v.* for other notes and editions.

Page de titre en rouge et noir. ¶ P. de t. supplémentaire avec gravure : Cosmography in foure bookes . . . . ¶ The 7th edition . . . . Quatre livres en cinq part., chacun comportant une p. de t. distincte. Les livres 1 à 3 sont datés de 1701, les deux part. du livre 4 le sont de 1702 ; l'annexe ne comporte qu'un titre de départ. ¶ Pagination irrégulière. ¶ Édition révisée et augm. de *Microcosmus* du même auteur, Oxford, 1621, *q.v.* ¶ Première édition sous le titre ci-dessus : Londres, 1642 (*q.v.*) ; aussi publ. à Londres en 1652, *q.v.* pour d'autres notes et éditions.

Lahontan, Louis Armand de Lom d'Arce, *baron de*, 1666–1715? New Voyages to North-America. Containing an account of the several nations of that vast continent ... the several attempts of the English and French to dispossess one another ... and the various adventures between the French, and the Iroquese confederates of England, from 1683–1694. A geographical description of Canada ... with remarks upon their government, and the interest of the English and French in their commerce. Also a dialogue between the author and a general of the savages ... with an account of the authors retreat to Portugal and Denmark ... to which is added, a dictionary of the Algonkine language, which is generally spoke in North-America.... Written in French by the Baron Lahontan, Lord Lieutenant of the French colony at Placentia in Newfoundland, now in England. Done in English .... A great part of which never printed in the original. London: printed for H[enry]. Bonwicke in St. Paul's Church-yard; T[imothy]. Goodwin, M[atthew]. Wotton, B[enjamin]. Tooke, in Fleetstreet; and S[amuel]. Manship in Cornhil, 1703. 2 v. in 1. front., plates (part fold.), maps (part fold.). 8°

NUC(Pre–56)312:55*

Form of author's name as in NUC; in DCB the form is: Lom d'Arce de Lahontan, Louis-Armand de, baron de Lahontan. ¶ The author professes great sincerity and impartiality and pretends he has all the qualities necessary to an impartial historian; but now his work is entirely out of credit, through the observations of modern travellers, his own countrymen as well as others; and instead of being one of the truest, he is found to be one of the falsest of all writers. Father Charlevoix, in particular, is very free in censuring him. *See* Ruben Gold Thwaites, editor, *New Voyages to North America*, by Lahontan (Chicago, A.C. McClurg, 1905), which contains a full bibliography of all editions of Lahontan, with exact descriptions, by Victor Hugo Paltsits, vol. 1, p. li–xciii. ¶ Vol. 2 has title as follows: *New voyages to North-America. Giving a full account of the customs, commerce, religion, and stronge*

C'est une forme du nom de l'auteur qui est identique à celle figurant dans le NUC ; pour sa part, le DBC a retenu : Lom d'Arce de Lahontan, Louis-Armand de, baron de Lahontan. ¶ L'auteur affiche sincérité et impartialité, et il prétend posséder toutes les qualités qui font un historien impartial ; pourtant son oeuvre est entièrement dépréciée de nos jours du fait des observations de voyageurs modernes, tant ses propres concitoyens que d'autres ; et on le juge comme l'un des écrivains les plus mensongers au lieu de le tenir pour l'un des plus dignes de foi. Le père Charlevoix en particulier ne se prive pas de le critiquer. *Voir* Ruben Gold Thwaites, éditeur, *New Voyages to North America*, par Lahontan (Chicago, A.C. McClurg, 1905), qui comprend une bibliographie complète de toutes les éditions de Lahontan, avec des descriptions exactes, par Victor Hugo Paltsits, vol. 1, p. li–xciii. ¶ Le titre du vol. 2 se lit comme suit : *New voyages to North-America. Giving a full account of the customs, commerce, religion, and stronge opinions of the*

opinions of the savages of that country. With political remarks upon the Courts of Portugal and Denmark, and the present state of the commerce of those countries. Never printed before. Written by the Baron Lahontan .... Vol. II. London: 1703. ¶ *First published as:* Nouveaux voyages de M^r le baron de Lahontan, dans l'Amerique Septentrionale. *La Haye, 1703; above is the first English ed.; second ed.: London, 1735, various issues, q.v.; 1703 English ed. reprinted Chicago, 1905 (cf. NUC). ¶ OTP*

savages of that country. With political remarks upon the Courts of Portugal and Denmark, and the present state of the commerce of those countries. Never printed before. Written by the Baron Lahontan .... Vol. II. Londres, 1703. ¶ *D'abord publié sous le titre* Nouveaux voyages de M^r le baron de Lahontan, dans l'Amerique Septentrionale. *La Haye, 1703 ; le titre anglais susmentionné est celui de la première éd. anglaise ; deuxième éd. : Londres, 1735, divers tirages, q.v. ; l'éd. anglaise de 1703 a été réimprimée à Chicago en 1905 (cf. NUC). ¶ OTP*

[Renneville, René Augustin Constantin de], 1650–1723. A collection of voyages undertaken by the Dutch East-India Company, for the improvement of trade and navigation. Containing an account of several attempts to find out the North-East Passage .... Tr. into English, and illustrated with several charts. London, printed for W[illiam]. Freeman [etc.] 1703. 16 p.l., 336 p. 10 maps (8 fold.). 8°

NUC(Pre–56)488:549

Transl. from his Recueil des voyages qui ont servi à l'établissement . . . de la Compagnie des Indes Orientales, *vol. 1, Amsterdam, 1702, which was in turn a transl. and adaptation by de Renneville mostly from Izaäk Commelin's* Begin ende voortgangh, van de Vereenighde Nederlantsche geoctroyeerde Oost-Indische Compagnie. *[Amsterdam] 1645 (cf. NUC, above and 117:427, and BLC(to 1975) 233:155). ¶ The four voyages given here correspond to the first found in Commelin's compilation.* ¶ "Other voyages in quest of a passage to China by the North": p. 68–70 (Henry Hudson, 1609); "A dissertation of the learned

Trad. de son ouvrage Recueil des voyages qui ont servi à l'établissement . . . de la Compagnie des Indes Orientales, *vol. 1, Amsterdam, 1702, cet ouvrage étant lui-même une trad. et une adaptation que de Renneville avait réalisée surtout à partir de l'écrit d'Izaäk Commelin,* Begin ende voortgangh, van de Vereenighde Nederlantsche geoctroyeerde Oost-Indische Compagnie. *[Amsterdam] 1645 (cf. NUC, plus haut et 117:427, et BLC(to 1975)233:155). ¶ Les quatre voyages dont il est question ici correspondent au premier qui figure dans la compilation de Commelin.* ¶ « Other voyages in quest of a passage to China by the North » : p. 68–70 (Henry Hudson, 1609) ; « A dissertation of the learned Isaac Pontanus, wherein he answers the objections

Isaac Pontanus, wherein he answers the objections that are made against finding passage ry [*sic*] the North; and proposed the most certain way to find it": p. 89–93.

that are made against finding passage ry [*sic*] the North ; and proposed the most certain way to find it » : p. 89–93.

1704

[**Churchill, Awnsham**], *d./déc.* 1728, *comp.* A collection of voyages and travels, some now first printed from original manuscripts. Others translated out of foreign languages, and now first publish'd in English. To which are added some few that have formerly appear'd in English, but do now for their excellency and scarceness deserve to be reprinted. In four volumes. With a general preface, giving an account of the progress of navigation, from its first beginning to the perfection it is now in, . . . the whole illustrated with a great number of useful maps, and cuts, all engraven on copper . . . . London, printed for Awnsham and John Church-hill . . . 1704. 4 v. front. (port., v. 2) illus., plates (part double, part fold.), maps (part fold.), indexes. fol.

NUC(Pre–56)109:263*

Compiled by Awnsham and John Chur-chill. ¶ *Vol. 2 has added t.-p., engraved.* ¶ Contents relating to Canada: "An account of a most dangerous voyage perform'd by the famous Capt. John Monck, in the years 1619, and 1620. By the special command of Christian IV, King of Denmark, Norway, &c. to Hudson's Straits, in order to discover a passage on that side, betwixt Greenland and America to the West-Indies. With a description of the Old and New Greenland, for the better elucidation of the said Treatise. Translated from the High-Dutch original, printed at Frankford upon the Maine, 1650.": v. 1, p. 541–69.

Compilé par Awnsham et John Churchill. ¶ *Le vol. 2 comporte une p. de t. supplémentaire, avec gravure.* ¶ Qui portent sur le Canada : « An account of a most dangerous voyage perform'd by the famous Capt. John Monck, in the years 1619, and 1620. By the special command of Christian IV, King of Denmark, Norway, &c. to Hudson's Straits, in order to discover a passage on that side, betwixt Greenland and America to the West-Indies. With a description of the Old and New Greenland, for the better elucidation of the said Treatise. Translated from the High-Dutch original, printed at Frankford upon the Maine, 1650. » : vol. 1, p. 541–69, planches, carte ; « Captain Thomas James's strange and dangerous voyage, *etc.* » : vol. 2,

plates, map; "Captain Thomas James's strange and dangerous voyage, etc.": v. 2, p. 479–544. ¶ First edition (NUC has a 1703 edition, evidently in error, and another in 1706); vols. 5 and 6 appeared in 1732 (cf. DNB, "A. Churchill"), and the first four vols. reissued the same year. Other editions: 1744–46 (6 v.), 1744–47 (8 v.), and 1752 (8 v.), q.v. Waldon notes a two-vol. set, the Harleian (Earl of Oxford) collection, 1745, issued as vols. 7 and 8 in the later editions (cf. also DNB, "A. Churchill," and 1744–47 edition). ¶ BVIPA

p. 479–544. ¶ *Première édition (le NUC mentionne une édition de 1703, une erreur de toute évidence, et une autre de 1706) ; les vol. 5 et 6 parurent en 1732 (cf. DNB, « A. Churchill »), et les quatre premiers vol. furent réimprimés la même année. Autres éditions : 1744–46 (6 vol.), 1744–47 (8 vol.), et 1752 (8 vol.), q.v. Waldon indique une série de deux vol., la collection Harleian (comte d'Oxford), 1745, qui furent publiés comme les vol. 7 et 8 dans les éditions ultérieures (de plus, cf. DNB, « A. Churchill », et l'édition de 1744–47). ¶ BVIPA*

Crouch, Nathaniel, 1632?–1725? The English empire in America .... The fourth edition. London, 1704.

Sabin:9499

First edition: 1685, q.v. for other information.

Première édition : 1685, q.v. pour d'autres renseignements.

Dennis, John, 1657–1734. Liberty asserted. A tragedy. As it is acted at the New Theatre in Little Lincoln's-Inn-Fields. Written by Mr. Dennis. London, printed by G[eorge]. Strahan ... and Bernard Lintott ... 1704. 8 p.l., 68 p. 21 cm. 4°

NUC(Pre–56)139:386*

Dedicated to Anthony Henley, Esq. ¶ Five-act play in blank verse, the scene laid in Angie (*i.e.*, Agnie, the chief place of the Agnies, one of the Five Nations Indians) in Canada. Frontenac, the English general Beaufort,

Dédicace à Monsieur Anthony Henley. ¶ Pièce en cinq actes écrite en vers non rimés, dont l'action se passe à Angie (*c.-à-d.*, Agnie, le principal village des Agniers, l'une des nations indiennes faisant partie des Cinq-Nations) au Canada. Parmi les personnages

Indians, etc., are among the characters. ¶ *First edition; another issue(?) appeared in the same year "with more lines to a page on p. 25–64 (signatures E–I) than on p. 1–24 (signatures B–D)" (cf. NUC); a microprint edition appeared in* Three centuries of drama: English, 1701–1750. *Henry W. Wells, ed. (New York, Readex, 1953 and ff., cf. NUC).* ¶ *OOP*

de la pièce, on retrouve Frontenac, le général anglais Beaufort, les Indiens, etc. ¶ *Première édition ; « doté d'un plus grand nombre de lignes par page aux p. 25–64 (signatures E–I) qu'aux p. 1–24 (signatures B–D) » (cf. NUC), un autre tirage(?) fut publié la même année ; une édition « microprint » parut dans* Three centuries of drama : English, 1701–1750. *Henry W. Wells, éd. (New York, Readex, 1953 et suiv., cf. NUC).* ¶ *OOP*

*Echard, Laurence, 1670?–1730. A most compleat compendium of geography, general and special . . . . The 6th ed., corrected and much improved. London, 1704.

Taken from Waldon's note to the first edition, 1691, *q.v.* for further information.

Tiré de la note de Waldon pour la première édition, 1691, *q.v.* pour d'autres renseignements.

Society for the Propagation of the Gospel in Foreign Parts, London. An account of the propagation of the gospel in foreign parts, what the Society establish'd in England by royal charter hath done since their incorporation, June the 16th 1701, in Her Majesty's plantations, colonies, and factories: as also what they design to do upon further encouragement from their own members and other well disposed Christians, either by annual subscriptions, present benefactions, or future legacies. [London, 1704.] 4 p. fol.

NUC(Pre–56)554:448*

Caption title. ¶ First report issued by the Society. ¶ "The Five Nations of Iroquois, commonly call'd, The Praying Indians of Canada": p. 10; Newfoundland: p. 15. ¶ See *the second report, this entry under 1705, for other notes.* ¶ Reprinted by Richard Clay &

Titre de départ. ¶ Premier rapport émis par la Société. ¶ « The Five Nations of Iroquois, commonly call'd, The Praying Indians of Canada » : p. 10 ; Terre-Neuve : p. 15. ¶ Voir *autres notes dans le deuxième rapport, dont la notice est répertoriée sous 1705.* ¶ Réimpression par Richard Clay & Sons à Londres

Sons, London, 1850, 1851, and 1886, where it is stated that the compiler was Philip Stubbs.

en 1850, 1851 et 1886, avec mention du nom du compilateur : Philip Stubbs.

1705

*Echard, Laurence, 1670?–1730. A most compleat compendium of geography, general and special .... The 7th ed. cor. and much improved. London, 1705. 236 p. maps. 12°(?)

NUC(Pre–56)154:608*

See first ed., 1691, for notes.

Voir notes à la première éd., 1691.

Harris, John, 1667?–1719. Navigantium atque itinerantium bibliotheca: or, A compleat collection of voyages and travels: consisting of above four hundred of the most authentick writers; beginning with Hackliut, Purchass, &c. in English; Ramusio in Italian; Thevenot, &c. in French; De Bry, and Grynæi Novus Orbis in Latin; the Dutch East-India Company in Dutch; and continued with others of note, that have publish'd histories, voyages, travels, or discoveries, in the English, Latin, French, Italian, Spanish, Portuguese, German, or Dutch tongues; relating to any part of Asia, Africa, America, Europe, or the islands thereof, to this present time .... Throughout the whole all original papers are printed at large .... To which is prefixed, a history of the peopling of the several parts of the world, and particularly of America.... By John Harris, A.M. Fellow of the Royal Society. In two volumes. London, printed for Thomas Bennet ... John Nicholson ... and Daniel Midwinter, 1705. 2 v.: [14], lxvii, 862 [14] p.; [6], 928, 56, [12] p. fronts. (ports.), 21 illus., 9 maps, indexes. fol.

NUC(Pre–56)232:71*

Contents relating to Canada: Vol. 1, bk. 4, chap. 21 — A journal of Mr.

Qui portent sur le Canada : vol. 1, livre 4, chap. 21 – A journal of Mr. Hudson's last

governor general, against the Iroquese. Chap. 18 — The expedition of the Marquess Denonville against the Iroquese. Chap. 19 — The author is sent with his detachment to Fort St. Joseph. . . . Chap. 20 — The author's journal of his voyage from Missilimekinac to the River Missisipi. Chap. 21 — Giving an account of Mr. de Frontenac's arrival. Chap. 22 — Containing an account of the author's departure from Rochel to Quebec. Chap. 24 — A short view of the manners and customs and of the diseases and remedies of the savages. Chap. 25 — Of the beasts, birds, fishes, insects, trees, and fruits of the Northern America. Chap. 26 — Of the interest of the French and English in North America. ¶ *First edition; rev. ed., London, 1744–48* (q.v.), *and London, T. Osborne, 1764 (cf. NUC).* ¶ *OTP · BVIPA*

account of Mr. de Frontenac's arrival. Chap. 22 – Containing an account of the author's departure from Rochel to Quebec. Chap. 24 – A short view of the manners and customs and of the diseases and remedies of the savages. Chap. 25 – Of the beasts, birds, fishes, insects, trees, and fruits of the Northern America. Chap. 26 – Of the interest of the French and English in North America. ¶ *Première édition ; éd. rév., Londres, 1744–48* (q.v.), *et Londres, T. Osborne, 1764 (cf. NUC).* ¶ *OTP · BVIPA*

[Society for the Propagation of the Gospel in Foreign Parts, London]. An account of the propagation of the gospel in foreign parts. Continued to . . . 1705, representing what the Society . . . hath done since their incorporation June 16, 1701 . . . as also what they design to do . . . either by annual subscriptions, present benefactions, or future legacies. [Comp. by P. Stubs.] [London, 1705.] 4 p. fol.

NUC(Pre–56)554:448*

Caption title. ¶ *The second report issued by the Society.* ¶ Except for the figures, this is practically the same as the first report, 1704. ¶ "The Five Nations of Iroquois, Commonly call'd, the Praying Indians of Canada": p. 2; Newfoundland: p. 3. ¶ The importance of converting the Indians to the

Titre de départ. ¶ *Le deuxième rapport émis par la Société.* ¶ Si ce n'est des chiffres, ce rapport est pratiquement identique au premier, 1704. ¶ « The Five Nations of Iroquois, Commonly call'd, the Praying Indians of Canada » : p. 2 ; Terre-Neuve : p. 3. ¶ On insiste sur l'importance de convertir les Indiens à la religion protestante et de les ·

Protestant religion and the English interest is urged. If not instructed, the Indians will "probably espouse the French and Popish interest." ¶ See also *other reports for the Society, under 1704 and 1706.*

rallier à la cause des Anglais. Si l'on ne les éduque pas, les Indiens « serviront probablement les intérêts des Français et des papistes ». ¶ Voir aussi *sous 1704 et 1706 d'autres rapports produits pour le compte de la Société.*

1706

*The English pilot. The fourth book. Describing the West-India navigation from Hudson's-Bay to the River Amazones . . . . Also a new description of Newfound-Land, New-England, New-York . . . . The whole being very much enlarged and corrected, with the additions of several new charts and descriptions, not before published. By the information of divers able navigators . . . . London, J[ohn]. Thornton, 1706. 69 p. illus., charts (part fold.). fol.

NUC(Pre–56)160:373*

First edition: 1689, *q.v.* for other editions; the 1698 edition has a somewhat similar title, and is transcribed more fully.

Première édition : 1689, *q.v.* pour d'autres éditions ; l'édition de 1698 comporte un titre à peu près identique et a fait l'objet d'une transcription plus complète.

Society for the Propagation of the Gospel in Foreign Parts, London. An account of the Society for propagating the gospel in foreign parts, established by the royal charter of King William III. With their proceedings and success, and hopes of continual progress under the happy reign of Her most Excellent Majesty Queen Anne. London, printed by Joseph Downing, in Bartholomew-close near West-Smithfield, 1706. 1 p.l., 97 p. front. 4°

NUC(Pre–56)554:449*

Third report; for the first and second reports and other notes, see this entry under 1704 and 1705. ¶ "Printed by order of the Society, John Chamberlayne, Secretary." ¶ A microcard edition appeared after World War II (cf. NUC). ¶ BVAU(MF)

Troisième rapport ; pour le premier rapport et le deuxième ainsi que pour d'autres notes, voir cette notice sous 1704 et 1705. ¶ « Imprimé sur ordre de la Société, John Chamberlayne, secrétaire. » ¶ Une édition sur microcartes a été publiée après la Seconde guerre mondiale (cf. NUC). ¶ BVAU (mic.)

1707

The English pilot . . . . London: printed for Rich. Mount, and Tho. Page. 1707. 58 p. 22 maps and woodcuts. fol.

Sabin:22617

Waldon says from Sabin, but Sabin's title starts: The fourth part of the general English pilot. Describing the sea-coasts . . ., continuing much as in the 1698 edition (q.v.), but including references to "the East Coast of America," "Baffin's Bay, Hudson's Bay, New Brittanie, New-found-Land, Canada and New-France, New-Scotland" (Nova Scotia), etc. ¶ First edition: 1689, q.v. for other editions.

Waldon donne le Sabin comme source de renseignements, bien que le titre dans le Sabin débute comme suit : The fourth part of the general English pilot. Describing the sea-coasts . . ., et continue de façon très semblable à l'édition de 1698 (q.v.), sans toutefois mentionner « la côte orientale de l'Amérique », « la mer de Baffin, la Baie d'Hudson, la Nouvelle-Bretagne, Terre-Neuve, le Canada et la Nouvelle France, la Nouvelle-Écosse » (Nova Scotia), etc. ¶ Première édition : 1689, q.v. pour d'autres éditions.

[Mather, Cotton], 1663–1728. A memorial of the present deplorable state of New-England, with the many disadvantages it lyes under by the male-administration of their present governour, Joseph Dudley, esq., and his son Paul, &c. Together with the several affidavits of people of worth relating to several of the said governour's mercenary and illegal proceedings but particularly his private treacherous correspondence with Her Majesty's enemies the French and Indians. To which is added, a faithful, but melancholy account of several barbarities lately committed upon Her Majesty's subjects by the said French and Indians in the east and west parts of New-England. Faithfully digested from the several original letters, papers, and MSS. by Philopolites. [London?] Printed in the year, 1707 and sold by S. Phillips [etc.] booksellers in Boston. 2 p.l., 41 p. 4°

NUC(Pre–56)369:77

"A letter from a captive at Port-Royal," dated Sept. 18, 1703, signed "W.C.": p. 38–46. Deals also with conflicts with the French and Indians. ¶ *NUC has only the reprint: Boston, Mass. Hist. Soc. Collections, 1879, series 5, vol. 6, p. 31–64.*

« Lettre d'un prisonnier à Port-Royal », daté du 18 sept. 1703, signé « W.C. » : p. 38–46. Traite également des conflits avec les Français et les Indiens. ¶ *Le NUC mentionne une seule réimpression : Boston, Mass. Hist. Soc. Collections, 1879, collection 5, vol. 6, p. 31–64.*

1708

Clarke, Samuel, 1599–1683. A new description of the world . . . . With an account of the natures of the people, in their habits, customs, wars, religions and policy, &c. As also, of the rarities, wonders and curiosities, of fishes, beasts, birds, rivers, mountains, plants, &c. With several remarkable revolutions, and delightful histories. By S. Clark. London, printed for Henry Rhodes . . ., 1708. 3 p.l., 218 p. front. 12°

NUC(Pre–56)111:361*

Signature G4 incorrectly signed F4. ¶ Originally pub., 1657, under title: A geographicall description (q.v., under Clarke); first ed. under this title: 1689 (q.v.).

Erreur de signature : F4 au lieu de G4. ¶ Initialement publ. en 1657 sous le titre A geographicall description (q.v.Clarke) ; première éd. sous ce titre : 1689 (q.v.).

The deplorable state of New-England, by reason of a covetous and treacherous governour, and pusillanimous counsellors with a vindication of the Honble Mr. Higginson, Mr. Mason, and several other gentlemen from the scandalous and wicked accusation of the votes, ordered by them to be published in their Boston news-letter. To which is added, an account of the shameful miscarriage of the late expedition against Port-Royal. London, printed in the year 1708. 4 p.l., 39 p. 8°

NUC(Pre–56)139:623*

Dedication signed: A.H. [i.e. Alex Holmes?] ¶ An arraignment of the administration of Governor Joseph Dudley. Authorship variously attributed to Alexander Holmes, Rev. John Higginson, Cotton Mather, and Rev. John Wise (cf. Evans, American bibliography, v. 1, no. 2214). British Museum enters under A.H., which it believes stands for Sir Henry Ashurst, "who had been agent for Massachusetts from the year 1688, and was the enemy of Gov. Dudley. From Bishop Kennet's remark" (Ms. note in BM 1061.g.72, cited by Waldon). ¶ Sect. V, p. 32–38, relates to the Port-Royal expeditions of 1707. ¶ First edition; reprinted Boston, 1720 and 1721, and by the Mass. Hist. Soc., Boston, 1879 (Collections, 5th ser., v. 6, p. [97]–131). ¶ BVAU(MF)

Dédicace signée : A.H. [c.-à-d. Alex Holmes ?] ¶ Une critique sévère de l'administration du gouverneur Joseph Dudley. La paternité de cet ouvrage est diversement attribuée à Alexander Holmes, au Rév. John Higginson, à Cotton Mather, ainsi qu'au Rév. John Wise (cf. Evans, American bibliography, vol. 1, n° 2214). Le British Museum répertorie cet écrit sous A.H., initiales désignant, selon cette institution, sir Henry Ashurst, « qui avait été mandataire pour le Massachusetts à compter de 1688 et était l'ennemi du gouverneur Dudley. Tiré de l'observation de l'évêque Kennet » (note manuscrite dans le BM 1061.g.72, citée par Waldon). ¶ La part. V, p. 32–38, se rapporte aux expéditions de Port-Royal de 1707. ¶ Première édition ; réimpression à Boston en 1720 et 1721, puis par la Mass. Hist. Soc. en 1879 (Collections, 5e coll., vol. 6, p. [97]–131). ¶ BVAU (mic.)

Geare, Allen. Ebenezer; or, A monument of thankfulness. Being a true account of a late miraculous preservation of nine men in a small boat which was inclosed within islands of ice about seventy leagues from land, and continued in distress twenty-eight days. Drawn up by Allen Geare, who was a principal sharer both in the misery and mercy; and attested by Mr. Joseph Hurlock .... London: printed for A[rthur]. Bettesworth ... and sold by J[ohn]. Morphew. 1708. 23 p. 8°

Copy seen or unknown bibliographical source

Waldon's sources are Sabin, which is different; BM, which is too short a title; and LC, but this is not in NUC. ¶ Heading, p. 3: "A brief relation of the most remarkable passages which hapned in our voyage from Plymouth to the Newfoundland, in the Langdon Frigate, Capt. Arthur Holdworth, Commander." ¶ *First edition? A variant appeared in the same year:* see next entry; reprinted in: Thomas Osborne, A collection of voyages and travels. *London, 1745, vol. 2, p. [787]–92,* q.v.; *and in: Awnsham Churchill, A* collection of voyages and travels. *London, 1752, vol. 8, p. 787–94,* q.v.

*Geare, Allen. Eben Ezer; or, A monument of thankfulness: being a true account of . . . 9 men in a small boat . . . continuing in distress 20 days; with the most remarkable passages which happened in their voyage from Plymouth to Newfoundland, in the ship called the Langdon frigate, Capt. Arthur Holdsworth Commander; with a list of the names of those that survived, and can witness to the truth of this relation. Written by Allen Geare, Chief Mate of the ship, who was a principal sharer both in the misery and the mercy. London: printed by Sam. Smith. 1708. 8 p. 8°

Sabin:26818

For other notes and editions, *see* preceding entry.

Great Britain. Sovereigns, etc., 1702–1714 (Anne). By the Queen, a proclamation [26 June 1708]. Anne R. Whereas by Act of Parliament made in the tenth and eleventh years of the reign of the late King William the Third, intituled, an act to encourage the trade to Newfoundland . . . . London, printed by Charles Bill and the executrix of Thomas Newcomb, deceas'd; printers to the Queens most Excellent Majesty. 1708. (Price two pence.) Broadside. fol.

NUC(Pre–56)215:414

Printed in the London *Gazette*, 12 July 1708; reprinted Worcester, Mass., American Antiquarian Society *Transactions*, 1911, v. 12, p. 163–67. ¶ *A similar (probably the same) work appears in BLC(to 1975)95:284, under title.*

Publié dans la *Gazette* de Londres le 12 juillet 1708 ; réimpression à Worcester (Mass.), dans *Transactions* de la American Antiquarian Society, 1911, vol. 12, p. 163–67. ¶ *Un ouvrage semblable (probablement le même) est répertorié dans le BLC(to 1975)95:284, suivant le titre.*

[Oldmixon, John], 1673–1742. The British empire in America, containing the history of the discovery, settlement, progress and present state of all the British colonies on the continent and islands of America. In two volumes. Being an account of the country, soil, climate, product and trade of them, viz. Vol. I, New-foundland, New-Scotland . . . Hudson's Bay . . . . With curious maps of the several places, done from the newest surveys. By Herman Moll, geographer. London, printed for John Nicolson, B[enjamin]. Tooke [etc.] 1708. 2 v.: xxxviii, [2], 412 p.; 1 p.l., 382 [2, books], [32, index] p. 8 fold. maps. 8°

NUC(Pre–56)429:309*

Dedication signed: J. Oldmixon. ¶ *Waldon notes that transls. were pub. in Hamburg, 1715; Amsterdam, 1721 and 1727; Lemgo, 1744; and Sorau, 1761.* ¶ Contents: v. 1, Newfoundland, New-England, New-Scotland, New-York, New-Jersey, Pennsylvania, Maryland, Virginia, Carolina, Georgia, Hudson's Bay; v. 2, Barbados, St. Lucia, St. Vincents, Dominico,

Dédicace signée : J. Oldmixon. ¶ *Waldon relève que des trad. furent publ. à Hambourg en 1715, à Amsterdam en 1721 et 1727, à Lemgo en 1744, ainsi qu'à Sorau en 1761.* ¶ Titres : vol. 1, Terre-Neuve, Nouvelle-Angleterre, Nouvelle-Écosse, New York, New-Jersey, Pennsylvanie, Maryland, Virginie, Caroline, Georgie, Baie d'Hudson ; vol. 2, la Barbade, Sainte-Lucie, Saint-Vincent, Saint-Domingue, Antigua, Montserrat,

Antego, Montserrat, Nevis, St. Christophers, Barbuda, Anguilia, Jamaica, Bahama, and Bermudas. ¶ *First ed.; rev. and enl. ed.: London, 1741 (q.v.). NUC also has a London, 1740 ed.; reprinted in MF, Ann Arbor, Mich., University Microfilms, after World War II (American culture ser., 22:8), and Toronto Public Library, post-World War II (Canadiana in the Toronto Public Library ser.).* ¶ OTP · BVAU · BVIP · BVIPA

Nevis, Saint-Christophe, Barboude, Anguilia, la Jamaïque, les îles Lucayes (l'archipel des Bahamas), et les Bermudes. ¶ *Première éd. ; éd. rév. et augm. : Londres, 1741 q.v. Le NUC indique également une éd. à Londres en 1740 ; reproduction sur mic., Ann Arbor (Mich.), University Microfilms, après la Seconde guerre mondiale (collection American Culture, 22:8), et à Toronto, Public Library, après la Seconde guerre mondiale (dans Canadiana, de la collection de la Toronto Public Library).* ¶ OTP · BVAU · BVIP · BVIPA

1709

The compleat geographer: or, The chorography and topography of all the known parts of the earth. To which is premis'd an introduction to geography and a natural history. The whole containing the substance of at least an hundred and fifty books of modern travels, faithfully abstracted. To which are added maps of every country most engrav'd by Herman Moll. The 3d edition. London, printed for Awnsham and John Churchill . . . and Timothy Childe . . . 1709. 2 vols. in 1: 1 p.l., [22], lv, [5], 482 p.; 1 p.l., 341, [1], xxii p. front., maps. fol.

NUC(Pre–56)118:223*

Vol. 2 has title: *Thesaurus geographicus: or, The compleat geographer. The third edition.* ¶ At the end of vol. 2, the [1] p. is a list of books published, and the xxii p. constitute an index. ¶ "The Polar or Arctick countries": Pt. 2, chap. 2, p. 229; "Canada or New France": Pt. 2, chap. 3, p. 230–37 (maps). ¶ *The first and second eds. do not appear in NUC or BLC, and DNB ("Moll") lists only the third and fourth eds.; fourth ed.: 1723 (q.v.).*

Titre du vol. 2 : *Thesaurus geographicus : or, the compleat geographer. The third edition.* ¶ À la fin du vol. 2, la p. [1] est une liste de livres publiés, et les xxii p. constituent un index. ¶ « The Polar or Arctick countries » : Part. 2, chap. 2, p. 229 ; « Canada or New France » : Part. 2, chap. 3, p. 230–37 (cartes). ¶ *La première et la deuxième éd. n'apparaissent pas dans le NUC ni dans le BLC, et le DNB (« Moll ») répertorie seulement la troisième et la quatrième éd. ; quatrième éd. : 1723 (q.v.).*

The Britiſh Empire

IN

AMERICA,

Containing

The HISTORY of the Diſcovery, Settlement, Progreſs and preſent State of all the

𝕭𝖗𝖎𝖙𝖎𝖘𝖍 𝕮𝖔𝖑𝖔𝖓𝖎𝖊𝖘,

ON THE

Continent and Iſlands of *America.*

In Two VOLUMES.

Being an Account of the Country, Soil, Climate, Product and Trade of them, *Viz.*

Vol. I.	Carolina,	Montſerrat,
Newfoundland,	and	*Nevis,*
New-Scotland,	Hudſon's-Bay.	St. *Chriſtophers,*
New-England,	Vol. II.	*Barbuda,*
New-York,	*Barbados,*	*Anguilla,*
New-Jerſey,	St. *Lucia,*	*Jamaica,*
Penſylvania,	St. *Vincents,*	The *Bahama*
Maryland,	*Dominico,*	and
Virginia,	*Antego,*	*Bermudas*

} *Iſlands.*

With curious Maps of the ſeveral Places, done from
the neweſt Surveys. By *Herman Moll,* Geographer.

LONDON, Printed for *John Nicholſon* at the King's Arms in
Little Britain, Benjamin Tooke at the *Middle-Temple-Gate,*
Fleetſtreet, and *Richard Parker* and *Ralph Smith* under the
Piazza of the *Royal Exchange.* 1708.

John Oldmixon. *The British empire in America.* London/Londres, 1708.

1710

*The four Indian kings. Part I. How a beautiful lady conquered one of the Indian kings. Part II. The lady's answer to the Indian king's request. [London, 1710.] [2] p. 4°(?)

NUC(Pre–56)179:299

A broadside folded to form two pages; printed in four columns. In verse. ¶ Printed while the four chiefs of the Iroquois Confederacy of the Five Nations were visiting Queen Anne in London. A more extensive "Bibliography of Contemporary Sources" was compiled by Dr. Waldon, and published in the *Canadian historical review*, vol. 16, 1935, p. 266–75, but no titles on the subject of the Indian kings were found in the Waldon typescript. Another work, *The four Indian kings*, appears under the date 1760.

In-plano plié pour former deux pages ; imprimé sur quatre colonnes. En vers. ¶ Imprimé pendant la visite des quatre chefs de la confédération iroquoise des Cinq-Nations à la reine Anne à Londres. Waldon a compilé une « Bibliographie des sources contemporaines » plus détaillée, qui a paru dans la *Canadian historical review*, vol. 16, 1935, p. 266–75 ; toutefois, aucun titre au sujet des rois indiens ne figure dans le tapuscrit de Waldon. Un autre ouvrage, *The four Indian kings*, est répertorié sous la date 1760.

*The four kings of Canada. Being a succint account of the four Indian princes lately arriv'd from North America. With a particular description of their country, their strange and remarkable religion, feasts, marriages, burials, remedies for their sick, customs, manners, constitution, habits, sports, war, peace, policy, hunting, fishing, utensils belonging to the savages, with several other extraordinary things worthy [of] observation, as to the natural or curious productions, beauty, or fertility, of that part of the world. Enter'd in the Hall-Book of the Company of Stationers, pursuant to Act of Parliament. London printed: and sold by John Baker, at the Black Boy in Pater-Noster-Row, 1710. Price sixpence. 47 p. 12°

Casey:63

Refers to the four chiefs of the Five Nations — *see* preceding entry. ¶ Casey notes a reprint of 1891; Waldon's *CHR* article notes a one-page list of books following p. 47, and gives the format as 8°(in 4s). This latter work is clear evidence of Dr. Waldon's bibliographical thoroughness (full citation in preceding entry).

Se rapporte aux quatre chefs des Cinq-Nations – *voir* la notice précédente. ¶ Le Casey donne une réimpression en 1891 ; dans son article publié dans la *CHR*, Waldon signale une liste de livres tenant sur une page après la p. 47, et indique le format in-8° (4 f.). Cette recherche de Waldon est une preuve manifeste de la minutie avec laquelle celle-ci effectuait ses travaux bibliographiques (citation complète à la notice précédente).

A general collection of treatys, declarations of war, manifestos, and other publick papers, relating to peace and war, among the potentates of Europe, from 1648 to the present time .... To which is prefix'd, An historical account of the French King's breach of the most solemn treatys. London: printed by J[ohn]. Darby for Andrew Bell in Cornhill, and E[gbert]. Sanger at the Post-house in Fleetstreet. 1710. 35, [9], 448, [3] p. 8°

NUC(Pre–56)194:275*

NUC notes "Edited by S.W.," gives the date as 1710 and, in the collation, leaves the number of volumes open. ¶ *List of books: [3] p. at end.* ¶ Partial contents: "The Treaty of Peace between Lewis XIV. of France, and Charles II. King of England; concluded at Breda, July 21. 1667": p. 127–35 (Acadia restored to France); "A Treaty of Peace, Good Correspondence and Neutrality, in America, between ... James II. ... and ... Lewis XIV. ... on the 16th day of November, 1686. N.S.": p. 246–52; "King William and Queen Mary's Declaration of War against France,

Le NUC indique « Édité par S.W. », donne comme date 1710 et, dans la collation, ne tranche pas catégoriquement au sujet du nombre de volumes. ¶ *Liste de livres : [3] p. à la fin.* ¶ Liste partielle des titres : « The Treaty of Peace between Lewis XIV. of France, and Charles II. King of England; concluded at Breda, July 21. 1667 » : p. 127–35 (l'Acadie est rendue à la France) ; « A Treaty of Peace, Good Correspondence and Neutrality, in America, between ... James II. ... and ... Lewis XIV. ... on the 16th day of November, 1686. N.S. » p. 246–52 ; « King William and Queen Mary's Declaration of War against France, May 7. 1689. » : p. 281–83

May 7. 1689.": p. 281–83 (Encroachments of the French on Newfoundland and in Hudson's Bay territory among the causes); "Articles of Peace between . . . William III . . . and . . . Lewis XIV. . . . at Reswick, the $^{10}/_{20}$ day of Sept. 1697": p. 302–08; "The Queen of England's Declaration of War against France, May 4. 1702": p. 421–22; "A Deduction of the Right and Title of the Crown of Great Britain, and therein of our most Gracious Sovereign Lady Queen Anne, to all the Straits, Bays, Seas, Rivers, Lakes, Creeks, Islands, Shores, Lands, Territorys, and Places whatsoever, within Hudson's-Straits and Hudson's Bay; and of the Right and Property of the Hudson's-Bay Company, deriv'd from the Imperial Crown of Great Britain, by Letters Patent of Incorporation, and a free Grant of all the Premises from King Charles the Second, Anno 1670": p. 443–48. ¶ *First edition; another edition: London, 1732,* q.v.

(déclaration motivée entre autres par les empiétements des Français à Terre-Neuve et dans le territoire de la Baie d'Hudson) ; « Articles of Peace between . . . William III . . . and . . . Lewis XIV. . . . at Reswick, the $^{10}/_{20}$ day of Sept. 1697 » : p. 302–08 ; « The Queen of England's Declaration of War against France, May 4. 1702 » : p. 421–22 ; « A Deduction of the Right and Title of the Crown of Great Britain, and therein of our most Gracious Sovereign Lady Queen Anne, to all the Straits, Bays, Seas, Rivers, Lakes, Creeks, Islands, Shores, Lands, Territorys, and Places whatsoever, within Hudson's-Straits and Hudson's Bay; and of the Right and Property of the Hudson's-Bay Company, deriv'd from the Imperial Crown of Great Britain, by Letters Patent of Incorporation, and a free Grant of all the Premises from King Charles the Second, Anno 1670 » : p. 443–48. ¶ *Première édition ; une autre édition : Londres, 1732,* q.v.

---

*The history and progress of the four Indian kings, to the kingdom of England: giving a particular description of the country they came from, their government, customs, religion, and manners . . . . Together with their effigies at large in the habits they now wear . . . . Also the four Indian king's [*sic*] speech to Her Majesty. With the epilogue spoken to them at the Playhouse. London, printed by A. Hinde, 1710. 6, [2] p. 8°

NUC(Pre–56)248:54

Title-page illus. with four woodcuts of the Indian kings "in the habits they

Quatre gravures xylographiées des rois indiens « vêtus comme ils le sont de nos

now wear"; one in each corner. ¶ *See* preceding entries for other information.

jours » illustrent chacune un coin de la page de titre. ¶ *Voir* autres renseignements aux notices précédentes.

1711

Clüver, Philipp, 1580–1622. Philippi Cluverii Introductio in universam geographiam .... Londini, typis M. Jenour, impensis Joannis Nicholsoni, 1711. 4 p.l., 429, [44] p.l., 1 l. 6 fold. plates, 35 fold. maps. 4°

NUC(Pre–56)113:120*

Added t.-p., engraved. ¶ *Waldon has collation: [14], 429, [45, index] p.* ¶ America: p. 334–41; Canada, Nova Francia: p. 417–18. ¶ Originally published Lugduni Batavorium [Batavorum? Leyden, Holland], 1624. *See* Sabin [and NUC(Pre–56)114:120ff.] for list of editions, including one with imprint: Oxoniae, 1657; also an English translation: Oxford, Rob. Blagrave, 1657. 2 l., 341 p. [and: Oxford, L. Lichfield, 1657; cf. NUC]. ¶ *OTP (1676 ed.)*

P. de t. supplémentaire, avec gravure. ¶ *Collation de Waldon : [14], 429, [45, index] p.* ¶ America : p. 334–41 ; Canada, Nova Francia : p. 417–18. ¶ Initialement publié avec l'adresse bibliographique Lugduni Batavorium [Batavorum ? Leyde, Hollande], 1624. *Voir* le Sabin [et le NUC (Pre–56)114:120 et suiv.] pour une liste des éditions, y compris celle portant l'adresse bibliographique : Oxoniae, 1657 ; également traduite en anglais : Oxford, Rob. Blagrave, 1657. 2 f., 341 p. [et : Oxford, L. Lichfield, 1657 ; cf. NUC]. ¶ *OTP (éd. de 1676)*

Collins, John, *fl.* 1708–1712. The case of John Collins, Esq; Governour of Newfoundland, Jan. 21. 1711. [London? 1711 O.S.] Broadside. fol.

BLC(to 1975)66:215

Title from endorsation on back. ¶ *Waldon gives imprint: [London? 1711?].* ¶ Contents: Joseph Taylour's commission to John Collins to be Governor of St. John's, etc.; petition of J. Collins to the Queen [Queen Anne]; petition of inhabitants of Newfoundland to continue John Collins in office.

Titre tiré de l'inscription officielle au verso. ¶ *Adresse bibliographique indiquée par Waldon : [Londres ? 1711 ?].* ¶ Qui portent sur le Canada : Joseph Taylour's commission to John Collins to be Governor of St. John's, etc. ; petition of J. Collins to the Queen [la reine Anne] ; petition of inhabitants of Newfoundland to continue John Collins in office.

[**Crouch, Nathaniel**], 1632?–1725?   The English empire in America .... By R.B. [*pseud.*]. The fifth edition. London: printed for Nath. Crouch, at the Bell against Grocers-alley in the Poultry, near Cheapside, 1711.   191 p. illus., 2 maps (incl. front.). 12°

NUC(Pre–56)128:174*

Plates printed on versos. ¶ *First edition: 1685,* q.v. *for other information.*

Planches imprimées au verso. ¶ *Première édition : 1685,* q.v. *pour d'autres renseignements.*

Hudson's Bay Company. Reasons for the Hudson Bay Company against their being included in the clause for suppressing insurance offices. [London? 1711?]   Broadside. fol.

NUC(Pre–56)258:450

Waldon has a variant title: Reasons humbly offered in behalf of the Hudson-Bay Company, that they may be exempted in the clause that will be offer'd for suppressing the insurance offices. *The NUC title (above) has imprint: n.p. [c1710].* ¶ Text states

Waldon indique une variante de titre : Reasons humbly offered in behalf of the Hudson-Bay Company, that they may be exempted in the clause that will be offer'd for suppressing the insurance offices. *Le titre du NUC (ci-dessus) comporte une adresse bibliographique : s.l. [c1710].* ¶ Le texte précise que la Compagnie

that the Company has taken no new contracts since 8 March 1710. ¶ See also *other works relating to this controversy under 1690, and the notes appended to those entires (which refer also to other publication dates).*

n'a conclu aucun nouveau contrat depuis le 8 mars 1710. ¶ *Sous 1690,* voir aussi *d'autres ouvrages relatifs à cette controverse, et se reporter aux notes annexées à ces notices (qui se rapportent aussi à d'autres dates de publication).*

Hudson's Bay Company. Reasons humbly offered in behalf of the Hudson-Bay Company . . . . [London? 1711?]

See preceding entry.

Voir la notice précédente.

A letter from an old Whig in town, to a modern Whig in the country, upon the late expedition to Canada. London, printed: and sold by J[ohn]. Morphew near Stationers-Hall. <Price two pence.> [1711.] 8 p. 4°

NUC(Pre–56)328:680

Dated: 23 October 1711; signed: X.Z. ¶ The expedition referred to was against Quebec in August 1711, and was led by Sir Hovenden Walker (cf. DNB, "Walker"), as part of the so-called Queen Anne's War, 1702–13.

Daté du 23 octobre 1711 ; signé : X.Z. ¶ L'expédition dont il est question avait à sa tête sir Hovenden Walker (cf. DNB « Walker ») et fut menée contre Québec au mois d'août 1711 dans le cadre de la guerre dite « de la reine Anne », 1702–13.

Nicholson, Sir Francis, 1660–1728. Journal of an expedition performed by the forces of our Sovereign Lady Anne, By the Grace of God, of Great Britain, France and Ireland, Queen, Defender of the Faith, &c. under the command of the Honourable Francis Nicholson, general and commander in chief, in the year 1710. for the reduction of Port Royal in Nova Scotia, or any other place in those parts in America, then in the possession of the French. London, printed for R.S. and sold by J[ohn]. Morphew near Stationer's Hall. 1711. 24 p. 4°

NUC(Pre–56)418:241

[Thompson, Thomas], *fl.* 1711. Considerations on the trade to Newfoundland; giving reasons for which it may be proper to petition Her Majesty that no peace may be concluded with the enemy, unless the French king will restore to her crown of Great-Britain all Newfoundland and the islands that belong to it, as her undoubted right and property. [London, printed for Andrew Bell, 1711.] 4 p. fol.

NUC(Pre–56)592–12

Caption title. ¶ Waldon has author and imprint without square brackets, and the collation and format as "one sheet, fol.," citing Kennett:212 as her only source. ¶ Refers to the Spanish Succession War, and England's early peace negotiations with France. The war ended with the Peace of Utrecht, 1713. ¶ What seems to be another edition appeared the same year, q.v., next entry, for other notes.

Titre de départ. ¶ Waldon indique le nom de l'auteur et l'adresse bibliographique sans crochets, donne « une feuille, fol. » comme collation et format, ainsi que le Kennett:212 comme son unique source. ¶ Se rapporte à la guerre de la Succession d'Espagne et au début des négociations de paix entre l'Angleterre et la France. Le traité d'Utrecht, 1713, mit fin à la guerre. ¶ Une édition distincte, semble-t-il, parut la même année, q.v. notice suivante pour d'autres notes.

[Thompson, Thomas], *fl.* 1711. Considerations on the trade to Newfoundland. [London, 1711.] 3 p. fol.

Sabin:54979

Sabin lists under title, with note: "Perhaps by Thomas Whately?"; he gives the imprint as [n.p., about 1748]. BM attributes to Thomas Thompson. ¶ Endorsed, p. [4] [but Sabin collation has only 3 p.]: "Considerations on the trade to Newfoundland." BM copy bound with ms.: Copy of a memorial concerning Cape Breton and the Newfoundland fishery delivered the 31st January 1744 to Andrew Stone Esq. Secretary to the Duke of Newcastle... [with additions by Sir Peter Thompson, 1751, and a map, 1677] (Ms. Add. 13972). ¶ The writer believes the French should be excluded from the trade to Newfoundland. ¶ *What appears to be a different edition or issue appeared the same year (cf. preceding entry); Waldon says "Reprinted: A collection of voyages and travel, 1745, vol. 2, p. 793–94 (this might be: Thomas Osborne, A collection of voyages and travels. London, Osborne, 1745, q.v.).*

Pour répertorier l'ouvrage, le Sabin utilise le titre, avec la note : « Peut-être de Thomas Whately ? » ; il donne comme adresse bibliographique [s.l., vers 1748]. Le BM attribue la paternité de l'ouvrage à Thomas Thompson. ¶ Inscription officielle, p. [4] [tandis que la collation du Sabin ne comporte que 3 p.] : « Réflexions sur le commerce vers Terre-Neuve ». L'exemplaire du BM relié avec manuscrit : Copy of a memorial concerning Cape Breton and the Newfoundland fishery delivered the 31st January 1744 to Andrew Stone Esq. Secretary to the Duke of Newcastle... [with additions by Sir Peter Thompson, 1751, and a map, 1677] (aj. de man. 13972). ¶ L'auteur estime qu'il faut exclure les Français du commerce vers Terre-Neuve. ¶ *Il semble qu'une édition ou un tirage distinct parut la même année (cf. notice précédente) ; Waldon précise « Réimpression : A collection of voyages and travel, 1745, vol. 2, p. 793–94 (il peut s'agir de : Thomas Osborne, A collection of voyages and travels. Londres, Osborne, 1745, q.v.).*

1711–12

[Hare, Francis, *bp. of Chichester/év. de Chichester*], 1671–1740. The allies and the late ministry defended against France, and the present friends of France. In answer to a pamphlet, entitled, The conduct of the allies. London, printed for E[gbert]. Sanger. 1711–12. 4 v. in 1. 8°(?)

NUC(Pre–56)231:77*

Pt. 1: third ed. London, printed for E[gbert]. Sanger, 1712; pt. 2: London, printed for A[nn]. Baldwin, 1711; pt. 3: London, printed for A[nn]. Baldwin, 1711; pt. 4: London, printed for E[gbert]. Sanger, 1712. ¶ *A reply to Jonathan Swift,* The conduct of the Allies. *London, 1711.* ¶ *Refers to peace negotiations in the War of the Spanish Succession (1701–14), which in Canada involved Quebec, Acadia, Newfoundland, and the Hudson Bay forts.* ¶ *NUC indicates a second ed. of pt. 2 (same imprint), but no other editions.*

Part. 1 : troisième éd. Londres, imprimé pour E[gbert]. Sanger, 1712 ; part. 2 : Londres, imprimé pour A[nn]. Baldwin, 1711 ; part. 3 : Londres, imprimé pour A[nn]. Baldwin, 1711 ; part. 4 : Londres, imprimé pour E[gbert]. Sanger, 1712. ¶ *Réplique à Jonathan Swift,* The conduct of the Allies. *Londres, 1711.* ¶ *Se rapporte aux négociations de paix durant la guerre de la Succession d'Espagne (1701–14), ces négociations visant au Canada le Québec, l'Acadie, Terre-Neuve, et les forts de la Baie d'Hudson.* ¶ *Le NUC indique une deuxième éd. de la part. 2 (même adresse bibliographique), mais aucune autre édition.*

1712

A calculation of the species and value of the manufactures and products of Great-Britain, Newfoundland, and Ireland, annually exported to the port of Leghorn. [s.l.; London? 1712.] Broadside. fol.

cf. NUC(Pre–56)84:403*

NUC(Pre–56)89:403 has [1700?] and [1715?] editions. ¶ Endorsed on back: A calculation of the yearly export to Leghorn. ¶ "The above-mentioned, are particulars of goods annually exported to Leghorn, exclusive of what goes to Genoa, Naples, Venice, and all other ports in the Streights." Leghorn was a free port, no customs were paid. ¶ The value of the fish was as follows:

Le NUC(Pre–56)89:403 indique une édition de [1700 ?] et une autre de [1715 ?]. ¶ Inscription officielle au verso : Un calcul des exportations annuelles à destination de Livourne. ¶ « Les données susmentionnées constituent le détail des marchandises exportées annuellement à Livourne, à l'exclusion des produits à destination de Gênes, de Naples, de Venise, ainsi que de tout autre port dans le détroit. » Livourne était un port franc, sans droits de douane. ¶ La valeur du poisson s'établissait comme suit :

5000	Hogsheads of Pilchards	£20000	5 000	barriques de sardines	20 000 £
30000	Quintals of Dry'd Codd	50000	30 000	quintaux de morue séchée	50 000
25000	Barrels of Red and White Herrings	40000	25 000	caques de harengs saurs et de harengs salés	40 000
2000	Teirce of Salmon	12000	2 000	tierçons de saumon	12 000

Clarke, Samuel, 1599–1683. A new description of the world: or, A compendious treatise . . . . With an account of the natures of the people . . . . [*see* 1708 ed.] By S. Clark. London, H. Rhodes, 1712. 3 p.l., 220 p. front. 12°(?)

NUC(Pre–56)III:361*

"Books printed for H. Rodes": p. 219–20. ¶ *Originally pub., under this title, in 1689* (q.v.).

« Livres imprimés pour le compte de H. Rodes » : p. 219–20. ¶ *Initialement publ. sous ce titre, en 1689* (q.v.).

[Dummer, Jeremiah], 1681–1739. A letter to a friend in the country, on the late expedition to Canada: with an account of former enterprizes, a defence of that design, and the share the late M——rs [Ministers] had in it. London, printed for A[nn]. Baldwin, near the Oxford Arms in Warwick-Lane. 1712. 22 [1] p. 4°

BLC(to 1975)89:36

Attributed to Dummer by *Halkett and Laing*, on the authority of Sabin and Evans. ¶ List of books: [1] p. at end. ¶ The author defends both those who planned and those who carried out the expedition, pointing out the value of Canada to the English colonies and the necessity of conquering it.

Attribué à Dummer dans le *Halkett et Laing*, sur la foi de Sabin et Evans. ¶ Liste de livres : [1] p. à la fin. ¶ Défendant à la fois ceux qui planifièrent l'expédition et ceux qui y participèrent, l'auteur souligne l'atout que représente le Canada pour les colonies anglaises et la nécessité de s'en emparer.

[**Dummer, Jeremiah**], 1681–1739. A letter to a noble lord, concerning the late expedition to Canada. London, printed for A[nn]. Baldwin, 1712. 26 p. 8°

NUC(Pre–56)151:443*

Attributed to Dummer by *Halkett and Laing*, on the authority of Sabin. Signed: J.D. ¶ *Concerns the Quebec expedition of 1711, and answers three questions: "I. Of what importance the conquest of that country would have been to the crown . . . . II. Whether the expedition was well concerted? And [III.], lastly, If the ill success of it ought wholly to be charg'd on New-England, as people here are made to believe."* ¶ Written in defence of the people of New England against criticism for the failure of the expedition. ¶ Reprinted Boston, 1712 and 1746, and also in the *American magazine*, June 1746, p. 241–88. The latter contains also the speech of Peter Warren to the American troops drawn up on the parade at Louisbourg, 19 May 1746, and other contemporary material.

Attribué à Dummer dans le *Halkett et Laing*, sur la foi de Sabin. Signé : J.D. ¶ *Traite de l'expédition de Québec de 1711 et répond à trois questions : « I. Quelle importance la conquête de cette contrée revêt-elle pour la Couronne . . . II. L'expédition fut-elle bien montée ? Et [III.], enfin, faut-il en attribuer entièrement l'échec à la Nouvelle-Angleterre, comme on le fait croire aux gens d'ici. »* ¶ Rédigé à la défense du peuple de la Nouvelle-Angleterre contre les critiques relatives à l'échec de l'expédition. ¶ Réimpression à Boston en 1712 et en 1746, ainsi que dans le *American magazine* au mois de juin 1746, p. 241–88. Cette dernière édition comprend également le discours de Peter Warren aux troupes américaines prêtes à défiler à Louisbourg le 19 mai 1746, ainsi que d'autres documents de l'époque.

Great Britain. Sovereigns, etc., 1702–1714 (Anne). By the Queen. A Proclamation, declaring the suspension of arms, as well by sea as land, agreed upon between Her Majesty and the Most Christian King, and enjoyning the observance thereof. Given at our castle of Windsor this eighteenth day of August, in the eleventh year of our reign . . . . London, printed by John Baskett . . . and the assigns of Thomas Newcomb, and Henry Hills, diceas'd. 1712 (Price one peny.) Broadside. fol.

BLC(to 1975)95:286

Great Britain. Sovereigns, etc., 1702–1714 (Anne). By the Queen. A proclamation, declaring the continuation of the cessation of arms, as well by sea as land, agreed on between Her Majesty and the Most Christian King and enjoyning the observance thereof. [Text.] Given at our Court at St. James's, the eleventh day of December, 1712. In the eleventh year of our reign . . . . London, printed by John Baskett . . . and the assigns of Thomas Newcomb, and Henry Hills, deceas'd. 1712. (Price one penny.) Broadside. fol.

BLC(to 1975)95:286

The history of the peace, from the arrival of M. Mosnager, Sept. 18, 1711, to the return of the Earl of Strafford from Utrecht, May 15. 1712. Wherein, the proceedings of both Houses of Parliament are inserted, and the reasons for and against it fully consider'd. Done out of French. London: printed in the year 1712. Price 6d. 1 p.l., 49, [1] p. 8°(?)

NUC(Pre–56)248:183

Errata: p. [50]. ¶ Waldon has no place of publication, nor collation, but her edition was that published in Somers tracts, 1751 (see note below), and is thus listed under that date by her. ¶ The settlement in America was not mentioned in the Preliminary articles offered by France and published in the *Daily courant,* London, Oct. 1711. When proposals were submitted in writing, Articles 3–4 dealt with Hudson Bay, Acadia, Newfoundland, *etc.* ¶ *The French source has not been determined, but this appears to be the first ed. in English; the text was reprinted in Somers tracts, A* fourth Collection of . . . tracts. *London, 1751, vol. 4, p. 61–95; the tracts appeared in a second ed., London, 1809–15, 13 vols.*

Errata : p. [50]. ¶ Waldon n'indique aucun lieu de publication et ne donne aucune collation, mais l'édition qu'elle mentionne est celle qui fut publiée dans le cadre des tracts de Somers, 1751 (voir la note plus loin), et elle est en effet répertoriée sous cette date par Waldon. ¶ Le règlement en Amérique n'était pas mentionné dans les Préliminaires proposés par la France et publiés dans le *Daily courant* de Londres en oct. 1711. Lors du dépôt des propositions par écrit, les Préliminaires 3 et 4 concernaient la Baie d'Hudson, l'Acadie, Terre-Neuve, *etc.* ¶ *La source française n'a pas été déterminée, mais il s'agirait de la première éd. en anglais ; le texte fut repris dans les tracts de Somers,* A fourth Collection of . . . tracts. *Londres, 1751, vol. 4, p. 61–95 ; les tracts parurent dans une deuxième éd., Londres, 1809–15, 13 vol.*

The history of the Treaty of Utrecht. In which is contain'd, a full account of all the steps taken by France, to bring the allies to a treaty during the war, and by that means to divide them. Her several offers to the confederates jointly and separately, from the Elector of Bavaria's, after the Ramilles campaign, to Monsieur Mesnager's at London. Her intrigues to procure the congress at Utrecht, and during the negotiations there. To which is occasionally added, a brief relation of the progress of the arms of the Allies, and a state of their affairs at the commencement of the Treaty. London: printed and sold by the booksellers of London and Westminster. 1712. Price 5s. [7], 426, [14] p. Index. 8°

NUC(Pre–56)248:198*

NUC has collation as: 426 p.; Waldon's source is given as BM, but her collation starts the same as that in the second ed., 1713. ¶ Refers to the peace negotiations which culminated in the Treaty of Utrecht (11 April 1713), ending British participation in the War of the Spanish Succession (1701–14) which in Canada involved Quebec, Acadia, Newfoundland, and the forts on Hudson Bay. ¶ This appeared in a second ed. in 1713 with a different title, but beginning with the same seven first words (q.v.).

Collation du NUC : 426 p. ; Waldon indique BM comme source, bien que sa collation débute comme celle de la deuxième éd., 1713. ¶ Se rapporte aux négociations de paix qui aboutirent au traité d'Utrecht (11 avril 1713) mettant fin à la participation anglaise à la guerre de la Succession d'Espagne (1701–14) qui, au Canada, touchait le Québec, l'Acadie, Terre-Neuve, et les forts de la Baie d'Hudson. ¶ Cet écrit parut dans une deuxième éd. en 1713 sous un titre différent mais débutant par les mêmes sept premiers mots (q.v.).

The offers of France explain'd .... London, printed for A[nn]. Baldwin ... 1712. price 3d. Where may be had, *The allies and the late ministry defended*. 1 p.l., 26 p. 8°(in 4s).

NUC(Pre–56)427:403

Waldon enters this under Francis Hare, bp. of Chichester, but this is not supported in NUC, nor Morgan, BBH:0507. ¶ The author is critical of the proposed treaty. The question of Hudsons Bay, Nova Scotia, and Newfoundland dealt with p. 7–9. ¶ Refers to the preliminaries of peace at Utrecht in the War

Waldon répertorie ce sujet sous Francis Hare, év. de Chichester, en l'absence toutefois de toute donnée justificative dans le NUC aussi bien que dans Morgan, BBH:0507. ¶ L'auteur se montre critique à l'égard de la proposition de traité. Il aborde la question de la Baie d'Hudson, de la Nouvelle-Écosse et de Terre-Neuve aux p. 7–9. ¶ Se rapporte aux

of the Spanish Succession, which led to the Peace of Utrecht, 1713.

préliminaires de paix à Utrecht au cours de la guerre de la Succession d'Espagne, qui aboutirent au traité d'Utrecht, 1713.

A West-India merchant, *pseud.* A letter from a West-India merchant to a gentleman at Tunbridg, concerning that part of the French proposals, which relates to North-America, and particularly Newfoundland. With some thoughts on their offers about our trade to Spain and the West-Indies: and an abstract of the Assiento. London, printed in the year 1712. Price four pence. 1 p.l., 34 p. 8°

BM(to 1955)657:241

1713

*Echard, Laurence, 1670?–1730. A most complete compendium of geography, general and special.... The eighth edition corrected and much improved. By Laurence Echard .... London, printed for J[ohn]. Nicholson ... and S[amuel]. Ballard ... 1713. 7 p.l., 236, [9] p. 12°

NUC(Pre–56)154:608*

Pages 45, 51 incorrectly numbered 4, 15, respectively. ¶ Adverts.: last 3 p. ¶ *See* first ed., 1691, for notes.

Erreurs de pagination : pages 45 et 51 respectivement numérotées 4 et 15. ¶ Réclame : 3 dernières p. ¶ *Voir* notes à la première éd. de 1691.

Great Britain. Sovereigns, etc., 1702–1714 (Anne). By the Queen, a proclamation, for a publick thanksgiving. To be observed in England, Wales and the Town of Berwick upon Tweed, for the conclusion of the war. Given at our Court at St. James's, the eighteenth day of May, 1713. In the twelfth year of our reign . . . . London, printed for John Baskett, printer to the Queens most Excellent Majesty, and by the assigns of Thomas Newcomb, and Henry Hills, deceas'd. 1713. Broadside. fol.

BLC(to 1975)95:286

Proclaims a general thanksgiving for the Treaty of Utrecht, which terminated the War of the Spanish Succession, and under which the Hudson Bay territory, Acadia, and Newfoundland were ceded by France. The date was postponed by a subsequent proclamation (8 June) — see next entry but one. ¶ A variant of this, for Scotland, appeared the same day — see next entry.

Proclamation d'une fête générale d'action de grâces à l'occasion de la signature du traité d'Utrecht qui mit fin à la guerre de la Succession d'Espagne et par lequel la France céda ses territoires de la Baie d'Hudson, de l'Acadie et de Terre-Neuve. La date fut reportée dans une proclamation ultérieure (8 juin) – voir deux notices plus bas. ¶ Une variante de cette proclamation parut le même jour en Écosse –voir la notice suivante.

Great Britain. Sovereigns, etc., 1702–1714 (Anne). By the Queen, a proclamation, for a publick thanksgiving. [To be observed in Scotland, on June 16, for the conclusion of the war.] Given at our Court at St. James's the eighteenth day of May, 1713. In the twelfth year of our reign . . . . London, printed by John Baskett . . . and by the assigns of Thomas Newcomb, and Henry Hills, deceas'd. 1713. Broadside. fol.

BLC(to 1975)95:286

For notes, see preceding entry. ¶ This thanksgiving was deferred to 7 July in a subsequent proclamation (8 June) — see next entry.

Voir *notes à la notice précédente. ¶ La fête d'action de grâces fut reportée au 7 juillet dans une proclamation ultérieure (8 juin) –voir la notice suivante.*

Great Britain. Sovereigns, etc., 1702–1714 (Anne). By the Queen, a proclamation, for a publick thanksgiving. [To be observed throughout England, Wales, and the Town of Berwick upon Tweed, on July 7, instead of on June 16.] Given at our Court at Kensington, the eighth day of June, 1713. In the twelfth year of our reign . . . . London, printed by John Baskett, printer to the Queens most Excellent Majesty, and by the assigns of Thomas Newcomb, and Henry Hills, deceas'd. 1713. Broadside. fol.

NUC(Pre–56)215:418

Sets a later date for the thanksgiving for the end of the War of the Spanish Succession, by the Treaty of Utrecht. For the original proclamation, see preceding entry but one.

Remet la date de la fête de l'action de grâces à l'occasion de la fin de la guerre de la Succession d'Espagne par le traité d'Utrecht. Proclamation originale : voir deux notices plus haut.

Great Britain. Sovereigns, etc., 1702–1714 (Anne). By the Queen. A proclamation, for the publishing the peace, between Her Majesty, and His most Christian Majesty the French King . . . . Given at our Court at St. James's, the fourth day of May, in the twelfth year of our reign . . . . London, printed for John Baskett, printer to the Queens most excellent Majesty, and by the assigns of Thomas Newcomb, and Henry Hills, deceas'd. 1713. Broadside. fol.

BLC(to 1975)95:286

Refers to the Peace of Utrecht, 1713, which ended the War of the Spanish Succession, and under which France ceded the territories of Hudson Bay, Acadia, and Newfoundland to Britain.

Renvoie au traité d'Utrecht (1713) qui mit fin à la guerre de la Succession d'Espagne et par lequel la France céda les territoires de la Baie d'Hudson, de l'Acadie et de Terre-Neuve à la Grande-Bretagne.

*Great Britain. Treaties, etc., 1702–1714 (Anne). Tractatus navigationis et commerciorum inter Serennissimam ac Potentissimam Principem Annam, Dei Gratiâ, Magnae Britanniae, Franciae, & Hibernae, Reginam, & Serenissimum ac Potentissimum Principem Ludovicum XIV. Dei Gratiâ, Regem Christianissimum, conclusus trajecti ad Rhenum die 31 Martii/11 Aprilis anno 1713. Treaty of navigation and commerce between the most serene and most potent Princess Anne, by the Grace of God, Queen of Great Britain, France, and Ireland, and the most serene and most potent Prince Lewis the XIVth, the Most Christian King, concluded at Utrecht the 31/11 day of March/Apr. 1713. By Her Majestie's special command. London, printed by John Baskett, printer to the Queen's most excellent Majesty, and by the assigns of Thomas Newcomb, and Henry Hills, deceas'd, 1713. 47 p. 23 cm.

NUC(Pre–56)215:510*

Latin and English; or French and English in parallel columns; in the three languages. ¶ Part of the Treaty of Utrecht, by which Britain gained from France Acadia, Hudson Bay territory, and Newfoundland. *See also Tractatus pacis & amicitiae.* London, 1713, under the same entry. ¶ An apparent variant appears in NUC with the dates in the titles given as "21/11 day of March/April, 1713," and with 55 p., otherwise the same.

Latin et anglais ou français et anglais disposés en colonnes parallèles ; en trois langues. ¶ Partie du traité d'Utrecht par lequel la France céda l'Acadie, le territoire de la Baie d'Hudson et Terre-Neuve à la Grande-Bretagne. *Voir aussi Tractatus pacis & amicitiae.* Londres, 1713, sous la même date. ¶ Le NUC donne une variante supposée dont les dates dans les titres donnés apparaissent comme suit : « 21/11 day of March/April, 1713 », et 55 p. Le reste est identique.

*Great Britain. Treaties, etc., 1702–1714 **(Anne).** Tractatus pacis et amicitiae inter serenissimam ac potentissimam principem Annam, Dei gratiâ, Magnae Britanniae, Franciae, & Hibernae, reginam, & serenissimum ac potentissimum principem Ludovicum XIV. Dei gratiâ regem Christianissimum, conclusus trajecti ad Rhenum die 31 Martii/11 Aprilis anno 1713. Treaty of peace and friendship between the most serene and most potent Princess Anne, by the Grace of God, Queen of Great Britain, France, and Ireland, and the most serene and most potent Prince Lewis the XIVth, the most Christian King, concluded at Utrecht the 31/11 day of March/April 1713. By Her Majesties special command. London, printed by John Baskett, printer to the Queens most excellent Majesty, and the assigns of Thomas Newcomb, and Henry Hills, deceas'd. 1713. 80 p. 4°(?)

NUC(Pre–56)215:510*

French, Latin, and English in parallel columns. ¶ Treaty of Utrecht, 11 April (N.S.) 1713, under which France ceded Acadia, Newfoundland, and the Hudson Bay territory to Britain. *See also Tractatus navigationis et commerciorum.* London, 1713, under the same entry. Note that the separate treaties with Spain, and other countries, did not directly affect Canada. ¶ Waldon lists, in abridged form, a similar work, but with 84 p. This in turn is similar to the NUC entry which follows the above (215:510, col. 2), but differs again in having "21/11 day of March/April" in the title, and in being printed in Latin, English, French, and Spanish. A copy of this latter is in BVIPA. Sabin:96541 is another variant, with "concluded at Utrecht the 2/13 day of July, 1713" in the title, and a collation of 115 p., 4°.

Français, latin et anglais disposés en colonnes parallèles. ¶ Traité d'Utrecht, 11 avril 1713 (c.g.), par lequel la France cèda l'Acadie, Terre-Neuve et le territoire de la Baie d'Hudson à la Grande-Bretagne. *Voir aussi* l'ouvrage *Tractatus navigationis et commerciorum.* Londres, 1713, sous la même année. Notez bien que les traités distincts signés avec l'Espagne et d'autres pays n'eurent pas d'effets directs sur le Canada. ¶ Waldon signale, sous forme abrégée, un ouvrage similaire qui ne contient toutefois que 84 p., ce qui correspond à la notice du NUC pour ce qui précède (215:510, col. 2), mais qui en diffère puisque son titre donne « 21/11 day of March/April » et qu'il fut imprimé en latin, en anglais, en français et en espagnol. Il existe un exemplaire de ce même ouvrage au BVIPA. L'ouvrage répertorié dans le Sabin:96541 est une autre variante qui renferme dans son titre « 2/13 day of July, 1713 » et dont la collation est la suivante : 115 p., in-4°.

*A history of the Treaty of Utrecht. Wherein is contain'd, a particular state of the affairs of the allies at the commencement of that treaty. And the negotiations at large. With all the acts, memorials, representations, offers, demands, letters, speeches. And the treaties of peace and commerce between Great Britain and France, &c. The second edition, with addition. London, printed for J. Pemberton, 1713. 4 p.l., 426, [14], [8], [42] p. 8°(?)

NUC(Pre–56)248:198*

Title-page and preface of the first ed. are inserted between the Index and the Appendix (cf. NUC). ¶ First ed.: London, 1712 (*q.v.* for other notes), has a different title except for the first seven words.

La page de titre et la préface de l'édition originale ont été insérées entre l'index et l'annexe (cf. NUC). ¶ La première édition : Londres, 1712 (*q.v.* pour d'autres notes) porte un titre différent sauf pour les sept premiers mots.

[Kennett, White, *bp. of Peterborough/év. de Peterborough*], 1660–1728. Bibliothecae americanae primordia. An attempt towards laying the foundation of an American library, in several books, papers, and writings, humbly given to the Society for the Propagation of the Gospel in Foreign Parts for the perpetual use and benefit of their members, their missionaries, friends, correspondents, and others concern'd in the good design of planting and promoting Christianity within Her Majesties colonies and plantations in the West-Indies. By a member of the said Society. London, printed for J[ohn]. Churchill, at the Black Swan in Pater-Noster-Row, 1713. 2 p.l., xvi, 275 p. (incl. index); t.-p., iii, advertisement; xvi; 3–275; 220 p. (incl. index). 4°

NUC(Pre–56)293:371*

NUC has "Printed for G. Church" (not in Plomer) and collation as: 1 p.l., iii, xvi, 3–275 (i.e. 283) p., 112 l. Paging is irregular: nos. 125–32 repeated. Index pages not numbered. ¶ Only 250 copies printed. ¶ "Advertisement," "Auctarium Bibliothecae americane. An addition of some other books and papers humbly given to the Society . . . ," and

Le NUC donne « Printed for G. Church » (pas dans le Plomer) et la collation suivante : 1 f. l., iii, xvi, 3–275 (c.-à-d. 283) p., 112 f. Pagination irrégulière, les n°s 125–32 se répètent. Index non paginé. ¶ Tirage limité de 250 exemplaires. ¶ « Réclame », « Auctarium Bibliothecae americane. An addition of some other books and papers humbly given to the Society. . . », et « Index » de Robert Watts. ¶

"*Index*" *by Robert Watts.* ¶ *The dedication is dated 20 Oct. 1713, but the Advertisement has date 1 Nov. 1714, and the "addition" contains entries of books published in 1714.* ¶ This is the first catalogue of Americana in English, and a very excellent one. Bishop Kennett made a collection of books, charts, maps, and documents, with the intention, never carried out, of writing a history of the propagation of the gospel in the English colonies. He gives titles in full, imprint and pagination. The items are arranged chronologically [by date of pub., and extracts from Purchas and Hakluyt are entered under date of voyage described], with analytics for collections of voyages, etc. Kennett's library was left by his will to the S.P.G.F.P., which still has part of it [though the greater part has been lost. The remnant consists of about 300 vols., chiefly historical, theological, and polemical works]. Many vols. are now in other hands. Cf. Church, v. 4, p. 1787–88 and Charles Dean, *An account of the White Kennett library of the Society for the Propagation of the Gospel in Foreign Parts.* Cambridge, J. Wilson & Sons, 1883. 8 p. ¶ The Bishop's name is spelt "Kennett" by NUC, Sabin, DNB, and Church; "Kennet" by BLC. ¶ Other eds.: London, J. Debrett, 1789, 4° (this was based on Kennett's work, but entries are neither as accurate nor as full as in the original; attributed to one Homer), and London, Dryden Press, J. Davey & Sons, 1917, cf. NUC.

La dédicace est datée du 20 octobre 1713, mais la réclame, du premier novembre 1714. De plus, le « supplément » renferme des titres de livres publiés en 1714. ¶ Il s'agit ici du premier catalogue d'ouvrages portant sur des sujets américains en langue anglaise, catalogue d'excellente qualité d'ailleurs. L'évêque Kennett colligea livres, plans, cartes et documents dans l'espoir, jamais réalisé, d'en faire un livre racontant l'histoire de la propagation de l'évangile au sein des colonies anglaises. Il donne les titres complets ainsi que l'adresse bibliographique et la pagination. Les articles sont présentés chronologiquement [par date de publication ; cependant, des extraits tirés de Purchas et de Hakluyt sont ordonnés selon la date des voyages décrits] ainsi que des analyses logiques pour les collections de voyages, etc. Kennett légua sa bibliothèque à la S.P.G.F.P. [Société pour l'évangélisation des régions étrangères] qui en possède toujours une partie [bien que la plus grande partie ait été perdue. Les trois cents volumes qui ont pu être conservés sont principalement des ouvrages historiques, théologiques et polémiques]. Bon nombre de ces volumes ont depuis changé de mains. Cf. Church, vol. 4, p. 1787–1788 et Charles Dean, *An account of the White Kennett library of the Society for the Propagation of the Gospel in Foreign Parts.* Cambridge : J. Wilson & Sons, 1883. 8 p. ¶ Dans le NUC, le Sabin, le DNB et le Church, Kennett s'écrit avec deux « t » tandis qu'il n'en retient qu'un dans le BLC. ¶ Autres éditions : Londres, J. Debrett, 1789, in-4° (ouvrage rédigé à partir de celui de Kennett, mais les notices ne sont ni aussi précises ou ni aussi complètes que dans l'original ; attribué à un certain Homer), et Londres, Dryden Press, J. Davey & Sons, 1917, cf. NUC.

A true list of the several ships arrived at Leghorn from Great Britain, Ireland, and Newfoundland, in one year, commencing at Lady-Day, 1712, to Lady-Day, 1713. [London? 1713?] 2 p. fol.

Kennett:215

Endorsed with same title at bottom of p. 2. ¶ *Kennett's entry concludes with the note: "Printed Half-sheet."* ¶ There were ten ships from Newfoundland with cargoes of "Dried Fish."

Inscription officielle tirée du même titre au bas de la p. 2. ¶ *La notice de Kennett se termine par la note suivante : « Printed Half-sheet ».* ¶ Il y avait dix bateaux en provenance de Terre-Neuve chargés de « poisson séché ».

1714

Jesuits. Letters from missions. The travels of several learned missioners of the Society of Jesus, into divers parts of the archipelago, India, China, and America. Containing a general description of the most remarkable towns; with a particular account of the customs, manners and religion of those several nations, the whole interspers'd with philosophical observations and other curious remarks. Translated from the French original publish'd at Paris in the year 1713. London, printed for R[obert]. Gosling, 1714. 8 p.l., 335, [12] p. 2 fold. plates. 8°

NUC(Pre–56)280:199

Waldon has collation as: [16], 335, [1, books, 12, 4, books] p. index. ¶ Twenty letters transl. and abridged from Lettres edifiantes et curieuses ... 9–10 recueil. *Paris, 1711–13, and a condensed transl. of Sieur de Dièreville,* Relation du voyage du Port Royal de l'Acadie. *Amsterdam, 1710, entitled "Extract of an account of the country of Accadia . . ."* (see *below*). ¶ "A letter from Father Gabriel Marest, missioner of the Society of Jesus, to F. de Lamberville, of the same society, procurator of the

Collation de Waldon : [16], 335, [1, livres, 12, 4, livres] p., index. ¶ *Vingt lettres abrégées et traduites tirées de l'ouvrage :* Lettres edifiantes et curieuses ... 9–10 recueil. *Paris, 1711–1713, plus une traduction condensée du livre* Relation du voyage du Port-Royal de l'Acadie *de Sieur de Dièreville. Amsterdam, 1710, intitulée « Extract of an account of the country of Accadia. . . » (voir plus loin).* ¶ « A letter from Father Gabriel Marest, missioner of the Society of Jesus, to F. de Lamberville, of the same society, procurator of the missions of Canada [of the settlement

missions of Canada [of the settlement of the French at Hudson's Bay; their war with the English; the French abandon that settlement, etc.]": p. 254–77; "Extract of an account of the country of Accadia, in North America, yielded up in the last treaty of peace by the King of France to the Crown of England .... Written in the year 1710, by a French gentleman, and sent to a missioner of the Society of Jesus.": p. 277–318. ¶ *See also* the notes for *Travels of the Jesuits*, London, 1743, under the above entry for a different translation. ¶ *NSWA · BVAU · BVIPA*

of the French at Hudson's Bay; their war with the English; the French abandon that settlement, etc.] » : p. 254–77 ; « Extract of an account of the country of Accadia, in North America, yielded up in the last treaty of peace by the King of France to the Crown of England .... Written in the year 1710, by a French gentleman, and sent to a missioner of the Society of Jesus » : p. 277–318. ¶ *Voir aussi* les notes pour l'ouvrage *Travels of the Jesuits* à la notice ci-dessus, Londres, 1743, pour obtenir une traduction différente. ¶ *NSWA · BVAU · BVIPA*

Joutel, Henri, 1640?–1735. A journal of the last voyage perform'd by Monsr. de La Sale, to the Gulph of Mexico, to find out the mouth of the Mississippi River; containing an account of the settlements he endeavour'd to make on the coast of the aforesaid bay, his unfortunate death, and the travels of his companions for the space of eight hundred leagues across that inland country of America, now call'd Louisiana ... till they came into Canada. Written in French by Monsieur Joutel, a commander in that expedition; and translated from the ed. just publish'd at Paris. With an exact map of that vast country, and a copy of the letters patents granted by the K. of France to M. Crozat. London, printed for A[ndrew]. Bell at the Cross-Keys and Bible in Cornhill, B[ernard]. Lintott at the Cross Keys in Fleet-street, and J. Baker, in Pater-noster-Row, 1714. 1 p.l., xxi, [9], 205, [5] p. fold. map. 8°

NUC(Pre-56)285:565*

Index at the end. ¶ *Transl. from his Journal historique du dernier voyage que feu M. de La Sale fit dans le golfe de Mexique. Paris, 1713.* ¶ *Concerns the 1684–87 voyage of Robert Cavelier, Sieur de La Salle.* ¶ *First edition in English; reissued London, 1719, q.v.; reprinted in Historical Collections of*

Index à la fin. ¶ *Traduction de Journal historique du dernier voyage que feu M. de La Sale fit dans le golfe de Mexique du même auteur. Paris, 1713.* ¶ *Traite du voyage de Robert Cavelier, Sieur de La Salle en 1684–1687.* ¶ *Première édition en anglais ; nouveau tirage, Londres, 1719, q.v. ; réimpression dans Historical Collections of Louisiana,*

Louisiana, ed. by Benjamin F. French, New York, 1846–53, vol. 1 (1846), p. [85]–193, and again in Chicago, The Caxton Club, 1896 (see NUC). ¶ OTP

dir. par Benjamin F. French, New York, 1846–1853, vol. 1 (1846), p. [85]–193, et de nouveau à Chicago par The Caxton Club en 1896 (voir le NUC). ¶ OTP

*A letter to the Honourable A——r M——re, Com—ner of Trade and Plantation. London, printed for J[ames]. Roberts, 1714. 39 p. fold. table. 8°

NUC(Pre–56)329:85

Dated: "Royal Exchange 26 May 1714." ¶ Discusses British trade with France, the Newfoundland fishery, and the French cession of Hudson Bay territory, Acadia, and Newfoundland under the Treaty of Utrecht (1713, ending the Spanish Succession War), and opposes the terms of the treaty. The letter is addressed to Arthur Moore, Commissioner of Trade and Plantations.

Date : Royal Exchange 26 May 1714. ¶ Traite du commerce entre l'Angleterre et la France, des pêches à Terre-Neuve et de la cession par la France des territoires de la Baie d'Hudson, de l'Acadie et de Terre-Neuve conformément au traité d'Utrecht (de 1713, mettant fin à la guerre de la Succession d'Espagne) et s'oppose aux termes du traité. Lettre adressée à M. Arthur Moore, Commissaire au Commerce et aux Colonies.

*The present ministry justify'd: or, An account of the state of the several treaties of peace, between Her Majesty and her allies, and France and Spain: with an account of the obstructions of peace; and of what was done relating to the Catalans, as laid before both Houses of Parliament. London, printed and sold for J[ohn]. Morphew, near Stationers-hall, 1714. Price one shilling. 76 p. 8°

NUC(Pre–56)470:282

Erroneously attributed in Morgan, BBH:Q549 to George Ridpath, and NUC states that there is no evidence to support Swift as author. ¶ Relates to several treaties concerning England gaining possession of Hudson Bay and Hudson Straits, Nova Scotia, and Newfoundland, and the freedom of the Five Nations Indians to trade with England under the Treaty of Utrecht, which ended the War of the Spanish Succession.

Ouvrage attribué par erreur, dans le Morgan, BBH:Q549, à George Ridpath. Le NUC soutient que rien ne permet de croire que Swift en soit l'auteur. ¶ Porte sur les différents traités régissant l'acquisition par l'Angleterre de la Baie d'Hudson et de ses détroits, de la Nouvelle-Écosse et de Terre-Neuve, et sur la liberté, pour les cinq nations indiennes, de commercer avec l'Angleterre conformément au traité d'Utrecht qui mit fin à la guerre de la Succession d'Espagne.

Withall, Benjamin, *fl.* 1697–1717. The case of Benjamin Withall, Gent. [London? 1714?] Broadside. fol.

BM(to 1955)259:783

Endorsed: Case of Benjamin Withall, Gent. Newfoundland. ¶ Begins: That Liuetenant [*sic*, in Waldon] Collonel (now the honourable Major General) Handasyd, (who succeeded Collonel Gibson as Commander in Chief of his late Majesties Land Forces, in St. John's, Newfoundland . . .) did the 8th October, 1697. constitute and appoint the said Withall as Agent or Storekeeper of Provisions to the said Garrison . . . . ¶ BM supplies after Withall in title: [Being a petition to the House of Commons that B. Withall and General Handasyd be relieved from the charge of having purloined provisions sent out for His Majesty's forces in Newfoundland, in 1697 and 1698. London, 1700?] ¶ *I*

Inscription officielle : Case of Benjamin Withall, Gent. Newfoundland. ¶ Commence ainsi : Que le lieutenant-colonel [en anglais, Liuetenant, *sic*, dans Waldon] (maintenant honorable major-général) Handasyd (successeur du colonel Gibson en tant que commandant en chef des armées de terre de feu Sa Majesté à St. John's, Terre-Neuve) ait, le 8 octobre 1697, constitué le dénommé Withall agent ou gardien des provisions à ladite garnison . . . . ¶ Le BM donne après Withall dans le titre : [Being a petition to the House of Commons that B. Withall and General Handasyd be relieved from the charge of having purloined provisions sent out for His Majesty's forces in Newfoundland, in 1697 and 1698. Londres, 1700 ?]. ¶ *Nous avons utilisé le titre et l'adresse bibliographique de Waldon tirés de ses deux*

have used Waldon's title and imprint because, from her first two notes, she appears to have seen a copy of this broadside, probably the BM copy, the location she cites. ¶ The next entry is a 1714 work on the same subject; Waldon also has a "see also" reference to the dates 1711, 1713, 1715, and 1717, but the first one has not been found amongst her sheets — although there are several Newfoundland titles under 1711, none concerns the Withall case; and the 1713 sheet is identical with this 1714 entry, and may be a confusion; the 1715 and 1717 works are different, and appear below under Withall.

premières notes, parce qu'elle semble avoir consulté un exemplaire de cet in-plano, sans doute l'exemplaire du BM, qu'elle cite comme localisation. ¶ La notice suivante porte sur un ouvrage de 1714 traitant du même thème ; Waldon renvoie également aux dates suivantes : 1711, 1713, 1715 et 1717, mais la première ne se trouve pas dans ses feuilles – malgré les nombreux titres sur Terre-Neuve en 1711, aucun ne traite de la cause Withall ; la feuille datée 1713 est identique à la présente notice de 1714, et il peut y avoir eu confusion ; les ouvrages de 1715 et 1717 sont différents et apparaissent ci-dessous sous Withall.

Withall, Benjamin, *fl.* 1697–1717. The case of Benjamin Withall, Gent. In His Majesty's victualling-office, &c. [London? 1714?] Broadside. fol.

Waldon's source is the Bodleian Library, fol. 591(23). ¶ Begins: Humbly sheweth, That in the Year, 1697, he the said Withall, was (by ample Authority, joyn'd with Necessity) constituted and appointed Storekeeper of his late Majesty King William's Provisions in St. John's, Newfoundland. ¶ Dated in ms.: 1714. Withall applied to the Commissioners of Public Accounts in 1712. In the second paragraph of this "case" he asserts that he applied to the Commissioners "about two years since." "Twice" is inserted in ms. in the margin before "two." It was written after Anne's death. ¶ Ms. note at foot of page: "This case is not yet laid before the Gent. Coms. because the foregoing Ordnance Matters has

La source de Waldon est la Bodleian Library, fol. 591(23). ¶ Commence ainsi : Il a été établi qu'en l'an 1697, le dénommé Withall fut (par grande autorité et nécessité) constitué gardien des provisions de feu Sa Majesté le roi William à St. John's, Terre-Neuve. ¶ Date manuscrite : 1714. Withall fit une demande aux Commissaires des comptes publics en 1712. Dans le deuxième paragraphe de ce « cas », Withall affirme qu'il présenta sa demande aux Commissaires « il y a environ deux ans ». « Twice » a été inséré à la main dans la marge devant le « two ». Texte rédigé après la mort de la reine Anne. ¶ Note manuscrite en bas de page : « This case is not yet laid before the Gent. Coms. because the foregoing Ordnance Matters has had such cold entert [?] with them. But to do their predecessors

had such cold entert[?] with them. But to do their predecessors justice they were very Ready (not to state & Report but) to get in & give. Will [? end of line cut off] Copies of books &c. Requested (which Could be Little or No hindrance to other matters then before them) as [?] these [?] the Gent. Honble Gent. can't be spoke to in the first six Months altho' Earnestly Begg'd." ¶ *Quite evidently Waldon saw an original of this, probably the Bodleian copy, if indeed any other is extant.* ¶ See *related works under other dates, notes in preceding entry.*

justice they were very Ready (not to state & Report but) to get in & give. Will [? fin de la ligne supprimée] Copies of Books &c. Requested (which Could be Little or No hindrance to other matters then before them) as [?] these [?] the Gent. Honble Gent. can't be spoke to in the first six Months altho' Earnestly Begg'd. » ¶ *De toute évidence, Waldon a consulté un ouvrage original, probablement l'exemplaire de la Bodleian, puisqu'on ne connaît pas d'autres exemplaires.* ¶ Voir *les ouvrages connexes sous d'autres dates et les notes à la notice précédente.*

1715

Davenant, Charles, 1656–1714. An account of the trade between Great-Britain, France, Holland, Spain, Portugal, Italy, Africa, Newfoundland, &c., with the importations and exportations of all commodities, particularly of the woollen manufactures. Deliver'd in two reports made to the Commissioners for publick accounts. By Charles Davenant, L.L.D. Late inspector general of the exports and imports. London: printed for A[rchibald]. Bell . . . W. Taylor and J. Baker . . . 1715. (Price 2s.) 1 p.l., 5–78, 75, [3] p. 8°

NUC(Pre–56)134:72

Waldon has collation: t.-p., 5–78, 75 [1 blank; 3, Index] p.

Collation de Waldon : p. de t., 5–78, 75 [1 blanche ; 3, index] p.

The dismal state of the nation, with remarks on the articles of Gertruydenberg and Utrecht.... London, printed and sold by J[ames]. Roberts, J[I? Israel?]. Harrison, and A. Boulter, 1715. (Price 1s.) 80 p. 8°

NUC(Pre–56)144:528

The terms of both treaties relating to America are given (p. 24, 37–41, 49) but the chief criticism is directed against the European settlement and American affairs are little discussed. ¶ *The War of the Spanish Succession won Hudson Bay, Acadia, and Newfoundland from France.*

Les conditions des deux traités touchant l'Amérique (p. 24, p. 37–41 et p. 49) sont décrites, mais la critique touche surtout le règlement européen et il est très peu question des affaires américaines. ¶ *La guerre de la Succession d'Espagne dépossède la France de la Baie d'Hudson, de l'Acadie et de Terre-Neuve.*

*[Freschot, Casimir], 1640?–1720. The compleat history of the Treaty of Utrecht, as also that of Gertruydenberg; containing all the acts, memorials, representations, complaints, demands, letters, speeches, treaties and other authentick pieces relating to the negotiations there. To which are added, the treaties of Radstat and Baden .... London, A[bel]. Roper and S. Butler, 1715. 2 v. tables (part fold.). 8°(?)

NUC(Pre–56)185:6*

Concerns the termination of the War of the Spanish Succession, and the treaties of 1713 and 1714. ¶ This edition was reproduced on microfilm from the University of Kansas original, in 1964 (cf. NUC).

Porte sur la fin de la guerre de la Succesion d'Espagne et sur les traités de 1713 et de 1714. ¶ Cette édition fut reproduite sur microfilm à partir de l'original de l'Université du Kansas en 1964 (cf. NUC).

Great Britain. Parliament, 1715. House of Commons. Articles of impeachment of high treason, and other high crimes and misdemeanours, against the Right Honourable Robert, * * * * * . London: sold at all the pamphlet shops. [1715?] (Price one shilling.) 1 p.l., 72 p. 8°

No bibliographical citations found.

Dr. Waldon's source was the copy in the Hamilton Public Library. ¶ Quebec expedition, 1711: p. 49–52. ¶ *Similar works have title:* ... against Robert Earl of Oxford ... 1715 (see *below*). ¶ *From the context (e.g., Matthew Prior, p. 14–15, as Harley's emissary), the subject is Robert Harley, earl of Oxford, who instituted peace negotiations with France in 1711, leading to the Peace of Utrecht, ending the War of Spanish Succession.* ¶ *Answered by: Robert Harley,* The Answer of Robert, Earl of Oxford ... to the articles exhibited ... against him for high treason .... London, 1715 *(q.v.), in which Harley defends (for example) his part in the Quebec expedition and the negotiations relative to Newfoundland.* ¶ *Several other editions appear in NUC(Pre–56) 436:229, under:* "Oxford, Robert Harley, 1st Earl of, 1661–1724, defendent" *(see below), though he is the subject, not the author, and the sixteen Articles were prepared by Robert Walpole (DNB), drawn up by the House of Commons (NUC, loc. cit.), and moved in Parliament by Thomas, Lord Coningsby (DNB), June 1715. Morgan,BBH:4275 has first ed. as a folio, and with "July 9, 1715" in the title; Morgan,BBH:T448 is a London, 1717 ed., not confirmed elsewhere; there were also 1727 (under above entry) and 1739 (under Great Britain. Parliament, 1739. House of Commons) editions, q.v.* ¶ *OH*

La source de Waldon était l'exemplaire de la bibliothèque publique de Hamilton. ¶ Quebec expedition, 1711: p. 49–52. ¶ *Des oeuvres similaires portent les titres:* ... against Robert Earl of Oxford ... 1715 (voir *plus bas*). ¶ *Selon le contexte (p. ex., Matthew Prior, p. 14–15, comme l'émissaire d'Harley), le sujet en est Robert Harley, comte d'Oxford, qui institua les négociations de paix avec la France en 1711, aboutissant à la paix d'Utrecht, terminant ainsi la guerre de Succession d'Espagne.* ¶ *Réplique de: Robert Harley,* The Answer of Robert, Earl of Oxford ... to the articles exhibited ... against him for high treason .... Londres, 1715 *(q.v.), dans laquelle Robert Harley défend (par exemple) sa part dans l'expédition au Québec et les négociations concernant Terre-Neuve.* ¶ *Plusieurs autres éditions figurent dans le NUC(Pre–56)436:229 comme:* "Oxford, Robert Harley, 1st Earl of, 1661–1724, defendent" *(voir plus bas), quoiqu'il soit le sujet, non l'auteur, et les seize articles en question furent préparés par Robert Walpole (DNB), rédigés par la Chambre des Communes (NUC, loc. cit.), et proposés au parlement par Thomas, comte de Coningsby (DNB) en juin 1715. Morgan,BBH:4275 répertorie la première édition comme folio comportant dans le titre la date "le 9 juillet 1715; Morgan,BBH:T448 est une édition faite à Londres en 1717, non confirmée ailleurs; il existait également celle de 1727 (sous la notice précédente), et de 1739 (sous Great Britain. Parliament, 1739. House of Commons), q.v.* ¶ *OH*

*Great Britain. Parliament, 1715. House of Commons. Articles of impeachment of high treason ... against Robert Earl of Oxford and Earl Mortimer. ... London: printed for T. Wright, near Fleetstreet. 1715. 9 p. fol.

Waldon cites "Harmsworth" only (cf. NUC(Pre–56)231:282–83).

Perhaps from Sir R.L. Harmsworth, Catalogue of Americana *(unavailable to the editor); not found in* The Northcliffe Collection, *in* PAC *(Ottawa, 1926); but* NUC *lists many other catalogues of parts of the Harmsworth Library.* ¶ *Imprint at end.* ¶ *Article XVII charges Oxford with cheating the nation of £20,000 because the expedition of 1711 against Canada was a failure.* ¶ *Several other editions appear in NUC(Pre–56)436:229 under "Oxford, Robert Harley, 1st Earl of, 1661–1724, defendent," see following.*

Peut-être en provenance du Catalogue of Americana *de sir R.L. Harmsworth (non disponible à l'éditeur); introuvable dans* The Northcliffe Collection *de* PAC *(Ottawa, 1926); cependant le* NUC *mentionne de nombreux autres catalogues de parties de la Harmsworth Library.* ¶ *Adresse bibliographique à la fin.* ¶ *L'article XVII accuse Oxford d'avoir escroqué la nation de 20 000 £ puisque l'expédition contre le Canada a échoué.* ¶ *Plusieurs autres éditions sont répertoriées dans le NUC(Pre–56)436:229 sous "Oxford, Robert Harley, 1st Earl of, 1661–1724, defendent," voir notice suivante.*

*Great Britain. Parliament, 1715. House of Commons. Articles of impeachment .... [London, 1715?] 6 p. fol.

NUC(Pre–56)436:229*

Caption title.

Titre de départ.

*Great Britain. Parliament, 1715. House of Commons. Articles of impeachment .... [Colophon: Printed and sold by J. Baker and the booksellers of London and Westminster. 1715.] 17, [1] p. fol.

NUC(Pre–56)436:229*

Caption title. ¶ Includes "Additional articles," with separate colophon.

Titre de départ. ¶ Comprend des « articles supplémentaires » portant un colophon distinct.

*Great Britain. Parliament, 1715. House of Commons. Articles of impeachment . . . against Robert Earl of Oxford and Mortimer. [Colophon: London and Westminster, J. Baker, 1715.] 12 p. fol.

NUC(Pre–56)436:229*

[Caption title?]

[Titre de départ?]

*Great Britain. Parliament, 1715. House of Commons. The articles of impeachment against Robert, Earl of Oxford, and Earl Mortimer: together with His Lordship's Answer; and the Commons replication. London, printed for John Morphew, near Stationers-hall. 1715. 28 p. [8°?]

NUC(Pre–56)436:229*

Harley's *Answer* was also published separately: *see* below, 1715.

L'ouvrage *Answer* de Harley fut également publié séparément, *voir* 1715, plus bas.

*Great Britain. Parliament, 1715. House of Commons. The articles of impeachment of high treason, and other crimes and misdemeanors, against Robert Earl of Oxford .... London, printed; reprinted [in Dublin] by E[dward]. Waters, 1715. 1 p.l., 41 p. [8°?]

NUC(Pre–56)436:229*

*Great Britain. Parliament, 1715. House of Commons. Articles of impeachment .... [Colophon: Dublin, re-printed by Edwin Sandys, for George Grierson, 1715.] 24 p. 16°

NUC(Pre–56)436:229*

Caption title. ¶ Format from Morgan, BBH:R275.

Titre de départ. ¶ Format tiré du Morgan, BBH:R275.

Instructions by the citizens of London, to their representatives for the ensuing Parliament .... London: printed for John Clark ... 1715. Price one penny or 9d. a dozen. Broadside. fol.

cf. NUC(Pre–56)268:393

"We desire that you enquire ... How the expedition on Canada came to miscarry, how the French were allowed to keep their interest in Canada and Newfoundland." ¶ *Concerns the Treaty of Utrecht (1713), under which France ceded Hudson Bay, Acadia, and Newfoundland, but kept present P.E.I., Cape Breton, and her Newfoundland fishing rights. ¶ Reprinted in Boston in the same year, and that is the edition listed in NUC.*

« Nous souhaitons que vous fassiez enquête ... sur l'échec de l'expédition au Canada, sur le fait que les Français ont pu conserver leurs intérêts au Canada et à Terre-Neuve. » ¶ *Porte sur le traité d'Utrecht (1713) par lequel la France dut céder la Baie d'Hudson, l'Acadie et Terre-Neuve, mais put conserver le territoire actuel de l'Île-du-Prince-Édouard, du Cap-Breton ainsi que ses droits de pêche à Terre-Neuve. ¶ Réimpression à Boston la même année, c'est d'ailleurs l'édition donnée dans le NUC.*

*Oxford, Robert Harley, *1st earl of/1ᵉʳ comte de*, 1661–1724, *defendent/défendeur*. The answer of Robert Earl of Oxford and Earl Mortimer, to the articles exhibited by the knights, citizens and burgesses in Parliament assembled in the name of themselves and of all the commons of Great Britain, in maintenance of their impeachment against him for high treason and other high crimes and misdemeanors, supposed to have been by him committed. [London, printed for J[ohn]. Morphew, 1715.] 12 p. fol.

NUC(Pre–56)436:229*

Caption title. ¶ A reply to: Great Britain. Parliament, 1715. House of Commons. *Articles of impeachment of high treason* . . . . London, 1715 [etc.]: *see* above. ¶ Harley defended his part in the expedition against Quebec and the negotiations as to Newfoundland (cf. Morgan, BBH:R274). ¶ Other editions: *see* following entries; also pub. with: Great Britain. Parliament, 1715. House of Commons. *Articles of impeachment*, 1727, *q.v.*

Titre de départ. ¶ Réplique au document issu de la Chambre des Communes de Grande-Bretagne. *Articles of impeachment of high treason* . . . . Londres, 1715 [etc.] : *voir plus haut*. ¶ Harley défend sa participation dans l'expédition contre Québec et les négociations à l'égard de Terre-Neuve (cf. Morgan, BBH:R274). ¶ Autres éditions : *voir* notices suivantes ; publié également avec *Articles of impeachment* rédigé par la Chambre des Communes britannique, 1727, *q.v.*

*Oxford, Robert Harley, *1st earl of/1ᵉʳ comte de*, 1661–1724, *defendent/défendeur*. The answer of Robert Earl of Oxford . . . . [Dublin, printed by A[aron]. Rhames, and sold by the booksellers, 1715.] 27 p. fol.

NUC(Pre–56)436:229*

Caption title.

Titre de départ.

*Oxford, Robert Harley, 1st earl of/1ᵉʳ comte de, 1661–1724, *defendent/défendeur*. The answer of Robert Earl of Oxford . . . . [Colophon: Dublin, reprinted, and are to be sold by Thomas Humes, 1715.] 52 p. [8°?]

NUC(Pre–56)436:229*

Caption title.   Titre de départ.

Withall, Benjamin, *fl.* 1697–1717. The case of Great-Britain, in relation to His Majᵞˢ Office of Ordnance, represented by Benjamin Withall, engineer. [London?] 1715. [Broadside?] fol.

"London. Br."

Waldon's source [Br: broadsides?] has not been further identified; it is not in the BM(to 1955), nor the London Library and Suppl. ¶ The imprint, or at least the place, should evidently be given in square brackets. Waldon does not indicate that this is a broadside, but Withall's earlier works were, and the endorsement further suggests this. ¶ Endorsed: The case of the nation, in his Majesty's Office of Ordnance. ¶ Similar works by Withall appear under 1714 and 1717, q.v. ¶ NFSM

La source de Waldon (Br. : broadsides [in-plᵒ] ?) n'a pu être retracée ; elle ne se trouve ni dans le BM(to 1955) ni dans la London Library et Suppl. ¶ L'adresse bibliographique ou, à tout le moins, le lieu de publication, devrait évidemment être placé entre crochets. Waldon ne précise pas s'il s'agit d'un in-plᵒ, mais c'était le cas des ouvrages précédents de Withall et c'est ce que suggère également l'inscription officielle. ¶ Inscription officielle : The case of the nation, in his Majesty's Office of Ordnance. ¶ D'autres ouvrages similaires de Withall font l'objet de notices sous 1714 et 1717, q.v. ¶ NFSM

THE

TRAVELS

Of several

Learned MISSIONERS

OF THE

Society of *JESUS,*

INTO

DIVERS PARTS

OF THE

ARCHIPELAGO,

India, China, and *America.*

Containing a general Defcription of the moft remarkable
Towns; with a particular Account of the Cuftoms,
Manners and Religion of thofe feveral Nations, the
whole interfpers'd with Philofophical Obfervations and
other curious Remarks.

Tranflated from the *French* Original publifh'd at *Paris*
in the Year 1713.

LONDON:

Printed for *R. Gofling,* at the *Mitre and Crown,* over aginft
St. *Dunftan's* Church, in *Fleet-ftreet,* M DCC XIV.

Jesuits. *The travels of several learned missioners of the Society of Jesus* . . . . London/Londres,

*The English pilot. The fourth book. Describing the West-India navigation, from Hudson's-Bay to the River Amazones . . . . The whole being very much enlarged and corrected . . . . London: printed for Rich. and Will. Mount, and Tho. Page, in Postern-Row on Tower-Hill, 1716. 1 p.l., 66 p. illus., 20 maps on 18 plates (part fold., part double). fol.

NUC(Pre–56)160:373*

Title vignette (British arms). ¶ First edition: 1689, *q.v.* for other editions; the 1698 edition has a similar title, and is transcribed more fully there.

Titre vignette (armoiries britanniques). ¶ Première édition : 1689, *q.v.* pour autres éditions ; l'édition de 1698 possède un titre très similaire, transcrit de façon plus complète dans la notice pour cette date.

Marsh, Henry, *fl.* 1716. A proposal for raising a stock not exceeding forty thousand pounds sterling; by subscription for forming a settlement, in a large and convenient river in Acadia. And to improve a great space of land on each side of the said river. London, printed for the Author, in the year 1716. (Price 1s.) 15 p. fol.

?Waldon

Waldon gives BM *and Sabin as her sources, but both list only the 1720 edition,* q.v. *for a variant (the stock proposed has been raised to two million pounds) and more detailed title; also the* BLC *entry has no pagination, while Sabin:66020 has 10 p., and neither gives the price. So, Waldon evidently saw (or read of) a different work or (as she says, next note) edition.* ¶ Another edition, 1720, signed: Henry Marsh, author.

Waldon cite le BM *et le Sabin comme sources, mais ces derniers ne citent que l'édition de 1720,* q.v. *pour une variante (le fonds proposé a été augmenté à 2 millions de livres) et un titre plus détaillé ; le* BLC *ne donne aucune pagination tandis que le Sabin:66020 donne 10 p. Cependant, ni l'un ni l'autre ne mentionnent de prix. Waldon a donc, de toute évidence, vu (ou lu sur) un ouvrage différent ou (comme elle le dit dans la notice suivante) une édition différente.* ¶ Autre édition de 1720 signée : Henry Marsh, auteur.

1717

Tipton, William, *fl.* 1716. The case of William Tipton. [London, 1717?] [2] p. Broadsheet.

NUC(Pre–56)595:42

Caption title. ¶ Endorsed: The case of Serjeant Tipton. ¶ "A serjeant to Captain John Williams, Independent Company at Annapolis-Royal in America" charges that Gen. Nicholson and other officers discharged 232 men, whose names were left on the muster-rolls. Also that powder was sold by the officers to French and Indians. ¶ Waldon notes within her title: [respecting false musters and other abuses in certain detachments of the Army in America].

Titre de départ. ¶ Inscription officielle : The case of Serjeant Tipton. ¶ « Un sergent du capitaine John Williams, compagnie indépendante à Annapolis-Royal en Amérique », accuse le général Nicholson et d'autres officiers d'avoir démis 232 hommes dont les noms étaient présents sur la liste des effectifs. Il soutient aussi que les officiers vendaient de la poudre aux Français et aux Indiens. ¶ Waldon note dans son titre : [respecting false musters and other abuses in certain detachments of the Army in America].

Withall, Benjamin, *fl.* 1697–1717. A detection of the exhorbitant oppressions, publick frauds, and mismanagements, that for a long time has been perpetrated, nay, and is now acting (order, frugality and justice being trampled underfoot) in His Majesty's Victualling and Ordnance Offices. These, and the like notorious abuses, unredressed, being the prime and multiply'd causes of the heavy public debts the nation now groans under; contrary to His Majesty's repeated declarations and royal example: all which is here faithfully represented, &c. By Benj. Withall, engineer, who now does, and for many years past has belong'd to one or both the abovesaid offices. London, printed: and sold by J[ames]. Roberts, at the Oxford Arms in VVarwick-Lane. 1717. (Price 18d.) [4], 96 p. 4°

BM(to 1955)259:783

This full title is from Waldon, who must have seen the work. Both BM and Morgan, BBH:T1258 give brief titles only. ¶ A complete review of Withall's experiences in Newfoundland and his subsequent dealings with the Victualling Office and the Commissioners of Public Accounts, over his accounts as storekeeper, with transcripts of the documents in the case. Withall applied to the Com. of P.A. in 1712 (p. 11). ¶ *Similar works by Withall appear under 1714 and 1715,* q.v.

1718

*Child,** Sir **Josiah,** 1630–1699. A new discourse of trade, wherein is recommended several weighty points relating to companies of merchants .... And our woollen manufactures. The ballance of trade .... And some proposals for erecting a court of merchants for determining controversies, relating to maritine [*sic*] affairs, and for a law for transferrance [*sic*] of bills of debts, are humbly offer'd. By Sir Josiah Child. 3d edition. London, printed and sold, by the assigns of J[ane]. Sowle, 1718. 24 p.l., 238 p. 8°[?]

NUC(Pre–56)106:637*

Otherwise, same title as 1692 edition. ¶ "A small treatise against usury," by Sir Thomas Culpeper, first pub. London, 1641: p. 217–38. ¶ Concerns Newfoundland fisheries, and is opposed to settlement. ¶ First pub. under this title: London, 1692, *q.v.* for other notes and editions.

Great Britain. Board of Trade. Copy of a representation of the Lords Commissioners for Trade and Plantations to his Majesty, relating to the Newfoundland trade and fishery. London. 1718. 23 p. 4°

Sabin:54981

This might well be the same as NUC(Pre–56)212:34, where the title continues after "fishery": dated 19th Dec. 1718. Ordered to be printed 11th March 1793. [London? 1793]. folio. pp. 22+. The date of the *Representation* would explain Dr. Waldon's date, but the NUC publication date should exclude it from this work, as would the "later" editions noted by Waldon: 1766, 1786, 1790.

Ceci pourrait très bien être un ouvrage identique à celui que donne le NUC(Pre–56)212:34, pour lequel le titre continue après « fishery »: dated 19 Dec. 1718. Commande d'impression : 11 mars 1793. [Londres ? 1793], fol., p. 22+. La date de la *Representation* explique la date donnée par Waldon, mais la date de publication du NUC devrait l'exclure du présent ouvrage, comme d'ailleurs les éditions « ultérieures » de 1766, 1786 et 1790 notées par Waldon.

*[Wood, William], 1679–1765. A survey of trade; in four parts . . . . Together with considerations on our money and bullion . . . . London, W. Hinchlieffe, 1718. xiv p., 1 l., 373 p. 8°

NUC(Pre–56)672:410*

The author obtained a patent for minting coins for circulation in the British colonies in America. Includes passages on the Newfoundland fishery, the Assiento contract for Negroes under the Treaty of Utrecht (1713), etc. Part three concerns the advantages the colonies and plantations have for Britain, and that country's interest in preserving and encouraging them. ¶ First edition; other editions: London, 1719, and London, 1722, *q.v.*

L'auteur obtint un brevet pour frapper la monnaie qui sera mise en circulation dans les colonies britanniques d'Amérique. Inclut certains passages sur les pêcheries de Terre-Neuve, le contrat Assiento concernant les Noirs conformément au traité d'Utrecht (1713), etc. La partie 3 traite des avantages qu'apportent les colonies et les établissements à la Grande-Bretagne et souligne qu'il est dans l'intérêt du pays de les préserver et de les encourager. ¶ Première édition ; autres éditions : Londres, 1719 et Londres, 1722, *q.v.*

1719

*Clarke, Samuel, 1599–1683. A new description of the world . . . . London, 1719.

NUC(Pre–56)111:361*

No further information in NUC. ¶ *See* 1689, *the first ed. under this title.*

Aucun autre renseignement dans le NUC. ¶ *Voir* 1689, *la première édition portant ce titre.*

Joutel, [Henri], 1640?–1735. Mr. Joutel's journal of his voyage to Mexico: his travels eight hundred leagues through forty nations of Indians in Louisiana to Canada: his account of the great river Missasipi. To which is added, a map of that country; with a description of the great water-falls in the river Misouris. Transl. from the French pub. at Paris. London, printed for B[ernard]. Lintot, 1719. 1 p.l., xxi, [9], 205, [5] p. fold. map. 8°

NUC(Pre–56)285:566*

This is identically the same as the 1714 edition with a new title-page and the list of Lintot books. Lintot was one of the publishers of the 1714 ed., and he probably took over the unsold copies and printed a new title-page. ¶ *First ed. in English: London,* 1714, q.v. *for other notes and later editions.*

Exemplaire en tout point identique à l'édition de 1714, sauf pour une nouvelle p. de t. et une liste des ouvrages imprimés chez Lintot. Ce dernier fut l'un des éditeurs de l'édition de 1714 et l'on suppose que cette version est en fait le stock non vendu du premier ouvrage, auquel il a ajouté une nouvelle p. de t. ¶ *Première édition en langue anglaise : Londres,* 1714, q.v. *pour d'autres notes et les éditions ultérieures.*

*[Wood, William], 1679–1765. A survey of trade. In four parts . . . . 2d ed. London, printed by W.W. and sold by W. Mears [etc.] 1719. xiv p., 1 l., 373 p. 8°

NUC(Pre–56)672:410*

Author's name signed to dedication. ¶ First edition: 1718, *q.v.* for other notes.

Dédicace signée par l'auteur. ¶ Première édition : 1718, *q.v.* pour d'autres notes.

1720

Burchett, Josiah, 1666?–1746. A complete history of the most remarkable transactions at sea from the earliest accounts of time to the conclusion of the last war with France . . . . London, printed by W.B. for J. Walthoe and J. Walthoe, junior, 1720. 28 p.l., 800, [33] p. front., 9 fold. maps. fol.

NUC(Pre–56)84:487*

Map of world showing America: between p. 182 and 183. Bk. IV, Chap. XXII, An account of Monsieur Ponty's coming with a French squadron to Newfoundland while Sir John Norris was with a squadron of English ships there: p. 559–62. Bk. V, Chap. XI, Captain John Leake's proceedings with a squadron of ships at Newfoundland: p. 631–34. Bk. V, Chap. XXXII, The unsuccessful expedition against Quebec, with a squadron under the command of Sir Hovenden Walker, and a body of troops commanded by General Hill: p. 775–81. ¶ *Parts four and five rewritten from the author's* Memoirs of transactions at sea . . . . *London, 1703,* q.v.

Mappemonde représentant l'Amérique : entre les pages 182 et 183. Livre IV, Chap. XXII, Récit de l'arrivée de M. Ponty avec une escadrille française à Terre-Neuve où sir John Norris se trouvait déjà avec sa flotte anglaise : p. 559–62. Livre V, Chap. XI, L'avance du capitaine John Leake et de son escadrille vers Terre-Neuve : p. 631–34. Livre V, Chap. XXXII, L'échec de l'expédition contre Québec entreprise par sir Hovenden Walker et le général Hill commandant respectivement une escadrille et un corps de troupes : p. 775–81. ¶ *Parties 4 et 5 réécrites à partir de* Memoirs of transactions at sea . . . . *du même auteur. Londres, 1703,* q.v.

[Hennepin, Louis], *1626–ca./vers 1705*. A discovery of a large, rich, and plentiful country, in the North America; extending above 4000 leagues.Wherein, by a very short passage, lately found out, thro' the Mer-Barmejo into the South-Sea; by which a considerable trade might be carry'd on, as well in the northern as the southern parts of America. London, printed for W. Boreham . . . 1720. (Price six-pence.) 2 p.l., 22 (*i.e.* 30), 2 p. 8°(in 4s).

NUC(Pre–56)240:546*

An abridgement of Hennepin's A new discovery of a vast country in America. *London, 1698 (first English edition)*, q.v., *and transl. from his* Nouvelle découverte d'un trés grand pay situé dans l'Amerique. *Utrecht, 1697. This was an enlargement of his* Description de la Louisiane. *Paris, 1683.* ¶ Pages 25–30 wrongly numbered 17–22. ¶ *List of books available: last 2 p.* ¶ *NUC has imprint: London, printed for W. Boreham [1720].* ¶ Begins with his arrival at Quebec and voyage to Fort Frontenac (p. 1–7), followed by the journey to the Mississippi and back, and his return to Montreal by way of Michilimackinac (p. 21–22). ¶ *BVIPA*

Version abrégée de A new discovery of a vast country in America *de Hennepin, Londres, 1698 (première éd. angl.)*, q.v., *et traduction de son ouvrage* Nouvelle découverte d'un trés grand pay situé dans l'Amerique. *Utrecht, 1697. Ce dernier ouvrage est une version augmentée de* Description de la Louisiane *du même auteur, Paris, 1683.* ¶ Erreur de pagination : pages 25–30 numérotées 17–22. ¶ *Liste des livres disponibles : 2 dernières pages.* ¶ *Adresse bibliographique du NUC : London, printed for W. Boreham [1720].* ¶ Commence avec son arrivée à Québec et son voyage vers Fort Frontenac (p. 1–7), suivi de son expédition sur le Mississippi et de son retour à Montréal en passant par Michilimackinac (p. 21–22). ¶ *BVIPA*

Marsh, Henry, *fl. 1716*. A proposal for raising a stock of two millions of pounds sterling; by subscriptions for forming a settlement . . . [on each side of a: BLC; in a: Sabin] large and convenient river in Acadia on the continent of North-America. And to improve a great space of land on each side of said river for growth of hemp and flax, and for importing mastyards, deals, staves and other timber, with pitch and tar, &c. in greater quantities. Likewise for carrying on the Acadia fishery in those parts. London, printed for the Author in the year 1720. 10 p. fol.

Sabin:66020 and BLC(to 1975)212:228

Signed at end: Henry Marsh, author. ¶ *BLC title ends with "North America," lacks pagination, and has "on each side of a," as above, while Sabin has "in a."* ¶ *"He first laid his scheme before the public in 1716, after having spent some time in the country [i.e., Acadia, or Nova Scotia]": Sabin:66020.* ¶ *An earlier edition, or possibly only a similar work, appeared in London, 1716, q.v.*

Signature en fin de livre : Henry Marsh, auteur. ¶ *Le titre de ce même ouvrage dans le BLC se termine par « North America » ; pas de pagination ; le BLC donne « on each side of a », comme ci-dessus, et le Sabin, « in a ».* ¶ *« Il dévoila son plan en 1716 après avoir passé quelque temps dans le pays [c.-à-d. l'Acadie ou la Nouvelle-Écosse] » : Sabin:66020.* ¶ *Une édition plus ancienne, ou encore un ouvrage similaire, parut à Londres en 1716, q.v.*

[Smith, James], *judge advocate/avocat de juge*. Some considerations on the consequences of the French settling colonies on the Mississippi, with respect to the trade and safety of the English plantations in America and the West-Indies. From a gentleman of America, to his friend in London .... London: printed for J[ames]. Roberts near the Oxford-Arms in Warwick-Lane. 1720. 1 p.l., 60 p. fold. map. 8°

NUC(Pre–56)551:348*

Also attributed to Richard Berresford (cf. Justin Winsor, Narrative and critical history of America. *vol. 5, Boston, 1887, p. 76, 80).* ¶ *Waldon has 2 p.l. in the collation, in place of 1 p.l. in NUC.* ¶ *The author warns that John Law's scheme is furthering French expansion.* ¶ The writer fears a union of the French forces on the St. Lawrence and on the Mississippi to drive the English into the sea. French encroachments on Nova Scotia are also discussed. ¶ Reprinted by the Historical and Philosophical Society of Ohio, with preface by Beverly W. Bond, Cincinnati, 1928. front. (fold. map).

Aussi attribué à Richard Berresford (cf. Justin Winsor, Narrative and critical history of America. *vol. 5, Boston, 1887, p. 76 et 80).* ¶ *Contrairement au NUC, Waldon donne 2 f. l. au lieu d'un.* ¶ *L'auteur dénonce le plan de John Law comme étant un encouragement à la croissance des colonies françaises.* ¶ Il craint une union des forces françaises sur le Saint-Laurent et le Mississippi qui ferait reculer les Anglais jusqu'à la mer. On y parle aussi des déprédations des Français en Nouvelle-Écosse. ¶ Réimpression par la Historical and Philosophical Society of Ohio, avec une préface de Beverly W. Bond à Cincinnati en 1928. Front. (carte pl.).

Walker, Sir **Hovenden**, 1656?–1728. A journal: or full account of the late expedition to Canada. With an appendix containing commissions, orders, instructions, letters, memorials, courts-martial, councils of war, &c. relating thereto. By Sir Hovenden Walker, kt. . . . London: printed for D[aniel]. Browne at the Black-Swan, W. Mears at the Lamb, without Temple Bar, and G[eorge]. Strahan at the Golden Ball against the Exchange in Cornhil, 1720. 2 p.l., 304 p. 8°

NUC(Pre–56)645:675*

The author was in charge of the naval forces in the disastrous [Quebec] expedition of 1711. He was arraigned for his conduct, and his name was struck from the list of admirals. This volume was published in self-justification. ¶ *Reprinted in Gerald Graham, The Walker expedition to Quebec, 1711. Toronto, Champlain Soc., 1953, and in MFiche (negative) of typescript, in the Canadiana in the Toronto Public Library series, Toronto, ca. 1960; another ed., 1720: next entry. Faribault:665 suggests a 1712 edition, but this has not been confirmed.* ¶ NSHPL · OONL · AEU · BVA

L'auteur commandait les forces navales lors de la désastreuse expédition de 1711 [Québec]. Il fut poursuivi en justice en raison de sa conduite et son nom fut rayé de la liste des amiraux. Walker publia ce livre pour justifier ses actes. ¶ *Réimpression dans l'ouvrage de Gerald Graham The Walker expedition to Quebec, 1711. Toronto, Champlain Society, 1953, et reproduction sur mic. (négatifs) à partir de tapuscrits, dans Canadiana de la collection de la Toronto Public Library, vers 1960 ; autre éd. : 1720, notice suivante. Faribault:665 suppose l'existence d'une autre édition de 1712, qui, toutefois, n'a pas été confirmée.* ¶ NSHPL · OONL · AEU · BVA

Walker, Sir **Hovenden**, 1656?–1728. A full account of the late expedition to Canada. With an appendix . . . . By Sir Hovenden Walker, kt. London: printed for G[eorge]. Strahan, at the Golden Ball, over against the Royal Exchange in Cornhill [1720?] [4], 304 p. 8°

Sabin:101051

Sabin has "[n.d.]" in the imprint, while for collation Waldon has "t.-p., 304 p.," and the Canadian Union Catalogue has 309 p. ¶ Running title: A journal of the Canada expedition. ¶ NSWA · QMBN · OTY · MWP · BVA

Le Sabin donne « [s.d.] » dans l'adresse bibliographique, alors que la collation de Waldon est « p. de t., 304 p. ». Le Catalogue collectif canadien donne 309 p. ¶ Titre courant : A journal of the Canada expedition. ¶ NSWA · QMBN · OTY · MWP · BVA

A
JOURNAL:
Or FULL
ACCOUNT
Of the late
EXPEDITION
TO
C A N A D A.

WITH AN
A P P E N D I X
Containing

Commiffions, Orders, Inftructions, Letters, Memorials, Courts-Martial, Councils of War, &c. relating thereto.

By Sir *HOVENDEN WALKER*, K.

Rebus anguftis animofus atque
Fortis appare! Sapienter idem
Contrahes vento nimium fecundo
Turgida Vela.

Hor. Lib. 1. Ode 10.

LONDON:
Printed for D. Browne at the *Black-Swan*, W. Mears at the *Lamb;* without *Temple Bar*, and G. Strahan at the *Golden Ball* againft the *Exchange* in *Cornhil*, 1720.

Sir Hovenden Walker. *A journal: or full account of the late expedition to Canada.* London/Londres,

1721

*Abstract of the scheme of government** so far as it relates to the grantees in trust, for settling the land lying between Nova-Scotia and the province of Maine in New-England, in America. [London? 1721.] [4] p. fol.

NUC(Pre–56)2:221

Caption title; endorsed title (p. [1]) repeats caption title. ¶ The words "in trust" have been deleted in ms. in both title and text — perhaps the reason for their omission in Sabin:56101. ¶ Reprinted in the Photostat Americana, second series, no. 130, Boston, Mass. Hist. Soc., 1941.

Titre de départ ; le titre tiré de l'inscription officielle (p. 1) est une reprise du titre de départ. ¶ Les mots « in trust » ont été supprimés du manuscrit aussi bien dans le titre que dans le texte – la raison de cette omission se trouve peut-être dans le Sabin:56101. ¶ Réimpression dans Photostat Americana, deuxième collection, n° 130, Boston, Mass. Hist. Soc., 1941.

The British merchant; or, Commerce preserv'd. In three volumes. By Mr. Charles King, Chamber-Keeper to the Treasury, and late of London, merchant. London: printed by John Darby in Bartholomew-Close, 1721. 3 v. fold. tables. 8°

NUC(Pre–56)76:436*

Consists of the most important numbers of this periodical, collected and edited by Charles King (fl. 1721), originally pub. semi-weekly in London, as no. 1–103, 7 Aug. 1713–30 July 1714. ¶ First edition in book form of weekly papers which appeared 1713–14 [NUC has "twice a week during the summer of 1713"], in opposition to the [proposed treaty of commerce with

Composé des numéros les plus importants de ce périodique ; recueillis et édités par Charles King (fl. 1721) ; à l'origine, publiés séparément deux fois par semaine, n°ˢ 1–103, du 7 août 1713 au 30 juillet 1714. ¶ Première édition sous forme de livre réunissant les journaux hebdomadaires parus en 1713–1714 [le NUC donne deux fois par semaine pendant l'été de 1713] en signe de protestation contre [le traité de commerce avec la France, soutenu

France, supported by Defoe's] *Mercator; or, Commerce retrieved* (incomplete file in BM: no. 38–92, 11 Dec. 1713–22 June 1714). ¶ Contains account of the Newfoundland fishery. *See* long note relative to this work in [John R.] McCulloch, *The literature of political economy*, [London, 1845], p. 142–44. ¶ *Second edition: 1743, third, 1748, q.v.; another ed., 1787; French transl.: Le négotiant anglois (Paris, 1753). NUC also has: "Ed 2. Lond., 1744," which is suspect.*

par l'ouvrage de Defoe] *Mercator; or, Commerce retrieved* (fichier incomplet dans le BM : n°s 38–92, du 11 déc. 1713 au 22 juin 1714). ¶ Présente un bilan des pêcheries de Terre-Neuve. Consulter la longue note relative à cet ouvrage dans *The literature of political economy* de [John R.] McCulloch, [Londres, 1845], p. 142–44. ¶ *Deuxième édition : 1743, troisième : 1748, q.v. ; autre édition : 1787 ; traduction française : Le négotiant anglois (Paris, 1753). Le NUC donne également : « deuxième éd. Londres, 1744 », ce qui paraît douteux.*

---

*The English pilot. The fourth book. Describing the West-India navigation, from Hudson's-Bay . . . . London, R[ichard]. and W[illiam]. Mount, and T[homas]. Page, 1721. 66 p. illus., charts (part fold.). fol.

NUC(Pre–56)160:373*

"From the east-part of the Grand Bank of Newfoundland . . . to the east-part of bank Queco . . . [by] Peter Kenwood of Topham": leaf (14 x 17 cm) mounted on back of fold. chart entitled "A large draught of New England, New York and Long Island." Perhaps in NUC copy only? ¶ First edition: 1689, *q.v.* for other editions; the 1706 edition has a similar title, and is there transcribed more fully.

« From the east-part of the Grand Bank of Newfoundland . . . to the east-part of bank Queco . . . [by] Peter Kenwood of Topham » : feuillet (14 cm sur 17 cm) monté au dos d'un plan pl. intitulé « A large draught of New England, New York and Long Island ». Peut-être uniquement dans l'exemplaire du NUC. ¶ Première édition : 1689, *q.v.* pour d'autres éditions ; l'édition de 1706 possède un titre similaire, transcrit toutefois de façon un peu plus complète.

1722

*Wood, William, 1679–1765. A survey of trade. In four parts . . . . 2d ed. By William Wood, esq. London, J[ohn]. Walthoe, 1722. xiv, 373 p. 8°(?)

NUC(Pre–56)672:410*

First edition: 1718, and another so-called second ed.: 1719, *q.v.* ¶ For other notes, *see* first edition.

Première édition : 1718, et une prétendue deuxième édition : 1719, *q.v.* ¶ Pour d'autres notes, *voir* la première édition.

1722–23

*The compleat geographer: . . . To which is premis'd an introduction to geography, and a natural history of the earth and the elements. Containing a true and perfect account of I. the situation, bounds and extent . . . of all the countries on the earth. II. the several provinces that every kingdom or state is divided into. III. the principal cities . . . . The whole containing . . . maps of every country, fairly engraven on copper . . . most engrav'd by Herman Moll. The fourth edition. Wherein the descriptions of Asia, Africa and America are compos'd a-new from the relations of travellers of the best repute. . . . London, printed for J[ames]. Knapton, R[obert]. Knaplock [and twenty-one others]. 1723. Pt. I. 402 p. fol.; 1722. Pt. II. 288, xx [index] p. fol. (collation from Sabin:49905).

NUC(Pre–56)118:223*

Part two has separate t.-p.: Thesaurus geographicus: or, The compleat geographer. Part the second . . . . The fourth edition, much amended. London: printed in the year 1722. "A general and particular description of America": pt. two, p. 189–280. ¶ The text of pt. one largely follows that of H. Moll's *A system of geography.*

La partie 2 a sa propre p. de t. : « Thesaurus geographicus : or, The compleat geographer. Part the second . . . . The fourth edition, much amended. London: printed in the year 1722 ». « A general and particular description of America » : partie 2, p. 189–280. ¶ Le texte de la partie 1 suit en général celui de H. Moll dans son ouvrage *A system of geography.* Londres, 1701. Dans

London, 1701. Sabin enters under: Moll. ¶ Fourth ed.; third ed. pub. 1709, *q.v.* Sabin has third ed., 1719, and another ed. 1709.

le Sabin, cette notice est placée sous Moll. ¶ Quatrième éd. ; troisième éd. publiée en 1709, *q.v.* Le Sabin donne 1719 pour la troisième éd. et signale une autre édition de 1709.

1724

Philips, Miles, *fl.* 1568–1582. The voyages and adventures of Miles Philips, a West-country sailor. Containing a relation of his various fortune both by sea and land; the inhuman usage he met with from the Spaniards at Mexico, and the salvage Indians of Canada and other barbarous nations; and the sufferings he and his companions underwent by their confinement and sentence in the Spanish inquisition. Together with a natural description of the countries he visited, and particular observations on the religion, customs and manners of their respective inhabitants. Written by himself in the plain stile of an English sailor. London, printed for T. Payne and T. Butler, 1724. 6 p.l., 216 p. 12°

NUC(Pre–56)455:669

"The second voyage of Miles Philips" (Adventures in Canada): p. [102]–216.

« The second voyage of Miles Philips » (Aventures au Canada) : p. [102]–216.

1725

*The English pilot. The fourth book. Describing the West-India navigation, from Hudson's-Bay .... London, R[ichard]. and W[illiam]. Mount, and T[homas]. Page, 1725. 66 p. illus., charts (part fold.). fol.

NUC(Pre–56)160:373*

First edition: 1689, *q.v.* for other editions; the 1706 and 1721 editions have similar titles, and the 1706 is there transcribed more fully.

1726

Ker, John, 1673–1726. The memoirs of John Ker, of Kersland in North Britain, esq; containing his secret transactions and negotiations in Scotland, England, the courts of Vienna, Hanover and other foreign parts. With an account of the rise and progress of the Ostend company in the Austrian Netherlands. Published by himself. . . . London, printed in the year 1726. 3 v. in 2. front. (port.), fold. map. 8°

NUC(Pre–56)90:91*

Printed by Edmund Curll. ¶ Title-pages vary slightly. ¶ Transl. into French as: Memoires de Mr. Jean Ker de Kersland. *Rotterdam, 1726–28, 3 v.; and into Dutch as:* Memorien van Johan Ker van Kersland, in Noord-Brittanien. *Rotterdam, 1727, 3 v. (cf. NUC). ¶ Pt. 2 has title:* The memoirs and secret negotiations of John Ker, of Kersland Esq; Part II. *¶ Pt. 2 relates to the French possessions in America. The map of Louisiana and the River Mississippi shows the Great Lakes and part of Ontario. ¶ First edition; Waldon notes that a second ed. was pub. in the same year, 1726; third ed.: London, 1727, q.v. ¶ BVAU*

1727

Colliber, Samuel, *fl.* 1718–1737. Columna Rostrata: or, A critical history of the English sea-affairs: wherein all the remarkable actions of the English nation at sea are described, and the most considerable events (especially in the account of the three Dutch wars) are proved, either from original pieces, or from the testimonies of the best foreign historians. By Samuel Colliber. London, printed for R[anew]. Robinson, 1727. 312, [8] p. 8°

NUC(Pre–56)115:468*

Waldon notes that the work is replete with index. ¶ Contains references to Cabot, Frobisher, Davis, actions against the French in Newfoundland, the capture of Quebec, the Treaty of Ryswick, the capture of Port Royal, 1709, the attack on Quebec, 1711, the Treaty of Utrecht [1713], etc. ¶ *First edition; second ed., 1739, second ed., improved, 1742* (q.v.).

Waldon note que l'ouvrage contient un index. ¶ Contient des mentions sur Cabot, Frobisher et Davis, sur les attaques contre les Français de Terre-Neuve, la prise de Québec, le traité de Ryswick, la prise de Port-Royal en 1709, l'attaque de Québec en 1711, le traité d'Utrecht [1713], etc. ¶ *Première édition ; deuxième éd. : 1739 ; deuxième éd. améliorée : 1742* (q.v.).

*Great Britain. Parliament, 1715. House of Commons. Articles of impeachment . . . against Robert Earl of Oxford and Earl Mortimer. July 9. 1715. With His Lordship's answer, paragraph by paragraph. To which is added, A short state of the war and the peace. London, printed for J. Roberts [etc.] 1727. 2 p.l., 165 p. 8°

NUC(Pre–56)436:229*

Format from Morgan, BBH:R275. ¶ The *Answer* was also pub. separately, under: Oxford, Robert H., *The answer of Robert Earl of Oxford*, 1715. ¶ First edition of the *Articles*, 1715, *q.v.* for other notes and editions, under: Great Britain. Parliament, 1715. House of Commons.

Format tiré du Morgan, BBH:R275. ¶ L'ouvrage *Answer* fut également publié séparément sous : Oxford, Robert H., *The answer of Robert Earl of Oxford*, 1715. ¶ Édition originale des *Articles* : 1715, *q.v.* pour d'autres notes et éditions sous : Great Britain. Parliament, 1715. House of Commons.

Ker, John, 1673–1726. The memoirs of John Ker, of Kersland . . . relating to politicks, trade, and history . . . . Containing his secret transactions . . . . Published by himself . . . . The third edition. London: printed in the year 1727. Price 3s. 6d. 3 v. in 2. front. (port.), fold. map. 8°

NUC(Pre–56)90:91*

The first part of the title is abridged as in NUC; from "Containing" on is as in first ed., 1726 (q.v. for other notes), excepting as indicated.

Comme dans le NUC, la première partie du titre est abrégée ; à partir de « Containing » , le titre est le même que dans l'édition originale de 1726 (q.v. pour d'autres notes) sauf indication contraire.

1728

Crouch, Nathaniel, 1632?–1725? The English empire in America; or, A view of the dominions of the Crown of England in the West-Indies . . . . by Robert Burton [*pseud.*]. The sixth edition. London: printed for A[rthur]. Bettesworth . . . and J. Batley, 1728. 192 p. incl. front. (map). 5 illus. 12°

NUC(Pre–56)128:174*

Illus. are from plates of the first ed., 1685, *q.v.* for other information.

Illustrations tirées des planches de la première éd. de 1685, *q.v.* pour d'autres renseignements.

1729

[Crouch, Nathaniel], 1632?–1725? The English empire in America. Or, A view of the dominions of the Crown of England in the West-Indies. . . . By Robert Burton [*pseud.*]. The seventh edition. London: printed and Dublin: reprinted by S[amuel]. Fuller, 1729. 180 p. illus. (incl. front., map). 12°

NUC(Pre–56)128:174*

Dublin, 1735, and London, 1739, are also called the seventh eds. ¶ First edition: 1685, q.v. *for other information.*

Les éditions de Dublin 1735 et de Londres 1739 sont également appelées septième éd. ¶ Première édition : 1685, q.v. *pour d'autres renseignements.*

*The English pilot. The fourth book, describing the West-India navigation, from Hudson's Bay . . . . Enlarged and corrected, with the additions of several new charts . . . not published before this edition . . . . London, printed for Thomas Page and William Mount, 1729. [2], 66 p. illus., 23 maps (part. fold.). fol.

NUC(Pre–56)160:373*

Possibly lacking one or two maps (NUC). ¶ First edition: 1689, *q.v.* for other editions; the 1706 edition is there transcribed more fully.

Il manque probablement 1 ou 2 cartes (NUC). ¶ Première édition : 1689, *q.v.* pour d'autres éditions ; l'édition de 1706 est transcrite de façon beaucoup plus détaillée.

Great Britain. Treaties, etc., 1727–1760 **(George II).** The treaty of peace, union, friendship, and mutual defence, between the crowns of Great-Britain, France, and Spain, concluded at Seville on the 9th of November N.S. 1729. London, printed by S[amuel]. Buckley, 1729. 16 p. 4°

NUC(Pre–56)215:512*

French and English in parallel columns.
¶ *Refers to the Treaty of Seville, 1729.*
¶ Spain was forced by Great Britain
and France to grant full recognition
of the consequences of the Treaty of
Utrecht, 1713. ¶ *Other editions of the
same year: see next entries; also reprinted
Dublin, 1730 (q.v.).*

*Textes en français et en anglais disposés en
colonnes parallèles.* ¶ *Renvoie au traité de Séville
de 1729.* ¶ La Grande-Bretagne et la France
forcèrent l'Espagne à reconnaître entièrement les conséquences du traité d'Utrecht,
1713. ¶ *Autres éditions de la même année :* voir
*les notices suivantes ; également réimprimé à
Dublin en 1730 (q.v.).*

*Great Britain. Treaties, etc., 1727–1760 (George II). A treaty of peace, union,
friendship, and mutual defence . . . . London, A. Moore, 1729. 12 p.

NUC(Pre–56)215:512*

See preceding entry for notes.

Voir notes plus haut.

*Great Britain. Treaties, etc., 1727–1760 (George II). A treaty of peace . . . N.S.
1729. Taken from the Daily Post-Boy of January 8, 1729. To which are added, the two
separate articles. (In: Robert Walpole, *Observations upon the treaty between the crowns of
Great-Britain, France and Spain.* London, 1729. 8° Occupies the last 23 p.)

NUC(Pre–56)215:512*

See preceding entry but one for notes.

Voir notes deux notices plus haut.

1730

Dobbs, Arthur, 1689–1765. Table of meteorological observations from 1721 to 1729 in nine voyages to Hudson's Bay. London, 1730. 8 p. 4°

Sabin:48858n.

Not found in NUC or BLC. From the biography of Dobbs in DNB, the observations do not appear to have been made by Dobbs; his voyages occurred later.

Introuvable dans le NUC ou le BLC. D'après la biographie de M. Dobbs tirée du DNB, les observations ne semblent pas avoir été faites par Dobbs, ses voyages s'étant déroulés plus tard.

*Great Britain. Treaties, etc., 1727–1760 **(George II).** The treaty of peace, union, friendship, and mutual defence, between . . . Great-Britain, France, and Spain . . . 9th November, N.S. 1729. Dublin: printed by S[amuel]. Powell, for George Risk, at the Shakespear's Head, George Ewing, at the Angel and Bible, And, William Smith, at the Hercules, booksellers in Dame's-street, 1730. [2], 23, [1] p. 8°

NUC(Pre–56)215:512*

Refers to the Treaty of Seville, 1729, and further to the Treaty of Utrecht, 1713. ¶ First pub. London, 1729, *q.v.* under same entry and title, for other notes and editions. ¶ (Information supplied by RPJCB, from its copy, gratefully acknowledged.)

Renvoie au traité de Séville de 1729 et au traité d'Utrecht de 1713. ¶ Publié pour la première fois à Londres en 1729, *q.v.* le même auteur et le même titre pour d'autres notes et éditions. ¶ (Renseignements fournis par RPJCB à partir de son exemplaire gracieusement prêté.)

1731

[**Hall, Fayrer**], *fl.* 1731–1735.   The importance of the British plantations in America to this kingdom; with the state of their trade, and methods for improving it; as also a description of the several colonies there. London, printed for J[ohn]. Peele. 1731. (Price one shilling and six pence.) 3 p.l., 114 p. 8° (in 4s).

NUC(Pre–56)227:235*

Dedication unsigned. ¶ New England (including Canso, or Nova Scotia): p. 101–11; Cape Breton, Newfoundland, Hudson's Bay: p. 111–12. ¶ *Another issue, 1731:* see *next entry. Reprinted on microcards, [Louisville, Ky., Lost Cause Press, 1959 (Travels in the Old South, vol. 1, no. 92), 2 cards].*

Dédicace non signée. ¶ Nouvelle Angleterre (y compris Canso ou Nouvelle-Écosse) : p. 101–11. Cap-Breton, Terre-Neuve et Baie d'Hudson : p. 111–12. ¶ *Autre tirage : 1731,* voir *notice suivante. Réimprimé sur microcartes, [Louisville (Kentucky), Lost Cause Press, 1959 (Travels in the Old South, vol. 1, n° 92), 2 cartes].*

[**Hall, Fayrer**], *fl.* 1731–1735.   The importance of the British plantations in America . . . . London, printed for J[ohn]. Peele. 1731. (Price 1s and 6s [*sic*].) 8°

Another issue, with new title-page. Dedication signed: F. Hall. ¶ *For other notes* see *preceding entry.*

Autre tirage avec page de titre différente. Dédicace signée : F. Hall. ¶ Voir *autres notes à la notice précédente.*

1732

Britannia major: the new scheme, or essay, for discharging the debts, improving the lands, and enlarging the trade, of the British dominions in Europe and America .... London: printed for J. Noon ... 1732. viii, 70 p. 8°(in 4s).

NUC(Pre–56)76:195

Books for sale: [2] p. at end. ¶ New-foundland, Nova Scotia: p. 16–17, 26, 35–38, 47–51.

Livres en vente : [2] p. à la fin. ¶ Terre-Neuve et Nouvelle-Écosse : p. 16–17, p. 26, p. 35–38, p. 47–51.

The case of the merchants of London, and manufacturers of wheat and biscuit. [London? 1732.] fol.

Petitions for a bounty on biscuit made of wheat exported, particularly to Newfoundland "to which last Place we have formerly sent all the Biscuit, &c. that the Planters and others concerned in the Fishery used to consume." Complains that the ships going from France to Newfoundland ballast with salt "and fill up with Biscuit &c. which they are frequently capable of supplying on lower Terms than we." ¶ [Endorsed as above.] ¶ *No other information discovered.*

Pétitions pour obtenir des compensations sur la vente des biscuits faits de blé d'exportation, particulièrement à Terre-Neuve « dernier endroit où nous avons envoyé tous les biscuits et autres aliments que les colons et les pêcheurs avaient l'habitude de consommer ». Les marchands anglais se plaignent que les bateaux français en route vers Terre-Neuve se lestent de sel « et chargent leurs cales de biscuits et d'autres choses qu'ils sont habituellement capables de fournir à des prix plus bas ». ¶ [Inscription officielle comme ci-dessus.] ¶ *Aucun autre renseignement.*

[Churchill, Awnsham], *d./déc.* 1728, *comp.* A collection of voyages and travels . . . . London, J[ohn]. Walthoe [etc.], 1732. 6 v. front. (v. 2) illus., plates (part fold.), maps (part fold.). Indexes. fol.

NUC(Pre–56)109:264*

Compiled by Awnsham and John Churchill. ¶ *Vol. 2 and 3 have added t.-p. engraved.* ¶ Contents relating to Canada: "An account of a most dangerous voyage performed by a famous Captain John Monck": v. 1, p. 487–514, plates, map; "Captain Thomas James's strange and dangerous voyage": v. 2, p. 429–88; "A voyage into the North-West Passage, undertaken in the year 1612. By the merchants adventurers of London, Sir George Lancaster, Sir Thomas Smith, Mr. Ball, Mr. Cocken, and Mr. James Hall, being venturer with them, and General of both ships. Written by John Gatonbe": v. 6, p. 241–56, illus., map. Gatonbe's narrative was reprinted as follows: *The voyages of W. Baffin, 1612–1622. Journals and letters of Baffin, with the narratives of J. Gatonbe and R. Fotherbye.* London, Hakluyt Soc., 1881 (cf. BM). ¶ *Vol. 1–4 first pub.: London, 1704 (q.v. for notes and other editions); they are here reissued, with the first publication of vols. 5–6 added.* ¶ OTP

Documents compilés par Awnsham et John Churchill. ¶ *Les vol. 2 et 3 ont chacun une p. de t. gravée qui a été ajoutée.* ¶ Qui portent sur le Canada : « An account of a most dangerous voyage performed by a famous Captain John Monck » : vol. 1, p. 487–514 (planches, carte) ; « Captain Thomas James's strange and dangerous voyage » : vol. 2, p. 429–88 ; « A voyage into the North-West Passage, undertaken in the year 1612. By the merchants adventurers of London, Sir George Lancaster, Sir Thomas Smith, Mr. Ball, Mr. Cocken, and Mr. James Hall, being venturer with them, and General of both ships. Written by John Gatonbe » : vol. 6, p. 241–56 (illus., carte). Le récit de Gatonbe fut réimprimé de différentes façons : *The voyages of W. Baffin, 1612–1622. Journals and letters of Baffin, with the narratives of J. Gatonbe and R. Fotherbye.* Londres : Hakluyt Soc., 1881 (cf. BM). ¶ *Les vol. 1 à 4 furent d'abord publiés à Londres en 1704 (q.v. pour d'autres notes et éditions) ; il s'agit ici de réimpressions avec l'ajout de la première édition des vol. 5 et 6.* ¶ OTP

*The English pilot. The fourth book describing the West-Indian navigation from Hudson-Bay [*sic* in NUC] . . . . London, 1732. 66 p. fol.(?)

NUC(Pre–56)160:373*

First edition: 1689, *q.v.* for other editions; NUC has a brief entry only, but the 1706 edition appears to have a similar title, and is more fully transcribed.

Première édition : 1689, *q.v.* pour d'autres éditions ; le NUC ne donne qu'une notice très courte, mais il semble que l'édition de 1706 possède un titre similaire, dont la transcription est plus complète.

A general collection of treatys, declarations of war, manifestos, and other public papers, relating to peace and war. In four volumes . . . . The second edition. London: printed for J[ames]. J[ohn]. and P[aul]. Knapton [and others] 1732. 4 v. 8°

NUC(Pre–56)194:275*

Dedication, vol. 3, signed: S.W. ¶ The preliminary matter has been reset, but the main text of vol. 1 is the same as the first ed., 1710. ¶ *"Catalogue of the several treatys and other publick papers contain'd in the four volumes of this collection, in a chronological order": vol. 4, at end.* ¶ Partial contents: "A Treaty between Lewis XIII. King of France, and Charles I. King of Great Britain, for the Restitution of New France, Acadia and Canada, and the Ships and Merchandizes taken on both sides. March 29. 1632": v. 2, p. 305–09; "The Treaty of Peace between the Kingdom of France, and the Republick of England, Scotland and Ireland. Done at Westminster the 3d of November 1655": v. 3, p. 149–61 (The question of "Pentacoet, St. Jan, and Port Royal" was referred to commissioners); "Treaty of Peace . . . between . . . Anne . . . and . . . Lewis XIV . . . at Utrecht, the 31/11 Day of March/April, 1713": v. 3, p. 398–440

Dans le vol. 3, dédicace signée : S.W. ¶ Les pages liminaires ont été recomposées, mais le texte principal du vol. 1 est le même que dans l'édition originale de 1710. ¶ *« Catalogue of the several treatys and other publick papers contain'd in the four volumes of this collection, in a chronological order » : vol. 4 à la fin.* ¶ Qui portent sur le Canada : « A Treaty between Lewis XIII. King of France, and Charles I. King of Great Britain, for the Restitution of New France, Acadia and Canada, and the Ships and Merchandizes taken on both sides. March 29. 1632 » : vol. 2, p. 305–09 ; « The Treaty of Peace between the Kingdom of France, and the Republic of England, Scotland and Ireland. Done at Westminster the 3d of November 1655 » : vol. 3, p. 149–61 (On adresse la question des forts de « Pentacoet, St. Jan, and Port Royal » aux commissaires) ; « Treaty of Peace . . . between . . . Anne . . . and . . . Lewis XIV . . . at Utrecht, the 31/11 Day of March/April, 1713 » : vol. 3, p. 398–440 (Canada, p. 431–34). ¶ *Première édition : Londres, 1710, q.v. pour d'autres notes*

(Canada, p. 431–34). ¶ *First edition: London, 1710*, q.v. *for other notes and contents relating to Canada.*

et titres portant sur le Canada.

The Natural probability of a lasting peace in Europe; shewn from the circumstances of the great powers, as they are now situated; compared with the state of affairs when the treaties of Ryswick and Utrecht were severally concluded. London, printed for J[ohn]. Peele, 1732. (Price six-pence.) xviii, 22 p. 8°(in 4s).

NUC(Pre–56)408:261

The Treaty of Utrecht [1713, ending the Spanish Succession War] criticized as admitting a dangerous rival to the Newfoundland fisheries: p. 10. [The Treaty of Ryswick, 1697, gave Acadia and Hudson's Bay forts to France, at the end of the War of the Grand Alliance.]

Le traité d'Utrecht [1713, qui mit fin à la guerre de la Succession d'Espagne] fut critiqué parce qu'il permettait l'établissement d'un dangereux rival des pêcheries de Terre-Neuve : p. 10. [Le traité de Ryswick de 1697 donna à la France l'Acadie et les forts de la Baie d'Hudson à la fin de la guerre dite « de la Ligue d'Augsbourg ».]

Popple, Henry, *d./déc.* 1743. A map of the British empire in America, with the French and Spanish settlements adjacent thereto; engraved on twenty sheets. By Henry Popple. London: Stephen Austen. [1732.] 20 maps, 1 l. [index]. fol.

Sabin:64140

"Engraved by William Henry Toms, and up to its date the largest and best map of America. The Index map forms the 21st sheet . . . . The maps also contain views of Niagara Falls, New York, Quebec, etc. Reissued in 1733, and again in 1740 [*q.v.*]": Sabin. Also published in Amsterdam, 1735, with Dutch settlements added (cf.

« Gravée par William Henry Toms, et à l'époque la meilleure carte de l'Amérique, et la plus grande. La carte d'index constitue la 21 ᵉ page . . . . Les cartes comportent également des vues des chutes du Niagara, de New York, de Québec, etc. Édition revue en 1733, puis en 1740 [*q.v.*] » : Sabin. Également publiée à Amsterdam en 1735, avec l'ajout des établissements hollandais (cf.

NUC). ¶ *"This map was undertaken 'with the patronage of the Lords of Trade and Plantations from authentic records and government surveys.' At the time it was published it was considered the best of its kind . . . ."* JCB(1)3:489.

NUC). ¶ « *Le tracé de cette carte fut entrepris 'sous les auspices des Lords of Trade and Plantations, à partir de documents authentiques et de levés du gouvernement.' À l'époque de sa publication, elle fut considérée comme la meilleure du genre . . . . »* JCB(1)3:489.

1733

*Popple, Henry, *d./déc.* 1743. A map of the British empire in America with the French and Spanish settlements adjacent thereto, by Hen. Popple. [London, sold by S[amuel]. Harding on the pavement in St. Martin's Lane, and by W.H. Toms engraver in Union Court near Hatton Garden Holborn, 1733.] 2 p.l., fold. map (engr. and col.), 20 plates (15 double). fol.

NUC(Pre–56)465:571*

Imprint from map 17; on map 20: London, engraved by Willm. Henry Toms, 1733. ¶ The twenty plates are enlargements of sections of the key map. Another 1733 entry in NUC has twenty-six maps. ¶ Transl. into French as: *Nouvelle carte particulière de l'Amerique* . . . (in G. Delisle, *Atlas nouveau.* Amsterdam [1741?]). ¶ Insets include views of Niagara Falls, Quebec, and New York. ¶ First pub. 1732, *q.v.* for other notes and editions.

Adresse bibliographique provenant de la carte 17 ; à la carte 20 : London, engraved by Willm. Henry Toms, 1733. ¶ Les vingt planches sont des agrandissements de certaines parties de la carte principale. Une autre notice du NUC (1733) compte 26 cartes. ¶ Trad. en français : *Nouvelle carte particulière de l'Amerique. . .* (dans G. Delisle, *Atlas nouveau.* Amsterdam [1741 ?]). ¶ Les illustrations en cartouche comportent des vues des chutes du Niagara, de Québec et de New York. ¶ Première publ. 1732, *q.v.* pour d'autres notes et éditions.

*Popple, Henry, *d./déc.* 1743. A map of the British empire in America with the French and Spanish settlements adjacent thereto, by Hen. Popple. [London: W[illiam]. H[enry]. Toms and R.W. Seale, 1733.] 21 plates. fol.

NUC(Pre–56)465:571*

The map is in twenty sheets, preceded by a general key sheet. ¶ For other notes and editions, *see* first edition, 1732. ¶ BVAU

La carte comprend vingt f. précédées d'une f. principale. ¶ Pour d'autres notes et éditions, *voir* la première édition, 1732. ¶ BVAU

1734

Great Britain. Board of Trade. Representation of the Board of Trade relating to the laws made, manufactures set up, and trade carried on, in His Majesty's plantations in America. [London, 1734.] 20 p. fol.

NUC(Pre–56)212:79*

Dated: Whitehall, January 23, 1733–34 (O.S./N.S.); Waldon places under 1733.
¶ Waldon states (in a note similar to one in NUC): This representation was laid before the Lords Spiritual and Temporal in Parliament assembled on the 23rd of January 17 $^{33}/_{34}$ in obedience to the King's command pursuant to their Lordships' address to his Majesty of June 13, 1733. It covers the colonies of Nova Scotia, New Hampshire [*etc.*]. It was ordered to be printed on the 21st of February, 1733, but, judging from its appearance, for official use only, and not for

Datation : Whitehall, 23 janvier 1733–1734 (c.j.-c.g.) ; classée par Waldon sous 1733. ¶ Selon Waldon (dans une note semblable à celle du NUC) : cette illustration fut soumise aux membres ecclésiastiques et laïques de la Chambre des Lords siégeant au Parlement le 23 janvier 17 $^{33}/_{34}$ conformément à l'ordre du Roi suite à l'adresse de leurs Seigneuries à sa Majesté le 13 juin 1733. Elle couvre les colonies de la Nouvelle-Écosse, du New Hampshire [*etc.*]. L'ordre de l'imprimer fut donné le 21 février 1733, mais sa présentation laisse croire qu'elle était uniquement vouée à un usage officiel, et non à une diffusion générale. ¶ *Reproduction sur microcarte*

general circulation. ¶ *Also appeared in a microcard edition, and in* MF, *Washington, D.C., Microcard Editions, 196– (cf. NUC).*

et sur microfiche, Washington (D.C.), Microcard Editions, 196– (cf. NUC).

1735

Crouch, Nathaniel, 1632?–1725? The English empire in America . . . . The seventh edition. Dublin, 1735. 12°

Sabin:9499

Dublin, 1729, and London, 1739, are also called seventh eds. ¶ *First edition: 1685,* q.v. *for other information.*

Dublin, 1729, et Londres, 1739, sont aussi dénommées Septième éd. ¶ *Première édition : 1685,* q.v. *pour d'autres renseignements.*

Lahontan, Louis Armand de Lom d'Arce, *baron de,* 1666–1715? New Voyages to North America . . . written in French by the Baron Lahontan, Lord Lieutenant of the French colony at Placentia in Newfoundland, at that time in England. Done into English. The second edition. In two volumes. A great part of which never printed in the original. Vol. I. London: printed for J[ohn]. Osborn, at the Golden-Ball, in Pater-noster-Row. 1735. 2 v.: 1 p.l., 22, 280 p. 9 plates, 4 maps (incl. front., 2 fold.); 1 p.l., 3–304 p. front., 9 plates. 8°(?)

NUC(Pre–56)312:56*

Vol. 2 has title: *New voyages to North America.* Giving a full account of the customs, commerce, religion and strange opinions of the savages of that country. With political remarks upon the courts of Portugal and Denmark, and the present state of the commerce

Titre du vol. 2 : *New voyages to North America.* Fournit un récit détaillé des coutumes, du commerce, de la religion et des convictions étranges des sauvages de cette contrée. Comporte des observations politiques sur les cours du Portugal et du Danemark, ainsi que sur l'état actuel du

of those countries. The second edition. Written by the Baron Lahontan, Lord Lieutenant of the French colony at Placentia, in Newfoundland: now in England. Vol. II. London: printed for J[ohn]. Walthoe, R. Wilkin, J[ames?]. and J. Bonwicke, J[ohn]. Osborn, S[amuel]. Bert [*i.e.* Birt], T. Ward and E. Wicksteed. 1735. ¶ *First English edition: London, 1703,* q.v. *for other notes; other 1735 issues follow, their order of appearance not determined.* ¶ *BVA · BVAU*

commerce de ces pays. Deuxième édition. Par le baron de Lahontan, représentant de la Couronne dans la colonie française à Placentia, Terre-Neuve : à l'heure actuelle en Angleterre. Vol. II. Londres : imprimé pour J[ohn]. Walthoe, R. Wilkin, J[ames ?]. et J. Bonwicke, J[ohn]. Osborn, S[amuel]. Bert [*c.-à-d.* Birt], T. Ward et E. Wicksteed. 1735. ¶ *Première édition anglaise : Londres, 1703,* q.v. *pour d'autres notes ; autres tirages de 1735 ci-dessous, ordre de parution indéterminé.* ¶ *BVA · BVAU*

*Lahontan, Louis Armand de Lom d'Arce, *baron de*, 1666–1715? New voyages to North-America. Containing an account of the several nations of that vast continent . . . . Illustrated with twenty-three maps and cuts. Written in French by the Baron Lahontan . . . . Done into English. The 2d ed . . . . A great part of which never printed in the original . . . . London, printed for John Brindley, bookseller, at the King's Arms in New-bond-street, bookbinder to Her Majesty, and His Royal Highness the Prince of Wales; and Charles Corbett, at Addison's-head, Temple-bar, 1735. 2 vols., fronts., plates (part fold.), maps (part fold.). 8°(?)

NUC(Pre–56)312:56*

Vol. 2 has title: *New voyages to North-America.* Giving a full account of the customs, commerce, religion, and strange opinions of the savages of that country. With political remarks upon the courts of Portugal and Denmark, and the present state of the commerce of those countries. The 2d ed. . . . ¶ First English edition: London, 1703, *q.v.*; another issue follows.

Titre du vol. 2 : *New voyages to North-America.* Relate en détail les coutumes, le commerce, la religion ainsi que les convictions étranges des sauvages de cette contrée. Comporte des observations politiques sur les cours du Portugal et du Danemark, ainsi que sur l'état actuel du commerce de ces pays. Deuxième éd. . . . ¶ Première édition anglaise : Londres, 1703, *q.v.* ; autre tirage ci-dessous.

*Lahontan, Louis Armand de Lom d'Arce, *baron de,* 1666–1715? New voyages . . . .
Illustrated with twenty three maps and cuts . . . . The second edition . . . . London,
printed for J[ames?]. and J. Bonwicke, R. Wilkin, S[amuel]. Birt, T. Ward, E.
Wicksteed; and J[ohn]. Osborn, 1735. 2 vols., fronts., plates (part fold.), maps (part
fold.). 8°(?)

NUC(Pre–56)312:55–56*

First English edition: London, 1703,
q.v. ¶ NSWA · BVIPA

Première édition anglaise : Londres, 1703,
q.v. ¶ NSWA · BVIPA

1737

*The English pilot. The fourth Book. Describing the West-India navigation, from
Hudson's-Bay . . . . London, W[illiam]. Mount and T[homas]. Page, 1737. 66 p. illus.,
charts (part fold.). fol.

NUC(Pre–56)160:373*

First edition: 1689, *q.v.* for other
editions; the 1706 edition has a similar
title, and is there transcribed more
fully.

Première édition 1689, *q.v.* pour d'autres
éditions ; l'édition de 1706 porte un titre
identique et comporte une transcription
plus détaillée.

1739

*Colliber, Samuel, *fl.* 1718–1737. A critical history of the English sea-affairs .... By Samuel Colliber. The second edition. London: printed for R[anew]. Robinson, 1739. 312, [8] p. 8°

NUC(Pre–56)115:468*

See first ed., 1727.　　　　　　　　*Voir* première éd., 1727.

[Crouch, Nathaniel], 1632?–1725? The English empire in America or, A view of the dominions of the Crown of England in the West-Indies.... By Robert Burton [*pseud.*]. The seventh edition. London: printed for A[rthur]. Bettesworth and C. Hitch at the Red-Lion in Pater-noster-row; and James Hodges at the Looking-Glass on London-bridge. 1739. 192 p. incl. front. (map), illus. (incl. map). small 8° or 12°

NUC(Pre–56)128:174*

Page [1] advertising matter; p. [2] is frontispiece. ¶ Two woodcut maps, and woodcuts in the text. ¶ Dublin 1729 and 1735 (q.v.) are also called seventh eds. ¶ First edition: 1685, q.v. for other information.

La page [1] comporte des réclames ; la p. [2] est le frontispice. ¶ Deux cartes xylographiées et gravures xylographiées dans le texte. ¶ Dublin 1729 et 1735 (q.v.) sont également dénommées Septième éd. ¶ Première édition : 1685, q.v. pour d'autres renseignements.

[Douglass, William], 1691?–1752. A discourse concerning the currencies of the British plantations in America. Especially with regard to their paper money: more particularly in relation to the province of the Massachusetts-Bay, in New England. London: printed for T[homas]. Cooper, R[obert]. Amey, and Mrs. [Sarah] Nutt [1739]. 54 p. 8°

NUC(Pre–56)147:673*

Attributed to Thomas Hutchinson (cf. NUC). ¶ Includes references to Newfoundland and Nova Scotia — cf. 1751 ed. ¶ First edition; reprinted London, 1741 (q.v.), and in Boston, Mass., 1740 (reprinted London, 1751, q.v., and London, 1857, in John R. MacCulloch, A select collection of tracts on paper currency and banking, p. 1–56), and New York, 1897, and in 1911 (as Colonial currency reprint, vol. 3, p. 307–63 — cf. NUC).

Attribué à Thomas Hutchinson (cf. NUC). ¶ Comprend des mentions se rapportant à Terre-Neuve et à la Nouvelle-Écosse – cf. éd. de 1751. ¶ Première édition ; réimpressions Londres, 1741 (q.v.), Boston (Mass.), 1740 (réimpressions Londres, 1751, q.v., et Londres, 1857, dans l'ouvrage de John R. MacCulloch, A select collection of tracts on paper currency and banking, p. 1–56), ainsi que New York, 1897, et 1911 (sous le titre Colonial currency reprint, vol. 3, p. 307–63 – cf. NUC).

*Great Britain. Parliament, 1739. House of Commons. Articles of impeachment of high treason, and other high crimes and misdemeanours, against Robert, &c. London: printed for John Trott. 1739. (Price one shilling.) viii, 72 p. [8°?]

NUC(Pre–56)436:229*

NUC(Pre–56)214:567 (under above entry) gives Robert Walpole, 1st Earl of Oxford, as the subject of this work, instead of Robert Harley, 1st Earl of Oxford, as given in above NUC location. ¶ First edition, 1715, q.v. for other notes and editions, under: Great Britain. Parliament, 1715. House of Commons.

Le NUC(Pre–56)214:567 (sous la notice ci-dessus) donne comme sujet de cet ouvrage Robert Walpole, premier comte d'Oxford, au lieu de Robert Harley, premier comte d'Oxford, comme cela est indiqué à la référence NUC susmentionnée. ¶ Première édition, 1715, q.v. pour d'autres notes et éditions, sous : Great Britain. Parliament, 1715. House of Commons.

1740

Child, Sir **Josiah,** 1630–1699. A new discourse of trade: wherein are recommended several weighty points relating to companies of merchants; the act of navigation, naturalization of strangers, and our woollen manufactures. The balance of trade, and nature of plantations; with their consequences, in relation to the kingdom . . . . The reduction of interest of money to 4 l. per cent. is recommended . . . . To which is added, a short, but most excellent treatise of interest. By Sir Josiah Child, Baronet. The 4th ed. London, printed for J[ames]. Hodges, on London Bridge [etc.]. [1740?] Price bound 3s. 2 p.l., xlvi, 232 (*i.e.* 262) p. 12°

NUC(Pre–56)106:637*

Same title as 1692 ed., but with the treatise added. ¶ Waldon has collation: 2 p.l., xlvi, 260, 2 (ads.) p. ¶ Newfoundland: p. 221–29. ¶ "A small treatise against usury," by Sir Thos. Culpepper, first pub. London, 1641: p. 235–57. ¶ First pub. under this title: London, 1692, q.v. for other notes. Waldon indicates another edition: "London or Dublin? 1740? 12° Varies slightly from the above in printer's devices and line-endings. '232' at head of verso of advertisement leaf omitted"; source: BM

Même titre que l'éd. de 1692, mais avec l'ajout du traité. ¶ Collation de Waldon : 2 f. l., xlvi, 260, 2 p. (de réclame). ¶ Terre-Neuve ; p. 221–29. ¶ « A small treatise against usury » , par sir Thos. Culpepper, première publ. Londres, 1641 : p. 235–57. ¶ Première publ. sous ce titre : Londres, 1692, q.v. pour d'autres notes. Waldon mentionne une autre édition : « Londres ou Dublin ? 1740 ? in–12°. Diffère légèrement de l'édition susmentionnée en ce qui a trait à la marque d'imprimeur et aux fins de ligne. '232' en tête du verso du feuillet publicitaire a été omis » ; source : BM.

James, Thomas, 1593?–1635? The dangerous voyage of Capt. Thomas James, in his intended discovery of a north west passage into the South Sea . . . . To which is added, a map for sailing in those seas: also divers tables of the author's of the variation of the compass, &c. With an appendix concernng the longitude, by Master Gellibrand . . . . 2d ed., rev. and corr. London: printed in 1633, and now reprinted for O[liver]. Payne, 1740. (Price bound two shillings and six pence.) 5 p.l., 142 p. front. (fold. map). 8°

NUC(Pre–56)276:645*

Waldon's collation: t.-p., [6], 142 p. ¶ "The copie of the letter I left at Charleston, fastened to the Crosse the first of July, 1632" (p. 112–20, in 1633 ed.) and the "Advise" by William Watts (22 p. at end) are omitted in this edition. ¶ *First ed.:* The strange and dangerous voyage .... *London, 1633,* q.v. *for other notes.* ¶ *OTU · BVIPA*

Collation de Waldon : p. de t., [6], 142 p. ¶ « The copie of the letter I left at Charleston, fastened to the Crosse the first of July, 1632 » (p. 112–20, dans l'éd. de 1633) et « Advise » de William Watts (22 p. à la fin) ne figurent pas dans cette édition. ¶ *Première éd. :* The strange and dangerous voyage .... *Londres, 1633,* q.v. *pour d'autres notes.* ¶ *OTU · BVIPA*

*Popple, Henry, *d./déc.* 1743. A map of the British empire in America .... [London?] 1740. 20[?] maps. fol.

Sabin:64140n.

Not verified, but noted in Sabin; *see* first edition, 1732, for other notes and editions.

Non vérifié mais noté dans le Sabin ; *voir* la première édition, 1732, pour d'autres notes et éditions.

1741

Coxe, Daniel, 1673–1739, *ed./rév.* A collection of voyages and travels in three parts. Part I. The dangerous voyage of Capt. Thomas James .... Part II. Sieur Pointis's voyage to America .... Part III. A description of the English province of Carolana .... By Daniel Coxe, Esq; to which is added, a large and accurate map of Carolana .... [London] Printed for and sold by Olive Payne, 1741. <Price bound 5s.> N.B. Either part may be had separate. 3 v. in 1: t.-p., [James:] [10], 142 p. front., fold. map; [Pointis:] viii, 86 p. front., fold. map. (list of books: 2 p.); [Carolana:] [54], 122 p. front., fold. map. 8°

NUC(Pre–56)125:696

Contents: pt. I. *The dangerous voyage of Capt. Thomas James, in his intended discovery of a north west passage into the South Sea. Second ed.* 1740; pt. II. *[The taking of Cartagena by the French, 1697, by Sieur Pointis. Second ed.* 1740]; pt. III. *A description of the English province of Carolana by the Spaniards call'd Florida and by the French La Louisiane.* 1741. ¶ James's narrative [of his voyage to Hudson's and James Bay, 1631–32] is the same as [in] the 1740 ed. ¶ The map of "Carolana" shows the Great Lakes and some of the rivers of Canada.

Qui portent sur le Canada : part. I. *The dangerous voyage of Capt. Thomas James, in his intended discovery of a north west passage into the South Sea. Deuxième éd.* 1740 ; part. II. *[The taking of Cartagena by the French, 1697, by Sieur Pointis. Deuxième éd.* 1740] ; part. III. *A description of the English province of Carolana by the Spaniards call'd Florida and by the French La Louisiane.* 1741. ¶ Le récit de James [récit de sa traversée jusqu'à la Baie d'Hudson et la Baie James, 1631–1632] est identique dans l'éd. de 1740. ¶ Les Grands Lacs et certains fleuves du Canada sont indiqués sur la carte de la « Carolana ».

*[Douglass, William], 1691?–1752. A discourse concerning the currencies of the British plantations in America . . . . London: printed for T[homas]. Cooper, at the Globe in Pater-noster-row; R[obert]. Amey, in the Court of Requests, and Mrs. [Sarah] Nutt, at the Royal-Exchange. [1741.] <Price 1s.> 54 (*i.e. 56*) p. 8°(?)

NUC(Pre–56)147:673*

Errors in paging: nos. 9–10 repeated. ¶ First pub. London, 1739, *q.v.* for other notes.

Erreurs de pagination : répétition des n°s 9 et 10. ¶ Première publ. Londres, 1739, *q.v.* pour d'autres notes.

[Oldmixon, John], 1673–1742. The British Empire in America, containing the history of the discovery, settlement, progress and state of the British colonies on the continent and islands of America . . . . 2d ed., corr. and amended. With the continuation of the history, and the variation in the state and trade of those colonies, from the year 1710 to the present time. Including occasional remarks, and the most feasible and useful methods for their improvement and security. London, printed for J[ohn]. Brotherton, J[ohn]. Clarke [etc.] 1741. 2 v.: xxxiv, 567 p.; 1 p.l., 478 p. 8 fold. maps (incl. front.). Index. 8°

NUC(Pre–56)439:309*

Dedication signed (in ms.): John Oldmixon (in at least one copy, cf. NUC). ¶ First ed.: 1708, q.v. for other notes. ¶ OTP · BVAU · BVIP · BVIPA

Dédicace signée (dans le man.) : John Oldmixon (au moins dans un exemplaire, cf. NUC). ¶ Première éd. : 1708, q.v. pour d'autres notes. ¶ OTP · BVAU · BVIP · BVIPA

Wotton, Thomas, d./déc. 1766. The English baronetage: containing a genealogical and historical account of all the English baronets, now existing . . . to which are added, an account of such Nova-Scotia baronets as are of English families, now resident in England . . . . London, printed for Tho. Wotton, 1741. 4 v. in 5. plates. 8°

NUC(Pre–56)674:624*

Wotton was a London bookseller (cf. Plomer). ¶ Title pages in red and black. ¶ Vol. 4 contains the section on Nova Scotia baronets. ¶ "Of the institution of Nova Scotia's baronets": p. 330–61. ¶ The Nova Scotia baronetcies were originated by Charles I, in 1625, to facilitate settlement. ¶ This was published also in 1727 (cf. NUC), but presumably without the Nova Scotia section, and again in 1771. ¶ OTP · OTU

Wotton était un libraire londonien (cf. Plomer). ¶ Pages de titre en rouge et noir. ¶ Le vol. 4 comprend la partie sur les baronnets de Nouvelle-Écosse. ¶ « Of the institution of Nova Scotia's baronets » : p. 330–61. ¶ Charles Ier institua les titres de baronnets de Nouvelle-Écosse en 1625 pour encourager la colonisation. ¶ Cet ouvrage fut également publié en 1727 (cf. NUC), mais vraisemblablement sans la partie sur la Nouvelle-Écosse, puis à nouveau en 1771. ¶ OTP · OTU

Colliber, Samuel, *fl.* 1718–1737. Columna Rostrata: or, A critical history of the English sea-affairs. With an account of the most remarkable sea-fights, &c. between the English, French, Dutch, Spaniards, &c. Containing, among many other curious particulars, the following: the sea-fight between Admiral Blake and Van Trump, the Dutch Admiral . . . . By Samuel Colliber. The second edition, improved. London: printed for F[rancis]. Noble . . . T[homas?]. Wright . . . J. Duncan. 1742. 312, [8] p. 8°

BLC(to 1975)66:112*

Not found in NUC. ¶ Waldon notes that this contains an index. ¶ *See* first ed., 1727.

Introuvable au NUC. ¶ Waldon note que cet ouvrage comprend un index. ¶ *Voir* la première éd., 1727.

The English pilot. The fourth book, describing the West-India navigation, from Hudson's-Bay . . . . London, printed for William Mount and Thomas Page, 1742. 1 p.l., 16 p. maps, illus., diagr. fol.

NUC(Pre–56)160:374*

NUC has collation: 2, 66 p.; Waldon has illus. statement (from Sabin: 22618): 16 maps. ¶ First edition: 1689, *q.v.* for other editions; the 1706 edition has a similar title, and is more fully transcribed.

Collation du NUC : 2, 66 p. ; mention d'illustr. par Waldon (d'après le Sabin:22618) : 16 cartes. ¶ Première édition : 1689, *q.v.* pour d'autres éditions ; l'édition de 1706 porte un titre identique, et a fait l'objet d'une transcription plus complète.

Great Britain. Parliament, 1742. House of Commons. Report relating to the finding a North-west Passage. [London, 1742.] 7 p. fol.

NUC(Pre–56)214:568

Waldon dates this 1745, citing BM, Sabin, and JCB as sources, but both Sabin:69938 and JCB(I)3:717 list this under 1742 (not found in BLC). In fact, Waldon notes: "JCB:1742, copied by Sabin, possibly a misprint"; it is not clear from JCB and Sabin, nor from Waldon's further note (which follows; taken from Sabin) why a misprint is suspected. ¶ *NUC has collation as: 7, [1] p.* ¶ Report of a Committee of the House of Commons appointed to inquire into the discoveries made by the *Furnace* [and] *Discovery*. The first was commanded by Capt. Christopher Middleton [for notes on the Dobbs-Middleton controversy, *see* Middleton's *A vindication*. London, 1743]. The expedition reached Churchill River 7 August 1741, and explored in 1742. ¶ Report of John Rankin, Rob. Wilson, dated 1 August 1742: p. 6–7. ¶ *Printed docket on last page: Report relating to the finding a north-west passage.*

Citant le BM, le Sabin et le JCB comme sources, Waldon date cet ouvrage de 1745 ; toutefois, le Sabin:69938 et le JCB(I)3:717 le répertorient tous deux pour l'année 1742 (renseignement introuvable dans le BLC). En fait, Waldon note : « JCB:1742, reproduit par le Sabin, peut-être une coquille » ; pas plus Waldon, dans sa note (ci-après ; tirée du Sabin), ni le JCB ni le Sabin n'indiquent clairement pourquoi on soupçonne l'existence d'une coquille. ¶ *Collation du NUC : 7, [1] p.* ¶ Rapport d'un Comité de la Chambre des communes nommé pour s'enquérir des découvertes du *Furnace* [et] du *Discovery*. Le premier navire fut commandé par le cap. Christopher Middleton [pour des notes sur la querelle Dobbs-Middleton, *voir* l'écrit de Middleton intitulé *A vindication*. Londres, 1743]. L'expédition atteignit le fleuve Churchill le 7 août 1741 et entreprit l'exploration en 1742. ¶ Rapport de John Rankin, Rob. Wilson, en date du 1er août 1742 : p. 6–7. ¶ *Fiche imprimée à la dernière page : Rapport sur la découverte du passage du Nord-Ouest.*

Remarks on a pamphlet, intitled, An inquiry into the revenue, credit and commerce of France, exposing the false-quotations and false reasonings of the author, and the evil tendency of his pamphlet. To which are added, some political reflections on the present situation of our affairs. As also some remarks on a pamphlet, intitled, A letter to the author of An inquiry, &c. wherein the design of the latter is pointed out . . . . London, sold by Jacob Robinson, 1742. <Price one shilling.> 1 p.l., 62 p. 8°

NUC(Pre–56)44:45

A reply to: An inquiry into the revenue, credit and commerce of France. *London, 1742, and* A letter to the author of An enquiry into the revenue

Réplique à An inquiry into the revenue, credit and commerce of France. *Londres, 1742, et à* A letter to the author of An enquiry into the revenue . . . of France. *Londres, 1742.* ¶

... of France. *London, 1742.* ¶ The *Inquiry* was written to prove that there was nothing to fear from France. *A letter*, which may be by the same hand as the *Remarks*, does not discuss the American trade, but the *Remarks* advocates, among other measures, driving the French out of Newfoundland. The author sees grave danger from France, but considers the English case not so hopeless as it seems at first sight, provided proper precautions are taken. The pamphlet is chiefly concerned with the woollen trade, the state of the navy, the possibility of war with France [the Seven Years War broke out in 1756], and trade in general.

An Inquiry fut rédigé afin de prouver qu'il n'y avait rien à craindre de la France. *A letter*, dont l'auteur est peut-être le même que celui des *Remarks*, ne traite pas du commerce américain, tandis que les *Remarks* recommandent de bouter les Français hors de Terre-Neuve. L'auteur croit que la France constitue une grave menace, mais il ne considère pas la cause des Anglais aussi désespérée qu'il y paraît de prime abord, pourvu que des précautions adéquates soient prises. Le pamphlet vise principalement le commerce de la laine, la situation de la marine, l'état de guerre virtuel avec la France [la guerre de Sept Ans a éclaté en 1756], ainsi que le commerce en général.

1742-44

*Campbell, John, 1708-1775. Lives of the admirals, and other eminent British seamen. Containing their personal histories, and a detail of all their public services. Including a new and accurate naval history from the earliest account of time .... Interspersed with many curious passages relating to our discoveries, plantations, and commerce .... By John Campbell .... London: printed by J[ohn]. Applebee, for J[ohn]. and H[enry]. Pemberton [etc.], 1742-44. 4 v. 8°(?)

NUC(Pre-56)92:210*

First edition. ¶ *See* second ed., 1750, for notes.

Première édition. ¶ *Voir* notes de la deuxième édition, 1750.

1743

The British merchant: a collection of papers relating to the trade and commerce of Great Britain and Ireland. First published by Mr. Charles King, from the originals of Sir Theodore Janssen. . . and others, the most eminent merchants of the city of London . . . . The second edition. London: printed for Charles Marsh and T. Davies, 1743. 3 v. 12°

NUC(Pre–56)76:436*

Letter on the fisheries: v. 2, p. 248–65. ¶ *See* first ed., 1721, for other notes.

Lettre sur les pêcheries : vol. 2, p. 248–65. ¶ *Voir* autres notes à la première éd., 1721.

Burrington, George, *ca.* 1680–1759. Seasonable considerations on the expediency of a war with France; arising from a faithful review of the state of both Kingdoms. To which are added a postscript, on the list of the French Army, a short comparison, between the British and French Dominions; and a state of the French revenues, and forces in the year 1701. By George Burrington, Esq. London, printed for F[rancis]. Cogan, 1743. (Price one shilling.) 1 p.l., 60 p. 8°

NUC(Pre–56)86:300

The author advocates a sea-war against France, but not a land-war except to give financial assistance to the Queen of Hungary and the King of Sardinia. ¶ "A short comparison between the British and French dominions; formerly publish'd by the same author": p. 46–52.

Contre la France, l'auteur préconise une guerre maritime mais ne recommande pas une guerre sur terre, si ce n'est un appui financier à la Reine de Hongrie et au Roi de Sardaigne. ¶ « A short comparison between the British and French dominions; formerly publish'd by the same author » : p. 46–52.

Jesuits. Letters from missions. Travels of the Jesuits, into various parts of the world; compiled from their letters. Now first attempted in English. Intermix'd with an account of the manners, government, religion, &c. of the several nations visited by those fathers: with extracts from other travellers, and miscellaneous notes. By Mr. Lockman. Illustrated with maps and sculptures. Vol. 2. London, printed for John Noon, 1743. 1 p.l., 4, [4], 507, [1, list of books], 24, [21] p. 1 fold. plate, 3 fold. maps, index. 8°

NUC(Pre–56)280:197

A two-volume work. ¶ Nothing in v. 1 relating to Canada. "Father Gabriel Marest to Father de Lamberville, procurator of the missions of Canada": v. 2, p. 474–507. A different translation [mainly of *Lettres edifiantes et curieuses*, Paris, 1711–13] from the 1714 ed., with editorial footnotes not in the earlier work [*q.v.* under same entry, with title: *The travels of several learned missioners* . . . . London, 1714].

Ouvrage en deux volumes. ¶ Rien dans le vol. 1 ne concerne le Canada. « Father Gabriel Marest to Father de Lamberville, procurator of the missions of Canada » : vol. 2, p. 474–507. Une autre traduction de l'éd. de 1714 [principalement des *Lettres edifiantes et curieuses*. Paris, 1711–1713] comporte des notes explicatives en bas de page qui ne figuraient pas dans l'ouvrage précédent [*q.v.* à la même vedette, sous le titre *The travels of several learned missioners* . . . . Londres, 1714].

Middleton, Christopher, *d./déc.* 1770. A vindication of the conduct of Captain Christopher Middleton, in a late voyage on board His Majesty's ship the Furnace, for discovering a north-west passage . . . . In answer to certain objections and asperisons of Arthur Dobbs . . . . By Christopher Middleton, late commander of the Furnace, and F.R.S. London: printed by the author's appointment; and sold by Jacob Robinson, at the Golden-Lion in Ludgate-Street. 1743. 2 p.l., [ii], 206 p., 1 l., 48 p. 8°(in 4s).

NUC(Pre–56)382:583*

This is the opening shot in the Dobbs-Middleton controversy on the existence of a northwest passage. It is explained in DNB ("Dobbs"): Dobbs was active in promoting the search for a northwest passage to India and China, and persuaded the Admiralty to provide two

C'est la première salve de la querelle opposant Dobbs à Middleton au sujet de l'existence du passage du Nord-Ouest. L'explication suivante figure au DNB (« Dobbs ») : Dobbs militait activement en faveur d'une expédition pour découvrir le passage du Nord-Ouest vers l'Inde et la Chine et persuada l'Amirauté de fournir

279

small vessels, the Furnace and the Discovery, for the purpose. Dobbs recommended Middleton, a Hudson's Bay Company captain who had commanded a voyage for the Company in 1737, to lead the expedition. It left in May 1741, wintered in Hudson Bay, and explored further north than anyone before, returning to England in September 1742. Middleton reported that the opening which had given Dobbs hopes of a passage was only a large river, whose tide was from the east not the north. Dobbs later challenged Middleton's report, accusing him of making false statements at the behest of the Hudson's Bay Company. The Admiralty requested Middleton to explain, which he attempted to do in his A vindication. An acrimonious dispute followed. The public sided with Dobbs, and a company was formed to send out a new expedition. Two small vessels were placed under Captain G. [i.e. William] Moor, who had commanded the Discovery in 1741 with Middleton, and they sailed in 1746. The results, disproving the existence of a northwest passage in the area supposed and restoring Middleton in public favour, were published by Henry Ellis as Voyage to Hudson's-Bay, by the Dobbs galley and California. London, 1748, and Charles Swaine, An account of a voyage . . . in the ship California. London, 1748–49, 2 v. (q.v.). Some earlier remarks by Moor are appended to Dobbs's Reply to Capt Middleton's Answer to the Remarks on his Vindication. 1745, q.v. ¶ Answered by: Arthur Dobbs, Remarks upon Capt. Middleton's defence. London, 1744 (q.v.), which was in turn answered by:

deux petits navires dans ce but, le Furnace et le Discovery. Dobbs recommanda que l'expédition fût dirigée par Middleton, capitaine au service de la Compagnie de la Baie d'Hudson, pour laquelle il avait assuré le commandement d'une traversée en 1737. La présente expédition partit au mois de mai 1741, passa l'hiver dans la Baie d'Hudson, s'aventura plus au nord que quiconque auparavant, puis regagna l'Angleterre au mois de septembre 1742. Middleton rapporta que l'échancrure sur laquelle Dobbs avait fondé ses espoirs d'un passage était en fait l'embouchure d'un grand fleuve, dont le courant allait vers l'est et non vers le nord. Dobbs contesta par la suite les conclusions de Middleton, qu'il accusa d'avoir fait de fausses déclarations sur l'ordre de la Compagnie de la Baie d'Hudson. L'Amirauté demanda à Middleton de s'expliquer, ce qu'il s'efforça de faire dans son ouvrage A vindication. Une dispute acerbe s'ensuivit. Le public prit fait et cause pour Dobbs, et l'on forma une compagnie afin d'organiser une nouvelle expédition. On confia le commandement de deux petits bâtiments au capitaine G. [c.-à-d. William] Moor, qui avait commandé le Discovery en 1741 avec Middleton, et cette nouvelle expédition partit en 1746. Elle permit de confirmer l'inexistence du passage du Nord-Ouest dans la région présumée et de rétablir la réputation de Middleton auprès du public. Henry Ellis et Charles Swaine publièrent respectivement Voyage to Hudson's-Bay, by the Dobbs galley and California. Londres, 1748, et An account of a voyage . . . in the ship California. Londres, 1748–1749, 2 vol. (q.v.), qui traitent des résultats de l'expédition. Certaines observations antérieures de Moor sont annexées au texte de Dobbs intitulé Reply to Capt Middleton's Answer to the Remarks on his Vindication. 1745, q.v. ¶ À l'écrit de Middleton, A Vindication, Arthur Dobbs répondit en publiant Remarks upon Capt.

Christopher Middleton, *A reply to the Remarks*. London, 1744 (*q.v.* for further titles in the controversy). ¶ *[Waldon's notes, mainly incompletely verified quotations, are here omitted.]* ¶ *OKQ · OTP · OTU · BVIPA*

Middleton's defence. Londres, 1744 (*q.v.*), auquel Christopher Middleton répliqua à son tour par : *A reply to the Remarks.* Londres, 1744 (*q.v.* pour d'autres titres concernant la querelle entre les deux hommes). ¶ *[Les notes de Waldon, principalement des citations partiellement vérifiées, sont omises ici.]* ¶ *OKQ · OTP · OTU · BVIPA*

Middleton, Christopher, *d./déc.* 1770. A vindication of the conduct of Captain Christopher Middleton . . . . Dublin, printed by and for [Isaac] Jackson, [J.?] Kinnear [etc., etc.], 1744. 168, 48 p. tables. 8°(?)

NUC(Pre–56)382:583*

For notes, see *preceding entry.* ¶ *NSWA*

Voir *notes à la notice précédente.* ¶ *NSWA*

A N

ACCOUNT

Of the COUNTRIES adjoining to

HUDSON's BAY,

IN THE

NORTH-WEST PART of *AMERICA:*

CONTAINING

A DESCRIPTION of their LAKES and RIVERS, the Nature of the SOIL and CLIMATES, and their Methods of COMMERCE, &c. Shewing the Benefit to be made by settling COLONIES, and opening a TRADE in these Parts; whereby the *French* will be deprived in a great Measure of their TRAFFICK in FURS, and the Communication between *Canada* and *Missisippi* be cut off.

WITH

An ABSTRACT of Captain *Middleton's* Journal, and OBSERVATIONS upon his Behaviour during his Voyage, and since his Return.

To which are added,

I. A Letter from *Bartholomew de Fonte,* Vice-Admiral of *Peru* and *Mexico*; giving an Account of his Voyage from *Lima* in *Peru,* to prevent, or seize upon any Ships that should attempt to find a North-west Passage to the *South Sea.*

II. An Abstract of all the Discoveries which have been publish'd of the Islands and Countries in and adjoining to the *Great Western Ocean,* between *America, India,* and *China,* &c. pointing out the Advantages that may be made, if a short Passage should be found thro' *Hudson's* Streight to that Ocean.

III. The *Hudson's Bay* Company's Charter.

IV. The Standard of Trade in those Parts of *America*; with an Account of the Exports and Profits made annually by the *Hudson's Bay* Company.

V. Vocabularies of the Languages of several *Indian* Nations adjoining to *Hudson's Bay.*

The whole intended to shew the great Probability of a NORTH-WEST PASSAGE, so long desired; and which (if discovered) would be of the highest Advantage to these Kingdoms.

By *ARTHUR DOBBS,* Esq;

LONDON:
Printed for J. ROBINSON, at the *Golden Lion* in *Ludgate-Street,*
M DCC XLIV.

Arthur Dobbs. *An account of the countries adjoining to Hudson's bay* .... London/Londres,

1744

Dobbs, Arthur, 1689–1765. An account of the countries adjoining to Hudson's bay, in the north-west part of America: containing a description of their lakes and rivers, the nature of the soil and climates, and their methods of commerce, &c. shewing the benefit to be made by settling colonies, and opening a trade in these parts; whereby the French will be deprived in a great measure of their traffick in furs, and the communication between Canada and Mississippi be cut off. With an abstract of Captain Middleton's journal, and observations upon his behaviour during his voyage, and since his return. To which are added, I. A letter from Bartholomew de Fonte . . . giving an account of his voyage from Lima in Peru, to prevent, or seize upon any ships that should attempt to find a north-west passage to the South Sea. II. An abstract of all the discoveries which have been publish'd of the islands and countries in and adjoining to the great Western Ocean between America, India, and China, &c. pointing out the advantages that may be made, if a short passage should be found thro' Hudson's Streight to that ocean. III. The Hudson's Bay Company's charter. IV. The standard of trade in those parts of America; with an account of the exports and profits made annually by the Hudson's bay company. V. Vocabularies of the languages of several Indian nations adjoining to Hudson's bay. The whole intended to shew the great probability of a north-west passage, so long desired; and which (if discovered) would be of the highet advantage to these kingdoms. By Arthur Dobbs, Esq. London: printed for J[acob]. Robinson, at the Golden Lion in Ludgate-Street. 1744. 1 p.l., ii, 211 p. front. (fold. map). 4°

NUC(Pre–56)145:252

Errata: p. 211. ¶ "A new map of Part of North America from the latitude of 40 to 68 degrees. Including the late discoveries made on board the *Furnace* bomb ketch in 1742. And the western rivers & lakes falling into Nelson River in Hudson's Bay, as described by Joseph La France a French Canadese Indian, who travaled thro those countries and lakes for 3 years; from 1739 to 1742." [This map] sometimes missing. BM. 213.CII (King's library) has map in ms., somewhat fuller than the original.

Errata : p. 211 ¶ « Une nouvelle carte de l'Amérique du Nord, allant du 40ᵉ au 68ᵉ degré de latitude. Comprend les dernières découvertes réalisées à bord de la galiote à bombes *Furnace* en 1742. Indique de plus les rivières et lacs occidentaux tributaires du fleuve Nelson à la Baie d'Hudson comme les décrivit l'Indien canadien français Joseph La France, qui avait parcouru ces régions et vogué sur ces lacs pendant trois ans, de 1739 à 1742 ». [Cette carte] manque parfois. Le BM:213.CII (King's library) en possède un exemplaire manuscrit un peu plus détaillé que l'original. [Le titre de la carte indiqué

[Waldon's map title corrected against actual copy.] ¶ An important work on the early history of Hudson Bay. Dobbs strongly urged that the monopoly of the Hudson's Bay Company should be broken and the trade thrown open, alleging that the rapacity of the Company in dealing with the Indians was throwing the trade into the hands of the French [cf. DNB, "Dobbs," which also says that this was compiled from the published French accounts and private communications from Hudson Bay residents]. ¶ *See also* his controversy with Middleton, 1743, 1744, 1745 [under Dobbs, and Christopher Middleton], and the notes under Middleton's *Vindication*, 1743; also *Reasons to shew, that there is a great probability of a navigable passage to the Western American Ocean* . . . . London, 1749. ¶ *OKQ · OTU · OTP · BVAU · BVIPA*

par Waldon a été corrigé d'après l'original.] ¶ Un ouvrage important sur les premiers événements de la Baie d'Hudson. Dobbs recommanda fortement de démanteler le monopole de la Compagnie de la Baie d'Hudson et de libéraliser le commerce car, soutenait-il, la rapacité dont la Compagnie faisait preuve dans ses activités commerciales avec les Indiens incitait ces derniers à se tourner vers les Français, qui s'accaparaient ainsi du commerce [cf. DNB, « Dobbs », selon lequel ces renseignements furent compilés à partir de récits français publiés et de communications privées des habitants de la Baie d'Hudson]. ¶ *Voir aussi* sa querelle avec Middleton, 1743, 1744, 1745 [sous Dobbs, et Christopher Middleton], et les notes sous *A vindication* par Middleton, 1743 ; voir aussi *Reasons to shew, that there is a great probability of a navigable passage to the Western American Ocean* . . . . Londres, 1749. ¶ *OKQ · OTU · OTP · BVAU · BVIPA*

Dobbs, Arthur, 1689–1765. Remarks upon Capt. Middleton's defence: wherein his conduct during his late voyage for discovering a passage from Hudson's-Bay to the South-Sea is impartially examin'd; his neglects and omissions in that affair fully prov'd; the falsities and evasions in his defence expos'd; the errors of his charts laid open, and his accounts of currents, streights, and rivers, confuted; whereby it will appear, with the hightest probability, that there is such a passage as he went in search of. With an appendix of original papers . . . . By Arthur Dobbs, Esq. London, printed by the author's appointment, and sold by Jacob Robinson, at the Golden Lion in Ludgate-street, 1744. 6 p.l., 171, [8] p. (incl. map, p. 145), fold. map. 8°(in 4s).

NUC(Pre–56)145:253

"Books printed and sold by Jacob Robinson": [8] p. at end. ¶ A reply to: Christopher Middleton, A vindication of the conduct of Captain Christopher Middleton. London, 1743, q.v. ¶ Answered by: Christopher Middleton, A reply to the Remarks of Arthur Dobbs. London, 1744; and also by his Forgery detected. London, 1745 (q.v.). ¶ For other notes on the Dobbs-Middleton controversy, see Middleton's A vindication. London, 1743. ¶ NSWA · OKQ · OTU · BVIP · BVIPA

« Livres imprimés et vendus par Jacob Robinson » : [8] p. à la fin. ¶ Réplique à l'écrit de Christopher Middleton, A vindication of the conduct of Captain Christopher Middleton. Londres, 1743, q.v. ¶ Ce document a suscité les répliques de Christopher Middleton suivantes : A reply to the Remarks of Arthur Dobbs. Londres, 1744, et Forgery detected. Londres, 1745 (q.v.). ¶ Pour d'autres notes sur la querelle Dobbs-Middleton, voir l'ouvrage de Middleton A vindication. Londres, 1743. ¶ NSWA · OKQ · OTU · BVIP · BVIPA

Great Britain. Sovereigns, etc., 1727–1760 (George II). His Majesty's declaration of war against the French King. [Text] Given at our Court at St. James's, the twenty ninth day of March, 1744, in the seventeenth year of our reign . . . . London, printed by Thomas Baskett and Robert Baskett, printers to the King's most Excellent Majesty, 1744. Broadside. fol.

BLC(to 1975)95:291

This declaration added war between France and England to the Austrian Succession War (1740–48), and resulted in the capture of the French fortress of Louisbourg (1745), on Cape Breton Island. ¶ Reprinted Boston, New England, the same year — NUC (Pre–56)215:426; and in the London Gazette, 31 March 1744. Also in the American Antiquarian Society Transactions, Worcester, Mass., 1911, v. 12, p. 196–99 (Waldon).

Par cette déclaration, la guerre de la Succession d'Autriche (1740–1748) se double d'un conflit armé entre la France et l'Angleterre et se solde par la prise de la forteresse française de Louisbourg (1745) au Cap-Breton. ¶ Réimpressions à Boston, Nouvelle-Angleterre, la même année – NUC(Pre–56)215:426, dans la Gazette de Londres, 31 mars 1744, ainsi que dans Transactions de l'American Antiquarian Society, Worcester (Mass.), 1911, vol. 12, p. 196–99 (Waldon).

Middleton, Christopher, *d./déc.* 1770. A reply to the Remarks of Arthur Dobbs, Esq; on Capt. Middleton's Vindication of his conduct on board his Majesty's ship Furnace, when sent in search of a north-west passage, by Hudson's-Bay, to the Western American Ocean. Humbly inscribed to the Right Honourable the Lord's Commissioners for executing the office of Lord High Admiral of Great-Britain and Ireland, &c. By Christopher Middleton, Esq; London: printed for George Brett, at the Three Crowns on Ludgate-Hill. 1744. (Price 3s 6d unbound.) x, 192, 93, [9] p. 8°

NUC(Pre–56)382:582

Errata: p. [2–3], third count; this is followed by "An Alphabetical Index." ¶ A reply to: Arthur Dobbs, Remarks upon Capt. Middleton's defence. *London, 1744* (q.v.). ¶ *Further to this is: Christopher Middleton,* Forgery detected. *London, 1745* (q.v.). ¶ *Answered by: Arthur Dobbs,* A reply to Capt. Middleton's answer to the Remarks. *London, 1745* (q.v.). ¶ *For other notes on this Dobbs-Middleton controversy, see Middleton's* A vindication. *London, 1743.* ¶ *OTU · OKQ (facsim.) · BVAU · BVIPA*

Errata : p. [2–3], troisième numérotation , suivi d'un index alphabétique. ¶ Réplique à Arthur Dobbs, Remarks upon Capt. Middleton's defence. *Londres, 1744* (q.v.). ¶ *Suivie par Christopher Middleton,* Forgery detected. *Londres, 1745* (q.v.). ¶ *Ce document a suscité la réponse de Arthur Dobbs,* A reply to Capt. Middleton's answer to the Remarks. *Londres, 1745* (q.v.). ¶ *Pour d'autres notes sur la querelle Dobbs-Middleton,* voir A vindication *par Middleton. Londres, 1743.* ¶ *OTU · OKQ (fac-sim.) · BVAU · BVIPA*

1744–46

[Churchill, Awnsham], *d./déc.* 1728, *comp.* A collection of voyages and travels . . . . To which is prefixed, an introductory discourse (supposed to be written by the celebrated Mr. Locke) intitled, The whole history of navigation from its original to this time. Illustrated with . . . maps and cuts, curiously engraved . . . . The third edition. London, printed by assignment from Messrs. Churchill, for Henry Lintot; and John Osborn . . . 1744–46. 6 v. fronts. (v. 1, 2) illus., plates (part fold.) ports., maps (part fold.). Index (v. 6). fol.

NUC(Pre–56)109:264*

Compiled by Awnsham and John Chur-chill. ¶ Contents relating to Canada: "An account of a most dangerous voyage performed by the famous Captain John Monck, in the years 1619 and 1620 etc.": v. 1, p. 419–44, plates, map; "Captain James's strange and dangerous voyage etc.": v. 2, p. 407–66; "A voyage into the North-West Passage . . . 1612 . . . by John Gatonbe": v. 6, p. 257–69. ¶ *Volumes 1–4 first pub.: London, 1704 (q.v. for notes and other editions).*

Compilé par Awnsham et John Churchill. ¶ Qui portent sur le Canada : « An account of a most dangerous voyage performed by the famous Captain John Monck, in the years 1619 and 1620 etc. » : vol. 1, p. 419–44, planches, carte ; « Captain James's strange and dangerous voyage etc. » : vol. 2, p. 407–66 ;« A voyage into the North-West Passage . . . 1612 . . . by John Gatonbe » : vol. 6, p. 257–69. ¶ *Volumes 1–4 première publ. : Londres, 1704 (q.v. pour d'autres notes et éditions).*

Oldys, William, 1696–1761, *comp. and ed./et rév.* The Harleian miscellany: or, A collection of scarce, curious and entertaining pamphlets and tracts, as well in manuscript as in print, found in the late Earl of Oxford's library. Interspersed with historical, political and critical notes. With a table of the contents, and an alphabetical index. London: printed for T[homas]. Osborne, in Gray's-Inn. 1744–46. 8 v. 4°

NUC(Pre–56)231:252*

NUC enters this under title. ¶ *Osborne, the bookseller and publisher, secured the library of Edward Harley, the 2d Earl of Oxford, in 1742 (for £13,000), but sold it again in Feb. 1744; meanwhile, he arranged for the selection and editing of the pamphlets by Oldys, and for the preface by Dr. Samuel Johnson (cf. Plomer, 1726–75: p. 185–86, and DNB).* ¶ *The items are not classified. For a chronological arrangement, see the edition of 1808–11.* ¶ "Proposals for carrying on an effectual war in America . . . <from a quarto edition, printed at London, in the year 1702>": vol. 1, p. 379–85. ¶ *First edition; second ed., London, 1753 (q.v.).*

Le NUC répertorie cet ouvrage sous le titre sus-mentionné. ¶ *Le libraire et éditeur Osborne acquit la bibliothèque d'Edward Harley, deux-ième comte d'Oxford, en 1742 (pour la somme de 13 000 £), mais la revendit au mois de février 1744 ; dans l'intervalle, il sélectionna et publia les pamphlets d'Oldys, qu'il fit préfacer par Samuel Johnson (cf. Plomer, 1726–1775 : p. 185–86, et DNB).* ¶ *Les documents ne sont pas classifiés. Pour une classification par ordre chronologique, voir l'édition de 1808–1811.* ¶ « Proposals for carrying on an effectual war in America . . . <from a quarto edition, printed at London, in the year 1702> » : vol. 1, p. 379–85. ¶ *Première édition ; deux-ième éd., Londres, 1753 (q.v.). Une autre édition en douze vol. parut à Londres (1808–1811),*

Another edition, in twelve vols., appeared in London, 1808–11, chronologically arranged by John Malham, and with a complete index in vol. 12; this edition appeared in the twentieth century on 154 microcards (cf. NUC). Other editions were published in London, 1808–13, with a selection in 1924, and an indexed list of the contents of the miscellany in Sydney, in 1885. ¶ BVAU (1924 selection)

dotée d'un index complet au vol. 12 et d'un classement par ordre chronologique effectué par John Malham ; au vingtième siècle, cette édition a été publiée sur 154 microcartes (cf. NUC). D'autres éditions furent publiées à Londres, 1808–1813, ainsi que des oeuvres choisies en 1924 et une table des matières du recueil, classée par ordre alphabétique, à Sydney en 1885. ¶ BVAU (1924, oeuvres choisies)

1744–47

*[Churchill, Awnsham], d./déc. 1728, comp. A collection of voyages and travels . . . . 3d ed. . . . London, printed by assignment from Messrs. Churchill, for H[enry]. Lintot [etc.], 1744–47. 8 v. fronts. (v. 1, 2) illus., plates (part fold.) ports., maps (part fold.). fol.

NUC(Pre–56)109:264*

Compiled by Awnsham and John Churchill. ¶ Volumes 1–4 first pub.: London, 1704 (*q.v.* for notes and other editions). Vols. 7–8, compiled by Thomas Osborne (from the Earl of Oxford's library) as a continuation of the collection by A. and J. Churchill, was also issued in 1745 as a separate two vol. work, *q.v.* under Osborne.

Compilé par Awnsham et John Churchill. ¶ Volumes 1–4 première publ. : Londres, 1704 (*q.v.* pour d'autres notes et éditions). Vol. 7–8, compilés par Thomas Osborne (à partir de la bibliothèque du comte d'Oxford) comme une suite de la collection publiée par A. et J. Churchill ; fut également publiée en 1745 sous forme d'un ouvrage distinct en deux vol., *q.v.* Osborne.

1744–48

Harris, John, 1667?–1719. Navigantium atque itinerantium bibliotheca. Or, A complete collection of voyages and travels. Consisting of above six hundred of the most authentic writers, beginning with Hackliut, Purchass, &c. in English; Ramusio, Alamandini, Carreri, &c. in Italian; Thevenot, Renaudot, Labat, &c. in French; De Brye, Grynæus, Maffeus, &c. in Latin; Herrera, Oviedo, Coreal, &c. in Spanish; and the voyages under the direction of the East-India company in Holland, in Dutch. Together with such other histories, voyages, travels, or discoveries, as are in general esteem; whether published in English, Latin, French . . . or in any other European language. Containing whatever has been observed worthy of notice in Europe, Asia, Africa, and America . . . . To which is prefixed a copious introduction . . . . By John Harris, D.D. and F.R.S. Now carefully revised, with large additions, and continued down to the present time; including particular accounts of the manufactures and commerce of each country. London, printed for T. Woodward [and others] 1744–48. 2 v.: [12], xvi, [4], 984 p.; [10], 1056, [22] p. front. (ports., v. 2), 40 illus., 20 maps, index. fol.

NUC(Pre–56)232:71*

Continued down to the present time by John Campbell [but Sabin inserts "By Dr. John Campbell," while NUC notes "Edited by John Campbell"]. ¶ Contents relating to Canada not found in 1705 ed.: Vol. 2, bk. 1, chap. 3, sect. 18 — The history of the discoveries, settlements, and other transactions of the English nation in America, from the accession of King James I to the Restoration. Chap. 3, sect. 19 — An account of the charter granted to the Hudson's-Bay Company for facilitating the discovery of a North-west passage, and of the settlements that have been made under it (p. 286–93). Sect. 20 — The history of the British colonies in America, from the Revolution to the death of his late Majesty King George I. Sect. 22 — A succinct history of the

De nos jours, John Campbell poursuit cette entreprise [le Sabin indique toutefois « Par le Dr John Campbell » tandis que le NUC note « Dirigé par John Campbell »]. ¶ Titres relatifs au Canada qu'on ne trouve pas dans l'éd. de 1705 : Vol. 2, liv. 1, chap. 3, part. 18 – L'histoire des découvertes, des colonies et des autres activités de la nation anglaise en Amérique, de l'accession au trône du roi Jacques Ier à la Restauration. Chap. 3, part. 19 –Un récit traitant, d'une part, de la charte accordée à la Compagnie de la Baie d'Hudson afin de faciliter la découverte du passage du Nord-Ouest et, d'autre part, des colonies établies en vertu de ladite charte (p. 286–93). Part. 20 – L'histoire des colonies britanniques en Amérique, de la Révolution à la mort de feu Sa Majesté le roi George Ier. Part. 22 – Une brève histoire des découvertes, des colonies et des conquêtes françaises en Amérique.

discoveries, settlements, and conquests made by the French in America. Vol. 2, bk. 2, chap. 1 — The discoveries made directly towards the North, and the attempts hitherto made for finding the North-east and North-west passages. Sect. 2 — The rational and philosophical motives for seeking a passage into the South Seas, by the North-west . . . together with the history of the attempts made with that view for the space of one hundred and thirty years. Sect. 3 — Voyage of Captain Thomas James. Sect. 4 — The late attempts made for the discovery of a passage to the South Seas from Hudson's Bay; more particularly that of Captain Christopher Middleton. ¶ *First edition: London, 1705, q.v. for other notes; also published: London, T. Osborne, 1764.* ¶ *BVA · BVIPA*

Vol. 2, liv. 2, chap. 1 – Les découvertes directement effectuées vers le Nord, et les tentatives entreprises jusqu'ici pour trouver des passages nord-est et nord-ouest. Part. 2 – Les motifs logiques et philosophiques de la recherche d'un passage vers la mer du Sud, par le Nord-Ouest. . . ainsi que l'histoire des tentatives entreprises dans ce but durant une période de cent trente ans. Part. 3 – Traversée du capitaine Thomas James. Part. 4 – Les dernières tentatives pour découvrir un passage vers la mer du Sud à partir de la Baie d'Hudson ; plus particulièrement celle du capitaine Christopher Middleton. ¶ *Première édition : Londres, 1705, q.v. pour d'autres notes ; publication ultérieure : Londres, T. Osborne, 1764.* ¶ *BVA · BVIPA*

1745

Articles of agreement, for carrying on an expedition, by Hudson's Streights, for the discovery of a North-West passage to the Western and Southern Ocean of America. Dated March 30, 1745. London: Printed in the year 1745. 16 p. 8°

NUC(Pre–56)23:46*

The expedition was undertaken at the instance of Arthur Dobbs [1689–1765]. ¶ First edition; other editions: 1746, (*q.v.*), 1940 (facsim.).

L'expédition fut entreprise à la demande d'Arthur Dobbs [1689-1765]. ¶ Première édition ; autres éditions : 1746 (*q.v.*), 1940 (fac-sim.).

Auchmuty, Robert, *fl.* 1745–1746. The importance of Cape Breton to the British nation. Humbly represented by Robert Auckmuty, judge of His Majesty's court of vice-admiralty for the provinces of Massachuset's-Bay and New-Hampshire, in New-England. N.B. Upon the plan laid down in this representation, the island was taken by Commodore Warren and General Pepperill, the 14th of June, 1745. London: printed for W. Bickerton, in the Temple-Exchange, near the Inner-Temple-Gate, Fleet-street. 1745. <Price sixpence.> 7 p. fol.

NUC(Pre–56)25:485

Though the author's name is given as "Auckmuty" in the title, BM and Sabin [and NUC] use "Auchmuty." ¶ *Concerns the Siege of Louisbourg, 1745.* ¶ *Another edition: 1798 (Mass. Hist. Soc., Boston. Collections, vol. 5, p. 202–06; further reprinted, M.H.S., Boston, 1816). A different work from* The importance and advantage of Cape Breton, *1746, by William Bollan,* q.v. See also *Auchmuty's* The importance of Cape Breton consider'd, *1746.*

Bien que le nom de l'auteur soit orthographié « Auckmuty » dans le titre, le BM et le Sabin [et le NUC] utilisent la graphie « Auchmuty ». ¶ *Traite du siège de Louisbourg en 1745.* ¶ *Autre édition : 1798 (Mass. Hist. Soc., Boston. Collections, vol. 5, p. 202–06 ; réimpression, M.H.S., Boston, 1816). Constitue un ouvrage distinct de* The importance and advantage of Cape Breton, *1746, par William Bollan,* q.v. Voir aussi The importance of Cape Breton consider'd, *1746, par Auchmuty.*

*Chauncy, Charles, 1705–1787. Marvellous things done by the right hand and holy arm of God in getting him the victory. A sermon preached the 18th of July, 1745. Being a day set apart for solemn thanksgiving to almighty God, for the reduction of Cape-Breton by His Majesty's New-England forces under the command of the Honourable William Pepperrell . . . and covered by a squadron of His Majesty's ships from Great Britain, commanded by Peter Warren, esq.; by Charles Chauncy . . . . Boston: printed and sold by T. Fleet, at the Heart and Crown in Cornhill. 1745. 23 p. 8°(?)

NUC(Pre–56)104:680*

The sermon refers to the British Siege of Louisbourg, 1745. ¶ First edition; reprinted London, 1745 (next entry).

Le sermon traite du siège de Louisbourg par les Britanniques en 1745. ¶ Première édition ; réimpression à Londres en 1745 (notice suivante).

*Chauncy, Charles, 1705–1787. Marvellous things done by the right hand and holy arm of God in getting him the victory . . . . under the command of the Honourable William Pepperell, Esq; Lieutenant-General and Commander in chief; and cover'd by a squadron of His Majesty's ships . . . by Charles Chauncy, D.D. Pastor of a church in Boston. [Text from *Judg.* 5:2, 20.] Boston: printed. London: reprinted for M[ary]. Cooper at the Globe in Pater-noster Row. 1745. Price 6d. 31 p. 8°(in 4s).

NUC(Pre–56)104:681*

See preceding entry.

Voir la notice précédente.

Considerations on the state of the British fisheries in America, and their consequence to Great Britain. With proposals for their security, by the reduction of Cape-Breton, &c., which were humbly offer'd by a gentleman of a large trade of the city of London, to His Majesty's ministers, in January 1744–5. London: printed for W[eaver]. Bickerton, in the Temple-Exchange, near the Inner-Temple-Gate, Fleet-street, 1745. <Price six-pence.> 8 p. fol.

NUC(Pre–56)120:399

Sets forth a plan for taking Cape Breton from the French. A letter at the end from an engineer at Cape Breton mentions the taking of Louisbourg by the English in June.

Établit un plan pour enlever le Cap-Breton des mains des Français. Placée à la fin, la lettre d'un ingénieur se trouvant au Cap-Breton mentionne la prise de Louisbourg par les Anglais au mois de juin.

Dobbs, Arthur, 1689–1765. A reply to Capt. Middleton's answer to the Remarks on his Vindication of his conduct, in a late voyage made by him in the Furnace sloop, by orders of the Lords Commissioners of the Admiralty, to find out a passage from the north-west of Hudson's Bay, to the Western and Southern Ocean of America. Shewing the art and evasions he makes use of to conceal his mis-conduct and neglect in prosecuting that discovery: as also the false currents, tides, straits, and rivers he has laid down in his chart and journal to conceal the discovery; with remarks upon some extraordinary affidavits he has published in his favour. To which is added, a full answer to a late pamphlet published by Capt. Middleton, called Forgery detected. By Arthur Dobbs, Esq; London printed: and sold by J[acob]. Robinson, at the Golden Lion, in Ludgate-street. 1745. 2 p.l., [8], 128 p. 8°

cf. NUC(Pre–56)145:253

Errata: p. 120. ¶ *Contents: 1. A reply, p. 1–104; An answer to Forgery detected (caption title), p. 105–20;* "This letter [from William Moor, commander of the Discovery *in 1741, under Middleton] was sent to me after the foregoing sheets were printed off. To Arthur Dobbs, Esq; Sir, . . ."* [complaining of Middleton's "ungenerous treatment" of him (Moor) in Middleton's *Forgery detected], p. 121–28.* ¶ *A reply to: Christopher Middleton,* A reply to the Remarks of Arthur Dobbs. *London, 1744; and to Middleton's* Forgery detected. *London, 1745 (q.v.).* ¶ *Answered by: Christopher Middleton,* A reply to Mr. Dobbs's Answer. *London, 1745; and by Middleton's* A rejoinder to Mr. Dobb's Reply. *London, 1745 (q.v.).* ¶ *For other notes on the Dobbs-Middleton controversy, see Middleton's* A vindication. *London, 1743.* ¶ *OKQ · OTU*

Errata : p. 120. ¶ *Qui portent sur le Canada : 1. A reply, p. 1–104 ; An answer to Forgery detected (titre de départ), p. 105–20 ;* « *Cette lettre* [de William Moor, commandant du Discovery *en 1741 sous Middleton] m'est parvenue après l'impression des feuilles précédentes. À M. Arthur Dobbs ; Monsieur, . . .* » [se plaignant du « traitement partial » que *Middleton lui inflige (à Moor) dans son écrit* Forgery detected], p. 121–28. ¶ *Réplique à Christopher Middleton,* A reply to the Remarks of Arthur Dobbs. *Londres, 1744 ; et à* Forgery detected *(du même auteur). Londres, 1745 (q.v.).* ¶ *Ce document a suscité les répliques suivantes de Christopher Middleton :* A reply to Mr. Dobbs's Answer. *Londres, 1745 ; et* A rejoinder to Mr. Dobbs's Reply. *Londres, 1745 (q.v.).* ¶ *Pour d'autres notes sur la querelle Dobbs-Middleton, voir* A vindication *par Middleton, Londres, 1743.* ¶ *OKQ · OTU*

Durell, Philip, *d./déc.* 1766. A particular account of the taking cape Breton from the French, by Admiral Warren, and Sir William Pepperell, the 17th of June, 1745. With a description of the place and fortifications; the loss it will be to the French trade, and the advantage it will be to Great Britain and Ireland; with the articles of the capitulation of fort Louisbourg. By Philip Durell, Esq., capt. of His Majesty's ship Superbe. To which is added a letter from an officer of marines to his friend in London, giving an account of the siege of Louisbourg and a description of the town, harbour, batteries, number of guns, &c. Also the happy situation of that country; and an account of M. Chambon, governor of Louisbourg, being laid in irons for surrendering it; in a letter from a gentleman in London, to a merchant in the west of England. London, printed for W[eaver]. Bickerton, 1745. 8 p. fol.

NUC(Pre–56)152:637

The Account is dated "in Louisbourgh harbor, June 20, 1745."	*Le récit est daté comme suit : « port de Louisbourg, le 20 juin 1745 ».*

*The English pilot. The fourth book. Describing the West-India navigation, from Hudson's-Bay.... London, W[illiam]. Mount and T[homas]. Page, 1745. 66 p. illus., charts (part fold.). fol.

NUC(Pre–56)160:374*

First edition: 1689, *q.v.* for other editions; the 1706 edition has a similar title, and is more fully transcribed.	Première édition : 1689, *q.v.* pour d'autres éditions ; l'édition de 1706 porte un titre identique, mais a fait l'objet d'une transcription plus complète.

*Galvão, Antonio, *d./déc.* 1557. The discoveries of the world.... Corrected, quoted, and now published in English, by Richard Hakluyt.... London, 1745. (In [Thomas Osborne], *A collection of voyages and travels,* vol. 2, p. [353–402].)

NUC(Pre–56)190:64*

First pub.: London, 1601, *q.v.* for notes and other editions.

Première publ. : Londres, 1601, *q.v.* pour d'autres notes et éditions.

*Geare, Allen. Ebenezer; or, A monument of thankfulness, being a true account . . . . London, 1745. (In [Thomas Osborne], *A collection of voyages and travels,* vol. 2, p. [787]–92.)

NUC(Pre–56)193:287*

First pub.: London, 1708, *q.v.* for other notes and editions.

Première publ. : Londres, 1708, *q.v.* pour d'autres notes et éditions.

Gibson, James, 1690?–1752. A journal of the late siege by the troops from North America, against the French at Cape Breton, the city of Louisbourg, and the territories thereunto belonging. Surrendered to the English, on the 17th of June, 1745, after a of [*sic*] siege forty-eight days. By James Gibson, gentleman volunteer at the above siege. London, printed for J[ohn]. Newbery, at the Bible and Sun, in St. Paul's Church-Yard. 1745. 1 p.l., viii, 9–49 p. front. (fold. plan). 8°(in 4s).

NUC(Pre–56)198:664*

NUC has "after a siege of forty-eight days" and "gentleman voluntier" in the title. ¶ Concerns the Siege of Louisbourg, 1745. ¶ First edition; reprinted [Washington,] J.B. Johnson, 1894. ¶ NSWA

Le titre du NUC comporte les mentions « after a siege of forty-eight days » et « gentleman voluntier ». ¶ Traite du siège de Louisbourg, 1745. ¶ Première édition ; réimpression [Washington], J.B. Johnson, 1894. ¶ NSWA

*Great Britain. Laws, statutes, etc., 1625–1649 **(Charles I).** A commission for the well-governing of our people inhabiting in Newfoundland; or, trafficking in bays, creeks, or fresh rivers there. London, 1745. (In [Thomas Osborne], *A collection of voyages and travels*, vol. 2, p. [783]–85. map.)

NUC(Pre–56)213:437*

Dated: 10 Feb. [1634]. ¶ First pub. 1634, *q.v.* for other variants and editions.

Datation : 10 février [1634]. ¶ Première publ. 1634, *q.v.* pour des variantes et d'autres éditions.

Le Sage, [Alain René], 1668–1747. The adventures of Robert Chevalier, call'd De Beauchêne. Captain of a privateer in New-France. By Monsieur Le Sage, author of Gil-Blas. . . . London: printed and sold by T[homas]. Gardner . . . R[obert]. Dodsley . . . and M[ary]. Cooper . . . 1745. 2 v.: [8], 307 p.; [8], 287 p. 12°

NUC(Pre–56)328:41; Sabin:40158

Transl. from his: Les avantures de Monsieur Robert Chevalier, dit de Beauchêne. *Paris, 1732, 2 vols., and many subsequent editions (cf. NUC (Pre–56)328:43, and Sabin:4163 and 40157).* ¶ " 'Ce n'est point une fiction, mais l'histoire singulière d'un capitaine de flibustiers, qui fut tué à Tours, par des Anglais, en 1731, rédigé d'après les mémoires fournis par sa veuve.' — Quérard," from catalogue of the Burton Historical Collection, Detroit Public Library [and from Sabin:4163n]. In spite of this assurance, the book is found under the subject "Canada — History — To 1763 — Fiction." ¶ Contains an account of Beauchêne's residence among the Indians and his being sold as a slave in New England.

Trad. de son ouvrage : Les avantures de Monsieur Robert Chevalier, dit de Beauchêne. *Paris, 1732, 2 vol. et nombreuses éditions ultérieures (cf. NUC(Pre–56)328:43, Sabin: 4163 et 40157).* ¶ « 'Ce n'est point une fiction, mais l'histoire singulière d'un capitaine de flibustiers, qui fut tué à Tours, par des Anglais, en 1731, rédigé d'après les mémoires fournis par sa veuve.' –Quérard », tiré du catalogue de la Burton Historical Collection, Detroit Public Library [et du Sabin:4163n]. En dépit de cette précision, le livre se trouve sous le sujet « Canada – History –To 1763 –Fiction ». ¶ Comprend le récit du séjour de Beauchêne chez les Indiens et l'épisode durant lequel il fut vendu comme esclave en Nouvelle-Angleterre. L'intrigue de la pièce française « Les mariages de Canada », d'abord produite en 1734, est tirée de l'histoire de M.

The plot of the French play, "Les mariages de Canada," first produced in 1734, is taken from M. de Mouneville's story in Beauchêne's "Mémoires" — cf. Sabin:40157–58. ¶ Les Mariages de Canada. *Paris, 1783, appears in NUC under Le Sage (NUC(Pre–56)328:82) in a Louisville, Ky., 1959 microcard reprint, as v. 15 of Le Sage's Oeuvres choisies. The same source refers from both Beauchêne and Chevalier to Le Sage (41:494 and 106:33), and Sabin:4163 has only, under Beauchêne:* Les avantures de Monsieur Robert Chevalier dit de Beauchêne. *Paris, 1732. Possibly this is Beauchêne's "Mémoires," and "Les Mariages" may not have been published separately in the eighteenth century.* ¶ *OTP*

de Mouneville dans les « Mémoires » de Beauchêne – cf. Sabin:40157–58. ¶ Les mariages de Canada. *Paris, 1783, est inscrit au NUC sous Le Sage (NUC(Pre–56)328:82) dans une reproduction sur microfiche à Louisville (Ky.), 1959, qui constitue le 15ᵉ vol. des* Oeuvres choisies *de Le Sage. La même source mentionne à la fois Beauchêne et Chevalier à la notice Le Sage (41:494 et 106:33), et le Sabin:4163 indique seulement, sous Beauchêne :* Les avantures de Monsieur Robert Chevalier dit de Beauchêne. *Paris, 1732. On peut supposer qu'il s'agit bien des « Mémoires » de Beauchêne et que « Les Mariages » n'a pas été publié séparément au dix-huitième siècle.* ¶ *OTP*

---

*[Lescarbot, Marc], *ca./vers* 1570–1642. Nova Francia: or, The description of that part of New France which is one continent with Virginia . . . . Translated out of the French into English, by P[ierre]. E[rondelle]. London, 1745. (In [Thomas Osborne], *A collection of voyages and travels*, vol. 2, p. [795]–917. map. fol.)

NUC(Pre–56)328:113*

Waldon refers to this under the Osborne title in a note to the London, Andrew Hebb, 1609 edition, and in a brief title entry (added later) under 1745. ¶ For other notes and editions, *see* the 1609 editions.

Waldon fait mention de cet ouvrage sous le titre Osborne dans une note visant l'édition londonienne de 1609 d'Andrew Hebb, ainsi que dans une courte notice de titre (ajout ultérieur) sous 1745. ¶ Pour d'autres notes et éditions, *voir* les éditions de 1609.

Middleton, Christopher, *d./déc.* 1770. Forgery detected. By which is evinced, how groundless are all the calumnies cast upon the editor, in a pamphlet published under the name of Arthur Dobbs, Esq; By Capt. Christopher Middleton, late commander of his Majesty's ship *Furnace*, when sent upon the search of a north-west passage to the Western American Ocean. London: printed for M[ary]. Cooper, at the Globe in Pater-noster-Row; and G[eorge]. Brett, at the Three Crowns on Ludgate-Hill. 1745. <Price 6d.> 1 p.l., v, 33, [2] p. maps (p. 5, 15). 8°

NUC(Pre–56)382:583

Further to his: A reply to the Remarks of Arthur Dobbs. *London, 1744* (q.v.). ¶ *Answered by: Arthur Dobbs*, A reply to Capt. Middleton's answer to the Remarks. *London, 1745* (q.v.). ¶ *For other notes on the Dobbs-Middleton controversy, see Middleton's* A vindication. *London, 1743.* ¶ *Middleton further defends himself against Dobbs's charges, in his* A reply, *1744, perhaps thinking he'd still not cleared his name with his countrymen (cf.* A reply, *p. 3).* ¶ *OKQ · BVIPA(MF)*

À la suite de son écrit : A reply to the Remarks of Arthur Dobbs. *Londres, 1744* (q.v.). ¶ *Ce document a suscité la réplique d'Arthur Dobbs,* A reply to Capt. Middleton's answer to the Remarks. *Londres, 1745* (q.v.). ¶ *Pour d'autres notes sur la querelle Dobbs-Middleton,* voir A vindication *par Middleton. Londres, 1743.* ¶ *Dans son écrit* A reply, *1744, Middleton présentera d'autres arguments pour se disculper des accusations portées contre lui par Dobbs – peut-être pensait-il que ses concitoyens ne l'avaient pas encore lavé de tout soupçon (cf.* A reply, *p. 3).* ¶ *OKQ · BVIPA (mic.)*

Middleton, Christopher, *d./déc.* 1770. A rejoinder to Mr. Dobbs's Reply to Captain Middleton; in which is expos'd, both his wilful and real ignorance of tides; &c. his Jesuitical prevarications, evasions, falsities, and false reasoning; his avoiding taking notice of facts, formerly detected and charged upon him as inventions of his or his witnesses; the character of the latter, and the present views of the former, which gave rise to the present dispute. In a word, an unparalelled disingenuity, and (to make use of a verodobbsical flower of rhetoric) a glaring impudence, are set in a fair light. By Christopher Middleton, Esq. ... [6 lines "From the Veradobbsical Miscellany."] London: printed for M[ary]. Cooper, at the Globe in Paternoster-Row; G[eorge]. Brett, at the Three Crowns on Ludgate-Hill; and R[obert]. Amey in the Court of Requests. 1745. <Price two shillings.> 2 p.l., 156 p. 8°(in 4s).

NUC(Pre–56)382:583

"Errors of the press": p. 156. ¶ A reply to Arthur Dobbs, A reply to Capt. Middleton's answer to the Remarks. London, 1745 (q.v.). ¶ For other notes on the Dobbs-Middleton controversy, see Middleton's A vindication. London, 1743. ¶ NSWA · OKQ (facsim.) · BVIPA

« Fautes d'impression » : p. 156. ¶ Réplique à Arthur Dobbs, A reply to Capt. Middleton's answer to the Remarks. Londres, 1745 (q.v.). ¶ Pour d'autres notes sur la querelle Dobbs-Middleton, voir A vindication par Middleton. Londres, 1743. ¶ NSWA · OKQ (fac-sim.) · BVIPA

Middleton, Christopher, *d./déc.* 1770. A reply to Mr. Dobbs's answer to a pamphlet, entitled, Forgery detected . . . . By Christopher Middleton, Esq. London: printed for M[ary]. Cooper, at the Globe in Pater-noster Row; and G[eorge]. Brett, at the Three Crowns on Ludgate-Hill. 1745. 1 p.l., 28 p. 8°(in 4s).

NUC(Pre–56)382:582

Caption title: A reply to Mr. Dobbs's answer to my pamphlet . . . . ¶ Includes letters and affidavits by others, presented as supporting evidence. ¶ "N.B. My Rejoinder to Mr. Dobbs's Reply is now in the press, and will speedily be published" (see Middleton, A rejoinder. London, 1745): p. 28. ¶ A reply to: Arthur Dobbs, A reply to Capt. Middleton's answer to the Remarks . . . . To which is added, a full answer to . . . Forgery detected. London, 1745 (q.v.). ¶ Sabin confused this with Middleton's Reply to the remarks of Arthur Dobbs. 1744 (q.v.). ¶ For other notes on the Dobbs-Middleton controversy, see Middleton's A vindication. London, 1743. ¶ OKQ (facsim.)

Titre de départ : A reply to Mr. Dobbs's answer to my pamphlet . . . . ¶ Comprend des lettres et des déclarations sous serment, qui étaient le fait de tiers et furent présentées comme pièces justificatives. ¶ « N.B. Ma répartie à la réplique de M. Dobbs est présentement sous presse et sera incessamment publiée » (voir Middleton, A rejoinder. Londres, 1745) : p. 28. ¶ Réplique à Arthur Dobbs, A reply to Capt. Middleton's answer to the Remarks . . . . To which is added, a full answer to . . . Forgery detected. Londres, 1745 (q.v.). ¶ Le Sabin a confondu cet écrit avec celui de Middleton intitulé Reply to the remarks to Arthur Dobbs. 1744 (q.v.). ¶ Pour d'autres notes sur la querelle Dobbs-Middleton, voir A vindication par Middleton, Londres, 1743. ¶ OKQ (fac-sim.)

[**Osborne, Thomas**], *d./déc.* 1767, *comp.* A collection of voyages and travels, consisting of authentic writers in our own tongue, which have not before been collected in English, or have only been abridged in other collections. And continued with others of note, that have published histories, voyages, travels, journals or discoveries in other nations and languages, relating to any part of the continent of Asia, Africa, America, Europe, or the islands thereof, from the earliest account to the present time . . . . Comp. from the curious and valuable library of the late Earl of Oxford . . . . London, printed and sold by Thomas Osborne, 1745. 2 v.: 4, xii, lxiii, 873 p.; 1 p.l., 931, 30 p. fronts., illus., plates (part fold.), maps (part fold.), fold. tables. fol.

NUC(Pre–56)434:44*

Paging irregular. ¶ *For contents, see the* Catalogue of the Royal Geographical Society. *London.* ¶ Contents relating to Canada, vol. 2: "The discoveries of the world, from their first original, unto the year of our Lord 1555 . . . . By Antony Galvano . . . . Corrected, quoted, and now published in English, by Richard Hakluyt . . .": p. 353–402; "A short discovery of the coast and continent of America, from the equinoctial northward; and of the adjacent isles. By William Castle": p. 665–781; "A commission for the well-governing of our people inhab- iting in Newfoundland; or, trafficking in bays, creeks, or fresh rivers there": p. 783–85; "Ebenezer: or, A monu- ment of thankfulness . . . by Allen Geare": p. 787–92; "Considerations on the trade to Newfoundland . . . . By Thomas Thompson": p. 793–94; "Nova Francia: or, The description of that part of New France, which is one continent with Virginia . . . . Trans- lated out of the French into English, by P.E. [i.e., Pierre Erondelle]": p. 795–917, map. ¶ *Comp. by Osborne from books in Robert Harley's library (Harleian Collection).* ¶ *First edition;*

Pagination irrégulière. ¶ *Pour la table des matières,* voir *le* Catalogue of the Royal Geographical Society. *Londres.* ¶ Qui por- tent sur le Canada, vol. 2 : « The discoveries of the world, from their first original, unto the year of our Lord 1555 . . . . By Antony Galvano . . . . Corrected, quoted, and now published in English, by Richard Hakluyt . . . » : p. 353–402 ; « A short discovery of the coast and continent of America, from the equinoctial northward; and of the adjacent isles. By William Castle » : p. 665–781 ; « A commission for the well-governing of our people inhabiting in Newfoundland; or, trafficking in bays, creeks, or fresh rivers there » : p. 783–85 ; « Ebenezer: or, A monument of thankfulness . . . by Allen Geare » : p. 787–92 ; « Considerations on the trade to Newfoundland . . . . By Thomas Thompson » : p. 793–94 ; « Nova Francia: or, The description of that part of New France, which is one continent with Virginia . . . . Translated out of the French into English, by P.E. [*c.-à-d.,* Pierre Eron- delle] » : p. 795–917, carte. ¶ *Compilé par Osborne à partir des livres de la bibliothèque de Robert Harley (Harleian Collection).* ¶ *Pre- mière édition ; autres éditions publiées en 1747 et en 1752,* q.v. *Ce sont les vol. 7–8 d'une col- lection entamée par A. et J. Churchill avec les*

other editions appeared in 1747 and 1752, q.v. These are vols. 7–8 of a collection begun by A. and J. Churchill with vols. 1–4 in 1704, q.v. under Awnsham Churchill, Collection of voyages. ¶ *BVA*

vol. 1–4 en 1704, q.v. Awnsham Churchill, Collection of voyages. ¶ *BVA*

The present state of the British and French trade to Africa and America consider'd and compar'd: with some propositions in favour of the trade of Great Britain .... London, printed for E[dmund]. Comyns, 1745. (Price one Shilling.) 56 p. 8°

NUC(Pre–56)470:290

Title vignette. ¶ *"Perhaps by John Ashley": Sabin:65327.* ¶ Chiefly deals with the West Indies and the southern colonies, but Cape Breton, Nova Scotia, Hudson Bay, and Newfoundland are included in the discussion.

Titre vignette. ¶ *« Peut-être de John Ashley » : Sabin:65327.* ¶ Traite principalement des Antilles et des colonies méridionales, mais le Cap-Breton, la Nouvelle-Écosse, la Baie d'Hudson et Terre-Neuve sont aussi abordés.

1746

Articles of agreement, for carrying on an expedition, by Hudson's Streights, for the discovery of a North-West Passage .... Dublin: Printed in the year 1746. BVIP.

See 1745.

Voir 1745.

Auchmuty, Robert, *fl.* 1745–1746. The importance of Cape Breton consider'd; in a letter to a member of Parliament, from an inhabitant of New-England. London: printed for R[obert]. Dodsley and sold by M[ary]. Cooper, 1746. Price one shilling. 1 p.l., 73 p. 8°(in 4s).

Signed: Massachusettensis. ¶ *NUC has collation:* [1], *73 p., but Waldon has:* t.-p., *73 p., so evidently 1 p.l.* ¶ *Concerns the Siege of Louisbourg, 1745.* ¶ *A different work from* The importance and advantage of Cape Breton, *1746, by William Bollan,* q.v. See also *Auchmuty's* The importance of Cape Breton to the British Nation, *1745.* ¶ *OONL(MF) · NBFU(MF) · QMBM(? title) · OOA · OOU(MF) · AEU(MF)*

Signé : Massachusettensis. ¶ *Collation du NUC :* [1], *73 p., tandis que Waldon signale :* p. de t., *73 p., de toute évidence 1 f. l.* ¶ *Traite du siège de Louisbourg en 1745.* ¶ *Constitue un ouvrage distinct de* The importance and advantage of Cape Breton, *1746, par William Bollan,* q.v. Voir aussi The importance of Cape Breton to the British Nation, *1745, par Auchmuty.* ¶ *OONL (mic.) · NBFU (mic.) · QMBM (? titre) · OOA · OOU (mic.) · AEU (mic.)*

[Bollan, William], *d./déc.* 1776. The importance and advantage of Cape Breton, truly stated, and impartially considered. With proper maps . . . . London, printed for John and Paul Knapton, 1746. vi p., 1 l., 156 p. 2 fold. maps. 8°

NUC(Pre–56)64:627

Attributed by BM to Sir William Pepperell. ¶ Maps: "Map of the Island of Cape Breton as laid down by the Sieur Bellin 1746"; "A map of North America as far as relates to the English settlements, taken from Sieur Bellin, 1746." ¶ Supports Great Britain's claim to Cape Breton, and gives reasons for the desirability of enforcing that right. Includes chapters on Canada, Nova Scotia and the Siege of Louisbourg. "The descriptive part is taken from Charlevoix's *Histoire et description générale de la Nouvelle*

Attribué par le BM à sir William Pepperell. ¶ Cartes : « Carte de l'île du Cap-Breton tracée par le sieur Bellin 1746 » ; « Une carte de l'Amérique du Nord, dans la mesure où il s'agit des colonies anglaises, inspirée de celle du sieur Bellin, 1746 ». ¶ Étaye les visées territoriales de la Grande-Bretagne quant au Cap-Breton, et explique les avantages résultant de l'application de ces droits. Comprend plusieurs chapitres sur le Canada, la Nouvelle-Écosse, et le siège de Louisbourg. « La partie narrative est tirée de l'*Histoire et description générale de la Nouvelle France* par Charlevoix » (NUC). ¶ *En*

France" (NUC). ¶ *Waldon also has an entry for* The importance and advantage of Cape Breton truly and impartially considered. *London, 1757, but concedes that possibly the date "is an error for 1746." NUC has an entry for a "microcard edition" (undated) of this 1746 edition. ¶ A different work from* The importance of Cape Breton consider'd, *1746, and* The importance of Cape Breton to the British Nation, *1745, both by Robert Auchmuty, q.v. ¶ NSWA · OTP · OKQ · BVAU*

outre, *Waldon présente une notice pour* The importance and advantage of Cape Breton truly and impartially considered. *Londres, 1757, mais admet la possibilité d'une erreur, la présente date étant indiquée « au lieu de 1746 ». Le NUC donne une notice pour une « reproduction sur microfiches » (non datée) de cette édition de 1746. ¶ Constitue un ouvrage distinct des deux écrits de Robert Auchmuty, q.v., soit* The importance of Cape Breton consider'd, *1746, et* The importance of Cape Breton to the British Nation, *1745. ¶ NSWA · OTP · OKQ · BVAU*

A description of the coast, tides, and currents, in Button's Bay and in the [Roes] Welcome: being the north-west coast of Hudson's Bay, from Churchill River, in 58° 56′ north latitude, to Wager River or strait, in 65° 24′ taken from Scrog's [*sic*], Crow's, Napier's [*sic*], and Smith's journals, made in the years 1722, 1737, 1740, 1742, 1743, and 1744. Also, from the discoveries made in 1742, in the voyage in the Furnace Bomb, and Discovery Pink, commanded by Captain Middleton and Captain Moor; shewing from these journals, a probability, that there is a passage from thence to the Western Ocean of America. London, printed for J[acob]. Robinson, at the Golden Lion in Ludgate-street. [1746.] 24 p. 8°

NUC(Pre–56)140:328*

The date is from Waldon; NUC has a shorter title and [1745?], and BM has [1750], but presumably all the same edition. ¶ Half the pamphlet is devoted to Middleton's voyage (q.v., 1743), the author supporting the Dobbs viewpoint (see Middleton and Dobbs, 1744–45). ¶ Another edition the same year: next entry.

La date est de Waldon ; le NUC présente un titre plus court et répertorie cet ouvrage sous [1745 ?], tandis que BM indique [1750], mais on suppose qu'il s'agit de la même édition. ¶ La moitié du pamphlet est consacrée au voyage de Middleton (q.v., 1743), l'auteur appuyant le point de vue de Dobbs (voir Middleton et Dobbs, 1744–1745). ¶ Une autre édition la même année : notice suivante.

A description of the coast, tides, and currents, in Button's Bay . . . . Dublin: printed in the year 1746. 27 p. 8°

For notes, see *preceding entry.*   Voir *notes à la notice précédente.*

- - -

The great importance of Cape Breton, demonstrated and exemplified, by extracts from the best writers, French and English, who have treated of that colony. The whole containing, besides the most accurate descriptions of the place, a series of the arguments that induced the French court to settle and fortify it; the plan laid down for making the establishment, and the great progress made in execution of that plan: with the reasons that induced the people of New-England to subdue this formidable and dangerous rival, and that should determine the British nation never to part with it again, on any consideration whatever. In this pamphlet is included all that Father Charlevoix says of this island in his celebrated History of New-France, lately published, in three volumes in quarto, and Savary, in his Dictionary of commerce, (a new edition of which was not long since published, in French likewise, in four volumes folio.) Also additional remarks by the compiler, with a map and plan from Charlevoix, and references giving a distinct idea of the siege. London, printed for John Brindley, and sold by C[harles]. Corbett; M[ary]. Cooper; and by the booksellers and pamphlet shops of London and Westminster, 1746. viii, 72 p. fold. map. 8°(in 4s).

NUC(Pre–56)216:174

"A map of the Island of Cape Breton, with Part of Newfoundland, Acadia, St. Lawrence's Bay, &c. and a Plan of the City and Port of Louisbourg." ¶ *OTP*

« Une carte de l'île du Cap-Breton, montrant une partie de Terre-Neuve, de l'Acadie, du golfe du Saint-Laurent, etc., et un plan de la ville et du port de Louisbourg ». ¶ *OTP*

Pepperell, Sir William, 1696–1759. An accurate journal and account of the proceedings of the New-England land-forces, during the late expedition against the French settlements on Cape Breton, to the time of the surrender of Louisbourg. Containing a just representation of the transactions and occurrences, and of the behaviour of the said forces. Dated, Louisbourg, Oct. 20, 1745, and in form attested by Lieut. General Pepperell, commander in chief of the forces, Brigad. General Waldo, Col. Moore, Lieut. Col. Lothrop, and Lieut. Col. Gridley of the train of artillery; all under their own hands. Exhibiting a more authentic, correct, and perfect account, than any before made publick. With a computation of the French fishery on the Banks of Newfoundland, Acadia, Cape Breton, and neighbouring shores, gulphs, harbours, &c. as it was carried on before the present war: the whole of which did then depend, in a great manner, on the port of Louisbourg, as a cover and protection to it, &c. All sent over, by General Pepperell himself, to his friend, Capt. Hen. Stafford, at Exmouth, Devon. Printed from the original manuscript, at the desire of Capt. Stafford, as well in justice to the general, as for the better information of the publick. Exon [*i.e.*, Exeter], printed by and for A[ndrew]. and S. Brice and sold by M[ary]. Cooper, in London, 1746. Price 6d. 40 p. 8°

NUC(Pre–56)449:540

Entered under title in NUC(Pre–56) 2:598, as also in JCB(1)3:824, but this must be the same work. ¶ The expedition was of New England land forces under Pepperell in 1745, against Louisbourg; the fortress fell, but was restored to France under the Treaty of Aix-la-Chapelle (Aachen), which ended the War of the Austrian Succession in Europe. ¶ Prepared at the behest of the Massachusetts colonial government, under the direction of Gov. William Shirley at the time of his visit to Louisbourg, Aug.–Oct. 1745, it was, in Shirley's words, "the joint account of the commanding officers of the three colonies, and settled by the agreement of 'em all," attested by signatures of Pepperell and four others: cf. "William Shirley to Benning Wentworth," a letter dated Boston, 1 January 1745, in Mass. Hist. Soc. Collections, 6th ser., vol. 10, p. 418. ¶ This is apparently the first

Répertorié selon le titre dans le NUC (Pre–56)2:598, ainsi qu'au JCB(1)3:824, mais il doit s'agir du même ouvrage. ¶ L'expédition contre Louisbourg fut menée par les forces terrestres de la Nouvelle-Angleterre sous le commandement de Pepperell en 1745 ; la forteresse tomba mais fut rendue à la France en vertu du traité d'Aix-la-Chapelle (Aachen en allemand), qui mit fin à la guerre de la Succession d'Autriche en Europe. ¶ Rédigé sur l'ordre du gouvernement colonial du Massachusetts, sous la direction du gouverneur William Shirley à l'époque de sa visite à Louisbourg, du mois d'août au mois d'octobre 1745, ce fut, au dire de Shirley, « le récit conjoint des chefs militaires des trois colonies, auquel tous les intéressés ont donné leur consentement », ce dont les signatures de Pepperell et de quatre autres personnes attestent : cf. « William Shirley to Benning Wentworth », lettre datée du 1ᵉʳ de janvier 1745 à Boston et se trouvant dans les Collections de la Mass. Hist. Soc., 6ᵉ coll., vol. 10, p. 418. ¶ Il s'agit,

printed edition of the account, published in Apr. 1746. It was next issued as an appendix to A letter from William Shirley . . . to . . . the Duke of Newcastle. *London, 1746, etc. (cf. NUC). Another ed.: London, 1758, with title:* An accurate and authentic account, *q.v.* ¶ *OTP*

semble-t-il, de la première édition imprimée du récit, qui a été publiée au mois d'avril 1746. Elle fut ensuite publiée comme annexe à A letter from William Shirley . . . to . . . the Duke of Newcastle. *Londres, 1746, etc. (cf. NUC). Autre éd.: Londres, 1758, intitulée:* An accurate and authentic account, *q.v.* ¶ *OTP*

[Philolaos], *pseud.* Two letters, concerning some farther advantages and improvements that may seem necessary to be made on the taking and keeping of Cape Breton. Humbly offer'd to public consideration. London: printed in the year 1746. 12 p. 12°

NUC(Pre–56)456:339

Addressed: "To the Author of the Tradesman's Journal"; signed: "Philolaos."

Adressées: « À l'auteur du Tradesman's Journal »; signées: « Philolaos ».

Prince, Thomas, 1687–1758. Extraordinary events the doings of God, and marvelous in pious eyes. Illustrated in a sermon at the South church in Boston, N. E. on the general thanksgiving, Thursday, July 18, 1745. Occasion'd by taking the city of Louisbourg on the isle of Cape-Breton, by New-England soldiers, assisted by a British squadron. By Thomas Prince . . . . Boston, printed; London, reprinted and sold by J[ohn]. Lewis [etc.], 1746. 32 p. 8°

NUC(Pre–56)471:453*

Waldon has some title variations, including "Boston, (New-England)," "City of Louisburg," and collation as: 1 p.l., [5]–32 p., which she says includes a half-title probably wanting in other copies. ¶ *First edition: Boston (N. E.), 1745; the second to fifth eds. all have edition number on t.-p., and imprint:*

Waldon relève quelques variantes du titre, notamment « Boston, (New-England) », « City of Louisburg », et établit la collation suivante: 1 f. l., [5]–32 p., qui comprend à son avis un faux-titre probablement manquant dans d'autres exemplaires. ¶ *Première édition: Boston (N.-A.), 1745; les éd. ultérieures, de la deuxième à la cinquième, comportent toutes un*

Boston, printed, London, reprinted, sold by J. Lewis, 1746 (q.v., following); and Edinburgh, 1746 (q.v.). Subsequent editions in NUC all pub. in Boston. ¶ BVAU

numéro d'édition sur la p. de t., ainsi qu'une adresse bibliographique : Boston, printed, London, reprinted, sold by J. Lewis, 1746 (q.v. ci-dessous) ; et Édimbourg, 1746 (q.v.). Toutes les éditions ultérieures répertoriées au NUC furent publiées à Boston. ¶ BVAU

Prince, Thomas, 1687–1758. Extraordinary events the doings of God.... By Thomas Prince.... 2d ed. Boston, printed: London, reprinted; and sold by J[ohn]. Lewis, 1746. 32 p. 8°

NUC(Pre–56)471:453*

Format from Sabin:65596. ¶ See the *preceding edition for other notes.* ¶ NSWA

Format d'après le Sabin:65596. ¶ Voir *notes dans l'édition précédente.* ¶ NSWA

*Prince, Thomas, 1687–1758. Extraordinary events the doings of God.... By Thomas Prince.... 3d ed. Boston, printed: London, reprinted; and sold by J[ohn]. Lewis, 1746. 32 p. 8°

NUC(Pre–56)471:453*

For a fuller title, and notes, *see* preceding entries. ¶ OTP

Voir notes et titre plus complet aux notices précédentes. ¶ OTP

*Prince, Thomas, 1687–1758.   Extraordinary events the doings of God . . . . By Thomas Prince. The 4th ed. Boston, printed; London, reprinted; and sold by J[ohn]. Lewis, in Bartholomew-close, near West-Smithfield; and at the pamphlet shops in London and Westminster, 1746. <Price four-pence.> 32 p. 8°

NUC(Pre–56)471:453*

For fuller title, and notes, *see* preceding entries.	*Voir* notes et titre plus complet aux notices précédentes.

*Prince, Thomas, 1687–1758.   Extraordinary events . . . in a sermon at . . . Boston, (New-England) . . . . By Thomas Prince . . . . 5th ed. Boston, printed: London reprinted; and sold by J[ohn]. Lewis, 1746. 32 p. 8°

NUC(Pre–56)471:454*

For a fuller title, and notes, *see* preceding entries.	*Voir* notes et titre plus complet aux notices précédentes.

Prince, Thomas, 1687–1758.   Extraordinary events . . . in a sermon at . . . Boston, N. E. . . . . By Thomas Prince . . . . Edinburgh, printed by R[obert]. Fleming and Company, 1746. 3 p.l., [5]–38 p. 8°

NUC(Pre–56)471:454*

For a fuller title, and notes, see *preceding entries.*	Voir *notes et titre plus complet aux notices précédentes.*

Shirley, William, 1694–1771. A letter from William Shirley, Esq.; governor of Massachuset's Bay, to his Grace the Duke of Newcastle: with a Journal of the Siege of Louisbourg, and other operations of the forces, during the expedition against the French settlements on Cape Breton; drawn up at the desire of the Council and House of Representatives of the Province of Massachuset's Bay; approved and attested by Sir William Pepperrell, and the other principal officers who commanded in the said expedition. Published by authority. London: printed by E[dward]. Owen, 1746. (Price six-pence.) 32 p. 8°(in 4s).

NUC(Pre–56)544:190*

Signatures of subscribers to attest the truth of this account, at end: Wm. Pepperrell, S. Waldo, Sam. Moore, Simon Lothrop, Richard Gudley. ¶ *Concerns the Siege of Louisbourg, 1745.* ¶ Reprinted twice in Boston, 1746, and in New York the same year, and in London, 1748, *q.v.* "Letters relating to the expedition against Cape Breton (1744–52), including Shirley's instructions to Pepperrell, and several letters signed 'W. Shirley' and 'W. Pepperrell,' " were published in the Mass. Hist. Soc. Coll., Boston, 1792, v. 1, p. 5; this was reprinted 1806.

En apposant leur signature à la fin du document, les signataires attestèrent de la véracité de ce récit : Wm. Pepperrell, S. Waldo, Sam. Moore, Simon Lothrop, Richard Gudley. ¶ *Traite du siège de Louisbourg, 1745.* ¶ Réimprimé à deux reprises à Boston, 1746, ainsi qu'à New York la même année, puis à Londres, 1748, *q.v.* Des « Letters relating to the expedition against Cape Breton (1744–52), including Shirley's instructions to Pepperrell, and several letters signed ' W. Shirley ' and ' W. Pepperrell ' » furent publiées dans la collection de la Mass. Hist. Soc., Boston, 1792, vol. 1, p. 5 ; réimpression en 1806.

1747

Colden, Cadwallader, 1688–1776. The history of the Five Indian nations of Canada, which are dependent on the province of New-York in America, and are the barrier between the English and French in that part of the world. With accounts of their religion, manners, customs, laws, and forms of government; their several battles and treaties with the European nations; particular relations of their several wars with the other Indians; and a true account of the present state of our trade with them. In which are shewn the great advantage of their trade and alliance to the British nation, and the intrigues and attempts of the French to engage them from us; a subject nearly concerning all our American plantations, and highly meriting the consideration of the British nation at this juncture. By the Honourable Cadwallader Colden, Esq; one of his Majesty's counsel, and surveyor-general of New York. To which are added, accounts of the several other nations of Indians in North-America, their numbers, strength, &c. and the treaties which have been lately made with them. A work highly entertaining to all, and particularly useful to the persons who have any trade or concern in that part of the world. London: printed for T[homas]. Osborne, 1747. xvi, [4], 90, iv, 91–204, 283 p. front. (fold. map). 8°

NUC(Pre–56)114:531*

For list of contents, see NUC entry. ¶ The first historical work printed in New York and the first general history of the Iroquois Indians (cf. Church, v. 4, p. 1867). ¶ *The Iroquois, or Five (later Six) Nations Indians, were the barrier between the English and French on the New York–New France frontier.* ¶ First pub., with shorter title, as: *The history of the five Indian nations depending on the province of New-York in America.* New York: printed and sold by W[illiam]. Bradford, 1727. 1 p.l., xvii, [i], 119 p. (NUC(Pre–56)114:531), a facsim. of which was pub. "With an introduction and notes by John Gilmary Shea. New York, T. H. Morrell, 1866"; other eds. 1750, 1755 (*q.v.*),

Voir *la liste des titres à la notice du NUC.* ¶ Le premier ouvrage d'histoire imprimé à New York et la première histoire générale des Iroquois (cf. Church, vol. 4, p. 1867). ¶ *Les Iroquois, qui s'étaient regroupés en une confédération appelée les Cinq-Nations (laquelle deviendra plus tard les Six-Nations), servaient de tampon entre les Anglais et les Français dans les régions frontalières entre le territoire de New York et la Nouvelle France.* ¶ Première publ. sous le titre abrégé : *The history of the five Indian nations depending on the province of New-York in America.* New York : imprimé et vendu par W[illiam]. Bradford, 1727. 1 f. l., xvii, [i], 119 p. (NUC(Pre–56)114:531), dont un facsimilé fut publié : « With an introduction and notes by John Gilmary Shea. New York. T.H. Morrell, 1866 » ;

and later editions. ¶ *NSWA · OTP · BVAU · BVIPA · BVILSB*

autres éd. 1750, 1755 (*q.v.*), ainsi que des éditions ultérieures. ¶ *NSWA · OTP · BVAU · BVIPA · BVILSB*

*Galvão, Antonio, *d./déc.* 1557. The discoveries of the world . . . . Corrected . . . and . . . published . . . by Richard Hakluyt. London, 1747. (In [Thomas Osborne], *A collection of voyages and travels*, vol. 2, p. 353–402.)

NUC(Pre–56)190:64*

First pub.: London, 1601, *q.v.* for notes and other editions.

Première publ. : Londres, 1601, *q.v.* pour des notes et d'autres éditions.

*Great Britain. Laws, statutes, etc., 1625–1649 (Charles I). A commission for the well-governing of our people inhabiting in Newfoundland . . . . London, 1747. (In [Thomas Osborne], *A collection of voyages and travels*, vol. 2, p. [783]–85. map.)

NUC(Pre–56)213:437*

First pub. 1634, *q.v.* for other variants and editions.

Première publ. 1634, *q.v.* pour d'autres variantes et éditions.

[Osborne, Thomas], *d./déc.* 1767, *comp.* A collection of voyages and travels . . . . London, Thomas Osborne, 1747. 2 v. front., illus., plates (part fold.), maps (part fold.), tables. fol.

NUC(Pre–56)434:44*

Reissue of the 1745 edition, with new t.-p. ¶ *First edition: 1745, q.v. for a fuller title and contents notes, one of which describes this as vol. 7–8 of A. and J. Churchill's* Collection of voyages; *a microfiche format of this edition was issued by the Toronto Public Library in its Canadiana series, about 1960, and the 1747 is there called the second ed.; another edition: 1752, q.v.*

Nouveau tirage de l'édition de 1745, avec une nouvelle p. de t. ¶ *Première édition : 1745, q.v. pour un titre plus complet et plusieurs notes sur le contenu. L'une des notes en question désigne cet ouvrage comme les vol. 7 et 8 de* Collection of voyages *par A. et J. Churchill ; vers 1960, la Toronto Public Library a fait paraître cette édition sur microfiche dans la collection Canadiana, dans laquelle l'édition de 1747 est appelée Deuxième éd. ; autre édition : 1752, q.v.*

1748

*The British merchant: containing the sentiments of the most eminent and judicious merchants of the city of London, concerning the trade and commerce of these kingdoms; more particularly that which relates to France, Spain, and Portugal . . . . Originally composed by a body of merchants, and pub. by Mr. Charles King . . . . 3d ed. London, T[homas?]. Osborn, 1748. 3 v. 8°(?)

NUC(Pre–56)76:436*

See first ed., 1721, for other notes.

Voir notes à la première éd., 1721.

Ellis, Henry, 1721–1806. A voyage to Hudson's-Bay, by the Dobbs galley and California, in the years 1746 and 1747, for discovering a North west passage; with an accurate survey of the coast, and a short natural history of the country. Together with a fair view of the facts and arguments from which the future finding of such a passage is rendered probable. By Henry Ellis, gent., agent for the proprietors in the said expedition. To which is prefixed, an historical account of the attempts hitherto made for the finding a passage that way to the East-Indies. Illustrated with proper cuts, and a new and correct chart of Hudson's Bay, with the countries adjacent. London: printed for H[enry]. Whitridge, 1748. xxviii, 336 p. front. (fold. map), 9 plates (1 double, 3 fold.). 8°

NUC(Pre–56)158:501*

Further to this is: James Isham, Observations on Hudson's Bay, 1743, and Notes and observations on a book entitled A voyage to Hudson's Bay. Toronto, Champlain Society, 1949 (but from contemporary originals). ¶ Ellis here publishes the results of William Moor's voyage of 1746 (see notes to Christopher Middleton, A vindication of the conduct . . . . London, 1743). ¶ Ellis speaks with "much Assurance of the Probability and Possibility of determining by another Expedition" the much desired passage. ¶ First edition; second ed., 1749 (q.v.), and another ed., Dublin, 1749 (q.v.); also a Dutch transl., Leiden, 1750; a German transl., Goettingen, 1750; and three French transls., Paris, 1749, and another of Leide, 1750; it also appeared in The world displayed. London, 1762–90 (etc.), vol. 10 (1773), p. [203]–258. ¶ OKQ · OTP · BVAU · BVIPA

Cet ouvrage fut suivi de Observations on Hudson's Bay, 1743, and Notes and observations on a book entitled A voyage to Hudson's Bay. Toronto, Champlain Society, 1949 (néanmoins d'après des originaux d'époque), de James Isham. ¶ Dans son ouvrage, Ellis fait connaître au public les résultats de la traversée de William Moor en 1746 (voir les notes sous Christopher Middleton, A vindication of the conduct . . . . Londres, 1743). ¶ Ellis parle avec « beaucoup d'assurance de la probabilité et de la possibilité qu'une autre expédition permette de trouver » le passage tant désiré. ¶ Première édition ; deuxième éd., 1749 (q.v.), et une autre éd., Dublin, 1749 (q.v.) ; également une traduction hollandaise, Leiden, 1750 ; une trad. allemande, Goettingen, 1750 ; et trois trad. françaises, Paris, 1749, auxquelles s'ajoute celle de Leide, 1750 ; de plus, parution dans The world displayed. Londres, 1762–1790 (etc.), vol. 10 (1773), p. [203]–258. ¶ OKQ · OTP · BVAU · BVIPA

*The English pilot; describing the West-India navigation from Hudson's Bay . . . .
London, 1748. vol. 4. fol.(?)

NUC(Pre–56)160:374*

First edition: 1689, *q.v.* for other editions; the 1706 edition has a similar title, and is more fully transcribed.

Première édition : 1689, *q.v.* pour d'autres éditions ; l'édition de 1706 a un titre identique et a fait l'objet d'une transcription plus complète.

Great Britain. Lords Justices. By the Lords Justices, a proclamation . . . . Whereas Preliminaries for restoring a General Peace were signed at Aix la Chapelle . . . . London; printed by Thomas Baskett . . . and by the assigns of Robert Baskett. 1748. Broadside. fol.

NUC(Pre–56)214:117

The Peace of Aix-la-Chapelle (Aachen), October 1748, ended the War of the Austrian Succession. ¶ Reprinted: Philadelphia, Benjamin Franklin, 1748.

Le traité de paix d'Aix-la-Chapelle (Aachen), octobre 1748, mit fin à la guerre de la Succession d'Autriche. ¶ Réimpression : Philadelphie, Benjamin Franklin, 1748.

Great Britain. Treaties, etc., 1727–1760 (George II). The definitive treaty of Christian, universal, and perpetual peace, friendship and union, concluded at Aix-la-Chapelle, on the 7/18th October, 1748. Between the crowns of Great-Britain and France, and the States General of the United Provinces; and afterwards acceded to by the powers interested in the war, thereby put an end to. Together with a translation of the Acts of cession of the Empress Queen, and King of Sardinia, as they stand in this treaty, the former in Latin, and the latter in the Italian language; and also the separate articles annexed to the said treaty. London: printed by E[dward]. Say, in Ave-Mary-Lane, 1748. 1 p.l., 25 p. 8°

NUC(Pre–56)215:511*

Refers to the Peace of Aix-la-Chapelle (or Aachen), 18 October (N. S.) 1748, under which Britain returned Louisbourg to France. ¶ Reprinted London, 1749 (q.v.), and in Boston, Mass., 1749, 23 p., 16°, and in a microcard edition about 1950 (cf. NUC).

Mentionne le traité de paix d'Aix-la-Chapelle (ou Aachen), 18 octobre (c.g.) 1748, en vertu duquel la Grande-Bretagne rendit Louisbourg à la France. ¶ Réimprimé à Londres, 1749 (q.v.), et à Boston (Mass.), 1749, 23 p., in–16°, puis reproduit sur microcarte vers 1950 (cf. NUC).

Hudson's Bay Company. The case of the Hudson's-Bay Company. [London, 1748?] 3, [1] p. fol.

NUC(Pre–56)258:448

Caption title. ¶ This may be the same work as in the similar entry under 1749 (q.v.), to which Waldon gives the imprint, from BLC: [London, 1749?]. ¶ Argues in support of the Company's claim to exclusive right of trade. ¶ See also other works relating to this controversy under 1690, and the notes appended to those entries (which refer to other publication dates also).

Titre de départ. ¶ Cet ouvrage est peut-être le même que celui dont il est question dans la notice identique sous 1749 (q.v.), et auquel Waldon attribue l'adresse bibliographique provenant du BLC : [Londres, 1749 ?]. ¶ Présente des arguments à l'appui de la demande de la Compagnie pour l'obtention d'un droit de commerce exclusif. ¶ Voir aussi d'autres ouvrages sous 1690 concernant cette controverse, ainsi que les notes annexées à ces notices (qui renvoient aussi à d'autres dates de publication).

*Hudson's Bay Company. A short view of the countries and trade carried on by the Company in Hudson's Bay; shewing the prejudice of that exclusive trade, and benefit which will accrue to Great Britain, by opening and extending that trade, etc. [London, 1748?] Broadside? fol.

BLC(to 1975)154:302

BLC does not indicate pagination. ¶ *See also* other works relating to this controversy under 1690, and the notes appended to those entries (which refer to other publication dates also).

Le BLC ne fournit aucune indication de pagination. ¶ *Voir aussi* d'autres ouvrages sous 1690 au sujet de cette controverse, ainsi que les notes annexées à ces notices (qui renvoient en outre à d'autres dates de publication).

---

*Jones, John, 1700–1770. A letter to a friend in the country, upon the news of the town. London, J. Raymond [1748]. 47 p. 8°(?)

NUC(Pre–56)284:45*

For notes, *see* the 1755 edition.

Voir notes à l'édition de 1755.

A letter from a gentleman in London to his friend in the country, concerning the treaty at Aix-la-Chapelle, concluded on the 8th of October, 1748. London, printed for W. Webb, near St. Paul's, 1748. <Price one shilling.> 1 p.l., 45 p. 8°(in 4s).

NUC(Pre–56)328:660

The writer denounces all the terms of the Treaty [ending the Austrian Succession War] as advantageous to France. Though the English were defeated by land, their success at sea should have brought better terms. Cape Breton is "infinitely more valuable than all the Conquests made by France" and should not be given up. [Louisbourg *was* returned to France.]

L'auteur dénonce toutes les conditions du traité [qui mit fin à la guerre de la Succession d'Autriche] parce qu'il donne l'avantage à la France. Bien que les Anglais furent défaits sur terre, leurs succès maritimes auraient dû amener de meilleures conditions. Le Cap-Breton a « infiniment plus de valeur que toutes les conquêtes remportées par la France » et ne doit pas être abandonné. [Louisbourg *fut* rendue à la France.]

[Little, Otis], 1712–1754. The state of trade in the northern colonies considered; with an account of their produce, and a particular description of Nova Scotia . . . . London: printed by G[eorge]. Woodfall at the King's Arms, near Charing-Cross. 1748. 84 p. 8°

NUC(Pre–56)336:214*

Waldon has collation: t.-p., [v]–viii, [9]–84 p.; NUC has: viii, [9]–84 p. ¶ Preface signed: Otis Little. ¶ Points out the value of the North American colonies and the desirability of encouraging trade with them, and recommends the fortifying and settlement of Nova Scotia. ¶ *Reprinted: Boston [New England], 1749 (Hazard pamphlets, v. 24, no. 2), and in facsimile: Boston, 1937 (Photostat Americana, 2d series; Mass. Hist. Soc., no. 32), and in the Readex Microprint edition of Early American Imprints, Worcester, Mass., American Antiquarian Soc. (cf. NUC). ¶ NSWA · OTU*

Collation de Waldon : p. de t., [v]–viii, [9]–84p.; collation du NUC : viii, [9]–84 p.¶ Avant-propos signé par Otis Little. ¶ Souligne la valeur des colonies nord-américaines et l'intérêt d'encourager le commerce avec elles ; recommande en outre de coloniser la Nouvelle-Écosse et d'y établir des places fortes. ¶ *Réimpressions : Boston [Nouvelle-Angleterre], 1749 (Hazard pamphlets, vol. 24, n° 2), et Boston, 1937, en facsimilé (Photostat Americana, deuxième collection ; Mass. Hist. Soc., n° 32), ainsi que dans l'édition Readex Microprint, Early American Imprints, Worcester (Mass.), American Antiquarian Soc. (cf. NUC). ¶ NSWA · OTU*

National prejudice, opposed to the national interest, candidly considered in the detention or yielding up Gibraltar and Cape-Breton by the ensuing treaty of peace: with some observations on the natural jealousy of the Spanish nation, and how far it may operate to the prejudice of the British commerce if not removed at this crisis. In a letter to Sir John Barnard, knight. London, printed for W[illiam]. Owen [etc.], 1748. 2 p.l., 9–50 p. 8°

NUC(Pre–56)407:412

Half-title and t.-p.: 2 p.l. ¶ The "ensuing treaty of peace" was the Peace of Aix-la-Chapelle (or Aachen), 18 Oct. 1748, ending the Austrian Succession War. ¶ The writer urges that both conquests be given up for the sake of peace.

Faux-titre et p. de t. : 2 f. l. ¶ Le « traité de paix qui s'ensuivit » fut celui d'Aix-la-Chapelle (ou d'Aachen), 18 octobre 1748, qui mit fin à la guerre de la Succession d'Autriche. ¶ L'auteur recommande instamment d'abandonner les deux conquêtes en question dans l'intérêt de

Unless the French can be driven from Canada, Cape Breton is useless.

la paix. À moins de bouter les Français hors du Canada, le Cap-Breton ne présente aucune espèce d'utilité.

Observations on the probable issue of the congress at Aix la Chapelle. In a letter to a friend . . . . London, printed for R[ichard]. Montagu, and sold by M[ary]. Cooper, 1748. <Price one shilling.> 52 p. 8°

NUC(Pre–56)426:64

Cape Breton: p. 11–15. ¶ Whatever is done, peace or war, whatever the terms, the ministry will be criticized. Cape Breton (like everything else) will be valuable if given up, but worthless if kept. ¶ *Refers to the Peace of Aix-la-Chapelle (or Aachen), 18 Oct. 1748, which ended the Austrian Succession War.*

Cap-Breton : p. 11–15. ¶ Quoiqu'on fasse, la paix ou la guerre, quelles que soient les conditions, le gouvernement sera critiqué. Le Cap-Breton (comme tout le reste) deviendra précieux si on l'abandonne, mais sans aucun intérêt si on le garde. ¶ *Concerne le traité d'Aix-la-Chapelle (ou d'Aachen) du 18 octobre 1748, qui mit fin à la guerre de la Succession d'Autriche.*

The pr...t...st of the m....ch....ts of G...t B.....n, against the pr..l..m.....ry a..t.....s for a peace, lately signed at A..x-la-Ch...pp...le. London: printed for R. Freeman, 1748. 2 p.l., 23 p. 8°

NUC(Pre–56)468:614

Amplified title: The protest of the merchants of Great Britain against the preliminary articles for a peace, lately signed at Aix-la-Chappelle. ¶ Refers to the Peace of Aix-la-Chapelle (or Aachen), Oct. 1748. ¶ Relates chiefly to the settlement in America. The writer considers that Peace should have

Titre restitué : The protest of the merchants of Great Britain against the preliminary articles for a peace, lately signed at Aix-la-Chappelle. ¶ Se rapporte au traité d'Aix-la-Chapelle (ou d'Aachen), octobre 1748. ¶ Traite principalement de la colonisation en Amérique. L'auteur considère que le traité aurait dû comporter « un article donné, reconnaissant

included "some Article, acknowledging the sole Right of Possession in the Crown of G—t B—n, of all that Territory called Nova Scotia, or Accadie, in North America, together with all the Dominions thereto belonging": p. 11. ¶ OONL · NBFL · OOA · OTP · AEU

à la Couronne de G——e-B——e le droit de possession exclusif de tout le territoire nommé Nouvelle-Écosse, ou Acadie, en Amérique du Nord, aussi bien que de toutes les colonies qui appartiennent à ce territoire » : p. 11. ¶ OONL · NBFL · OOA · OTP · AEU

The preliminaries productive of a premunire: or, Old England caught in a trap. Plainly shewing, by observations on every particular article of the preliminary treaty of Convention, how far it is conducive to the welfare and advantage of Great Britain, or subservient to the interests of other powers. With some particular remarks on ... the Assiento treaty ... to be considered ... by all merchants, or others that have an interest in commerce .... London: printed for H[enry]. Carpenter [1748?]. (Price one shilling.) 52 p. 8°

NUC(Pre–56)469:610

The treaty under consideration became known as the Treaty of Aix-la-Chapelle (or Aachen, 1748) ending the Austrian Succession War, and it included the renewal of the Asiento (British monopoly of the slave trade with the Spanish colonies). ¶ The war has been mismanaged by a corrupt administration which is now making a detrimental peace. The author denounces the cession of Cape Breton, but is chiefly concerned with the settlement in Europe.

Le traité dont il est question devint connu comme le traité d'Aix-la-Chapelle (ou d'Aachen, 1748) qui mit fin à la guerre de la Succession d'Autriche ; il stipulait le renouvellement de l'asiento (monopole britannique de la traite des esclaves dans les colonies espagnoles). ¶ La guerre a été mal conduite par une administration corrompue qui est en train de conclure un traité préjudiciable. L'auteur dénonce la cession du Cap-Breton, mais il se soucie surtout du règlement visant l'Europe.

Shirley, William, 1694–1771. A letter from William Shirley, esq. . . . London: printed by E[dward]. Owen, 1748. 32 p. plan. 8°

Sabin:80549

For the first ed., and the complete title (same as the 1748 ed.) and notes, *see* 1746.

Pour la première éd., ainsi que pour le titre complet (identique au titre de l'éd. de 1748) et des notes, *voir* 1746.

A short view of the countries and trade carried on by the company in Hudson's-Bay; shewing the prejudice of that exclusive trade, and benefit which will accrue to Great-Britain, by opening and extending that trade, and settling those countries. [London, 1748?] 3 p. fol.

NUC(Pre–56)544:453

Waldon has imprint, without brackets: London, 1749? But NUC and BLC have as above. ¶ Endorsed with above title: p. 4.

Adresse bibliographique indiquée par Waldon, sans crochets : Londres, 1749 ? En revanche, l'adresse ci-dessus figure dans le NUC et le BLC. ¶ Inscription officielle tirée du titre susmentionné : p. 4.

*The state of the nation, with a general balance of the publick accounts . . . . London, printed for M[ary]. Cooper, 1748. 2 p.l., 55 p. fold. tab. 8°

NUC(Pre–56)565:328*

Refers mainly to the cost of the War of the Austrian Succession (between England and France, etc.), and the Treaty of Aix-la-Chapelle (or Peace of Aachen), in which England returned Louisbourg to France. ¶

Traite principalement des dépenses de la guerre de la Succession d'Autriche (entre l'Angleterre et la France, etc.), et du traité d'Aix-la-Chapelle (ou traité de paix d'Aachen), par lequel l'Angleterre rendit Louisbourg à la France. ¶ Première édition ;

First edition; a second ed. appeared the same year (*see* next entry), and another: Dublin, 1749, *q.v.*

une deuxième éd. parut la même année (*voir* la notice suivante), puis une autre : Dublin, 1749, *q.v.*

*The state of the nation with a general balance of the publick accounts. Ed. 2 [*sic*] London, [Mary] Cooper, 1748. 55 p. 8°(?)

NUC(Pre–56)565:328*

The "Ed. 2" in NUC is assumed to mean "2d edition." ¶ For other notes, *see* preceding entry.

On présume que la mention « Ed. 2 » dans le NUC signifie « 2ᵉ édition ». ¶ *Voir* d'autres notes à la notice précédente.

1748–49

Swaine, Charles, *fl.* 1746–1766, *supposed author/auteur présumé.* An account of a voyage for the discovery of a North-West Passage by Hudson's Streights, to the Western and Southern Ocean of America. Performed in the year 1746 and 1747, in the ship California, Capt. Francis Smith, commander. By the clerk of the California. Adorned with cuts and maps. London, printed; and sold by Mr. [John] Jolliffe, in St. James's-street; Mr. [Charles?] Corbett, in Fleet-street; and Mr. [John] Clarke, under the Royal Exchange. 1748[–49]. 2 v.: 1 p.l., vii, 237 p.; 1 p.l., 326, 18 p. 4 plates, 5 fold. maps. 8°

NUC(Pre–56)578:95* and 148:362*

NUC cites evidence for Swaine as clerk of the California, *but notes one authority who names Theodorus Swaine Drage as the clerk of the* California. ¶ *Imprint,*

Le NUC cite des documents tendant à prouver que Swaine était greffier à bord du California, *mais signale une source qui désigne le greffier du* California *sous le nom Theodorus Swaine*

vol. 2, has addition: "And Mr. R[obert]. Baldwin, Jun. in Pater-Noster-Row." ¶ Index: 18 p. at end. NUC has: 3 plates (1 fold.). ¶ This expedition was sent out as a result of the Dobbs-Middleton controversy [*see* notes under: Christopher Middleton, *A vindication*, 1743, and Arthur Dobbs, *An account*, 1744]. Middleton's statements were proved correct. ¶ *This appeared in microfiche in the Canadiana in the Toronto Public Library series, about 1970; another issue; see next entry; Waldon also has an edition of two vols., both pub. London, 1749, with six maps, four plates, otherwise apparently identical.* ¶ *OTP · BVAU · BVIPA*

Drage. ¶ L'adresse bibliographique, vol. 2, comporte un ajout : « And Mr. R[obert]. Baldwin, Jun. in Pater-Noster-Row ». ¶ Index : 18 p. à la fin. Indication du NUC : 3 planches (1 pliée). ¶ Cette expédition fut mise sur pied à la suite de la querelle Dobbs-Middleton [*voir* les notes sous : Christopher Middleton, *A vindication*, 1743, et Arthur Dobbs, *An account*, 1744]. La justesse des déclarations de Middleton fut prouvée. ¶ *Cet ouvrage a été reproduit sur microfiche dans la collection Canadiana de la Toronto Public Library vers 1970 ; autre édition : voir la notice suivante ; Waldon signale également une édition en deux vol., comportant quatre planches et six cartes, lesquelles différencient cette édition de la précédente, toutes deux publiées à Londres en 1749.* ¶ *OTP · BVAU · BVIPA*

Swaine, Charles, *fl.* 1746–1766, *supposed author/auteur présumé*. An account of a voyage for the discovery of a North-West Passage . . . . By the clerk of the California. Adorned with cuts and maps. London: Jonah Warens, 1748[–49]. 2 v.: 2 p.l., vii, 237; 1 p.l., 326 p., 9 l. 4 plates, 5 maps. 8°

Sabin:20808

In her note to the preceding entry, Waldon notes that apart from the imprint this is identical.

Dans sa note à la notice précédente, Waldon signale que les deux notices sont identiques, si ce n'est de l'adresse bibliographique.

1749

The advantages of the Definitive treaty, to the people of Great-Britain, demonstrated. To which is added, a copy of our Treaty of commerce with Spain in the year 1715, which has been omitted in our late treaty. 2d ed. London: printed for W. Webb, Junior, 1749. 32 p. 8°

NUC(Pre–56)4:391*

Waldon has the spelling "Difinitive" in the title, as in the first ed. ¶ See first ed., next entry.

Waldon a conservé l'orthographe du mot « Difinitive » dans le titre comme il est écrit dans la première éd. ¶ Voir la première éd., notice suivante.

The advantages of the Difinitive [*sic*] **treaty,** to the people of Great-Britain, demonstrated. London: printed for W. Webb, Junior, 1749. 1 p.l., 26 p. 8°

NUC(Pre–56)4:391*

NUC has "26 p.," omitting the p.l. ¶ The writer chiefly deplores the settlement in Europe, but also criticizes the government for not supporting the New England expedition against Canada. The war should have been continued and all North America subdued. It is a mistake to give up Cape Breton (which is worth the Netherlands and all the conquests France has made since the beginning of the war) and to allow the French to retain fortifications in Newfoundland. ¶ *First edition; another edition appeared later the same year (q.v., above). NUC has also an edition of 1744,*

Le NUC omet le f. l. et indique « 26 p. ». ¶ L'auteur déplore surtout la conclusion du traité en ce qui a trait à l'Europe, mais il critique également le gouvernement parce que celui-ci n'a pas soutenu l'expédition de la Nouvelle-Angleterre contre le Canada. Il fallait poursuivre la guerre et conquérir toute l'Amérique du Nord. C'est une erreur d'abandonner le Cap-Breton (qui vaut les Pays-Bas et toutes les conquêtes que la France a faites depuis le début de la guerre) et de permettre aux Français de conserver leurs places fortes à Terre-Neuve. ¶ *Première édition ; une autre édition parut plus tard la même année (q.v., plus haut). Le NUC mentionne également une édition de 1744, mais il*

but if this work refers to the Treaty of Aix-la-Chapelle in Oct. 1748, that earlier work must be a ghost.

doit s'agir d'une édition supposée si cet ouvrage concerne le traité d'Aix-la-Chapelle signé au mois d'octobre 1748.

A defence of the Dutch, against the imputations of fraud, cruelty, and perfidiousness. Shewing how Dutch industry may become profitable to Great Britain in the herring fishery; and this kindom restored to a prosperous condition, by good oeconomy, and a more spirited policy: particularly with regard to the encroachments of France, and the untractableness of Spain. To which is added, A supplement, relative to the settlement of Nova Scotia. London, printed for R. Spavan, at the Crown in Ivy-Lane, near Paternoster-Row. 1749. 35, [1] p. 8°(in 4s).

NUC(Pre–56)136:474

Plomer has only the bookseller-publisher George Spavan at this address. ¶ List of books: [1] p. at end. ¶ "A supplement relative to the settlement of Nova Scotia": p. [25]–35. ¶ The writer advances suggestions to prevent mistakes made in the older colonies, especially to prevent monopoly of the land by a few rich people. Nova Scotia, in his opinion, might become the most powerful province in North America, the barrier for all the other British colonies against the French and the bulwark of the greatest and most valuable British fisheries. The writer suggests settlement by fishermen from Boston to prevent draining men from Great Britain.

Plomer signale seulement le libraire-éditeur George Spavan à cette adresse. ¶ Liste de livres : [1] p. à la fin. ¶ « A supplement relative to the settlement of Nova Scotia » : p. [25]–35. ¶ L'auteur avance des propositions visant à prévenir certaines erreurs commises dans les colonies plus anciennes, notamment celle d'empêcher quelques personnes fortunées d'exercer un monopole sur la terre. À son avis, la Nouvelle-Écosse pourrait devenir la province la plus puissante en Amérique du Nord, le rampart qui protégerait toutes les autres colonies britanniques contre les Français et le château fort qui abriterait les pêcheries britanniques les plus importantes et les plus précieuses. L'auteur suggère que des pêcheurs de Boston entreprennent la colonisation de ce territoire, de sorte que la Grande-Bretagne ne soit pas privée d'hommes.

[Dobbs, Arthur], 1689–1765. A short narrative and justification of the proceedings of the Committee appointed by the adventurers, to prosecute the discovery of the passage to the Western Ocean of America; and to open and extend the trade, and settle the countries beyond Hudson's Bay. With an apology for their postponing at present their intended application to Parliament. To which are annexed, the report and petitions referred to in the narrative; and the papers prepared to be delivered to the Lords and Commons, upon presenting the petition, as the foundation for a parliamentary enquiry, and the facts they were prepared to support: now laid before the publick, for their future consideration. London: printed for J[acob]. Robinson . . . 1749. 30 p. 8°

NUC(Pre–56)145:253

Concerns the North West Committee and the rights of its claim for support in seeking a northwest passage, and proposing that it be granted land and trading rights. This challenged, therefore, the exclusivity of the rights granted to the Hudson's Bay Company by its charter. ¶ For notes on the Dobbs-Middleton controversy, see Middleton's A vindication. London, 1743. ¶ OTP · BVAU · BVIP

Traite du Comité du Nord-Ouest et du bien-fondé de sa demande de soutien pour la recherche du passage du Nord-Ouest, ainsi que de sa proposition visant l'obtention de terres et de droits commerciaux. Par conséquent, cet ouvrage contestait le caractère exclusif des droits accordés à la Compagnie de la Baie d'Hudson conformément à sa charte. ¶ Pour des notes sur la querelle Dobbs-Middleton, voir A vindication. Londres, 1743, de Middleton. ¶ OTP · BVAU · BVIP

Douglass, William, 1691?–1752. Consideration on the state of British fisheries in America. London, 1749.

"*From* C. H. C., p. 883."

No other information available.

Aucun autre renseignement.

Ellis, Henry, 1721–1806. A voyage to Hudson's Bay .... 2d ed. London, H[enry]. Whitridge, 1749. map. 8°

Sabin:22312

See *first ed., 1748, for other notes.*   Voir *autres notes à la première éd., 1748.*

Ellis, Henry, 1721–1806. A voyage to Hudson's-Bay .... Dublin: printed for George and Alexander Ewing, at the Angel and Bible in Dame-street. 1749. xvi, 152 p. map. 8°

NUC(Pre–56)158:501*

JCB and Sabin indicate 162 p. ¶ See *first ed., 1748, for other notes.*   *Le JCB et le Sabin indiquent 162 p.* ¶ Voir *autres notes à la première éd., 1748.*

*The English pilot. The fourth book. Describing the West-India navigation, from Hudson's-Bay .... London, W[illiam]. and J[ohn]. Mount and T[homas]. Page, 1749. 4, 66 p. illus., charts (part fold.). fol.

NUC(Pre–56)160:374*

First edition: 1689, *q.v.* for other editions; the 1706 edition (and those subsequent) has a similar title, and is more fully transcribed.   Première édition : 1689, *q.v.* pour d'autres éditions ; l'édition de 1706 (ainsi que les éditions ultérieures) porte un titre identique et a fait l'objet d'une transcription plus complète.

A geographical history of Nova Scotia. Containing an account of the situation, extent and limits thereof, as also of the various struggles between the two crowns of England and France for the possession of that province. Wherein is shewn, the importance of it, as well with regard to our trade, as to the securing of our other settlements in North America. To which is added, an accurate description of the bays, harbours, lakes, and rivers, the nature of the soil, and the produce of the country. Together with the manners and customs of the Indian inhabitants. London: printed for Paul Vaillant, facing Southampton-Street, in the Strand, 1749. <Price one shilling and six pence.> 1 p.l., [7]–110, [1] p. 8°(in 4s).

NUC(Pre–56)198:88

Errata: [1] p. at end. ¶ *NUC has collation: 110 p., 1 l., but Waldon notes: there are two blank preliminary leaves, which are included in pagination and signatures.* ¶ *First (?) edition; transl. into German: Frankfurt, Leipzig, H. L. Bronner, 1750, and also into French as* Histoire géographique de la Nouvelle Écosse. *Londres, 1749 and 1755, (q.v.). Waldon notes that some sources indicate a 1754 edition in French, though another source suggests that the 1749, 1754, and 1755 eds. are all the same; also "Nouvelle éd., rev. & corr.," in Étienne de Lafargue,* Oeuvres mêlées de M. de Lafargue. *Paris, 1765.* ¶ *NSWA · OTP*

Errata : [1] p. à la fin. ¶ *Collation du NUC : 110 p., 1 f. ; toutefois Waldon signale l'existence de deux feuillets liminaires vierges, qui sont compris dans la pagination et les signatures.* ¶ *Première (?) édition ; trad. en allemand : Francfort, Leipzig, H.L. Bronner, 1750, et aussi en français sous le titre* Histoire géographique de la Nouvelle Écosse. *Londres, 1749 et 1755, (q.v.). Waldon indique que certaines sources mentionnent une édition de 1754 en français, bien qu'une autre source avance que les éd. de 1749, 1754 et 1755 sont toutes identiques ; en outre, il est fait mention d'une « Nouvelle éd., rev. & corr. » dans les* Oeuvres mêlées de M. de Lafargue. *Paris, 1765, d'Étienne de Lafargue.* ¶ *NSWA · OTP*

Great Britain. Parliament, 1749. House of Commons. Committee Appointed to Inquire into the State and Condition of the Countries Adjoining to Hudson's Bay. Papers presented to the Committee appointed to inquire into the state and condition of the countries adjoining to Hudson's Bay and of the trade carried on there. London printed in the year 1749. 49 p. 2 maps. fol.

Sabin:58462

This title follows Waldon's entry; Sabin has "Enquire" and "Hudson's Bay," and a colon after "London." ¶ "A Journal of Henry Kelsey in the Years 1691, and 1692. sent by the Hudson's-Bay Company to make Discoveries, and increase their Trade Inland from the Bay" (signed: Henry Kellsey): p. 52–70. ¶ *This is similar to (and may be identical with, described erroneously) the work of 60, xxxi pages, in the following entry.*

Ce titre suit la notice de Waldon ; le Sabin indique « Enquire » et « Hudson's Bay », ainsi qu'un deux-points après « London ». ¶ « A Journal of Henry Kelsey in the Years 1691, and 1692. sent by the Hudson's-Bay Company to make Discoveries, and increase their Trade Inland from the Bay » (signé : Henry Kellsey) : p. 52–70. ¶ *Cet ouvrage est semblable (et peut-être identique quoique mal désigné) à l'ouvrage de 60, xxxi pages, à la notice suivante.*

Great Britain. Parliament, 1749. House of Commons. Committee Appointed to Inquire into the State and Condition of the Countries Adjoining to Hudson's Bay. Papers presented to the Committee appointed to inquire into the state and condition of the countries adjoining to Hudson's Bay, and of the trade carried on there. [London] printed in the year 1749. 60, xxxi p. fol.

NUC(Pre–56)214:569

Appendix: His Majesty's Royal Charter to the Governor and Company of Hudson's Bay <2d May, 1670>; <Report of statements by Joseph La France>. ¶ *Reprinted the same year (see next entry), and also in* Reports from committees of the House of Commons, *1803, vol. 2, p. 213–86.* ¶ *This is similar to, and perhaps the same as, the preceding entry, given as having 49 p.* ¶ *OTP*

Annexe : His Majesty's Royal Charter to the Governor and Company of Hudson's Bay <2 mai 1670> ; <rapport sur les dépositions de Joseph La France>. ¶ *Réimprimé la même année (voir la notice suivante), ainsi que dans les* Reports from committees of the House of Commons. *1803, vol. 2, p. 213–86.* ¶ *Cet ouvrage est semblable, et peut-être identique, à celui de la notice précédente, présentée comme ayant 49 p.* ¶ *OTP*

Great Britain. Parliament, 1749. House of Commons. Committee Appointed to Inquire into the State and Condition of the Countries Adjoining to Hudson's Bay. Report of the Committee, appointed to enquire into the state and condition of the countries adjoining to Hudson's Bay, and of the trade carried on there. Together with an appendix. Reported by Lord Strange, 24 April, 1749. [London? 1749?] p. [213–86]. fol.

BLC(to 1975)96:743

This is the complete work, although the pagination starts at p. 213. [Waldon does not indicate where it ends. BLC notes — "In: Reports from Committees of the House of Commons, etc. vol. 2. pp. 213–86."] ¶ *Waldon gives imprint as "n.p., n.d."* ¶ See also *preceding entries.*

Il s'agit de l'ouvrage complet, bien que la pagination débute à la p. 213. [Waldon n'indique pas à quelle page il se termine. Le BLC signale – « Dans : Rapports des Comités de la Chambre des communes, etc. vol. 2, p. 213–86 ».] ¶ *Waldon donne comme adresse bibliographique « s.l., s.d. ».* ¶ Voir aussi *les notices précédentes.*

Great Britain. Treaties, etc., 1727–1760 (George II). A definitive treaty of peace and friendship, between His Britannick Majesty, the most Christian King, and the States General of the United Provinces. Concluded at Aix la Chapelle, the 18th day of October N. S. 1748. To which the Empress Queen of Hungary, the Kings of Spain and Sardinia, the Duke of Modena, and the Republick of Genoa, have acceded. Published by authority. London: printed by Edward Owen, 1749. 64 p. 4°

cf. NUC(Pre–56)215:511*

In English and French. ¶ Great Britain restored Cape Breton and her conquests in the West Indies to France. ¶ *First published as:* The definitive treaty of Christian, universal, and perpetual peace, friendship and union .... *London, 1748, q.v., under the same entry, for other notes; a variant appeared the same year: see next entry; the above work does not appear in NUC, but something similar is*

En anglais et en français. ¶ La Grande-Bretagne rendit à la France le Cap-Breton et les territoires qu'elle avait conquis dans les Antilles. ¶ *D'abord publié sous le titre :* The definitive treaty of Christian, universal, and perpetual peace, friendship and union .... *Londres, 1748, q.v., sous la même notice, pour d'autres notes ; une variante parut la même année :* voir *la notice suivante ; l'ouvrage susmentionné ne figure pas dans le NUC, mais le BLC(to 1975) désigne un ouvrage semblable à la*

described in BLC(to 1975)95:325, with 65 p., and one copy (?) "Wanting the last leaf."

cote 95:325, avec 65 p., et un exemplaire (?) « auquel il manque le dernier feuillet ».

*Great Britain. Treaties, etc., 1727–1760 (George II). The definitive treaty of peace . . . 18th day of October N. S. 1748. London, E[dward]. Owen, 1749. 65 p. 4°(?)

NUC(Pre–56)215:511*

In English, French, Italian, and Latin. ¶ *See* preceding entry for other notes.

En anglais, en français, en italien et en latin. ¶ *Voir* d'autres notes à la notice précédente.

Histoire géographique de la Nouvelle Ecosse; contenant le détail de sa situation, de son étendue & de ses limites; ainsi que des différens démêles entre l'Angleterre & la France, au sujet de la possession de cette province . . . . A Londres [Paris?]. 1749. vi, 164 p. 8°

NUC(Pre–56)247:515*

Transl. (by Étienne de Lafargue) from: A geographical history of Nova Scotia. *London, 1749,* q.v. *for other notes.* ¶ *Waldon notes that some sources indicate a* 1754 *edition in French, though another source suggests that the* 1749, 1754, *and* 1755 *eds. in French are all the same; also:* "Nouvelle éd., rev. & corr.," *in Étienne de Lafargue,* Oeuvres mêlées de M. de Lafargue. *Paris, 1765.* ¶ NSWA · BVAU

Trad. (par Étienne de Lafargue) de : A geographical history of Nova Scotia. *Londres, 1749,* q.v. *pour d'autres notes.* ¶ *Waldon signale que certaines sources mentionnent une édition de* 1754 *en français, bien qu'une autre source suggère que les éd. en français de* 1749, 1754 *et* 1755 *sont toutes identiques ; en outre, il est fait mention d'une « Nouvelle éd., rev. & corr. »* dans les Oeuvres mêlées de M. de Lafargue. *Paris, 1765, d'Étienne de Lafargue.* ¶ NSWA · BVAU

Hudson's Bay Company. The case of the Hudson's-Bay Company. [London, 1749?] 3 p. fol.

NUC(Pre–56)258:448

BLC, Waldon's source, has imprint: [London, 1749?], as above, but this may be the same work as in the similar entry under 1748 (q.v.), from NUC, which has the imprint: [London, 1748?]. ¶ Endorsed with above title: p. 4 [presumably a ms. endorsement on an otherwise blank page, since only 3 p. given in collation]. ¶ Case presented to the House of Commons in support of their claim to exclusive right of trade. ¶ See also *other works relating to this controversy under 1690, and the notes appended to those entries (which refer also to other publication dates).*

Adresse bibliographique du BLC, qui est la source de Waldon : [Londres, 1749 ?], comme plus haut, mais il peut s'agir du même ouvrage que celui qui est indiqué dans la notice semblable sous 1748 (q.v.), du NUC, qui donne l'adresse : [Londres, 1748 ?]. ¶ Inscription officielle tirée du titre susmentionné : p. 4 [on suppose une annotation man. sur une page qui autrement serait vierge, puisque la collation n'indique que 3 p.]. ¶ Affaire présentée à la Chambre des communes, à l'appui de la demande des intéressés visant des droits commerciaux exclusifs. ¶ Voir aussi *d'autres ouvrages sous 1690 au sujet de cette controverse, ainsi que les notes annexées à ces notices (qui renvoient également à d'autres dates de publication).*

*Hudson's Bay Company. Report from the Committee appointed to inquire into the state . . . of the countries adjoining to Hudson's Bay, and of the trade carried on there. (His Majesty's [Charles II's] Royal Charter to the Governor and Company of H.'s B.) [London?] 1749. fol.

BLC(to 1975)154:300

Included here for the presence of the Royal Charter to the Company, originally granted in 1670 to Prince Rupert and seventeen other promoters, for all the lands draining into Hudson Bay. These territorial rights

Ci-inclus en raison de la Chartre royale de la Compagnie, initialement accordée en 1670 au prince Rupert et à dix-sept autres fondateurs pour toutes les terres aboutissant à la Baie d'Hudson. La Compagnie a cédé ces droits territoriaux au gouvernement du

were surrendered by the Company in 1869 to the Government of Canada, for £300,000.

Canada en 1869 pour la somme de 300 000 £.

Miscellaneous reflections upon the peace, and its consequences. More especially on a just, as well as real and national oeconomy, the regard due to subjects, who have served in quality of soldiers . . . . Addressed to the more considerate and disinterested part of the nation. London, printed for J[ames]. Roberts, 1749. 63 p. 8°(in 4s).

NUC(Pre–56)387:121

The importance of Cape Breton: p. 30–36. Having given it up [at the Treaty of Aix-la-Chapelle, ending the War of Austrian Succession], England should now develop the other colonies and make herself independent of the rest of the world. "If at length we should take this salutary step, and convince them that their Countries produce nothing which we could not have from our own, they <other countries> would alter their Conduct . . . shewing them that Great Britain, when her Councils are rightly directed, need depend for Timber and Naval Stores on no other Countries in the World, but what are in her own possession": p. 34. ¶ *BVAU*

L'importance du Cap-Breton : p. 30–36. Ayant renoncé à ce territoire [au traité d'Aix-la-Chapelle, qui mit fin à la guerre de la Succession d'Autriche], l'Angleterre doit désormais développer les autres colonies et se rendre indépendante du reste du monde. « Si nous prenons enfin cette décision salutaire, et convainquons ces pays qu'ils ne produisent rien que nous ne puissons obtenir par nos propres moyens, ils <les autres pays> modifieront leur conduite . . . nous leur montrerons ainsi que la Grande-Bretagne, lorsque ses instances dirigeantes prennent les bonnes décisions, ne doit dépendre d'aucun autre pays au monde, si ce n'est des territoires qui lui appartiennent, pour le bois-d'oeuvre et l'approvisionnement de ses entrepôts maritimes » : p. 34. ¶ *BVAU*

Reasons to shew, that there is a great probability of a navigable passage to the western American ocean, through Hudson's Streights, and Chesterfield Inlet; from the observations made on board the ships sent upon the late discovery; supported by affidavits, which coincides with several former accounts. Humbly offered to the consideration of the Lords and Commons assembled in Parliament. London: printed for J[acob]. Robinson, at the Golden Lion on Ludgate-Street, 1749. 23 p. 8°(in 4s).

NUC(Pre–56)483:526

Attributed (in a NUC note) to Arthur Dobbs; see his An account of the countries adjoining to Hudson's Bay .... London, Jacob Robinson, 1744, for numerous other titles on this subject. ¶ *OTP · BVAU (facsim.) · BVIPA*

Attribué (dans une note du NUC à Arthur Dobbs ; voir son ouvrage An account of the countries adjoining to Hudson's Bay .... Londres, Jacob Robinson, 1744, pour de nombreux autres titres sur ce sujet. ¶ *OTP · BVAU (fac-sim.) · BVIPA*

A short state of the countries and trade of North America. Claimed by the Hudson's Bay company, under a pretence of a charter for ever, of lands without bounds or limits, and an exclusive trade in those unbounded seas and countries; shewing the illegality of the said grant, and the abuse they have made of it; and the great benefit Britain may obtain by settling those countries, and extending the trade amongst the natives by civilizing and incorporating with them, and laying a foundation for their becoming Christians and industrious subjects of Great-Britain; and the necessity there is of a parliamentary enquiry into the pretended rights and exclusive monopoly claimed by the said Company, and their abuse of the grant. That these countries may be settled, either by fixing a company under proper regulations and restrictions, or by laying open the trade to all the British merchants, and settling them, at the publick expence, or by a moderate tax upon that trade. London, printed for J[acob]. Robinson . . . 1749. 44 p. 8°

NUC(Pre–56)544:446*

Standard of trade: p. 25–28; An abstract of the weather taken at Montague-House, near York-Fort, in Hay's-River in Hudson's-Bay in latitude 57° 20; and on board the California, Aug. 1746 – Sept. 1747: p. 29–44. ¶ *A microcard*

Situation du commerce : p. 25–28 ; Un résumé d'observations climatiques effectuées à Montague-House, près de Fort York, à l'embouchure de la rivière Hay dans la Baie d'Hudson par 57° 20' de latitude ; et à bord du California, août 1746 –sept. 1747 : p. 29–44.

edition (two cards) was published after World War II (copy in BVAU). ¶ OTP · BVIP · BVIPA

¶ *Une édition sur microcartes (deux cartes) a été publiée après la Seconde guerre mondiale (exemplaire au BVAU). ¶ OTP · BVIP · BVIPA*

*The state of the nation, with a general balance of the publick accounts . . . . Dublin, printed by S[amuel]. Powell, for G[eorge]. Faulkner [etc.] 1749. 48 p. fold. tab. 8°(?)

NUC(Pre–56)565:329*

The NUC copy is bound with another, later work. ¶ First edition: London, 1748, *q.v.*

L'exemplaire du NUC est relié avec un ouvrage postérieur. ¶ Première édition : Londres, 1748, *q.v.*

Swaine, Charles, *fl.* 1746–1766, *supposed author/auteur présumé.* An account of a voyage for the discovery of a North-West Passage . . . . By the clerk of the California. London, 1749. 2 v. 4 plates, 6 maps. 8°

For notes, *see* the 1748–49 edition.

Voir notes de l'édition de 1748–1749.

*[Tucker, Josiah], 1712–1799. A brief essay on the advantages and disadvantages, which respectively attend France and Great Britain, with regard to trade. With some proposals for removing the principal disadvantages of Great Britain. In a new and concise method. London, printed for the author, and sold by T[homas]. Trye, 1749. v, [1], 79 p. 8°(?)

NUC(Pre–56)603:615*

First edition; second ed., 1750, *q.v.* for notes and other editions.

Première édition ; deuxième éd., 1750, *q.v.* pour des notes et d'autres éditions.

334

THE

HISTORY

OF THE

FIVE Indian NATIONS

OF

CANADA,

WHICH ARE

The BARRIER between the ENGLISH and
FRENCH in that Part of the World.

WITH

Particular Accounts of their Religion, Manners, Customs, Laws,
and Government; their several Battles and Treaties with the
European Nations; their Wars with the other *Indians*;

AND

A true Account of the present State of our TRADE with them.

In which are shewn,

The great Advantage of their Trade and Alliance to the *British* Nation;
and the Intrigues and Attempts of the *French* to engage them from us;
a Subject nearly concerning all our *American* Plantations, and highly
meriting the Consideration of the *British* Nation.

By the Honourable CADWALLADER COLDEN, *Esq;*
One of his Majesty's Counsel, and Surveyor-General of New-York.

To which are added,

Accounts of the several other Nations of *Indians* in *North-America*, their
Numbers, Strength, &c. and the Treaties which have been lately
made with them.

The SECOND EDITION.

LONDON:

Printed for JOHN WHISTON at Mr. *Boyle's Head*, and
LOCKYER DAVIS at Lord *Bacon's Head*, both in, *Fleet-
street*, and JOHN WARD opposite the *Royal Exchange*.

MDCCL.

Cadwallader Colden. *The history of the Five Indian nations of Canada . . . .*
London/Londres,

1750

Campbell, John, 1708–1775. Lives of the admirals and other eminent British seamen. Containing their personal histories, and a detail of all their public services . . . . By John Campbell. . . . The second edition, carefully revised, corrected, and enlarged. London, printed for T. Waller, 1750. 4 v. 8°

NUC(Pre–56)92:211*

See *first ed., 1742–44, for a more complete title.* ¶ Contents relating to Canada: Sir John Cabot: v. 1, p. 326–31; Sebastian Cabot: v. 1, p. 385–99; Sir Humphrey Gilbert: v. 1, p. 490–99; Sir Martin Frobisher: v. 1, p. 531–32; Sir Wm. Phips: v. 3, p. 168–70; Newfoundland: v. 3, p. 206–11; Nova Scotia & Newfoundland, v. 4, p. 129–33; Cape Breton: v. 4, p. 216. ¶ Second edition; first ed., 1742–44 (*q.v.*); third ed., 1761 (*q.v.*); other eds.: London, 1779, 1781, 1785 (two, plus Edinburgh), and into the nineteenth century (twelfth ed., 1873). ¶ *1781 ed.: BVIP · BVIPA*

Voir *la première éd., 1742–1744, pour un titre plus complet.* ¶ Qui portent sur le Canada : sir Jean Cabot : vol. 1, p. 326–31 ; Sébastien Cabot : vol. 1, p. 385–99 ; sir Humphrey Gilbert : vol. 1, p. 490–99 ; sir Martin Frobisher : vol. 1, p. 531–32 ; sir Wm. Phips : vol. 3, p. 168–70 ; Terre-Neuve : vol. 3, p. 206–11 ; Nouvelle-Écosse et Terre-Neuve, vol. 4, p. 129–33 ; Cap-Breton : vol. 4, p. 216. ¶ Deuxième édition ; première éd., 1742–1744 (*q.v.*) ; troisième éd., 1761 (*q.v.*) ; autres éd. : Londres, 1779, 1781, 1785 (deux à Londres, plus une autre à Édimbourg), puis au XIXe siècle (douzième éd., 1873). ¶ *Éd. de 1781 : BVIP · BVIPA*

Colden, Cadwallader, 1688–1776. The history of the Five Indian nations of Canada, which are the barrier between the English and French in that part of the world. With particular accounts of their religion, manners, customs, laws and government; their several battles and treaties with the European nations; their wars with the other Indians; . . . highly meriting the consideration of the British nation. By the Honourable Cadwallader Colden, Esq. . . . To which are added, accounts of the several other nations of Indians . . . and the treaties which have been lately made with them. The second edition. London: printed for John Whiston . . . and Lockyer Davis . . . and John Ward . . . 1750. xvi, [4], 204, 283 p. fold. map. 8°

NUC(Pre–56)114:532*

Waldon notes (from Sabin): Some copies of this issue are without date. ¶ This is the second London ed., with variant title. ¶ See *1747 (first London edition)*. ¶ *OTP*

Observation de Waldon (tirée du Sabin) : Certains exemplaires de ce tirage ne sont pas datés. ¶ Il s'agit de la deuxième éd. de Londres, avec une variante de titre. ¶ Voir *1747 (première édition de Londres)*. ¶ *OTP*

*Ellis, Henry, 1721–1806. Considerations on the great advantages which would arise from the discovery of the North west passage, and a clear account of the most practicable method for attempting that discovery. By Capt. Henry Ellis. [London], 1750. 8 p. fold. map. fol.

NUC(Pre–56)158:501

Proposes to begin the search for a northwest passage from the Pacific side, where the seas are clear of ice. ¶ OTP

Propose de commencer l'exploration pour trouver le passage du Nord-Ouest à partir du Pacifique, là où il n'y a pas de glace flottante. ¶ OTP

A genuine account of Nova Scotia: containing, a description of its situation, air, climate, soil and its produce; also rivers, bays, harbours, and fish, with which they abound in very great plenty. To which is added, His Majesty's proposals, as an encouragement to those who are willing to settle there. London printed; Dublin, re-printed for Philip Bowes, 1750. 16 p. 8°

NUC(Pre–56)195:29

[Lambert, Claude François], 1705–1765. A collection of curious observations on the manners, customs, usages, different languages, government, mythology, chronology, ancient and modern geography, ceremonies, religion, mechanics, astronomy, medicine, physics, natural history, commerce, arts, and sciences, of the several nations of Asia, Africa, and America. Translated from the French, first printed at Paris in 1749, by John Dunn . . . . London, printed for the translator, 1750. 2 vols. 8°(?)

NUC(Pre–56)313:30*

Waldon has title: Curious observations upon the manners . . ., *with imprint* London: printed for G. Woodfall [1750?], *taken from Sabin:38730; but Sabin has date as* [1751], *and this is proper for that title* — q.v. *under 1751.* ¶ *Transl. from his:* Recueil d'observations curieuses sur les moeurs . . . . *Paris, 1749 (cf. BLC(to 1975)12:402).* ¶ Volume 1, chap. 28, "The different languages of the Hurons, of the Abnakis, the Algonkins, the Illinese, the Outaouacks, and several other nations of New France; their employments, dresses [etc.]": p. 277–87. ¶ *Apparently the first English edition; other editions, London, 1751, 1754, 1755, and 1760, q.v.*

Waldon donne le titre Curious observations upon the manners . . ., *avec pour adresse bibliographique :* London: printed for G. Woodfall [1750 ?], *tiré du Sabin :38730 ; mais la date mentionnée par le Sabin est* [1751], *et c'est la bonne date pour ce titre* –q.v. *1751.* ¶ *Trad. de son ouvrage :* Recueil d'observations curieuses sur les moeurs . . . . *Paris, 1749 (cf. BLC(to 1975)12:402).* ¶ Volume 1, chap. 28, « The different languages of the Hurons, of the Abnakis, the Algonkins, the Illinese, the Outaouacks, and several other nations of New France; their employments, dresses [etc.] » : p. 277–87. ¶ *Apparemment la première édition anglaise ; autres éditions, Londres, 1751, 1754, 1755 et 1760, q.v.*

The Nova Scotia's garland; furnished with three merry new songs. I. The weavers wives resolution, not to go to Nova Scotia. II. An invitation to the famous and plentiful island of pleasure, call'd New Scotland, in the Northren parts of America. III. Gently touch the warbling lyre. Licensed and entred according to order. [Newcastle, 1750?] 8 p. 8°

BLC(to 1975)239:84

The third song has no connection with Nova Scotia, but the first two are evidently occasioned by the founding of Halifax in 1749. "The weavers wives resolution" (tune, *Rakes of London*) begins: ¶ Sister dear, I pray be minding, / What in Care I have design'd ye: / Not like Cape Breton to be foil'd in, / The glorious Nova Scotia. ¶ The wife declines to emigrate, but her spinster sister is inclined to try her chance of finding a husband in the new land. ¶ "An

La troisième chanson n'a aucun rapport avec la Nouvelle-Écosse, mais la fondation d'Halifax en 1749 a manifestement inspiré les deux premières. Sur l'air de *Rakes of London*, la chanson intitulée « The weavers wives resolution » commence ainsi : ¶ Chére soeur, je vous prie d'écouter / Ce que j'ai mûrement conçu pour vous : / Non pas le Cap-Breton trompeur, / Mais la glorieuse Nouvelle-Écosse. ¶ L'épouse refuse d'émigrer, mais sa soeur célibataire est encline à tenter sa chance pour trouver un mari sur le nouveau continent. ¶ La chanson intitulée

Invitation" is reminiscent of a popular ballad of our own day, *The big Rock Candy Mountains*, with such sentiments as these: ¶ The Rivers run with Claret Wine, / The Brooks with rich Canary, / The Ponds with other Sorts of Wine, / To make your Heart full merry: / Nay, more than this, you may behold / The Fountains flow with Brandy, / The Rocks are all refined Gold, / The Hills are Sugar-Candy. / There is nothing there but Holidays, / With Musick out of Measure; / Who can forbear to speak the Praise / Of such a Land of Pleasure.

« An Invitation » rappelle une balade populaire contemporaine, *The big Rock Candy Mountains*, et exprime des sentiments comme ceux-ci : ¶ Dans les rivières, coule du vin de Bordeaux, / Dans les ruisseaux, du vin des Canaries, / Dans les étangs, d'autres sortes de vin, / Afin de réjouir les coeurs : / On peut encore apercevoir / Du cognac jaillissant des fontaines / Des pierres faites d'or pur / Des collines, de sucre candi. / Là-bas chaque jour est jour de vacances / Ponctué d'une musique endiablée ; / Qui ne chanterait les louanges / De cette terre de plaisirs.

Trevor, Richard, *bp. of Durham/év. de Durham*, 1707–1771. A sermon preached before the incorporated Society for the Propagation of the Gospel in Foreign Parts; at their anniversary meeting in the parish church of St. Mary-le-Bow, on Friday February 16, 1749 [1750 N. S.]. By the Right Reverend Father in God, Richard, Lord Bishop of St. Davids. London, printed by Edward Owen ... and sold by J[ames]. Roberts ... and A[ndrew]. Millar ... 1750. 71 p. 8°(in 4s).

NUC(Pre–56)601:197

Proceedings of the Society, 17 Feb. 1748 to 16 Feb. 1749 [*etc.*]: p. 23–71. (Newfoundland: p. 33, 38; Nova Scotia: p. 38–41.) ¶ Until 1853 the annual report of the Society was usually printed as an appendix to the anniversary sermon (*cf.* Sabin: 85933n.).

Actes de la Société, du 17 fév. 1748 au 16 fév. 1749 [*etc.*]: p. 23–71. (Terre-Neuve : p. 33, 38 ; Nouvelle-Écosse : p. 38–41.) ¶ Jusqu'en 1853, le rapport annuel de la Société était habituellement imprimé sous forme d'annexe au sermon d'anniversaire (*cf.* Sabin:85933n.).

[Tucker, Josiah], 1712–1799. A brief essay on the advantages and disadvantages which respectively attend France and Great Britain, with regard to trade. With some proposals for removing the principal disadvantages of Great Britain. In a new method. 2d ed. corr., with large additions. London, T[homas]. Trye, near Gray's Inn Gate, Holborn. 1750. <Price two shillings.> viii, xii, [13]–166, [2] p. 8°(in 4s).

NUC(Pre–56)603:615*

List of books: final [2] p. ¶ The writer is critical of exclusive companies and proposes to remove restrictions: p. 65–85. (Case of the Hudson's Bay Company considered: p. 75–85.) ¶ *First ed.: 1749; third ed., London, 1753, and Dublin, 1757; fourth ed., under title:* An essay on the advantages. *Glasgow, 1756; reprinted in David Hume,* Three essays. *London, 1787 (Waldon; not found in NUC or BLC under Hume, but NUC(Pre–56) 603:615 under Tucker,* A brief essay, *1787, notes that the Hume work reprints Tucker's third ed.), and, from the third ed., in J. R. MacCulloch,* A select collection of tracts on commerce [etc.], *1859 (Waldon; presumably John R. McCulloch,* A select collection of scarce and valuable economical tracts. *London, 1859).* ¶ *BVIPA*

Liste de livres : les [2] dernières pages. ¶ L'auteur se montre critique à l'égard des compagnies jouissant de droits exclusifs et propose de lever les restrictions : p. 65–85. (Case of the Hudson's Bay Company considered: p. 75–85.) ¶ *Première éd. : 1749 ; troisième éd., Londres, 1753, et Dublin, 1757 ; quatrième éd., sous le titre* An essay on the advantages. *Glasgow, 1756 ; réimpression dans l'ouvrage de David Hume,* Three essays. *Londres, 1787 (Waldon ; introuvable au NUC ou au BLC sous Hume, mais il est noté à la cote NUC(Pre–56)603:615 sous Tucker,* A brief essay, *1787, que l'ouvrage de Hume reproduit la troisième éd. de Tucker), puis, à partir de la troisième éd., dans* A select collection of tracts on commerce [etc.], *1859, par J. R. MacCulloch (Waldon ; on présume qu'il s'agit de l'ouvrage de John R. McCulloch,* A select collection of scarce and valuable economical tracts. *Londres, 1859).* ¶ *BVIPA*

1751

An account of the colony of Nova Scotia. [s.l., London? s.d., 1751.] 2 p.l., 21 p. 8°

NUC(Pre–56)2:559

Waldon has (evidently from Sabin): half-title, [2], 21 p.; the [2] p. here assumed to be the title leaf.

Indication de Waldon (de toute évidence tirée du Sabin) : faux-titre, [2], 21 p. ; on présume que les [2] p. en question constituent le feuillet de titre.

Bartram, John, 1699–1777. Observations on the inhabitants, climate, soil, rivers, productions, animals, and other matters worthy of notice. Made by Mr. John Bartram, in his travels from Pensilvania to Onondago, Oswego and the Lake Ontario, in Canada. To which is annex'd, a curious account of the cataracts at Niagara. By Mr. Peter Kalm, a Swedish gentleman who travelled there. London: printed for J[ohn]. Whiston and B[enjamin]. White, in Fleet-Street, 1751. (Price one shilling and six-pence.) 1 p.l., viii, [9]–94 p. front. (fold. plan). 8°

NUC(Pre–56)38:101*

A famous and interesting work. Kalm's account (p. 79–94) is the first scientific description in English of Niagara Falls. The plan is of Oswego. ¶ *Waldon gives Bartram's year of birth as 1701.* ¶ *Another edition: [Geneva, N. Y., 1895]; also MF of 1751 ed., Ann Arbor, Mich., University Microfilms (American Culture series no. 146, roll 13).*

Un ouvrage réputé et intéressant. Le récit de Kalm (p. 79–94) est la première description scientifique en anglais des chutes Niagara. Le plan est d'Oswego. ¶ *Waldon indique 1701 comme année de naissance de Bartram.* ¶ *Autre édition : [Geneva (N. Y.), 1895] ; également reproduction sur mic. de l'éd. de 1751, Ann Arbor (Mich.), University Microfilms (collection American Culture, n° 146, rouleau 13).*

Child, Sir **Josiah**, 1630–1699. A new discourse of trade: wherein are recommended several weighty points; relating to companies of merchants. The act of navigation, naturalization of strangers, and our woollen manufactures. The balance of trade, and nature of plantations; with their consequences, in relation to the kingdom . . . . The reduction of interest of money to 4 l. per cent. is recommended . . . . By Sir Josiah Child, baronet. To which is added, a small treatise against usury. By the same author. The fifth edition. Glasgow, printed and sold by Robert and Andrew Foulis. 1751. xxix, 184 p. 8°

NUC(Pre–56)106:638*

Same title as the 1740 edition. ¶ NUC notes under the 1718 and 1740 editions that the treatise on usury is by Sir Thomas Culpeper, and first pub. London, 1641. ¶ Newfoundland: p. 154–60. ¶ First pub. under this title: London, 1692, q.v. for other notes.

Titre identique à celui de l'édition de 1740. ¶ Le NUC signale aux éditions de 1718 et 1740 que sir Thomas Culpeper est l'auteur du traité sur l'usure, qui fut publié la première fois à Londres en 1641. ¶ Terre-Neuve : p. 154–60. ¶ Première publ. sous ce titre : Londres, 1692, q.v. pour d'autres notes.

[Douglass, William], 1691?–1752. A discourse concerning the currencies of the British plantations in America . . . . With a postscript thereto. Boston: printed, 1740. And London: reprinted, 1751. 62 p. 8°

NUC(Pre–56)147:673*

Newfoundland, Nova Scotia: p. 8. ¶ First pub. London, 1739, *q.v.* for other notes.

Terre-Neuve, Nouvelle-Écosse : p. 8. ¶ Première publ. Londres, 1739, *q.v.* pour d'autres notes.

*The English pilot. The fourth book. Describing the West-India navigation, from Hudson's-Bay . . . . London: printed for W[illiam]. and J[ohn]. Mount and T[homas]. Page, on Tower-Hill, 1751. 66 [*i.e.* 68] p. incl. illus., maps. 24 maps (incl. front.). fol.

NUC(Pre–56)160:374*

First edition: 1689, *q.v.* for other editions; the 1706 edition (and those later) has a similar title, and is more fully transcribed.

Première édition : 1689, *q.v.* pour d'autres éditions ; l'édition de 1706 (ainsi que les éditions ultérieures) porte un titre similaire, et a fait l'objet d'une transcription plus complète.

The importance of settling and fortifying Nova Scotia: with a particular account of the climate, soil, and native inhabitants of the country. By a gentleman lately arrived from that colony. London, printed for J[ohn]. Scott, in Exchange Alley. 1751. <Price one shilling.> 2 p.l., [3]–37 p. fold. map. 8°

NUC(Pre–56)265:255

Waldon omits the fold. map. ¶ The writer traces the history of Nova Scotia, emphasizing its fertility and value, and urges the necessity of keeping it — the key to North America. It is also a nursery for seamen, the fish, fur, and timber trades are profitable and ships of war stationed at Halifax will be available against the French fisheries. "By settling and fortifying Nova Scotia, and keeping a squadron there, we may easily make ourselves masters of all North America, and engross all the cod-fishery and fur-trade to ourselves": p. 36. This optimistic view of the new colony is in marked contrast to the depressing picture painted by the authors of *An account of the present state of Nova-Scotia*. London, 1756, *q.v.*

Waldon omet la carte pliée. ¶ L'auteur reconstitue l'histoire de la Nouvelle-Écosse, dont il souligne la fertilité et la valeur, et fait valoir qu'elle doit rester – la clé donnant accès à l'Amérique du Nord. C'est aussi une pépinière de marins ; le commerce du poisson comme ceux de la fourrure et du bois d'oeuvre y sont rentables, et les navires de guerre en rade à Halifax pourront servir contre les pêcheries françaises. « En colonisant la Nouvelle-Écosse, en établissant des places fortes et en entretenant une escadrille dans ses eaux, nous pouvons facilement nous rendre maîtres de toute l'Amérique du Nord, et nous approprier toute la pêche à la morue et tout le commerce de la fourrure » : p. 36. Cette vision optimiste de la nouvelle colonie contraste de façon marquée avec la situation désolante dépeinte par les auteurs de *An account of the present state of Nova-Scotia*. Londres, 1756, *q.v.*

*Lambert, Claude François, 1705–1765. Curious observations upon the manners, customs, usages, ... antient and modern geography.... Translated from the French of M. l'abbe Lambert.... London: G[eorge]. Woodfall [1751]. 2 v.: 1 p.l., iv, 411; 1 p.l., vi, 404, [16] p. 8°

NUC(Pre–56)313:31*

Pagination from Sabin:38730. ¶ First pub. in English as: *A collection of curious observations*. London, 1750, *q.v.* for other notes and editions.

Pagination du Sabin:38730. ¶ Première publ. en anglais sous le titre *A collection of curious observations*. Londres, 1750, *q.v.* pour d'autres notes et éditions.

Wilson, John, *inspector of stores/inspecteur de provisions*. Address'd to the merchants of London. A genuine narrative of the transactions in Nova Scotia, since the settlement, June 1749, till August the 5th, 1751; in which the nature, soil, and produce of the country are related, with the particular attempts of the Indians to disturb the colony. By John Wilson, late inspector of the stores. London: printed and sold by A. Henderson, J[oseph]. Fox, B[arnes]. Tovey, Westminster-Hall; J[acob]. Robinson, Ludgate-Street; J. James, and H. Cook, at the Royal-Exchange. [1751?] (Price sixpence.) 21 p. 8°(?)

NUC(Pre–56)667:17–18

Waldon gives no format, but JCB(1)3:966 has 8°, and also quotes the Monthly Review, 5:458, *thus: "Mr. Wilson pours out his spleen upon this new colony, which he represents in a very unpromising way; but ... he deserves little notice and less credit."* ¶ *NSHPL · OOA · SSU*

Waldon n'indique aucun format, tandis que le JCB(1)3:966 donne in–8° et cite en outre la Monthly Review, 5:458, *comme suit : « Monsieur Wilson décharge sa bile sur cette nouvelle colonie, qu'il dépeint sous un jour très peu prometteur ; mais ... ses dires sont de peu d'intérêt, et il convient encore moins d'y ajouter foi. »* ¶ *NSHPL · OOA · SSU*

1752

[Churchill, Awnsham], *d./déc.* 1728, *comp.* A collection of voyages and travels . . . . London, printed by assignment from Messieurs Churchill for Thomas Osborn in Gray's-Inn. 1752. 8 v. plates, maps (part fold.). fol. (?)

NUC(Pre–56)109:264*

Contents relating to Canada: Capt. John Monck's voyage: v. 1, p. 419–44. plates, map; Capt. Thomas James's voyage: v. 2, p. 407–66; John Gatonbe's voyage: v. 6, p. 257–69. illus., plate, map. ¶ *Volumes 1–4 first pub.: London, 1704 (q.v. for notes and other editions). Vols. 5–6 were added in 1732 edition (q.v.), and vols. 7–8 in 1744–47 edition (q.v.).* ¶ *BVAU*

Qui portent sur le Canada : voyage du cap. John Monck, vol. 1, p. 419–44. Planches, carte ; voyage du cap. Thomas James, vol. 2, p. 407–66; voyage de John Gatonbe, vol. 6, p. 257–69. illustr., planche, carte. ¶ *Première publ. des volumes 1–4 : Londres, 1704 (q.v. pour des notes et d'autres éditions). Vol. 5–6 furent ajoutés à l'édition de 1732 (q.v.) et les vol. 7–8 à l'édition de 1744–1747 (q.v.).* ¶ *BVAU*

An epistle to the Hon. Arthur Dobbs, Esq.; in Europe. From a clergyman in America. Part I . . . . London: printed for the author, and sold by R[obert]. Dodsley and M[ary]. Cooper . . ., 1752. 2 p.l., iii–v, 7–95, [1] p. 4°

NUC(Pre–56)160:684*

Advertisement (promising a second epistle, "speedily to be published"): [1] p. at end. ¶ Verse, in praise of Dobbs [1689–1765] for his efforts to find the Northwest Passage, written in Maryland after the return of the *Dobbs* and *California* [galleys] and before the news of the signing of the Treaty of Aix-la-Chapelle [Oct. 1748, ending the War of the Austrian Succession] reached the author. It contains some war-like references to

Réclame (promettant une deuxième épître « qui sera publiée sous peu ») : [1] p. à la fin. ¶ Apologie de Dobbs [1689–1765] pour les efforts qu'il a déployés afin de trouver le passage du Nord-Ouest, écrite en vers au Maryland après le retour du *Dobbs* et du *California* [galères] et avant que la nouvelle de la signature du traité d'Aix-la-Chapelle [octobre 1748, traité qui mit fin à la guerre de la Succession d'Autriche] ne parvînt à l'auteur. Cet ouvrage comporte quelques remarques guerrières sur le Canada et la

Canada and the taking of Cape Breton. ¶ *Reprinted Dublin, the same year:*
see *next entry.*

prise du Cap-Breton. ¶ *Réimpression à
Dublin, la même année :* voir *la notice suivante.*

*An epistle to the Hon. Arthur Dobbs, Esq.; in Europe, from a clergyman in America.
Dublin, printed for J[ohn]. Smith, 1752. 52 p. 4°(?)

NUC(Pre–56)160:684*

BVIPA

BVIPA

*Galvão, Antonio, *d./déc.* 1557. The discoveries of the world . . . . Corrected . . . and
. . . published . . . by Richard Hakluyt. London, 1752. (In Awnsham Churchill, *A
collection of voyages and travels,* vol. 8, p. 353–402.)

NUC(Pre–56)190:64*

First pub.: London, 1601, *q.v.* for
notes and other editions.

Première publ. : Londres, 1601, *q.v.* pour
des notes et d'autres éditions.

*Geare, Allen. Ebenezer; or, A monument of thankfulness, being a true account . . . .
London, 1752. (In Awnsham Churchill, *A collection of voyages and travels,* vol. 8,
p. 787–94.)

NUC(Pre–56)193:288*

First pub.: London, 1708, *q.v.* for
notes and other editions.

Première publ. : Londres, 1708, *q.v.* pour
des notes et d'autres éditions.

[Kennedy, Archibald], 1685?–1763. The importance of gaining and preserving the friendship of the Indians to the British interest considered. London: printed for E[dward]. Cave, jun., 1752. 1 p.l., 46 p. 8°

NUC(Pre–56)293:229*

The writer points out that the French keep Canada by cultivating the friendship of the Indians. He wants a strong fort at Wood-Creek to protect the English colonies and serve as a base of attack on Canada. He also suggests a confederacy of the English colonies for defence. ¶ Reprinted from the first ed.: New York: printed and sold by James Parker, 1751, 31 p., 8°; also issued in a microcard edition, cf. NUC.

L'auteur souligne que les Français conservent le Canada grâce aux relations amicales qu'ils entretiennent avec les Indiens. Il veut qu'on établisse une solide place forte à Wood-Creek pour protéger les colonies anglaises et servir de base offensive contre le Canada. De plus, il suggère de confédérer les colonies anglaises en vue de leur défense. ¶ Réimpression de la première éd. : New York, imprimée et vendue par James Parker, 1751, 31 p., in-8° ; aussi reproduction sur microcarte, cf. NUC.

*[Lescarbot, Marc], *ca./vers* 1570–1642. Nova Francia; or, The description of that part of New France, which is one continent with Virginia . . . . Translated out of the French into English by P[ierre]. E[rondelle]. London, 1752. (In Awnsham Churchill, *A collection of voyages and travels*, vol. 8, p. 795–917.)

NUC(Pre–56)328:113*

This has the same page-span as the Thomas Osborne *Collection of voyages*. London, 1745, *q.v.* ¶ Waldon lists only the Churchill *Collection*, under 1752, noting the Canadian contents but not Lescarbot. ¶ For other notes and editions, *see* the 1609 editions.

Les dimensions (pages) de cet ouvrage sont identiques à celles de l'écrit de Thomas Osborne, *Collection of voyages*. Londres, 1745, *q.v.* ¶ Sous 1752, Waldon énumère seulement les documents de la *Collection* de Churchill, dont elle établit les titres portant sur le Canada, mais elle ne mentionne pas Lescarbot. ¶ Pour d'autres notes et éditions, *voir* les éditions de 1609.

Osbaldeston, Richard, *successively bp. of Carlisle and London/év. de Carlisle et ensuite de Londres,* 1690–1764. A sermon preached before the incorporated Society for the Propagation of the Gospel in Foreign Parts; at their anniversary meeting in the parish church of St. Mary-le-Bow, on Friday February 21, 1752. By the Right Reverend Father in God, Richard, Lord Bishop of Carlisle. London, printed by Edward Owen . . . and sold by J[ames]. Roberts . . . and A[ndrew]. Millar . . . 1752. 71 p. 8°(in 4s).

NUC(Pre–56)433:638–39

Proceedings of the Society, 15 Feb. 1750–51, to 21 Feb. 1752 [etc.]: p. 21–71. (Newfoundland, Nova Scotia: p. 35–36.)

Actes de la Société, du 15 fév. 1750–51 au 21 fév. 1752 [etc.] : p. 21–71. (Terre-Neuve, Nouvelle-Écosse : p. 35–36.)

[Osborne, Thomas], *d./déc.* 1767, *comp.* A collection of voyages and travels, some now first printed from original manuscripts, others now first published in English. With a general preface, giving an account of the progress of trade and navigation, from its first beginning. Illustrated with several hundred useful maps and cuts . . . all elegantly engraved on copper plates. Vol. VII[–VIII]. London: printed by assignment from Messieurs Churchill, for Thomas Osborne, 1752. 2 v. fronts., illus., maps, plates. fol.

NUC(Pre–56)434:44*

First edition, which has a variant title: 1745, q.v. for contents and other notes; reissued 1747 (q.v.). This is vols. 7–8 of A. and J. Churchill's Collection of voyages, *vols. 1–4 pub. first in 1704 (q.v.).*

Première édition, comportant une variante de titre : 1745, q.v. pour titres et autres notes ; réimprimée en 1747 (q.v.). Il s'agit des vol. 7–8 de l'ouvrage de A. et J. Churchill intitulé Collection of voyages, *vol. 1–4 publiés pour la première fois en 1704 (q.v.).*

Robson, Joseph, *fl.* 1733–1763. An account of six years residence in Hudson's-Bay, from 1733 to 1736, and 1744 to 1747. By Joseph Robson, late surveyor and supervisor of the buildings to the Hudson's-Bay Company. Containing, a variety of facts, observations, and discoveries, tending to shew, I. The vast importance of the countries about Hudson's Bay to Great-Britain, on account of the extensive improvements that may be made there in many beneficial articles of commerce particularly in the furs and in the whale and seal fisheries. And, II. The interested views of the Hudson's bay Company; and the absolute necessity of laying open the trade and making it the object of national encouragement, as the only method of keeping it out of the hands of the French. To which is added an Appendix: containing, I. A short history of the discovery of Hudson's-bay; and of the proceedings of the English there since the grant of the Hudson's-bay charter: Together with remarks upon the papers and evidence produced by that company before the committee of the honourable House of Commons, in the year 1749. II. An estimate of the expence of building the stone fort, called Prince of Wales's-fort, at the entrance of Churchill-river. III. The soundings of Nelson-river. IV. A survey of the course of Nelson-river. V. A survey of Seal and Gillam's Islands, and, VI. A journal of the winds and tides at Churchill-river, for part of the years 1746 and 1747. The whole illustrated, by a draught of Nelson and Hayes's Rivers; a draught of Churchill-River; and plans of Yorkfort, and Prince of Wales's Fort. London: printed for J[ohn]. Payne and J. Bouquet . . . Mr. Kincaid . . . Mr. Barry . . . and Mr. Smith . . . 1752. 1 p.l., vi, 84, 95 p. 3 fold. maps. (incl. front.). 8°

cf. NUC(Pre–56)499:114*

The NUC entry seems to have a muddled and incomplete title. ¶ *Robson, a stonemason for the Hudson's Bay Company at Fort Prince of Wales (Churchill, Man.), kept a personal journal (cf. DCB 3:561–62).* ¶ Some copies contain also a preliminary leaf with advertisements of books. The recto is dated: London, April 15th, 1752, and the first item, "Just published," is a description of the first four volumes of *The Rambler.* [The 95 p. at end are the Appendix.] ¶ *Another ed., London, 1759, q.v.; reissued in fiche form, Toronto, ca. 1960s (in Canadiana in the Toronto Public Library series).* ¶ *NSWA · OKQ · OTU · BVA · BVAU · BVIPA*

La notice du NUC semble comporter un titre embrouillé et incomplet. ¶ *Robson, tailleur de pierre au service de la Compagnie de la Baie d'Hudson à Fort Prince of Wales (Churchill (Man.)), tenait un journal personnel (cf. DBC 3:561–62).* ¶ Certains exemplaires comprennent aussi un feuillet liminaire avec des réclames de livres. Le recto est daté : Londres, le 15 avril 1752, et le premier article, « qui vient d'être publié », consiste en une description des quatre premiers volumes de *The Rambler.* [Les 95 p. à la fin constituent l'annexe.] ¶ *Autre éd., Londres, 1759, q.v. ; reproduction sous forme de fiches, Toronto, vers 1960 (dans la collection Canadiana de la Toronto Public Library).* ¶ *NSWA · OKQ · OTU · BVA · BVAU · BVIPA*

Some considerations on the importation and exportation of beaver; with remarks on the hatter's case. [London, 1752.] Broadsheet. fol.

NUC(Pre–56)555:658

Caption title. ¶ The hatters, who wish to discourage the exportation of beaver so as to reduce its price, have declared, untruthfully, that their trade has declined. To prohibit the exportation of beaver would have a contrary effect to that intended by the hatters, since all the beaver which is imported from America is purchased by the produce, labour, and manufacture of Great Britain.

Titre de départ. ¶ Voulant décourager l'exportation des peaux de castor afin d'en faire baisser le prix, les chapeliers ont faussement déclaré que leur commerce décline. L'interdiction d'exporter des peaux de castor produirait l'effet contraire à celui que veulent les chapeliers, puisque toutes les peaux de castor qui sont importées d'Amérique sont achetées par les boutiquiers, les façonniers et les fabricants de Grande-Bretagne.

1753

*Oldys, William, 1696–1761. The Harleian miscellany: or, A collection of scarce, curious, and entertaining pamphlets . . . . With a table of contents, and an alphabetical index. Vol. I. The 2d ed. London, printed for T[homas]. Osborne, 1753. viii, 168, viii, 608 p. 4°(?)

NUC(Pre–56)231:252* (under title)

No more published? ¶ Includes "A copious and exact catalogue of pamphlets in the Harleian library" (168 p.) by William Oldys. ¶ Waldon has this as 8 vols., 4°; the above is from

Aucune autre édition ? ¶ Comprend « A copious and exact catalogue of pamphlets in the Harleian library » (168 p.) par William Oldys. ¶ Indication de Waldon pour cet ouvrage : 8 vol., in–4° ; les renseignements

NUC. ¶ First ed.: London, 1744 (*q.v.* for other notes).

susmentionnés proviennent du NUC. ¶ Première éd. : Londres, 1744 (*q.v.* pour d'autres notes).

Tucker, Josiah, 1712–1799. A brief essay on the advantages and disadvantages which respectively attend France and Great Britain, with regard to trade. With some proposals . . . . In a new method. By Josiah Tucker . . . . The 3d ed. corr., with additions. London: T[homas]. Trye, 1753. <Price two shillings.> 1 p.l., [vi]–viii, xii, [13]–168 p. 8°

NUC(Pre–56)603:615*

Waldon has collation as: viii, 168 p. ¶ *For other notes and editions,* see *second ed., 1750.* ¶ *BVIPA*

Collation de Waldon : viii, 168 p. ¶ *Pour d'autres notes et éditions,* voir *la deuxième éd., 1750.* ¶ *BVIPA*

1754

Histoire géographique de la Nouvelle Ecosse . . . . London, 1754.

This edition not verified, *see* first ed., 1749, for notes.

Cette édition n'a pas été vérifiée; *voir* notes de la première éd., 1749.

[Jefferys, Thomas], *d./déc.* 1771. The conduct of the French, with regard to Nova Scotia; from its first settlement to the present time. In which are exposed the falsehood and absurdity of their arguments made use of to elude the force of the Treaty of Utrecht, and support their unjust proceedings. In a letter, to a member of Parliament. London: printed for T[homas]. Jefferys ... 1754. (Price one shilling.) 1 p.l., 77 p. 8°

NUC(Pre–56)279:25*

Waldon indicates a list of books on one extra page at the end. ¶ *Under the Treaty of Utrecht (1713), France retained certain rights and regions, including Cape Breton, on which she was now building the mighty fortress of Louisbourg.* ¶ Answered by: Gilbert A. F. S. de La Grange de Chessieux, *La conduite des François justifiée.* Utrecht, 1756; and, Mathieu F. P. de Mairobert, *Lettre de Monsieur de M***, au sujet des écrits anglois, sur les limites de l'Amerique.* [Paris? 1755]. ¶ *Transl. into French as:* Conduite des François, par rapport a la Nouvelle Ecosse. *À Londres, 1755,* q.v. ¶ *NSWA · BVIP*

Waldon mentionne une liste de livres sur une page supplémentaire à la fin. ¶ *Aux termes du traité d'Utrecht (1713), la France conservait certains droits et gardait plusieurs territoires, y compris le Cap-Breton, où elle construisit alors la puissante forteresse de Louisbourg.* ¶ Ce document a suscité la réponse de Gilbert A. F. S. de La Grange de Chessieux, *La conduite des François justifiée.* Utrecht, 1756 ; et de Mathieu F. P. de Mairobert, *Lettre de Monsieur de M***, au sujet des écrits anglois, sur les limites de l'Amerique.* [Paris ? 1755]. ¶ *Trad. en français sous le titre* Conduite des François, par rapport a la Nouvelle Ecosse. *À Londres, 1755,* q.v. ¶ *NSWA · BVIP*

*Lambert, Claude François, 1705–1765. Curious observations upon ... ancient and modern geography ... arts and sciences of the several nations .... Translated from the French. London, printed for J. Wren, 1754. 2 vols. 8°(?)

NUC(Pre–56)313:31*

First pub. in English as: *A collection of curious observations.* London, 1750, *q.v.* for other notes and editions.

Première publ. en anglais sous le titre *A collection of curious observations.* Londres, 1750, *q.v.* pour d'autres notes et éditions.

A letter from a Russian sea-officer, to a person of distinction at the court of St. Petersburgh: containing his remarks upon Mr. de L'Isle's chart and memoir, relative to the new discoveries northward and eastward from Kamtschatka. Together with some observations on that letter. By Arthur Dobbs, Esq; Governor of North-Carolina. To which is added, Mr. de L'Isle's explanatory memoir on his chart published at Paris, and now translated from the original French. London: printed for A[ndreas]. Linde, and sold by J[acob]. Robinson, in Ludgate-Street. 1754. 2 p.l., 83, [1] p. 8°

NUC(Pre–56)328:673*

Sometimes attributed to Gerhard Müller. ¶ Waldon has only 1 p.l., and NUC omits final p. (list of books). ¶ Contents: A letter from a Russian sea-officer [signed: N. N.]; Observations upon the Russian discoveries, &c. By Governor Dobbs; An explanation of the map of the new discoveries northward of the South-sea. By Mr. de L'Isle; A letter by Admiral Barthelemi de Fonte . . . in which he gives an account of . . . his expedition for discovering whether there be any passage from the north-west of the Atlantic-ocean to the South-sea, and that of Great Tartary. Tr. from the Spanish. ¶ Also issued in microfilm, in History of the Pacific Northwest series, no. 191, reel 19 (cf. NUC).

Parfois attribué à Gerhard Müller. ¶ Waldon indique 1 f. l., et le NUC omet la p. finale (liste de livres). ¶ Qui portent sur le Canada : A letter from a Russian sea-officer [signed: N. N.]; Observations upon the Russian discoveries, &c. By Governor Dobbs; An explanation of the map of the new discoveries northward of the South-sea. By Mr. de L'Isle; A letter by Admiral Barthelemi de Fonte . . . in which he gives an account of . . . his expedition for discovering whether there be any passage from the north-west of the Atlantic-ocean to the South-sea, and that of Great Tartary. Tr. from the Spanish. ¶ Également reproduit sur microfilm dans la collection History of the Pacific Northwest, n° 191, bobine 19 (cf. NUC).

[Plumard de Dangeul, Louis Joseph], *b./n.* 1722. Remarks on the advantages and disadvantages of France and of Great-Britain with respect to commerce, and to the other means of encreasing the wealth and power of a state. Being a (pretended) translation from the English, written by Sir John Nickolls [*pseud.*], and printed at Leyden 1754. Translated from the French original. London, printed for T[homas]. Osborne, 1754. xi, 273 p. 12°

NUC(Pre–56)462:120*

The author is "a young gentleman, who has an employ at the court of Versailles, who travelled about two years ago, into the different provinces of England and even into Scotland.... On his return to France, he published the result of his observations, under the fictitious name of Sir John Nickolls": "Advertisement," p. v–vi. ¶ Transl. from his: Remarques sur les avantages et les désavantages de la France et de la Gr. Bretagne.... Traduction de l'anglois du chevalier John Nickolls [pseud.] 2d éd. Leyde, 1754 (this and the first ed., Leyde, 1754, were pretended transls., having been written first in French). ¶ "Of fisheries": p. 93–100 (Cape Breton and Newfoundland: p. 99–100); Hudson's Bay Company: p. 150–53. (An attack on the administration of the Company. Trade is not fully developed and profits are concealed in order not to have to share the benefits of the monopoly with the nation. The country is not opened up as it should be.) ¶ BVAU

L'auteur est « un jeune seigneur, qui sert à la cour de Versailles. Voici environ deux ans, il a voyagé dans les diverses provinces d'Angleterre et même en Écosse.... À son retour en France, il a publié, sous le nom d'emprunt sir John Nickolls, le résultat de ses observations » : « Advertisement », p. v–vi. ¶ Trad. de son ouvrage : Remarques sur les avantages et les désavantages de la France et de la Gr. Bretagne.... Traduction de l'anglois du chevalier John Nickolls [pseud.] deuxième éd. Leyde, 1754 (cette édition et la première éd., À Leyde, 1754, étaient considérées comme des trad., puisqu'elles avaient été rédigées d'abord en français). ¶ « Of fisheries » : p. 93–100 (Cap-Breton et Terre-Neuve : p. 99–100) ; Compagnie de la Baie d'Hudson : p. 150–53. (Une attaque contre l'administration de la Compagnie. Le commerce n'a pas pris son plein essor, et la Compagnie dissimule ses profits afin de ne pas devoir partager avec la nation les avantages que lui procure le monopole. Le pays ne s'épanouit pas comme il le devrait.) ¶ BVAU

Remarks on the present proceedings of the French in America, with respect to the British colonies in general, &c. [No imprint or collation.]

Source: see note.

Not found in NUC, BM, BLC, JCB. ¶ From a list of books "in a few days to be published" by T. Jefferys, p. [78] of his The conduct of the French, with regard to Nova Scotia. London, 1754.

Introuvable dans le NUC, le BM, le BLC et le JCB. ¶ Tiré d'une liste de livres « devant être publiés d'ici quelques jours », à la p. [78] de l'ouvrage de T. Jefferys, The conduct of the French, with regard to Nova Scotia. Londres, 1754.

354

A scheme to drive the French out of all the continent of America. Humbly offered to the consideration of ⸺ ⸺, Esq. [London?] printed in the year 1754. 23 p. 12°

NUC(Pre–56)525:20*

Page 18 incorrectly numbered 81. ¶ Signed at end: T. C.; dated: 5 September 1754. ¶ Reprinted: Boston, New-England, 1755.

Page 18 incorrectement numérotée 81. ¶ Signé à la fin : T. C. ; daté du 5 septembre 1754. ¶ Réimpression : Boston (Nouvelle-Angleterre), 1755.

[Smith, William], 1727–1803. Some account of the North-America Indians; their genius, characters, customs, and dispositions, towards the French and English nations. To which are added, Indian miscellanies . . . . Collected by a learned and ingenious gentleman in the province of Pensylvania . . . . London, printed for R[alph]. Griffiths [1754]. viii, [9]–68 p. 8°

NUC(Pre–56)552:315

Mainly concerns the Iroquois and Creek Indians.

Traite principalement des Iroquois et des Creeks.

1755

An accurate description of Cape Breton, with respect to its situation, soil, climate, ports, harbours, forces, and productions both natural and artificial. The political reasons, that induced the French ministry to settle and fortify it. From all which may be seen, its great importance to France, but of how much greater it might have been to England. With a circumstantial account of the taking and surrendering of the city and garrison by the New-England forces, &c. commanded by General Pepperell in 1745. A work especially at this critical juncture, the more interesting, as the French seem to be ardently desirous of dispossessing us of Nova Scotia also. Illustrated with an exact map of the island, and a plan of the city and port of Louisbourg, taken from an actual survey, and references to the Journal of the siege. To which are added notes and observations by a gentleman, who resided there several years. Most humbly inscribed to the Hon. Edward Boscawen, esq; London: printed for M. Cooper [etc.] 1755. viii, 72 p. fold. map. 8°

NUC(Pre–56)2:598

Gent. Mag. 1755. From Sabin:10724. ¶ *Concerns the Siege of Louisbourg, 1745, under General Pepperell.* ¶ *NSWA*

Gent. Mag. 1755. D'après le Sabin:10724. ¶ *Traite du siège de Louisbourg, 1745, sous le commandement du général Pepperell.* ¶ *NSWA*

An answer to an invidious pamphlet, intituled, A brief state of the province of Pennsylvania. Wherein are exposed the many false assertions of the author or authors, of the said pamphlet, with a view to render the Quakers of Pennsylvania and their government obnoxious to the British Parliament and ministry; and the several transactions, most grossly misrepresented therein, set in their true light. London, printed for S[amuel]. Bladon . . . , 1755. 1 p.l., 80 p. 8°

NUC(Pre–56)17:581

Possibly by an attorney's clerk named Cross(?) — cf. Wm. Smith, A brief view of the conduct of Pennsylvania. London, 1756, p. 13n. ¶ A reply to:

Peut-être écrit par un certain Cross (?) clerc chez un avocat, – cf. Wm. Smith, A brief view of the conduct of Pennsylvania. Londres, 1756, p. 13n. ¶ Réplique à William Smith, A brief

William Smith, A brief state of the province of Pennsylvania. *London, 1755.* ¶ A number of pamphlets arising out of the controversy over the part played by Pennsylvania in the defence of the English colonies against the French [and Indians] were published in 1755 and the following years. Not all are included here as their relevance to our subject is sometimes slight.

state of the province of Pennsylvania. *Londres, 1755.* ¶ La controverse au sujet du rôle joué par la Pennsylvanie dans la défense des colonies anglaises contre les Français [et les Indiens] a suscité la publication de plusieurs pamphlets en 1755 et les années suivantes. Ces pamphlets ne figurent pas tous ici, car leur pertinence est parfois minime par rapport à notre propos.

Anville, Jean Baptiste Bourguignon d', 1697–1782. North America from the French of M^r D'Anville improved with the back settlements of Virginia and course of Ohio [River]. [London.] [Thomas] Jefferys, 1755. map. fol.

NUC(Pre–56)18:296*

Dr. Waldon takes her entry (given under 1754, Bourguignon d'Anville) from a list of books to be pub. "in a few days" on p. 78 of Jefferys's The conduct of the French, with regard to Nova Scotia. *London, 1754 (q.v.); but this is the earliest ed. found in NUC, and title and pub. date may not have been as announced in the list. Waldon's title, from the list, is: A map of North America; from the French of Mr. D'Anville, containing the English, French and Spanish settlements, improved in the back settlements of Virginia and course of the Ohio, illustrated with geographical and historical remarks. Price 1s 6d.* ¶ *First (?) edition; other appearances: 1756 and 1762, q.v., and 1775 and 1786 (cf. NUC).*

Waldon tire sa notice (sous 1754, Bourguignon d'Anville) d'une liste de livres devant être publiés « d'ici quelques jours », à la p. 78 de l'ouvrage de Jefferys, The conduct of the French, with regard to Nova Scotia. *Londres, 1754 (q.v.) ; mais il s'agit de l'éd. la plus ancienne qui soit inscrite dans le NUC, et dont le titre et la date de publication peuvent différer des indications fournies dans la liste. Tiré de la liste, le titre de Waldon est : A map of North America; from the French of Mr. D'Anville, containing the English, French and Spanish settlements, improved in the back settlements of Virginia and course of the Ohio, illustrated with geographical and historical remarks. Price 1s 6d.* ¶ *Première (?) édition ; autres publications : 1756 et 1762, q.v., ainsi que 1775 et 1786 (cf. NUC).*

[Butel-Dumont, Georges Marie], 1725–1788. Histoire et commerce des colonies angloises, dans l'Amerique Septentrionale, où l'on trouve l'état actuel de leur population, & des détails curieux sur la constiution, de leur gouvernement, principalement sur celui de la Nouvelle-Angleterre, de la Pensilvanie, de la Caroline & de la Géorgie. A Londres, et se vend à Paris, chez Le Breton [etc.] 1755. xxiv, 336 p. 12°

NUC(Pre–56)87:286*

First edition; another ed. pub. same year: *see* next entry. ¶ OTP

Première édition ; autre éd. publ. la même année : *voir* la notice suivante. ¶ OTP

[Butel-Dumont, Georges Marie], 1725–1788. Histoire et commerce des colonies angloises, dans l'Amerique Septentrionale . . . . Nouv. ed. La Haye, aux depens de la compagnie, 1755. xvi, 246 p. 12°(?)

NUC(Pre–56)87:286*

NUC entry notes BN attributes also to de Forbonnais. ¶ See *preceding entry (first ed.).*

La notice du NUC indique que le BN attribue également cet ouvrage à de Forbonnais. ¶ Voir *la notice précédente (première éd.).*

[Chauncy, Charles], 1705–1787. A letter to a friend; giving a concise, but just account, according to the advices hitherto received, of the Ohio-defeat; and pointing out also the many good ends, this inglorious event is naturally adapted to promote: or, shewing wherein it is fitted to advance the interest of all the American British colonies. To which is added, some general account of the New-England forces, with what they have already done, counter-ballancing the above loss. Boston, printed: Bristol, re-printed by Edward Ward on the Tolzey, 1755. <Price six-pence.> 30 p. 8°

Sabin:12320 and 40382

Signed: T. W.; dated: Boston, August 25th, 1755. "Also attributed to Timothy Walker": Evans:7381. ¶ *Con-*

Signé : T. W. ; daté : Boston, le 25 août 1755. « Également attribué à Timothy Walker » : Evans:7381. ¶ *Traite de la cam-*

cerns the "inglorious" campaign of General Edward Braddock, defeated by an inferior force of French, Canadians, and Indians, at Fort Duquesne, 1755. ¶ This, and the London edition (q.v., following), were reprinted from the first edition: A letter to a friend; giving a concise, but just account . . . . Boston: N. E. printed and sold by Edes and Gill, at their printing office, next to the prison in Queen-Street, 1755. 15 p. 4°(?) OTP (NUC(Pre–56)104:680). It was followed by A second letter to a friend; giving a more particular narrative of the defeat of the French army at Lake-George by the New-England troops . . . . Boston, N. E., Edes and Gill, 1755 (NUC(Pre–56)104:682). Both Letters were reprinted together as Two letters to a friend, on the present critical conjuncture of affairs in North America. Boston (reprinted same year, London, q.v.), 1755; the first ed. was repub. in MF, Ann Arbor, Mich., University Microfilms, 1960 (NUC).

pagne « peu glorieuse » du général Edward Braddock, qui fut défait à Fort Duquesne en 1755 par des forces inférieures composées de Français, de Canadiens et d'Indiens. ¶ Cet écrit ainsi que l'édition londonienne (q.v., plus loin) constituent de nouvelles éditions de la suivante, qui fut la première : A letter to a friend ; giving a concise, but just account . . . . Boston : N.E. printed and sold by Edes and Gill, at their printing office, next to the prison in Queen-Street, 1755. 15 p. in–4°(?) OTP (NUC(Pre–56) 104:680). Il fut suivi de A second letter to a friend ; giving a more particular narrative of the defeat of the French army at Lake-George by the New-England troops . . . . Boston (N.E.), Edes and Gill, 1755 (NUC (Pre–56)104:682). Ces deux ouvrages furent réimprimés ensemble sous le titre Two letters to a friend, on the present critical conjuncture of affairs in North America. Boston (réimprimé la même année à Londres, q.v.), 1755 ; la première éd. a été reproduite sur mic., Ann Arbor (Mich.), University Microfilms, 1960 (NUC).

*[Chauncy, Charles], 1705–1787. A letter to a friend: giving a concise, but just, account . . . . Boston, New-England, printed; London, re-printed and sold by J. Noon, 1755. 2 p.l., 28 p. 8°

Waldon (from Sabin) has bookseller as "J. Nunn," but no such name found in Plomer. ¶ See preceding entry.

Waldon (d'après le Sabin) nomme le libraire « J. Nunn », mais ce nom est introuvable dans Plomer. ¶ Voir la notice précédente.

[Chauncy, Charles], 1705–1787. Two letters to a friend, on the present critical conjuncture of affairs in North America; particularly on the vast importance of the victory gained by the New-England militia under the command of General Johnston [!] at Lake-George. Being the most genuine account of this action yet published. Boston, printed: London, reprinted, for T. Jefferys, 1755. 1 p.l., 54 p. 8°

NUC(Pre–56)104:682

NUC has only 54 p. ¶ Waldon has not indicated if she had found a separate Boston edition of this Two letters. *¶ A reprint of two letters published separately (Boston, 1755) over the pseudonymous signature T. W., with the following titles: (1)* A letter to a friend; giving a concise, but just, account ... of the Ohio-defeat *(dated 25 August 1755; see Bristol ed., above); (2)* A second letter to a friend; giving a more particular narrative of the defeat of the French army at Lake-George *(dated 29 September 1755).*

Le NUC indique seulement 54 p. ¶ Au sujet de cet ouvrage, Two letters, *Waldon n'a pas mentionné si elle avait trouvé une édition distincte publiée à Boston. ¶ Les deux lettres, signées du pseudonyme T.W., furent imprimées et publiées séparément (Boston, 1755) sous les titres respectifs : 1)* A letter to a friend ; giving a concise, but just, account ... of the Ohio-defeat *(daté du 25 août 1755 ; voir l'éd. de Bristol, plus haut) ; 2)* A second letter to a friend ; giving a more particular narrative of the defeat of the French army at Lake-George *(daté du 29 septembre 1755).*

Clarke, William, *fl.* 1755. Observations on the late and present conduct of the French, with regard to their encroachments upon the British colonies in North America. Together with remarks on the importance of these colonies to Great-Britain. By William Clarke, M. D., of Boston, in New England. To which is added, wrote by another hand, Observations concerning the increase of mankind, peopling of countries, &c. Boston: printed: London: reprinted for John Clarke. ... 1755. 5 p.l. 54 p. 8°

NUC(Pre–56)111:390*

Waldon has collation: t.-p., [8], 54 p. ¶ "Observations concerning the increase of mankind" *was written by Benjamin Franklin, in 1751. ¶* "Observations" *on the Seven Years' War, called the French and Indian War in*

Collation de Waldon : p. de t., [8], 54 p. ¶ « Observations concerning the increase of mankind » *a été écrit par Benjamin Franklin en 1751. ¶* « Observations » *sur la guerre de Sept Ans, appelée la guerre des Français et des Indiens en Amérique du Nord. ¶* Première

North America. ¶ First pub., anonymously, as: *Observations on the late and present conduct of the French* .... *To which is added ... Observations concerning the increase of mankind* .... Boston, printed and sold by S. Kreeland ... , 1755. 4 p.l., iv, 47, 15 p. 4° (NUC(Pre–56)111:389); reprinted: Tarrytown, N.Y., W. Abbatt, 1917. vi, [3]–31 p., omitting Franklin's "Observations"; and in an undated microcard edition (cf. NUC).

publ. anonyme sous le titre *Observations on the late and present conduct of the French* .... *To which is added ... Observations concerning the increase of mankind* .... Boston, printed and sold by S. Kreeland ... , 1755. 4 f. l., iv, 47, 15 p. in–4° (NUC(Pre–56)111:389) ; réimpressions : Tarrytown (N.Y.), W. Abbatt, 1917. vi, [3]–31 p., sans les « Observations » de Franklin ; et dans une édition non datée sur microcarte (cf. NUC).

Colden, Cadwallader, 1688–1776. The history of the Five Indian nations of Canada .... With particular accounts of their religion ... their wars with other Indians ... and the treaties which have been lately made with them. In two volumes. The third edition. London, printed for Lockyer Davis ... 1755. 2 v.: [xvi], 260 p.; 2 l., 251 p. fold. map (front., v. 1). 12°

NUC(Pre–56)114:532*

For list of contents, see entry in NUC. ¶ *This is the third London ed., with variant title. See* 1747 *for first London edition.* ¶ *OKQ · BVAU*

Voir *table des matières à la notice du NUC.* ¶ *Il s'agit de la troisième éd. de Londres, qui comporte une variante de titre.* Voir *sous* 1747 *la première édition de Londres.* ¶ *OKQ · BVAU*

[Cross, ———], *counselor/conseiller.* An answer to an invidious pamphlet, intituled, A brief state of the province of Pennsylvania. Wherein are exposed the many false assertions of the author or authors, of the said pamphlet, with a view to render the Quakers of Pennsylvania and their government obnoxious to the British Parliament and ministry; and the several transactions, most grossly misrepresented therein, set in their true light. London: printed for S[amuel]. Bladon, in Pater–noster–Row. 1755. 1 p.l., 80 p. 8°

NUC(Pre–56)128:67

A reply to: *William Smith*, A brief state of the Province of Pennsylvania .... London, *1755* (q.v.), *where there is a note on this controversy.*

Ce texte constitue une réplique à : A brief state of the Province of Pennsylvania .... *Londres, 1755,* de William Smith (q.v.), *ouvrage dans lequel se trouve une note sur cette controverse.*

*A description of the English and French territories, in North America: being, an explanation of a new map of the same. Shewing all the encroachments of the French, with their forts, and usurpations on the English settlements; and the fortifications of the latter. Done with the newest maps published in London. And compared with Dr. Mitchell's . . . and every omission carefully supplied from it. Dublin: printed for J[ohn]. Exshaw, 1755. 28 p. 8°

NUC(Pre–56)140:329

Another edition: Dublin, *1756, q.v.* for notes.

Autre édition : Dublin, 1756, *q.v.* pour des notes.

Douglass, William, 1691?–1752. A summary, historical and political, of the first planting, progressive improvements, and present state of the British settlements in North-America. Containing I. Some general account of ancient and modern colonies, the granting and settling of the British continent and West-India Island colonies, with some transient remarks concerning the adjoining French and Spanish settlements, and other remarks of various natures. II. The Hudson's Bay Company's lodges, furr and skin trade. III. Newfoundland harbours and cod-fishery. IV. The province of L'Accadie or Nova Scotia; with the vicissitudes of the property and jurisdiction thereof, and its present state. V. The several grants of Sagadahock, province of Main, Massachusetts-Bay, and New-Plymouth, united by a new charter in the present province of Massachusetts-Bay, commonly called New-England. By William Douglass, M. D. Vol. I. [Vol. II.] Boston, New-England, printed: London, re-printed for R[obert]. Baldwin, 1755. 2 v.: iv, [4], 568 p.; 1 p.l., [4], 416 p. fold. map. 8°

NUC(Pre–56)147:674*

Advertised in *Public advertiser*, 30 July 1755: "This day is published." First pub. Boston, 1747–52 [copy in BVIPA] as by W. D., M. D., in numbers [v. 1, Jan. 1747–May 1749; v. 2, April 1750–Aug(?) 1752, but not printed in the *American magazine* as first announced by the publisher. Unfinished at author's death, October 1752. The subtitle of the two volumes specifying the content varies accordingly — cf. NUC for details]. First edition in book form, without map: Boston, Rogers and Fowle, v. 1, 1749, v. 2, 1751. Reprinted London, 1760, *q.v.* ¶ *OKQ · BVILSB*

Annoncé à la rubrique : « This day is published » dans le *Public advertiser* du 30 juillet 1755. Première publ. Boston, 1747–1752 [exemplaire au BVIPA] par numéros sous la signature W.D., M.D. [vol. 1, janvier 1747–mai 1749 ; vol. 2, avril 1750–août (?) 1752, mais la parution dans l'*American magazine* que l'éditeur avait initialement annoncée n'a pas eu lieu. Inachevée à la mort de l'auteur au mois d'octobre 1752. Le sous-titre des deux volumes, qui en précise le contenu, diffère donc –cf. NUC pour des détails]. Première édition en livre, sans carte : Boston, Rogers et Fowle, vol. 1, 1749, vol. 2, 1751. Réimprimé à Londres, 1760, *q.v.* ¶ *OKQ · BVILSB*

The English pilot. The fourth book. Describing the West-India navigation, from Hudson's-Bay . . . . London, W[illiam]. and J[ohn]. Mount, T[homas]. Page, 1755. 4, 66 p. illus., charts (part fold.). fol.

NUC(Pre–56)160:374*

First edition: 1689, *q.v.* for the dates of the many other editions, including the 1706, which has a similar title and is more fully transcribed.

Première édition : 1689, *q.v.* pour les dates des nombreuses autres éditions , y compris celle de 1706, qui porte un titre identique et a fait l'objet d'une transcription plus complète.

French policy defeated. Being, an account of all the hostile proceedings of the French, against the inhabitants of the British colonies in North America, for the last seven years. Also, the vigorous measures pursued both in England and America, to vindicate the rights of the British subjects, and the honour of the crown, from the insults and invasions of their perfidious enemies. With an authentic account of the naval engagement off Newfoundland, and the taking of the forts in the bay of Fundy. Embellished with two curious maps, describing all the coasts, bays, lakes, rivers, soundings, principal towns and forts, confining on the British plantations in America. London: printed for M[ary]. Cooper, 1755. (Price two shillings.) 2 p.l., 114 p. 2 fold. maps (incl. front.). 8°

NUC(Pre–56)184:609*

Caption title: Gallica fides: or, French policy. ¶ Events preceding the Seven Years' War. ¶ First edition; reprinted London, 1760, q.v. (variant subtitle).

Titre de départ : Gallica fides : or, French policy. ¶ Événements qui précèdent la guerre de Sept Ans. ¶ Première édition ; réimprimé à Londres en 1760, q.v. (variante de sous-titre).

Great Britain. Commissioners for Adjusting the Boundaries for the British and French Possessions in America. The memorials of the English and French commissaries concerning the limits of Nova Scotia or Acadia. London: printed in the year 1755. 2 v.; v. 1: 2 p.l., 771 p. (v. 2 relates to St. Lucia) front. (fold. map). 4°

NUC(Pre–56)212:321

Vol. 2 has title: The memorials of the English and French commissaries concerning St. Lucia. ¶ Waldon has the entry as: Great Britain. Commissioners for Adjusting the Boundaries of the British and French Possessions in North America. ¶ Further to this is: A fair representation of His Majesty's right in Nova Scotia. London, 1756, and Remarks on the French memorials. London, 1756, q.v. ¶ The English commissioners were William Shirley, Governor of Massachusetts Bay, and Sir William Mildmay, bart.; the

Titre du vol. 2 : The memorials of the English and French commissaries concerning St. Lucia. ¶ Waldon note ainsi le titre : Great Britain. Commissioners for Adjusting the Boundaries of the British and French Possessions in North America. ¶ Ouvrages consécutifs : A fair representation of His Majesty's right in Nova Scotia. Londres, 1756, et Remarks on the French memorials. Londres, 1756, q.v. ¶ Les commissaires anglais étaient William Shirley, gouverneur de Massachusetts Bay, et le baronnet sir William Mildmay ; les Français étaient R.M. Barrin, marquis de la Galissonnière, et E. de Silhouette. On

French were R. M. Barrin, Marquis de La Galissonnière, and E. de Silhouette. Because some of the Memorials had been published in Paris, it was thought necessary to publish all the documents in London [see also the notes to *A fair representation*. London, 1756]. ¶ *Similar works were pub., in French, in Paris, and in Germany and the Netherlands, in 1755–57 (cf. NUC).*

estima nécessaire de publier tous les documents à Londres [*voir aussi* les notes sous *A fair representation*, Londres, 1756] parce que certaines des chroniques en question avaient été publiées à Paris. ¶ *Des ouvrages semblables en français furent publiés à Paris ainsi qu'en Allemagne et aux Pays-Bas en 1755–1757 (cf. NUC).*

Great Britain. Sovereigns, etc., 1727–1760 (George II). His Majesty's most gracious speech to both Houses of Parliament, on Thursday, the thirteenth day of November, 1755. London, printed by Thomas Baskett ... and by the assigns of Robert Baskett. 1755. 4 p. fol.

NUC(Pre–56)215:428

The King, while anxious to preserve peace, has been preparing to protect his American colonies and prevent further French encroachments. Spain has promised neutrality. ¶ *Events presaging the Seven Years' War; six months later France and Britain were at war.*

Bien que désireux de préserver la paix, le roi se prépare à protéger ses colonies américaines et à empêcher tout autre empiétement de la part des Français. L'Espagne s'est engagée à rester neutre. ¶ *Événements présageant la guerre de Sept Ans ; six mois plus tard, la France et la Grande-Bretagne étaient en guerre.*

*****Histoire géographique de la Nouvelle Ecosse.... À Londres, 1755. vi, 164 p. 8°(?)

NUC(Pre–56)247:515*

Transl. (by Étienne de Lafargue) from: *A geographical history of Nova*

Trad. (par Étienne de Lafargue) de *A geographical history of Nova Scotia*. Londres,

Scotia. London, 1749 (*q.v.*), and first pub. in French: À Londres, 1749 (*q.v.*).

1749 (*q.v.*), et première publ. en français : À Londres, 1749 (*q.v.*).

[Huske, John], 1721?–1773.   The present state of North America, &c. Part I. London: printed for, and sold by R[obert]. and J[ames]. Dodsley, 1755.   2 p.l., 88 p. 4°

NUC(Pre–56)261:579*

Also attributed to Ellis Huske. ¶ Table of contents covers eight chapters, but only three appeared; no more published. ¶ *Rich, Sabin, and JCB(1) catalogues, following* Gentleman's magazine, *1755, v. 25, p. 238, state that this work is principally taken from G. M. Butel-Dumont's* Histoire et commerce des colonies angloises dans l'Amerique Septentrionale, 1755. *The two are somewhat similar in plan, the French work having eight chapters, as Huske's was planned to have, but the headings of the chapters are entirely different, and though the same facts are sometimes made use of by the two writers, their points of view are directly opposed to each other (cf. NUC).* ¶ Contents: Chap. I, The discoveries, rights and possessions of Great Britain; Chap. II, The discoveries, rights and possessions of France; Chap. III, The encroachments and depredations of the French upon His Majesty's territories, [etc.]. ¶ *First edition; reprinted Dublin, 1755 (q.v., following) and Boston, New England, D. Fowle, 1755 (cf. NUC); the*

Aussi attribué à Ellis Huske. ¶ La table des matières comprend huit chapitres, mais trois seulement furent publiés. Aucune autre édition. ¶ *Les catalogues Rich, Sabin et JCB(1), tout comme le* Gentleman's magazine, *1755, vol. 25, p. 238, notent que cet ouvrage est principalement tiré de l'ouvrage de G.M. Butel-Dumont,* Histoire et commerce des colonies angloises dans l'Amerique Septentrionale, 1755. *Les deux oeuvres possèdent une structure similaire ; l'ouvrage français contient huit chapitres, soit le même nombre de chapitres que devait avoir celui de Huske. Toutefois, les titres de chapitre sont complètement différents et bien que les deux auteurs utilisent parfois les mêmes faits, leurs idées sont diamétralement opposées (cf. NUC).* ¶ Qui portent sur le Canada : Chap. I, The discoveries, rights and possessions of Great Britain ; Chap. II, The discoveries, rights and possessions of France ; Chap. III, The encroachments and depredations of the French upon His Majesty's territories, [etc.]. ¶ *Première édition ; réimpression, Dublin, 1755 (q.v., notice suivante) et Boston (Nouvelle-Angleterre), D. Fowle, 1755 (cf. NUC ; la deuxième éd. avec corrections et contenant aussi « Une carte récente*

second ed., with emendations and containing also "A new and accurate map of North America," was pub. London, 1755 — see next entry but one.

et exacte de l'Amérique du Nord », fut publ. à Londres, en 1755 – voir deux notices plus loin.

*[Huske, John], 1721?–1773.   The present state of North America; lately presented to the Lords of the Regency of Great Britain. Pt. 1. Dublin, G[eorge]. Faulkner, 1755. 72 p. 4°(?)

NUC(Pre–56)261:579*

No more published. ¶ First ed.: London, 1755, q.v. (preceding) for other notes.

Aucune autre édition. ¶ Première éd. : Londres 1755, q.v. (note précédente) pour d'autres notes.

*[Huske, John], 1721?–1773.   The present state of North America, &c. Part I. The 2d ed., with emendations. London: printed for, and by R[obert]. and J[ames]. Dodsley in Pall-mall. 1755.   2 p.l., 88 p. fold. map. 4°

NUC(Pre–56)261:579*

Table of contents covers eight chapters, but pt. 1 contains chapters 1–3 only; no more published. ¶ The map, engraved by Thos. Kitchin, was published separately for the first ed., with title: "A new and accurate map of North America . . . . Inscribed to the Honorable Charles Townshend . . . by . . . [John] Huske. Tho; Kitchin sculpt. Published for The present state of North America . . . ." NYP [New York Public Library?] copy has ms. note: "As no more were published the fine map was clapped into this 2d editn." [NUC notes that a detached copy of

La table des matières comprend huit chapitres, mais la part. 1 ne comprend que les chapitres 1–3 ; aucune autre édition. ¶ La carte, gravée par Thos. Kitchin, a été publiée séparément pour la première éd., sous le titre suivant : « A new and accurate map of North America . . . . Inscribed to the Honorable Charles Townshend . . . by . . . [John] Huske. Tho ; Kitchin sculpt. Published for The present state of North America . . . . » L'exemplaire de la NYP [New York Public Library (?)] comporte la note manuscrite suivante : « Comme aucune autre édition n'a été publiée, cette excellente carte fut ajoutée dans cette deuxième éd. » [Le NUC note

this map is found in the Library of Congress.] ¶ *For other notes, see first ed.; London, 1755, entry before last.* ¶ BVAU

qu'un exemplaire détaché de cette carte se trouve à la Library of Congress.] ¶ Voir *autres notes dans la première éd. ; Londres, 1755, deux notices plus haut.* ¶ BVAU

[Jefferys, Thomas], *d./déc.* 1771. Conduite des François, par rapport a la Nouvelle Ecosse, depuis le premier établissement de cette colonie jusqu'à nos jours. Ouvrage où l'on expose la foiblesse des arguments dont ils se servent pour éluder la force du Traité d'Utrecht & pour justifier leurs procédés illégitimes, dans une lettre à un membre du Parlement. Tr. de l'anglois, avec des notes d'un François [par G. M. Butel-Dumont] .... A Londres, Chez les freres Vaillant, 1755. 1 p.l., xiv, 281 p. 12°

NUC(Pre–56)279:25*

English edition: The conduct of the French .... *London, 1754,* q.v. *for replies to this, and other notes.* ¶ OTU · BVAU

Édition anglaise : The conduct of the French .... *Londres, 1754,* q.v. *pour les répliques à cet ouvrage et d'autres notes.* ¶ OTU · BVAU

[Jones, John], 1700–1770. A letter to a friend in the country, upon the news of the town. London, printed for J. Raymond [1755]. <Price one shilling.> 2 p.l., 47 p. 8°(in 4s).

NUC(Pre–56)284:45*

[One source gives the] date [1756?], but it was apparently written before Braddock's defeat in 1755. The writer is of the opinion that French encroachments should be checked. The British have a chance to defeat France in America and should take it, instead of wasting money on a hopeless continental war. ¶ *Other editions:*

[Une source donne la] date [1756 ?], mais cette dernière fut apparemment écrite avant la défaite de Braddock en 1755. L'auteur est d'avis que les incursions par les Français devraient être contrées. Les Britanniques devraient profiter de la possibilité qu'ils ont de vaincre la France en Amérique au lieu de gaspiller de l'argent dans une guerre continentale perdue d'avance. ¶ *Autres éditions :*

see *under 1748, and second ed., [1756?]*
(perhaps the edition referred to by Wal-
don in her note, preceding).

voir *sous 1748, et deuxième éd., [1756 ?]*
(peut-être l'édition à laquelle réfère Waldon
dans la note précédente).

Lambert, Claude François, 1705–1765. Curious observations . . . . London, Lockyer Davis, 1755. 2 vols.: xii, [4], 260 p.; 1 p.l., 251, [18] p. 8°

Sabin:38730

First pub. in English as: A collection of
curious observations. *London, 1750,*
q.v. *for other notes and editions.*

Première publ. en anglais sous le titre A collection of curious observations. *Londres,*
1750, q.v. *pour d'autres notes et éditions.*

[LaRoche, —— de]. A letter from Quebeck, in Canada, to M. L'Maine, a French officer. Which contains a particular account of the present designs of the French upon the English in North-America; what force the French have collected, their several divisions, and the place destin'd for each. Likewise an account of the defenceless condition of the English provinces and colonies, and the method made use of by the French to procure such intelligence. Boston printed: Edinburgh: reprinted; sold by W[illiam]. Gray and W. Peter, at their shop opposite to the Cross. 1755. 11, [1, advert.] p. 12°

NUC(Pre–56)316:426*

Signed: De Roche, Quebeck, February 6,
1753. ¶ *First pub. Boston, 1754, 8 p.,*
and in Newport, R. I., the same year,
13 p.; reprinted Boston, Mass. Hist. Soc.,
1942 (Photostat Americana, 2d ser., no.
145). ¶ *OTP (Newport, 1754)*

Signé : De Roche, Quebeck, 6 février 1753. ¶
Première publ. Boston, 1754, 8 p., et Newport
(R.I.), la même année, 13 p. ; réimpression
Boston, Mass. Hist. Soc., 1942, (Photostat
Americana, deuxième coll., n° 145). ¶ *OTP*
(Newport, 1754)

A letter from a member of Parliament to . . . the Duke of ***** upon the present situation of affairs. London, printed for M[ary]. Cooper . . . 1755. 1 p.l., 13 [*i.e. 25*] p. 8°(in 4s).

NUC(Pre–56)328:668*

NUC has collation: 1 p.l., 25 p. ¶ Deals with the war in America, the writer wishing that the war could be confined to America and the sea. The English right to Nova Scotia is upheld (p. 4–6) and the ability of the English to conquer the French in America maintained (p. 22–25). ¶ *This was reproduced in microfiche, as part of the project of reproducing the texts of all titles in the Public Archives (Ottawa)* Catalogue of Pamphlets, *Ottawa, 1968 (cf. NUC).* ¶ *OOA · BVAU (facsim.)*

Collation du NUC : 1 f. l., 25 p. ¶ Traite de la guerre en Amérique ; l'auteur espère que celle-ci soit limitée à l'Amérique et sur mer. Il défend les droits de l'Angleterre sur la Nouvelle-Écosse (p. 4–6) et soutient que les Anglais peuvent vaincre les Français en Amérique (p. 22–25). ¶ *Réimpression sur microfiche dans le cadre du projet de reproduction du texte de tous les titres des Archives publiques du Canada, Ottawa,* Catalogue of Pamphlets, *Ottawa, 1968 (cf. NUC).* ¶ *OOA · BVAU (facsim.)*

Letters to the people of England, on the present situation and conduct of national affairs. London, 1755. [Not collated.] 8°

Sabin:40651

Includes an account of General Braddock's march to Fort Duquesne on the Ohio River [in the Seven Years' War], to dislodge the French. ¶ *This may be one in a group of pamphlets, some of which are described in NUC (Pre–56)542:463, under [John Shebbeare],* Letters to the people of England. *London, 1756–57: "6 pamphlets in 1 v." In the same place a similar but different work is listed, by Shebbeare:* Letters on the English nation, *and several works whose titles begin* A letter to the people of England. *One of these*

Contient un compte rendu de l'expédition du général Braddock entreprise [pendant la guerre de Sept Ans] afin de chasser les Français de Fort Duquesne, situé sur les rives de l'Ohio. ¶ *Ce document fait peut-être partie d'une série de pamphlets, dont quelques-uns sont décrits dans le NUC(Pre–56)542:463; sous [John Shebbeare],* Letters to the people of England. *Londres, 1756–1757 : « 6 pamphlets en 1 v. ». Au même endroit, un ouvrage similaire, quoique différent, par Shebbeare est noté :* Letters on the English nation, *ainsi que plusieurs ouvrages dont les titres commencent par* A letter to the people of England. *L'une*

is A letter to the people of England. On the present situation and conduct of national affairs. Letter I .... 6th ed. *London, 1756. 34 p. 8°. It is cited as Sabin:80052,* q.v. *under Shebbeare, 1755.*

d'elles est A letter to the people of England. On the present situation and conduct of national affairs. Letter I .... 6th ed. *Londres, 1756. 34 p., in–8°. Elle est citée dans le Sabin:80052,* q.v. *Shebbeare, 1755.*

[McCulloh, Henry], *d./déc.* 1778. A miscellaneous essay concerning the courses pursued by Great Britain in the affairs of her colonies: with some observations on the great importance of our settlements in America, and the trade thereof. London, R[obert]. Baldwin .... 1755. <Price eighteen pence.> 1 p.l., 134 p. 8°(?)

NUC(Pre–56)349:611*

The author's name is also spelled: McCulloch. ¶ The author advocates more direct control over colonial affairs by the Crown, a fund for use in America to win the Indians to the British side, etc., and the better regulation of the existing colonies before more are conquered from the French. ¶ *Reprinted in microfiche: Ottawa, Public Archives of Canada, 1968 (in Canada. Archives.* Pamphlets in the Public Archives of Canada*).* ¶ *BVAU*

Variante orthographique du nom de l'auteur : McCulloch. ¶ L'auteur préconise une intervention plus directe de la Couronne dans les affaires coloniales et la mise sur pied d'un fonds pour rallier les Indiens à la cause anglaise. Il prône aussi la mise en place d'une meilleure réglementation dans les colonies existantes avant que les Français n'en conquièrent d'autres. ¶ *Reproduction sur microfiches : Ottawa, Archives publiques du Canada, 1968 (au Canada. Archives.* Pamphlets in the Public Archives of Canada*).* ¶ *BVAU*

[McCulloh, Henry], *d./déc.* 1778. The wisdom and policy of the French in the construction of their great offices, so as best to answer the purposes of extending their trade and commerce, and enlarging their foreign settlements. With some observations in relation to the disputes now subsisting between the English and French colonies in America. London, printed for R[obert]. Baldwin . . . 1755. <Price eighteen pence.> 1 p.l., 134 p. 8°(?)

NUC(Pre–56)349:612*

The author's name is also spelled: McCulloch. ¶ NUC has collation: 1 p.l., 133 p. ¶ Discusses attacks on Canada and alliance with the Indians [in events leading to the Seven Years' War]. These papers contain interesting suggestions and opinions in regard to Canada. ¶ McCulloh's papers were published as follows: Miscellaneous representations relative to our concerns in America submitted <in 1761> to the Earl of Bute, by Henry McCulloh. Now first printed from the original ms., with biographical and historical introduction by Wm. A. Shaw . . . . London, George Harding [1905]. xvi, 22 p. 8° ¶ Also appeared in MF: Washington, D. C., Microcard Editions, 196– (cf. NUC). ¶ OTP · BVAU

Variante orthographique du nom de l'auteur : McCulloch. ¶ Collation du NUC : 1 f. l., 133 p. ¶ Traite des attaques contre le Canada et de l'alliance conclue avec les Indiens [dans le cadre des événements précédant la guerre de Sept Ans]. Ces documents contiennent des suggestions et opinions intéressantes sur le Canada. ¶ Les documents de McCulloh furent publiés ainsi : Miscellaneous representations relative to our concerns in America submitted <in 1761> to the Earl of Bute, by Henry McCulloh. Now first printed from the original ms., with biographical and historical introduction by Wm. A. Shaw . . . . Londres, George Harding, [1905]. xvi, 22 p., in–8°. ¶ Aussi reproduit sur mic. : Washington (D.C.), Microcard Editions, 196– (cf. NUC). ¶ OTP · BVAU

Mitchell, John, *d./déc.* 1768. A map of the British and French dominions in North America, with the roads, distances, limits and extent of the settlements . . . . [London] printed for [Thomas] Jefferys and [William?] Faden. Pub. by the author, Febry, 13th, 1755. col., fold. map. fol.

NUC(Pre–56)388:28*

This is the closest entry (next to a photostat, noted below) to Dr. Waldon's to be found in NUC, with Jefferys and Faden

Il s'agit de la notice du NUC qui se rapproche le plus de celle de Waldon (après la photocopie notée ci-dessous) ; elle donne les noms de Jefferys et de

named and the Feb. 13th date in the imprint; but after "settlements" Waldon has a period and "By John Mitchell. London:," while NUC has "humbly inscribed . . . Jno. Mitchell. [London]." Moreover, Waldon has collation "Atlas folio, 8 sheets." Her sources (q.v.) are JCB(I)3:1079 and (derivatively) Sabin: 49695. ¶ Inset: A new map of Hudson's Bay and Labrador. ¶ "A variant of the second ed. of Mitchell's map of the British colonies in North America, pub. the same year" (NUC), i.e., John Mitchell, A map of the British colonies. London, 1755. ¶ What is possibly the first ed., and a variant under this same title, follow; an undated photostat copy appears in NUC: "A map . . . of the settlements . . . by Jno. Mitchell. London, printed for Jeffery [sic] and Faden, 1755, photostat copy in thirty-one parts; known as the John Jany map." There was also an Amsterdam, 1755 edition, and a reprint in N. Sanson, Atlas nouveau, Amsterdam [n. d.], with inset plans of Quebec, Louisbourg, and Halifax (cf. NUC).

*Mitchell, John, d./déc. 1768. A map of the British and French dominions in North America . . . . Engraved by Thos. Kitchin. [London] 1755. map. fol.

NUC(Pre–56)388:28*

NUC notes map received at Trades and Plantations Office 13 Feb. 1755. ¶ See preceding entry for other notes.

*Mitchell, John, *d./déc.* 1768. A map of the British and French dominions . . . . Jno. Mitchell. [London.] The author, Febry 13th, 1755. col. map. fol.

NUC(Pre–56)388:28*

A second ed. of Mitchell's *Map of the British colonies in North America.* London, 1755. ¶ For other notes and editions, *see* preceding entries.

Deuxième édition de la *Map of the British colonies in North America.* Londres, 1755, de Mitchell. ¶ *Voir* autres notes et éditions aux notices précédentes.

The naked truth . . . . London, printed for A. Price. 1755. <Price six pence.> viii, 31 p. 8°

NUC(Pre–56)404:559*

Attributed to Oglethorpe by the British Museum (cf. NUC). ¶ *The omission marks in the title may represent "Numb. 1," as in the succeeding editions.* ¶ An *"A. Price" in Plomer is "probably fictitious" (cf. Plomer, 1726–75:203).* ¶ *Also transl. into French as* La vérité révélée (see *below*). ¶ Address "To the people of Great Britain, Ireland, and America," signed in ms. "Oglethorpe" [presumably James Edward Oglethorpe, 1696–1785]: p. iii–viii. ¶ A protest against the proposed French War [the Seven Years' War, 1756–63] on the grounds that the French are stronger in numbers and wealth and the cost in taxes and loss of trade will be crippling. Britain could buy all the French possessions in North America for less than the war will cost. Even if the British succeed in taking them, can they be held for long? The author

Attribué à Oglethorpe par le British Museum (cf. NUC). ¶ *Les marques d'omission dans le titre représentent peut-être « Numb. 1 », que l'on retrouve dans les éditions ultérieures.* ¶ *Selon Plomer, « A. Price » est « probablement fictif » (cf. Plomer, 1726–1775:203).* ¶ *Aussi trad. en français sous le titre* La vérite révélée (voir *plus loin*). ¶ Discours « Au peuple de Grande-Bretagne, d'Irlande, et d'Amérique », signé dans le man. « Oglethorpe » [l'on présume qu'il s'agit de James Edward Oglethorpe, 1696–1785] : p. iii–viii. ¶ L'auteur s'élève contre la guerre devant être déclarée aux Français [la guerre de Sept Ans, 1756–1763] en soutenant qu'ils sont plus nombreux et plus riches, et que le prix de cette guerre, en impôts et en raison de perturbations du commerce, serait ruineux. Il serait moins coûteux pour la Grande-Bretagne d'acheter tous les territoires français en Amérique du Nord. Même si les Anglais réussissaient à conquérir ces territoires, seraient-ils en

also refers to the jingoism of "Hurlothrumb" in the *Publick advertiser*, Wed., 30 July 1755. The reference is to a letter, signed: T. C., which extols the "Benefits that will accrue to this Nation by driving the French out of all the Continent of America." The wars, in T. C.'s views, hinder trade. By driving the French out of Canada, Britain would gain millions in trade and her troops could then be sent against Florida. ¶ The same issue of the *Publick advertiser* contains despatches from Nova Scotia reporting the surrender of the French fort at Beausejour, the loss of HMS *Mars* at the mouth of Halifax Harbour through the fault of the pilot, and other news. ¶ *First edition; at least five editions followed in the same year:* see *next entries.*

mesure de les garder ? L'auteur fait aussi référence au chauvinisme de « Hurlothrumb » dans le *Publick advertiser* du mer. 30 juillet 1755. Il fait référence à une lettre signée : T. C., qui vante les « bénéfices que la Nation retirera en chassant les Français de tout le continent d'Amérique ». Les guerres, selon T. C., entravent le commerce. En chassant les Français du Canada, la Grande-Bretagne obtiendrait des bénéfices commerciaux se chiffrant en millions et ses troupes pourraient ensuite être dirigées contre la Floride. ¶ Le même numéro du *Publick advertiser* contient des dépêches de Nouvelle-Écosse décrivant la capitulation du fort français à Beausejour, la perte du HMS *Mars* à l'embouchure du port d'Halifax due à la négligence du pilote, ainsi que d'autres nouvelles. ¶ *Première édition ; la même année, au moins cinq éditions suivirent :* voir *les notices suivantes.*

*The naked truth. Numb. I. London, 1755. 2d ed., 8°(?)

NUC(Pre–56)404:559*

For notes, *see* preceding entry.

Voir notes à la notice précédente.

*The naked truth. Numb. I. . . . London, printed for A. Price, 1755. viii, 32 p. 4th ed. 8°

NUC(Pre–56)404:559*

First ed. appeared the same year, but with 31 p., *see* above.

Première éd. parue la même année mais avec 31 p., *voir* ci-dessus.

*The naked truth. Numb. 1 . . . 5th ed. London, printed for A. Price, in Fleet-street, 1755. viii, 32 p. 8°(?)

NUC(Pre–56)404:559*

First ed. pub. the same year (*see* above), but with 31 p., and no publisher's address; note that the "A. Price" in Plomer, 1726–75:203, given as "probably fictitious," has the address "near Temple Bar" (cf. first ed.).

Première édition parue la même année (*voir* ci-dessus) mais avec 31 p. et sans l'adresse de l'éditeur ; il y a lieu de noter que le « A. Price » « probablement fictif » que mentionne Plomer, 1726–1775:203 comporte l'adresse « near Temple Bar » (cf. première éd.).

*Reflections upon the present state of affairs at home and abroad, particularly with regard to subsidies, and the differences between Great Britain and France. In a letter from a Member of Parliament to a constituent. . . . London, printed for J[ohn]. Payne, 1755. 60 p. 8°

NUC(Pre–56)485:324

Events leading to the Seven Years' War (1756–63), especially French and English affairs in North America, and including encroachments on the English colonies from New France, the Indians, and Gen. Braddock's defeat by the French and Indians at Fort Duquesne, 1755.

Événements précédant la guerre de Sept Ans (1756–1763), et notamment les affaires anglaises et françaises en Amérique du Nord, y compris les incursions dans les colonies anglaises à partir de la Nouvelle France, les Indiens, et la défaite du général Braddock aux mains des Français et des Indiens à Fort Duquesne en 1755.

[Shebbeare, John], 1709–88. A letter to the people of England, on the present situation and conduct of national affairs. Letter I . . . . London: printed for J[ohn]. Scott, 1755. 1 p.l., 58 p. 8°(in 4s).

NUC(Pre–56)542:463*

Criticizes the conduct of the [Seven Years'] War in America [with particular reference to Braddock's Campaign, 1755]. ¶ *First edition; also reprinted as microcard edition (cf. NUC); second ed., 1755 (see next entry); other eds., 1756, q.v. This first letter also appeared in Shebbeare's* Three letters to the people of England *[Letters I, II, and III]. 6th ed. London, 1756 (NUC (Pre–56)542:466). Shebbeare wrote seven (DNB) or eight (NUC(Pre–56) 542:463) letters "to the people of England," published separately and also in collections, some with replies by others; all but this first and the fourth (1756, q.v.) concern only the war in Europe, the peace, and King George I and II; the others seem to have no direct bearing on Canada. ¶ This is probably the same as Waldon's entry under title, from Sabin:40651, q.v., for other notes:* Letters to the people of England, 1755.

Critique la façon dont est menée la guerre [de Sept Ans] en Amérique [en particulier la campagne du général Braddock, 1755]. ¶ *Première édition ; reproduction sur microcarte (cf.* NUC *; deuxième éd., 1755 (voir la notice suivante) ; autres éd., 1756, q.v. Cette première lettre parut aussi dans* Three letters to the people of England *[Lettres I, II et III], sixième éd. Londres, 1756 (NUC(Pre–56)542:466) de Shebbeare. Shebbeare écrivit sept (DNB) ou huit (NUC(Pre–56)542:463) lettres « au peuple d'Angleterre », publiées séparément et sous forme de recueil, dont quelques-unes avec les réponses ; toutes sauf cette première lettre et la quatrième (1756, q.v.) ne traitent que de la guerre en Europe, de la paix et des rois George Iᵉʳ et George II ; les autres semblent n'avoir aucun rapport direct avec le Canada. ¶ Il s'agit probablement de la même notice que celle de Waldon sous ce titre, du Sabin:40651, q.v., pour d'autres notes :* Letters to the people of England, 1755.

*[Shebbeare, John], 1709–1788. A letter to the people of England . . . . Letter I. 2d ed. London, J[ohn]. Scott, 1755. 56 p. 8°(?)

NUC(Pre–56)542:463*

Sabin:80052 has: [2], 58 p. ¶ *See* first ed., preceding entry, for other notes.

Le Sabin:80052 note : [2], 58 p. ¶ *Voir* première éd., notice précédente, pour d'autres notes.

[Smith, William], 1727–1803. A brief state of the province of Pennsylvania, in which the conduct of their assemblies for several years past is impartially examined, and the true cause of the continual encroachments of the French displayed, more especially the secret design of their late unwarrentable invasion and settlement upon the River Ohio. To which is annexed, an easy plan for restoring quiet in the public measures of that province, and defeating the ambitious views of the French in time to come. In a letter from a gentleman who has resided many years in Pennsylvania, to his friend in London. London, printed for R[alph]. Griffiths, at the Dunciad, in Pater-noster Row. 1755. 1 p.l., 45 p. 8°(in 4s).

NUC(Pre–56)552:309*

William Smith, provost of the College of Philadelphia, urges that measures should be taken against the encroachments of the French, who are building and strengthening forts on the Ohio, St. Lawrence, etc., and attacks the Quakers for opposing plans for the defence of the Province. ¶ *Answered by: Cross, [first name unknown], An answer to an invidious pamphlet . . . . London, 1755* (q.v.). ¶ *Further to this is: William Smith, A brief view . . . . London, 1756* (q.v.). ¶ *First edition; republished in microfilm: Ann Arbor, Mich., University Microfilms, 1960 (American Culture series, 77:8); second ed., 1755 (see next entry); third ed., 1756* (q.v.).

William Smith, doyen du College of Philadelphia, préconise la prise de mesures contre les déprédations des Français qui construisent et fortifient des forts sur l'Ohio, le Saint-Laurent, etc., et attaquent les Quakers qui s'opposent aux plans de défense de la province. ¶ *Cet ouvrage a suscité la réplique suivante : An answer to an invidious pamphlet . . . . Londres, 1755, de Cross, [prénom inconnu], (q.v.). ¶ Ultérieurement, publication de William Smith, A brief view . . . . Londres, 1756, (q.v.). ¶ Première éd. ; reproduction sur microfilm : Ann Arbor (Mich.), University Microfilms, 1960 (collection American Culture, 77:8) ; deuxième éd., 1755 (voir la notice suivante) ; troisième éd., 1756 (q.v.).*

[Smith, William], 1727–1803. A brief state of the province of Pennsylvania . . . . 2d ed. London, printed for R. Griffiths, 1755.

NUC(Pre–56)552:309*

For notes, see preceding entry. ¶ *Reprinted New York, for Joseph Sabin,*

Voir *les notes à la notice précédente.* ¶ *Réimpression New York, pour Joseph Sabin, 1865,*

1865, 44 p. (Sabin reprints, no. 4) and in a microcard edition (two cards), cf. NUC. BVAU

44 p. (réimpressions du Sabin, n° 4) et dans une édition sur microcartes (deux cartes), cf. NUC. BVAU

[Smith, William], 1727–1803. A brief state of the province of Pennsylvania .... London, printed for R. Griffiths, and Dublin, re-printed by R[ichard]. James, 1755. 47 p. 8°

NUC(Pre–56)552:309*

Waldon has collation: 47, [1] p. ¶ See foregoing entries for notes. ¶ Republished in microfiche edition, cf. NUC. BVAU

Collation de Waldon : 47, [1] p. ¶ Voir les notes des notices précédentes. ¶ Reproduit sur microfiche, cf. NUC. BVAU

State of the British and French colonies in North America, with respect to number of people, forces, forts, Indians, trade and other advantages. In which are considered, I. The defenceless condition of our plantations, and to what causes owing. II. Pernicious tendency of the French encroachments, and the fittest methods of frustrating them. III. What it was occasioned their present invasion, and the claims on which they ground their proceedings. With a proper expedient proposed for preventing future disputes. In two letters to a friend. London: printed for A[ndrew]. Millar, 1755. 1 p.l., 190 p. 8°

NUC(Pre–56)565:328*

Refers to conditions just prior to the Seven Years' War (1756–63). ¶ Probably first (and only 18th cent.) edition; NUC lists a microcard and a microfilm format, and this was reprinted New York, Johnson, 1967. ¶ NSHPL · OTP · OONL(1967) · SSU(MF)

Traite de la période précédant la guerre de Sept Ans (1756–1763). ¶ Probablement la première édition (et la seule du 18ᵉ s.) ; le NUC note un format microcarte et microfilm ; réimpression à New York, chez Johnson, en 1967. ¶ NSHPL · OTP · OONL(1967) · SSU(mic.)

*La vérité révélée. Ouvrage traduit de l'Anglois .... A Londres [*i.e.*, Paris], 1755. 164 p. 8°(?)

NUC(Pre–56)634:189

London imprint but actually pub. in Paris (cf. NUC). ¶ Transl. (by E. J. Genet?) from: *The naked truth. Numb. 1.* London, 1755 (attributed to [James Edward?] Oglethorpe), *q.v.* for other notes. ¶ Published just before the outbreak of the Seven Years' War, 1756–63, in protest against the proposed war.

Adresse bibliographique de Londres mais publ. à Paris (cf. NUC). ¶ Trad. (par E. J. Genet?) de : *The naked truth. Numb. 1.* Londres, 1755 (attribué à [James Edward?] Oglethorpe), *q.v.* pour d'autres notes. ¶ Publié juste avant la guerre de Sept Ans, 1756–1763, pour protester contre la guerre qui se préparait.

1756

An account of conferences held, and treaties made, between Major-General Sir William Johnson, bart. and the chief sachems and warriours of the . . . Indian nations in North America . . . at Fort Johnson, in the colony of New York, in the years 1755 and 1756. With a letter from the Rev. Mr. Hawley to Sir William Johnson . . . . And a preface giving a short account of the Six Nations, some anecdotes of the life of Sir William, and . . . an account of conferences between several Quakers in Philadelphia, and some of the heads of the Six nations, in April 1756. London: printed for A[ndrew]. Millar, 1756. <Price 1s. 6d.> 1 p.l., xii, 3–77 p. 8°

NUC(Pre–56)2:551*

These conferences were an attempt to follow the oft-given advice to win the Indians to the support of the British against the French. Johnson is said to

Ces conférences visaient à rallier les Indiens à la cause britannique dans cette guerre contre les Français. On a dit que Johnson avait à sa disposition 10 000 £ pour

have had £10,000 to use for this purpose within nine months of Braddock's arrival (cf. Church, v. 5, p. 2041–42). ¶ *Reprinted: Lancaster, Pa., Lancaster Press, 1930. 1 p.l., xii, 3–77, [1] p.* ¶ *OTP*

atteindre cet objectif dans les neuf mois suivant l'arrivée de Braddock (cf. Church, vol. 5, p. 2041–42). ¶ *Réimpression : Lancaster (Pa.), Lancaster Press, 1930. 1 f. l., xii, 3–77, [1] p.* ¶ *OTP*

An account of the present state of Nova-Scotia: in two letters to a noble lord: one from a gentleman in the navy lately arrived from thence. The other from a gentleman who long resided there. Made publick by his lordship's desire. London, Printed, 1756. 11, 31 p. 4°

NUC(Pre–56)2:573*

The first letter signed: J. B.; the second: W. M. ¶ Not to be confused with *An account of the present state of Nova Scotia* [By S. Hollingsworth]. Edinburgh, 1786. ¶ The writers paint a very gloomy picture of the state of the colony. In contrast to this, *see The importance of settling and fortifying Nova Scotia. London, 1751.*

La première lettre est signée : J. B. ; la deuxième : W. M. ¶ Ne pas confondre avec *An account of the present state of Nova Scotia.* Édimbourg, 1786, [de S. Hollingsworth]. ¶ Les auteurs tracent un portrait très sombre de l'état de la colonie. Pour un autre point de vue, *voir The Importance of settling and fortifying Nova Scotia.* Londres, 1751.

---

*Anville, Jean Baptiste Bourguignon d', 1697–1782. North America from the French of Mr d'Anville . . . . London: Thos. Jefferys, 1756. map. fol.

NUC(Pre–56)18:296*

Laid in William Douglass, *A summary, historical and political.* London, 1755, vol. 2 (cf. NUC). ¶ For fuller title and other notes and editions, *see* first (?) ed., 1755.

Exposé dans William Douglass, *A summary, historical and political.* Londres, 1755, vol. 2 (cf. NUC). ¶ Pour un titre plus complet et d'autres notes et éditions, *voir* première (?) éd., 1755.

An appeal to the sense of the people, on the present posture of affairs. Wherein the nature of the late treaties are inquired into, and the conduct of the M—i—y with regard to M—n—ca, A—r—ca, &c, is considered; with some remarks upon the light in which these, and other publick affairs have been lately represented. London: printed for David Hookham, 1756. <Price one shilling.> 1 p.l., 54 p. 8°

NUC(Pre–56)18:505

A reply to: John Shebbeare, A letter to the people of England. London, 1755 (q.v.). ¶ Concerns the Seven Years' War, 1756–63, and Minorca and America. ¶ Supports the ministry. The war in America discussed: p. 38–51.

Réplique à A letter to the people of England. Londres, 1755, de John Shebbeare (q.v.). ¶ Traite de la guerre de Sept Ans, 1756–1763, de Minorque et de l'Amérique. ¶ Appuie le ministère. Porte sur la guerre en Amérique : p. 38–51.

The conduct of the Ministry, impartially examined. In a letter to the merchants of London. London: printed for S[amuel]. Bladon, 1756. <Price one shilling.> 68 p. 8°

NUC(Pre–56)118:549

Answered by: John Shebbeare, An answer to a pamphlet call'd, The Conduct .... London, 1756 (q.v.). ¶ Deals with the conflict in America, with particular reference to the traders taken prisoner in the Ohio. ¶ First edition; second ed., see next entry. ¶ OTP

Cet ouvrage a suscité la réplique suivante : An answer to a pamphlet call'd, The Conduct .... Londres, 1756, de John Shebbeare (q.v.). ¶ Traite du conflit en Amérique, et insiste plus particulièrement sur les commerçants faits prisonniers sur l'Ohio. ¶ Première édition ; deuxième éd., voir la notice suivante. ¶ OTP

The conduct of the Ministry .... London, S[amuel]. Bladon, 1756. 68 p. 8° 2d ed.

Sabin:15207

See first edition, preceding entry.

Voir première édition, notice précédente.

A description of the English and French territories, in North America: With an account of the great fall of Niagara; and of the Five Indian nations; together with the plan and description of Crown Point. Being an explanation of a new map of the same. Shewing all the encroachments of the French, with their forts and usurpations on the English settlements; and the fortifications of the latter. Done from the newest maps published in London: and compared with Dr. Mitchell's F. R. S. and every omission carefully supplied from it. Dublin: Printed for J[ohn]. Exshaw, at the Bible, opposite Castle-Lane, in Dame-Street, 1756. Price of the map and description. Coloured, 2s 2d. Traced, 1s 7 1/2d. Plain, 1s. 4d. 32 p. fold. map. plan. 8°

BLC(to 1975)7:63

Plan between p. 12 and 13: "Plan of Fort Frederick at Crown Point," with "A more particular description of Crown Point" on verso. Map inserted between p. 6 and 7: "Nova Scotia drawn from survey by T. Kitchin Gr." ¶ New Britain (Hudson Bay territory): p. 4; Nova Scotia: p. 4–7; Canada: p. 23; Five Nations Indians in Canada: p. 24–27; Newfoundland: p. 29–30; Cape Breton: p. 30–31. ¶ For an earlier edition, *see* this title under 1755.

Plan inséré entre les p. 12 et 13 : « Plan of Fort Frederick at Crown Point », avec « A more particular description of Crown Point » au verso. Carte insérée entre les p. 6 et 7 : « Nova Scotia drawn from survey by T. Kitchin Gr. ». ¶ Nouvelle-Bretagne (territoire de la Baie d'Hudson) : p. 4 ; Nouvelle-Écosse : p. 4–7 ; Canada : p. 23 ; Les cinq nations indiennes du Canada : p. 24–27 ; Terre-Neuve : p. 29–30 ; Cap-Breton : p. 30–31. ¶ *Voir* ce titre sous 1755 pour une édition précédente.

Evans, Lewis, 1700?–1756. Geographical, historical, political, philosophical and mechanical essays. Number II. Containing a letter, representing the impropriety of sending forces to Virginia: the importance of taking Frontenac; and that the preservation of Oswego was owing to General Shirley's proceeding thither. Containing objections to those parts of Evans's General map and Analysis, which relate to the French title to the country, on the north-west side of St. Laurence River, between Fort Frontenac and Montreal, &c. Published in the New-York Mercury, no. 178. Jan. 5, 1756. With an answer to so much thereof as concerns the public: and the several articles set in a just light: by Lewis Evans. London, printed for R[obert]. and J[ames]. Dodsley in Pall-mall. 1756. v, 7–35 p. 4°

NUC(Pre–56)164:29*

Dated: New York, Jan. 10, 1756. ¶ *Number one of this, by Evans, appeared as:* Geographical, historical, political, philosophical and mechanical essays. The first, containing An analysis of A general map of the Middle British colonies in America. *Philadelphia, 1755, with the addition in some versions of:* "and sold by R. and J. Dodsley in Pall-Mall, London." *It was not reprinted in London.* "So great was the demand in London, however," *says Waldon* "that the second part, published in Philadelphia in 1756 was immediately reprinted in London ... with the 2d Philadelphia edition of the first part." ¶ The first part, published in the summer of 1755, provoked an attack by the New York *Mercury* of 5 Jan. 1756, because part of it appeared to favour the claim of France to the country from Fort Frontenac [now Kingston, Ontario] to Montreal. This occasioned the publication of the second part, in which Evans makes his defence. The map [in the first part, 1755] is regarded as embodying the best geographical knowledge of the time. For many years afterwards it was used as a basis for all maps of the regions west of the Alleghenies. [Waldon is paraphrasing Church:1011.] ¶ *First pub. Philadelphia, 1755; reprinted, with no. 1 and facsims. of Evans's maps, Philadelphia, 1939.*

Datation : New York, le 10 janv. 1756. ¶ *Le premier de ces essais, par Evans, parut sous le titre* Geographical, historical, political, philosophical and mechanical essays. The first, containing An analysis of A general map of the Middle British colonies in America. *Philadelphie, 1755, avec, dans certaines versions,* « and sold by R. and J. Dodsley in Pall-Mall, London ». *Il ne fut pas réimprimé à Londres. Waldon note* « qu'a Londres, la demande était telle que la deuxième partie, publiée à Philadelphie en 1756, fut aussitôt réimprimée à Londres ... avec la deuxième édition, de Philadelphie, de la première partie ». ¶ La publication de la première partie, au cours de l'été 1755, provoqua une attaque de la part du *Mercury* de New York le 5 janv. 1756. Cette attaque fut suscitée par le fait que cette première partie semblait appuyer les revendications de la France sur les territoires s'étendant de fort Frontenac [maintenant Kingston (Ontario)] à Montréal. Evans publia alors la deuxième partie dans laquelle il défendait sa position. La carte [dans la première partie, 1755] est considérée comme représentative des connaissances géographiques les plus avancées de l'époque. Plusieurs années après, cette carte servait toujours de base pour toutes les cartes des régions à l'ouest des Alleghenies. [Waldon paraphrase Church:1011.] ¶ *Première éd. Philadelphie, 1756 ; réimpression, avec n° 1 et fac-sim. des cartes d'Evans, Philadelphie, 1939.*

A fair representation of His Majesty's right to Nova-Scotia or Acadie. Briefly stated from the memorials of the English commissaries; with an answer to the objections contained in the French memorials, and in a treatise, entitled, Discussion sommaire sur les anciennes limites de l'Acadie. London, printed by Edward Owen, in Warwick-Lane, 1756. 64 p. 8°(in 4s).

NUC(Pre–56)165:601

The *Discussion sommaire*, by Mathieu François Pidanzat de Mairobert, 1727–1779, was published at Basle, 1755 (cf. Sabin:62694). [It was also answered in: *Remarks on the French memorials.* London, 1756 (q.v.).] ¶ Sabin:56129 *quotes* Monthly review, *14:365, as follows: "The French Commissioners having, besides their voluminous 'Mémoires,' published a pamphlet 'in order to prejudice all the courts of Europe in favour of their unjustifiable pretensions,' the English Commissioners thought proper, 'to obviate the wrong impressions that these might create, briefly to recapitulate what had been offered in support of H. M.'s claim, collected from the English memorials.' " ¶ The memorials of the English commissaries appeared in: Great Britain. Commissioners for Adjusting the Boundaries for the British and French Possessions in America.* The memorials of the English and French commissaries. *London, 1755.* (q.v. *for further notes).* ¶ *Reprinted Dublin, in the same year* (see *next entry).* ¶ *OTP · BVAU*

La *Discussion sommaire* de Mathieu François Pidanzat de Mairobert, 1727–1779, fut publiée à Bâle, 1755 (cf. Sabin:62694). [On y répondit aussi dans : *Remarks on the French memorials.* Londres, 1756 (q.v.).] ¶ *Le Sabin: 56129 cite la* Monthly review, *14:365, « Les Délégués français ayant publié, en plus de leurs volumineux 'Mémoires', un pamphlet 'dans le but de rallier toutes les cours d'Europe à leurs injustifiables prétentions', les Délégués anglais crurent bon 'de récapituler brièvement les arguments en faveur des revendications de S. M. contenus dans les mémoires anglais afin de corriger les fausses impressions que pourraient laisser ces publications' ». ¶ Les mémoires des délégués anglais ont paru dans : Great Britain. Commissioners for Adjusting the Boundaries for the British and French Possessions in America.* The memorials of the English and French commissaries. *Londres, 1755* (q.v. *pour d'autres notes).* ¶ *Réimpression à Dublin, la même année* (voir *la notice suivante).* ¶ *OTP · BVAU*

A fair representation .... Dublin: re-printed by Richard James. 1756. 48 p. 8°

Sabin:56129

Originally printed in London the same year: see *preceding entry.*

Originalement imprimé à Londres la même année : voir *la notice précédente.*

[Fauquier, Francis], 1704?–1768. An essay on ways and means for raising money for the support of the present war, without increasing the public debts. Inscribed to the Right Honourable George Lord Anson, first Lord Commissioner of the Admiralty, &c. By F. F. London, printed for M[ary]. Cooper, 1756. 4 p.l., iv, 35 p. 8°

NUC(Pre–56)167:560*

Answered by: Joseph Massie, *Observations upon Mr Fauquier's Essay* .... London, 1756 (*q.v.*). ¶ The author assumes that the war has been undertaken on behalf of the American colonies, to check French aggression, and estimates that it will last seven years and cost £3,000,000 per year. He proposes a tax on houses to pay the whole of this. ¶ *First edition; second ed., pub. same year (see next entry); third ed., 1757 (q.v.); reprint of the first ed. appeared as:* Francis Fauquier on An essay on ways and means. *Baltimore, Md., 1915.*

Cet ouvrage a suscité la réplique suivante : *Observations upon Mr Fauquier's Essay* .... Londres, 1756, de Joseph Massie (*q.v.*). ¶ L'auteur postule que la guerre a été entreprise pour contrer les aggressions françaises à l'égard des colonies américaines. Il estime qu'elle durera sept ans et coûtera 3 000 000 £ par année. Il propose un impôt foncier pour défrayer la totalité des coûts. ¶ *Première édition ; deuxième éd. publ. la même année* (voir *la notice suivante*) *; troisième éd., 1757* (q.v.) *; une réimpression de la première éd. parut sous le titre* Francis Fauquier on An essay on ways and means. *Baltimore (Md.), 1915.*

[Fauquier, Francis], 1704?–1768. An essay on ways and means .... By Francis Fauquier. The 2d ed. London, 1756. 4 p.l., iv, 58 p. 22 cm.

NUC(Pre–56)167:560*

First ed. pub. same year: *see* preceding entry.

Première éd. publ. la même année : *voir* la notice précédente.

A full and particular answer to all the calumnies, misrepresentations, and falsehoods, contained in a pamphlet, called A fourth letter to the people of England. London, printed for T. Harris . . . 1756. <Price one shilling.> 1 p.l., 61 p. 8°

NUC(Pre–56)187:487

A reply to: John Shebbeare, A fourth letter to the people of England. *London, 1756.* ¶ An ironical defence of the Ministry, reinforcing Shebbeare's arguments [for peace with France (Seven Years' War), and against Whig policy].

Réplique à John Shebbeare, A fourth letter to the people of England. *Londres, 1756.* ¶ Une défense ironique du Ministère, renforçant les arguments de Shebbeare [en faveur de la paix avec la France (guerre de Sept Ans) et contre la politique des Libéraux].

Great Britain. Sovereigns, etc., 1727–1760 **(George II).** His Majesty's declaration of war against the French King. Given at our Court at Kensington, the seventeenth day of May, 1756, in the twenty ninth year of our reign . . . . London: printed by Thomas Basket, printer to the King's most Excellent Majesty; and by the assigns of Robert Baskett. 1756. Broadside. fol.

BLC(to 1975)95:291

This marks Britain's entry into the Seven Years' War, 15 May 1756. ¶ Begins: "The unwarrantable proceedings of the French in the West Indies, and North America . . . . Encroachments . . . particularly in our Province of Nova Scotia." ¶ "This edition was suppressed on account of the typographical error 'from North America' instead of 'for North America,' and an

Elle signale pour la Grande-Bretagne, le début de la guerre de Sept Ans, le 15 mai 1756. ¶ Début : « Les actions injustifiées des Français aux Antilles et en Amérique du Nord . . . . Les déprédations . . . particulièrement dans notre Province de Nouvelle-Écosse ». ¶ « Cette édition fut interdite à cause de l'erreur typographique ' from North America ' au lieu de ' for North America', et une édition corrigée fut

emended edition was despatched to the colonies and plantations." [BLC] By this error the French were said to have despatched troops from instead of to America. ¶ *Probably the first edition; others: Edinburgh, 1756, as a pamphlet (see next entry), the London Gazette, 18 May 1756; New York, J. Parker, 1756, and Transactions of the American Antiquarian Soc., Worcester, Mass., 1911, v. 12, p. 203–06.*

envoyée dans les colonies et plantations. » [BLC] Cette erreur laissait entendre que les Français avaient dépêché des troupes en provenance d'Amérique au lieu de vers ce continent. ¶ *Probablement la première édition ; autres éd. : Édimbourg, 1756, sous forme de pamphlet (voir la notice suivante) ; la Gazette de Londres, le 18 mai 1756 ; New York, J. Parker, 1756, et Transactions de l'American Antiquarian Soc., Worcester (Mass.), 1911, vol. 12, p. 203–06.*

Great Britain. Sovereigns, etc., 1727–1760 (George II). His Majesty's declaration of war against the French King. Edinburgh, printed by the assigns of Robert Basket His Majesty's printer, 1756. 7 p. 8°

NUC(Pre–56)215:426

Caption title. ¶ "Given at our Court at Kensington, the seventeenth day of May, 1756." ¶ For other notes and editions, *see* preceding entry.

Titre de départ. ¶ « Déclaration faite devant la Cour à Kensington, le dix-septième jour de mai 1756. » ¶ Pour d'autres notes et éditions, *voir* la notice précédente.

An humble apology for the Quakers, addressed to great and small. Occasioned by certain gross abuses and imperfect vindications of that people, relative to the late public fast. To which are added Observations on a new pamphlet, intituled A brief view of the conduct of Pennsylvania for the year 1755 .... And also a much fairer method pointed out, than that contained in the Brief state of Pennsylvania, to prevent the incroachments of the French, and restore quiet to the province. London, printed for and sold by Stanley Crowder, and Henry Woodgate, 1756. 38 p., 1 l. 4°

NUC(Pre–56)260:80

*Waldon's entry varies slightly: "...
restore quiet in the province"; "London:
printed for Stanley Crowder, 1756"; and
format is small 8°; but she appears not to
have seen the original.* ¶ The Observations *are a reply to:* William Smith, A
brief view of the conduct of Pennsylvania. *London, 1756, and also his* A
brief state of the province of Pennsylvania. *London, 1755.* ¶ *The year
1756 marks the beginning of the Seven
Years' War, which ended in the fall of
New France and the Treaty of Paris,
1763.*

*La notice de Waldon diffère légèrement : « ...
restore quiet in the province » ; « London :
printed for Stanley Crowder, 1756 » ; et le
format est petit in–8° ; mais Waldon ne semble
pas avoir vu le document original.* ¶ *Les*
Observations *sont une réplique à* William
Smith, A brief view of the conduct of
Pennsylvania. *Londres, 1756, ainsi qu'à son
écrit* A brief state of the province of Pennsylvania. *Londres, 1755.* ¶ *L'année 1756 signale le début de la guerre de Sept Ans qui se
termina par la capitulation de la Nouvelle
France et le traité de Paris en 1763.*

An impartial view of the conduct of the M——ry [Ministry], in regard to the war
in America; the engagements entered into with Russia, Hesse-Cassel, and Prussia; the
cause of throwing out the Militia bill; and the affairs of the Mediterranean. In answer
to the many inviduous [*sic*] attacks of pamphleteers, &c . . . . London: printed in the
year 1756. 52 p. 8°(in 4s).

NUC(Pre–56)265:200

*Refers to the Seven Years' War,
1756–63, which resulted in the fall of
Louisbourg, Quebec, and Montreal.* ¶
First edition; second ed.: see next entry.

*Traite de la guerre de Sept Ans, 1756–1763, qui
provoqua la chute de Louisbourg, Québec et
Montréal.* ¶ *Première édition ; deuxième éd. :
voir la notice suivante.*

An impartial view of the conduct of the Ministry, in regard to the war in America,
the engagement with Hesse Cassel and Prussia, the cause of throwing out the Militia
bill, and the affairs of the Mediterranean; in answer to the many attacks of pamphleteers.
London, J. Robinson, 1756. 52 p. 8°

Sabin:34386

For first ed., see preceding entry.   Voir *la notice précédente, pour la première éd.*

*Jones, John, 1700–1770. A letter to a friend in the country, upon the news of the town. 2d ed. London [1756?]. [Collation not given.]

NUC(Pre–56)284:45*

For notes, *see* the 1755 edition. ¶ OOA · BVAU

Voir l'édition de 1755 pour les notes. ¶ OOA · BVAU

A letter from a Frenchman at Paris, to his countryman at The Hague; on the present dispute between France and Great Britain. Translated from the French. London, printed for S[amuel]. Bladon . . . 1756. <Price one shilling.> 1 p.l., 56 p. 8°(in 4s).

NUC(Pre–56)328:656*

"Purporting to be translated from the French" (BLC). No French edition found in NUC. ¶ Supports the English claim to Acadia and refers to "partial and mutilated memorials" printed in 1754 at the Louvre. ¶ *BVAU*

« *Présentée comme une traduction du français* » *(BLC). Édition française introuvable dans le NUC.* ¶ Appuie les revendications anglaises sur l'Acadie et fait référence aux « mémoires partiaux et tronqués » imprimés au Louvre en 1754. ¶ *BVAU*

A letter from a gentleman in Nova-Scotia, to a person of distinction on the Continent. Describing the present state of government in that colony. [Signed J. W.] With some seasonable remarks. [London?] Printed in 1756. 12 p. 4°

NUC(Pre–56)328:660(?)

Dated: Halifax, 1 March 1756. ¶ NUC omits the last sentence of the title, but that may be a different work from this.

Datation : Halifax, le 1ᵉʳ mars 1756. ¶ Le NUC omet la dernière phrase du titre, mais il s'agit peut-être d'une oeuvre différente.

A letter to the King of ****** [*i.e.* France]. By an Englishman; not a member of the House of Commons. London, printed for A[nn?]. and C[harles]. Corbett, at Addison's Head, opposite St. Dunstan's church in Fleet-street. 1756. 2 p.l., 39 p. 8°

NUC(Pre–56)329:88

Charges France with responsibility for the differences with Britain. ¶ Relates to Canada, etc.

Accuse la France d'être responsable du différend avec l'Angleterre. ¶ Traite du Canada, etc.

[Massie, Joseph], *d./déc.* 1784. Observations upon Mr. Fauquier's Essay on ways and means for raising money to support the present war without increasing the public debts. To which is added, An account of several national advantages derived from the nobility and gentry of the present age living in London a greater part of the year than their ancestors used to do. By J. M. London: printed by Thomas Payne, 1756. 2 p.l., 67 p. 8°

NUC(Pre–56)368:356

NUC omits the 2 p.l. in the collation. ¶ *A reply to: Francis Fauquier,* An essay on ways and means .... *London, 1756* (q.v.). ¶ *Further to this is his:* Ways and means .... *London, 1757,* q.v. ¶ *Concerns the Seven Years' War, 1756–63.* ¶ The author questions the practicability of Fauquier's scheme without proposing any other.

Le NUC omet les 2 f. l. de la collation. ¶ *Réplique à* An essay on ways and means .... *Londres, 1756, de Francis Fauquier* (q.v.). ¶ *Ultérieurement :* Ways and means .... *Londres, 1757,* (q.v.). ¶ *Traite de la guerre de Sept Ans, 1756–1763.* ¶ L'auteur remet en question la viabilité du plan de Fauquier sans toutefois proposer d'autres solutions.

[A new and complete history of the British empire in America.] [London? 1756?]
3 v.: xlvi, 402; 496; 272 p. illus., maps. 8°

NUC(Pre–56)412:184

Issued in numbers of 24 p. each, without any title-pages, the title given above being taken from the first page of two of the three volumes. The work ends abruptly on p. 272 of the third volume. The first volume contains an account of Hudson Bay, Newfoundland, Nova Scotia, and New England (Rich, 1756:12).

Tirage en numéros de 24 p. chacun, sans pages de titre ; le titre donné ci-dessus est de la première page de deux des trois volumes. L'oeuvre se termine brusquement à la p. 272 du troisième volume. Le premier volume contient un exposé sur la Baie d'Hudson, Terre-Neuve, la Nouvelle-Écosse, et la Nouvelle-Angleterre (Rich, 1756:12).

[Newcastle, Thomas Pelham-Holles, *1st duke of/1ᵉʳ duc de*], 1693–1768. The resignation: or, The fox out of the pit, and the geese in, with B——g at the bottom. London, printed in the year 1756. 24 p. 8°(in 4s).

NUC(Pre–56)416:697

"Relates to Braddock's defeat of the Ohio, and Admiral Byng's failure in the Mediterranean," cf. *Sabin:70065.* ¶ War in America: p. 4–10. ¶ *BVAU*

« Traite de la défaite du général Braddock sur l'Ohio et de l'échec de l'amiral Byng sur la Méditerrannée », cf. *Sabin:70065.* ¶ La guerre en Amérique : p. 4–10. ¶ *BVAU*

Palairet, Jean, 1697–1774. Description abrégée des possessions angloises et françoises du continent septentional de l'Amérique . . . . 3e éd. A Londres, Chez Messrs. J[ohn]. Nourse, P[aul]. Vaillant [etc.] A Dublin, Chez Mr. J. Rocque. A La Haye [etc.] 1756. <Le prix est de 12 sous.> 72 p. 8°

NUC(Pre–56)438:252*

First French ed.: À Londres, 1755, q.v. *for other notes; second ed. also pub. 1755.*

Première éd. française : À Londres, 1755, q.v. *pour d'autres notes ; deuxième éd. aussi publ. 1755.*

[Payne, J——], *fl.* 1756. The French encroachments exposed; or, Britain's original right to all that part of the American continent claimed by France fully asserted; wherein it appears, that the honour and interest of Great-Britain are equally concerned, from the conduct of the French, for more than a century past, to vindicate her right; the practibility of which, at this juncture, is manifestly proved. In two letters, from a merchant retired from business, to his friend in London .... London, printed for George Keith. 1756. 44 p. 8°

NUC(Pre–56)446:136

The events referred to were part of the Seven Years' War, 1756–63.

Fait référence à des événements survenus durant la guerre de Sept Ans, 1756–1763.

Reasons humbly offered to prove that the letter printed at the end of the French memorial of justification is a French forgery, and falsely ascribed to His R——l H——ss .... London, printed for M. Collyer, at the Royal-Exchange, and in 'Change-Alley. 1756. <Price one shilling.> 1 p.l., 61 p. 8°(in 4s).

NUC(Pre–56)483:517*

An ironical defence of the Duke of Cumberland. The letter referred to has title "Lettre de M. Robert Napier, écrite à M. Braddock par ordre de M. le duc de Cumberland. À Londres, le 25 novembre 1754," and is included in a collection of documents published by order of the French government: Jacob Nicolas Moreau, comp., Mémoire contenant le précis des faits, avec leurs piéces

Une défense ironique du duc de Cumberland. La lettre à laquelle il est fait référence s'intitule : « Lettre de M. Robert Napier, écrite à M. Braddock par ordre de M. le duc de Cumberland. À Londres, le 25 novembre 1754 ». Elle est incluse dans un recueil de documents publié à la demande du gouvernement français : Jacob Nicolas Moreau, comp., Mémoire contenant le précis des faits, avec leurs piéces justificatives, pour servir de réponse aux

justificatives, pour servir de réponse aux Observations envoyées par les ministres d'Angleterre, dans les cours de l'Europe. *Paris, 1756. The letter also appeared in the English transl. of the book, and (says Waldon) in the* Public advertiser, *London, and attempted to show that the English began the hostilities (now called the Seven Years' War, 1756–63). ¶ Transl. into English as:* The conduct of the late ministry. *London, 1757, q.v., under Moreau. ¶ BVAU(MF)*

Observations envoyées par les ministres d'Angleterre, dans les cours de l'Europe. *Paris, 1756. La lettre, ayant aussi paru dans la trad. anglaise du livre et (selon Waldon) dans le* Public advertiser *de Londres, tentait de démontrer que les Anglais avaient engagé les hostilités (maintenant appelées la guerre de Sept Ans, 1756–1763). ¶ Trad. en anglais sous le titre* The conduct of the late ministry. *Londres, 1757,* q.v. Moreau. *¶ BVAU(mic.)*

Remarks on the French memorials concerning the limits of Acadia; printed at the royal printing-house at Paris, and distributed by the French ministers at all the foreign courts of Europe. With two maps, exhibiting the limits: one according to the system of the French, as inserted in the said memorials; the other conformable to the English rights, as supported by the authority of treaties, continual grants of the French kings, and express passages of the best French authors. To which is added, An answer to the summary discussion, &c. London, printed for T. Jefferys, 1756. <Price 2s. 6d.> 2 p.l., 110 p., 1 l. 2 fold. maps. 8°(in 4s).

NUC(Pre–56)488:65

The Addition is a reply to: Mathieu F. P. de Mairobert, Discussion sommaire sur les anciennes limites de l'Acadie. *Basle, 1755; it was also answered in:* A fair representation of His Majesty's right to Nova-Scotia. *London, 1756 (q.v.). ¶ The "French Memorials" appeared in:* Great Britain. Commissioners for Adjusting the Boundaries for the British and French Possessions in America. The memorials of the English and French commissaries. *London, 1755 (q.v. for further notes). ¶ BVAU*

L'ajout est une réplique à Mathieu F. P. de Mairobert, Discussion sommaire sur les anciennes limites de l'Acadie. *Bâle, 1755 ; une autre réponse se trouve aussi dans* A fair representation of His Majesty's right to Nova-Scotia. *Londres, 1756 (q.v.). ¶ Les « French Memorials » parurent dans:* Great Britain. Commissioners for Adjusting the Boundaries for the British and French Possessions in America. The memorials of the English and French commissaries. *Londres, 1755 (q.v. pour notes supplémentaires). ¶ BVAU*

The royal conference or a dialogue between their Majesties. G. . . .E the II^d. of E. . . . . .D. and L. . . . . .s the XV. of F. . . . .E. With some notes critical and explanatory . . . . In the year 1756. 28 p. 12°

Casey:214

Casey (PAC) is Dr. Waldon's only source, but she gives asterisks instead of dots for omissions, and 8° for format. ¶ Account of an imaginary conference to prevent war. The limits of Acadia are the chief point at issue. The King of France will give no satisfactory answer to the pacific arguments of George II. ¶ *The Seven Years' War, 1756–63, was not prevented.*

Le Casey (APC) est la seule source de Waldon, mais elle utilise des astérisques au lieu de points pour indiquer les omissions et elle note in–8° comme format. ¶ Compte rendu d'une conférence imaginaire pour éviter la guerre. Les frontières de l'Acadie en constituent le point essentiel. Le roi de France ne veut donner aucune réponse satisfaisante aux arguments pacifistes de Georges II. ¶ *La guerre de Sept Ans, 1756–1763, ne put être évitée.*

[Shebbeare, John], 1709–1788. An answer to a pamphlet call'd, The conduct of the Ministry impartially examined. In which it is proved, that neither imbecillity nor ignorance in the M——r have been the causes of the present unhappy situation of this nation. By the author of the four letters to the people of England . . . . London: printed for M[ary]. Cooper . . . 1756. <Price one shilling and sixpence.> 100 p. 8°(in 4s).

NUC(Pre–56)542:461*

A reply to: The conduct of the Ministry impartially examined. In a letter to the merchants of London. *London, 1756* (q.v.). ¶ *For Shebbeare's letters, see his* A letter to the people of England. *London, 1755.* ¶ The conduct of the [Seven Years'] War in America was severely criticized by Shebbeare in his first and fourth letters [1755 and 1756]. This continues the attack. ¶ *This edition only, though NUC lists an undated microcard edition of this work.* ¶ *BVAU*

Réplique à The conduct of the Ministry impartially examined. In a letter to the merchants of London. *Londres, 1756* (q.v.). ¶ *Pour les lettres de Shebbeare, voir* A letter to the people of England. *Londres, 1755.* ¶ La façon dont fut menée la guerre [de Sept Ans] en Amérique fut sévèrement critiquée par Shebbeare dans ses première et quatrième lettres [1755 et 1756]. Cet ouvrage constitue une suite à ses premières critiques. ¶ *Il n'existe que cette édition, quoique le NUC donne une édition non datée de cet ouvrage, sur microcarte.* ¶ *BVAU*

[Shebbeare, John], 1709–1788. A fourth letter to the people of England. On the conduct of the M——rs [Ministers] in alliances, fleets, and armies, since the first differences on the Ohio, to the taking of Minorca by the French . . . . London: printed for M. Collier, bookseller at the Royal-Exchange, 1756. 2 p.l., III p. 8°(in 4s).

NUC(Pre–56)542:463*

Errata: 2 l., verso of t.-p. ¶ Another attack on the government for the conduct of affairs in America. Refers to the British traders taken prisoner on the Ohio, carried to Quebec, and neglected by the Ministers, the fight for the Ohio, Braddock's expedition, and the reduction of Nova Scotia. ¶ Another *Fourth Letter to the people of England* . . . . London, printed by M. Cooper . . . 1756. 42 p. 8°(in 4s), is erroneously ascribed to Shebbeare by Sabin. This is a reply to Shebbeare's first three letters by someone who confesses that he has assumed the character of the "public's favourite author." ¶ See also *Shebbeare's* A letter to the people of England, *1755, the first such letter; that and the present fourth letter are the only ones in the series "to the people of England" which concern Canada.* ¶ *First edition; second to sixth eds. published in the same year (cf. NUC).* ¶ *OTP*

Errata : 2 f., verso de la p. de t. ¶ Une autre critique du gouvernement et de sa gestion des affaires en Amérique. Fait référence aux commerçants britanniques capturés sur l'Ohio, transportés à Québec et oubliés par les ministres , à la bataille pour l'Ohio, à l'expédition de Braddock et à la perte de territoires en Nouvelle-Écosse. ¶ Par erreur, le Sabin attribue à Shebbeare une autre *Fourth Letter to the people of England* . . . . Londres, imprimée par M. Cooper . . . 1756. 42 p. in–8° (4 feuilles). C'est une réplique aux trois premières lettres de Shebbeare rédigée par quelqu'un qui avoue s'être fait passé pour « l'auteur préféré du public ». ¶ Voir aussi *de Shebbeare*, A letter to the people of England, *1755, la première de la série ; celle-ci et la présente lettre sont les seules de la série « au peuple d'Angleterre » qui traitent du Canada.* ¶ *Première édition ; deuxième à sixième éditions la même année (cf. NUC).* ¶ *OTP*

[Shebbeare, John], 1709–1788. A fourth letter to the people of England . . . . 2d ed. London, printed for M. Collyer, 1756. 1 p.l., III p. 8°(in 4s).

NUC(Pre–56)542:463*

Title-page reset and errata in first edition corrected. Sabin:80047 has same title, edition unspecified: London, printed for M. Collier. 1756. 49 p. [Waldon entry has 2 p.l., confirmed in Sabin:80046, undoubtedly a half-title and title-page.] ¶ See preceding entry for other notes.

P. de t. recomposée et correction des errata de la première édition. Le Sabin:80047 donne le même titre, sans spécifier l'édition : London, printed for M. Collier. 1756. 49 p. [La notice de Waldon donne 2 f. l. et est corroborée par le Sabin:80046, sans doute un faux-titre et une page de titre.] ¶ Voir autres notes à la notice précédente.

*[Shebbeare, John], 1709–1788. A fourth letter to the people of England, on the conduct . . . . 6th ed. London, printed for M. Collier, 1756. 88 p. 8°(?)

NUC(Pre–56)542:463*

Another "6th ed." in NUC has collation: [1–2], 3–84 p. ¶ There were, presumably, third, fourth, and fifth eds. prior to this. NUC(Pre–56) 542:462 has other 1756 editions without edition number, with 49 p., 56 p., 69 p., and 80 p. respectively. ¶ See preceding entries for other notes.

Collation du NUC pour une autre « sixième édition » : [1–2], 3–84 p. ¶ Il y eut probablement une troisième, quatrième et cinquième éd. avant celle-ci. Le NUC (Pre–56)542:462 donne d'autres éditions pour 1756 sans en donner la succession, avec 49, 56, 69 et 80 p. respectivement. ¶ Voir autres notes aux notices précédentes.

[Shebbeare, John], 1709–1788. A letter to the people of England . . . . Letter I. 3d ed. London: printed in the year, 1756. 56 p. 8°

NUC(Pre–56)542:463*

Format: Sabin:80052. ¶ First edition: 1755, q.v. for notes; subsequent editions: see next entries. ¶ BVAU

Format : Sabin:80052. ¶ Première édition : 1755, q.v. pour d'autres notes ; éditions ultérieures : voir les notices suivantes. ¶ BVAU

[Shebbeare, John], 1709–1788. A first letter to the people of England .... 4th ed. London, printed in the year, 1756. 56 p. 8°

Sabin:80045*

See *first ed., 1755, for other information.* ¶ *OTP*

Voir *première éd., 1755, pour d'autres renseignements.* ¶ *OTP*

[Shebbeare, John], 1709–1788. A letter to the people of England .... 6th ed. London, printed in the year, 1756. 34 p. 8°

NUC(Pre–56)542:463*

See *first ed., 1755, for other information; by inference, a fifth edition must have appeared in 1756, but it is not found in NUC or Sabin, though Sabin:80045 and 80052 are for the first, second, third, fourth, and sixth editions.*

Voir *la première éd., 1755, pour d'autres renseignements ; on suppose qu'une cinquième édition a paru en 1756, mais il n'en est pas fait mention dans le NUC ou dans le Sabin, bien que dans le Sabin:80045 et 80052, on retrouve les première, deuxième, troisième, quatrième et sixième éd.*

[Smith, William], 1727–1803. A brief state of the province of Pennsylvania, in which ... the true cause of the continual encroachments of the French displayed .... 3d ed. London, R[alph]. Griffiths, 1756. 47 p. 8°

NUC(Pre–56)552:309*

Reprinted from the second ed., but from a new setting of type. ¶ *See* first ed., 1755, f·r further information.

Réimpression à partir de la deuxième éd., mais avec une nouvelle composition typographique. ¶ *Voir* première éd., 1755, pour d'autres renseignements.

[Smith, William], 1727–1803. A brief view of the conduct of Pennsylvania, for the year 1755; so far as it affected the general service of the British colonies, particularly the expedition under the late General Braddock. With an account of the shocking inhumanities, committed by incursions of the Indians upon the province in October and November; ... being a sequel to a late well-known pamphlet, intitled, A brief state of Pennsylvania. In a second letter to a friend in London .... London, printed for R[alph]. Griffiths in Pater-noster row; and sold by Mr. Bradford in Philadelphia. 1756. <Price one-shilling and six-pence.> 88 p. 8°

NUC(Pre–56)552:309*

Further to: William Smith, *A brief state of the province of Pennsylvania.* London, 1755 (*q.v.*). ¶ Further to this is: William Smith, *A true and impartial state of the province of Pennsylvania.* Philadelphia, 1759 (Sabin:97096), which does not appear to be of Canadian interest. ¶ First edition; reprinted in microfilm: Ann Arbor, Mich., University Microfilms, 1960 (American Culture series, 77:9). ¶ BVAU(MF)

Suite à l'ouvrage de William Smith, *A brief state of the province of Pennsylvania.* Londres, 1755 (*q.v.*). ¶ Pour faire suite à ce document, William Smith a écrit *A true and impartial state of the province of Pennsylvania.* Philadelphie, 1759 (Sabin:97096), lequel ne semble contenir aucune information relative au Canada. ¶ Première édition ; reproduction sur mic., Ann Arbor (Mich.), University Microfilms, 1960 (collection American Culture, 77:9). ¶ BVAU(mic.)

Tucker, Josiah, 1712–1799. An essay on the advantages and disadvantages which respectively attend France and Great Britain, with regard to trade. With some proposals .... By Mr. Josiah Tucker .... 4th ed. Glasgow, 1756. vii, [3]–194 p. 12°

NUC(Pre–56)603:617

NUC has author entry in square brackets, and notes first ed. as London, 1750. ¶ *First ed.: London, 1749, with title:* A brief essay, q.v.; *for other notes and editions,* see *second ed., 1750, with title* A brief essay.

Le NUC met la notice de l'auteur entre crochets et donne comme première éd. : Londres, 1750. ¶ *Première éd. : Londres, 1749, sous le titre* A brief essay, q.v. ; *pour d'autres notes et éditions,* voir *deuxième éd., 1750, sous le titre* A brief essay.

1757

[Burke, Edmund], 1729?–1797. An account of the European settlements in America. In six parts. I. A short history of the discovery of that part of the world. II. The manners and customs of the original inhabitants. III. Of the Spanish settlements. IV. Of the Portuguese. V. Of the French, Dutch and Danish. VI. Of the English. Each part contains an accurate description of the settlements in it, their extent, climate, productions, trade, genius and disposition of their inhabitants: the interests of the several powers of Europe with respect to those settlements; and their political and commercial views with regard to each other. In two volumes.... London, printed for R[obert]. and J[ames]. Dodsley, 1757. 2 v.: 5 p.l., 3–312 p. map; 2 p.l., 3–300 p., 10 l. (Contents). map. 8°

NUC(Pre–56)85:275*

Probably the joint work of William and Edmund Burke, but usually attributed to the latter, although he calls himself merely the reviser of his kinsman's work (cf. DNB). ¶ First edition; other editions: 1758, 1760, 1762, 1765–66, 1770, 1777, 1808, and (first American) 1835. ¶ *NSWA · OTP*

Probablement l'oeuvre commune de William et d'Edmund Burke, mais habituellement attribuée à ce dernier, bien qu'il dise simplement être le réviseur de l'oeuvre de son parent (cf. DNB). ¶ Première édition ; autres éditions : 1758, 1760, 1762, 1765–1766, 1770, 1777, 1808, et (la première éd. américaine) 1835. ¶ *NSWA · OTP*

Davies, Samuel, 1724–1761. The crisis: or, The uncertain doom of kingdoms at particular times, considered with reference to Great-Britain and her colonies in their present circumstances. A sermon preached in Hanover, Virginia, Oct. 28, 1756; a day appointed by the Synod of New-York, to be observed as a general fast, on account of the present war with France. By the Rev. Mr. Samuel Davies, A. M. With a preface by the Reverend Mr. Thomas Gibbons. London, printed for J[ames]. Buckland; J[ohn]. Ward [etc.], 1757. viii, 36 p. 8°(in 4s).

NUC(Pre–56)134:448*

Contains curious particulars relating to the loss of Oswego, Braddock's defeat, etc. [Sabin]. ¶ *First edition; also*

Contient des détails curieux sur la perte d'Oswego, la défaite de Braddock, etc. [Sabin]. ¶ *Première édition ; aussi reproduit sur*

issued in a microcard edition, and in microfilm: Washington, D. C., Microcard Editions, 196–? (see NUC); Sabin: 18757 has an identical entry but for the date, 1758 (q.v.).

microcarte et sur microfilm : Washington (D. C.), Microcard Editions, 196– ? (voir le NUC) . Le Sabin:18757 donne une notice identique sauf pour la date, qui est 1758 (q.v.).

*Entick, John, 1703?–1773. A new naval history: or, Compleat view of the British marine. In which the Royal Navy and the merchant's service are traced through all their periods and different branches . . . . To which are added our right and title to the British colonies in North-America: and an abstract of the laws now in force for regulating our trade and commerce . . . . By John Entick, M. A. London, R[ichard]. Manby [etc.], 1757. 2 p.l., 887, [10] p. front., 2 plates, 2 ports., fold. map. fol.

NUC(Pre–56)160:544

Waldon notes, under Entick's *A general history*, 1763, that this "contains some account of discoveries, etc., in Canada."

Waldon note, sous l'ouvrage d'Entick, *A general history*, 1763, que celle-ci contient des comptes rendus de découvertes, etc., faites au Canada.

[Fauquier, Francis], 1704?–1768. An essay on ways and means for raising money for . . . the present war . . . . By Francis Fauquier. The 3d ed. London: printed for J[ohn]. Wilkie, 1757. [5], iv, 58 p. 8°

NUC(Pre–56)167:560*

NUC has collation as: [7], iv, 35 p. This is the collation of the first and second eds. ¶ First edition:1756, q.v. for other notes.

Collation du NUC : [7], iv, 35 p. Ceci est la collation des première et deuxième éd. ¶ Première édition : 1756, q.v. pour d'autres notes.

A letter from a merchant of the city of London, to the R——t H——ble W—— P—— esq.; upon the affairs and commerce of North America, and the West-Indies; our African trade; the destination of our squadrons and convoys; new taxes, and the schemes proposed for raising the extraordinary supplies for the current year .... London, printed for J[ohn]. Scott, 1757. 98 p. 8°

NUC(Pre–56)328:670

Signed: *A merchant of London.* ¶ The disputes in America are acknowledged as the cause of the war. The author discusses the financing of the war and a plan of campaign. Nova Scotia: p. 11–12, 22–23; Newfoundland: p. 23–24. ¶ *Waldon notes that a second edition appeared with the same imprint in the same year. (Not found in NUC.)* ¶ *BVAU*

Signée : *Un marchand de Londres.* ¶ L'on y admet que les querelles en Amérique sont la cause de la guerre. L'auteur discute du financement de la guerre et d'un plan stratégique. Nouvelle-Écosse : p. 11–12, 22–23 ; Terre-Neuve : p. 23–24. ¶ *Waldon note que la deuxième édition a paru la même année avec la même adresse bibliographique (introuvable dans le NUC).* ¶ *BVAU*

A letter to a Member of Parliament, on the importance of the American colonies, and the best means of making them most useful to the mother country. London: printed for J[ohn]. Scott ... 1757. 24 p. 8°(in 4s).

NUC(Pre–56)329:32

The author is of the opinion that the American colonies are not of as much benefit to England as they should be because of wrong politics. He speaks, p. 5, of "The Insensibility of those who grumble at the Expence of *Nova Scotia*; a Settlement of as much Importance to the *American*, as *Gibraltar* is to the *Mediterranean* Trade, and infinitely more beneficial from its Situation, and Conveniency for the Fishery and Consumption of *English* Manufactures."

L'auteur pense, qu'à cause de mauvaises politiques, les colonies américaines ne profitent pas à l'Angleterre autant qu'elles le devraient. Il parle, à la p. 5, de « l'inconscience de ceux qui rechignent contre les dépenses que représente la *Nouvelle-Écosse*, celle-ci étant, en matière de commerce avec *l'Amérique*, ce qu'est *Gibraltar* à la *Méditerrannée* ; de plus, la Nouvelle-Écosse est beaucoup plus intéressante à cause de sa situation et des avantages qu'elle représente pour les pêcheries et la consommation de produits *anglais* ».

[Livingston, William], 1723–1790. A review of the military operations in North-America; from the commencement of the French hostilities on the frontiers of Virginia in 1753, to the surrender of Oswego, on the 14th of August, 1756. Interspersed with various observations, characters, and anecdotes; necessary to give light into the conduct of American transactions in general; and more especially into the political management of affairs in New York. In a letter to a nobleman. London: printed for R[obert]. and J[ames]. Dodsley, 1757. 2 p.l., 144 p. 4°

NUC(Pre–56)336:617*

A defence of General Shirley's conduct of operations during the Seven Years' War. It has been attributed to various persons. Samuel Jones, in the New York Historical Society Collections, *v. 3, 1821, p. 361, says: "This pamphlet was written in New York, and it is believed . . . that William Smith [1728–1793] afterwards chief justice of Canada, was the author: that he copied it himself, never permitting either of the clerks to see a word of it: that the manuscript was carefully nailed up . . . and sent to London to be printed. The pamphlets when received from London were not publicly distributed. . . ." (Cited in* Documentary history of the State of New York, *1849–51, v. 4, p. 1054.) In Smith's posthumous* History of the late Province of New York, *1829, v. 2, p. 255–56, it is stated that William Alexander (who later called himself Lord Stirling) acknowledged having given the manuscript to the printer, but denied the authorship, but Smith neither hints at himself being the author, nor offers any suggestions as to who wrote the pamphlet. It is now generally believed that Alexander had the manuscript from his brother-in-law Livingston, to whom it is attributed by his biographer Sedgwick (cf.* American quarterly review, *1833, v. 14, p. 12–13), by Halkett and Laing,*

Constitue une défense de la conduite, par le général Shirley, des opérations pendant la guerre de Sept Ans. Elle a été attribuée à plusieurs personnes. Samuel Jones, dans Collections de la New York Historical Society, *vol. 3, 1821, p. 361, dit que : « Ce pamphlet fut écrit à New York et l'on pense . . . que William Smith [1728–1793], plus tard juge en chef du Canada, en était l'auteur. L'on pense aussi qu'il a lui-même préparé le manuscrit en interdisant à tous les clercs d'en voir un mot et que le manuscrit fut soigneusement déposé dans une caisse clouée . . . et envoyé à Londres pour y être imprimé. Lorsque les pamphlets revinrent de Londres, ils ne furent pas distribués publiquement . . . . » (cité dans* Documentary history of the State of New York, *1849–1851, vol. 4, p. 1054). Dans l'oeuvre posthume de Smith,* History of the late Province of New York, *1829, vol. 2, p. 255–56, il est dit que William Alexander (qui, par la suite, se fit appeler lord Stirling) admettait avoir donné le manuscrit à l'imprimeur, mais niait en être l'auteur. Smith ne donne aucun indice comme quoi il en serait l'auteur et ne suggère rien sur l'identité de celui-ci. Il est maintenant généralement admis qu'Alexander tenait le manuscrit de son beau-frère, Livingston, auquel le manuscrit est attribué par son biographe, Sedgwick (cf.* American quarterly review, *1833, vol. 14, p. 12–13), et par Halkett et Laing,* Sabin, *et d'autres autorités en la matière. ¶ Première édition ; réimpression la*

Sabin, and other authorities. ¶ First edition; reprinted the same year in Dublin (see *next entry*); also Boston, *1758* and *1801*, and New York, *1770* (*cf. NUC*). ¶ *NSWA · OTU*

même année à Dublin (voir *la notice suivante*) ; *aussi Boston, 1758 et 1801, et New York, 1770* (*cf. NUC*). ¶ *NSWA · OTU*

[Livingston, William], 1723–1790. A review of the military operations in North America. . . . In a letter to a nobleman. To which are added, Col. Washington's journal of his expedition to the Ohio, in 1754, and several letters . . . found in the cabinet of Major General Braddock, after his defeat near Fort Du Quesne . . . . Dublin, P[eter]. Wilson and J[ohn]. Exshaw, 1757. 276 p. 12°

NUC(Pre–56)336:616*

Concerns events in North America in the Seven Years' War. ¶ *First edition: London, 1757* (see *preceding entry*). ¶ *OTU*

Traite des événements en Amérique du Nord pendant la guerre de Sept Ans. ¶ *Première édition : Londres, 1757* (voir *la notice précédente*). ¶ *OTU*

[McCulloh, Henry], d./déc. 1778. Proposals for uniting the English colonies on the continent of America, so as to enable them to act with force and vigour against their enemies. London, printed for J[ohn]. Wilkie, 1757. 1 p.l., vi, 38, [1] p. 8°(in 4s).

NUC(Pre–56)349:612

List of books: [1] p. at end. ¶ The author compares the organization of the French and English colonies, including the situation in Nova Scotia, Cape Breton, and Newfoundland, to the advantage of the former (p. 36–37), and advocates a uniform currency. He concludes: "Upon the whole, if we compare the Number of the *French* Settlers on the Continent

Liste des livres : [1] p. à la fin. ¶ L'auteur compare défavorablement l'organisation des colonies anglaises à celle des colonies françaises, incluant la situation en Nouvelle-Écosse, au Cap-Breton et à Terre-Neuve (p. 36–37) ; il préconise l'utilisation d'une même monnaie. Il conclut : « Dans l'ensemble, si l'on compare le nombre de colons *français* en Amérique au nombre et à la situation des nôtres, et que

404

of America, with our Number and Situation, and the many Resources we have, if properly exerted, it is matter of Wonder and Amazement to consider the Advantages they have gained over us, and the Danger we are still exposed to from the Want of System in the Conduct of publick Affairs: As we are at present circumstanced, we cannot reasonably hope for Redress, unless it be thought agreeable to the Wisdom of our Senators to appoint a Committee to examine into the State and Condition of our Colonies; to create a new Fund, and to establish a Militia, for the general Security of our Settlements and to apply such further Remedies, as may be thought necessary in so interesting a matter."

l'on tient compte de nos grandes ressources et de leur utilisation potentielle, il est étonnant et stupéfiant de voir, d'une part, tous les avantages qu'ils ont pu remporter sur nous et, d'autre part, le danger auquel nous expose encore le manque d'organisation dans la conduite des affaires publiques : Étant donné les circonstances auxquelles nous faisons face, on ne peut raisonnablement espérer redresser la situation, à moins que nos sénateurs, dans leur sagesse, nomment un comité chargé d'étudier l'état et la condition de nos colonies, créent un nouveau Fonds, mettent sur pied une milice afin d'assurer la sécurité générale de nos colonies et appliquent toute autre mesure jugée nécessaire à cette entreprise vitale ».

[Massie, Joseph], *d./déc.* 1784. Ways and means for raising the extraordinary supplies to carry on the war for seven years, if it should continue so long; without doing any prejudice to the manufacturies or trade of Great Britain: also an account of the ancient and present states of the most considerable branches of manufactury and trade belonging to these kingdoms. Extracted from the commercial writings of various authors, &c. and digested in order of time. Part I. London, printed for Thomas Payne, 1757. <Price one shilling and sixpence.> 4 p.l., 88 p. tables (2 fold.). 8°

NUC(Pre–56)368:356

Waldon has collation: [5], 88 p. ¶ Dedication signed: J. Massie. ¶ No more published. ¶ Further to his: Observations upon Mr. Fauquier's Essay. *London, 1756,* q.v. ¶ The author proposes a tax on bachelors and childless widowers.

Collation de Waldon : [5], 88 p. ¶ Dédicace signée : J. Massie. ¶ Aucune publication ultérieure. ¶ Fait suite à ses Observations upon Mr. Fauquier's Essay. *Londres, 1756,* q.v. ¶ L'auteur propose d'imposer une taxe aux célibataires et aux veufs sans enfants.

The Military history of Great Britain, for 1756, 1757. Containing a letter from an English officer at Canada, taken prisoner at Oswego; exhibiting the cruelty and infidelity of the French, and their savage Indians, in times of peace and war; shewing their superior advantages, and the only means of redress: and impartially delineating the present state of our colonies in America, with some hints for their future regulation. Also, A journal of the siege of Oswego, and the articles of capitulation; with a particular table of their inhabitants . . . . London: printed for J. Millan, 1757. iv, [5], 125 p. front. (fold. map). 8°

NUC(Pre–56)383:578

Waldon has collation: 125 p. ¶ *The conflict is the Seven Years' War, 1756–63.*

Collation de Waldon : 125 p. ¶ *Le conflit en question est la guerre de Sept Ans, 1756–1763.*

[Mitchell, John], *d./déc.* 1768. The contest in America between Great Britain and France, with its consequences and importance; giving an account of the views and designs of the French, with the interests of Great Britain, and the situation of the British and French colonies, in all parts of America: in which a proper barrier between the two nations in North America is pointed out, with a method to prosecute the war, so as to obtain that necessary security for our colonies. By an impartial hand . . . . London, printed for A[ndrew]. Millar in the Strand. 1757. 2 p.l., iii–xlix,[1, errata], [17]–244 (*i.e.* 260) p. 8°(in 4s).

NUC(Pre–56)388:27*

The contest referred to is the Seven Years' War, 1756–63. ¶ *[Waldon notes variations in make-up of the preliminary pages, and that the BM copy has a coloured folding map]:* "A new and Accurate Map of the English Empire in North America: Representing their Rightful Claim as confirm'd by Charters, and the formal Surrender of their Indian Friends; Likewise the encroachments of the French, with the several Forts they have unjustly erected therein. By a Society of Anti-Gallicans. Publish'd

Le conflit en question est la guerre de Sept Ans, 1756–1763. ¶ *[Waldon note des variantes dans la composition des pages liminaires, et la présence d'une carte pliante en couleurs dans l'exemplaire du BM] :* « Une carte récente et exacte de l'Empire anglais en Amérique du Nord : présentant leurs revendications légitimes, confirmées par les Chartres et la capitulation officielle de leurs amis indiens ; représentant aussi les déprédations des Français, ainsi que les divers forts qu'ils y ont illégitimement construits. Par une Société des Anti-français. Publiée en vertu de la Loi de déc.

according to Act of Parliament Decr. 1755 And Sold by W^m. Herbert on London Bridge & Robt. Sayer over against Fetter Lane in Fleet Street." The map leaves French possessions and encroachments white, *i.e.*, Quebec, Anticosti, and the N. E. Coast of Newfoundland. The Great Lakes are entirely within British territory, and all the West and North. A line, however, shows that the Mississippi valley, Nova Scotia, and what is now New Brunswick and Ontario were claimed by the French. ¶ *This appeared in* MF: *Ann Arbor, Mich., University Microfilms, 1960 (American Culture series, 77:6); cf. NUC.* ¶ *OTP · BVAU*

1755, et vendue par W^m. Herbert, situé sur le Pont de Londres & Robt. Sayer, situé près de l'allée Fetter, sur la rue Fleet ». La carte laisse en blanc les possessions et empiétements français, c.-à-d., Québec, Anticosti et la côte n.-e. de Terre-Neuve. Les Grands Lacs, tout comme l'ensemble du Nord et de l'Ouest, sont entièrement situés en territoire britannique. Toutefois, une ligne indique que la vallée du Mississippi, la Nouvelle-Écosse, et ce qui constitue maintenant le Nouveau-Brunswick et l'Ontario, étaient revendiqués par les Français. ¶ *Reproduction sur mic., Ann Arbor (Mich.), University Microfilms, 1960 (collection American Culture, 77:6) ; cf. NUC.* ¶ *OTP · BVAU*

[Moreau, Jacob Nicolas], 1717–1804, *comp.* The conduct of the late ministry; or, A memorial; containing a summary of facts with their vouchers, in answer to the Observations, sent by the English ministry, to the courts of Europe. Wherein (among many curious and interesting pieces, which may serve as authentic memoirs towards a history of the present quarrel between Great-Britain and France) several papers are to be seen at full length . . . . London, printed for W[illiam]. Bizet, 1757. vi, 319 p. 8°(in 4s).

NUC(Pre–56)394:301

Transl. from his *Mémoire contenant le précis des faits, avec leurs piéces justificatives, pour servir de réponse aux Observations envoyées par les ministres d'Angleterre, dans les cours de l'Europe.* Paris, 1756. The "Lettre de M. Robert Napier" (p. 127–31) called forth the ironical defence of the Duke of Cumberland, published as: *Reasons humbly offered* . . . . London, 1756, *q.v.* ¶ *NUC has collation: 1 p.l., 319 p.* ¶

Trad. de son *Mémoire contenant le précis des faits, avec leurs piéces justificatives, pour servir de réponse aux Observations envoyées par les ministres d'Angleterre, dans les cours de l'Europe.* Paris, 1756. La *Lettre de M. Robert Napier* (p. 127–31) provoqua la défense ironique du duc de Cumberland, publiée sous le titre *Reasons humbly offered* . . . . Londres, 1756, *q.v.* ¶ *Collation du NUC : 1 f. l., 319 p.* ¶ « Lettre de M. Robert Napier, écrite à M. Braddock, par ordre de Son Altesse Royale,

"Letter from M. Robert Napier, written to M. Braddock, by order of his Royal Highness the Duke of Cumberland. London, Nov. 25, 1754": p. 188–94. ¶ The first part contains a statement of affairs from the Treaty of Utrecht [1713, ending the War of the Spanish Succession] to some time after Braddock's defeat [1755]. The second part contains documents in support of the narrative, including letters that passed between English and French officers in Canada and Nova Scotia [during the Seven Years' War, 1756–63]. ¶ Two editions appeared in New York the same year, 1757, under the title: *A memorial containing a summary view of the facts*; it was also republished in London, 1759, under title: *The mystery revealed, q.v.*

le duc de Cumberland, Londres, le 25 nov. 1754 » : p. 188–94. ¶ La première partie fait état des événements à partir du traité d'Utrecht [1713, qui mit un terme à la guerre de la Succession d'Espagne] jusqu'à peu de temps après la défaite de Braddock [1755]. La deuxième partie contient des documents appuyant le récit, incluant des lettres échangées entre officiers anglais et français au Canada et en Nouvelle-Écosse [pendant la guerre de Sept Ans, 1756–1763]. ¶ Deux éditions ont paru à New York la même année, 1757, sous le titre *A memorial containing a summary view of the facts* ; l'ouvrage fut également réédité à Londres en 1759, sous le titre *The mystery revealed, q.v.*

Postlethwayt, Malachy, 1707?–1767. Britain's commercial interest explained and improved; in a series of dissertations on several important branches of her trade and police; containing a candid enquiry into the secret causes of the present misfortunes of the nation. With proposals for their remedy. Also the great advantages which would accrue to this kingdom from an union with Ireland. By Malachy Postlethwayt, Esq; . . . . London: printed for D[aniel]. Browne [etc.] . . . 1757. 2 v.: xviii, [6], 548; vi, [6], 551 p. fold. tables. 8°

NUC(Pre-56)467:396*

Dissertations XVI–XVIII deal with the American colonies, with some reference to Canada; Dissertations XIX–XX deal with the policy and conduct of France in America. ¶ *First edition; reprinted Dublin, 1758 (q.v.), and as*

Les Dissertations XVI–XVIII traitent des colonies américaines, avec quelques mentions concernant le Canada ; les Dissertations XIX–XX traitent de la politique et de la conduite de la France en Amérique. ¶ *Première édition ; réimpression à Dublin en 1758*

Great-Britain's commercial interest .... 2d ed. London, 1759 (q.v.).

(q.v.), et sous le titre Great-Britain's commercial interest .... deuxième éd., Londres, 1759 (q.v.).

Proposals for carrying on the war with vigour, raising the supplies within the year, and forming a national militia. To which are added, considerations in respect to manufacturers and labourers, and the taxes paid by them; the inconveniences of credit for small sums, and the courts lately erected to recover them. Intended to demonstrate, that it is not the dearness of the labour of the poor, but the profits and expences of higher classes of people, which are the real clog on the foreign trade and commerce of England. London, printed for M[ary]. Cooper, 1757. 2 p.l., 54 p. tables. 8°

NUC(Pre–56)472:670

Dr. Waldon notes: Sometimes attributed to [Owen] Ruffhead [cf. DNB]. ¶ An early advocate of economic nationalism, the writer agrees with [Francis] Fauquier [e.g., *An essay on ways and means for raising money*, 1756, *q.v.*] and [Malachy] Postlethwayt [e.g., *Britain's commercial interest explained*, 1757, *q.v.*] that it would be ruinous to increase the national debt, and considers various proposals for taxation .... He approves luxury taxes for the duration of the war. ¶ *The war referred to in the title and the note is the Seven Years' War, 1756–63.*

Selon Waldon, ouvrage parfois attribué à [Owen] Ruffhead [cf. DNB]. ¶ Défenseur avant-gardiste du nationalisme économique, l'auteur est du même avis que [Francis] Fauquier [p. ex. *An essay on ways and means for raising money*, 1756, *q.v.*] et [Malachy] Postlethwayt [p. ex. *Britain's commercial interest explained*, 1757, *q.v.*], à savoir qu'il serait ruineux d'augmenter la dette nationale, et il examine divers schémas de taxation .... Il est en faveur d'une taxe sur les produits de luxe pendant la durée de la guerre. ¶ *La guerre à laquelle le titre et la note font allusion est la guerre de Sept Ans, 1756–1763.*

Remarks upon a letter published in the London Chronicle, or Universal evening post, no. 115. Containing an enquiry into the causes of the failure of the late expedition against Cape Breton. In a letter to a member of Parliament. London, printed for M[ary]. Cooper in Pater-noster-Row, 1757. 2 p.l., [5]–30 p. 8°(in 4s).

NUC(Pre–56)488:84

The writer considers Cape Breton very important, and the failure of the expedition [against Louisbourg, 1757] a grave matter. He blames the Admiral and General in charge for delay. The letter in the London *Chronicle* had blamed the Ministry, and justified the men on the spot for abandoning the expedition on Aug. 4. ¶ *OTP*

L'auteur considère que le Cap-Breton est très important, et que l'échec de la campagne [contre Louisbourg, 1757] est un sujet grave. Il accuse l'amiral et le général chargés des opérations d'être responsables du retard. La lettre parue dans le *Chronicle* de Londres accusait le ministère et déculpait les hommes qui, le 4 août, avaient abandonné la campagne. ¶ *OTP*

[Shirley, William], 1694–1771. Memoirs of the principal transactions of the last war between the English and French in North America. From the commencement of it in 1744, to the conclusion of the treaty at Aix la Chapelle. Containing in particular an account of the importance of Nova Scotia or Acadie and the island of Cape Breton to both nations. London, printed for R[obert]. and J[ames]. Dodsley . . . 1757. <Price one shilling and six pence.> viii, 102 p. 8°

NUC(Pre–56)375:237*

Authorship: TPL:276, and Sabin:80550; but more cautiously only "Attributed sometimes to [William] Shirley": Justin Winsor, Narrative and critical history of America. Boston, 1884–89, 8 vols., v. 5, p. 568. Waldon (and TPL) notes: Possibly written by Shirley's Secretary, William Alexander. ¶ Concerns the Austrian Succession War, ended by the Treaty of Aix-la-Chapelle, 18 Oct. 1748. ¶ Another issue of same year differs only in omitting the price after the publication

Identification de l'auteur : TPL:276, et Sabin: 80550 ; mais avec avertissement : Parfois attribué à [William] Shirley : Justin Winsor, Narrative and critical history of America. Boston, 1884–1889, 8 vol., vol. 5, p. 568. Waldon (et le TPL) note : probablement écrit par William Alexander, secrétaire de Shirley. ¶ Traité de la guerre de la Succession d'Autriche, à laquelle mit fin le traité d'Aix-la-Chapelle, le 18 oct. 1748. ¶ Une autre édition parue la même année diffère de celle-ci seulement en ce qu'elle omet le prix après la date de publication (cf.

date (*cf. NUC); it was reprinted, Boston, New England, 1758, third ed. (cf. TPL and Sabin), and also as the third ed. in Bath, 1759 (cf. NUC), q.v.; also issued in a microcard edition (cf. NUC).* ¶ *NSWA*

NUC); réimpression, Boston (Nouvelle-Angleterre), 1758, troisième éd. (cf. TPL et Sabin), et Bath, 1759, comme troisième édition (cf. NUC), q.v. ; aussi reproduction sur micro-carte (cf. NUC). ¶ *NSWA*

*Tucker, Josiah, 1712–1799. A brief essay on the advantages and disadvantages which respectively attend France and Great Britain, with regard to trade. With some proposals .... In a new method. By Josiah Tucker .... 3d ed. corr., with additions. Dublin, printed by G[eorge]. Faulkner, 1757. v, viii, [9]–110 p. 8°(?)

NUC(Pre–56)603:615*

The London third ed., 1753, *q.v.*, has a different collation. ¶ For other notes and editions, *see* second ed., 1750.

La collation de la troisième édition, Londres, 1753, *q.v.*, est différente. ¶ *Voir* la deuxième éd., 1750, pour d'autres notes et éditions.

Williamson, Peter, 1730–1799. French and Indian cruelty; exemplified in the life and various vicissitudes of fortune, of Peter Williamson, a disbanded soldier. Containing a particular account of the manners, customs, and dress, of the savages; of their scalping, burning, and other barbarities, committed on the English, in North-America, during his residence among them: Being at eight years of age, stolen from his parents and sent to Pensylvania, where he was sold as a slave: Afterwards married and settled as a planter, 'till the Indians destroy'd his house and every thing he had, and carried him off a captive; from whom, after several months captivity, he made his escape, and serv'd as a volunteer and soldier in many expeditions against them. Comprehending in the whole, a summary of the transactions of the several provinces of Pensylvania (including Philadelphia), New-York, New-England, New-Jersey, &c &c. From the commencement of the war in these parts; particularly, those relative to the intended attack on Crown Point and Niagara. And, an accurate and succinct detail, of the operations of the French and English forces, at the Siege of Oswego, where the author was wounded and taken prisoner; and being afterwards sent to England, was, on his arrival at Plymouth, discharg'd, as incapable of further service. Written by himself. York, printed for the author, by N[icholas]. Nickson, 1757. <Price one shilling.> iv, 103 p. 8°

BM(to 1955)665:615*

The full title is from Waldon, who cites BM —evidently from a personal examination of the BM copy. ¶ *The incidents occurred during the Seven Years' War, 1756–63.* ¶ "Homer [says Waldon] has an entry under 1759: No French and Indian cruelty in the Life of Peter Williamson. 1759. 12° 1s., which was not found in BM, Bodleian, NYP, nor Sabin." ¶ The first edition ends with his return to Plymouth and failure to get a pension on being discharged. ¶ *First edition; second and third eds., 1758; fourth ed., 1759; fifth, 1762, q.v.; also Dublin, 1766; Edinburgh, 1787 and 1792; also 1794, 1801, 1803, 1807, 1820, 1821, 1822, 1840, 1841, 1867 (cf. BM, and NUC(Pre–56) 665:612–13).*

Le titre complet est de Waldon, qui cite l'exemplaire du BM – qu'elle a de toute évidence personnellement examiné. ¶ *Ces incidents se produisirent pendant la guerre de Sept Ans, 1756–1763.* ¶ « [Selon Waldon], Homer catalogue une notice sous 1759 que l'on ne trouve ni dans le BM, le Bodleian, le NYP ni dans le Sabin : No French and Indian cruelty in the Life of Peter Williamson. 1759. 12°, 1 s. » ¶ La première édition se termine sur son retour à Plymouth et sur l'échec des démarches entreprises pour obtenir une pension au moment de sa réforme. ¶ *Première édition ; deuxième et troisième éd., 1758 ; quatrième éd., 1759 ; cinquième éd., 1762, q.v. ; aussi, Dublin, 1766 ; Édimbourg, 1787 et 1792 ; aussi, 1794, 1801, 1803, 1807, 1820, 1821, 1822, 1840, 1841, 1867 (cf. BM, et NUC(Pre–56)655:612–13).*

1758

An accurate account of the taking of Cape Breton, in the year 1755. London, Staples, 1758. 8°

Waldon has taken this from Faribault:849, but it is probably an error for: An accurate and authentc [sic] account *(same imprint)*, q.v., *1758*, under Pepperell.

Waldon s'inspire ici de Faribault :849, mais il s'agit probablement d'une erreur; la version correcte serait An accurate and authentc [sic] account *(même adresse bibliographique)*, q.v., *1758*, Pepperell.

[Alexander, William], 1726–1783. The conduct of Major Gen. Shirley, late general and commander in chief of His Majesty's forces in North America. Briefly stated. London: printed for R[obert]. and J[ames]. Dodsley . . . and sold by M[ary]. Cooper . . . 1758. viii, 130, 1 p. 8°(in 4s).

BLC(to 1975)5:172

Sometimes attributed to Shirley himself, but probably written by his secretary, William Alexander ["an American general who claimed to be the sixth Earl of Stirling" (DNB)]. ¶ The preface refers to Shirley's services in the previous war in Nova Scotia, but this narrative deals only with the miscarriage of plans in the present war [the Seven Years' War], in vindication of Shirley. ¶ NSWA · BVAU

Parfois attribué à Shirley lui-même, mais probablement écrit par son secrétaire, William Alexander [« un général américain prétendant être le sixième comte de Stirling » (DNB)]. ¶ Pour défendre Shirley, la préface fait référence aux services qu'il a rendus pendant la guerre en Nouvelle-Écosse, mais ce récit ne traite que des échecs stratégiques de la guerre actuelle [la guerre de Sept Ans]. ¶ NSWA · BVAU

*Amherst, Jeffery Amherst, *1st/1ᵉʳ baron,* 1717–1797. A journal of the landing of His Majesty's forces on the island of Cape-Breton, and of the siege and surrender of Louisbourg: extracted from Major-General Amherst's and Admiral Boscawen's letters to the Right Honourable Mr. Secretary Pitt. The third edition. Boston, New-England: printed and sold by Green & Russell, in Queen-street. Sold also by Edes & Gill, in Queen-street [1758]. 22 p. 4°(?)

NUC(Pre–56)14:390

Records the events of the Siege of Louisbourg, June 1758 (surrendered, 26 July), in the Seven Years' War. ¶ Nothing has been found on earlier editions, though they must also have appeared after June, in 1758; but Dr. Waldon's entry is for a journal article (as such, now excluded from this work) from *London magazine*, Aug. 1758, p. 379–84, entitled: "Journal of the landing of H. M.'s forces on the Island of Cape-Breton & of the siege of Louisbourg ... with a plan of the city & fortifications of Louisbourg & a map of the harbour." Later editions (or versions) of Lord Amherst's *Journal* appeared in 1927 and 1931 (cf. TPL: 307 and 356).

Relate les événements du siège de Louisbourg, juin 1758 (capitulation, le 26 juillet), pendant la guerre de Sept Ans. ¶ Aucun renseignement n'a été trouvé sur les éditions précédentes bien qu'elles aient également dû paraître après juin 1758 ; mais la notice de Waldon concerne un article de journal (qui, comme tel, est exclu de cet ouvrage) du *London magazine*, août 1758, p. 379–84, intitulé : « Journal of the landing of H. M.'s forces on the Island of Cape-Breton & of the siege of Louisbourg ... with a plan of the city & fortifications of Louisbourg & a map of the harbour ». Des éditions (ou versions) ultérieures du *Journal* de lord Amherst ont paru en 1927 et en 1931 (cf. TPL:307 et 356).

An authentic account of the reduction of Louisbourg, in June and July 1758 .... By a spectator. London, printed for W[illiam]. Owen, near Temple-Bar. 1758. <Price one shilling.> 60 p. 8°(in 4s).

NUC(Pre–56)27:242

The Library of Congress copy is described as having a portrait and maps, but these may have been inserted later, for JCB, Sabin, and MiU-C collations do not call for them.

On décrit pour l'exemplaire de la Library of Congress un portrait et des cartes, mais ceux-ci ont pu être insérés à une date ultérieure ; les collations notées par le JCB, le Sabin, et le MiU-C n'en font pas mention.

[Burke, Edmund], 1729?–1797. An account of the European settlements in America .... The second edition, with improvements. London, R[obert]. and J[ames]. Dodsley, 1758. 2 v. fronts. (fold. maps). 8°

NUC(Pre–56)85:275*

First edition: 1757, q.v. for full title and notes. ¶ NSWA

Première édition : 1757, q.v. pour le titre complet et d'autres notes. ¶ NSWA

*Candid reflections on the Report (as published by authority) of the General-Officers, appointed by His Majesty's warrant of the first of November last, to enquire into the causes of the failure of the late expedition to the coasts of France. In a letter to a friend in the country .... London, printed for S[amuel]. Hooper and A. Morley, 1706 [i.e., 1758]. 2 p.l., 3–44 p., 1 l. 8°

NUC(Pre–56)93:609

The writer's contention is that the best method of successfully attacking France would be through an attack on Cape Breton, not on the French coasts. Such an attack was made, that very year, when the English took Louisbourg, in the Seven Years' War.

L'auteur postule que la meilleure façon d'attaquer la France consisterait à lancer une offensive sur le Cap-Breton plutôt que sur les côtes françaises. Une telle offensive eut lieu, cette même année, et les Anglais prirent Louisbourg, pendant la guerre de Sept Ans.

Church of England. Liturgy and Ritual. A form of prayer and thanksgiving to Almighty God; to be used at morning and evening service, after the general thanksgiving, throughout the cities of London and Westminster, and elsewhere within the weekly bills of mortality, on Sunday the twentieth day of August, 1758; and in all churches and chapels throughout England on the Sunday following; for the taking of Louisbourg by His Majesty's forces. By His Majesty's special command. London: printed by Thomas Baskett, and by the assigns of Robert Baskett, 1758. 4 p. 4°

NUC(Pre–56)109:164

Louisbourg fell to the English 26 July 1758, during the Seven Years' War, 1756–63.

Louisbourg tomba aux mains des Anglais le 26 juillet 1758, pendant la guerre de Sept Ans, 1756–1763.

The conduct of a noble commander in America, impartially reviewed. With the genuine causes of the discontents at New-York and Hallifax. And the true occasion of the delays in that important expedition. Including a regular account of all the proceedings and incidents in the order of time wherein they happened. London: printed for R[obert]. Baldwin, in Pater-noster-Row. 1758. 1 p.l., 45 p. 8°

NUC(Pre–56)118:547*

Heading, p. 1: The conduct of the Earl of Loudon [*i.e.*, John Campbell, 4th Earl of Loudoun, 1705–1782, the subject of this work (though BLC(to 1975)52:155 incorrectly places this under the 1st Earl), appointed Commander-in-Chief of the British forces in America, 1756. "Hallifax" is the present Halifax, N. S., founded seven years earlier]. ¶ A vindication of Campbell, 4th Earl of Loudoun. ¶ *First edition; the second and another ed. pub. same year;* see *next entry.* ¶ *NSWA · BVAU*

En-tête, p. 1 : The conduct of the Earl of Loudon [*c.-à-d.* John Campbell, 4ᵉ comte de Loudoun, 1705–1782, sujet de cette oeuvre (bien que le BLC(to 1975)52:155 catalogue incorrectement l'ouvrage sous le 1ᵉʳ comte), nommé commandant en chef des forces britanniques en Amérique en 1756. *Hallifax* est la ville d'Halifax (N.-É.), fondée sept ans plus tôt.] ¶ Une défense de Campbell, 4ᵉ comte de Loudoun. ¶ *Première édition ; les deuxième et troisième éd. publ. la même année ;* voir *la notice suivante.* ¶ *NSWA · BVAU*

The conduct of a noble commander in America . . . . The second edition. London, printed for R[obert]. Baldwin . . . 1758. 1 p.l., 45 p. 8°

Waldon

The conduct of a noble commander in America . . . . London, printed for R[obert]. Baldwin, in Pater-noster-Row. 1758. <Price six pence.> 2 p.l., [3]–41 p. 8°(in 4s).

Waldon

Half-title: The conduct of the Earl of Loudon impartially reviewed. ¶ NUC(Pre–56)118:547 also lists a microcard reprint of a London, Baldwin, 1758, edition.	Faux-titre : The conduct of the Earl of Loudon impartially reviewed. ¶ NUC (Pre–56)118:547 note aussi une reproduction sur microcarte d'une édition Baldwin, Londres, 1758.

*Davies, Samuel, 1724–1761. The crisis:, or The uncertain doom of kingdoms . . . . London, printed for J[ames]. Buckland; J[ohn]. Ward [etc.], 1758. viii, 36 p. 8°

Sabin:18757

See first ed., 1757, for other information.	*Voir* première éd., 1757, pour d'autres renseignements.

The English pilot. The fourth book. Describing the West-India navigation, from Hudson's-Bay . . . . London, W[illiam]. and J[ohn]. Mount, T[homas]. Page, 1758. 4, 66 p. illus., charts (part fold.). fol.

NUC(Pre–56)160:374*

Waldon has only "W. & J. Mount" as booksellers, 66 p. in the collation, and "maps and woodcuts" as illustration statement. ¶ First edition: 1689, q.v. for the dates of the many other editions, including the 1706 which has a similar title, and is more fully transcribed.	*Collation de Waldon : 66 p. Elle nomme seulement « W. & J. Mount » comme libraires, et n'indique que « cartes et gravures » comme mention d'illustration. ¶ Première édition : 1689, q.v. pour les dates des nombreuses autres éditions, y compris celle de 1706, qui porte un titre identique et a fait l'objet d'une transcription plus complète.*

*[Fauques, Marianne Agnès (Pillement), *dame de*], *d./déc.* 1773. La derniere guerre des betes. Fable pour servir a l'histoire du XVIII. siecle. Par l'auteur d'Abassai . . . . A Londres; Chez C. G. Seyffert, libraire dans Dean-street, vis à vis St. Ann's-church, Soho [*i.e.* Genève]. 1758. 4 p.l., 110 p., 1 l., [111]–218 p. 8°(?)

NUC(Pre–56)167:557*

NUC indicates that this is a false imprint, the work actually being published in Geneva. ¶ "La clef de la guerre des bêtes": p.l. 3–4. ¶ An allegory on the disputes between Great Britain and France over Acadia (now Nova Scotia, and parts of adjacent areas). ¶ NUC has a second entry for a work differing apparently only in having 2 p.l.; another edition, with quite different pagination, follows. No titles are presented in NUC with diacritical marks.

Le NUC indique que l'adresse bibliographique est erronée, l'ouvrage ayant paru en réalité à Genève. ¶ « La clef de la guerre des bêtes » : f. l. 3–4. ¶ Une allégorie sur les conflits entre la Grande-Bretagne et la France au sujet de l'Acadie (l'actuelle Nouvelle-Écosse, plus une partie des territoires adjacents). ¶ Le NUC donne une deuxième notice au sujet d'un ouvrage dont la seule différence, semble-t-il, consiste à avoir 2 f. l. ; une autre édition comportant une pagination assez différente est présentée ci-dessous. Les titres donnés par le NUC n'ont pas de signes diacritiques.

*[Fauques, Marianne Agnès (Pillement), *dame de*], *d./déc.* 1773. La derniere guerre des betes . . . . A londres, chez C. G. Seyffert, libraire dans Dean-street, vis à vis St. Ann's-church-Soho. 1758. 96, [2] p. 8°(?)

NUC(Pre–56)167:558*

"Clef ": last 2 pages. ¶ For other notes, *see* preceding entry.

« Clef » : les 2 dernières pages. ¶ *Voir* autres notes à la notice précédente.

[Maillard, Antoine Simon], *d./déc.* 1768. An account of the customs and manners of the Micmakis and Maricheets savage nations, now dependent on the government of Cape-Breton. From an original French manuscript-letter, never published, written by a French abbot, who resided many years, in quality of missionary, amongst them. To which are annexed, several pieces, relative to the savages, to Nova-Scotia, and to North-America in general. London: printed for S[amuel]. Hooper and A. Morley . . . 1758. 2 p.l., viii, 138, [1] p. 8°

NUC(Pre–56)356:123

Published anonymously. ¶ *List of books (frequently missing, says Waldon): 1 p. at end.* ¶ *The opening paragraphs of this letter of Abbé Maillard are a translation of the first part of his letter to M. de Lalane, Superior of the Seminaire des Missions Étrangères in Paris, published from the original ms. in v. 3 of* Les soirées canadiennes. *Quebec, 1863, p. [299]–426. Except in the first paragraph, the two letters are entirely different.* ¶ "Memorial of the motives of the savages, called Mickmakis and Maricheets, for continuing the war with England since the last Peace. Dated Isle-Royal, 175–": p. [61]–72; "Letter from Mons. De La Varenne, to his friend at Rochelle. Louisbourg, the 8th of May, 1756": p. [73]–130; "Character of the savages of North-America. Extracted from a Letter of the Father Charlevoix to a Lady of distinction": p. [131]–38. ¶ *No other edition or issue found, though Faribault:853 has:* An account of the Micmacs and Marakeets (savage nations). *London, Hooper, 1759, no doubt in error.*

Publication anonyme. ¶ *Liste de livres (manquant souvent, selon Waldon) : 1 p. à la fin.* ¶ *Les paragraphes d'introduction de cette lettre de l'abbé Maillard sont une traduction de la première partie de sa lettre à M. de Lalane, Supérieur du Séminaire des Missions Étrangères à Paris, lettre qui fut publiée d'après le man. original dans le vol. 3 de* Les soirées canadiennes. *Québec, 1863, p. [299]–426. Les deux lettres diffèrent entièrement, à l'exception du premier paragraphe.* ¶ « Memorial of the motives of the savages, called Mickmakis and Maricheets, for continuing the war with England since the last Peace. Dated Isle-Royal, 175– »: p. [61]–72 ; « Letter from Mons. De La Varenne, to his friend at Rochelle. Louisbourg, the 8th of May, 1756 » ; p. [73]–130 ; « Character of the savages of North-America. Extracted from a Letter of the Father Charlevoix to a Lady of distinction » : p. [131]–38. ¶ *Aucune trace d'une autre édition ou d'un autre tirage, bien que Faribault:853 indique :* An account of the Micmacs and Marakeets (savage nations). *Londres, Hooper, 1759, renseignements manifestement erronés.*

Pepperell, Sir **William**, 1696–1759. An accurate and authentic account of the taking of Cape-Breton, in the year MDCCXLV.: together with a computation of the French fishery in that part of the world; both sent over by General Pepperell, who commanded in that expedition, in a letter to his friend Captain Henry Stafford, at Exmouth, Devon. From whence will appear the importance of that island, and the danger we shall be in of losing our superiority at sea, should it now again be restored to France. London: printed for J. Staples ... & T[homas]. Atkinson, at York, 1758. <Price one shilling.> 1 p.l., 41 p. 8°

BLC(to 1975)251:241

A new edition of the 1746, *Accurate journal and account, q.v.*, to enlighten the public as to the importance of Cape Breton and to prevent its being returned to France [after the new hostilities (the Seven Years' War, 1756–63)] as it was [under the Treaty of Aix-la-Chapelle] in 1748. ¶ *BLC title ends with "that part of the world, etc.," and the entry has a briefer collation and imprint than that given by Waldon, here. NUC(Pre–56)2:597 has what must be a variant of the same work listed under title (just as it has the 1746 edition under both title and Pepperell), with a misspelling in the title:* An accurate and authentc [sic] account, *1758. Waldon also has:* An accurate account of the taking of Cape Breton in the year 1755 *(London, Staples, 1758), under title, from Faribault:849, but probably the same work with incorrect title and date in the title.*

Une nouvelle édition de *Accurate journal and account*, 1746, *q.v.*, pour éclairer le public quant à l'importance du Cap-Breton et pour empêcher que l'île ne soit rendue à la France [à la fin des nouvelles hostilités (la guerre de Sept Ans, 1756–1763)] comme ce fut le cas [aux termes du traité d'Aix-la-Chapelle] en 1748. ¶ *Le titre du BLC se termine par « that part of the world, etc. », et la notice comporte une collation et une adresse bibliographique plus courtes que celles de Waldon ici. NUC (Pre–56)2:597 indique ce qui doit être une variante du même ouvrage répertorié d'après le titre (comme c'est le cas de l'édition de 1746 qui est répertoriée à la fois sous le titre et Pepperell), mais dont le titre est mal orthographié :* An accurate and authentc [sic] account, *1758. Waldon indique également :* An accurate account of the taking of Cape Breton in the year 1755 *(Londres, Staples, 1758), répertorié suivant le titre, tiré de Faribault:849, mais il s'agit probablement du même ouvrage, quoique le titre et la date soient erronés.*

*Postlethwayt, Malachy, 1707?–1767. Britain's commercial interest explained and improved . . . . Also the great advantages which would accrue to this kingdom from an union with Ireland. By Malachy Postlethwayt . . . . Dublin, printed for L[aurence]. Flin, 1758. 2 v. tables. 8°(?)

NUC(Pre–56)467:369*

First printed London, 1757, *q.v.* for other notes; second ed., London, 1759, *q.v.*

D'abord imprimé à Londres en 1757, *q.v.* pour d'autres notes ; deuxième éd., Londres, 1759, *q.v.*

Things as they are. [pt. 1] . . . . 2d ed. London, printed for S[amuel]. Hooper, and A. Morley [etc.] 1758. 2 p.l., 112 p., 1 l. 8°

NUC(Pre–56)590:166*

Attributed to John Perceval, 2d Earl of Egmont (cf. NUC), and concerns the political relations of the country. ¶ *Part two pub. London, 1761.* ¶ *Format from BM.* ¶ Contains references to affairs in Canada and Cape Breton. ¶ *The first ed. is not in NUC, but the third ed., pub. the same year, follows.* ¶ *OTP*

Attribué à John Perceval, 2ᵉ comte d'Egmont (cf. NUC), traite des relations politiques du pays. ¶ *Partie deux publ. à Londres, 1761.* ¶ *Format tiré du BM.* ¶ Fait mention de certaines affaires au Canada et au Cap-Breton. ¶ *La première éd. ne figure pas dans le NUC, mais on trouvera ci-dessous la troisième éd., qui fut publiée la même année.* ¶ *OTP*

*Things as they are. [pt. 1] . . . . 3d ed. corrected. London, printed for S[amuel]. Hooper, and A. Morley [etc.] 1758. 2 p.l., 112 p., 1 l. 8°

NUC(Pre–56)590:166*

Format from BM. ¶ Second edition also pub. 1758, *q.v.*, preceding entry, for other notes.

Format tiré du BM. ¶ Deuxième édition également publiée en 1758, *q.v.*, notice précédente, pour d'autres notes.

*Towgood, Michaijah, 1700–1792. Britons invited to rejoice and to thank God, for national blessings. A sermon preach'd at Exeter August the 27th, 1758 The Lord's-day after receiving the account of the taking of the islands of Cape-Breton and St. John [P. E. I.]. By Mic. Towgood. London, printed for J. Noon, in the Poultry; sold by Aaron Tozer, in Exeter. [1758.] 30 p. 12°

Casey:254

Williamson, Peter, 1730–1799. French and Indian cruelty; exemplified in the life . . . of Peter Williamson . . . . Written by himself. (The 2d ed., with corrections and amendments.) York, printed and sold by J[ohn]. Jackson, 1758. iv, 104 p. 8°

NUC(Pre–56)665:612*

The title is the same as in the first ed., except that "including Philadelphia" is omitted after "Pensylvania" [in the title]. ¶ *The incidents occurred during the Seven Years' War, 1756–63.* ¶ *First edition: 1757, q.v. for other notes and editions; another edition of the same year follows.*

Le titre est identique à celui de la première éd., si ce n'est que l'expression « including Philadelphia » n'apparaît pas après le mot « Pensylvania » [dans le titre]. ¶ *Les incidents dont il est question se produisirent durant la guerre de Sept Ans, 1756–1763.* ¶ *Première édition : 1757, q.v. pour d'autres notes et éditions ; autre édition de la même année ci-dessous.*

Williamson, Peter, 1730–1799. French and Indian cruelty; exemplified in the life . . . of Peter Williamson, containing, a particular account of the manners . . . of the savages . . . . Comprehending . . . the transactions of the several provinces of Pensylvania, . . . New-Jersey, &c . . . . And an accurate . . . detail of the operations . . . at the siege of Oswego, where the author was wounded . . . and . . . discharged . . . . Also, a curious discourse on kidnapping, with proper directions for tradesmen and others, to avoid slavery, when transported from their native country. Together with a description of the most convenient roads for the British forces to invade Canada in three divisions, and make themselves masters of it the next campaign, 1759. Dedicated to the Rt. Hon. Willim Pitt, Esq; written by himself. The 3d ed., with considerable improvements. Glasgow, printed by J[ohn]. Bryce and D[avid]. Paterson for the benefit of the unfortunate author, 1758. <Price one shilling.> iv, 112 p. 8°

NUC(Pre–56)665:612*

NUC title extended from Waldon. ¶ The preface of the first ed., York, 1757 (*q.v.*) is omitted, and a dedication to Pitt substituted. Before the conclusion some descriptive matter has been inserted: "Of New-England" (p. 84–86) etc.; "Of Nova-Scotia" (p. 91–92); "Of Canada" (p. 92–93). His plan for conquering Canada occupies p. 105–08. ¶ *First edition: 1757, q.v. for other notes and editions; the second ed., pub. in the same year, is described in the preceding entry; this third ed. also appeared in MFiche in the Canadiana in the Toronto Public Library series, Toronto, ca. 1960.* ¶ *NFSM(MF) · QMBN · OTP*

Titre du NUC augmenté a partir de celui donné par Waldon. ¶ L'avant-propos de la première éd., York, 1757 (*q.v.*) est omis et est remplacé par une dédicace à Pitt. Avant la conclusion, des sujets descriptifs ont été insérés : « Of New-England » (p. 84–86) etc. ; « Of Nova-Scotia » (p. 91–92) ; « Of Canada » (p. 92–93). Son plan pour la conquête du Canada se trouve aux pages 105 à 108. ¶ *Première édition : 1757, q.v. pour d'autres notes et éditions ; la deuxième éd., qui fut publiée la même année, est décrite dans la notice précédente ; cette troisième éd. a également été reproduite sur microfiches dans la collection Canadiana de la Toronto Public Library, vers 1960.* ¶ *NFSM(mic.) · QMBN · OTP*

Williamson, Peter, 1730–1799, *supposed author/auteur présumé.* Occasional reflections on the importance of the war in America, and the reasonableness and justice of supporting the King of Prussia, &c. in defence of the common cause. Founded on a general view of the state and connections of this country; the general system of Europe; and the ambitious designs of French policy for overturning the ballance of power and liberties of Europe. In a letter to a member of Parliament. London: printed for J[ohn]. Whiston and B[enjamin]. White . . . 1758. 2 p.l., 139 p. 8°

NUC(Pre–56)665:614

Refers to the Seven Years' War (1756–63), in its American theatre. ¶ NFSM(MF) · QSHERU(MF) · OOU(MF) · OTP

Traite du contexte américain de la guerre de Sept Ans (1756–1763). ¶ NFSM (mic.) · QSHERU (mic.) · OOU (mic.) · OTP

Williamson, Peter, 1730–1799. Some considerations on the present state of affairs. Wherein the defenceless situation of Great-Britain, is pointed out, and an easy rational and just scheme for its security, at this dangerous crisis; proposed, in a militia formed on an equal plan, that can neither be oppressive to the poor nor offensive to the rich, as practised by some of His Majesty's colonies abroad; interspersed with an account of the first settlement of the province of Pennsylvania . . . . Likewise a short description of the air, soil, produce, &c. of the several colonies on the continent of North-America. The whole concluded with a summary detail of the education, manners, and religion of the Indians, not heretofore mention'd. Written by Peter Williamson . . . . York: printed for the author and sold by all the booksellers in town, 1758. iv, 56 p. 8°

NUC(Pre–56)665:615

Description of the colonies (including Nova Scotia and Canada, p. 54–56) is taken from his *French and Indian cruelty.* York, 1758, second ed.

La description des colonies (y compris la Nouvelle-Écosse et le Canada, p. 54–56) est tirée de son ouvrage *French and Indian cruelty.* York, 1758, deuxième éd.

[Young, Arthur], 1741–1820. The theatre of the present war in North America: with candid reflections on the great importance of the war in that part of the world. By A. Y****, Esq. London: printed for J. Coote . . . 1758. Price one shilling and sixpence. 2 p.l., vii, 56 p. 8°(in 4s).

NUC(Pre–56)679:207

Written when Young was aged only seventeen; DNB refers to "the precocity of his intelligence." ¶ Waldon has only 1 p.l. (the title-page) in the collation. ¶ The conflict referred to is the Seven Years' War, 1756–63. ¶ OTU

Young n'était âgé que de dix-sept ans lorsqu'il écrivit cet ouvrage ; le DNB mentionne « son intelligence précoce ». ¶ Collation de Waldon : 1 f. l. (la page de titre). ¶ Le conflit dont il est question est la guerre de Sept Ans, 1756–1763. ¶ OTU

1759

An accurate and authentic journal of the siege of Quebec, 1759. By a gentleman in an eminent station on the spot. London, Printed for J. Robinson . . . . 1759. 1 p.l., 44 p. 8°(in 4s).

NUC(Pre–56)2:597

Refers to an event in the Seven Years' War, 1756–63. ¶ Other editions: Dublin, 1759, 12° (Waldon), and 16° under title *An accurate journal, q.v.,* (and Faribault:854 has: London, Owen, 1759), and 1901 (in Sir Arthur Doughty, *The siege of Quebec.* Quebec, 1901–02, 6 v., v. 4, p. [279]–94).

Traite d'un événement de la guerre de Sept Ans, 1756–1763. ¶ Autres éditions : Dublin, 1759, in–12° (Waldon), et in–16° sous le titre *An accurate journal, q.v.,* (tandis que Faribault:854 indique : Londres, Owen, 1759), ainsi que 1901 (dans l'ouvrage de sir Arthur Doughty, *The siege of Quebec.* Québec, 1901–1902, 6 vol., vol. 4, p. [279]–94).

*An accurate journal of the siege of Quebec, 1759. By a gentleman in an eminent station on the spot. Dublin, Printed for J[ohn]. Exshaw [etc.] 1759. 34 p. 16°

NUC(Pre–56)2:598

See 1759: *An accurate and authentic journal,* for notes.

Voir notes sous 1759, *An accurate and authentic journal.*

[Bradstreet, John], 1711–1774. An impartial account of Lieut. Col. Bradstreet's expedition to Fort Frontenac. To which are added, a few reflections on the conduct of that enterprize, and the advantages resulting from its success. By a volunteer on the expedition. London, printed for T. Wilcox [etc.], 1759. 2 p.l., 60 p. 8°

NUC(Pre–56)71:616*

Concerns the capture of Fort Frontenac (Kingston) in 1758, described by an anonymous eye-witness, identified in the 1940 edition as Col. Bradstreet himself. ¶ First edition; reprinted Toronto, 1940. ¶ NSWA · OTU (1940)

Traite de la prise du Fort Frontenac (Kingston) en 1758, racontée par un témoin oculaire anonyme que l'édition de 1940 identifie comme le colonel Bradstreet lui-même. ¶ Première édition ; réimpression à Toronto en 1940. ¶ NSWA · OTU (1940)

Bulkley, Charles, 1719–1797. The signs of the times, illustrated and improved. In a sermon preached at the evening-lecture in the Old-Jewry, on Sunday, October 21, 1759. On occasion of the surrender of Quebec to His Majesty's forces, September 18, 1759. By Charles Bulkley. London, printed for J. Noon, and C. Henderson, 1759. 30 p. 8°(in 4s).

NUC(Pre–56)83:582

NUC has collation: 30 p., 1 l.

Collation du NUC : 30 p., 1 f.

Church of England. Liturgy and Ritual. A form of prayer and thanksgiving to Almighty God; to be used in all churches and chapels throughout that part of Great Britain called England, the dominion of Wales, and the town of Berwick upon Tweed, on Thursday the twenty ninth day of November next, being the day appointed by proclamation for a general thanksgiving to God; for vouchsafing such signal successes to His Majesty's arms, both by sea and land, particularly by the defeat of the French army in Canada, and the taking of Quebec, and for most seasonably granting us at this time an uncommonly plentiful harvest. By His Majesty's special command. London: printed by Thomas Baskett, and by the assigns of Robert Baskett, 1759. 15 p. 4°

NUC(Pre–56)109:164

Refers to the taking of Quebec at the Battle of the Plains of Abraham, by the English under Wolfe, 1759, during the Seven Years' War, 1756–63.

Traite de la prise de Québec par les Anglais sous le commandement de Wolfe en 1759 à la bataille des Plaines d'Abraham, durant la guerre de Sept Ans, 1756–1763.

Church of England. Liturgy and Ritual. A form of prayer and thanksgiving .... London: printed in the year, 1759: <Price one penny.> 8 p. 8°

"Harmsworth"

Perhaps from Sir R. L. Harmsworth, Catalogue of Americana *(typescript; unavailable to the Editor); not found in* The Northcliffe Collection, *in* PAC *(Ottawa, 1926); but* NUC *lists many other catalogues of parts of the great Harmsworth Library. Not found in* NUC, BLC, Sabin, *or* JCB.

Peut-être de sir R. L. Harmsworth, Catalogue of Americana *(tapuscrit, auquel l'éditeur n'a pu avoir accès) ; introuvable dans* The Northcliffe Collection, *aux* APC *(Ottawa, 1926) ; mais le* NUC *répertorie de nombreux autres catalogues de documents de l'importante Harmsworth Library. Introuvable dans le* NUC, *le* BLC, *le* Sabin, *aussi bien que dans le* JCB.

Church of England. Liturgy and Ritual. A form of prayer and thanksgiving to Almighty God; to be used at morning and evening service, after the general thanksgiving, throughout the cities of London and Westminster, and elsewhere within the bills of mortality, on Sunday the twenty first of October, 1759; and in all churches and chapels throughout England, Wales, and the town of Berwick upon Tweed, on the Sunday after the ministers thereof receive the same; for the defeat of the French army in Canada, and the taking of Quebeck by His Majesty's forces, and for the other successes and blessings of the year. By His Majesty's special command. London: printed by Thomas Baskett . . .; and by the Assigns of Robert Baskett. 1759. 4 p. 4°

NUC(Pre–56)109:164

Text in black-letter. ¶ See the entry before the preceding for a note.

Texte en écriture gothique. ¶ Voir note à la première notice.

Considerations on the importance of Canada, and the Bay and River of St. Lawrence; and of the American fisheries dependant on the Islands of Cape Breton, St. John's, Newfoundland, and the seas adjacent. Address'd to the Right Hon. William Pitt. London, printed for W[illiam]. Owen, near Temple-Bar, 1759. 4 p.l., 23 p. 8°(in 4s).

NUC(Pre–56)120:394

Waldon has collation: t.-p. [4], 23 p. ¶ To deprive the French of the fisheries would be a fatal blow. The writer holds that Canada is valuable for the fur and timber trade and necessary to the British for the security of their other colonies. Nova Scotia is to be valued for the fisheries. ¶ Waldon also lists Address to the Rt. Hon. Wm. Pitt. Considerations on the importance of the American fisheries, etc. London, 1759. Her source is "C.H.C., p. 883," but she notes: Possibly the same as Considerations on the importance of

Collation de Waldon : p. de t., [4], 23 p. ¶ On aurait porté un coup fatal aux Français en leur enlevant les pêcheries. L'auteur soutient que le Canada est précieux en ce qui a trait au commerce de la fourrure et du bois d'oeuvre, et qu'il constitue un atout indispensable aux Britanniques pour la sécurité de leurs autres colonies. Les pêcheries confèrent à la Nouvelle-Écosse une valeur appréciable. ¶ Waldon répertorie également l'ouvrage intitulé Address to the Rt. Hon. Wm. Pitt. Considerations sur the importance of the American fisheries, etc. Londres, 1759. Comme source, elle indique « C.H.C.,

Canada . . . , *1759.* ¶ *NFSM*

p. 883 », mais note : peut-être le même ouvrage que Considerations on the importance of Canada . . . , *1759.* ¶ *NFSM*

Daphnis and Menalcas: a pastoral. Sacred to the memory of the late General Wolfe. And humbly inscribed to the Right Honourable William Pitt, Esquire . . . . London, printed for R[obert]. and J[ames]. Dodsley, in Pall-mall; and J[ohn]. Scott, at the Black Swan in Pater-noster-row. 1759. 2 p.l., 20 p. 9 engravings (incl. 7 ports.). 4°

NUC(Pre–56)133:98

At foot of half-title: Price One Shilling. ¶ No plates noted in Bodleian copies [nor in NUC copies].

Mention au-dessous du faux-titre : Prix un shilling. ¶ On n'a trouvé aucune planche dans les exemplaires relevés par la Bodleian Library [ni dans ceux du NUC].

A dialogue betwixt General Wolfe, and the Marquis Montcalm, in the Elysian Fields. Printed in the year 1759 and sold by E. Jopson [widow of Jas. Jopson, d. 1759], in Coventry; Messrs. [James] Rivington and [James] Fletcher . . . London; and the other booksellers in town and country. Price six-pence. 20 p. 8°

BM(to 1955)260:158

Bookseller information from Plomer.

Les renseignements sur les libraires sont de Plomer.

*The English pilot. The fourth book. Describing the West-India navigation, from Hudson's-Bay.... London, W[illiam]. J[ohn]. Mount, T[homas]. Page, 1759. 4, 66 p. illus., charts (part fold.). fol.

NUC(Pre–56)160:374*

First edition: 1689, *q.v.* for the dates of the many other editions, including the 1706, which has a similar title, given in more extended detail.

Première édition : 1689, *q.v.* pour les dates des nombreuses autres éditions, y compris celle de 1706, qui porte un titre similaire mais plus détaillé.

Great Britain. Sovereigns, etc., 1727–1760 **(George II).** By the King. A proclamation for a publick thanksgiving. [Oct. 23, 1759.] London: printed by Thomas Baskett, Printer to the King's most Excellent Majesty; and by the Assigns of Robert Baskett. 1759. 1 l. fol.

"A. A. S. Trans. 1911. v. 12, p. 207–208."

Source: American Antiquarian Society, Worcester, Mass. Transactions and collections, *vol. 12, 1911, p. 207–08.*¶ Printed *London gazette*, 27 Oct. 1759. ¶ A similar proclamation was issued for Scotland, also printed in *London gazette*, 27 Oct. 1759. 1 p. fol. . . . The Privy Council ordered that the Thanksgiving should also be celebrated in Ireland . . . .

Source : American Antiquarian Society, Worcester (Mass.), Transactions and collections. *vol. 12, 1911, p. 207–08.*¶ Publié dans la *London gazette*, le 27 octobre 1759. ¶ Une proclamation semblable fut publiée à l'intention de l'Écosse et parut également dans la *London gazette*, le 27 octobre 1759. 1 p. fol. . . . Le Conseil privé ordonna que l'Action de grâces fût également célébrée en Irlande . . . .

Hitchin, Edward, *the elder/père.* A sermon preached at the new meeting, in White-Row Spital Fields, on Thursday 29 November 1759. Being the day appointed by His Majesty for a general thanksgiving. By Edward Hitchin .... [Text from Psalm 136:3–4.] London, printed; and sold by J[ames]. Buckland ... T[homas]. Field ... E[dward]. Dilly ... and G[eorge]. Keith ... [1759?] 2 p.l., [2], 30 p. 8°(in 4s).

cf. NUC(Pre–56)248:281

NUC has title variant (. . . on 29 Nov. 1759. Being the day appointed for a general thanksgiving), and has imprint: London, 1759, and collation: 30 p. Waldon has no date in her imprint. The thanksgiving is for the British victory at Quebec (and elsewhere).

Dans le NUC : variante de titre (. . . on 29 Nov. 1759. Being the day appointed for a general thanksgiving) ; adresse bibliographique : Londres, 1759 ; collation : 30 p. L'adresse bibliographique donnée par Waldon ne comporte aucune date. ¶ L'Action de grâces commémore la victoire remportée par les Britanniques à Québec (et ailleurs).

A letter to the Right Honourable William Pitt, Esq; from an officer at Fort Frontenac. London: printed for J[ames]. Fleming, opposite Norfolk-Street, in the Strand. 1759. 2 p.l., 38 p. 8°(in 4s).

Sabin:40533

"Fort Frontenac was a French fort at the entrance to the St. Lawrence from Lake Ontario, on the site of the present town of Kingston." The writer describes the fort, considers it one of the most important in Canada, and recommends improved fortifications and frigates to patrol the lake: Sabin, and JCB(1)3:1223.

« Fort Frontenac était un fort français bâti sur la rive du Saint-Laurent, à l'endroit où le fleuve est émissaire du lac Ontario, c.-à-d. sur le site actuel de la ville de Kingston. » L'auteur décrit le fort, qu'il considère comme l'un des plus importants au Canada ; il recommande que les fortifications soient améliorées et que des frégates s'y trouvent en station pour patrouiller sur le lac : Sabin et JCB(1)3:1223.

Miscellaneous correspondence 1759–60, containing Miscellaneous correspondence, in prose and verse. For April, 1759. 1759–60. p. 73–74 [and] American news. p. 235–39 [and] A chronological memoir of occurrences, for November, 1759. Foreign affairs. p. 255–58. London, 1759. [No total collation.]

Casey:286

This is the present Editor's interpretation of Casey. ¶ "A description of Quebec": p. 73–74. The volume also contains a number of extracts, relating to Canada, dated Oct. 1759 to Dec. 1760, with running-title: "A chronological memoir of occurences." ¶ *Relates to the Seven Years' War, 1756–63.*

L'éditeur s'est inspiré de Casey pour rédiger la présente notice. ¶ « A description of Quebec » : p. 73–74. Le volume comprend également plusieurs extraits concernant le Canada ; il est daté du mois d'octobre 1759 au mois de décembre 1760 et comporte un titre courant : « A chronological memoir of occurences ». ¶ *Traite de la guerre de Sept Ans, 1756–1763.*

*A monody on the death of Major-Gen¹ James Wolfe. To which is added, some particulars of his life .... London: printed for M. Thrush, at the King's Arms, in Salisbury-Court, Fleet-Street, 1759. 19 p. 4°

NUC(Pre–56)391:170

[Moreau, Jacob Nicolas], 1717–1804, *comp.* The mystery reveal'd; or, Truth brought to light. Being a discovery of some facts, in relation to the conduct of the late M——y [Ministry], which however extraordinary they may appear, are yet supported by such testimonies of authentick papers and memoirs; as neither confidence, can outbrave; nor cunning invalidate. By a patriot .... London: printed and sold by W[illiam]. Cater ... R[obert]. Withy ... and T[homas]. Hope ... 1759. 1 p.l., 319 p. 8°(in 4s).

NUC(Pre–56)394:303

Transl. from his: Mémoire contenant le précis des faits, avec leurs piéces justificatives. *Paris, 1756. It was also transl. into English as:* The conduct of the late ministry; or, A memorial; containing a summary of facts. *London, 1757,* q.v. *for other notes.*

Trad. anglaise de son ouvrage intitulé Mémoire contenant le précis des faits, avec leurs piéces justificatives. *Paris, 1756. Autre trad. anglaise :* The conduct of the late ministry; or, A memorial; containing a summary of facts. *Londres, 1757,* q.v. *pour d'autres notes.*

Morris, Charles, 1711–1781. A chart of Halifax in Nova-Scotia, with Jebucto's Bay and Cape Sambrô, also the islands, ledges of rocks, shoals, and soundings. Surveyed by His Excellency Brigadier General Laurence, governor of the province of Nova-Scotia. By Charles Morris, chief surveyor, 1759. Published by command of the Right Honourable the Lords of Trade and Plantations, for the benefit of the trade and navigation of Great Britain and its colonies. [London, 1759.] map. fol.(?)

Jefferys (see note).

Waldon's source is a list of books "Just published, by Thomas Jefferys," at the end of A journal of the siege of Quebec. *London, 1760* (q.v.), *but no bibliographical citation has been found: perhaps never pub.? Morris, however, published similar maps in 1749 (cf. NUC(Pre–56) 395:656).*

La source de Waldon consiste en une liste de parutions récentes, « Just published, by Thomas Jefferys », à la fin de A journal of the siege of Quebec. *Londres, 1760* (q.v.), *mais aucune citation bibliographique n'a été trouvée : peut-être cet ouvrage n'a-t-il jamais été publié ? Morris a toutefois fait paraître des cartes semblables en 1749 (cf. NUC(Pre–56)395:656).*

Postlethwayt, Malachy, 1707?–1767. Great-Britain's commercial interest explained and improved: in a series of dissertations on the most important branches of her trade and landed interest. With an essay, shewing the great advantages which would certainly accrue to England, from an union with Ireland. Also a clear view of the state of our plantations in America, their constitution, trade, and revenues, with a certain method to encrease their commerce and strength. By Malachy Postlethwayt. . . . 2d ed. London, W[illiam]. Owen, 1759. 2 v.: xviii, [6], 548; vi, [6], 551 p. fold. tables. 8°

NUC(Pre–56)467:397*

First ed. pub. under title: Britain's commercial interest .... *London, 1757,* q.v. *for other notes.*

Première éd. publ. sous le titre Britain's commercial interest.... *Londres, 1757,* q.v. *pour d'autres notes.*

Robson, Joseph, *fl.* 1733–1763. An account of six years residence in Hudson's Bay.... Containing a variety of facts, observations, and discoveries, tending to shew, I. The vast importance of ... Hudson's-Bay .... To which is added an appendix .... London, printed for T. Jefferys, 1759. 1 p.l., vi, 84, 95 p. 2 fold. maps (incl. front.), fold. plan. 8°(?)

NUC(Pre–56)499:114*

First pub. 1752, q.v. *for fuller title and notes; probably from the same stand of type, the slight differences in the two NUC entries being ones of transcription only. Waldon says they collate the same, but that the t.-p. has been reset, with these differences: seventeenth line, "And" omitted after "Seal Fisheries"; eighteenth line, comma in place of semi-colon after "Company"; twenty-ninth line, hyphen omitted in "Wales's Fort" and "E" capitalized in "Entrance" (information from Newberry Library).* ¶ *BVIPA*

Première publ. 1752, q.v. *pour un titre plus complet et des notes ; probablement la même composition typographique, les légères différences entre les deux notices du NUC relevant uniquement de la transcription. Selon Waldon, le contenu est le même mais la p. de t. a été recomposée comme suit : à la dix-septième ligne, le mot « And » a été omis après l'expression « Seal Fisheries » ; à la dix-huitième ligne, une virgule remplace un point-virgule après le mot « Company » ; à la vingt-neuvième ligne, trait d'union n'apparaît pas dans l'expression « Wales's Fort » et le premier « E » du mot « Entrance » est une majuscule (renseignements provenant de la Newberry Library).* ¶ *BVIPA*

***[Shirley, William],** 1694–1771. Memoirs of the principal transactions of the last war between the English and French in North America. 3d ed. Bath, 1759. [Pagination?] 8°

NUC(Pre–56)375:237*

For an earlier edition and other notes, *see* 1757.

Pour une édition antérieure et d'autres notes, *voir* 1757.

Smith, William, 1727–1803. Discourses on several public occasions during the war in America. Preached chiefly with a view to the explaining the importance of the Protestant cause, in the British colonies; and the advancement of religion, patriotism and military virtue. Among which are a discourse on adversity; and also a discourse on planting the sciences, and the propagation of Christianity, in the untutored parts of the earth. With an appendix, containing some other pieces. By William Smith . . . . London, printed for A[ndrew]. Millar . . . R[alph]. Griffiths . . . and G[eorge]. Keith. 1759. xii, ix, [11]–246 p. 8°

NUC(Pre–56)552:310*

Appendix I: "An earnest address to the colonies, particularly those of the southern district, on the opening of the campaign 1758." ¶ *Six discourses on various subjects.* ¶ *First edition; second ed., London, 1762, q.v. Reprinted with other works by Smith, London, 1803 (cf. Rich, 1759:5).* ¶ *BVAU*

Annexe I : « An earnest address to the colonies, particularly those of the southern district, on the opening of the campaign 1758 ». ¶ *Six discours sur des sujets variés.* ¶ *Première édition ; deuxième éd., Londres, 1762, q.v. Réimpression avec d'autres ouvrages de Smith, Londres, 1803 (cf. Rich, 1759:5).* ¶ *BVAU*

Townley, James, 1774–1833. A sermon preached before the Right Honourable the Lord-Mayor, the court of aldermen, and the liveries of the several companies of the city of London, in the cathedral church of St. Paul, on Thursday, November 29, 1759; being the day appointed by proclamation for a general thanksgiving to God; for vouchsafing such signal successes to His Majesty's arms, both by sea and land, particularly by the defeat of the French army in Canada, and the taking of Quebec; and for most seasonably granting us at this time an uncommonly plentiful harvest. By James Townley .... London: printed for H[enry]. Kent, in Finch-lane near the Royal Exchange; T[homas]. Field, in Cheapside; and J. Walter, at Charing-Cross. 1759. <Price six-pence.> 19 p. 4°

NUC(Pre–56)599:112

Apparently the first and only edition.　　　*Apparemment la première et seule édition.*

Williamson, Peter, 1730–1799. French and Indian cruelty: exemplified in the life . . . of Peter Williamson. Containing, a particular account of the manners . . . of the savages; . . . many expeditions against them. Comprehending . . . a summary of the transactions of the several provinces in America; particularly, those relative to the intended attack on Crown Point and Niagara. And an accurate . . . detail of the operations . . . at the siege of Oswego, where the author was wounded and taken prisoner. Also, a curious discourse on kidnapping. Written by himself. The fourth edition, with considerable improvements. London: printed for the unfortunate author and sold by R[alph]. Griffiths, 1759. iv, 5–120 p. front. (port.). 12°

NUC(Pre–56)665:612–13*

NUC title extended from Waldon. ¶ Text the same as the third ed., 1758, *q.v.* ¶ *First ed.: 1757, q.v. for other notes and editions.* ¶ *OONL*

Titre du NUC augmenté à partir de celui que donne Waldon. ¶ Texte identique à celui de la troisième éd. 1758, *q.v.* ¶ *Première éd. : 1757, q.v. pour d'autres notes et éditions.* ¶ *OONL*

[**Young, Arthur**], 1741–1820. Reflections on the present state of affairs at home and abroad. By A. Y**** esq; author of the Theatre of the present war in North America. London, printed for J. Coote, 1759. 2 p.l., v p., 1 l., 51 p. 8°

NUC(Pre–56)679:205

Young's The theatre of the present war in North America *(London, 1758) appears above.* ¶ The war in America [*i.e.*, the Seven Years' War, 1756–63]: p. 23–51. ¶ *QQL · OTP*

L'ouvrage de Young, The theatre of the present war in North America *(Londres, 1758), est répertorié plus haut.* ¶ La guerre en Amérique [*c.-à-d.*, la guerre de Sept Ans, 1756–1763] : p. 23–51. ¶ *QQL · OTP*

1760

An answer to the Letter to two great men. Containing remarks and observations on that piece, and vindicating the character of a noble lord [*i.e.* John Campbell, Earl of Loudoun] from inactivity. London: printed for A. Henderson, in Westminster Hall. 1760. (Price six-pence.) 1 p.l., 22 p. 8°(in 4s).

NUC(Pre–56)17:592*

In part a defence of the Earl of Loudoun's American campaign. ¶ A reply to: John Douglas, *A letter addressed to two great men.* London, 1760 (*q.v.*). ¶ *First edition; reprinted: Providence, R. I., John Carter Brown Library, 1934.*

Constitue en partie une défense de la campagne américaine menée par le comte de Loudoun. ¶ Réplique à John Douglas, *A letter addressed to two great men.* Londres, 1760 (*q.v.*). ¶ *Première édition ; réimpression : Providence (R. I.), John Carter Brown Library, 1934.*

*An authentic register of the British successes; being a collection of all the extraordinary and some of the ordinary gazettes, from the taking of Louisbourgh, July 26, 1758, by the honourable Admiral Boscawen and Gen. Amhurst [*sic*]; to the defeat of the French fleet under M. Conflans, Nov. 21, 1759, by Sir Edward Hawke. To which is added, a particular account of M. Thurot's defeat, by Captain John Elliott. London, printed for G[eorge]. Kearsly, 1760. vi, 126 p. 12°

NUC(Pre–56)27:253

Plomer gives this publisher's name as George Kearsley. ¶ The events described were part of the Seven Years' War, 1756–63, called the French and Indian War in North America. ¶ First edition; a second ed. appeared the same year: *see* next entry. ¶ *NBFU(MF) · OTMCL · SSU(MF)*

Selon Plomer, cet éditeur s'appelle George Kearsley. ¶ Les événements qui y sont décrits eurent lieu pendant la guerre de Sept Ans, 1756–1763, appelée la guerre des Français et des Indiens en Amérique du Nord. ¶ Première édition ; une deuxième éd. parue la même année : *voir* la notice suivante. ¶ *NBFU(mic.) · OTMCL · SSU(mic.)*

*An authentic register of the British successes . . . from the taking of Louisbourg, July 26, 1758, by the Hon. Adm. Boscawen and Gen. Amherst, to the defeat of the French fleet, under M. Conflans . . . by Sir Edward Hawke. Also a particular account of M. Thurot's defeat, by Capt. John Elliott. The second edition. To which is now added, Gen. Wolfe's letter to Mr. Pitt, a few days before the taking of Quebec, in which glorious acquisition he died in honour to his country. London: printed for G. Kearsley, at the Golden-Lion, in Ludgate-Street, 1760. vi, 136 p. 12°

Waldon?

See preceding entry for first ed.

Voir la notice précédente pour la première éd.

[Belsham, Jacobus], *d./déc.* 1770. Canadia. Ode. Epinikios [transliterated from Greek characters]. . . . [9 lines, Latin quotation from Cicero] Cic. pro Rosc. Amer. Londini: impensis Auctoris. Prostant apud J[ohn]. Clarke, sub Bursa Regia [under the Royal Exchange], R. & J. Dodsley in Vico, Pall-Mall, et J[ames]. Buckland in Vico, Pater-noster Row. 1760. 3 p.l., 3–18 p. 4°

NUC(Pre–56)45:505

Dedication signed by the author: Jacobus Belsham; Waldon enters under James Belsham, and supplies the death date. NUC has only 2 p.l. in pagination. ¶ Latin verse. ¶ OTU

Dédicace signée par l'auteur : Jacobus Belsham ; pour sa part, Waldon a répertorié cet ouvrage sous James Belsham et indique la date de décès. Le NUC mentionne seulement 2 f. l. à la rubrique pagination. ¶ Vers en latin. ¶ OTU

[Burke, Edmund], 1729?–1797. An account of the European settlements in America . . . . Third edition, with improvements. London, R[obert]. and J[ames]. Dodsley, 1760. 2 v. 8°(?)

First edition: 1757, q.v. for full title and notes.

Première édition : 1757, q.v. pour des notes et le titre complet.

[Burke, William], *d./déc.* 1798, *supposed author/auteur présumé.* Remarks on the Letter addressed to two great men. In a letter to the author of that piece . . . . London: printed in the year 1760. Price eight pence. 38 p. 8°(in 4s).

NUC(Pre–56)85:360*

Authorship ascribed to Charles Townshend (1725–67) by Waldon, supported by BM and Halkett and Laing, but NUC and DNB attribute to Burke. ¶ The above title is taken from Waldon, but is assumed to be the same as the second entry under this title in NUC, where only "London,

Selon Waldon, l'auteur de cet ouvrage est Charles Townshend (1725–1767), hypothèse qui est appuyée par le BM et Halkett et Laing, tandis que le NUC et le DNB attribuent la paternité de cet écrit à Burke. ¶ Le titre ci-dessus provient de Waldon, mais on présume qu'il s'agit du même titre qu'à la deuxième notice sous cette vedette

1760" is given for imprint. ¶ *A reply to: John Douglas,* A letter addressed to two great men .... *London, 1760, which argued for the retention of both Canada and Guadeloupe in the peace treaty (Peace of Paris, 1763, ending The Seven Years' War). Waldon does not identify Burke's argument, but* DNB *("Burke") states that he strongly advocated retention of Guadeloupe, of which island he became Secretary in 1762.* ¶ *Answered by: Benjamin Franklin,* The interest of Great Britain considered. *London, 1760, which also favoured the keeping of Canada (but Franklin may not have been replying directly to William Burke),* General reflections .... *London, 1760, and* A letter to a great M——R. *London, 1761, q.v. The controversy continued in 1761; see, for example,* Reasons for keeping Guadaloupe. *London, 1761 (q.v.), which prefers keeping Guadeloupe to keeping Canada, in the terms of peace ending the Seven Years' War.* ¶ *Probably the first edition; other editions, appearing in the same year, follow; also reprinted in Boston, New England [1760], 40 p.*

dans le NUC, *qui n'indique que « London, 1760 » comme adresse bibliographique.* ¶ *Réplique à John Douglas,* A letter addressed to two great men .... *Londres, 1760, qui milite pour que le Canada et la Guadeloupe demeurent tous deux territoires anglais aux termes du traité de paix (traité de Paris, 1763, qui mit fin à la guerre de Sept Ans). Waldon n'indique pas la nature des arguments de Burke, mais le* DNB *(« Burke ») précise que ce dernier défendait vigoureusement le maintien sous domination anglaise de l'île de la Guadeloupe, dont il devint « Secretary » en 1762.* ¶ *Réplique de Benjamin Franklin,* The interest of Great Britian considered. *Londres, 1760, qui lui aussi favorisait le maintien du Canada sous la houlette de l'Angleterre (mais il est possible que Franklin n'ait pas directement répliqué à William Burke),* General reflections .... *Londres, 1760, et* A letter to a great M——R. *Londres, 1761, q.v. La controverse s'est poursuivie en 1761 ; par exemple,* voir Reasons for keeping Guadaloupe. *Londres, 1761 (q.v.), dont l'auteur préfère conserver la Guadeloupe plutôt que le Canada, aux termes du traité mettant fin à la guerre de Sept Ans.* ¶ *Probablement la première édition ; parues la même année, d'autres éditions suivent ; en outre, réimpression à Boston (Nouvelle-Angleterre) [1760], 40 p.*

[Burke, William], *d./déc.* 1798, *supposed author/auteur présumé.* Remarks on the Letter address'd to two great men .... London, printed for R[obert]. and J[ames]. Dodsley [1760]. 64 p. 8°

NUC(Pre–56)85:360*

For notes, see preceding entry. ¶ This also appeared as a microcard edition, cf. NUC. ¶ OTP

Voir notes à la notice précédente. ¶ Aussi, reproduction sur microcartes, cf. NUC. ¶ OTP

[Burke, William], *d./déc.* 1798, *supposed author/auteur présumé.* Remarks on the Letter address'd to two great men .... 2d ed. London, printed for R[obert]. and J[ames]. Dodsley [1760]. 64 p. 8°

NUC(Pre–56)85:361*

The first ed. appeared earlier the same year; see above.

La première éd. parut plus tôt la même année ; voir ci-dessus.

[Burke, William], *d./déc.* 1798, *supposed author/auteur présumé.* Remarks on the Letter address'd to two great men .... 3d ed., corr. London, printed for R[obert]. and J[ames]. Dodsley, in Pall-Mall. [1760.] 1 p.l., [5]–72 p. 8°

NUC(Pre–56)85:361*

Waldon has only 1 p.l.; NUC has this as "With Douglas, John, bp. of Salisbury. A letter addressed to two great men. London, 1760," to which Remarks *is a reply. ¶ Postscript, p. 65–72, is not in the first ed. ¶ For other notes, see first ed., 1760, above.*

Collection de Waldon : 1 f. l. ; mention du NUC : « With Douglas, John, bp. of Salisbury. A letter addressed to two great men. London, 1760 », écrit auquel les Remarks *donne la réplique. ¶ La postface, p. 65–72, ne figure pas dans la première éd. ¶ Pour d'autres notes, voir la première éd., 1760, plus haut.*

*[Burke, William], *d./déc.* 1798, *supposed author/auteur présumé*. Remarks on a Letter addressed to two great men . . . . Dublin: printed for G[eorge]. Faulkner [etc.], 1760. 38 p. 8°(?)

NUC(Pre–56)85:360*

First edition: London, 1760, *q.v.*   Première édition : Londres, 1760, *q.v.*

[Cato], *pseud*. Reasons for not restoring Guadaloupe at a peace. In a letter addressed to the Right Honourable the Earl of Halifax, first Lord Commissioner of Trade and Plantations, &c. In answer to certain animadversions contained in A letter to two great men . . . . London: printed for John Williams, bookseller, on Ludgate-Hill. 1760. 46 p. 8°(in 4s).

NUC(Pre–56)100:131

Signed: Cato. ¶ *A reply to: John Douglas, A letter addressed to two great men. London, 1760* (q.v.). ¶ *Concerns the terms of peace ending the Seven Years' War, and the controversy over whether Canada or Guadeloupe should be held.* ¶ The controversy was continued the following year; *see: Reasons for keeping Guadaloupe* . . . . London, 1761.

Signé : Cato. ¶ *Réplique à John Douglas, A letter addressed to two great men. Londres, 1760* (q.v.). ¶ *Porte sur les conditions du traité mettant fin à la guerre de Sept Ans, et sur la controverse suscitée par le choix du territoire qu'il fallait garder, soit le Canada, soit la Guadeloupe.* ¶ La controverse se poursuivit l'année suivante; *voir : Reasons for keeping Gaudaloupe* . . . . Londres, 1761.

*Church of England. Liturgy and Ritual. A form of prayer and thanksgiving to Almighty God . . . on occasion of the late successes of His Majesty's arms in North America, and the surrender of Montreal and all Canada. London: printed by Thomas Baskett, 1760. [Pagination not given.] 4°

NUC(Pre–56)109:165

Refers to the surrender of Montreal, 8 Sept. 1760, and of Quebec the previous year, in the Seven Years' War, 1756–63. ¶ A similar work, Casey:288, is 12° with 4 p.

Traite de la capitulation de Montréal, le 8 sept. 1760, et de celle de Québec l'année précédente, durant la guerre de Sept Ans, 1756–1763. ¶ Un ouvrage semblable, répertorié dans Casey:288, existe en format in–12° comptant 4 p.

[Coade, George], *jr./fils*. A letter to a noble lord, wherein it is demonstrated that all the great and mighty difficulties in obtaining an honourable and lasting peace, &c. are for the most part chimerical and imaginary. By an Englishman. London, G[eorge]. Kearsly, 1760. 45, [1] p. 8°

NUC(Pre–56)113:185

Waldon enters under title, and notes: See *N.Y. Hist. Soc. Colls. III, 349.* ¶ On Canada. Smith or Livingston wrote it and Alexander had it printed in London. ¶ *"Books published by the same author": 1 p. at end.*

Waldon répertorie cet ouvrage selon le titre et note : voir *N.Y. Hist. Soc. Colls. III, 349.* ¶ Sur le Canada. Smith ou Livingston a rédigé cet ouvrage, et Alexander l'a fait imprimer à Londres. ¶ *« Livres publiés par le même auteur » : 1 p. à la fin.*

*Cockings, George, *d./déc.* 1802. War: an heroic poem. From the taking of Minorca by the French, to the raising of the siege of Quebec, by General Murray. By George Cockings. London: printed by C[harles Green]. Say, for the author; and sold by J[ohn]. Cook, 1760. xiv p., 1 l., 174 p. 8°

NUC(Pre–56)113:567*

Sabin:14111 states (of a later edition): Book I. Relates to the operations of the English in the West Indies, to the taking of Louisburg; II. To the operations of Lord Howe and Admiral Boscawen; III. To the fall of Quebec;

Le Sabin:14111 indique (au sujet d'une édition ultérieure) : Livre I. Se rapporte aux opérations militaires des Anglais dans les Antilles et à la prise de Louisbourg ; II. Traite des opérations menées par lord Howe et l'amiral Boscawen ; III. Concerne la chute

V. Gives a recapitulation of England's victories. . . . (These are events in the Seven Years' War, 1756–63.) ¶ First edition; second ed., London, 1762, *q.v.*; also London, 1765; reprinted Portsmouth, N.H., and Boston, Mass., 1762, *q.v.*

de Québec ; V. Récapitule les victoires de l'Angleterre. . . . (Il s'agit d'épisodes de la guerre de Sept Ans, 1756–1763.) ¶ Première édition ; deuxième éd., Londres, 1762, *q.v.* ; également Londres, 1765 ; réimpressions à Portsmouth (N.H.), et Boston (Mass.), 1762, *q.v.*

The cruel massacre of the Protestants, in North America; shewing how the French and Indians join together to scalp the English, and the manner of their scalping, &c. &c. London. [1760?] 8 p. 1 illus. (small woodcut, p. 8). small 8°

BLC(to 1975)7:63; NUC(Pre–56)128:355?

This contains a summary of the declaration of war, p. 3–6, and a justification of it. Begins: "We think good to let the Country know, that it could not be avoided, though all Means were used abroad and at home to bring the Enemy to terms of peace, to no purpose, were forced to declare war . . . ." ¶ Reference is made to the attack on Minorca (1756) as to a recent event but also to Simon Fraser, who was lieutenant-colonel commanding the 78th Foot in America, 1758–63. Dates given in other sources are 1756 and 1766. ¶ *This is probably the same as the ed. in NUC(Pre–56) 128:355, with imprint: London, printed and sold in Aldermary churchyard, Bow Lane [1759?], 8 p. ¶ First edition(?); another edition: 1761,* q.v.

Cet ouvrage comprend un résumé de la déclaration de guerre, p. 3–6, et sa justification. Débute par : « Nous croyons bon de faire savoir au pays que cette situation n'a pu être évitée malgré tous les moyens qui ont été mis en oeuvre, en vain, tant à l'étranger qu'à l'intérieur, pour amener l'ennemi à conclure un traité, et que nous avons été forcés de déclarer la guerre. . . . » ¶ On y fait mention de l'attaque sur Minorque (1756) à titre d'événement récent, mais aussi du lieutenant-colonel Simon Fraser, qui commandait le 78ᵉ d'infanterie en Amérique 1758–1763. D'autres sources indiquent 1756 et 1766. ¶ *Il s'agit probablement du même ouvrage que celui de l'éd. répertorié dans le NUC(Pre–56)128:355, avec l'adresse bibliographique : London, printed and sold in Aldermary churchyard, Bow Lane [1759 ?], 8 p. ¶ Première édition (?) ; autre édition :* 1761, q.v.

Dawson, Eli. A discourse, delivered at Quebec, in the chappel belonging to the convent of the Ursulins, September 27th, 1759; occasioned by the success of our arms in the reduction of that capital: at the request of Brigadier General Monckton, and by order of Vice-Admiral Saunders, commander in chief. By the Reverend Eli Dawson, chaplain of His Majesty's ship Sterling-Castle, on board of which the vice-admiral's [*sic*] hoisted his flag, during the siege. London: printed for R[alph]. Griffiths, opposite Somerset-House in the Strand. 1760. 2 p.l., 3–14 p. 4°

NUC(Pre–56)135:285*

Concerns the Quebec campaign of 1759. ¶ First edition; reprinted, with modern spelling, Quebec, "by the Nuns of the Franciscan Convent at their press on the Plains of Abraham," 1901. ¶ OTP

Concerne la campagne de Québec de 1759. ¶ Première édition ; réimpression à Québec selon les règles d'orthographe modernes « par les soeurs franciscaines dans leur imprimerie située sur les Plaines d'Abraham », 1901. ¶ OTP

[Douglas, John, *bp. of Salisbury/év. de Salisbury*], 1721–1807. A letter addressed to two great men, on the prospect of peace; and on the terms necessary to be insisted upon in the negociation. London, printed for A[ndrew]. Millar in the Strand, 1760. 2 p.l., 56 p. 8°(in 4s).

NUC(Pre–56)147:605*

The "two great men" were William Pitt and the Duke of Newcastle. The letter has been ascribed to the Earl of Bath, who was Douglas's patron and who undoubtedly inspired it. ¶ Douglas urged the retention of all Canada, except possibly Cape Breton, if Louisbourg were demolished. He wanted to keep Guadeloupe also, but thought it not valuable enough to be made a necessary condition of peace. This is probably the most famous and influential of all the pamphlets called forth by the controversy over the terms of peace [ending the Seven

Les « deux grands hommes » étaient William Pitt et le duc de Newcastle. La lettre a été attribuée au comte de Bath, qui protégeait Douglas, et a sans aucun doute inspiré ce document. ¶ Douglas conseillait vivement de garder tout le territoire du Canada, hormis éventuellement le Cap-Breton, si Louisbourg était démoli. Il voulait aussi garder la Guadeloupe, mais il ne croyait pas qu'elle fût suffisamment précieuse pour en faire une condition de paix obligatoire. C'est probablement le pamphlet le plus célèbre et celui qui a eu le plus d'influence, parmi tous ceux qu'avait suscités la controverse sur les termes du traité [qui mit fin à la guerre de

Years' War]. ¶ *Answered by:* An answer to the Letter to two great men. *London, 1760; William Burke,* Remarks on the Letter .... *London, 1760; Benjamin Franklin,* The interest of Great Britain. *London, 1760; and others* (q.v.). ¶ *First edition; three other editions appeared in 1760* (q.v., *following*) *as well as two Boston, 1760, editions.* ¶ *OTP*

Sept Ans]. ¶ *Cet ouvrage a suscité les répliques suivantes :* An answer to the Letter to two great men. *Londres, 1760 ; William Burke,* Remarks on the Letter .... *Londres, 1760 ; Benjamin Franklin,* The interest of Great Britain. *Londres, 1760 ; et d'autres* (q.v.). ¶ *Première édition ; en plus de deux éditions publiées à Boston en 1760, trois autres parurent cette même année* (q.v. *ci-dessous*). ¶ *OTP*

[Douglas, John, *bp. of Salisbury/év. de Salisbury***],** 1721–1807.   A letter addressed to two great men .... 2d ed., corrected. London, 1760. 2 p.l., 56 p. 8°

NUC(Pre–56)147:605*

See *preceding entry.* ¶ *OTP*

Voir *la notice précédente.* ¶ *OTP*

[Douglas, John, *bp. of Salisbury/év. de Salisbury***],** 1721–1807.   A letter addressed to two great men ... on the terms ... in the negotiation. London: printed for A. Millar, in the Strand. Sold by A[lexander]. Kincaid and J[ohn]. Bell, Edinburgh. 1760. 2 p.l., 55 p. 12°(in 4s).

Casey:297.

Third edition? Waldon has "J. Ball" and "8°(in 4s)." ¶ See *first ed., 1760.* ¶ *OOA · OKQ*

Troisième édition ? Waldon indique « J. Ball » et « in–8° (4 f.) ». ¶ Voir *première éd., 1760.* ¶ *OOA · OKQ*

[Douglas, John, *bp. of Salisbury/év. de Salisbury*], 1721–1807. A letter addressed . . . . 4th ed., enlarged. Dublin, 1760. 42 p. 8°

Sabin:40263

NUC(Pre–56)147:605 has: Dublin: for G[eorge]. and A[lexander]. Ewing, 1760, 41 p., but omits edition statement. ¶ See first ed., 1760.

Le NUC(Pre–56)147:605 indique : Dublin : pour G[eorge]. et A[lexander]. Ewing, 1760, 41 p., mais ne fournit aucun renseignement sur l'édition. ¶ Voir première éd., 1760.

Douglass, William, 1691?–1752. A summary, historical and political, of the first planting, progressive improvements, and present state of the British settlements in North-America . . . . London, R[obert]. and J[ames]. Dodsley, 1760. 2 v.: 1 p.l., viii, 568 p.; 1 p.l., iv, 416 p. fold. col. map. 8°

NUC(Pre–56)147:675*

First pub. Boston, Mass., 1747–52, in numbers; reprinted London, 1755, q.v. for other notes. ¶ OKQ · OTP · BVAU · BVIPA

Première publ. Boston (Mass.), 1747–1752, en fascicules ; réimpression à Londres, 1755, q.v. pour d'autres notes. ¶ OKQ · OTP · BVAU · BVIPA

*The English pilot. The fourth book. Describing the West-India navigation, from Hudson's-Bay . . . . London, W[illiam]. and J[ohn]. Mount, T[homas]. Page, 1760. 4, 66 p. illus., charts (part fold.). fol.

NUC(Pre–56)160:374*

First edition: 1689, *q.v.* for the dates of the many other editions, including the 1706, which has a similar title, given in more detail.

Première édition : 1689, *q.v.* pour les dates des nombreuses autres éditions, y compris celle de 1706, dont le titre est similaire mais comporte davantage de détails.

*The four Indian kings, in two parts. Tewkesbury [Gloucs.], S[amuel]. Harward [n. d., 1760?]. 7 p. 8°(?)

NUC(Pre–56)179:300

Harward printed in Tewkesbury from 1760 to 1809 (Plomer), and since the event referred to occurred in 1710 (*see The four Indian kings*, 1710), it seems likely that this would have appeared early in Harward's career.

Harward a imprimé à Tewkesbury de 1760 à 1809 (Plomer), et selon toute vraisemblance, il aurait fait paraître cet ouvrage au début de sa carrière puisque l'événement dont il est question se produisit en 1710 (*voir The four Indian kings*, 1710).

[Franklin, Benjamin], 1706–1790. The interest of Great Britain considered, with regard to her colonies, and the acquisitions of Canada and Guadaloupe. To which are added, Observations concerning the increase of mankind, peopling of countries, &c. London: printed for T[homas]. Becket . . . 1760. 1 p.l., 58 p. 8°(in 4s).

NUC(Pre–56)183:159*

Ascribed by certain bibliographical authorities to Franklin, by others to Richard Jackson; and by an editor of Franklin's Works *to both, as a joint production (cf. NUC). Waldon cites Verner W. Crane, "Certain writings of Benjamin Franklin . . ." (in Bibliog. Soc. of America,* Papers, *1934, v. 28, pt. 1, p. 1–27), as presenting conclusive evidence of Franklin's authorship. ¶ A reply to: John Douglas,* A letter addressed to two great men. *London, 1760; and William Burke,* Remarks on the Letter . . . . *London, 1760 (q.v.); further to this is:* Some hints to people in power. *London, 1763 (q.v.). NUC notes that " 'Observations concerning the increase of mankind' (p. 50–56) written by Franklin in 1751, was first pub. as an appendix to*

Selon certains experts en bibliographie, Franklin est l'auteur de cet ouvrage, que d'autres attribuent à Richard Jackson, tandis que pour sa part un éditeur de Works, *de Franklin, estime qu'il s'agit d'une production commune des deux auteurs (cf. NUC). Waldon cite l'ouvrage de Verner W. Crane, « Certain writings of Benjamin Franklin . . . » (dans* Papers, *1934, vol. 28, part. 1, p. 1–27, par la Bibliog. Soc. of America), comme preuve concluante qu'il s'agit bien d'un ouvrage de Franklin. ¶ Réplique à John Douglas,* A letter addressed to two great men. *Londres, 1760 ; et à William Burke,* Remarks on the Letter . . . . *Londres, 1760 (q.v.) ; suivi de :* Some hints to people in power. *Londres, 1763 (q.v.). Note du NUC : « L'ouvrage 'Observations concerning the increase of mankind' (p. 50–56) rédigé par Franklin en 1751 fut d'abord publié sous forme*

William Clarke's 'Observations on the late and present conduct of the French,' 1755." ¶ *Answered by:* An examination into the value of Canada and Guadaloupe. *London, 1761, and* A letter to a great M——R. *London, 1761,* q.v. ¶ *Concerns the terms of peace to end the Seven Years' War, and the controversy over whether Canada or Guadeloupe should be held.* ¶ Says Waldon, "With Bishop Douglas' *Letter* [cited above], this essay in favour of keeping Canada probably had the most influence of all these pamphlets" on the Canada-or-Guadeloupe controversy. ¶ *First edition; also issued the same year in Dublin, with a second in London, 1761 (q.v.); reprinted in both Boston and Philadelphia, 1760 (cf. NUC), and in Franklin's* Works, *John Bigelow, ed., New York, 1905 (vol. 3, p. 278–334).*

d'annexe de l'ouvrage de William Clarke, 'Observations on the late and present conduct of the French', 1755 ». ¶ *Cet ouvrage a suscité les répliques suivantes :* An examination into the value of Canada and Guadaloupe. *Londres, 1761, et* A letter to a great M——R. *Londres, 1761,* q.v. ¶ *Porte sur les conditions du traité devant mettre fin à la guerre de Sept Ans, et sur la controverse sur le choix du territoire qu'il convenait de garder, soit le Canada, soit la Guadeloupe.* ¶ Selon Waldon, « Avec *A letter* de l'évêque Douglas [précitée], cet essai en faveur du maintien du Canada comme territoire anglais fut probablement, de tous ces pamphlets, celui qui eut le plus d'influence » lors de la controverse Canada ou Guadeloupe. ¶ *Première édition ; également publié la même année à Dublin, suivi d'une deuxième édition à Londres en 1761 (q.v.) ; réimpressions à la fois à Boston et à Philadelphie, 1760 (cf. NUC), et dans l'ouvrage* Works *de Franklin, John Bigelow, éd., New York, 1905 (vol. 3, p. 278–334).*

[Franklin, Benjamin], 1706–1790. The interest of Great Britain considered .... Dublin, P[eter]. Wilson, 1760. 46 p. 8°(in 4s).

Sabin:35450

Waldon has publishers as "P. Wilson and J. Potts," and the collation as "46, [2, books] p." ¶ *First edition: London, 1760 (q.v.).*

« P. Wilson et J. Potts » sont identifiés comme les éditeurs par Waldon, dont la collation est : « 46, [2, livres] p. » ¶ *Première édition : Londres, 1760 (q.v.).*

*French policy defeated: being an account of the original and progress of the present war with France. The encroachments, depredations, insults, and cruelties of the French, and their Indian allies, on the British inhabitants in America. With a succinct narrative of all the battles, sieges, and naval engagements both by sea and land. Likewise an account of the several noble acquisitions made by our arms, and heroic exploits performed by our admirals and generals, in Europe, Asia, Africa, and America, to the conclusion of the year one thousand seven hundred and sixty . . . . London, M[ary]. Cooper, 1760. 2 p.l., 130 p. 2 fold. maps. 8°(?)

NUC(Pre–56)184:609*

Events in the Seven Years' War, 1756–63. ¶ First pub. under title beginning with same first three words (otherwise different), London, 1755, *q.v.*

Événements de la guerre de Sept Ans, 1756–1763. ¶ Première publ., dont le titre commence par les mêmes trois premiers mots (mais diffère pour le reste), Londres, *1755, q.v.*

General reflections occasioned by the Letter addressed to two great men, and the Remarks on that letter. London: printed for E[dward]. Dilly, and W[illiam]. Owen . . . 1760. <Price six-pence.> 22 p. 8°

NUC(Pre–56)194:412

A reply to: John Douglas, Bishop of Salisbury, A letter addressed to two great men. *London, 1760* (q.v.), *and to William Burke,* Remarks on the Letter addressed to two great men. *London, 1760* (q.v.). ¶ The author would keep Cape Breton in preference to Canada [in the terms of peace for ending the Seven Years' War], but considers neither Canada nor Guadeloupe alone sufficient.

Réplique à John Douglas, évêque de Salisbury, A letter addressed to two great men. *Londres, 1760* (q.v.), *et à William Burke,* Remarks on the Letter addressed to two great men. *Londres, 1760* (q.v.). ¶ L'auteur préférerait garder le Cap-Breton plutôt que le Canada [aux termes du traité devant mettre fin à la guerre de Sept Ans], mais estime que ni le Canada ni la Guadeloupe ne suffisent à eux seuls.

Genuine letters from a volunteer, in the British service, at Quebec . . . . London, printed for H[enry]. Whitridge, at the Royal-Exchange; and A. and [Sir] C[harles]. Corbett, opposite St. Dunstan's Church, Fleet-Street [1760?] viii, 39, [1] p. 8°

NUC(Pre–56)195:32

Contents. — Preface. — [Letter] To Mr. J—— W—— (dated on board the Sterling-Castle in the River St. Lawrence, two miles below the city of Quebec, Sept. 2, 1759). — Extracts from another letter of the same date, addressed to Mr. M. P. — [Letter] To Mr. J. W. (dated at Quebec, Sept. 20, 1759). ¶ Refers to the Quebec Campaign, 1759, in the Seven Years' War, 1756–63. ¶ Probably the first ed., but Faribault, p. 167, has imprint: London, Whitridge, 1759 (no brackets around date).

Qui portent sur le Canada : Avant-propos. – [Lettre] À M. J—— W—— (datée du 2 septembre 1759 à bord du Sterling-Castle sur le Saint-Laurent, à deux milles en aval de la ville de Québec). – Extraits d'une autre lettre de la même date, adressée à M. M. P. –[Lettre] À M. J. W. (datée du 20 septembre 1759 à Québec). ¶ Se rapporte à la campagne de Québec, 1759, durant la guerre de Sept Ans, 1756–1763. ¶ Probablement la première éd., bien que Faribault, p. 167, indique pour adresse bibliographique : London, Whitridge, 1759 (la date n'est pas entre crochets).

Hanson, Mrs. **Elizabeth,** *fl.* 1703–1741. An account of the captivity of Elizabeth Hanson, now or late of Kachecky, in New-England: who, with four of her children and servant-maid, were taken captive by the Indians, and carried into Canada. Setting forth the various remarkable occurrences, sore trials, and wonderful deliverances which befel them after their departure, to the time of their redemption. Taken in substance from her own mouth, by Samuel Bownas. London, printed and sold by S[amuel?]. Clark, 1760. 1 p.l., 28 p. 12°

NUC(Pre–56)230:243*

Waldon gives no printer or pagination. ¶ Publisher's advertisement: 1 leaf at end. ¶ Apparently first published, Philadelphia and New York, 1728, under title: God's mercy surmounting man's cruelty, exemplified in the captivity . . . of Elizabeth Hanson . . . . ¶ "The substance of the foregoing account was

Waldon ne nomme pas l'imprimeur et ne donne aucun renseignement sur la pagination. ¶ Réclame de l'éditeur : 1 feuillet à la fin. ¶ D'abord publié, semble-t-il, à Philadelphie et à New York en 1728 sous le titre God's mercy surrounding man's cruelty, exemplified in the captivity . . . of Elizabeth Hanson . . . . ¶ « L'essentiel dudit récit vient de sa propre

taken from her own mouth by Samuel Bownas. And in the seventh month, called September, 1741, Samuel Hopwood was with her, and received the relation much to the same purpose" (cf. note, p. 28). ¶ There were two editions this same year. The second edition so states on the title-page. ¶ NUC lists numerous other editions, under this and also under the original title, including those of London, 1782 and 1787; Cork, 1791; Leeds, 1810 and 1815(?); and many American editions.

bouche et a été recueilli par Samuel Bownas. Puis au cours du septième mois, soit le mois de septembre 1741, Samuel Hopwood était à ses côtés et, dans la même intention ou à peu près, a noté les propos qu'elle lui a confiés » (cf. note, p. 28). ¶ Il y eut deux éditions cette même année, ce qui est indiqué à la page de titre de la deuxième édition. ¶ Le NUC répertorie de nombreuses autres éditions sous ce titre et également sous le titre original, notamment les éditions de Londres, 1782 et 1787 ; Cork, 1791 ; Leeds, 1810 et 1815 (?) ; et bon nombre d'éditions américaines.

[Hanway, Jonas], 1712–1786. An account of the Society for the encouragement of the British troops, in Germany and North America. With the motives to the making a present to those troops, also to the widows and orphans of such of them as have died in defense of their country, particularly at the battles of Thornhausen, Quebec, &c. With an alphabetical list of the subscribers to this benevolent design; and a state of the receipts and disbursements of the society. London, 1760. viii, 91, 55 p. 8°

NUC(Pre–56)230:323

Title in red and black. ¶ "Dedication" signed: Jonas Hanway. The report was written at the request of the Society, to which the author was a subscriber. ¶ Section V deals with the importance of Quebec; Section VI deals with the presents sent to New York and Quebec. Boots, for example, cost 5/- [shillings] a pair. ¶ NSWA · OTU

Titre en rouge et noir. ¶ « Dédicace » signée : Jonas Hanway. Le rapport fut rédigé à la demande de la Société, dont l'auteur était un abonné. ¶ La partie V traite de l'importance de Québec ; la partie VI concerne les dons envoyés à New York et à Québec. Une paire de bottes, par exemple, coûtait 5/- [shillings]. ¶ NSWA · OTU

The importance of Canada considered, in two letters to a nobleman. London, [Robert] Dodsley, 1760. [No collation recorded.]

Faribault:856

Possibly an error for: Charles Lee, *The importance of Canada considered in two letters to a noble lord.* London, 1760 (*q.v.*). It seems likely that this present work is a ghost.

Il s'agit peut-être d'une erreur pour l'ouvrage de Charles Lee, *The importance of Canada considered in two letters to a noble lord.* Londres, 1760 (*q.v.*). Il semble que cette édition n'a jamais existé.

[Jefferys, Thomas], *d./déc.* 1771. Directions for navigating the gulf and river of St. Laurence, with a particular account of the bays, roads, rocks, sands, land-marks, depths of water, latitudes, bearings, and distances from place to place; the setting and flowing of the tides, &c. Founded on accurate observations and experiments, made by the officers of his Majesty's fleet. By order of Charles Saunders, Esq; Vice-Admiral of the Blue, and Commander in Chief of the British naval forces in the expedition against Quebec, in 1759. Published by command of the Right Hon. the Lords Commissioners of the Admiralty. London: printed for Thomas Jefferys, Geographer to His Royal Highness the Prince of Wales. 1760. 1 p.l., 31, [3] p. 4°

NUC(Pre–56)144:354

NUC has no author and only a short title, without collation; Sabin gives a longer title, with small variations in punctuation. Waldon indicates "t.-p." instead of "1 p.l." ¶ *List of books for sale: [3] p. at end.* ¶ Advertisement at end of *A journal of the siege of Quebec*, 1760 (*q.v.*), offers "Just published, by Thomas Jefferys": "A new chart of the River St. Laurence .... Also particular directions for navigating that river with safety. Taken by order of Cha. Saunders, Esq; .... Published by command of the Right Honourable the Lords of the Admiralty. Price 12s.

Le NUC n'indique pas l'auteur et donne seulement un titre abrégé, sans collation ; le Sabin fournit un titre plus long, comportant une ponctuation légèrement différente. Pour sa part, Waldon indique « p. de t. » au lieu de « 1 f. l. ». ¶ *Liste de livres à vendre : [3] p. à la fin.* ¶ Sous la rubrique des dernières parutions, « Just published, by Thomas Jefferys », une réclame à la fin de *A journal of the siege of Quebec*, 1760 (*q.v.*), annonce la publication d'« une nouvelle carte du Saint-Laurent ... Comprend en outre des instructions particulières pour naviguer sur cette voie d'eau. Relevé effectué par ordre de M. Cha. Saunders ; ... Publié sur l'ordre du très

in sheets, or 18s. on pasteboard."

honorable ministre de la Marine. Prix 12 shillings en feuilles volantes, ou 18 shillings montée sur carton ».

Jefferys, Thomas, *d./déc.* 1771. The natural and civil history of the French dominions in North and South America. Giving a particular account of the climate, soil minerals, animals, vegetables, manufactures, trade, commerce and languages, together with the religion, government, genius, character, manners and customs of the Indians and other inhabitants. Illustrated by maps and plans of the principal places, collected from the best authorities, and engraved by T[homas]. Jefferys, geographer to His Royal Highness the Prince of Wales. Part I. containing a description of Canada and Louisiana. London, printed for Thomas Jefferys . . . 1760. 2 pts. in 1 v.: [8], 168 p.; 2 p.l., 246 p. 9 fold. maps, 9 fold. plans. fol.

NUC(Pre–56)279:27*

Each part has separate t.-p. Part 1: Canada and Louisiana. ¶ First edition; another ed.: London, 1761, q.v. Reprinted on microcards: Louisville, Ky., Lost Cause Press, 1960. (Travels in the Old South series, 1, 263), 13 cards. ¶ NSWA · BVAU · BVIPA

Chaque partie comporte une p. de t. distincte. Partie 1 : le Canada et la Louisiane. ¶ Première édition ; autre éd. : Londres, 1761, q.v. Reproduction sur microcartes : Louisville (Ky.), Lost Cause Press, 1960. (collection Travels in the Old South, 1, 263), 13 cartes. ¶ NSWA · BVAU · BVIPA

A journal of the siege of Quebec. To which is annexed, a correct plan of the environs of Quebec, and of the battle fought on the 13th September, 1759: together with a particular detail of the French lines and batteries, and also of the encampments, batteries and attacks of the British army, and their investiture of that city under the commands of Vice Admiral Saunders, Major General Wolfe, Brigadier General Monckton, and Brigadier General Townshend. Drawn from the original surveys taken by the engineers of the army. Engraved by Thomas Jefferys, geographer to His Majesty. Price five shillings. [London, 1760.] 1 p.l., 16, [2] p. Large plan with "second plate" attached. 4°

NUC(Pre–56)285:512

List of books "*Just published, by Thomas Jefferys*": [2] p. at end. ¶ The plan measures 34 1/2 x 16 inches [89 x 43 cm in NUC] within the border lines. There is also a second plate overlying the first showing the altered positions [after the battle of 13 Sept.] as the engagement proceeded [size 14 1/2 x 24 cm]. ¶ "Plan of the City of Quebec, the capital of Canada, as it surrendered the 18th of September, 1759, to the British fleet and army, commanded by Vice Admiral Saunders and Brigadier General Townshend. Price 2s.," is advertised at end of list of books.

Liste de parutions récentes, « *Just published, by Thomas Jefferys* » : [2] p. à la fin. ¶ Le plan mesure 34,5 po sur 16 po [89 cm sur 43 cm dans le NUC] d'une bordure à l'autre. De plus, une deuxième planche superposée à la première indique les nouvelles positions [après la bataille du 13 sept.] en fonction du déroulement des combats [dimensions : 14,5 cm sur 24 cm]. ¶ Réclame à la fin de la liste de livres : « Plan de la ville de Québec, capitale du Canada, au moment de sa reddition, le 18 septembre 1759, à la flotte et à l'armée britanniques commandées par le vice-amiral Saunders et le brigadier général Townshend. Prix 2 shillings ».

Junius, *pseud., author of the "Letters"/auteur des "Letters."* A letter to an honourable brigadier general, Commander in Chief of His Majesty's forces in Canada. London, printed for J. Burd, opposite St. Dunstan's Church, Fleetstreet, 1760. 2 p.l., 31, [1] p. 8°

NUC(Pre–56)286:654*

Errata: [1] p. at end. ¶ Also ascribed to Charles Lee, Henry Fox, and others [but Waldon cites the study which first ascribed authorship to Junius]. ¶ *Answered by:* A refutation of the Letter to an hon^ble. brigadier-general. *London, 1760* (q.v.). *Further to this is:* Curious and authentic memoirs. *London, 1763* (q.v.). ¶ The writer accuses Lord George Townshend of taking undeserved credit for the capture of Quebec and then deserting his post because he believed Quebec indefensible against a counter-attack by the French. Townshend is advised

Errata : [1] p. à la fin. ¶ Fut aussi attribué à Charles Lee, à Henry Fox et à d'autres [mais Waldon cite l'étude qui a initialement désigné Junius comme l'auteur de cet écrit]. ¶ *Cet ouvrage a suscité la réplique* A refutation of the Letter to an hon^ble. brigadier-general. *Londres, 1760* (q.v.), puis, Curious and authentic memoirs. *Londres, 1763* (q.v.). ¶ L'auteur accuse lord George Townshend de s'attribuer le mérite de la prise de Québec et d'avoir ensuite déserté son poste parce qu'il croyait Québec indéfendable en cas de contre-attaque des Français. On intime à Townshend l'ordre de regagner Québec ou de démissionner. ¶ Première édition ;

to return to Quebec or resign his commission. ¶ First edition; reprinted, with *A refutation*, London, 1841 (which work Waldon uses as her entry, under 1760).

réimpression avec *A refutation*, Londres, 1841 (titre dont Waldon se sert pour sa notice, sous 1760).

[Lambert, Claude François], 1705–1765. Curious observations upon . . . antient and modern geography . . . . London, 1760. 2 v. 8°

NUC(Pre–56)313:31*

Waldon has imprint: London: Lockyer Davis, 1760, from Sabin:38730, but Sabin does not specify Lockyer Davis for his 1760 edition; cf. 1755 ed. ¶ First pub. in English as: A collection of curious observations. *London, 1750, q.v. for other notes and editions.*

Adresse bibliographique de Waldon : London : Lockyer Davis, 1760, d'après le Sabin:38730, bien que celui-ci ne désigne pas nommément Lockyer Davis pour son édition de 1760 ; cf. éd. de 1755. ¶ Première publ. en anglais sous le titre A collection of curious observations. *Londres, 1750, q.v. pour d'autres notes et éditions.*

Lavington, Samuel, 1726–1807. God the giver of victory: A sermon, preached at Bideford, Devon, on the 29th of November, 1759, being the day appointed for a general Thanksgiving, for the success of His Majesty's arms. Published at the earnest request of the congregation. By Samuel Lavington. London: printed for J[ames]. Buckland . . . J[ohn]. Ward . . . and A[aron]. Tozer, at Exeter. 1760. 2 p.l., 3–38 p. 8°(in 4s).

Casey:289

Casey is Dr. Waldon's only source, but Casey has 38 p. and 12°. ¶ Refers to events of the Seven Years' War, 1756–63.

Le Casey est la seule source de Waldon ; toutefois, le Casey donne les renseignements suivants : 38 p. et in–12°. ¶ Traite d'événements de la guerre de Sept Ans, 1756–1763.

A letter from a gentleman in the country to his friend in town. On his perusal of a pamphlet addressed to two great men. London: printed for R[obert]. Davis . . . 1760. 1 p.l., 20 p. 8°

NUC(Pre–56)328:662

Waldon has 2 p.l. in her collation. ¶ *A reply to: John Douglas, Bishop of Salisbury*, A letter addressed to two great men. *London, 1760 (q.v.), which pressed strongly for keeping Canada and weakly for Guadeloupe.* ¶ The author argues that the possession of Canada alone is not sufficient recompense for the cost of the [Seven Years'] war. ¶ *This appears to be the only edition.*

Collation de Waldon : 2 f. l. ¶ *Réplique à John Douglas, évêque de Salisbury,* A letter addressed to two great men. *Londres, 1760 (q.v.), qui réclamait le maintien du Canada et de la Guadeloupe comme territoires anglais, avec ardeur à l'égard du premier mais plutôt mollement pour le second.* ¶ L'auteur soutient que la seule possession du Canada ne constitue pas une contrepartie suffisante pour le coût de la guerre [de Sept Ans]. ¶ *Il s'agirait de la seule édition.*

A letter to the great man, occasioned by the Letter to two great men. In which many of that writer's absurdities, inconsistencies and contradictions are detected. And the fatal tendency of his propositions exposed. By a citizen of London, a disciple of Sidney and Locke . . . . London: printed for W. Bristow, 1760. 1 p.l., 61 p. 8°

NUC(Pre–56)329:85*

A reply to: John Douglas, Bishop of Salisbury, A letter addressed to two great men. *London, 1760 (q.v.), where it was strongly argued that Canada be kept at the treaty ending the Seven Years' War, and Guadeloupe too if possible.* ¶ *First edition; it was reprinted as a photostatic reproduction of the William L. Clements Library copy, University of Michigan, Ann Arbor, Mich., 1934.*

Réplique à John Douglas, évêque de Salisbury, A letter addressed to two great men. *Londres, 1760 (q.v.), dans laquelle il est fortement recommandé de garder le Canada à l'occasion de la signature du traité mettant fin à la guerre de Sept Ans, ainsi que la Guadeloupe le cas échéant.* ¶ *Première édition ; reproduction par photocopie de l'exemplaire de la William L. Clements Library, University of Michigan, Ann Arbor (Mich.), 1934.*

A letter to the people of England, on the necessity of putting an immediate end to the war; and the means of obtaining an advantageous peace . . . . London: printed for R[alph]. Griffiths . . . 1760. 1 p.l., 54 p. 8°(in 4s).

NUC(Pre–56)329:95*

Sometimes attributed to John Shebbeare. ¶ The writer refers to John Douglas, *A letter to two great men.* London, 1760 (*q.v.*), and also favours the retention of Canada [in the settlement of the Seven Years' War, 1756–63]. "I must give my Voice entirely for those who would rather give up Guadeloupe, with every other acquisition we have made, or may make, in the West-Indies, than part with one single foot of Canada": p. 47. His chief reasons are that surrendering Canada will lead to fresh wars, as the colonists will always encroach on any limits set, and the great expense of maintaining forces on the frontiers. ¶ *Reprinted in a microcard edition (cf. NUC), ca. 1950.* ¶ *BVAU*

Parfois attribué à John Shebbeare. ¶ L'auteur fait allusion à John Douglas, *A letter to two great men.* Londres, 1760 (*q.v.*). Il est, lui aussi, favorable à ce que l'Angleterre conserve le Canada [lors du règlement de la guerre de Sept Ans, 1756–1763]. « Je dois entièrement prendre parti pour ceux qui préféreraient abandonner la Guadeloupe, ainsi que tout autre territoire que nous possédons, ou que nous pourrions obtenir, dans les Antilles plutôt que se départir d'un seul pied de terre au Canada » : p. 47. Il invoque surtout le fait que l'abandon du Canada entraînera de nouvelles guerres, car les colons empiéteront toujours sur d'autres territoires en dépit des lignes de démarcation établies, et qu'il faut engager des sommes considérables pour maintenir des forces armées aux frontières. ¶ *Reproduction sur microcartes (cf. NUC), vers 1950.* ¶ *BVAU*

[Patrick, J.]. Quebec: a poetical essay, in imitation of the Miltonic stile: being a regular narrative of the proceedings and capital transactions performed by the British forces under the command of Vice-Admiral Saunders and Major-General Wolfe, in the glorious expedition against Canada, in the year 1759. The performance of a volunteer on board His Majesty's ship Somerset during the passage home from Quebec. The whole embellished with entertaining and explanatory notes . . . . London, printed for P. Whitridge, under the Royal-Exchange; and T[homas]. Becket, at Tully's-Head, near Surry-Street, in the Strand. 1760. 2 p.l., [vii]-viii, 30 p. 4°

NUC(Pre–56)444:631*

Dedication signed: J. Patrick. ¶ *Reprinted in microfiche: Washington, Microcard Editions, 1967 — (cf. NUC).* ¶ *OTP · BVAU*

Dédicace signée : J. Patrick. ¶ *Reproduction sur mic., Washington, Microcard Editions, 1967 –(cf. NUC).* ¶ *OTP · BVAU*

[Pichon, Thomas], 1700–1781. Genuine letters and memoirs, relating to the natural, civil, and commercial history of the islands of Cape Breton, and Saint John, from the first settlement there, to the taking of Louisburg by the English, in 1758. In which, among many interesting particulars, the causes and previous events of the present war are explained. By an impartial Frenchman . . . . Translated from the author's original manuscript. London, printed for J[ohn]. Nourse . . . 1760. xvi, 400 p. 8°

NUC(Pre–56)457:190

The island of Saint John is now called Prince Edward Island. ¶ *Transl. from his:* Lettres et mémoires pour servir à l'histoire naturelle, civile et politique du Cap Breton. *La Haye, 1760.*

De nos jours, l'île Saint-Jean s'appelle l'Île-du-Prince-Édouard. ¶ *Trad. de son ouvrage :* Lettres et mémoires pour servir à l'histoire naturelle, civile et politique du Cap Breton. *La Haye, 1760.*

[Pringle, Sir John], 1707–1782. The life of General James Wolfe, the conqueror of Canada: or, The elogium of that renowned hero, attempted according to the rules of eloquence. With a monumental inscription, Latin and English, to perpetuate his memory. By J*** P******, A. M. . . . London, printed for G[eorge]. Kearsly, successor to the late Mr. [Jacob] Robinson, 1760. 1 p.l., ii, 24 p. 4°

NUC(Pre–56)471:604*

For identification of "J. P." with Sir John Pringle, *see* "The first published life of James Wolfe," by J. Clarence Webster (in *Can. hist. rev.*, Dec. 1930, p. 328–32). ¶ *Waldon has this work, but gives "G. Kearsley" and "<Price one shilling.>" after the date; however, this*

Pour l'identification des initiales « J. P. » à sir John Pringle, *voir* « The first published life of James Wolfe », par J. Clarence Webster (dans *Can. hist. rev.*, déc. 1930, p. 328–32). ¶ *Waldon a répertorié cet ouvrage, mais indique « G. Kearsley », ainsi que « <Prix un shilling.> » après la date. Il s'agit toutefois*

is the closest entry to hers, though she does not cite LC, and this differs in details from all the sources she does cite; e.g. *JCB(1)3:1280* has "eulogium"; Casey: 293 has "eulogium" and "Kearsley," but does give the price; Sabin:58057 has "eulogium" and 8° format. It is not clear which variant Waldon saw (if any); but it is tempting, in the absence of a matching source, to think that Waldon's is a composite entry: all her details appear in one or the other source. ¶ Possibly the first appearance, though the variants cited above were all published in 1760, as were editions published in Portsmouth, N. H., (in OTP), and in Boston (Sabin:58057). ¶ *OOA(?) · OTP*

*[Pringle, Sir John], 1707–1782. Life of General James Wolfe . . . . London: printed for G[eorge]. Kearsley successor to the late Mr. Robinson at the Golden Lion in Ludgate Street. 1760. (Price one shilling.) 36 p. 8°

Casey:292

OOA notes: title-page missing, and gives authorship to: James Pearce. ¶ OOA

A refutation of the Letter to an Honble. Brigadier-General, commander of His Majesty's forces in Canada. By an officer . . . . London: printed for R[obert?]. Stevens, at Pope's Head, in Pater-Noster-Row. 1760. (Price one shilling.) 1 p.l., 52 p. 8°(in 4s).

NUC(Pre–56)485:444*

[Authorship has been] attributed to Lord Edward Thurlow; the author may be a friend of Lord [George] Townshend, or [even] Townshend himself [the brigadier-general referred to in the title]. He evidently regards the latter as the virtual conqueror of Quebec (cf. Church:1034). ¶ *A reply to: Junius*, pseud., A letter to an honourable brigadier general. *London, 1760 (q.v.), in which Townshend is charged with incompetency in his Canadian campaigns. ¶ First edition; second and fourth eds. pub. in the same year* — see *next entries; reprinted, with the* Letter, *London, 1841, and with other works, London, 1772, 1806, 1812, 1814, 1850, etc. (cf. Sabin:36906–10).*

[La paternité de cet ouvrage a été] attribuée à lord Edward Thurlow ; l'auteur est peut-être un ami de lord [George] Townshend, ou [même] Townshend lui-même [soit le brigadier général dont il est question dans le titre]. De toute évidence, l'auteur considère que ce dernier a virtuellement remporté la victoire à Québec (cf. Church:1034). ¶ *Réplique à Junius*, pseud., A letter to an honourable brigadier general. *Londres, 1760 (q.v.), dans laquelle Townshend est accusé d'incompétence lors de ses campagnes canadiennes. ¶ Première édition ; deuxième et quatrième éd. publ. la même année* – voir *les notices suivantes ; réimpressions avec la* Letter, *Londres, 1841, et avec d'autres ouvrages, Londres, 1772, 1806, 1812, 1814, 1850, etc. (cf. Sabin:36906–10).*

A refutation of the Letter . . . . By an officer . . . . The 2d ed. London, printed for R[obert?]. Stevens, 1760. 1 p.l., 52 p. 8°

NUC(Pre–56)485:444*

See first ed., above, for notes.

Voir notes à la première édition ci-dessus.

A refutation of the Letter .... The 4th ed. London: printed for R[obert?]. Stevens, 1760. Price one shilling. 40 p. 8°

Sabin:36904

See first ed., above, for notes.   *Voir* notes à la première édition ci-dessus.

Short, Richard, *fl.* 1759–1763. Proposals for engraving and publishing by subscription, twelve views of the principal buildings in Quebec, from drawings taken on the spot, at the command of Vice-Admiral Saunders. By Richard Short, purser to His Majesty's ship the Prince of Orange. [London, T[homas]. Jefferys, 1760?] [No collation.]

Source: *see* note.

From advertisement, p. [34], Thomas Jefferys, *Directions for navigating* .... London, 1760. ¶ *The views themselves appeared in Richard Short,* Twelve views in Quebec, in 1759. *London, 1761,* q.v.

Tiré d'une réclame, p. [34], Thomas Jefferys, *Directions for navigating* .... Londres, 1760. ¶ *Les vues elles-mêmes parurent dans l'ouvrage de Richard Short,* Twelve views in Quebec, in 1759. *Londres, 1761,* q.v.

Unanswerable arguments against a peace. By a British Freeholder .... Dublin, printed for S[amuel]. Smith, at Mr. Faulkner's in Essex-Street. 1760. 24 p. 8°(in 4s).

NUC(Pre–56)607:468

The [Seven Years'] war [1756–63] is just and necessary. The French taught the Indians to be "more cruel in the Use of Arms, than their barbarous Nature would have done" (p. 12). They must be punished and reduced to accepting the British terms. The

La guerre [de Sept Ans] [1756–1763] est juste et nécessaire. Les Français ont appris aux Indiens à se montrer « plus cruels dans le maniement des armes que leur nature barbare ne les y aurait poussés » (p. 12). Il faut les punir et les contraindre à accepter les conditions britanniques. De plus, l'auteur

author also quotes from [John] Douglas's *Letter addressed to two great men.* [London, 1760], *q.v.*

cite certains passages de l'ouvrage de [John] Douglas, *Letter addressed to two great men.* [Londres, 1760], *q.v.*

Williamson, Peter, 1730–1799. A brief account of the war in N. America: shewing the principal causes of our former miscarriages: as also, the necessity and advantage of keeping Canada, and the maintaining a friendly correspondence with the Indians. To which is added, a description of the natives, their manner of living, &c. The whole containing several remarkable particulars, relative to the natural dispositions, tempers and inclinations of the unpolished savages, not taken notice of in any other history. By Peter Williamson, formerly a planter in the back-settlements of Pensylvania. Edinburgh: printed for the author, and sold by R. Griffiths [and others, 1760]. 1 p.l., 38 p. 12°

NUC(Pre–56)665:612

The war referred to is the Seven Years' War, 1756–63.

La guerre dont il est question est la guerre de Sept Ans, 1756–1763.

1761

[Bath, William Pulteney, *earl of/comte de*], 1684–1764. Reflections on the domestic policy, proper to be observed on the conclusion of a peace . . . . London: Printed for A. Millar, in the Strand. 1761. 94 p. 8°

NUC(Pre–56)39:126*

This is one of the most interesting and original of the war pamphlets [Seven Years' War, 1756–63]. The writer advocates settlement of discharged soldiers, sailors, and carpenters (estimated at 84,000 men) in England rather than in America [more particularly Nova Scotia], as at the end of the last war. The expenses of the settlement of Nova Scotia for the first ten years, exclusive of the guards and garrisons, amount to £582,270 (p. 9). There are uncultivated lands at home and fisheries to be developed. Keep the men at home. They may be needed for war in Europe, but America is now secure. The writer has no fear of losing the colonies, as they are too widespread to unite and revolt. Canada should be retained. It is more important than Guadeloupe, but Great Britain should keep both (p. 71 ff.). Our author (p. 42 ff.) also attacks the stockholders: "The interest paid by the nation annually to our stockholders exceeds three millions sterling, which is more than five shillings in the pound of the computed rent of all the lands in England .... And, indeed, it is evident that the greatest enemies we have had during this war are ourselves, or rather our stockholders ... for if the war had continued two or three years longer, and our aims [arms?] had still been successful against our foreign enemies, the nation nevertheless would have been so exhausted by its domestic enemies, that we should have been obliged to conclude a peace upon any terms with the former, to get some respite from the dangerous

C'est l'un des pamphlets sur la guerre les plus intéressants et les plus originaux [guerre de Sept Ans, 1756–1763]. L'auteur préconise que soldats, marins et charpentiers rendus à la vie civile (on estime leur nombre à 84 000) s'établissent en Angleterre plutôt qu'en Amérique [plus particulièrement en Nouvelle-Écosse], comme ce fut le cas à la fin de la dernière guerre. Durant les dix premières années de la colonisation de la Nouvelle-Écosse, le pays a dépensé une somme de 582 270 £, sans compter les frais pour les soldats et les garnisons (p. 9). Le pays a des terres en friche à cultiver et des pêcheries à exploiter. Gardons les hommes sur la terre natale. Le pays peut avoir besoin d'eux en cas de guerre en Europe, tandis que l'Amérique n'est plus menacée à l'heure actuelle. L'auteur ne voit aucun risque de perdre les colonies, car leurs territoires sont trop vastes pour qu'elles puissent s'unir et se révolter. Il faut garder le Canada, qui est plus important que la Guadeloupe, quoique la Grande-Bretagne devrait garder les deux (p. 71 et suiv.). Notre auteur (p. 42 et suiv.) s'attaque également aux actionnaires : « L'intérêt que la nation paye annuellement à nos actionnaires dépasse les trois millions de livres sterling, ce qui représente, par rapport à la somme estimée de tous les fermages en Angleterre, plus de cinq shillings par livre .... De plus, il est en effet évident que nous sommes nous-mêmes nos plus grands ennemis depuis le début de cette guerre, ou plutôt nos actionnaires le sont... car si la guerre devait se poursuivre deux ou trois ans de plus, et que nous arrivions à nos fins [aims] malgré nos ennemis étrangers [et que nous remportions la victoire (arms) contre nos ennemis étrangers ?], la nation serait néanmoins tellement saignée à blanc par ses ennemis intérieurs que nous serions

encroachments made upon the national property by the latter." ¶ *Another edition: 1763.*

obligés de conclure un traité aux conditions des premiers afin de nous ménager un répit par rapport aux menées dangereuses des derniers visant à s'approprier les biens de la nation. » ¶ *Autre édition : 1763.*

*Campbell, John, 1708–1775. Lives of the admirals, and other eminent British seamen . . . . Including a new and accurate naval history, from the earliest account of time . . . proving our uninterrupted claim to and enjoyment of, the dominion of our seas. Interspersed with many curious passages, relating to our discoveries, plantations and commerce . . . . Carefully rev. and cor., with very considerable additions, by John Campbell. . . . 3d ed. London, T[homas]. Osborne, C. Hitch and L. Hawes [etc.], 1761. 4 v. ports., fol. maps. 8°(?)

NUC(Pre–56)92:211*

See: second ed., 1750.

Voir : deuxième éd., 1750.

A candid answer, to a pamphlet called Reasons for keeping Guadaloupe at a peace, preferable to Canada, explained, in five letters from a gentleman in Guadaloupe, to his friend in London. In a letter to the author. London: printed for Thomas Hope, opposite the North-Gate of the Royal-Exchange, Threadneedle-Street. 1761. (Price six-pence.) 1 p.l., 30 p. 8°

NUC(Pre–56)93:607

A reply to: Reasons for keeping Guadaloupe at a peace. *London, 1761* (q.v.). ¶ *A statement of the case for Canada. The author dismisses the possibility of the English colonies revolting, and refutes his opponent's Guadeloupe arguments with data from Jamaica* (NUC). ¶ *OTP*

Réplique à Reasons for keeping Guadaloupe at a peace. *Londres, 1761* (q.v.). ¶ *Un exposé des arguments en faveur du Canada. L'auteur écarte la possibilité d'une révolte des colonies anglaises et, à l'aide de données provenant de la Jamaïque, il réfute les arguments de son adversaire en faveur de la Guadeloupe (NUC).* ¶ *OTP*

*Charlevoix, Pierre François Xavier de, 1682–1761. Journal of a voyage to North-America. Undertaken by order of the French King. Containing the geographical description and natural history of that country, particularly Canada. Together with an account of the customs, characters, religion, manners and traditions of the original inhabitants. In a series of letters to the Duchess of Lesdiguières. Translated from the French of P. de Charlevoix. In two volumes. Vol. I. [Vol. II.] London: printed for R[obert]. and J[ames]. Dodsley, in Pall-Mall. 1761. 2 v.: viii, 128, 145–382 p. (nos. 129–44 omitted in paging). front. (fold. map); viii, 380, [26] p. (p. 82 numbered 83). 8°

NUC(Pre–56)104:169

Transl. from his: *Histoire et description générale de la Nouvelle France*. Paris, 1744. 3 v. (considered the first general history of Canada): vol. 3, *Journal d'un voyage*. ¶ This is the first English edition in English of the *Journal*, containing the "Preliminary discourse on the origin of the Americans" and the thirty-six Letters of the third volume of the *Histoire*, first 4° edition, Paris, 1744. ¶ This was possibly reissued in 1766 and 1772 (cf. Dionne 2:628n.), reprinted Chicago, 1923, 2 vols., and on microfilm (Dallas, Southwestern Microfilm Inc., ca. 1950); a new translation appeared as *Letters to the Dutchess of Lesdiguières*. London, 1763 (*q.v.*), and possibly in 1764 (Sabin:12140n.), and as *A voyage to North-America*. Dublin, 1766, 2 vols. The *Histoire*, cited above, was first transl. by John Gilmary Shea as *History and general description of New France*. New York, 1866–72, 6 vols. ¶ NSWA · OKQ · OTP · BVAU

Trad. de son ouvrage *Histoire et description générale de la Nouvelle France*. Paris, 1744. 3 vol. (considéré comme la première histoire générale du Canada) : vol. 3, *Journal d'un voyage*. ¶ C'est la première édition anglaise parue en anglais du *Journal*, comprenant le « Preliminary discourse on the origin of the Americans » et les trente-six Lettres du troisième volume de l'*Histoire*, première édition in–4°, Paris, 1744. ¶ Cet ouvrage a peut-être été réimprimé en 1766 et en 1772 (cf. Dionne 2:628n.), puis à Chicago en 1923, 2 vol., et, plus tard, reproduit sur microfilm (Dallas, Southwestern Microfilm Inc., vers 1950) ; une nouvelle traduction avait paru sous le titre *Letters to the Dutchess of Lesdiguières*. Londres, 1763 (*q.v.*), et peut-être en 1764 (Sabin:12140n.), ainsi que sous le titre *A voyage to North-America*. Dublin, 1766, 2 vol. L'*Histoire*, précitée, fut d'abord traduite par John Gilmary Shea sous le titre *History and general description of New France*. New York, 1866–1872, 6 vol. ¶ NSWA · OKQ · OTP · BVAU

[Choiseul-Stainville, Etienne François, *duc de*], 1719–1785. Memoire historique sur la negociation de la France & de l'Angleterre, depuis le 26 mars 1761, jusqu'au 20 Septembre de la même année; avec les pièces justificatives. Imprimée selon l'édition publiée à Paris, par l'autorité. A Londres, chez D. Wilson, T[homas]. Becket & P[eter]. A[braham]. de Hondt, 1761. 2 p.l., 60 p. 4°

NUC(Pre–56)107:602*

At end: Par ordre du roi. Signé le Duc de Choiseul. ¶ A collection of state papers [with connecting narrative by Choiseul], preliminary to the treaty of 1762 [Treaty of Paris, Feb. 1763?], relative to the cession [by France] of Canada, the limits of Louisiana, the Newfoundland fisheries, Cape Breton, Guadeloupe [and Nova Scotia, France retaining St. Pierre and Miquelon], etc. [ending the Seven Years' War]. ¶ *Waldon has a variant from BM Cat., etc., with collation: iv, 196 p. 8°* ¶ *Answered by:* Remarks upon the Historical memorial . . . . *London, 1761,* q.v. ¶ *The original was published under the same title, with imprint: Paris, Imprimerie Royale, 1761. Transl. into English as* An historical memorial . . . . *London, 1761, and Dublin, 1761, q.v.; also* Historischer Bericht. . . . *Leipzig, 1761, etc. (cf. NUC, BLC).* ¶ *BVAU*

À la fin : Par ordre du roi. Signé le Duc de Choiseul. ¶ Recueil de documents officiels [accompagnés de notes connexes rédigées par Choiseul] constituant des préliminaires du traité de 1762 [traité de Paris, fév. 1763 ?] visant les questions suivantes : la cession du Canada [par la France], les lignes de démarcation de la Louisiane, les pêcheries de Terre-Neuve, le Cap-Breton, la Guadeloupe [et la Nouvelle-Écosse, la France conservant Saint-Pierre et Miquelon], etc. [questions dont le règlement permit de mettre fin à la guerre de Sept Ans]. ¶ *Waldon mentionne une variante du Cat. du BM, etc., avec la collation : iv, 196 p. in–8°.* ¶ *Ce texte a suscité la réplique* Remarks upon the Historical memorial . . . . *Londres, 1761,* q.v. ¶ *L'original fut publié sous le même titre, avec l'adresse bibliographique : Paris, Imprimerie Royale, 1761. Trad. en anglais sous le titre* An historical memorial . . . . *Londres, 1761, et Dublin, 1761,* q.v. ; *également* Historischer Bericht. . . . *Leipzig, 1761, etc. (cf. NUC, BLC).* ¶ *BVAU*

[Choiseul-Stainville, Etienne François, *duc de*], 1719–1785. An historical memorial of the negotiation of France and England, from the 26th of March, 1761, to the 20th of September of the same year, with the vouchers. Translated from the French original, published at Paris by authority. London: printed for D. Wilson and T[homas]. Becket and P[eter]. A[braham]. Dehondt in the Strand. 1761. 63, [1] p. 4°

NUC(Pre–56)107:602*

Contents list occupies the final page. ¶ *Waldon has a variant from "Camb." and "NYP" catalogues, with collation: 107 p. 8°(in 4s). Signed: Le Duc de Choiseul.* ¶ See *preceding entry for other notes.* ¶ *OTU · BVIP*

Table des matières à la dernière page. ¶ *Waldon mentionne une variante des catalogues « Camb. » et « NYP », avec la collation : 107 p. in–8° (4 f.). Signé : Le Duc de Choiseul.* ¶ Voir *autres notes à la notice précédente.* ¶ *OTU · BVIP*

[Choiseul-Stainville, Etienne François, *duc de*], 1719–1785. An historical memorial . . . . Dublin: printed for H[enry]. Saunders in Castle-street; J[ames?]. Potts & S[amuel]. Watson, in Dame-street, booksellers, 1761. 79 p. 8°

BLC(to 1975)113:74*

See *preceding entries for notes.*

Voir *notes aux notices précédentes.*

A complete history of the present war, from its commencement in 1756, to the end of the campaign, 1760. In which, all the battles, sieges, and sea-engagements; with every other transaction worthy of public attention, are faithfully recorded; with political and military observations. London, printed for W[illiam]. Owen . . . L[ockyer]. Davis and C. Reymers [Reymer or Rymer] . . . and J. Scott . . . 1761. 2 p.l., 548 p. 8°

NUC(Pre–56)118:244

Concerns the Seven Years' War, 1756–63, which involved Anglo-French rivalry in North America. ¶ *BVAU*

Traite de la guerre de Sept Ans, 1756–1763, durant laquelle les Anglais et les Français se sont affrontés en Amérique du Nord. ¶ *BVAU*

The cruel massacre of the Protestants in North-America . . . . London: printed for Michael Adamson, 1761. 8 p. 1 illus. (woodcut). small 8°

NUC(Pre–56)128:355*

The type is more regular than in the 1760 edition; (q.v.) for notes.

La composition typographique est plus régulière que dans l'édition de 1760 ; (q.v.) pour notes.

A detection of the false reasons and facts, contained in the five letters, (entitled, Reasons for keeping Guadaloupe at a peace, preferable to Canada; from a gentleman in Guadaloupe to his friend in London.) In which the advantages of both conquests are fairly and impartially stated and compared. By a Member of Parliament. London: printed for Thos. Hope . . . 1761. <Price one shilling and six-pence.> 1 p.l., 58 p. 8°

NUC(Pre–56)140:697

A reply to: Reasons for keeping Guadaloupe at a peace. *London, 1761 (q.v.), which had argued for keeping Guadaloupe rather than Canada in the terms of peace ending the Seven Years' War.*

Réplique à Reasons for keeping Guadaloupe at a peace. *Londres, 1761 (q.v.), dont l'auteur plaidait pour le maintien de la Guadeloupe plutôt que celui du Canada, au titre des conditions du traité mettant fin à la guerre de Sept Ans.*

*The English pilot. The fourth book. Describing the West-India navigation, from Hudson's-Bay. . . . London, printed for W[illiam]. and J[ohn]. Mount, T[homas]. Page and Son, on Tower-Hill, 1761. 4, 3–66 p. illus., 25 maps on 23 plates (part fold., part double). fol.

NUC(Pre–56)160:374*

Title vignette (British arms). ¶ First edition: 1689, *q.v.* for the dates of the

Titre vignette (armoiries britanniques). ¶ Première édition : 1689, *q.v.* pour les dates

many other editions, including the 1706, which has a similar title, given in more detail.

des nombreuses autres éditions, y compris celle de 1706, dont le titre est similaire, quoique plus détaillé.

An examination into the value of Canada and Guadaloupe, with an impartial account of the latter, in answer to a late pamphlet, entituled, The interest of Great-Britain, considered with regard to her colonies. In a letter to a gentleman in England . . . . London: printed for William White, 1761. 1 p.l., 40 [*i.e.* 41], iv p. 8°(in 4s).

NUC(Pre–56)164:466

Page 41 wrongly numbered 40. ¶ *"Appendix. A specification of the sugar works in Guadaloupe and Grand-terre, and to whom they belong": iv p. at end.* ¶ *A reply to: Benjamin Franklin,* The interest of Great Britain considered. *London, 1760 (q.v.).* ¶ [In considering the terms of peace to end the Seven Years' War], Guadeloupe is more valuable than Canada in this writer's opinion [because of its sugar], and Canada is not necessary to the security of the American colonies. ¶ *No other edition discovered.*

La page 41 porte, par erreur, le numéro 40. ¶ « *Appendix. A specification of the sugar works in Guadaloupe and Grand-terre, and to whom they belong* » : *iv. p. à la fin.* ¶ *Réplique à Benjamin Franklin,* The interest of Great Britain considered. *Londres, 1760 (q.v.).* ¶ [À l'examen des conditions du traité pour mettre fin à la guerre de Sept Ans], la Guadeloupe est, d'après cet auteur, plus précieuse que le Canada [en raison de son sucre], et le Canada n'est pas indispensable à la sécurité des colonies américaines. ¶ *Aucune autre édition n'a été découverte.*

[Franklin, Benjamin], 1706–1790. The interest of Great Britain considered . . . . 2d ed. London, printed for T[homas]. Becket, 1761. 1 p.l., 58 p. 8°(in 4s) (?).

NUC(Pre–56)183:159*

First ed. pub. 1760, *q.v.* for other notes. ¶ BVAU

Première éd. publ. en 1760, *q.v.* pour d'autres notes. ¶ BVAU

Gardiner, Richard, 1723–1781. Memoirs of the siege of Quebec, capital of all Canada, and of the retreat of Monsieur de Bourlemaque, from Carillon to the Isle au Noix. From the journal of a French officer on board the Chezine frigate, taken by His Majesty's ship Rippon. Compared with the accounts transmitted home by Major-General Wolfe, and Vice-Admiral Saunders; with occasional remarks. By Richard Gardiner, Esq; Captain of Marines in the Rippon . . . . London: printed for R[obert]. and J[ames]. Dodsley . . . 1761. <Price one shilling and six pence.> 39 p. 3 double plates, 14 ports., 12 fold. maps (incl. front.), 1 double plan. 4°

NUC(Pre–56)191:177

The title given in NUC is inaccurately transcribed or else irregularly abridged. ¶ Concerns the Quebec Campaign of 1759. ¶ Waldon indicates the possibility of a 1762 edition, but this has not been verified beyond Faribault:252. ¶ OTP

Le titre donné dans le NUC est soit inexact, soit arbitrairement tronqué. ¶ Traite de la campagne de Québec de 1759. ¶ Waldon indique la possibilité d'une édition en 1762, mais l'existence de cette édition n'a pas été vérifiée au-delà de Faribault:252. ¶ OTP

Jefferys, Thomas, *d./déc.* 1771. The natural and civil history of the French dominions in North and South America. With an historical detail of the acquisitions, and conquests, made by the British arms in those parts. Giving a particular account of the climate . . . and languages. Together with the religion, . . . of the Indians and other inhabitants. Illustrated by maps . . . engraved by T[homas]. Jefferys, geographer to His Majesty. London: printed for T[homas]. Jefferys . . . 1761. 2 pts. in 1 v.: [8], 168 p.; 2 p.l., 246 p. 9 maps, 9 plans. fol.

NUC(Pre–56)279:27*

First edition: London, 1760, q.v. for notes. ¶ OTP · BVAU

Première édition : Londres, 1760, q.v. pour notes. ¶ OTP · BVAU

[Lee, Charles], 1731–1782.   The importance of Canada considered. In two letters to a noble lord. London, printed for R[obert]. and J[ames]. Dodsley, in Pall-mall. 1761. 2 p.l., 38 p. 8°(in 4s).

NUC(Pre–56)322:610

Concerns events of the Seven Years' War, 1756–63. ¶ OTP

Traite des événements de la guerre de Sept Ans, 1756–63. ¶ OTP

*A letter to a great M——R, on the prospect of a peace .... London: G[eorge]. Kearsly, 1761. 148 p. 12°

Casey:315

If this is the same as the issue noted by Dr. Waldon in the following entry, q.v., for fuller title and notes, then it also has a map, and is the first issue.

S'il s'agit du même document que celui indiqué par Waldon dans la notice suivante, q.v., pour un titre plus complet et des notes, il convient alors de signaler que c'est le premier tirage de cet ouvrage, qui, de plus, comprend une carte.

A letter to a great M——R, on the prospect of a peace; wherein the demolition of the fortifications of Louisbourg is shewn to be absurd; the importance of Canada fully refuted; the proper barrier pointed out in North America; and the reasonableness and necessity of retaining the French sugar islands. Containing remarks on some preceding pamphlets that have treated of the subject, and a succinct view of the whole terms that ought to be insisted on from France at a future negociation. By an unprejudiced observer .... London: printed for G[eorge]. Kearsley ... 1761. 2 p.l., 148 p. 8°(in 4s).

NUC(Pre–56)329:26

A reply to Benjamin Franklin, The interest of Great Britain considered. London, 1760, q.v., John Douglas, A

Réplique à Benjamin Franklin, The interest of Great Britain considered. Londres, 1760, q.v., à John Douglas, A letter addressed to two

letter addressed to two great men. London, 1760, *q.v.*, and Charles Townshend, *Remarks on the Letter addressed to two great men.* London, 1760, *q.v.* under William Burke, supposed author. Waldon says the author "also quotes from Lahontan, Charlevoix, Postlethwaite's *Great-Britain's commercial interest* [*explained* .... London, 1759, *q.v.* under Malachy Postlethwayt] and other works."

great men. Londres, 1760, *q.v.*, et à Charles Townshend, *Remarks on the Letter addressed to two great men.* Londres, 1760, *q.v.* William Burke, auteur présumé. Waldon indique que l'auteur « cite en outre Lahontan et Charlevoix, ainsi que d'autres ouvrages et celui de Postlethwaite, *Great-Britain's commercial interest* [*explained* .... Londres, 1759, *q.v.* Malachy Postlethwayt]. »

A letter to the Right Honourable the Earl of B* [*i.e.* Bute] on a late important resignation, and its probable consequences. London: printed for J. Coote, 1761. 2 p.l., 75 p. 8°

NUC(Pre–56)329:114*

NUC omits the 2 p.l. in the collation. ¶ *On the resignation of William Pitt, 1st Earl of Chatham.* ¶ The writer states that the [Seven Years'] war was begun to ensure the safety of the American colonies and in defence of trade. Canada should be kept, but Gaudeloupe might be restored for the sake of peace. *See also* various titles relating to this controversy, 1760, 1761. ¶ *First edition; second and third editions follow.*

La collation du NUC omet les 2 f. l. ¶ *À propos de la démission de William Pitt, 1ᵉʳ comte de Chatham.* ¶ L'auteur affirme que la guerre [de Sept Ans] avait débuté pour garantir la sécurité des colonies américaines et pour assurer la défense du commerce. Il faut garder le Canada, mais on pourrait restituer la Guadeloupe pour la sauvegarde de la paix. *Voir également* divers titres concernant cette controverse, 1760, 1761. ¶ *Première édition ; deuxième et troisième éditions ci-dessous.*

A letter to the Right Honourable the Earl of B* .... The second edition. London: printed for J. Coote, at the King's Arms, in Pater-noster-row, 1761. 1 p.l., 75 p. 8°

NUC(Pre–56)329:114*

First edition: 1761, see preceding entry.　　*Première édition : 1761, voir la notice précédente.*

A letter to the Right Honourable the Earl of B*** . . . . The third edition. London: printed for J. Coote, 1761. 2 p.l., 75 p. 8°(?)

NUC(Pre–56)329:114*

First edition: 1761, see above.　　*Première édition : 1761, voir ci-dessus.*

Massie, Joseph, *d./déc.* 1784. Brief observations concerning the management of the war, and the means to prevent the ruin of Great Britain. Most humbly offered to the consideration of the Parliament, and people thereof, by J. Massie. The second edition, with additions. [London] Sold at the pamphlet shops at the Royal-Exchange, Temple-bar, and Charing-cross, price three pence; but will be given with my calculations of the taxes yearly paid by a family of each rank, degree, or class; which may be had at the same places, price one shilling. [1761.] 12 p. 4°

NUC(Pre–56)368:354

Caption title; imprint on p. 12. ¶ Sabin:46180 has different title after "Great Britain": with notices of the gold mines of Peru and Mexico, the possessions of the French in America, 1761. London, 1761. folio. ¶ Critical of the government for not seizing the French sugar colonies, but, instead, keeping the troops icebound in Canada, also for spending too much on the navy and the European war in proportion to France's expenditures. The postscript denounces the West Indian sugar planters as tyrannical profiteers.

Titre de départ ; adresse bibliographique à la p. 12. ¶ Le Sabin:46180 mentionne un titre différent après « Great Britain » : with notices of the gold mines of Peru and Mexico, the possessions of the French in America, 1761. Londres, 1761. In-folio. ¶ Se montre critique à l'égard du gouvernement parce que, au lieu de s'être emparé des colonies sucrières françaises, il a laissé les glaces immobiliser les troupes au Canada, et parce qu'il a dépensé trop d'argent pour la marine et la guerre en Europe, en regard des sommes engagées par la France. La postface dénonce les planteurs de canne à sucre des Antilles

Massie also published a broadside, *General propositions relating to colonies,* dated at Westminster, 21 April 1761, comparing the North American continental colonies with the sugar islands, to show the greater value to England of the latter. ¶ *The work to which this calls itself the second ed. may be Massie's* Observations upon Mr. Fauquier's Essay. *London, 1756,* q.v.

comme des profiteurs tyranniques. Massie publia également, en format in-plano, *General propositions relating to colonies,* daté du 21 avril 1761 à Westminster, dans lequel il compare les colonies continentales nord-américaines aux îles sucrières afin de démontrer que ces dernières revêtent une importance supérieure pour l'Angleterre. ¶ *L'ouvrage de Massie, duquel la présente édition est désignée comme la deuxième éd., est peut-être :* Observations upon Mr. Fauquier's Essay. *Londres, 1756,* q.v.

Müller, Gerhard Friedrich, 1705–1783. Voyages from Asia to America, for completing the discoveries of the North West coast of America. To which is prefixed, a summary of the voyages made by the Rusians [*sic*] on the Frozen Sea, in search of a north east passage. Serving as an explanation of a map of the Russian discoveries, published by the Academy of sciences at Petersburgh. Translated from the High Dutch of S. [*i.e.* G.] Muller.... With the addition of three new maps: 1. A copy of part of the Japanese map of the world. 2. A copy of De Lisle's and Buache's fictitious map. And 3. A large map of Canada, extending to the Pacific Ocean, containing the new discoveries made by the Russians and French. By Thomas Jefferys Geographer to His Majesty. London, printed for T[homas]. Jefferys ... 1761. viii, xliii, 76 p. 4 maps (2 fold., incl. front.). 4°

NUC(Pre–56)399:598*

Waldon has only three maps (from Sabin:51285). ¶ *Transl. from his* Sammlung Russischer Geschichte. *Vol. 3. St. Petersburg, 1758 (cf. NUC).* ¶ Contains the original account of Capt. Behring's Polar expedition and discoveries — Sabin. The maps are interesting in tracing the progress of geographical discovery in the north-west portions of North America —

Waldon indique seulement trois cartes (d'après le Sabin:51285). ¶ *Trad. de son ouvrage* Sammlung Russischer Geschichte. *Vol. 3. St. Petersbourg, 1758 (cf. NUC).* ¶ Comprend le récit original de l'expédition polaire et des découvertes du cap. Behring – Sabin. Les cartes sont intéressantes parce qu'elles retracent l'évolution des découvertes géo-graphiques dans les parties nord-ouest de l'Amérique du Nord – JCB(I). ¶ *Première*

JCB(1). ¶ *First English edition; second ed. London, 1764.* ¶ *NSWA · OTP · BVA · BVAU · BVIPA*

édition anglaise ; deuxième éd. Londres, 1764. ¶ *NSWA · OTP · BVA · BVAU · BVIPA*

Reasons for keeping Guadaloupe at a peace, preferable to Canada, explained in five letters, from a gentleman in Guadaloupe, to his friend in London. London: printed for M[ary]. Cooper . . . 1761. <Price 1s. 6d.> 79 p. 8°

NUC(Pre–56)483:504

Sabin:68267 mentions a map. ¶ *Answered by:* A candid answer, to a pamphlet called Reasons . . . . *London, 1761, and* A detection of the false reasons . . . in the five letters . . . . *London, 1761* (q.v.); *various 1760 titles also bear on this controversy.* ¶ The writer says that the trade with Guadeloupe is extremely valuable, while our holding Canada will mean but little extension of the fur trade. He also foresees [unlike the author of *A candid answer*] that the removal of the French menace will enable the older colonies to become independent. ¶ *This pamphlet was unfavourably criticized in the* Monthly review, *v. 24, p. 440* (NUC(Pre–56)140:697, A Detection of the false reasons and facts . . .).

Le Sabin:68267 mentionne une carte. ¶ *Cet ouvrage a suscité les répliques suivantes :* A candid answer, to a pamphlet called Reasons . . . . *Londres, 1761, et* A detection of the false reasons . . . . in the five letters . . . . *Londres, 1761* (q.v.) ; *plusieurs titres de 1760 ont également trait à cette controverse.* ¶ Selon l'auteur, le commerce avec la Guadeloupe est extrêmement avantageux, tandis que notre possession du Canada n'implique qu'une faible expansion du commerce de la fourrure. De plus, il prévoit [contrairement à l'auteur de *A candid answer*] que la disparition de la menace française permettra aux anciennes colonies de devenir indépendantes. ¶ *Ce pamphlet fit l'objet de critiques défavorables dans la* Monthly review, *vol. 24, p. 440* (NUC(Pre–56)140:697, A Detection of the false reasons and facts . . .).

*Remarks upon the Historical memorial published by the Court of France. In a letter to the Earl Temple. London, printed for G[eorge]. Woodfall [etc.] 1761. 2 p.l., 46 p. 8°(in 4s).

NUC(Pre–56)488:91

A reply to: Étienne François, duc de Choiseul-Stainville, *Memoire historique* .... Londres, 1761, *q.v.* under: Choiseul-Stainville. ¶ Terms in regard to Canada: p. 35, 38–40.¶ First edition; second ed.: *see* next entry.

Réplique à Étienne François, duc de Choiseul-Stainville, *Memoire historique* .... Londres, 1761, *q.v.* Choiseul-Stainville. ¶ Conditions touchant le Canada : p. 35, 38–40. ¶ Première édition ; deuxième éd. : *voir* la notice suivante.

Remarks . . . by the Court of France, in a letter to the Earl Temple. By a Member of Parliament. The second edition. London: printed for G[eorge]. Woodfall, at Charing-Cross, and G[eorge]. Kearsley, in Ludgate-street. 1761.

Sabin:69530

See *preceding entry for notes.*

Voir *notes à la notice précédente.*

Sentiments relating to the late negotiation. London: printed for R[alph]. Griffiths in the Strand. 1761. 1 p.l., 44 p. 4°

NUC(Pre–56)538:465

Appendices: Numb. 2, Paper on the rights of the two nations to Canada: p. 37–38; Numb. 4, Extract from a memorial delivered by the Duke de Mirepoix to the British ministry, 1755. Of the limits of Canada: p. 38; Numb. 6, Paper on the importance of

Annexes : N° 2, Paper on the rights of the two nations to Canada : p. 37–38 ; n° 4, Extract from a memorial delivered by the Duke de Mirepoix to the British ministry, 1755. Of the limits of Canada : p. 38 ; n° 6, Paper on the importance of the New-foundland fishery, by Mr. Postlethwayte :

the Newfoundland fishery, by Mr. Postlethwayte: p. 40. ¶ The writer protests at concessions to France [in the British and French peace negotiations, in the Seven Years' War]. All North America should be ceded to Great Britain. Canada is not enough, the fur trade being a very inconsiderable thing. ¶ *OTP*

p. 40. ¶ L'auteur proteste contre les concessions faites à la France [lors des négociations de paix entre les Britanniques et les Français durant la guerre de Sept Ans]. Toute l'Amérique du Nord doit être cédée à la Grande-Bretagne. Le Canada n'est pas suffisant, le commerce de la fourrure étant de valeur insignifiante. ¶ *OTP*

Short, Richard, *fl.* 1759–1763. [Twelve views of Quebec, in 1759, from drawings taken on the spot by Richard Short, by command of Vice Admiral Saunders.] London. 1761. fol.

Sabin:80570

Twelve double-page engravings, each dated "London, Sept. 1, 1761." ¶ Proposals *for these views were pub. London, 1760, q.v. under Short.* ¶ *For titles and descriptions of the individual plates,* see *the eleven entries in NUC(Pre–56)544:386–87, or more conveniently and for twelve plates, in TPL:280 (nos. 3–14).*

Douze gravures sur double page, individuellement datées : « Londres, le 1er sept. 1761 ». ¶ *Visant ces vues, un ouvrage intitulé* Proposals *parut à Londres en 1760, q.v. Short.* ¶ *Pour des titres et des descriptions des planches individuelles,* voir *les onze notices du NUC(Pre–56)544:386–87, ou pour une consultation plus pratique,* voir *celles de TPL :280 (nos 3–14) qui traitent des douze planches.*

Wright, John, *fl.* 1761–1765. The American negotiator: or, The various currencies of the British colonies in America; as well the islands, as the continent. The currencies of Nova Scotia, Canada, New England, New York . . . and of the islands of Barbadoes, Jamaica, St. Christophers . . . reduced into English money, by a series of tables, suited to the several exchanges between the colonies and Britain . . . . With tables reducing the currency of Ireland into sterling, and the contrary . . . . Also, a chain of tables, for the interchangeable reduction of the currencies of the colonies . . . . By J. Wright, accomptant. London, printed by J. Everingham, for the author, 1761. 1 p.l., ii p., 1 l., 24, xvi, 464 p. 8°

NUC(Pre–56)675:293*

Waldon has collation as: 3 p.l., 464 p. ¶ First ed.; also pub. in MF, Ann Arbor, Mich., University Microfilms, 1970 (American Culture series, reel 440, no. 2); second ed. 1763, q.v.; third ed., 1765 (also MF), and another ed., 1767; Waldon also lists a variant 1761 issue, not found in NUC or Sabin — see next entry; but the locations of copies of the two variants are not distinguished here, all being given under this present issue. ¶ NSHPL · OOA · OKQ · OTMCL · OTLS · OH

Collation de Waldon : 3 f. l., 464 p. ¶ Première éd. ; également publ. sur mic., Ann Arbor (Mich.), University Microfilms, 1970 (collection American Culture, bobine 440, n° 2) ; deuxième éd. de 1763, q.v. ; troisième éd. de 1765 (également sur mic.), et une autre éd. de 1767 ; Waldon répertorie en outre une variante du tirage de 1761, introuvable dans le NUC aussi bien que dans le Sabin –voir la notice suivante ; toutefois, les endroits où se trouvent des exemplaires des variantes ne sont pas précisés ici, tous les renseignements étant donnés sous cette édition. ¶ NSHPL · OOA · OKQ · OTMCL · OTLS · OH

Wright, John, *fl.* 1761–1765. The American negotiator; or, Various currencies of the British colonies in America . . . . London: J. Everingham, 1761. 464 p. 8°

JCB(1)3:1311

Apparent variant of the first ed., preceding entry; but possibly the same work not precisely described.

Il s'agirait d'une variante de la première éd., notice précédente ; mais c'est peut-être le même ouvrage qui n'a pas été décrit avec précision.

1762

An address to the City of London . . . . London: printed for R[obert]. Davis, in Piccadilly, 1762. 1 p.l., 34 p. 8°(in 4s).

NUC(Pre–56)4:91*

Partly relates to the conquest of Canada — Sabin. The connection is very slight. ¶ *NUC has: 2 p.l., [3]–34 p., and notes: A defence of the ministry of the Duke of Newcastle. ¶ Further to this is:* A continuation of the address to the city of London. *London, 1762. ¶ First and probably the only edition; the other entry in NUC most likely refers to this same edition.*

Relate en partie la conquête du Canada – Sabin. Le lien entre ce sujet et cet ouvrage est ténu. ¶ *Collation du NUC : 2 f. l., [3]–34 p. ; note du NUC : Défense du ministère du duc de Newcastle. ¶ Suivi de* A continuation of the address to the city of London. *Londres, 1762. ¶ La première édition et probablement l'unique ; selon toute vraisemblance, l'autre notice du NUC se rapporte à cette même édition.*

[Almon, John], 1737–1805. A review of Mr. Pitt's administration . . . . London: printed for G[eorge]. Kearsly, 1762. 2 p.l., 5–141 p. 8°

NUC(Pre–56)10:273*

NUC has [1] p. at end. ¶ Attributed to John Almon by *Halkett and Laing.* ¶ Eulogistic of Pitt, but critical of the peace. Canada, "an almost barren province," Florida, Senegal, etc., are not worth keeping. The war in America (1759 Campaign against Canada: p. 88–103) is reviewed, and the negotiations of 29 July 1762 are discussed. ¶ *First edition; other editions: 1763 (two), 1764, and 1766; see also his* An appendix to the Review of Mr. Pitt's administration, *1763.*

Mention du NUC : [1] p. à la fin. ¶ Attribué à John Almon par *Halkett et Laing.* ¶ Élogieux à l'endroit de Pitt, mais critique à l'égard du traité. Le Canada, « une province presque déserte », la Floride, le Sénégal, etc., ne valent pas la peine de les conserver. La guerre en Amérique (campagne de 1759 contre le Canada : p. 88–103) y est examinée, et les négociations du 29 juillet 1762 y sont débattues. ¶ *Première édition ; autres éditions : 1763 (deux), 1764 et 1766 ;* voir aussi *son ouvrage intitulé* An appendix to the Review of Mr. Pitt's administration, *1763.*

[Bollan, William], *d./déc.* 1776. Observations on the preliminary articles of peace, so far as they relate to the fishery. [London, 1762.] 4 p. fol.

NUC(Pre–56)64:627*

Caption title. ¶ Endorsement for outside fold (same title) on p. 4. ¶ *This refers to the Newfoundland fishery, and the articles preliminary to the Treaty of Paris, Feb. 1763.* ¶ *Reprinted [Boston, 1941] in the second series, Photostat Americana, Mass. Hist. Soc., no. 128, from the original in the John Carter Brown Library, Providence, R. I.*

Titre de départ. ¶ Inscription officielle — pli extérieur (même titre) à la p. 4. ¶ *Cet ouvrage traite des pêcheries de Terre-Neuve, ainsi que des préliminaires du traité de Paris, fév. 1763.* ¶ *Réimpression [Boston, 1941] dans le cadre de la deuxième collection, Photostat Americana, Mass. Hist. Soc., n° 128, d'après l'original de la John Carter Brown Library, Providence (R. I.).*

[Britannicus], *pseud.* A letter to the Right Honourable the Lord Mayor, alderman, Common Council, and citizens, of London, concerning the peace now in agitation between Great Britain and France . . . . London, printed for J[ohn]. Hinxman [etc.] . . ., 1762. 1 p.l., 22 p. 8°

NUC(Pre–56)76:201

Signed: Britannicus. ¶ The writer wants England to withdraw from the destructive alliance with Germany [in the Seven Years' War], as concessions in America have to be made on that account. The French must be debarred from the fisheries, and the sugar islands, as well as Canada, should be retained.

Signé : Britannicus. ¶ L'auteur veut que l'Angleterre se retire de l'alliance néfaste qu'elle a conclue avec l'Allemagne [durant la guerre de Sept Ans], puisqu'à ce titre l'Angleterre est tenue de faire des concessions en Amérique. Il faut interdire les pêcheries aux Français et conserver les îles sucrières, ainsi que le Canada.

*[Burke, Edmund], 1729?–1797. An account of the European settlements in America .... The fourth edition, with improvements. Dublin: printed for Peter Wilson ..., 1762. 2 v. 12° (NUC has 16° in 12s).

NUC(Pre–56)85:275*

First edition: 1757, *q.v.* for full title and notes.	Première édition : 1757, *q.v.* pour le titre complet et des notes.

The comparative importance of our acquisitions from France in America. With remarks on a pamphlet, intitled, An examination of the commercial principles of the late negotiation in 1761. London: printed for J[ohn]. Hinxman ... 1762. <Price one shilling.> 2 p.l., 59 p. 8°

NUC(Pre–56)118:172

Written before the preliminary articles of peace were signed [leading to the Treaty of Paris, 1763, ending the Seven Years' War], urging in general the terms agreed upon (p. [iii]). ¶ *A reply, in part, to:* An examination of the commercial principles of the late negotiations between Great Britain and France in 1761 .... *London, Dodsley, 1762 (q.v.). ¶ First edition; second edition pub. London, J[ohn]. Hinxman, 1772. 59 p. 8° Sabin:15031.*	Rédigé avant la signature des préliminaires du traité [qui aboutirent au traité de Paris, 1763, mettant fin à la guerre de Sept Ans], cet ouvrage recommande en général d'accepter les conditions qui ont été convenues (p. [iii]). ¶ *En partie, une réplique à* An examination of the commercial principles of the late negotiations between Great Britain and France in 1761 .... *Londres, Dodsley, 1762 (q.v.). ¶ Première édition ; deuxième édition publ. à Londres, J[ohn]. Hinxman, 1772. 59 p. in–8° Sabin:15031.*

Comparative importance of the commercial principles of the late negotiation between Great Britain and France in 1761, in which the system of that negotiation with regard to our colonies and commerce is considered. The second edition. London: R[obert]. and J[ames]. Dodsley, 1762. 108 p. 8°

Sabin:15030

Sabin (and Waldon) has note: Attributed to Mr. [Edmund] Burke. ¶ Details of the first ed. not found, but Waldon suggests this is "possibly" another edition of *An examination of the commercial principles of the late negotiations.* London, 1762, *q.v.* However, the latter work has its own second ed. under the same title, *q.v.*

Note du Sabin (ainsi que de Waldon) : Attribué à M. [Edmund] Burke. ¶ Les détails de la première éd. restent introuvables, mais Waldon suggère qu'il s'agit « peut-être » d'une autre édition de *An examination of the commercial principles of the late negotiations.* Londres, 1762, *q.v.* Cependant, ce dernier ouvrage a sa propre deuxième éd. sous le même titre, *q.v.*

Considerations on the approaching peace . . . . London: printed for W. Morgan . . . 1762. vi, 33 p. 8°

NUC(Pre–56)120:390*

Waldon has collation: t.-p., v-vi, 33 p. ¶ Preliminary articles re Newfoundland and Canada discussed: p. 18–24. The writer is opposed to peace [terminating the Seven Years' War] until the French are utterly debased. The British are giving up too much — Canada and Senegal are not worth fighting for, Canada being a barren waste, the only value of holding it, to ensure peace to the fertile southern colonies. ¶ *Probably the first edition; the third edition (so presumably the second ed. also) appeared the same year,* see *next entry.*

Collation de Waldon : p. de t., v-vi, 33 p. ¶ Les préliminaires du traité concernant Terre-Neuve et le Canada sont débattus aux p. 18–24. L'auteur est contre le traité [mettant fin à la guerre de Sept Ans] jusqu'à ce que les Français soient totalement écrasés. La contrepartie consentie par les Britanniques est trop élevée – le Canada et le Sénégal ne valent pas la peine de se battre ; le Canada étant une étendue désertique, son maintien comme territoire anglais n'a qu'un seul intérêt : garantir la paix aux colonies prospères du sud. ¶ *Probablement la première édition ; la troisième édition (ainsi que très vraisemblablement la deuxième éd.) parut la même année;* voir *la notice suivante.*

*Considerations on the approaching peace . . . . 3d ed. London, 1762. [No imprint given.]

NUC(Pre–56)120:390*

See preceding entry for notes.   *Voir* notes à la notice précédente.

De la Mayne, Thomas Hallie, *fl.* 1718–1773.   The Oliviad. London, printed for J[ohn]. Scott, 1762. xii, 9–56 (and more?) p. 4°

NUC(Pre–56)137:384

NUC copy lacks all after p. 56. ¶ A scarce work on the old French war [Seven Years' War, 1756–63], and relates largely to the fall of Canada. It is possible that there were more than two cantos, although that is all that was originally designed for the poem. The pagination at the front is curious, and the signatures begin with "b" and "B."

Toutes les pages de l'exemplaire du NUC sont manquantes après la p. 56. ¶ Un ouvrage rare sur la vieille guerre avec les Français [guerre de Sept Ans, 1756–1763], qui se rapporte en grande partie à la chute du Canada. Il existait peut-être plus de deux chants, bien qu'à l'origine, le poème n'en comptât que deux. La pagination du frontispice est inusitée, et les signatures débutent par « b » et « B ».

An examination of the commercial principles of the late negotiations between Great Britain and France in MDCCLXI [1761].   In which the system of that negotiation with regard to our colonies and commerce is considered. London, printed for R[obert]. and J[ames]. Dodsley, 1762. 2 p.l., 100 p. 8°(in 4s).

NUC(Pre–56)164:469*

Attributed to William Burke, d. 1798, by Rev. William Hunt in DNB ("Wm. Burke, d. 1798"), and by Halkett and Laing (v. 9); to Edmund Burke, BLC(to 1975)7:63; to William Burke, BLC(to

Attribué à William Burke, déc. 1798, par le rév. William Hunt dans le DNB(« Wm. Burke, d. 1798 »), et par Halkett et Laing (vol. 9); attribué à Edmund Burke dans le BLC(to 1975)7:63 ; attribué à William Burke dans le

1975)48:163; and to Edward Burke in Sabin:23354. ¶ This pamphlet is a reply to Bishop Douglas's *Letter*, 1760, q.v., and to a work referred to as *Interest of the colonies* (possibly Franklin's *Interest of Great Britain*? q.v., 1760). The writer protests against the cession of the West Indian conquests to France as unnecessary. He does not propose to give up Canada, but minimizes its value. "Canada came at last to take an entire Possession of our Hearts and Understanding; and we were taught to believe, that no Cession was too great to purchase this inestimable Security .... This very groundless Opinion was the true source of our Neglect, in the late Negotiation, of such real commercial advantages as might augment the Resources of Great Britain" (p. 60–61, first ed.). ¶ *Answered by:* The comparative importance of our acquisitions from France in America. *London, 1762*, q.v., *and: Ignotus*, pseud., Thoughts on trade in general. *London, 1763*, q.v. ¶ *First edition; second edition published same year: see next entry; Sabin has first ed. published in 1761 (and second ed. 1762), but 1761 not confirmed elsewhere.*

BLC(to 1975)48:163 ; *attribué à Edward Burke dans le Sabin:23354.* ¶ Ce pamphlet est une réplique à l'écrit de l'évêque Douglas, *Letter*, 1760, q.v., et à un ouvrage désigné sous le titre *Interest of the colonies* (peut-être s'agit-il de *Interest of Great Britain* de Franklin ? q.v., 1760). L'auteur proteste contre la cession à la France des territoires conquis aux Antilles, cession qu'il juge inutile. Il ne propose pas d'abandonner le Canada mais minimise la valeur de ce territoire. « Le Canada s'est finalement emparé totalement de notre coeur et de notre esprit ; et nous avons appris à croire qu'aucune cession ne serait trop onéreuse pour acheter ce bien inestimable .... Cette opinion absolument non fondée fut, lors de la récente négociation, la véritable raison de notre négligence envers les avantages commerciaux réels susceptibles d'accroître les ressources de la Grande-Bretagne » (p. 60–61, première éd.). ¶ *Cet ouvrage a suscité les répliques suivantes :* The comparative importance of our acquisitions from France in America. *Londres, 1762*, q.v., *et : Ignotus*, pseud., Thoughts on trade in general. *Londres, 1763*, q.v. ¶ *Première édition ; deuxième édition publiée la même année :* voir *la notice suivante ; le Sabin indique 1761 comme année de publication de la première éd. (et 1762 pour la deuxième éd.), mais aucune autre source ne permet de confirmer cette date.*

An examination of... Gt. Britain and France in MDCCLXI [1761], in which the system ... is considered .... The 2d ed. .... London, Dodsley, 1762. 2 p.l., 108 p. 8°(?)

NUC(Pre–56)164:469*

First ed. published the same year: *see* preceding entry.

Première éd. publiée la même année : *voir* la notice précédente.

A full, clear and succinct discussion of the Preliminary articles of peace, as published by authority. Most humbly submitted to the King, the Senate, and the people. By an eminent citizen . . . . London: printed for S. Williams, on Ludgate-Hill. [1762?] <Price one shilling.> 2 p.l., [5]–20 p. 4°

NUC(Pre–56)187:492*

NUC has the pub. date unbracketed and unqueried. ¶ The articles are given in one column, with comments in the second, followed by a discussion of the whole. The writer is critical of some of the articles, but not all. The French should not be given such advantages in Newfoundland, and the boundaries of Canada are too vague. ¶ *The Preliminary Articles, between England, France, and Spain in the Seven Years' War, were signed at Fontainebleau, 3 Nov. 1762 (cf. BM). ¶ Apparently reissued in the following year, though NUC has the date for the 1763 entry (q.v.) in brackets. All else the same as this with each having different locations, so they may be the same edition.*

Le NUC indique la date de publ. sans crochets et sans point d'interrogation. ¶ Les préliminaires du traité sont inscrits dans la première colonne, tandis que les commentaires figurent dans la deuxième, ces deux colonnes étant suivies de débats sur l'ensemble. L'auteur se montre critique à l'égard de certains préliminaires, mais non de tous. Il ne faut pas accorder de tels avantages aux Français à Terre-Neuve, et les frontières du Canada sont trop vagues. ¶ *Les préliminaires conclus entre l'Angleterre, la France et l'Espagne lors de la guerre de Sept Ans furent signés à Fontainebleau le 3 nov. 1762 (cf. BM). ¶ Apparemment réimprimé l'année suivante, bien que la date soit indiquée entre crochets à la notice du NUC sous 1763 (q.v.). Tous les autres renseignements sont identiques à ceux de la présente, quoique les lieux diffèrent dans chaque cas, aussi s'agit-il peut-être de la même édition.*

Great Britain. Laws, statutes, etc. Anno regni Georgii III. secundo. An Act for importing salt from Europe into the colony of Nova Scotia in America. [London, printed by] Mark Baskett. 1762. fol.

"From Harmsworth ms. cat."

Most likely source is Sir Robert L. Harmsworth, *Catalogue of Americana.* [n.p., n.d.], a typescript with ms. additions (cf. NUC(Pre–56)231:382). No further infomation discovered.

La source la plus probable est sir Robert L. Harmsworth, *Catalogue of Americana* [s.l., s.d.], soit un tapuscrit comportant des ajouts man. (cf. NUC(Pre–56)231:382). Aucun autre renseignement.

Great Britain. Parliament, 1762. Papers relative to the rupture with Spain, laid before both Houses of Parliament, on Friday the twenty ninth day of January, 1762, by His Majesty's command. London: printed by Mark Baskett, printer to the King's most excellent Majesty; and by the assigns of Robert Baskett. 1762. 71 p. 4°

NUC(Pre–56)440:442*

NUC seems to indicate a preliminary leaf, before the 71 p., but BLC(to 1975)96:560 has 71 p. ¶ *Chiefly the correspondence of Mr. Pitt and the Earl of Bristol, then embassador [sic] to Spain (cf. NUC).* ¶ The Biscayans and Guipuscoans claimed the right to fish at Newfoundland, which cannot be allowed. ¶ *Sabin:58483 notes several replies, including:* Answer to the exposition of a pamphlet entitled Papers relative to the rupture with Spain. *1762, 8°, and* Answer to the Observations on the Papers relative to a rupture with Spain. *London, 1762, 35 p., 8° (respectively Sabin:1660 and 1662).* ¶ *Other editions: Dublin, 1762; with subtitle "In*

Le NUC semble indiquer un feuillet liminaire précédant les 71 p., mais le BLC(to 1975)96:560 mentionne 71 p. ¶ *Il s'agit principalement de la correspondance entre M. Pitt et le comte de Bristol, alors "embassador" [sic] auprès de l'Espagne (cf. NUC).* ¶ Les Basques des provinces de Biscaye et de Guipuzcoa ont réclamé le droit de pêcher à Terre-Neuve, ce qui ne peut être accordé. ¶ *Le Sabin:58483 mentionne plusieurs répliques, y compris :* Answer to the exposition of a pamphlet entitled Papers relative to the rupture with Spain. *1762, in-8°, et* Answer to the Observations on the Papers relative to a rupture with Spain. *Londres, 1762, 35 p., in-8° (respectivement Sabin:1660 et 1662).* ¶ *Autres éditions : Dublin, 1762 ; éd. avec sous-titre « In*

French and English," *1762; and in French as* Papiers relatifs, *1762,* q.v., *following.*

French and English », *1762 ; et en français sous le titre* Papiers relatifs, *1762,* q.v., *plus loin.*

---

*Great Britain. Parliament, 1762. Papers relative to the rupture with Spain .... Dublin, Boulter Grierson, 1762. 99 p. 8°

BLC(to 1975)96:560*

For notes and other editions, *see* preceding entry.

Voir notes et autres éditions à la notice précédente.

Great Britain. Parliament, 1762. Papers relative to the rupture with Spain. In French and English .... London: printed by E[dward]. Owen and T[homas]. Harrison, 1762. 2 p.l., 279 p. 8°

NUC(Pre–56)440:442*

Added t.-p. in French. ¶ For other notes, see preceding entries.

Ajout d'une p. de t. dans la version française. ¶ Voir *notes aux notices précédentes.*

---

*Great Britain. Parliament, 1762. Papiers relatifs á la rupture avec l'Espagne. En françois & en anglois. Publiés par autorité. Londres, T[homas]. Harrison, 1762. 279 p. 8°

BLC(to 1975)96:560*

For notes, *see* preceding entries.

Voir notes aux notices précédentes.

Great Britain. Sovereigns, etc., 1760–1820 (George III). By the King, a proclamation, declaring the cessation of arms, as well by sea as land, agreed upon between His Majesty, the Most Christian King, and the Catholick King, and enjoining the observance thereof. [26 Nov. 1762.] London: printed by Mark Baskett . . . and by the assigns of Robert Baskett. 1762. Broadside. fol.

NUC(Pre–56)215:433

Refers to the French and Spanish kings respectively, and the preliminaries to ending the Seven Years' War and the signing of the Treaty of Paris (Feb. 1763).

Se rapporte respectivement aux rois de France et d'Espagne, ainsi qu'aux préliminaires visant à mettre fin à la guerre de Sept Ans et à la signature du traité de Paris (fév. 1763).

Great Britain. Treaties, etc., 1760–1820 (George III). Preliminary articles of peace, between His Britannick Majesty, the Most Christian King, and the Catholick King. Signed at Fontainebleau, the 3d day of November, 1762. Published by authority. London, printed by E[dward]. Owen and T[homas]. Harrison, 1762. 23 p. 4°

NUC(Pre–56)215:517

French and English. ¶ These were the preliminary articles of the Treaty of Paris, 10 February 1763, q.v. under the same entry, with title: The definitive treaty of peace and friendship . . . . London, 1763. ¶ OTP

En français et en anglais. ¶ Il s'agit des préliminaires du traité de Paris, 10 février 1763, q.v. même notice dont le titre est The definitive treaty of peace and friendship . . . . Londres, 1763. ¶ OTP

[Heathcote, George]. A letter to the Right Honourable the Lord Mayor, the worshipful aldermen, and common-council; the merchants, citizens, and inhabitants, of the City of London. From an old servant . . . . London: printed for W[illiam]. Owen . . . R[obert]. Baldwin . . . and C. Pugh . . . 1762. 1 p.l., 90 p. 8°

NUC(Pre–56)237:373*

Signed, p. 79: George Heathcote. ¶ *Waldon omits the p.l. in the collation (half-title: cf. NUC).* ¶ Heathcote protests against the reported terms of peace [proposed in the Seven Years' War]. France should not be given so much in the West Indies, nor the right to fish in Newfoundland and trade in Canada. He assumes that Canada will be retained, and he is chiefly anxious over the sugar and fishery trades and France's restoration to naval power, comparing the whole trade and general position of France and England. The figures of the trade in Hudson Bay, Newfoundland, and Canada are given: p. 23–28. The appendix, p. 82–90, from the *British merchant* (v. 2, p. 284–96) is largely concerned with the fisheries of Newfoundland and Cape Breton. ¶ *A second and third edition appeared in the same year — see next entries.* ¶ *Answered by:* A reply to Mr. Heathcote's Letter. *London,* [*1762?*], q.v.

Signé, p. 79 : George Heathcote. ¶ *Waldon omet le f. l. dans la collation (faux-titre : cf. NUC).* ¶ Heathcote proteste contre les conditions du traité qui ont été annoncées [et proposées durant la guerre de Sept Ans]. La contre-partie consentie à la France dans les Antilles ne doit pas être aussi considérable, pas plus qu'il ne faut lui accorder le droit de pêcher à Terre-Neuve et de commercer au Canada. Il suppose que l'on gardera le Canada, et il s'inquiète surtout du commerce du sucre et de celui du poisson, ainsi que du rétablissement de la puissance navale de la France, ce qui l'amène à comparer la situation commerciale globale et la position générale de chaque partie, soit la France et l'Angleterre. Les chiffres relatifs au commerce à la Baie d'Hudson, à Terre-Neuve et au Canada sont fournis : p. 23–28. L'annexe, p. 82–90, tiré du *British merchant* (vol. 2, p. 284–96) traite en grande partie des pêcheries de Terre-Neuve et du Cap-Breton. ¶ *Une deuxième et une troisième éditions parurent la même année* –voir *les notices suivantes.* ¶ *Cet ouvrage a suscité la réplique suivante :* A reply to Mr. Heathcote's Letter. *Londres,* [*1762 ?*], q.v.

[**Heathcote, George**]. A letter to the Right Honourable the Lord Mayor . . . . From an old servant. The second edition . . . . London, printed for W. Nicoll, 1762. <Price one shilling and six-pence.> 1 p.l., 90 p. 8°

NUC(Pre–56)237:373*

First ed.: see preceding entry.

Première éd. : voir la notice précédente.

[Heathcote, George]. A letter .... From an old servant. The third edition ....
London, printed for W. Nicoll, 1762. 1 p.l., 90 p. 8°

NUC(Pre–56)237:373*

See *preceding entries for first and second ed., and for notes.*

Voir *première et deuxième éd., et notes aux notices précédentes.*

An impartial enquiry into the right of the French King to the territory west of the great river Mississippi, in North America, not ceded by the preliminaries, including a summary account of that river, and the country adjacent .... London, W. Nicoll, [1762.] 1 p.l., 58 p. 8°(in 4s).

NUC(Pre–56)265:191*

Waldon has pagination: t.-p., 56 p. ¶ Chiefly concerned with Louisiana, but the writer also holds that the value of the Canadian fur trade will be lessened by the French holding the Mississippi, as the Indians will still bring their furs to them from Canada. ¶ *NUC lists a microfilm reprint, undated, and a "micro-opaque," Louisville, Kentucky, Lost Cause Press, 196–? 1 card (Travels in the Old South, 1, 260).*

Pagination de Waldon : p. de t., 56 p. ¶ Traite principalement de la Louisiane, bien que l'auteur soutienne également que la possession française du Mississippi entraînera une diminution de la valeur du commerce canadien de la fourrure, puisque les Indiens continueront d'apporter aux Français des pelleteries provenant du Canada. ¶ *Le NUC répertorie une reproduction sur microfilm, non datée, et une édition sur microfiche opaque, Louisville (Kentucky), Lost Cause Press, 196– ? 1 carte (Travels in the Old South, 1, 260).*

An inquiry into the merits of the supposed preliminaries of peace, signed on the 3d instant. London, printed for John Bird, in Ave-Mary-Lane. 1762. (Price 6d.) 1 p.l., 30 p. 8°(in 4s).

NUC(Pre–56)160:470

NUC has collation: 30 p. ¶ The writer defends the Preliminary Articles [to the Treaty of Paris, 1763, to end the Seven Years' War] and considers Canada a valuable acquisition, though not one of the original objects of the war.

Collation du NUC : 30 p. ¶ L'auteur défend les préliminaires [du traité de Paris, 1763, devant mettre fin à la guerre de Sept Ans] et estime que le Canada constitue une possession de valeur, bien qu'il ne fût pas l'un des enjeux initiaux de la guerre.

A letter to a gentleman in the city. [London, 1762.] 4 p. 4°

NUC(Pre–56)329:26

Caption title. ¶ *Dated at end: Wandsworth, Sept. 5th, 1762.* ¶ *NUC has a query after the place of publication, but BLC has no such query.* ¶ The writer supports the ministry and the peace [ending the Seven Years' War, and signed in Paris in 1763], which "secured to this nation immense acquisitions, and terminated the most expensive and hazardous war we were ever engaged in with dignity and with glory." He suggests that as "the capital derives peculiar advantages from the war," the opposition to the peace on the part of some individuals may spring from motives "very different from love to their country."

Titre de départ. ¶ *Daté à la fin : Wandsworth, 5 sept. 1762.* ¶ *Le NUC marque le lieu de publication d'un point d'interrogation que, de son côté, le BLC n'indique pas.* ¶ L'auteur appuie le gouvernement et le traité [dont la signature à Paris en 1763 mit fin à la guerre de Sept Ans], qui « garantit à cette nation d'immenses possessions et met un terme à la guerre la plus onéreuse et la plus hasardeuse que nous ayons jamais faite et pour laquelle nous avons dignement et glorieusement livré bataille ». Il laisse entendre que, « compte tenu du fait que les capitalistes tirèrent particulièrement profit de la guerre », l'opposition que certaines personnes manifestent à l'égard du traité peut résulter de motifs « tout autres que l'amour de leur pays ».

A letter to the Right Honourable the Earl of Bute, on the preliminaries of peace. From neither a noble lord; a candid Member of Parliament; an impartial Briton, but, an Englishman. London, printed for W. Nicoll, 1762. 1 p.l., 60 p. 8°

"JR."

Source unidentified, and not found elsewhere. ¶ Article 2 (the acquisition of Canada, "the most material in the whole treaty"): p. 13–23. Article 3 (Newfoundland fisheries): p. 24–25. Cape Breton: p. 25–27. This writer supports the proposed peace [to end the Seven Years' War, 1756–63, which became the Peace of Paris]. ¶ *The negative phrases in the title refer to other titles on the same subject.*

Source non identifiée, introuvable ailleurs. ¶ Clause 2 (la possession du Canada, soit la question « d'importance primordiale de tout le traité ») : p. 13–23. Clause 3 (pêcheries de Terre-Neuve) : p. 24–25. Cap-Breton : p. 25–27. L'auteur appuie la proposition de traité [qui mit fin à la guerre de Sept Ans, 1756–1763, et fut appelé le traité de Paris]. ¶ *Les tournures négatives qui apparaissent dans le titre se rapportent à d'autres titres sur le même sujet.*

A letter to the Right Honourable William Pitt, esq; on the present negotiations for a peace with France and Spain . . . . London, printed for J. Coote, 1762. Price one shilling and six-pence. 1 p.l., 74 p. 8°(in 4s).

NUC(Pre–56)329:119

This is an attack on Pitt. The [Seven Years'] war was undertaken to fix the limits of Canada, not to conquer it, but Britain has gone on to conquest after conquest. The writer agrees to giving up Guadeloupe, peace on the best terms obtainable being more important than anything else. If all the French possessions in North America are taken, the result will be a general combination against Britain. ¶ *This*

Il s'agit d'une attaque dirigée contre Pitt. L'Angleterre est entrée en guerre [il s'agit de la guerre de Sept Ans] pour régler la question des frontières du Canada et non pour en faire la conquête, mais elle a remporté victoire après victoire. L'auteur consent à ce que l'Angleterre renonce à la Guadeloupe, la conclusion d'un traité aux meilleures conditions possibles primant sur toute autre considération. Si la France est dépouillée de toutes ses possessions en

edition only in NUC.

Amérique du Nord, cette situation engendrera une coalition générale contre la Grande-Bretagne. ¶ *Cette édition figure uniquement dans le NUC.*

[Marriott, Sir **James],** 1730?–1803. Political considerations; being a few thoughts of a candid man at the present crisis. In a letter to a noble lord retired from power. London, printed for J[ohn]. Hinxman . . . 1762. [4], 112 p. 8°(in 4s).

NUC(Pre–56)363:203

Title vignette. ¶ *The author was Advocate General, and judge in the Admiralty Court.* ¶ This writer urges moderation in the peace terms [to the Seven Years' War, signed in Paris the following year, 1763], lest the rest of Europe band against England as it had against France in the days of her arrogance. The colonies must be made secure, but not the whole of America seized. ¶ *OTP · BVAU*

Titre vignette. ¶ *L'auteur était Procureur général et juge à l'Admiralty Court.* ¶ L'auteur conseille vivement de faire preuve de pondération en ce qui a trait aux conditions du traité [qui mit fin à la guerre de Sept Ans et qui fut signé à Paris l'année suivante, en 1763], de crainte que le reste de l'Europe ne se ligue contre l'Angleterre, comme cela fut le cas contre la France à l'époque de son arrogance. Il faut assurer la sécurité des colonies, mais non accaparer toute l'Amérique. ¶ *OTP · BVAU*

Massie, Joseph, *d./déc.* 1784. An historical account of the naval power of France, from its first foundation to the present time. With a state of the English fisheries at Newfoundland for 150 years past. And various computations, observations, &c. proper to be considered at this decisive juncture. To which is added, a narrative of the proceedings of the French at Newfoundland, from the reign of King Charles the First to the reign of Queen Anne; shewing what measures were taken on the part of England, during that interval, in relation to the said French proceedings, &c. — First printed in the year 1712, and now reprinted for general information .... Most humbly submitted to the consideration of the Parliament and people of Great Britain. London: sold by T[homas]. Payne ... and W[illiam]. Owen, 1762. 19, 5 p. 4°

NUC(Pre–56)368:355

"A letter from a West-India merchant to a gentleman at Tunbridge, concerning that part of the French proposals, which relates to North-America, and particularly Newfoundland": 5 p. at end. ¶ *Waldon notes: second ed., 1763; but she does not further identify this, nor the 1712 printing noted on the t.-p.; neither work has been found in NUC or Sabin.*

« A letter from a West-India merchant to a gentleman at Tunbridge, concerning that part of the French proposals, which relates to North-America, and particulièrement Newfoundland » : 5 p. à la fin. ¶ *Waldon indique : deuxième éd., 1763, sans toutefois fournir davantage de précisions sur cette édition, ni sur l'édition de 1712 qui est inscrite sur la p. de t. ; ces deux ouvrages ne figurent ni dans le NUC ni dans le Sabin.*

Ogden, James, 1718–1802. The British lion rous'd; or, Acts of the British worthies, a poem in nine books, by James Ogden. Manchester: printed by R. Whitworth ... 1762. <Price five shillings.> [24], 223 p. 8°

NUC(Pre–56)427:561

Collation in NUC omits the preliminary 24 p., the separate contents of which are not identified by Waldon. ¶ The poem covers the principal events of the struggle between England and France for the possession of North America.

La collation du NUC ne mentionne pas les 24 p. liminaires, dont la table des matières distincte n'est pas indiquée par Waldon. ¶ Le poème couvre les principaux événements de la lutte que se sont livrée l'Angleterre et la France pour la possession de l'Amérique du Nord.

The proper object of the present war with France and Spain considered; and the independence of Great Britain vindicated from any connection with foreign politics. London: printed for W[illiam]. Johnston, 1762. 2 p.l., 68 p. 8°

Louisbourg: p. 27; the Newfoundland fisheries: p. 25–29; Canada: p. 53; French and English treatment of Indians: p. 58. To give up the Newfoundland fisheries for the demolition of Dunkirk is a mistake. If the French would keep the peace for thirty or forty years, their advantages in trade, etc., would gain them superiority over England: p. 23. ¶ *Concerns the Seven Years' War.*

Louisbourg : p. 27 ; les pêcheries de Terre-Neuve : p. 25–29 ; Canada : p. 53 ; le traitement des Indiens par les Français et par les Anglais : p. 58. C'est une erreur de renoncer aux pêcheries de Terre-Neuve en contrepartie du démantèlement de Dunkerque. Si la France maintient une situation de paix durant trente ou quarante ans, elle supplantera l'Angleterre grâce à sa position commerciale avantageuse, etc. : p. 23. ¶ *Se rapporte à la guerre de Sept Ans.*

A reply to Mr. Heathcote's Letter, from an honest man. In which the arguments are proved to be delusive; and the facts untrue. . . . London, printed for W. Morgan [1762]. (Price one shilling.) 39 p. 8°

NUC(Pre–56)489:55

Concerns the proposed peace terms with France in the Seven Years' War. ¶ The writer challenges not only Heathcote's opinions, but also his facts, denying that the French ever had as many fishing vessels as Heathcote states. Moreover, their trade depended on the possession of Cape Breton, now lost to them. What allowance the British now make them will be no great danger to Britain, and it is impossible to retain all conquests. If the Preliminaries, signed at Fontainebleau 3 November are correctly

Traite des conditions de la proposition de traité avec la France lors de la guerre de Sept Ans. ¶ L'auteur conteste non seulement les opinions de Heathcote, mais encore les faits rapportés par celui-ci. Il nie notamment que les Français aient jamais possédé un nombre de bateaux de pêche aussi élevé que Heathcote l'indique. En outre, leur commerce était subordonné à la possession du Cap-Breton, lequel ne leur appartient plus. Quelle que soit la compensation que les Britanniques leur consentent maintenant, cela n'est pas très dangereux pour la Grande-Bretagne, et il est impossible de

reported in the papers, this is the most glorious peace Britain ever made. Guadeloupe is not serviceable, the French share in the fisheries of no consequence, while Britain gains superiority in the East Indies, Louisbourg, all Canada, Florida, Louisiana west of the Mississippi, and other possessions. ¶ *A reply to: George Heathcote*, A letter to the Right Honourable the Lord Mayor. *London, 1762* (q.v.).

conserver toutes les conquêtes. Si les préliminaires signés à Fontainebleau le 3 novembre sont rapportés avec exactitude, c'est le traité le plus glorieux que la Grande-Bretagne ait jamais conclu. La Guadeloupe est de peu d'utilité, et la part de la France en ce qui a trait aux pêcheries est insignifiante, tandis que la Grande-Bretagne est avantagée dans les Indes orientales, à Louisbourg, dans tout le Canada, en Floride, en Louisiane à l'ouest du Mississippi, et dans d'autres possessions. ¶ *Réplique à George Heathcote*, A letter to the Right Honourable the Lord Mayor. *Londres, 1762* (q.v.).

[Shebbeare, John], 1709–1788, *supposed author/auteur présumé*. One more letter to the people of England. By their old friend . . . . London: printed for J[ohn]. Pridden, 1762. 1 p.l., 71 p. 8°

The "supposed author" added from NUC. ¶ Dated: London, Nov. 25, 1762. ¶ Shebbeare reviews the causes and course of the war, and outlines possible terms of peace. The sugar islands must be retained. Canada, in his view, is less valuable for the fur trade than is commonly supposed. It is a waste, but must be held to keep out "a most perfidious and perverse set of men." ¶ *For other works by Shebbeare*, see *under 1755 and 1756.*

L'ajout de la mention « auteur présumé » est tiré du NUC. ¶ Daté : Londres, le 25 nov. 1762. ¶ Shebbeare examine les causes et le déroulement de la guerre, puis il donne un aperçu des conditions possibles du traité. Il faut garder les îles sucrières. À son avis, le Canada a moins de valeur pour le commerce de la fourrure qu'on ne le suppose généralement. Ce ne sont que terres immenses et désolées, auxquelles il faut pourtant reconnaître le mérite d'être peu invitantes pour « toute une catégorie de traîtres et de gredins de la pire espèce ». ¶ Voir *d'autres ouvrages de Shebbeare sous 1755 et 1756.*

Smith, William, 1727–1803. Discourses on public occasions in America. By William Smith . . . . The second edition. Containing. I. Sundry discourses during the ravages of the French and Indians . . . . II. A thanksgiving-discourse . . . . With an Appendix, containing, I. *A letter to a clergyman on the frontiers of Pennsylvania, on Braddock's defeat . . . . II. An address to the colonies, on opening the campaign, 1758 . . . . London: printed for A[ndrew]. Millar, R[alph]. Griffiths [and others] 1762. xvi, 224, 160 p. 8°

NUC(Pre–56)552:310*

For the first edition and other notes, see *above, under 1759; a variant follows.* ¶ *NSWA · OTP*

Voir *première édition et autres notes plus haut, sous 1759 ; une variante est donnée ci-dessous.* ¶ *NSWA · OTP*

Smith, William, 1727–1803. Discourses on public occasions . . . . London: printed for A[ndrew]. Millar, D. Wilson and T[homas]. Becket and P[eter]. A[braham]. De Hondt, in the Strand; and G[eorge]. Keith, in Grace church Street. 1762. xvi, vi, [7]–115 p., 1 l., ii, [121]–224, 160 [Appendix] p. 8°

Sabin:84599.

Sabin explains the irregular paging as caused by cancellation. ¶ *From the same setting of type as the work in the preceding entry, except for the imprint (cf. Sabin: 84600n.).*

Le Sabin explique que la pagination irrégulière résulterait de la suppression de certains passages. ¶ *Tiré d'une composition identique à celle de l'ouvrage de la notice précédente, sauf en ce qui a trait à l'adresse bibliographique (cf. Sabin: 84600n.).*

Williamson, Peter, 1730–1799. French and Indian cruelty; exemplified in the life . . . of Peter Williamson, who was carried off from Aberdeen in his infancy, and sold as a slave in Pensylvania. Containing the history of the author's adventures in N. America; his captivity among the Indians, and manner of his escape; the customs, dress, &c. of the savages; military operations in that quarter; with a description of the British settlements, &c. &c. To which is added, an account of the proceedings of the magistrates of Aberdeen against him on his return to Scotland; a brief history of his process against them before the Court of Session, and a short dissertation on kidnapping. The fifth edition, with large improvements. Edinburgh: printed for the author, and sold by him, 1762. vi, 147 p. front. (port.). 12°

NUC(Pre–56)665:613*

The text has been revised after p. 138. The plan for conquering Canada is omitted. ¶ *First edition: 1757, q.v. (variant title but beginning the same) for other notes and editions.* ¶ *OTY*

Le texte a été revu après la p. 138. On a omis le plan pour la conquête du Canada. ¶ *Première édition : 1757, q.v. (variante de titre, dont le début est toutefois identique) pour d'autres notes et éditions.* ¶ *OTY*

1763

An address to the people of Great-Britain and Ireland, on the preliminaries of peace, signed November 3, 1762, between Great-Britain, France, and Spain. London: Printed for Mess. Whiston and White in Fleetstreet; and E. Dilly in the Poultry. 1763. <Price six-pence.> 24 p. 8°(in 4s).

NUC(Pre–56)4:105

Signed, p. 18: J. B. "Postscript," p. 19–24, is by Sir John Vanbrugh. ¶ The author is satisfied with the preliminaries [towards the peace settlement].

Signé, p. 18 : J. B. « Postface », p. 19–24, est de sir John Vanbrugh. ¶ L'auteur est satisfait des préliminaires [préludant à la conclusion du traité].

*[Almon, John], 1737–1805. An impartial history of the late war, deduced from the committing of hostilities in 1749, to the signing of the definitive treaty of peace in 1763. London, printed for J. Johnson, 1763. 388 p. illus. 12°

NUC(Pre–56)10:271*

The "treaty of peace" is the Treaty of Paris, Feb. 1763, which ended the Seven Years' War (1756–63). ¶ First edition (format from Sabin:34374); another edition appeared later the same year (*q.v.*, below).

Le « traité de paix » en question est le traité de Paris, qui fut signé au mois de février 1763 et mit fin à la guerre de Sept Ans (1756–1763). ¶ Première édition (format tiré du Sabin:34374) ; une autre édition parut plus tard la même année (*q.v.*, plus loin).

[Almon, John], 1737–1805. An impartial history of the late war. Deduced from the committing of hostilities in 1749, to the signing of the definitive treaty of peace in 1763. The second edition, with an index. London: printed for J. Johnson, opposite the Monument; and J. Curtis, in Fleet-Street. 1763. iv, [9]–421 p. plates, ports. (incl. front.). 12°(?)

NUC(Pre–56)10:272*

The Newberry copy is extra illustrated from the first edition. Attributed to John Almon by Sabin, accepted by *Halkett and Laing*. The Sabin entry is presumably the first edition in the same year, with collation: 12°, portraits and plates. OTP ¶ See *1763 (first ed.), above.*

L'exemplaire de Newberry comporte davantage d'illustrations que la première édition. Attribué à John Almon par le Sabin, et confirmé par *Halkett et Laing*. La notice du Sabin porte, on présume, sur la première édition de la même année, avec la collation suivante : in–12°, portraits et planches. OTP ¶ Voir *1763 (première éd.), plus haut.*

[Almon, John], 1737–1805. A review of Lord Bute's administration, by the author of the Review of Mr. Pitt's . . . . London: printed for I[ohn]. Pridden, 1763. (Price two shillings.) 116 p. 8°

NUC(Pre–56)10:273*

Critical of Lord Bute and the "disadvantageous and insecure" peace [of Feb. 1763, the Treaty of Paris]. Newfoundland: p. 43–51; terms of peace: p. 88–99.¶ *First edition; a third edition appeared the same year:* see *next entry.*

Se montre critique à l'égard de lord Bute et du traité « désavantageux et incertain » [traité de Paris, fév. 1763]. Terre-Neuve : p. 43–51 ; conditions de paix : p. 88–99. ¶ *Première édition ; une troisième édition parut la même année :* voir *la notice suivante.*

*[Almon, John], 1737–1805. A review of Lord Bute's Administration . . . . 3d ed. London: 1763. 152 p. 8°(in 4s).

NUC(Pre–56)10:273*

See first ed., above.

Voir première éd., plus haut.

[Almon, John], 1737–1805. A review of Mr. Pitt's administration . . . . 2d ed., with several alterations and additions. London, printed for G[eorge]. Kearsly, in Ludgate Street. 1763. viii, 7–150 p. 8°

NUC(Pre–56)10:273*

See *1762.* ¶ *OTP*

Voir *1762.* ¶ *OTP*

[Almon, John], 1737–1805. A review of Mr. Pitt's administration .... 3d ed., with several alterations and additions. London, 1763. viii, 9–152 p. 8°

NUC(Pre–56)10:273*

See *1762*.   Voir *1762*.

An appeal to knowledge: or, Candid discussions of the preliminaries of peace, signed at Fontainebleau, Nov. 3., 1762, and laid before both Houses of Parliament .... By a Member of Parliament. London: printed for J[ohn]. Wilkie ... 1763. 84 p. 8°(in 4s).

NUC(Pre–56)18:493

Title refers to the preliminaries to the peace ending the Seven Years' War, sealed by the Treaty of Paris, Feb. 1763. This work was thus published early in 1763.

Le titre se rapporte aux préliminaires du traité mettant fin à la guerre de Sept Ans. Ces préliminaires aboutirent à la conclusion du traité de Paris au mois de février 1763. Cet ouvrage fut donc publié au début de 1763.

[Bath, William Pulteney, *earl of/comte de*], 1684–1764. Reflections on the domestic policy .... London, 1763.

NUC(Pre–56)39:126

See 1761 for notes. ¶ OTP   *Voir* notes sous 1761. ¶ OTP

*Capitulations and extracts of treaties relating to Canada; with His Majesty's proclamation of 1763, establishing the government of Quebec. [London?] 1763. 41 p. 8°

Casey:358

In French and English.   En français et en anglais.

Charlevoix, Pierre François Xavier de, 1682–1761. Letters to the Dutchess of Lesdiguières; giving an account of a voyage to Canada, and travels through that vast country, and Louisiana, to the Gulf of Mexico. Undertaken by order of the present King of France, by Father Charlevoix. Being a more full and accurate description of Canada, and the neighbouring countries than has been before published; the character of every nation or tribe in that vast tract being given; their religion, customs, manners, traditions, government, languages, and towns; the trade carried on with them, and at what places; the posts or forts, and settlements, established by the French; the great lakes, water-falls, and rivers, with the manner of navigating them; the mines, fisheries, plants, and animals of these countries. With reflections on the mistakes the French have committed in carrying on their trade and settlements; and the most proper method of proceeding pointed out. Including also an account of the author's shipwreck in the Channel of Bahama, and return in a boat to the Mississippi, along the coast of the Gulf of Mexico, with his voyage from thence to St. Domingo, and back to France. Printed for R[obert]. Goadby, and sold by R[obert]. Baldwin in Pater-Noster-Row, London, 1763. xiv, [2], 384 p. front. (fold. map). 8°

NUC(Pre–56)104:170

Errata: first of [2] p. preceding p. 1. ¶ Transl. from his: Histoire et description générale de la Nouvelle France. *Paris, 1744. 3 v. (considered to be the first general history of Canada): vol. 3,* Journal d'un voyage. *¶ This is a new translation of the* Journal, *with a few footnotes added for English readers. It omits the Preliminary discourse found in vol. 3 of the first 4°edition, Paris, 1744, and contains only thirty-five of the*

Errata : la première de [2] p. précédant la p. 1. ¶ Trad. de son ouvrage : Histoire et description générale de la Nouvelle France. *Paris, 1744. 3 vol. (considéré comme étant la première histoire générale du Canada) : vol. 3,* Journal d'un voyage. *¶ Il s'agit d'une nouvelle traduction du* Journal, *assortie de quelques notes infrapaginales à l'intention des lecteurs anglais. On n'y retrouve pas le Discours préliminaire qui figure dans le vol. 3 de la première édition in–4°, Paris, 1744. Il ne comprend que trente-cinq des*

thirty-six Letters, beginning with Letter II, here numbered I. The "New map of North America," dated 1763, retains for the area west of the St. Lawrence the appellation "New France or Canada." ¶ "Advertisement of the translator" (second of [2] p. before p. 1) calls this "the most perfect Account of Canada that is extant"; and also "it is said that it was from this Work in particular that our Ministers formed their Notions of the Importance of Canada" — referring to the French original of Paris, 1744, and the British decision to invade Canada. ¶ First English transl.: Journal of a voyage. London, 1761, q.v. for notes on other editions of this, and for a transl. of the Histoire, cited above. ¶ NSWA · OKQ · BVIPA

trente-six Lettres et commence par la Lettre II, qui porte le numéro I dans cette édition. La « New map of North America » (nouvelle carte de l'Amérique du Nord), datée de 1763, conserve l'appellation « New France or Canada » (Nouvelle France ou Canada) pour désigner le territoire s'étendant à l'ouest du Saint-Laurent. ¶ À la rubrique « Advertisement of the translator » (note du traducteur) (deuxième de [2] p. avant la p. 1), cet ouvrage est qualifié de « description existante du Canada la plus achevée » ; puis le traducteur ajoute : « On dit que cet ouvrage en particulier a permis à nos ministres de juger de l'importance du Canada », – se rapportant à l'original en français, Paris, 1744, et à la décision des Britanniques d'envahir le Canada. ¶ Première trad. en anglais : Journal of a voyage. Londres, 1761, q.v. pour des notes sur d'autres éditions de cet ouvrage, et pour une trad. de l'Histoire, susmentionnée. ¶ NSWA · OKQ · BVIPA

Church of England. Liturgy and Ritual. A form of prayer and thanksgiving to Almighty God; to be used in all churches and chapels throughout England, the Dominion of Wales, and town of Berwick upon Tweed, on Thursday the fifth day of May next, being the day appointed by proclamation for a general thanksgiving to Almighty God, for putting an end to the late bloody and expensive war, by the conclusion of a just and honourable peace. By His Majesty's special command. London: printed by Mark Baskett, printer to the King's most Excellent Majesty; and by the assigns of Robert Baskett. 1763. 14 p. 12°

NUC(Pre–56)109:165

Waldon has collation: t.-p., 5–14 p. ¶ Marks the end of the Seven Years' War, 1756–63, and the Treaty of Paris, 1763. ¶ NBFU(MF) · QMU(MF) · OOA · OONL(MF) · AEU(MF)

Collation de Waldon : p. de t., 5–14 p. ¶ Atteste la fin de la guerre de Sept Ans, 1756–1763, ainsi que la signature du traité de Paris, 1763. ¶ NBFU(mic.) · QMU(mic.) · OOA · OONL(mic.) · AEU(mic.)

A Complete history of the origin and progress of the late war, from its commencement, to the exchange of the ratifications of peace between Great-Britain, France, and Spain: on the 10th of February, 1763, and to the signing of the treaty at Hubertsberg, between the King of Prussia the Empress-Queen, and the Elector of Saxony, on the 15th of the same month. In which, all the battles, sieges, sea-engagements, and every other transaction worthy of public attention, are faithfully recorded; with political and military observations . . . . London: printed for W. Nicol, 1763. 2 v. 8°

NUC(Pre–56)118:244*

Concerns the Treaty of Paris, 10 Feb. 1763, ending the Seven Years' War, 1756–63. ¶ First edition; second (?) ed. pub. 1764 (*q.v.*).

Se rapporte au traité de Paris, 10 fév. 1763, qui mit fin à la guerre de Sept Ans, 1756–1763. ¶ Première édition ; deuxième (?) éd. publ. 1764 (*q.v.*).

Considerations on the present peace, as far as it is relative to the colonies, and the African trade . . . . London: printed for W. Bristow, 1763. <Price one shilling.> 1 p.l., 68 p. 8°

NUC(Pre–56)120:396

Waldon has collation: t.-p., iv, 68 p. ¶ This defends the peace [Peace of Paris, Feb. 1763], holding that the conquests in North America are worth more than the sugar islands given up.

Collation de Waldon : p. de t., iv, 68 p. ¶ Cet ouvrage intervient en faveur du traité [traité de Paris, fév. 1763] et soutient que les conquêtes en Amérique du Nord ont plus de valeur que les îles sucrières auxquelles on a renoncé.

Curious and authentic memoirs concerning a late peace, concluded between the Rooks and Jackdaws. Extracted from the general history of the annual assembly of birds, and other undoubted authorities. London: printed for George Burnett...1763. <Price 1s. 6d.> 1 p.l., 70 p. 8°

BM(to 1955)157:727

BM notes: A political satire. ¶ *Further to: Junius,* pseud. A letter to an honourable brigadier general. *London, 1760* (q.v.). ¶ A fable eulogizing Pitt's conduct of the war and Bute's terms of peace. The Rooks represent the English and the Jackdaws the French. The contest in America is given prominence and there is a reference to Lord George Townshend's failure to mention Wolfe in his account of the conquest of Quebec.

Note du BM : Satire politique. ¶ *Fait suite à* A letter to an honourable brigadier general. *Londres, 1760, de Junius,* pseud. (q.v.). ¶ Une fable faisant l'éloge de Pitt pour la façon dont il a mené la guerre, et de Bute pour les conditions qu'il a obtenues lors de la conclusion du traité. Les Corneilles représentent les Anglais, et les Corbeaux incarnent les Français. Dans cette fable, la lutte en Amérique occupe une place prépondérante, et il est fait mention que lord George Townshend a omis de rapporter le rôle de Wolfe, dans son récit de la conquête de Québec.

Dobson, John, *fl.* 1760. Chronological annals of the war; from its beginning to the present time. In two parts. Part I. Containing from April 2, 1755, to the end of 1760. Part II. — From the beginning of 1761, to the signing of the preliminaries of the peace. With an introductory preface to each part, a conclusion, and a general index to the whole. By Mr. Dobson. Oxford, at the Clarendon Press. 1763. 1 p.l., xv, 327, [8] p. fold. table. 8°

NUC(Pre–56)145:349

Waldon's collation reads: t.-p., xv, 323, [13] p. ¶ *Concerns the Peace of Paris, ending the Seven Years' War (1756–63).* ¶ *Waldon notes Sabin:20415, which omits "By Mr. Dobson" and collates as xv, 327 p., as possibly another edition.*

Collation de Waldon : p. de t., xv, 323, [13] p. ¶ *Se rapporte au traité de Paris, qui mit fin à la guerre de Sept Ans (1756–1763).* ¶ *Waldon note que la cote du Sabin:20415, où ne figure pas la mention « By Mr. Dobson » et dont la collation est : xv, 327 p., correspond peut-être à une autre édition.*

Egmont, John Percival, *2d earl of/2ᵉ comte de,* 1711–1770.   To the King's Most Excellent Majesty, the memorial of John, Earl of Egmont, to the King [desiring "from his Majesty a grant of the whole island of Saint John's in the Gulph of Saint Laurence" etc.; presented in December, 1763. London, 1763?]. 32 p. 8°

NUC(Pre–56)156:510

NUC dates this 1764, which seems quite possible in view of the date of the presentation, late in 1763. ¶ Caption title. ¶ This contains a plan of settlement and a list of officers, etc., desirous of taking up grants. ¶ *A proposal for the settlement of the Island of St. John's (Prince Edward Island) under a system of feudal tenure. This memorial was the third drawn up on the subject by the Earl of Egmont.* ¶ NSWA · OTP

Le NUC date cet ouvrage de 1764, ce qui paraît tout à fait plausible par rapport à la date de présentation, soit à la fin de 1763. ¶ Titre de départ. ¶ On y trouve un plan de colonisation et une liste des officiers et autres qui étaient désireux d'obtenir des concessions. ¶ *Une proposition visant la colonisation de l'île Saint-Jean (Île-du-Prince-Édouard) selon un système de tenure féodale. C'est le troisième mémoire que le comte d'Egmont rédigea sur le sujet.* ¶ NSWA · OTP

*The English pilot; the fourth book describing the West-India navigation from Hudson's-Bay. . . . London, W[illiam]. and J[ohn]. Mount, and T[homas]. Page, 1763. 66 p. illus., fold. charts. fol.

NUC(Pre–56)160:374*

First edition: 1689, *q.v.* for dates of the many other editions, including the 1706, which has a similar title, but is given in more detail.

Première édition : 1689, *q.v.* pour les dates des nombreuses autres éditions, y compris celle de 1706, dont le titre est similaire bien que plus détaillé.

*A full, clear, and succinct discussion . . . . London, [1763]. 20 p. 4°(?)

NUC(Pre–56)187:492*

Preliminary articles, with remarks, in parallel columns: p. [5]–16. ¶ First pub. 1762, *q.v.* for other notes.

Préliminaires assortis d'observations, inscrits dans des colonnes parallèles : p. [5]–16. ¶ Première publ. 1762, *q.v.* pour d'autres notes.

Great Britain. Treaties, etc., 1760–1820 (George III). The definitive treaty of peace and friendship, between His Britannick Majesty, the most Christian King, and the King of Spain. Concluded at Paris, the 10th day of February, 1763. To which, the King of Portugal acceded on the same day. Published by authority. London: printed by E[dward]. Owen and T[homas]. Harrison, 1763. 48 p. 4°

NUC(Pre–56)215:516

French and English in parallel columns ("His Britannick Majesty's full power" in Latin and English; "His Catholick Majesty's full power" in Spanish and English; "His most faithful Majesty's full power" in Portuguese and English). ¶ This is the Treaty of Paris, which ended the Seven Years' War, under which France retained her fishing rights off Newfoundland and in the Gulf of St. Lawrence, with St. Pierre and Miquelon, while Britain received Canada, Nova Scotia, and Cape Breton.

Textes anglais et français en colonnes parallèles (« His Britannick Majesty's full power » en latin et en anglais ; « His Catholick Majesty's full power » en espagnol et en anglais ; « His most faithful Majesty's full power » en portugais et en anglais). ¶ Il s'agit du traité de Paris, qui mit fin à la guerre de Sept Ans, en vertu duquel la France conservait ses droits de pêche au large des côtes de Terre-Neuve et dans le golfe Saint-Laurent, ainsi que Saint-Pierre et Miquelon, tandis que la Grande-Bretagne recevait le Canada, la Nouvelle-Écosse et le Cap-Breton.

[Ignotus], *pseud.* Thoughts on trade in general, our West-Indian in particular, our continental colonies, Canada, Guadaloupe, and the preliminary articles of peace. Addressed to the community. London, printed for John Wilkie . . . 1763. <Price one shilling and six-pence.> 86 p. 8°

NUC(Pre–56)263:572

Homer, p. 145. ¶ Signed: Ignotus. December, 1762. ¶ A reply to *An examination of the commercial principles*. London, 1762, *q.v.* ¶ The writer is an advocate for Canada.

Homer, p. 145. ¶ Signé : Ignotus. Décembre 1762. ¶ Réplique à *An examination of the commercial principles*. Londres, 1762, *q.v.* ¶ L'auteur milite pour le Canada.

The late administration epitomised; an epistle in verse to the Right Honourable William Pitt, esq. London, printed: and sold by W[illiam]. Bathoe near Exeter-Change in the Strand. 1763. 32 p. 4°

NUC(Pre–56)317:437

The year 1763 marked the close of the Seven Years' War. ¶ A eulogy of Pitt, with reference to the glorious conquests of Canada, and the capture of Louisbourg and Quebec. The author regrets the concessions to France in regard to the Newfoundland trade, as he fears that the fisheries given to France will breed sailors.

L'année 1763 marque la cessation de la guerre de Sept Ans. ¶ Un panégyrique de Pitt, par rapport aux conquêtes glorieuses au Canada et aux prises de Louisbourg et de Québec. L'auteur regrette les concessions accordées à la France en ce qui a trait au commerce de Terre-Neuve, car il craint que les pêcheries données à la France n'augmentent le nombre des marins.

Reflections on the terms of peace . . . . London, printed for G[eorge]. Kearsly, in Ludgate-Street. 1763. 1 p.l., 50 p. 8°(in 4s).

NUC(Pre–56)485:320*

This writer is satisfied with the terms of peace [of the Treaty of Paris, ending the Seven Years' War, Feb. 1763]. Canada *vs.* Guadeloupe is discussed p. 5–7. The sugar islands may be of more immediate value, but

Cet auteur est satisfait des conditions de paix [du traité de Paris, qui mit fin à la guerre de Sept Ans en fév. 1763]. La controverse Canada *c.* Guadeloupe est débattue à la p. 5–7. Les îles sucrières représentent peut-être une valeur supérieure dans l'immédiat,

the continental acquisitions will prove more enduring gains. Concessions to the French in regard to the fisheries are of little consequence: p. 21–23, 35. ¶ *First edition; second ed., the same year, follows.*

mais les possessions continentales s'avéreront des gains plus durables. Les concessions accordées aux Français en ce qui a trait aux pêcheries importent peu : p. 21–23, 35. ¶ *Première édition ; deuxième éd., la même année, ci-dessous.*

Reflections on the terms of peace . . . . 2d ed. London, printed for G[eorge]. Kearsly, 1763. 2 p.l., 50 p. 8°(in 4s).

NUC(Pre–56)485:320*

See *preceding entry for first ed. and notes.*

Voir *première éd. et notes à la notice précédente.*

A review of the arguments for an immature peace in which they are refuted by a series of reasons entirely new; shewing, how we might have brought fifty thousand Russians, Danes, Swedes, &c. to our assistance without any expence to us, and thereby have kept our principal conquests. By a nobleman. Never turned in, nor turned out. London: printed for J. Lewis, Tower-Street; and sold by Mrs. Cooke . . . and others. 1763. (price 1s. 6d.) 1 p.l., 61 p. 8°(in 4s).

NUC(Pre–56)490:242

NUC has collation "2 pts. in 1 v.," and notes "No. 2 in vol. lettered: Historical tracts, Colonial, v. 8, 1762–70." ¶ The writer objects to giving up conquests [after the Seven Years' War], and fears that the English have so weakened themselves by giving up so much that they will not be able to hold the colonies they have retained.

Collation du NUC : « 2 part. en 1 vol. » ; note du NUC : « N°2 dans le vol. marqué comme suit : Historical tracts, Colonial, v. 8, 1762–70 ». ¶ L'auteur désapprouve l'abandon des conquêtes [à la suite de la guerre de Sept Ans] et craint que l'affaiblissement que les Anglais se sont eux-mêmes infligés en renonçant à autant de conquêtes ne les empêche de maintenir les colonies qu'ils ont conservées.

[Rocque, Jean], *d./déc.* 1762. A set of plans and forts in America, reduced from actual surveys. [London, Mary Ann Rocque] 1763. 1 l., 30 engraved double plans (1 fold.). 4°

NUC(Pre–56)499:546*

Illus. engraved double t.-p. ¶ The plans illustrate the campaign against Canada and Nova Scotia [in the Seven Years' War]. ¶ *Reprinted [London] 1765; issued in Microfilm, Ann Arbor, Mich., University Microfilms, 1950s? (American Culture series, no. 153). Waldon notes that there were three issues, two in 1763, one in 1765, "the only difference being in the title-page."*

Gravures sur p. de t. double. ¶ Les plans illustrent la campagne contre le Canada et la Nouvelle-Écosse [durant la guerre de Sept Ans]. ¶ *Réimpression [Londres] 1765 ; reproduit sur microfilm, Ann Arbor (Mich.), University Microfilms, vers 1950 ? (collection American Culture, n° 153). Waldon relève qu'il y eut trois tirages, dont deux en 1763 et un en 1765, « qui ne se distinguent l'un de l'autre que par la page de titre ».*

Short, Richard, *fl.* 1759–1763. [Six perspective views of Belle Isle, from drawings made by command of Admiral Keppell, by R. Short.] London. 1763. 6 plates. fol.

Sabin:80569

Reproduced in MF and MFiche in Selected Americana from Sabin's Dictionary series. ¶ *BVAU(MF)*

Reproduit sur microfilm et sur microfiches dans la collection Selected Americana, tiré du dictionnaire Sabin. ¶ *BVAU(mic.)*

Some hints to people in power, on the present melancholy situation of our colonies in North America . . . . London: Printed for J[ohn]. Hinxman, 1763. vi, [7]–47, [1] p. 8°

NUC(Pre–56)555:671*

Waldon has: 47 [i.e. 45], [1] p., but does not explain the discrepancy. Format is from Sabin:86649. ¶ The author, who

Waldon indique : 47 [c.-à-d. 45], [1] p., mais elle n'explique pas la disparité des renseignements. ¶ *Le format provient du Sabin:86649.*

claims to have had experience in the fur trade, wishes his work considered "an abstracted corollary" to the two great pamphlets, [Benjamin Franklin's] *Interest of Great Britain considered* [London, 1760] and [Charles Lee's] *The importance of Canada considered* [London, 1761, both *q.v.*]. He summarizes and quotes from these works and approves the peace [of Paris, ending the Seven Years' War, 1756–63], arguing that no West Indian acquisition could compare in importance with Canada. ¶ *A MF was made of the LC copy of this (cf. NUC).* ¶ *OTP*

¶ Affirmant posséder de l'expérience dans le commerce de la fourrure, l'auteur souhaite que son ouvrage soit considéré comme « un corollaire abrégé » des deux principaux pamphlets, soit [celui de Benjamin Franklin] *Interest of Great Britain considered* [Londres, 1760] et [celui de Charles Lee] *The importance of Canada considered* [Londres, 1761, q.v. les deux], pamphlets qu'il résume et qu'il cite. Il est partisan du traité [de Paris, qui mit fin à la guerre de Sept Ans, 1756–1763], et soutient qu'aucune possession des Antilles ne peut se comparer au Canada en fait d'importance. ¶ *On a reproduit une mic. de l'exemplaire de cet ouvrage qui se trouve à la LC (cf. NUC).* ¶ *OTP*

Wright, John, *fl.* 1761–1765. The American negotiator; or, The various currencies of the British colonies in America .... The 2d ed. London, printed for the proprietor, 1763. 1 p.l., ii, 24, xvi, 464 p. 8°

NUC(Pre–56)675:294*

Waldon has collation: 2 p.l., 464 p., and the plural word "proprietors" in the imprint, with "BM" as her source (confirmed in BM(to 1955)261:421). NUC indicates a variant spelling later in the title: "coarseness" in the 1761 edition and the misspelling "coareness" in this second ed. ¶ *For other notes, including editions, see first ed., 1761.* ¶ *OONL · OOU · BVAU*

Collation de Waldon : 2 f. l., 464 p., et le mot « proprietors » au pluriel dans l'adresse bibliographique, avec BM comme source (confirmée dans BM(to 1955)261:421). Le NUC indique une variante orthographique qui se trouve un peu plus loin dans le titre : « coarseness » dans l'édition de 1761 devient « coareness » dans la deuxième éd. ¶ Voir *autres notes, y compris des éditions dans la première éd., 1761.* ¶ *OONL · OOU · BVAU*

1763–64

Entick, John, 1703?–1773. The general history of the late war: containing it's [*sic*] rise, progress, and event, in Europe, Asia, Africa, and America. And exhibiting the state of the belligerent powers at the commencement of the war; their interests and objects in it's [*sic*] continuation; and remarks on the measures, which led Great Britain to victory and conquest. Interspersed with the characters of the able and disinterested statesmen, to whose wisdom and integrity, and of the heroes, to whose courage and conduct, we are indebted for that naval and military success, which is not equalled in the annals of this, or of any other nation. And with accurate descriptions of the seat of war, the nature and importance of our conquests, and of the most remarkable battles by sea and land. Illustrated with a variety of heads, plans, maps, and charts, designed and engraved by the best artists . . . . By the Rev. John Entick, M. A. and other gentlemen. London: printed for Edward Dilly, in the Poultry; and John Millan, at Charing-Cross. 1763–64. 5 v. fronts., ports., charts, maps, plans. 8°

NUC(Pre–56)160:542*

Title in red and black. Contains an index. ¶ Entick was also the author of *A new naval history: or, Compleat view of the British marine.* London, 1757 (*q.v.*), which contains some account of discoveries, etc., in Canada. ¶ Concerns the Seven Years' War, 1756–63. ¶ First edition; reprinted 1763–65, 1763–66, 1763–66 (vol. 5, second ed. rev. and corr.), 1763–66 (third ed.), 1764, 1764–65, 1764–66, 1765 (second ed. corr.), 1770 (third ed.), 1779 (fourth, corr.), etc. — cf. NUC. ¶ NSWA · OTP

Titre en rouge et noir. Comprend un index. ¶ Entick est également l'auteur de *A new naval history : or, Compleat view of the British marine.* Londres, 1757 (*q.v.*), qui comprend certains récits de découvertes, etc., au Canada. ¶ *Traite de la guerre de Sept Ans, 1756–1763.* ¶ *Première édition ; réimprimé en 1763–1765, 1763–1766, 1763–1766 (vol. 5, deuxième éd. rév. et corr.), 1763–1766 (troisième éd.), 1764, 1764–1765, 1764–1766, 1765 (deuxième éd. corr.), 1770 (troisième éd.), 1779 (quatrième éd. corr.), etc.* – cf. NUC. ¶ NSWA · OTP

Index

Abbot, George, *abp. of Canterbury/aev. de
Canterbury*, 1562–1633 § 41-42, 50, 52, 62,
64, 73, 97, 100, 102, 104, 112, 123
The abridgement of the English chronicle . . . .
[Stow] § 51–52 *[1607]*, 55–56 *[1611]*, 64
[1618]
*Abstract of the scheme of government so far as it
relates to the grantees in trust* . . . . § 249
[1721]
*An account of a voyage for the discovery of a
North-West Passage by Hudson's Streights*
. . . . [Swaine] § 321–22 *[1748–49, 2 entries]*,
334 *[1749]*
*An account of conferences held, . . . between
Major-General Sir William Johnson, bart.
and . . . Indian nations in North America*
. . . . § 380–81 *[1756]*
*An account of Monsieur de la Salle's last
expedition and discoveries in North America.*
§ 172 *[1698]*
An account of six years residence in Hudson's-Bay
. . . . [Robson] § 349 *[1752]*, 434 *[1759]*
*An account of the captivity of Elizabeth Hanson,
now or late of Kachecky, in New-England*
. . . . [Hanson] § 451–52 *[1760]*
An account of the colony of Nova Scotia. § 341
[1751]
*An account of the countries adjoining to Hudson's
bay* . . . . [Dobbs] § 282–84 *[1744]*
*An account of the customs and manners of the
Micmakis and Maricheets savage nations* . . . .
[Maillard] § 419 *[1758]*
*An account of the European settlements in
America* . . . . [Burke] § 400 *[1757]*, 415
[1758], 439 *[1760]*, 482 *[1762]*
*An account of the French usurpation upon the
trade of England* . . . . [Bethel] § 144 *[1679]*

*An account of the late action of the
New-Englanders, under the command of Sir
William Phips, against the French at Canada.*
[Savage] § 161–62 *[1691]*
An account of the present state of Nova-Scotia
. . . . § 381 *[1756]*
*An account of the propagation of the gospel in
foreign parts* . . . . [Society for the
Propagation of the Gospel in Foreign
Parts] § 193–94 *[1704]*, 196–97 *[1705]*
*An account of the Society for propagating the
gospel in foreign parts* . . . . [Society for the
Propagation of the Gospel in Foreign
Parts] § 197–98 *[1706]*
*An account of the Society for the encouragement
of the British troops, in Germany and North
America.* [Hanway] § 452 *[1760]*
*An account of the trade between Great-Britain,
France, Holland, Spain, Portugal, Italy,
Africa, Newfoundland, &c.* . . . . [Davenant] §
230 *[1715]*
An account of two voyages to New-England. . . . .
[Josselyn] § 140 *[1675]*
*An accurate account of the taking of Cape Breton,
in the year 1755.* § 413 *[1758]*
*An accurate and authentic account of the taking
of Cape-Breton, in the year MDCCXLV.*
[Pepperell] § 420 *[1758]*
*An accurate and authentic journal of the siege of
Quebec, 1759.* § 425 *[1759]*
An accurate description of Cape Breton . . . . §
356 *[1755]*
*An accurate journal and account of the
proceedings of the New-England land-forces*
. . . . [Pepperell] § 305–06 *[1746]*
An accurate journal of the siege of Quebec, 1759.
§ 426 *[1759]*